One Team...
A Commitment to Quality

There's just one reason our team is dedicated to producing quality travel publications—you, our reader.

Throughout our guides we offer **practical information**, **touring tips** and **suggestions** for finding the best places for a break.

Michelin driving tours help you hit the highlights and quickly absorb the best of the region. Our descriptive **walking tours** make you your own guide, armed with directions, maps and expert information.

We scout out the attractions, classify them with **star ratings**, and describe in detail what you will find when you visit them.

Michelin maps featured throughout the guide offer vibrant, detailed and easy-to-follow outlines of everything from close-up museum plans to international maps.

Places to stay and eat are always a big part of travel, so we research **hotels and restaurants** that we think convey the essence of the destination and arrange them by geographic area and price. We walk you through the best shopping districts and point you towards the host of entertainment and recreation possibilities available.

We **test**, **retest**, **check and recheck** to make sure that our guidebooks are truly just that: a personalized guide to help you make the most of your visit. And if you still want a speaking guide, we list local tour guides who will lead you on all the boat, bus, guided, historical, culinary, and other tours you shouldn't miss.

In short, we remove the guesswork involved with travel. After all, we want you to enjoy exploring with Michelin as much as we do.

The Michelin Green Guide Team

PLANNING YOUR TRIP

INTRODUCTION TO QUEBEC

© Malak, Ottawa

CONTENTS

DISCOVERING QUEBEC

5

HOW TO USE THIS GUIDE

PLANNING YOUR TRIP

The blue-tabbed PLANNING YOUR TRIP section at the front of the guide gives you **ideas for your trip** and **practical information** to help you organize it. You'll find tours, a host of breaks in the great outdoors, a calendar of events, information on shopping, sightseeing, kids' activities and more.

INTRODUCTION

The orange-tabbed INTRODUCTION section explores **Nature** and the Sea. The **History** section spans early human settlement in Quebec through today. The **Art and Culture** section covers architecture, art, literature, language,

traditions and folklore, while the **Country Today** delves into modern Quebec.

DISCOVERING

The green-tabbed DISCOVERING section features Quebec's Principal Sights, arranged alphabetically and by region, featuring the most interesting local **Sights**, **Walking Tours**, nearby **Excursions**, and detailed **Driving Tours**.

Contact information, admission charges, hours of operation, and a host of other **visitor information** is given wherever possible. Admission prices shown are normally for a single adult.

STAR RATINGS★★★

Michelin has given star ratings for more than 100 years. If you're pressed for time, we recommend you visit the ★★★, or ★★ sights first:

★★★   Highly recommended
★★   Recommended
★   Interesting

Sidebars

Throughout the guide you will find peach-colored text boxes (like this one), with lively anecdotes, detailed history and background information.

Address Books - Where to Stay, Eat and more...

WHERE TO STAY

We've made a selection of hotels and arranged them within the cities by price category to fit all budgets (*see the Legend on the cover flap for an explanation of the price categories*). For the most part, we've selected accommodations based on their unique regional quality, their regional feel, as it were. So, unless the individual hotel embodies local ambience, it's rare that we include chain properties, which typically have their own imprint.
See the back of the guide for an index of where hotels featured throughout the guide can be found.

WHERE TO EAT

We thought you'd like to know the popular eating spots in Quebec. So, we selected restaurants that capture the regional experience—those that have a unique regional flavor (*see the Legend on the cover flap for an explanation of the price categories*). We're not rating the quality of the food per se; as we did with the hotels, we selected restaurants for many towns and villages, categorized by price to appeal to all wallets.
See the back of the guide for an index of where restaurants featured throughout the guide can be found.

MAPS

- Regional **Driving Tours** map and **Regional Itinerary** map.
- Quebec map with the **Principal Sights** highlighted.
- Maps for major **cities** and **villages**.
- **Local tour** maps.

All maps in this guide are oriented north, unless otherwise indicated by a directional arrow. The term "Local Map" refers to a map within the chapter or Tourism Region. A complete list of the maps

found in the guide appears at the back of this book, as well as a comprehensive index and list of restaurants and accommodations.
See the map Legend at the back of the guide for an explanation of map symbols.

ORIENT PANELS

Vital statistics are given for each principal sight in the DISCOVERING section:

- **Information**: Tourist Office/Sight contact details.
- ▶ **Orient Yourself:** Geographic location of the sight with reference to surrounding boroughs, towns, and roads.
- **Parking:** Where to park.
- **Don't Miss:** Unmissable things to do.
- **Organizing Your Time:** Tips on organizing your stay; what to see first, how long to spend, crowd avoidance, market days and more.
- **Especially for Kids:** Sights of particular interest to children.
- **Also See:** Nearby PRINCIPAL SIGHTS featured elsewhere in the guide.

SYMBOLS

Spa	**Spa Facilities**		**Tours**
Kids	**Interesting for Children**	▯	**On-site Parking**
	Also See	▶	**Directions**
	Tourist Information	✕	**On-site eating Facilities**
◷	**Hours of Operation**		**Swimming Pool**
◷	**Periods of Closure**	△	**Camping Facilities**
☂	**Closed to the Public**		**Beaches**
	Entry Fees		**Breakfast Included**
	Credit Cards not Accepted		**A Bit of Advice**
	Wheelchair Accessible		**Warning**

Contact - Addresses, phone numbers, opening hours and prices published in this guide are accurate at the time of press. We welcome corrections and suggestions that may assist us in preparing the next edition. Please send your comments to:

UK
Michelin Maps and Guides
Hannay House
39 Clarendon Road
Watford, Herts WD17 1JA
travelpubsales@uk.michelin.com
www.michelin.co.uk

USA
Michelin Maps and Guides
Editorial Department
P.O. Box 19001
Greenville, SC 29602-9001
michelin.guides@us.michelin.com
www.michelintravel.com

Patisserie in La Minerve, Laurentides
© Benoît Desjardins

MICHELIN DRIVING TOURS

Local Drives

⟳Use the A–Z Discovering section and its maps to explore Quebec by car in:

- ÎLE D'ANTICOSTI
- BAS-SAINT-LAURENT
- BEAUCE
- CÔTE DE BEAUPRE
- CÔTE DE CHARLEVOIX
- CÔTE-NORD
- CANTONS DE L'EST
- GASPÉSIE
- LANAUDIÈRE

- ÎLES DE LA MADELEINE
- MAURICE
- LAC MEGANTIC
- ÎLE D'ORLEANS
- VALLÉE DU RICHELIEU
- FJORD DU SAGUENAY
- LAC SAINT-JEAN
- VALLÉE DU SAINT-LAURENT

Tourist Regions Map

REGIONAL ITINERARY MAPS

1 Bas-St-Laurent–Charlevoix
2 Bas-St-Laurent (inset)
3 Beauce
4 Beaupré, Côte de
5 Côte-Nord
6 Estrie
7 Gaspésie
8 Lanaudière
9 Laurentides
10 Mauricie
11 Mégantic, Lac
12 Orléans, Île d'
13 Richelieu, Vallée du
14 Saguenay, Fjord du
15 St-Jean, Lac
16 St-Laurent, Vallée du

Other regional maps
Anticosti, Île de
Gatineau, Parc de la
James, Baie
Madeleine, Îles de la

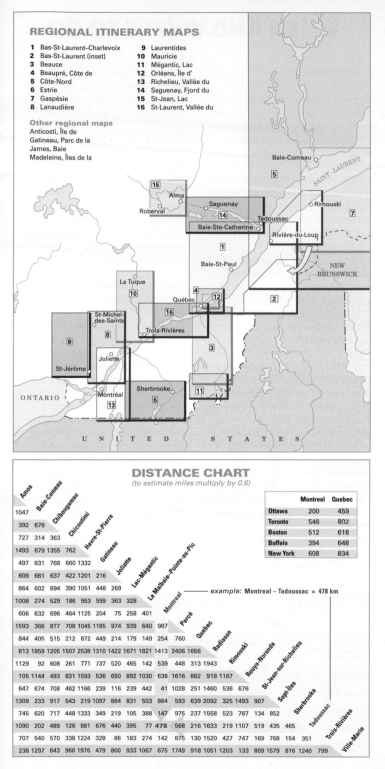

DISTANCE CHART
(to estimate miles multiply by 0.6)

	Montreal	Quebec
Ottawa	200	459
Toronto	546	802
Boston	512	618
Buffalo	394	648
New York	608	834

example: Montreal – Tadoussac = 478 km

Distance chart (diagonal matrix with locations: Amos, Baie-Comeau, Chibougameau, Chicoutimi, Havre-St-Pierre, Gatineau, Joliette, Lac-Mégantic, La Malbaie-Pointe-au-Pic, Montreal, Percé, Quebec, Radisson, Rimouski, Rouyn-Noranda, St-Jean-sur-Richelieu, Sept-Îles, Sherbrooke, Tadoussac, Trois-Rivières, Ville-Marie):

Amos																				
1047	Baie-Comeau																				
392	676	Chibougameau																			
727	314	363	Chicoutimi																		
1493	679	1355	762	Havre-St-Pierre																
497	831	768	660	1332	Gatineau															
609	661	637	422	1201	216	Joliette														
864	602	694	390	1051	448	269	Lac-Mégantic													
1008	274	529	186	953	599	363	328	La Malbaie-Pointe-au-Pic												
606	632	696	464	1125	204	75	258	401	Montreal											
1593	366	877	708	1045	1185	974	939	640	987	Percé										
844	405	515	212	872	449	214	179	149	254	760	Quebec									
813	1859	1205	1507	2538	1310	1422	1671	1821	1413	2406	1656	Radisson								
1129	92	608	261	771	737	520	465	142	539	448	313	1943	Rimouski							
105	1144	493	831	1593	536	650	892	1030	638	1616	882	918	1167	Rouyn-Noranda						
647	674	708	462	1166	239	116	239	442	41	1028	251	1460	536	676	St-Jean-sur-Richelieu					
1309	233	917	543	219	1097	864	831	503	864	593	639	2092	325	1493	907	Sept-Îles				
745	620	717	448	1333	349	219	105	388	147	975	237	1558	523	787	134	852	Sherbrooke			
1090	202	489	126	881	676	440	395	77	**478**	568	216	1633	219	1107	519	435	465	Tadoussac		
707	540	570	338	1224	328	86	183	274	142	875	130	1520	427	747	169	768	154	351	Trois-Rivières	
238	1297	643	966	1976	479	800	933	1067	675	1749	918	1051	1203	133	809	1579	816	1240	799	Ville-Marie

WHEN AND WHERE TO GO

When to Go

Quebec is a year-round vacation destination for sports enthusiasts, nature lovers, hunters and fishermen. Northern Quebec is subject to arctic temperatures, while the regions around the St. Lawrence are temperate in climate. Most cultural attractions are open from mid-May (Fête de Dollard, also called Fête des Patriotes) to the first weekend in September (Labor Day). *Sight descriptions contain more specific information.*

In March–April, the harvesting of maple syrup signals the coming of **spring** with sugaring-off parties. This season is brief with pleasant days and chilly evenings. In the southern part of Quebec, **summer**, extending from mid-June through mid-September, is hot and humid. Light, loose-fitting clothes are best for hot weather, but it is advisable to have a light jacket handy for cool evenings and excursions on lakes. Late May through June is mosquito and black fly season and insect repellent is a must, and virtually indispensable for those planning to camp or hike.

In **autumn**, beginning in early October, visitors can enjoy the many forest colors of the "Indian Summer." **Winter** can begin as early as November, with an abundance of snow. Temperatures often fall below freezing and during January and February can drop below 0°F (-17°C). Plenty of warm clothing will protect visitors from the cold. The Saint Lawrence Valley is warmer but more humid, so may feel just as cold.

Ideas for Your Visit

There is more to Quebec than long driving tours in the countryside, expeditions in the woods and fantastic urban festivals, although these are all strong points of travelling there. The following are ideas designed to help you appreciate Quebec in unusual, yet very accessible ways.

CYCLING IN AND AROUND MONTREAL

Surrounded by water, lined with an extensive network of safe cycling routes, **Montreal** (*see entry in the DISCOVERING section*) is an excellent city to experience the pleasure of urban cycling, especially on a quiet Sunday morning. Ride along the peaceful **Canal de l'Aqueduc** in the Lachine District and have a refined picnic purchased at the gourmet **Atwater Market**. Athletic types might seek the challenge of crossing the St. Lawrence River on the **Champlain Bridge Estacade** before touring the small islands lining the **St. Lawrence Seaway**. A refreshing option is the take a small ferry (no space for cars) with your bike from Old Montreal to Longueuil. www.velo.qc.ca.

Seasonal Temperatures (°F/°C)								
	April		July		October		January	
	min.	max.	min.	max.	min.	max.	min.	max.
Chicoutimi	25/-4	45/7	54/12	75/24	34/1	48/9	-9/-23	14/-10
Gaspé	27/-3	41/5	52/11	73/23	34/1	52/11	3/-16	21/-6
Kuujjuarapik	9/-13	28/-2	41/5	51/15	30/-1	41/5	18/-2	80/-18
Montreal	34/1	52/11	61/16	79/26	39/4	55/13	5/-15	21/-6
Quebec City	28/-2	19/7	55/13	77/25	36/2	52/11	0/-17	18/-8
Sherbrooke	28/-2	50/10	52/11	77/25	32/0	54/12	0/-17	21/-6

TRAIN TOURS AROUND MONTREAL

Some trains that bring stressed-out commuters to downtown Montreal also take holidays in summer by shuffling relaxed day-trippers on weekends and some weekdays. This clever idea is hugely successful, so reserve tickets in advance if you want to enjoy the countryside without driving to it and without having to make any research besides choosing between the day trips offered by the *Agence de transport métropolitain de Montréal*. You can sample maple liqueur in Mirabel, cheese and rabbit specialities in Saint-Sophie, apples in a Lower Laurentians orchard, etc. If your prefer a taste of history, you can visit the Trestler House in Vaudreui-Soulange, the Canadian Train Museum in Saint-Constant or the natural and historical features of **Île Perrot**. Many of these tours include lunch at a local restaurant. Some of these train tours go to **Laval**, north of Montreal, and allow to explore the worlds of space rockets, flowers, or ostriches. **For further information**: ☎514-287-7866. www.amt.qc.ca/escapades.

GHOST TOURS OF QUEBEC CITY

What qualification got you the job of Executioner in the 1600s in Quebec City? A stressful interview?, good refer-ences?, a practical skills test? How did the French terminate unwanted individuals before the guillotine? You'll have all these answers and more, as over 300 years of murders, executions, mysterious ghost sightings, tragedies and hauntings will be imprinted in your mind for ever... Seriously, it is a very highly rated ghost tour, well researched and expertly guided. Tours are in English or French, from May to October. And if it rains? It is even better and scarier, say organisers.
For further information: ☎418-692-9770, www.ghosttoursofquebec.com

CULTURAL AND HISTORICAL TOURS IN TROIS-RIVIERES

The city of **Trois-Rivières** (&see entry in the DISCOVERING section), between Montreal and Quebec City, on the St. Lawrence River, boasts an extremely vibrant cultural scene, favored by its geographic position and the low cost of making a living as an artist there. You can easily tour round the beautiful downtown **art galleries**, such as *illico, Maistre, St-Antoine* and *Oeil Tactile*.
Old Trois-Rivières is very compact, yet as old as the historic parts of Qubec City. So it is quite pleasant and easy to walk around Old Trois-Rivières, armed with a **self-guided tour** leaflet from the city tourism bureau, with the constant, soothing view of the river.

KNOW BEFORE YOU GO

Useful Websites

◆ www.bonjourquebec.com
  Official government tourist board
◆ www.quebecregion.com
  Events, accommodation, etc.
◆ www.hihostels.ca
  Hostelling information
◆ www.tourism-montreal.org
  Travel, accommodation, etc.
◆ www.skicentral.dom/quebec
  Ski resort directory, lodging, ski runs, pistes, etc.

Regional Tourist Offices

Contact the regional offices listed below for brochures giving details on points of interest, seasonal events and accommodation, as well as road and city maps. Regional offices, which distribute maps, brochures and other travel information free of charge, extend their operating hours from late June to September.

IN QUEBEC

Tourisme Québec:
C.P. 979, Montréal (QC) H3C 2W3;
www.bonjourquebec.com;
☎514-873-2015 & 1-877-266-5687

Abitibi-Témiscamingue:
155 Ave. Dallaire, bureau 100,
Rouyn-Noranda (QC) J9X 4T3;
www.tourisme-abitibi-
temiscamingue.org;
☎819-762-8181 & 1-800-808-0706

Bas-Saint-Laurent:
148 Rue Fraser, Rivière-du-Loup
(QC) G5R 1C8;
www.tourismebas-st-laurent.com;
☎418-867-1272 & 1-800-563-5268

Centre-du-Québec:
20, Blvd. Carignan Ouest,
Princeville (QC) G6L 4M4;
www.tourismecentreduquebec.com;
☎819-364-7177 & 1-888-816-4007

Charlevoix:
495 Blvd. de Comporté,
La Malbaie (QC) G5A 3G3;
www.tourisme-charlevoix.com;
☎418-665-4454 & 1-800-667-2276

Chaudière-Appalaches:
800 Autoroute Jean-Lesage,
Lévis (QC) G7A 1E3;
www.chaudiereppalaches.com;
☎418-831-4411 & 1-888-831-4411

Duplessis (Lower North Shore)**:**
312 Ave. Brochu,
Sept-Îles (QC) G4R 2W6;
www.tourismeduplessis.com;
☎418-962-0808 & 1-888-
463-0808

Eastern Townships/Cantons-de-l'Est:
20 Rue Don-Bosco Sud,
Sherbrooke (QC) J1L 1W4;
www.easterntowships.org;
☎819-820-2020 & 1-800-355-5755

Gaspésie:
357 Route de la Mer,
Sainte-Flavie (QC) G0J 2L0;
www.tourisme-gaspesie.com;
☎418-775-2223 & 1-800-463-0323

Lanaudière:
3568 Rue Church,
Rawdon (QC) J0K 1S0;
www.lanaudiere.ca; ☎450-834-
2535 & 1-800-363-2788

Laurentians/Laurentides:
14142 Rue de la Chapelle,
Mirabel (QC) J7J 2C8;
www.laurentides.com;
☎450-224-7007 & 1-800-561-6673

Laval:
2900 Blvd. Saint-Martin Ouest,
Laval (QC) H7T 2J2;
www.tourismelaval.qc.ca;
☎450-682-5522 & 1-877-465-2825

**Magdalen Islands/
Îles de la Madeleine:**
128 Chemin Principal,
Cap-aux-Meules (QC) G4T 1C5;
www.tourismeilesdela
madeleine.com;
☎418-986-2245 & 1-877-624-4437

Manicouagan (Upper North Shore)**:**
337 Blvd. La Salle, bureau 304,
Baie-Comeau (QC) G4Z 2Z1;
www.tourismemanicouagan.com
& www.routedesbaleines.ca;
☎418-294-2876 & 1-888-463-5319

Mauricie:
795, 5e Rue, bureau 102,
Shawinigan (QC) G9N 1G2;
www.tourismemauricie.com;
☎819-536-3334 & 1-800-567-7603

Montérégie:
2001, boul. de Rome, 3e étage,
Brossard (QC) J4W 3K5;
www.tourisme-monteregie.qc.ca;
☎450-466-4666 & 1-866-
469-0069

Montréal:
C.P. 979, Montréal (QC) H3C 2W3;
www.tourism-montreal.org;
☎514-873-2015 & 1-877-266-5687

Northern Quebec

James Bay/Baie-James:
1252 Route 167 Sud, C.P. 134,
Chibougamau (QC) G8P 2K6 ;
www.tourismebaiejames.com;
☎418-748-8140 & 1-888-748-8140

Eeyou Istchee:
203 Opemiska Meskino, C.P. 266,
Oujé-Bougoumou (QC) G0W 3C0;
www.creetourism.ca
☎418-745-2220 & 1-888-268-2682

Nunavik Tourism Association:
P.O. Box 779,
Kuujjuaq (QC) J0M 1C0;
www.nunavik-tourism.com;
☎819-964-2876 & 1-888-594-3424

Outaouais:
103 Rue Laurier,
Gatineau (QC) J8X 3V8;
www.outaouaistourism.com;
☎819-778-2222 & 1-800-265-7822

Quebec City and Area:
835 Ave. Wilfrid-Laurier,
Québec (QC) G1R 2L3;
www.quebecregion.com;
☎418-641-6290 & 1-877-783-1608

Saguenay–Lac-Saint-Jean:
412 Blvd. Saguenay Est, bureau
100, Chicoutimi District (QC)
G7H 7Y8;
www.saguenaylacsaintjean.net;
☎418-543-9778 & 1-877-253-8387

IN EUROPE

Belgium:
Tourisme Québec, www.bonjour
quebec.com; ☎0800 78 532

France:
Tourisme Québec, www.bonjour
quebec.com; ☎0800 90 77 77

United Kingdom:
Tourisme Québec, www.bonjour
quebec.com; ☎0800 051 70 55

International Visitors

CANADIAN EMBASSIES AND CONSULATES ABROAD

Atlanta:
1175 Peachtree St., 100 Colony
Square, Suite 1700, Atlanta GA
30361-6205; ☎404-532-2000

Chicago:
Two Prudential Plaza, 180 North
Stetson Avenue, Suite 2400,
Chicago IL 60601; ☎312-616-1860

Los Angeles:
550 S. Hope St., 9th Floor,
Los Angeles CA 90071-2627;
☎213-346-2700

New York:
1251 Avenue of the Americas,
New York NY 10020-1175;
☎212-596-1628

Washington DC:
501 Pennsylvania Ave., NW,
Washington DC 20001-2114;
☎202-682-1740

Australia:
Level 5, Quay West Building,
111 Harrington St., Sydney, N.S.W.
2000; ☎9364-3000

Germany:
Leipziger Platz 17, 10117 Berlin;
☎30 20 31 20

United Kingdom:

Canada House, Trafalgar Square,
London SW1Y 5BJ; ☎20 7258 6600

FOREIGN EMBASSIES AND CONSULATES IN QUEBEC

Consulates of most foreign countries
are located in Montreal. Embassies are
located in Ottawa, the capital of Canada.

Germany:
1250 Blvd. René-Lévesque Ouest,
Montréal (QC) H4B 4X1,
☎514-931-2277

Japan:
600 Rue de la Gauchetière Ouest, Montréal (QC) H3B 4L8;
☏514-866-3429

United Kingdom:
600 Rue de la Gauchetière Ouest, Suite 4200, Montréal (QC) H3B 4W5;
☏514-866-5863

United States:
1155 Rue Saint-Alexandre, Place Félix-Martin, Montréal (QC) H3B 3Z1; ☏514-398-9695 & 1-800-529-4410

Entry Requirements

United States citizens must show either a US passport or other proof of US citizenship - such as an original or certified birth certificate together with photo identification. US citizens entering Canada from a third country must have a valid passport. A visa is not required for US citizens for a stay up to 180 days. Permanent **US residents** who are not citizens must carry their Alien Registration Cards.

European Union citizens and all other international visitors to Canada (not US citizens or US permanent residents) must carry a valid passport and, if required, a visa. Citizens from the United Kingdom, France, Germany, Mexico, Japan, the Republic of Korea, Australia and others do not require a visa to enter Canada. Visit the Citizenship and Immigration Canada website (www.cic.gc.ca/english/visit/visas. asp) for a complete listing of countries whose citizens require visas to enter Canada You can also check with the Canadian embassy or consulate in your country regarding entry regulations. No vaccinations are necessary when entering Canada. All visitors admitted to Canada will be permitted to stay for a maximum of six months, unless otherwise notified in writing by an examining officer

Persons **under 18** who are not accompanied by an adult must have a letter from a parent or guardian stating the traveller's name and duration of trip. Students should carry a student ID; senior citizens (over 65) are required to present proof of age when requesting discounts at many attractions. **For further information** on all Canadian embassies and consulates abroad, contact the website of the Canadian Department of Foreign Affairs & International Trade: www.dfait-maeci.gc.ca.

Customs Regulations

Importation of **tobacco** is limited to 50 cigars or 200 cigarettes per adult. The limit for importing **alcoholic beverages** is 1.14 litres/1.2 quarts of liquor or wine, or 24 bottles of beer. Visitors to Canada can bring in personal goods without paying duty or tax, as long as they do not leave them in Canada. Visitors can bring in gifts without paying duty or tax, if they have a value of less than CAN$60 per gift. Gifts with a value over CAN$60 are subject to duty and tax on the amount over CAN$60.

Since Quebec has very strict laws concerning narcotics and other chemical substances, all prescription drugs should be identified; it is advisable to carry a copy of the prescription or a letter from your doctor.
Bringing **handguns** into Quebec is prohibited. Nonresidents must declare all firearms. **For further information** on entry of firearms contact the Canada Firearms Center, Ottawa (ON) K1A 1M6 ☏1-800-731-4000 or www.cfc-cafc.gc.ca.

Pets must be accompanied by a certificate of vaccination against rabies (within last 3 years). **For further information** contact the Canadian Food Inspection Agency (Animal Health Division), 2001 Rue University, Suite 746-S, Montréal (QC) H3A 3N2; ☏514-283-8888; www.inspection.gc.ca.

Health

Before leaving your country, it is advisable to check with your medical insurance provider to determine whether you are covered for doctor visits, medication, and hospital stays while visiting Quebec. A visitor insurance policy can be purchased either before leaving or within 30 days following the arrival in Canada ($3.50–$15 per day according to age and insurance limit -- $100,000 or $150,000 limit). However, Blue Cross recommends purchase to be made prior to arrival. If purchased after the arrival in Canada, the contract will be effective 72 hours after the purchase. Maximum coverage period is 180 days.Purchase of coverage can be made online. For more details contact Blue Cross of Quebec, 550 Rue Sherbrooke Ouest, Montréal (QC) H3A 3S3 ☎514-286-8403 or www.qc.croixbleue.ca.

US visitors travelling by car must have proof of automobile insurance with a liability coverage of at least $50,000 (♿ *see p 21*).

Accessibility

Sights accessible to disabled travelers are indicated by the ♿ symbol in this guide. Most public buildings, churches, restaurants and hotels provide wheelchair access. Parking spaces reserved for the disabled are strictly enforced. Passes issued by the International Transport Forum and by US authorities are recognised in Quebec and allow for parking in designated parking spaces for the disabled.

For further information or to obtain *The Accessible Road (downloadable free of charge on the Kéroul website)*, contact Kéroul, 4545 Ave. Pierre-de-Coubertin, C.P. 1000, Station M, Montréal (QC) H1V 3R2 ☎514-252-3104 and www.keroul.qc.ca. *Additional information* is available from the Canadian Rehabilitation Council for the Disabled, 90 Eglinton Ave. East, Toronto (ON) M4P 2Y3 ☎416-932-8382, www.esmodnc.org.

The **Autocars Orléans Express** inter-city bus lines offers transportation for persons with reduced mobility.

For further information, contact the nearest Orléans Express office or visit www.orleansexpress.com.

GETTING THERE AND GETTING AROUND

By Plane

In the province of Quebec, most international and domestic flights arrive at Montreal's **Pierre-Elliott-Trudeau International** airport (in the Dorval district) ☎514-394-7377. Some domestic and international flights land in Quebec City's **Jean-Lesage International** airport ☎418-640-2600. The **Mont-Tremblant International** airport (in the Laurentians Region) ☎819-275-9099 receives flights from Toronto and New York City. Canada's national airline, **Air Canada** (a Star Alliance member), serves major European cities,

the Caribbean, Asia and the Pacific, and provides service to most destinations within Canada and the US. Quebec is also serviced by a network of regional airlines (♿*see chart over page*). Canada's low-cost airline, **WestJet**, is an excellent option for the 45 destinations it serves in North America and the Caribbean.

Service to remote areas, provided by charter companies, may be offered once or twice a week only. For telephone numbers of local air carriers, consult your travel agent or contact the appropriate provincial or regional tourist office.

Airline	Local ☎	Toll-free ☎	Website
Air Canada and Air Canada Jazz	514-393-3333	1-888-247-2262	www.aircanada.ca
Air Inuit	514-636-9445	1-800-361-2965	www.airinuit.ca
First Air	613-254-6200	1-800-267-1247	www.firstair.ca
WestJet	403-539-7070	1-888-937-8538	www.westjet.com

By Ship

The Quebec government operates an extensive ferry boat system. **For further information** and schedules, contact the regional tourist office or Tourisme Québec, or the Société des Traversiers du Québec, 250 rue Saint-Paul, Québec (QC) G1K 9K9; ☎1-877-787-7483; www.traversiers.gouv.qc.ca.

By Train

Rail service within the province of Quebec and the rest of Canada is provided by **VIA Rail Canada.** Trains are relatively slow but fares are reasonable, service level is good, and trains are comfortable. The foreign visitor must be aware of the great distances within Quebec (travel time between Montreal and the Gaspé Peninsula, for example, is 19 hours). First class (called *VIA 1*, hot meals are included in the fares), coach (called *Comfort Class*) and sleeping accommodations are available for long trips. **For further information** and schedules, contact VIA Rail Canada, 895 Rue de la Gauchetière, Montréal (QC) H3B 4G1; ☎1-888-842-7245 (from anywhere in Canada and the US); www.viarail.ca. Significant discounts are offered for advance purchase, youth and senior citizens; students of all ages obtain particularly good rates and conditions if they can show an ISIC (International Student Identification Card). Reservations should be made well in advance, especially during the summer months. A **Canrailpass** (*Jun–mid-Oct $837; rest of the year $523*) gets you 12 days of unlimited travel in Comfort class (Economy) during a 30-day period. Just show your Canrailpass each time

you obtain a ticket for a trip during this 30-day period.

The card can be used anywhere that VIA goes, from the Atlantic to the Pacific, and up to Hudson Bay. You can make as many stops as you like during your journey. You can add up to three extra days' travel, which you can buy in advance or at any time during the 30-day validity period.

The United States train passenger service, **Amtrak**, provides daily service from Washington DC via New York City to Montreal; rates are excellent, but trains on the Montreal route are very slow. **For further information** and schedules in the US and Canada, call ☎1-800-872-7245 or visit www.amtrak.com.

By Car

Foreign **driver's licenses** are valid in Quebec for six months. Drivers must carry the **vehicle registration** information and rental contract at all times. The price of **gasoline**, sold in liters (3.78 liters to a US gallon), varies from province to province and is generally higher than in the US. **Service stations** are plentiful, except in isolated areas, and are usually full-service. Caution and lower speeds are recommended when driving on gravel and dust roads—common outside the

Rental Car Agency	Info ☎
Avis	1-800-321-3652
Budget	1-800-268-8900
Hertz	1-800-263-0678
Thrifty	1-800-367-2277
National	1-800-227-7368

main road network. Special precautions should be taken when driving in winter. Since 2008, **Winter tires** on all wheels are compulsory for Quebec vehicles from November 15 to April 1. Except during winter storms, most highways are cleared and open for traffic, but it is always advisable to check traffic conditions before leaving. For up-to-date reports on road conditions, call Transport Québec's "info-roads line" ☎1-888-355-0511 or check webcams at www.inforoutiere.qc.ca.

ROAD REGULATIONS

Transport Quebec maintains a network of four-lane, divided, controlled access expressways (called motorways in the UK, freeways in the US, and autoroutes in Quebec), of numbered provincial highways, and of secondary roads (often unpaved in remote areas). Most road signs are in French (some are also in English near borders with the US, Ontario, and New Brunswick, and around Montreal) and distances are posted in meters or kilometers. The speed limit on inter-city expressways is usually 100km/h (60mph), 90km/h (55mph) on highways and 50km/h (30mph) within city limits, unless otherwise posted. Turning right at a red light is prohibited in Montreal, but allowed in the rest of the province of Quebec, unless posted otherwise. The law requires that traffic in both directions halt for a stopped school bus. Seat belts are mandatory for all vehicle occupants. The possession or use of radar detection devices is illegal. Approach railroad crossings with caution; most do not have barriers, but are signaled with flashing lights and sound. Blue road signs indicate services and points of interest for tourists, and brown signs indicate national parks.

CANADIAN AUTOMOBILE ASSOCIATION (CAA)

CAA Québec, ☎514-861-1917 & 1-866-827-8801, www.caaquebec.com. All member services of this national motorclub are offered to the US tourist upon presentation of the membership card of the American Automobile Association (AAA). The CAA is also affiliated with the Alliance Internationale de Tourisme (AIT), the Fédération Internationale de l'Automobile (FIA), the Federation of Interamerican Touring & Automobile Clubs (FITAC) and the Commonwealth Motoring Conference (CMC). CAA provides helpful travel information, insurance coverage and emergency road service: **24-hour emergency road service** ☎514-861-1313 & 1-800-222-4357.

CAR RENTAL

The chart (☾see opposite page) presents a selection of rental car agencies operating in Quebec. The numbers listed are toll-free within Quebec: Major car rental companies operate offices in airports, train stations and larger cities. More favorable rates can usually be obtained with advance reservations. Minimum age for renting a car is 21; reservation and payment is easiest by credit card. Some agencies offer special packages, but be aware of drop-off charges if you return the car to a location other than the one from which you rented it. The rental price does not include collision coverage. Liability coverage is mandatory. **For any other information** about car insurance or coverage while in Quebec, contact the Insurance Bureau of Canada: ☎514-288-1563, www.ibc.ca; or Société de l'assurance automobile du Québec: ☎514 873-7620 & 1-800-361-7620, www.saaq.gouv.qc.ca.

CAMPER RENTAL

Families or groups of four to six people may prefer to rent a camper with amenities (beds, kitchenette, shower, toilet, etc.) to travel around the province of Quebec. Many campgrounds are operated by **Parks Canada** (www.pccamping.ca); numerous, easy-to-find private campgrounds offer more amenities (water and electrical hookups). **For further information**, see www.campsource.ca.

Be aware that travelling with a camper is very popular; it is best to make your reservations at least six months in advance. Minimum age to rent or drive a camper is 21, with a valid driver's license or international driver's permit. Check with your local travel agent for information; in Quebec, camper rentals are listed in the telephone book Yellow Pages under *"Véhicules Récréatifs."*

IN CASE OF ACCIDENT

First-aid stations are well marked on the major roads. Nonresidents sustaining vehicular damage and/or bodily injury should contact the local police and stay at the scene until an officer has completed an inspection. In certain cases, nonresidents may be entitled to compensation under the Quebec automobile insurance plan.

Société de l'assurance automobile du Québec ☎514 873-7620 & 1-800-361-7620, www.saaq.gouv.qc.ca.

By Coach/Bus

Autocars Orléans Express serves the Montreal-Quebec City-Gaspésie corridor. The **Rout-Pass** (May–Oct) is valid for 7, 14, or 18 consecutive days, costing respectively *$249, $301, and $385* (taxes included); additional days may be added at the time of purchase for an additional charge; www.routpass.com. The rest of Quebec is served by regional bus companies. **For further information** and schedules contact Orléans Express ☎514-842-2281 & 1-888-999-3977 and www.orleansexpress.com. No reservation is necessary.

WHERE TO STAY AND EAT

Where to Stay

Hotels and Restaurants are located in the Address Books throughout the *Discovering Quebec* section of this guide. *For coin ranges and for a description of the symbols used in the Address Books, see the Legend on the cover flap.* Quebec offers a wide range of accommodations, from luxurious hotels to campgrounds. Reservations should be made well in advance during the peak tourist season (late Jun–Sept).

However, this is not Venice: You can pretty much always find a bed/roof combination without reservations, but it will not always be what you hoped for. It is advisable to guarantee reservations with a credit card. Reserving on the internet often allows for the best prices. In remote areas, hotels often close during certain months of the year. Lower weekend rates may be available and many hotels offer packages that include some or all meals.

Hotel	Info ☎	Website
Best Western International	1-800-528-1234	www.bestwestern.com
Fairmont	1-800-441-1414	www.fairmont.com
Hilton	1-800-221-2424	www.hilton.com
Holiday Inn	1-800-465-4329	www.holidayinn.com
Hôtel des Gouverneurs	1-800-463-2820	www.gouverneurs.com
Radisson	1-800-333-3333	www.radisson.com
Ramada Inn	1-800-854-7854	www.ramadainn.com
Sheraton	1-800-325-3535	www.sheraton.com

Tourisme Charlevoix/Fairmont Le Manoir Richelieu

Fairmont Le Manoir Richelieu, Charlevoix

For price ranges and selection criteria used in this guide, see Montreal's Address Book.

HOTELS

The hotel chains listed below can be found in Quebec's larger cities. The accompanying telephone numbers are toll-free within Canada and the US. *For additional information* on hotels, contact Tourisme Québec, 1255 Rue Peel, Suite 100, Montréal; ☎514-873-2015 & 1-877-266-5687; www. bonjourquebec.com.

Small hotels, known for their ambience and excellent regional cuisine, are plentiful in urban areas and in the countryside. Quality accommodations at moderate prices is offered by **Comfort Inn, Quality Hotels & Suites** (reservations through Choice Hotels ☎1-877-424-6423; www.choicehotels. com) or **Days Inn** (☎1-800-329-7466, www.daysinn.com). Family-owned motels and guest houses provide basic accommodations, often without a restaurant.

YOUTH HOSTELS

In Quebec, Hostelling International–Canada (☎1-800-663-5777, www. hihostels.ca) has 12 youth hostels - clean, reliable, inexpensive lodging. Youth hostels are now designed and operated with all age groups in mind. Shared rooms (from $16/night, $20/night for non HI members) are the mainstay of "hostelling", but private rooms are increasingly available. Private rooms (for couples and families) in hostels are cheaper than similar rooms in hotels. Hostels are centrally located in cities, towns and villages, generally nearby tourist attractions and transportation terminals. Some "rustic" hostels provide an affordable access to nature areas. Hostelling International membership also translates into discounts on attractions, activities, food and travel gear.

BED & BREAKFASTS AND COUNTRY INNS

An alternative to small hotels, bed & breakfasts *(gîtes du passant)* and country inns promise a welcoming atmosphere and range from elaborate to modest. Yet owners generally seem to partake in a provincial home decoration contest. Usually family-owned, they may consist of an extra room in a Victorian house, a backyard cottage, a converted lighthouse, or a lovely town house on a quaint city street. Rates average $80/night (breakfast included); not all provide private bathrooms. Farm holidays for a day, a week or longer, are an especially appealing option for families with children who can participate in farm activities. The Fédération des Agricotours du Québec publishes a guide, *Gîtes du Passant au Québec* (*$29*), which lists establishments and provides detailed information on facilities and locations. **For further information**, contact the Fédération des Agricotours du Québec, 4545 Pierre-de-Coubertin Ave., C.P. 1000, Succursale M, Montréal (QC) H1V 3R2; ☎514-252-3138, www.agricotours.qc.ca or the Quebec association of resorts and country inns: Hôtellerie Champêtre, 1255 Rue University, Suite 430, Montréal (QC) H3B 3B6; ☎514-861-4024 & 1-800-861-4024, www.hotelleriechampetre.com.

CAMPING

Government-operated and private campgrounds rates range from $14–$35/night depending on services offered Situated in scenic locations, federal and provincial government campgrounds (operated by Parks Canada and Parcs Québec) are generally better maintained, situated in nicer natural environments, and fill up quickly. **For further information** on camping, caravanning, canoeing and to order the annually published *Guide Camping Québec* (free), contact Camping Québec ☎450-651-7396 & 1-800-363-0457, www.campingquebec.com.

UNIVERSITIES AND COLLEGES

Some universities and colleges rent dormitory space when school's out (*May–Aug*) at moderate rates. Contact Tourisme Québec or the institution's housing department. In Montreal: McGill University ☎514-398-6368; Université de Montréal ☎514-343-6531; Concordia University ☎514-848-2424. In Trois-Rivières: Université du Québec ☎819-376-5016. In Rimouski: Université du Québec ☎418-723-4311.

SKI RESORTS

Major ski resorts in Charlevoix, the Eastern Townships, the Laurentians and the Outaouais regions offer a complete range of accommodations, including slope-side lodgings, deluxe hotels and bed & breakfasts as well as condominium and chalet rentals. Some hotels offer their own ski schools and provide complete vacation packages. **For further information**, contact the Association des stations de ski du Québec ☎514-493-1810; www.maneige.com/en/.

Where to Eat

Certain sections of **Montreal**, including Old Montreal, Plateau Mt-Royal, Blvd. St-Laurent and downtown, are known for their restaurants. Yet the most pleasant, reasonably priced restaurants are often on small streets, hidden away (like the intimate restaurants of Rue Marie-Anne, running parallel to Ave. Mt-Royal in the Plateau). Such memorable restaurants often cannot afford to advertise in tourist publications.

Quebec City also boasts a wide assortment of fine restaurants, mostly along Rue Sainte-Anne, Rue Saint-Jean, Rue Saint-Louis, Avenue Cartier, and the Grande-Allée in the Upper Town, and along the Rue du Petit-Champlain area and Rue Saint-Paul in the Lower Town. **French food** (high class and bistro style) provides the most satisfying experiences. Service and décor is often better than in Montreal because Quebec City is so tourism-oriented, but beware the widespread "tourist food," the international fare made to please the average tourist at an average price with average results.

Many regions, including **Outaouais**, **Montérégie**, **Lanaudière**, **Charlevoix**, **Gaspésie**, and **Saguenay-Lac-Saint-Jean**, have developed modern regional *spécialités*. You could easily pass by this gastronomic bounty if you stick to chain restaurants.

🍃Some regional food producers have arrangements with specific restaurants, so look out for these places.

WHAT TO SEE AND DO

Outdoor Fun

For further information concerning the activities listed below, contact **Regroupement Loisir Québec** (RLQ), 4545 Ave. Pierre-de-Coubertin, Montréal (QC) H1V 3R2 ☎514-252-3126 & 1-800-932-3735, www.loisirquebec. qc.ca or contact the appropriate organizations directly.

WINTER ACTIVITIES

Due to abundant snowfall, a variety of winter sports attracts both Quebecers and visitors from afar. The winter sports season begins mid-November and ends mid-April, although certain northern regions have good snow conditions through mid-May. Popular ski areas are easily accessible from most major cities. National and provincial parks allow all winter sports, and many communities maintain skating rinks for ice hockey and recreational skating. **For further information** on winter activities, contact regional tourist offices, the ski resorts themselves, or Tourisme Québec.

Alpine Skiing

Quebec boasts four major ski areas: Charlevoix, the Eastern Townships, the Laurentians, and the Quebec City region. One of the largest concentrations of ski resorts is in the Laurentians, less than an hour's drive from Montreal, attracting a considerable number of Ontario skiers; favorable snow conditions (average snowfall of almost 300cm/118in), renowned ski schools, night skiing and excellent slope-side accommodations. The imposing Appalachian Mountains stretch across the Eastern Townships region and have long been favored by Americans and Quebecers for their cross-country trails and alpine ski slopes. Snowmaking equipment guarantees good skiing conditions all winter, although average snowfall is well above 350cm/138in. Four main resorts, located 60 minutes from Quebec City, provide slopes certified by the International Ski Federation. Snowfall averages 375cm/147in. **For further information**, contact the Association des stations de ski du Québec, 7665 rue Larrey, Suite 100, Anjou (QC) H1J 2T7 ☎514-493-1810; www.quebecskisurf.com.

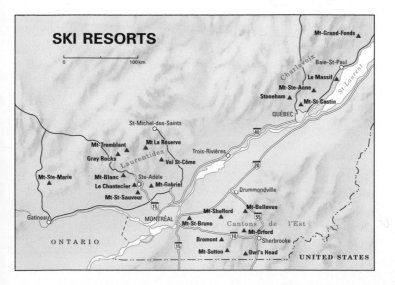

SKI RESORTS

Cross-country skiing

Quebec is renowned for cross-country skiing and offers a well-maintained network of trails totalling several thousand kilometers. Trails for every level of difficulty are patrolled and dotted with heated cabins. Lessons, guided tours and ski rentals are available in many areas. **For further information** on cross-country ski trails, maps and services offered along trails, contact the Fédération québécoise de ski: ☎514-252-3089, www.skiquebec.qc.ca.

Snowmobiling

Some 210 local clubs belong to the Fédération des clubs de moto-neigistes du Québec (☎514-252-3076, www.fcmq.qc.ca), which maintains 33,500km/20,938mi of marked trails crisscrossing the province. Heated cabins, other accommodations and repair services can be found along

Snowmobiling in Lanaudière

Vic Dennis/Tourisme Lanaudière

the Trans-Quebec trail network. It is important to follow safety rules: Exercise caution before crossing public roads, keep headlights on at all times,

	Info ☎	Vertical Drop		Total Runs	Runs			Total Lifts	Rooms
		M	ft		B	I	E		
Bromont	450-534-2200	**405**	1329	72	17	25	30	5	400
Gray Rocks	819-425-2771	**189**	620	22	4	10	8	4	240
Le Chantecler	888-916-1616	**201**	663	25	8	11	6	5	215
Le Massif	418-632-5876	**770**	2525	43	10	15	18	5	20
Mont-Bellevue	819-821-5872	**81**	266	6	3	3		3	
Mont-Blanc	819-688-2444	**300**	985	39	7	13	19	7	92
Mont-Gabriel	450-227-4671	**200**	655	18	2	8	8	6	0
Mont-Grand-Fonds	418-665-0095	**335**	1095	14	3	5	6	2	
Mont-Orford	819-843-6548	**589**	1945	56	20	14	22	8	1100
Mont-St-Bruno	450-653-3441	**134**	440	14	2	7	6	8	
Mont-St-Sauveur	450-227-4671	**213**	700	38	9	9	20	10	
Mont-Ste-Anne	418-827-4561	**625**	2050	63	15	27	21	12	1500
Mont-Ste-Marie	819-467-5200	**381**	1250	24	5	6	6	3	40
Mont-Sutton	450-538-2545	**460**	1500	53	17	15	21	9	75
Owl's Head	450-292-3342	**540**	1770	44	13	15	16	7	60
Stoneham	418-848-2411	**420**	1380	32	10	12	10	9	160
Tremblant	819-681-2000	**650**	2130	93	15	29	48	12	1200
Val St-Côme	450-883-0701	**305**	1000	21	8	8	5	4	66

Runs: B = *Beginner;* **I** = *Intermediate;* **E** = *Expert*

and travel with at least one other snowmobile.

A **registration card**, obtained by contacting the Federation, is required to operate a snowmobile. It is also advisable to acquire snowmobile liability insurance. The Federation publishes a yearly snowmobiler's guide to the Trans-Quebec trails, listing locations of service areas, repair shops, snowmobile dealers offering equipment rentals, and organized excursions. The Trans-Quebec Snowmobile Trail Network Map can be obtained by contacting Tourisme Québec or on the internet at www.fcmq.qc.ca.

SUMMER ACTIVITIES

Blessed with innumerable lakes, rivers, parks and reserves, Quebec is a marvelous place to participate in many forms of outdoor recreation during the summer months. A few are listed below.

Canoeing & Kayaking

These summer activities are enjoyed on most of the lakes and rivers across the province. You can also enjoy canoeing or kayaking in parks and rivers near cities. Canoe-camping trips are organized by several different organizations, including the Fédération québécoise du canot et du kayak: ☎514-252-3001, www.canot-kayak.qc.ca.

Cycling

Quebec is a model in terms of tourism cycling routes. Many parks include well-maintained cycling trails and offer bike rentals. Most cities have developed cycling networks. **For further information**, contact Vélo-Québec: 1251 Rue Rachel Est, Montréal (QC) H2J 2J9 ☎514-521-8356 & 1-800-567-8356, www.velo.qc.ca.

Golfing

Golfers can choose from nearly 300 golf courses in Quebec, most of them located in the Eastern Townships, Laurentians, Montérégie, Mauricie–Bois-Francs and Outaouais regions. Some are private clubs, while others allow visitors. Amenities include equipment rentals and use of club facilities. Advance reservation is recommended. For a listing, contact Golf Québec: 415 Bourke, Suite 110, Dorval (QC) H9S 3W9 ☎514-633-1088, www.golfquebec.org. Publications by the regional tourist offices give detailed information on location of courses, travel directions, facilities offered, availability to non-members, and rates.

Hiking

Nature lovers can escape the hustle and bustle of the city by hiking on well-marked trails over mountains, through dense forests or along windy seashores. The adventurous hiker may prefer off-the-beaten-path trails

Hiking in Parc des Grands-Jardins

Tourisme Charlevoix/ J.-F.Bergeron/ Enviro Foto

through undisturbed wilderness.
For further information, contact the Fédération québécoise de la marche: ☎514-252-3157 & 1-866-252-2065, www.fqmarche.qc.ca. To obtain topographic maps, contact Natural Ressources Canada in Ottawa, Ontario: ☎613-995-0947, http://maps.nrcan.gc.ca.

Horseback riding

Many reputable stables can be found in the Eastern Townships, **Gaspésie** and **Bas-Saint-Laurent** regions. Farms specializing in ranch vacations often offer accommodations and riding lessons. Horseback riding is also available in most Canada and Quebec national parks. **For further information**, contact Québec à cheval (in Blainville, north of Montreal): ☎450-434-1433, www.cheval.qc.ca.

Sailing

Enthusiasts can choose from a wealth of lakes in the Duplessis, Charlevoix, Laurentides, Manicouagan, and Montreal regions. A sail on the challenging St. Lawrence River should be on top of every serious sailor's list. **For further information**, contact the Fédération de voile du Québec ☎514-252-3097, www.voile.qc.ca.

Scuba diving

Popular diving spots include the coast of Forillon National Park (◐see entry), around Bonaventure (◐see Gaspésie) and the Magdalen Islands (◐see entry), as well as Côte-Nord (◐see entry). **For further information**, contact the Fédération des activités subaquatiques du Québec ☎514-252-3009 & 1-866-391-8835, www.fqas.qc.ca.

Rock-climbing

Many regions of Quebec offer excellent climbing. Charlevoix, Côte-Nord, Eastern Townships, Gaspésie, the Laurentians, as well as the Saguenay Fjord area have walls with drops from 30 to 300m (99 to 990ft). Rock-climbing season lasts from early May to late October. Ice climbing is also practised in these areas during the winter.

For further information, contact the Fédération québécoise de la montagne et de l'escalade ☎514-252-3004, www.fqme.qc.ca.

Windsurfing

This sport is popular on lakes, in parks and around the shores of the Gaspé Peninsula and the Magdalen Islands. The season runs from mid-June to the end of August. **For further information**, contact the Fédération de voile de Québec ☎514-252-3097, www.voile.qc.ca.

Hunting and Fishing

Southern Quebec boasts plentiful reserves of fish and game. Renowned for their salmon fishing, the rivers of the Gaspé Peninsula also teem with speckled trout and small-mouth bass. A permit is required to fish in fresh water. Daily fees for fishing vary with the season, location and type of fish. The central Quebec region abounds in moose, black bear, grouse, and white-tailed deer among other types of game, and is also well-known for its variety of fish species. Anticosti Island is a favorite with sport fishers. In northern Quebec, above the 52nd parallel, nonresidents are required to hire the services of an outfitter. Big game here includes caribou and moose. Regions known for their excellent hunting and fishing include Abitibi-Témiscamingue, Côte-Nord, Mauricie–Bois-Francs, Outaouais, Saguenay–Lac-Saint-Jean and Nunavik.

Hunting & Fishing Regulations

Hunting is prohibited in the parks; however, the wildlife reserves are open to hunters with permits, except in areas where hunting is subject to quotas. Fishing is permitted in most parks and reserves. Hunting and fishing **permits** (required for freshwater fishing) can be obtained from most local sporting goods stores and outfitters. The price varies according to season, location and type of game or fish. You are required by law to **register** your game within 48 hours after leaving the hunting area. Registration centers are generally found along major roads and in the airports of more isolated regions. Strict **safety regulations** are enforced and every hunter is asked to help fight poaching. To report violators, the Ministère des Ressources naturelles et de la Faune operates this 'poaching hot line' ☎1-800-463-2191 (Canada only). **For additional information** contact the Ministère des Ressources naturelles et Faune du Québec, 880 Chemin Sainte-Foy, RC 120-C, Québec (QC) G1X 4X4 ☎418-627-8600 & 1-866-248-6936, www.mrnfp.gouv.qc.ca.

Outfitters

Outfitters' lodges are easy to reach by land or air and offer packages for the experienced sports enthusiasts as well as the novice. There are two types of outfitters, or *pourvoiries:* some have leased territories, while others escort their expeditions to government-owned land. In addition to making all arrangements, including air transportation to remote locations, they provide accommodations and equipment needed to ensure a safe and carefree expedition. Furthermore, some outfitters offer fish and game storage, refrigeration and transport. **Registration Centers** are located along main roads and at airports in remote areas. A publication of **outfitters' lodges** is available at information kiosques or through the Fédération des pourvoyeurs du Québec, 5237 Blvd. Hamel, Québec (QC) G2E 2H2; ☎418-877-5191 & 1-800-567-9009, www.fpq.com.

Fishing at an outfitt ers, Saint-Zénon, Lanaudière

Cathy Beausoleil/Tourisme Lanaudière

Activities for Children

In this guide, numerous sights of particular interest to children, such as the Aquarium in Quebec City or the Zoo in Saint-Félicien, are indicated with the Michelin Green Guide KIDS symbol (KIDS). Most attractions offer discount fees for children and teenagers.

Quebec is an excellent place to travel with children. Hotel rooms are large and hotels often have a swimming pool. Outdoor activities that children adore, such as hiking, canoeing and fishing are cheaper and more easily accessible than practically anywhere in the world. And Quebec woods are safe. There are no killer insects or veninous plants looming in the bush. The only predator to watch for is the black bear, who is generally very afraid of humans, and for good reasons. **La TOHU** (in Montreal, ☎514 376-8648 & 1-888-376-8648, www.tohu. ca) is one of the world's largest gathering places for circus arts training, creation, production and performance. It was created in 2004 by the Quebec association of circus arts, the National Circus School and Cirque du Soleil. Children are fascinated by circus acts, a venue built for circus and the adjoining circus exhibition.
The **Canadian Children's Museum** (in Gatineau, just across from Ottawa, ☎819-776-7000 & 1-800-555-5621, www.civilization.ca) achieves the rare feat of entertaining and educating children at the highest levels possible. It is part of the Canadian Museum of Civilization, the most popular museum in Canada, so you really can't go wrong there.

Calendar of Events

Following is a selection of Quebec's popular annual events. Dates and duration of certain events may vary from year to year. **For further information**, contact the Société des fêtes et festivals du Québec: 4545 Pierre-De-Coubertin Ave., C.P. 1000, Succursale M, Montréal (PQ) H1V 3R2

☎514-252-3037 & 1-800-361-7688, www.festivals.qc.ca; the regional tourist offices; or Tourisme Québec via its website at www.bonjourquebec.com. Regional tourist offices can also suggest other cultural or sporting events.

SPRING

Mar — **Festival beauceron de l'érable** (maple sugar festival), *Saint-Georges, (Chaudière-Appalaches)*, *www.festivalbeauceron delerable.com*

mid-May —**Festival des harmonies et orchestres symphoniques du Québec** (classical music), *Sherbrooke (Eastern Townships)*, *www.festivaldesharmonies.com*

late May — **Montreal Bike Fest** (cycling race & festival), *Montreal, www.velo.qc.ca/feria*

SUMMER

mid-Jun — **Grand Prix du Canada - F1 car racing,** *Île Notre-Dame (Montreal), www.grandprix.ca*

mid-Jun — **Festival de la chanson** (Quebec song festival), *Tadoussac (Manicouagan), www.chanson tadoussac.com*

late-Jun-early-Aug — **L'International des feux Loto-Québec** (fireworks), *Île Sainte-Hélène (Montreal)*, *www.internationaldesfeuxloto quebec.com* **Just for Laughs Festival/ Festival Juste pour rire** (world's largest and most prestigious comedy festival), *Montreal, www.hahaha.com*

mid-Jun-late June — **James Bay Walleye Fishing Tournament, James Bay,** *www.festivaldudore.com*

mid-Jun–late Aug — **Festival Orford,** *Magog (Eastern Townships), www.arts-orford.org*

late June–early July — **Festival en chanson de Petite-Vallée** (singing), *Petite-Vallée (Gaspésie), www.festivalenchanson.com*

late Jun-late Aug — **Festival international du Domaine Forget** (classical music & jazz), *Saint-Irénée (Charlevoix), www.domaineforget.com*

end Jun-early Jul — **Festival International de Jazz de Montréal** *Montreal, www.montrealjazzfest.com*

early Jul — **Festirame,** *Alma (Saguenay–Lac-Saint-Jean), www.sagamie.org/alma/festivalma* **Festival d'été de Québec du Maurier** (international summer festival), *Quebec City, www.infofestival.com* **Mondial des cultures de Drummondville,** *Drummondville, (Centre-du-Québec), www.mondial descultures.com*

early July-early Aug — **Festival international de Lanaudière,** *Joliette (Lanaudière), www.lanaudiere.org*

mid-Jul —**Loto-Québec International Fireworks Competition,** *Quebec City,* over the Montmorency Falls, *www.lesgrandsfeux.com*

late Jul — **Exposition agricole,** *Saint-Hyacinthe (Montérégie), www.expo-agricole.com* **Grand Prix de Trois-Rivières** (F3 automobile racing), *Trois-Rivières (Mauricie), www.gp3r.com* **Traversée internationale du lac Saint-Jean,** *Roberval (Saguenay–Lac-Saint-Jean), www.traversee.qc.ca* **Traversée internationale du lac Memphrémagog** (international swim marathon), *Magog (Eastern Townships), www.traversee-memphremagog.com*

late Jul-early Aug — Francofolies de Montréal
(French music festival), *Montreal*, *www.francofolies.com*

early-Aug — Festival du bleuet de Dolbeau-Mistassini, *Mistassini (Saguenay–Lac-Saint-Jean)*, *www.festivaldubleuet.qc.ca*
Fêtes de la Nouvelle-France (heritage festival), *Quebec City*, *www.nouvellefrance.qc.ca*
Innu Nikamu (Amerindian music festival), *Réserve de Maliotenam (Duplessis)*, *www.innunikamu.net*

mid-Aug - Maski-Courons International (marathon), *Saint-Gabriel-de-Brandon (Lanaudière)*, *www.maskicourons.com*

mid-Aug — Concours de châteaux de sable
(sandcastle-building contest), *Havre Aubert (Magdalen Islands)*, *www.ilesdelamadeleine.com/chateaux*
Tennis Rogers Cup, a Tier 1 tournament (men's or women's, depending on the year), *Montreal, at Uniprix Stadium, www.rogerscup.com*
Festival de montgolfières de Saint-Jean-sur-Richelieu, *Saint-Jean-sur-Richelieu (Montérégie)*, *www.montgolfieres.com*

late Aug-early Sept — Festival des films du monde (international film festival), *Montreal*, *www.ffm-montreal.org*
Festival de montgolfières de Gatineau (hot air balloon festival), *Gatineau (Outaouais)*, *www.montgolfieresgatineau.com*

FALL

mid-Sept — Festival western de Saint-Tite (cowboy and Western music festival), *Saint-Tite (Mauricie)*, *www.festivalwestern.com*

early-mid-Oct — Festival de l'oie blanche (snow goose festival), *Montmagny (Chaudière-Appalaches)*, *www.festivaldeloie.qc.ca*

Tennis Challenge Bell, a Tier III women's indoor tournament, Quebec City, at Université Laval *www.challengebell.com*

WINTER

late Dec– mid-Feb — Festival des petits poissons des chenaux (tommy cod ice fishing festival), *Sainte-Anne-de-la-Pérade (Mauricie)*, *www.tourismemauricie.com*

late Jan–mid-Feb — Carnaval de Québec, *Quebec City winter carnival, www.carnaval.qc.ca*

Feb — Bal de Neige/Winterlude (winter festival), *Gatineau (Outaouais), www.winterlude.ca*

mid-Feb — Grand Prix de Valcourt (snowmobile festival), *Valcourt (Eastern Townships)*, *www.grandprixvalcourt.com*

Shopping

In Quebec, the obvious souvenir items are **Amerindian crafts**. Of course, there are no Amerindians in China, so beware 'made in China' bows and arrow sets! However, there are a lot of authentic Amerindian crafts on the Quebec market, even in touristy areas, that are worth purchasing at different price levels. The best experience is to buy Amerindian items on Amerindian reserves. This way you know exactly where the item was made, its significance, and its cultural value. This buying experience also allows for a genuine interaction with an Amerindian, something that is unfortunately rare. Do not be afraid to ask direct questions to Amerindian merchants: Amerindians are straight-talkers, they will appreciate your honesty and will in turn open themselves up to you. Buying in Indian reserves also brings about better prices. This is particularly true with **fur apparel**. A beaver hat costing $100 in an Indian reserve up North will cost double that in a Montreal department store.

Festival Western Saint-Tite, Mauricie

Mario Labonté/Tourisme Mauricie

Quebec is traditionally a land of winter, fashion, and apparel making. So it is perfectly logical that some of the best **winter clothing** in the world can be found there. The Kanuk™ brand is the benchmark of design, fabric ,and confectionery quality.

Traditional winter coats (*canadiennes*), wool scarfs, hats, and heavy bed sheets can be found at the Hudsons Bay Company flagship store in downtown Montreal. The store uses its historical stature to sell replicas of patterns apparel used by Metis "voyageurs" and frontier pioneers.

Winter sports gear is a Canadian specialty. Hockey players around Planet Ice use Quebec-made equipment. Snowshoes are also a good buy. The traditional snowshoes used for trapping fur animals make an outstanding discussion topic.

Jeans and CDs are consistently cheaper in Quebec than in Europe. The differential between the strength of the Canadian dollar and the Euro and other currencies greatly influences the relative merit of buying goods in Canada that are available elsewhere.

Maple products are always an interesting foodstuff proposition. You can buy maple syrup practically anywhere in the world but the variety of Quebec maple products is unparalleled.

In the course of the last few decades, Quebec has become a North American beacon of outstanding cheeses, meats, sweets and fine liqueurs, ice ciders, and Belgian-type beers. Some 7,000 of these crafts products and more can be found at the **Marché des Saveurs** (literally Market of Flavors) at pleasant Montreal's Marché Jean-Talon (in the north end, at the corner of Saint-Laurent and Jean-Talon Streets).

Sightseeing

The options for touring and discovering nature in Quebec are plentiful. Tourisme Québec's regional tourist guides are helpful when planning an itinerary, and there are a variety of escorted tours by bus, private car or on foot.

ORGANIZED NATURE TOURS

Organized nature tours are particularly popular. The Zoological Society of Montreal arranges a variety of field trips that involve visiting different regions throughout the Montreal area. Trips are usually one or two days.

For further information on reservations and available trips, contact the Zoological Society, 1117 Ste-Catherine Street West, Suite 525, Montréal (QC) H3B 1H9 ☎514-845-8317, http://zoologicalsocietymtl.org. Visitors may also participate in organized observation tours of harp seals and their young (whitecoats) on the giant ice floes in the Gulf of St. Lawrence. All-inclusive six-day excursions are led by expert guides. It is advisable to make reservations 6–9 months in advance due to limited group size (*late Feb–mid-Mar; from $4,695 US dollars, includes accommodations, meals & transportation; Natural Habitat Adventures, 2945 Center Green Court, Boulder, CO 80301, USA ☎303-449-3711 or 1-800-543-8917; www.nathab.com*).

ADVENTURE TRAVEL

Experienced sports enthusiasts can choose from a variety of excursions, including ski-mountaineering, dogsledding expeditions, snowmobile trekking, or ice- and rock-climbing, canoeing and kayaking. These expeditions into the hinterland of Quebec require careful planning; it is advisable to employ the services of experienced guides. **For further information** on adventure travel, contact **Passe Montagne** (ice- and rock-climbing only): 1760 Montée 2e rang, Val-David (QC) J0T 2N0 ☎819-322-2123 & 1-800-465-2123, www.passemontagne.com; **Randonnée Aventure**, Box 1102, Snowdon Stn, Montréal (QC) H3X 3Y2 ☎514-489-0339, www.randonnee.ca.

NATIONAL PARKS OF CANADA

Parks Canada, the Canadian parks service, operates three national parks in Quebec. **For further information**, trail maps and brochures, contact Parks Canada National Office, 25 Rue Eddy, Gatineau (QC) K1A 0M5; ☎*514-335-4813* (*international inquiries*) or *1-888-773-8888* (*enquiries from US & Canada*); *www.pc.gc.ca*.
All parks offer interpretation programs, some of which include guided hikes, slide and video presentations, exhibits and seasonal lecture programs, to help visitors understand the natural environments. Visitors are asked to respect wildlife and park rules. Most parks have camping facilities operated on a first-come-first-served basis. Camping facilities fill quickly during the summer; **for reservations** to any National Park of

Canada in Quebec, call ☎1-877-737-3783. The entrance fee varies from park to park, as do the fees charged for camping, fishing, or other activities. Contact the appropriate park service for opening season dates.

🔹 **Forillon National Park**
☎418-368-5505. Activities: hiking, backpacking, nature programs, biking trails, camping, swimming, sailing, scuba diving, boat tours, fishing, cross-country skiing.

🔹 **Mauricie National Park**
☎819-538-3232. Activities: hiking, backpacking, camping, canoeing, sailing, scuba diving, swimming, fishing, cross-country skiing.

🔹 **Mingan Archipelago**
1340 Rue de la Digue, Havre-Saint-Pierre (QC) G0G 1P0. ☎418-538-3285 (in season), ☎418-538-3331 (off-season). Activities: hiking, backpacking, camping, sailing, boat tours.

National Parks of Quebec and Nature Reserves

In the national parks operated by **Parcs Québec**, visitors can enjoy wildlife and forestry reserves year round. Hiking, climbing, cycling, canoeing, fishing and hunting, cross-country or alpine skiing, and snowmobiling are just some of the activities awaiting the outdoor enthusiast. A comprehensive guide (free) entitled *Découvrez votre vraie nature* covers the entire list of parks and their activities as well as detailed maps of park areas. 🔹Please note that some of these parks are closed off-season. Parcs Québec also operates **nature reserves**.
For further information on these parks, contact **SÉPAQ** (Société des établissements de plein air du Québec): Place de la Cité, Tour Cominar, 2640 Boulevard Laurier, Suite 250 (2nd floor), Quebec City (QC) G1V 5C2, ☎418-890-6527 or 1-800-665-6527, www.parcsquebec.com.

🔹 **Aiguebelle**
(*Abitibi-Témiscamingue*)

Mont-Brun Visitor Center
☎819-637-7322.

🐾 **Anticosti** (*Duplessis*)
Information Center:
☎418-535-0156.

🐾 **Bic** (*Bas-Saint-Laurent*)
Interpretation Center:
☎418-736-5035.

🐾 **Frontenac** (*Eastern Townships*)
Interpretation Center:
☎418-486-2300.

🐾 **Gaspésie** (*Gaspésie*)
Interpretation Center:
☎418-763-7494.

🐾 **Grands-Jardins** (*Charlevoix*)
Interpretation Center Château-
Beaumont: ☎418-439-1227.

🐾 **Hautes-Gorges-de-la-Rivière-
Malbaie** (*Charlevoix*)
Interpretation Center:
☎418-439-1227.

🐾 **Île-Bonaventure-et-
Rocher-Percé** (*Gaspésie*)
Interpretation Center:
418-782-2240.

🐾 **Îles-de-Boucherville**
(*Montérégie*)
Reception Center:
☎450-928-5088.

🐾 **Jacques-Cartier** (*Quebec*)
Reception Center: ☎418-848-3169
(summer); 418-528-8787 (winter).

🐾 **Miguasha** (*Gaspésie*)
Reception Center ☎418-794-2475.

🐾 **Mont-Mégantic**
(*Eastern Townships*)
Reception Center ☎819-888-2941.

🐾 **Mont-Orford** (*Eastern Townships*)
Reception Center ☎819-843-9855.

🐾 **Mont-Saint-Bruno** (*Montérégie*)
Reception Center:
☎450-653-7544.

🐾 **Mont-Tremblant** (*Laurentians*)
Reception Center: ☎819-688-
2281.

🐾 **Monts-Valin**
(*Saguenay–Lac-Saint-Jean*)
Information ☎418-674-1200.

🐾 **Oka** (*Laurentians*)
Reception Center ☎450-479-8365.

Camping in Parc national de la Jacques-Cartier, Quebec

Plaisance (*Laurentians*)
Reception Center ☎819-427-5334.

Pointe-Taillon (Saguenay–Lac-Saint-Jean) – Interpretation Center ☎418-347-5371.

Saguenay (*Saguenay–Lac-Saint-Jean*) Interpretation and Observation Centers☎418-237-4383; Parc Marin du Saguenay--Saint-Laurent ☎418-272-1556.

Yamaska (*Eastern Townships*) Reception Center ☎450-776-7182.

Entertainment

MUSIC

There are 13 professional symphony orchestras in the province of Quebec. Montreal alone boasts a few, the most renowned being the Montreal Symphony Orchestra (**Orchestre Symphonique de Montréal** ☎514-842-9951), under the direction of Kent Nagano, and l'**Orchestre métropolitain du Grand Montréal** (☎514-598-0870), under the direction of Yannick Nézet-Séguin. Canada's oldest symphony orchestra, l'**Orchestre Symphonique de Québec** (☎418-643-8486) plays under the direction of Yoav Talmi. Also in Québec City, Bernard Labadie conducts chamber orchestra **Les Violons du Roy** (☎418-692-3026). In Montreal, chamber orchestra **I Musici** (☎514-982-6038) is conducted by Yuli Turovsky.

The other professional symphony orchestras of the province of Québec are situated in Laval, Trois-Rivières, Shebrooke, Drummondville, Saguenay, Longueuil, and Rimouski. Also, classical music lovers traveling to Quebec in the summer can enjoy numerous festivals featuring symphony orchestras from around the world, the most important being **Le Festival de Lanaudière** (☎450-759-4343 & 1-800-561-4343), **Le Domaine Forget** (☎418-452-3535 & 1-888-336-7438), and **Le Festival Orford** (☎819-843-3981 & 1-800-567-6155). The prestigious **Place des Arts** (tickets ☎514-842-2112 & 1-866-842-2112) performing arts complex comprises five multi-purpose concert halls where the Montreal Opera Company (**Opéra de Montréal** ☎514-985-2258) and McGill University's **McGill Chamber Orchestra** (☎514-487-5190) perform. On the McGill University campus, the **Pollack Concert Hall** (☎514-398-4547) hosts classical, jazz and chamber music. The immensely popular **International Jazz Festival** (☎514-523-3378 or www.montrealjazzfest.com) held in June has become Montreal's flagship festival and musical event since its inception in 1977. The 21,270-seat **Bell Center** (☎514-932-2582) offers a variety of top performances throughout the year, including pop and rock concerts.

DANCE

Montreal's **Les Grands Ballets Canadiens** (☎514-849-8681), famous for its classical repertoire, performs nationally and abroad. Les Grands Ballets is one of the top three classical dance companies in Canada, along with The National Ballet of Canada (Toronto), and the Royal Winnipeg Ballet.

Montreal is the capital of modern dance in Canada, with a number of prestigious, innovative dance troupes such as **O Vertigo** (☎514-251-9177) and **La La La Human Steps** (☎514-277-9090) leading the way.

Quebec dance luminaries from the present and recent past include Ginette Laurin, Édouard Lock, Louise Lecavalier, Gilles Maheu, Paul-André Fortier, and Marie Chouinard.

THEATER

Internationally-renowned playwright/actor/director, Robert Lepage, was raised in a bilingual household in Quebec City. His dark, daring body of work is paradoxically appealing to people who generally dislike theater.

In 2004, the Conseil des Arts et des Lettres de Quebec (Quebec's arts and literature council) officially recognized the top seven theater companies in Quebec. The list includes Théâtre du Nouveau Monde, Théâtre d'Aujourd'hui, Théâtre du Rideau Vert, Théâtre Espace Go and Théâtre de la Manufacture, all French-language theaters from Montreal, as well as Quebec City's Théâtre du Trident. The only English-language theater in the elite group is Montreal's **Centaur Theater Company** (☎514-288-3161).

The Centaur Company bills itself as 'the voice of English-speaking Montreal.' Many of its plays are Montreal-based, and written by Montreal playwrights. Respected Québécois playwrights, such as Michel Tremblay, are translated into English and their plays are showcased at the Centaur.

Summer theaters are popular and can be enjoyed throughout the province. Repertory theaters and dinner theaters perform in both French and English. **For schedules**, see the arts and entertainment supplements in local newspapers (weekend editions) or free brochures distributed at hotels.

Books

SUGGESTED READING

20C LITERATURE

Home Truths, Selected Canadian Stories by Mavis Gallant (*Stoddart, 1956*)
The Watch that Ends the Night by Hugh MacLennan (*General Paperbacks, 1958*)
The Apprenticeship of Duddy Kravitz by Mordecai Richler (*McClelland & Stewart, 1959*)
The Favorite Game by Leonard Cohen (*McClelland & Stewart, 1963*)
Beautiful Losers by Leonard Cohen (*McClelland & Stewart, 1966*)
St. Urbain's Horseman by Mordecai Richler (*McClelland & Stewart, 1966*)

A North American Education by Clark Blaise (*General Paperbacks, 1973*)
Joshua Then and Now by Mordecai Richler (*McClelland & Stewart, 1980*)
Voices in Time by Hugh MacLennan (*Stoddart, 1980*)
Montréal mon amour, Short stories from Montreal ed. Michael Benazon (*Penguin, 1989*)
Solomon Gursky was Here by Mordecai Richler (*Penguin, 1989*)
Across the Bridge by Mavis Gallant (*McClelland & Stewart, 1993*)
Evil Eye by Ann Diamond (*Véhicule Press, 1994*)
Sonia and Jack by David Homel (*Harper Collins, 1995*)
The Tragedy Queen by Linda Leith (*NuAge Editions, 1995*)
True Copies by Monique LaRue (*NuAge Editions, 1996*)
Two Solitudes by Hugh MacLennan (*Fitzhenry & Whiteside Ltd., 1996*)
Myths, Memory and Lies by Esther Delisle (*Studio 9 Books, 1998*)
7 Waves: Quebec Women Writers by Clare Braux (*Morgaine House, 1999*)
Life of Pi by Yann Martel (*Knopf Canada, 2002*)

QUEBEC AUTHORS IN TRANSLATION

Maria Chapdelaine by Louis Hémon (*1916/Tundra Books, 2004*)
The Town Below by Roger Lemelin (*McClelland & Stewart, 1944*)
The Outlander by Germaine Guèvremont (*McClelland & Stewart, 1945*)
The Tin Flute by Gabrielle Roy (*McClelland & Stewart, 1945*)
The Madman, the Kite and the Island by Félix Leclerc (*Oberon Press, 1958*)
A Season in the Life of Emmanuel by Marie-Claire Blais (*McClelland & Stewart, 1965*)
Kamouraska by Anne Hébert (*General Paperbacks, 1970*)
The Alley Cat by Yves Beauchemin (*McClelland & Stewart, 1981*)
The Beothuk Saga by Bernard Assiniwi (*McClelland & Stewart, 2000*)

Thunder and Light by Marie-Claire Blais (*House Of Anansi, 2004*)

HISTORY AND ARCHITECTURE

Children of Aataentsic by Bruce Trigger (*McGill-Queen's University Press, 1976*)

Canada-Québec Synthèse Historique by Jacques Lacoursière and Denis Vaugeois (*Éditions du Renouveau Pédagogique, 1978*)

Inuit Stories by Nungak and Arima (*University of Toronto Press, 1988*)

Montreal Architecture, A Guide to Styles and Buildings by Francois Rémillard and Brian Merrett (*Méridian Press, 1990*)

Sauver Montréal, *Chroniques d'architecture et d'urbanisme, by Jean-Claude Marsan (1990),*

The Living Past of Montreal by R.O. Wilson and Eric McLean (*McGill-Queen's University Press, 1993*)

A Short History of Quebec, 2nd ed. by John A. Dickinson and Brian Young (*Copp Clark Pitman Ltd., 1993*)

Loin du Soleil: Architectural Practice in Quebec City during the French Regime by Marc Grignon (*Peter Lang, 1995*)

Making History in Twentieth-Century Quebec by Ronald Rudin (*University of Toronto Press, 1997*)

Canada and Quebec: One Country, Two Histories by Robert Bothwell (*University of British Columbia Press, 1998*)

Sacré Blues: An Unsentimental Journey Through Quebec by Taras Grescoe (*McFarlane Walter & Ross, 2000*)

PHOTOGRAPHIC ESSAYS

Wide Landscapes of Quebec (*Libre Expression, 1991*)

Montréal: a Scent of the Islands by François Poche (*Stanké, 1994*

Les croix de chemin au temps du Bon Dieu by Vanessa-Oliver Lloyd (*Éditions du Passage, 2007*)

Films

SELECTED FILMS

Titles listed below represent Quebec filmmaking highlights from 1970 through the present.

The Act of the Heart (1970) Paul Almond

The Apprenticeship of Duddy Kravitz (1974) Ted Kotcheff

Lies My Father Told Me (1975) Jan Kadar

The Street (1976) Caroline Leaf

Joshua Then and Now (1985) Ted Kotcheff

The Decline of the American Empire (1986) Denys Arcand

The Man Who Planted Trees (1988) Frédéric Back

Night Zoo (1987) Jean-Claude Lauzon

Train of Dreams (1987) John N. Smith

Jesus of Montréal (1989) Denys Arcand

Bethune, the Making of a Hero (1990) Phillip Borsos

The Company of Strangers (1990) Cynthia Scott

An Imaginary Tale (1990) André Fournier

Léolo (1992) Jean-Claude Lauzon

Love and Human Remains (1993) Denys Arcand

The Confessional (1995) Robert Lepage

Thirty-two short films about Glenn Gould (1995) François Girard

The Boys (1997) Louis Saia

The Red Violin (1998), François Girard

Un crabe dans la tête (2001) André Turpin

15 février 1839 (2001) Pierre Falardeau

The Far Side of the Moon (2003) Robert Lepage

Les invasions barbares (2003) Denys Arcand

Seducing Doctor Lewis (2003) Jean-François Pouliot

C.R.A.Z.Y. (2005) Jean-Marc Vallée

Congorama (2006) Pierre Falardeau.

L'âge des ténèbres (2007) Denis Arcand

Borderline (2008) Lyne Charlebois

BASIC INFORMATION

Business Hours

Regular business hours are Monday to Friday 9am–5pm. Retail stores are usually open Monday to Friday 9am–6pm (until 9pm Thursday and Friday). Saturday hours are 10am–5pm. In the larger towns, stores are open Sundays noon–5pm.

Communications

Quebec Province is divided into four telephone area codes: 514 (Montreal), 450 (Laval, North & South Shores, Laurentians, Richelieu Valley), 418 (Quebec City, Gaspé Peninsula and Eastern Quebec), 819 (Eastern Townships, Gatineau and northern Quebec). All numbers beginning with 1-800, 1-888 and 1-877 are toll-free. To call long distance within Canada and to the US, dial 1 + Area Code followed by the 7-digit number. For overseas calls, dial 011 + country code, or dial 0 for operator assistance, available in both English and French. Directory assistance can be reached by dialing 411; for numbers outside the local area dial 1 + Area Code + 555-1212. A local call at a public phone booth costs 50 cents. Credit card calls and collect calls can be made from public pay phones. You can also purchase calling cards, virtually anywhere, which allow you to call from telephone booths without using coins or a credit card.

Electricity

110 volts, 60 cycles. Electrical appliances from the United States can be used in Quebec. European appliances require plug adapters and current transformers. However, things can get a bit technical and complicated if you try to use appliances designed for 220 volts with 110 volts; electrical appliances may work poorly and electronic appliances may not work and could even be damaged.
It is probably best to stick to battery chargers and appliances that are designed to operate at 110 volts or at both 110 and 220 volts.

911 Emergencies

Anywhere in Quebec and in the rest of Canada, call 911 to report life-threatening emergency situations requiring the intervention of ambulance/paramedics, a fire department and/or the police. If dialing 911 does not allow you to reach emergency services, just dial "0" and press "0" again to ask an operator to connect you to the proper emergency number.

Languages

The official language of the province of Quebec is French, spoken by 80% of the population. The second language is English. Visitors can expect Quebecers in urban areas and in Southern Quebec to be bilingual. In much of the rest of the province, however, don't expect everyone to understand basic English. With some exceptions near borders and in the Montreal area, all road signs are in French. Tourist information is generally available in both languages. In Nunavik a majority of the Inuit speak Inuktitut, but English and French have become important in schools and public life there.

Liquor Laws

The minimum drinking age in Quebec is 18 (lower than in many Canadian provinces and parts of the US). The provincial government regulates the sale of wine and liquor sold in *"Société des Alcools du Québec"* or S.A.Q. stores. In Montreal and Quebec City, specially selected wine and liquor are also sold at Maisons des Vins. Stores are open during regular store hours, including on Sundays. Mainstream beers and lesser quality wines are also sold in grocery stores. When driving, the legal blood alcohol limit is 0.08%. Drinking alcohol or walking around with an open bottle of alcoholic beverage is prohibited everywhere except on a private property (including camping sites), or on a licensed site, restaurant or bar.

Mail/Post

Post offices are open Monday to Friday 9am–5.30pm. Some sample rates for first-class mail (letter or postcard):
- ⊠ within Canada, 52 cents (up to 30 grams);
- ⊠ to the US, 96 cents (up to 30 grams);
- ⊠ international mail, $1.60 (up to 30 grams).

Mail service for all but regional deliveries is by air. Postal facilities are located at regular post offices and other retailers (generally pharmacies and convenience stores) throughout the province. **For further information** regarding postal codes or locations of facilities call ☎1-866-607-6301 (within Canada) or 416-979-8822 (outside Canada); www.canada post.ca.

When writing to Quebec, use the following format:
Company or Name
Street Address
City (QC)
Postal Code
CANADA

Media

In large cities, international newspapers are generally available at airports, major hotels, and newsstands. The English-language paper, *The Gazette,* published daily in Montreal, is available in other towns throughout Quebec, as is the *Chronicle-Telegraph* published each Wednesday in Quebec City.

The Canadian Broadcasting Corporation (CBC) broadcasts in English and French throughout the Quebec territory, on the radio and on television.

Metric System

In 1980, Canada adopted the metric system. All distances and speed limits are posted in kilometers, (multiply by 5/8 or 0.625 to obtain the equivalent in miles). Gasoline is sold in liters. However, proximity to the United States, which still uses the Imperial measure system, brought about a form of 'measurement bilingualism' in the Quebec population. Quebecers know their height and weight in feet, inches and pounds better than in meters, centimeters and kilograms. They still buy pounds of meat at the grocery store, and they measure their apartments in square feet.

- ♦ **1 kilometer (km)** = 0.6 mile
- ♦ **1 metre (m)** = 3.3 feet
- ♦ **1 kilogram (kg)** = 1,000 grams (g) = 2.2 lbs
- ♦ **1 liter (l) = 33.8 fl.oz.** = 1 quart = 0.26 gallons
- ♦ **Celsius to Fahrenheit:** *multiply °C by 9, divide by 5, and add 32 = °F*

Money

The basic unit of currency is the Canadian dollar: one dollar = 100 cents. Bills (notes) are issued in denominations of $5, $10, $20, $50, and $100. Coins are minted in denominations of 1 cent (**un sou** in French), 5 cents, 10 cents, 25 cents, $1, and $2. Major credit cards (mainly Visa®, MasterCard® and American Express®) are widely accepted. Traveller's checks (mainly American Express®) are still generally accepted but are becoming a rarity. Visitors may also use their credit cards or bank cards 24hrs/day to withdraw cash from automatic teller machines (ATMs, *guichets automatiques*). If necessary, it is also possible to receive cash sent to Canada through Western Union®. The Canadian dollar fluctuates with the international money market.

Exchange facilities tend to be limited in rural or remote areas. It is generally recommended to exchange money in an area where exchange offices compete for customers, in order to receive the most favorable exchange rate.

BANKS

Banks are generally open Monday to Friday 10am–4pm; hours may vary in certain locations. Banks and foreign exchange counters at international airports have extended hours. Banks with ATMs, affiliated with American or European banking institutions, will allow withdrawal of Canadian funds. Some banks charge a fee for cashing traveller's checks.

In Canada, as in the US, **tax** is not usually included in the purchase price, but is added at the time of payment. In addition to the national tax (Goods and Services Tax, or GST) of 5%, there is a 7.5% provincial sales tax (taxe de vente du Québec, or TVQ) in Quebec.

Public Holidays

Most banks, government offices and schools are closed on the following legal holidays shown in the chart.

Reduced Rates

Reductions are omnipresent. Students (with ID, the ISIC card is best), children and youths (under 25), and seniors (over 60 or 65) get significant discounts. Sometimes couples get concessions for train tickets for example. Always look and ask for reductions.

Discount-coupons booklets are also distributed massively.

Smoking

Quebec used to be facetiously called "Canada's smoking zone." Not anymore:

New Year's Day	January 1
Good Friday	Friday before Easter Sunday
Easter Monday	Day following Easter Sunday
Fête de Dollard	3rd Monday in May
Québec National Holiday	June 24
Canada Day	July 1
Labor Day	1st Monday in September
Thanksgiving Day	2nd Monday in October
Christmas Day	December 25
Boxing Day	December 26

Smoking is most positively prohibited in every indoor venue (including bars), and there are no designated smoking rooms (in airports, etc.). If no police officer tells you to put out your cigarette, people around you will.

Smoking is even prohibited outdoors, near the entrance of public buildings, and in bus shelters.

Time Zones

Quebec is located in the Eastern Standard Time (EST) zone (like Toronto and New York City), with the exception of the Magdalen Islands, which are in the Atlantic Time zone (one hour ahead of the rest of Quebec). Daylight Savings Time (time advances one hour) is observed in Quebec (as in the United States) from the second Sunday in March to the first Sunday in November.

Tipping

Tips are not included in restaurant bills. It is customary to leave between 10–15% of the total as a tip for good service. Taxi drivers, bellboys and hairdressers are usually tipped at the customer's discretion, although the 10–15% rule seems to apply as well. There is no tipping in cinemas and theaters.

CONVERSION TABLES

Weights and Measures

🇪🇺	🇺🇸	🇬🇧	
1 kilogram (kg) 6.35 kilograms 0.45 kilograms	**2.2 pounds (lb)** 14 pounds 16 ounces (oz)	**2.2 pounds** 1 stone (st) 16 ounces	*To convert kilograms to pounds, multiply by 2.2*
1 metric ton (tn)	**1.1 tons**	**1.1 tons**	
1 litre (l) 3.79 litres 4.55 litres	**2.11 pints (pt)** 1 gallon (gal) 1.20 gallon	**1.76 pints** 0.83 gallon 1 gallon	*To convert litres to gallons, multiply by 0.26 (US) or 0.22 (UK)*
1 hectare (ha) **1 sq. kilometre (km²)**	**2.47 acres** 0.38 sq. miles (sq.mi.)	**2.47 acres** 0.38 sq. miles	*To convert hectares to acres, multiply by 2.4*
1 centimetre (cm) **1 metre (m)**	**0.39 inches (in)** 3.28 feet (ft) or 39.37 inches or 1.09 yards (yd)	**0.39 inches**	*To convert metres to feet, multiply by 3.28; for kilometres to miles, multiply by 0.6*
1 kilometre (km)	**0.62 miles (mi)**	**0.62 miles**	

Clothing

Women	🇪🇺	🇺🇸	🇬🇧
	35	4	2½
	36	5	3½
	37	6	4½
Shoes	38	7	5½
	39	8	6½
	40	9	7½
	41	10	8½
	36	6	8
	38	8	10
Dresses	40	10	12
& suits	42	12	14
	44	14	16
	46	16	18
	36	06	30
	38	08	32
Blouses &	40	10	34
sweaters	42	12	36
	44	14	38
	46	16	40

Men	🇪🇺	🇺🇸	🇬🇧
	40	7½	7
	41	8½	8
	42	9½	9
Shoes	43	10½	10
	44	11½	11
	45	12½	12
	46	13½	13
	46	36	36
	48	38	38
Suits	50	40	40
	52	42	42
	54	44	44
	56	46	48
	37	14½	14½
	38	15	15
Shirts	39	15½	15½
	40	15¾	15¾
	41	16	16
	42	16½	16½

Sizes often vary depending on the designer. These equivalents are given for guidance only.

Speed

KPH	10	30	50	70	80	90	100	110	120	130
MPH	6	19	31	43	50	56	62	68	75	81

Temperature

Celsius (°C)	0°	5°	10°	15°	20°	25°	30°	40°	60°	80°	100°
Fahrenheit (°F)	32°	41°	50°	59°	68°	77°	86°	104°	140°	176°	212°

To convert Celsius into Fahrenheit, multiply °C by 9, divide by 5, and add 32.
To convert Fahrenheit into Celsius, subtract 32 from °F, multiply by 5, and divide by 9.
NB: Conversion factors on this page are approximate.

Dogsledding at Hôtel Sacacomie,
St-Alexis-des-Monts, Mauricie
©Michel Julien/ATR Mauricie

NATURE

Quebec ranks as Canada's largest province, occupying roughly 15 percent of the country's landmass. With a total area of 1,542,056sq km/595,391sq mi, Quebec is slightly larger than Alaska and nearly three times the size of France. At its largest dimensions, Quebec's territory spans nearly 1,500km/930mi from east to west and 2,000km/1,240mi from north to south.

Regional Landscapes

This immense province boasts a striking range of landscapes and climates, from the often-steep shores of the mighty St. Lawrence River to the cultivated terraces of the Appalachian valleys to the wide-open spaces of the northern tundra.

THE CANADIAN SHIELD

The granitic and gneissic rocks of this immense craton, which covers over 80 percent of Quebec's territory, are the roots of ancestral mountain ranges that were repeatedly uplifted and eroded over billions of years. During the Paleozoic era, much of the ancient Shield surface was covered by shallow seas and buried under thick marine sediments. Today this expanse is generally flat and monotonous, rising no higher than 600m/1,968ft above sea level. The landforms of the Shield consist of extensive plateaus interrupted by a few mountain massifs. Only near the rim of the Shield is the land deeply incised by rivers flowing towards the surrounding lowlands. Within the Canadian Shield, the following subregions are commonly identified.

The Northern Plateaux

Known for its many lakes, this was the only area in Quebec still glaciated during the final stages of the last ice age, approximately 6,000 years ago. The Otish Mountain massif and its summits of over 1,000m/3,280ft dominate the plateau's southern half. Located to the southeast of the Otish Mountains, the Manicouagan Reservoir now fills the impact crater of a meteor. Westerly winds from Hudson Bay deposit over 1m/39cm of precipitation per year, nearly half of it as snow—a remarkable total for this high latitude. Separating Ungava Bay from the Labrador Sea, the imposing Torngat Mountains rise to Mt. Iberville (1,622m/5,320ft), the highest summit in Quebec.

Fjord du Saguenay

©Sépaq/ Jean-Pierre Huard

Abitibi-Témiscamingue

This area of the Shield lies along the border with Ontario between the Ottawa River and the Eastmain Plain, south of James Bay. To the south, the recurving upper Ottawa River frames the region of Témiscamingue, noted for its dairy farms nestled among spruce-covered hills.

The Laurentians

When viewed from a sufficiently high vantage point, the sea of well-rounded crests is remarkably even in elevation (600m/1,968ft–800m/2,624ft).

On the other side of the Saguenay fjord lies the sparsely inhabited expanse of Côte-Nord, the north shore of the Gulf of St. Lawrence. Stretching over 1,000km/620mi of wind-buffeted coast, a spruce-covered coastal plain lies in front of the Laurentian scarp into which tumultuous rivers have cut narrow, rock-strewn valleys.

Saguenay–Lac-Saint-Jean

The Saguenay–Lac-Saint-Jean region owes much of its economic dynamism to an oasis-like situation within the Shield. The basin has an extensive cover of fertile soils, a notably warm, if brief, summer as compared with the coastal areas farther south, and almost ubiquitous industrial power potential stored in the region's numerous rivers. From depths of 275m/902ft, the sheer rock faces of Cape Éternité and Cape Trinité form canyon-like walls, soaring many feet above the water surface.

THE ST. LAWRENCE LOWLANDS

Shaped like a triangle with its apex near Quebec City, the lowlands are lodged between the Canadian Shield to the north, and the Appalachian Mountains to the southeast. The lowlands rise gradually to the northeast so that the area around Quebec City has a higher elevation (100m/328ft above sea level) than the Montreal plain, which rarely surpasses the 70m/230ft mark.

Between Montreal and the first Appalachian ridges to the east, a string of isolated, massive outcrops known as the **Monteregian Hills** looms above an otherwise uniformly flat landscape.

Graced with fertile soils and a moderate climate, the lowlands have traditionally supported a variety of agricultural activities.

THE APPALACHIAN MOUNTAINS

Separated from the St. Lawrence lowlands by **Logan's Line**, the Appalachian Mountains cross into Quebec from Vermont and New Hampshire and run to the northeast along the boundary with the US and the province of New Brunswick.

Broadleaf forests cover the higher elevations and ridges, while mixed agriculture occupies the larger valleys. Towards the northeast and the Gaspé Peninsula, agricultural land use becomes increasingly marginal and forests of coniferous trees predominate.

Eastern Townships and Beauce

These two regions are the most populated areas in Appalachian Quebec. The Eastern Townships occupy the southwestern portion of the Appalachian region between the US border and the Chaudière River basin. The Beauce region is centered on the upper Chaudière River. While fruit orchards and even vineyards can be found among the pastures and dairy farms along the western margin of this region, forests of sugar maple predominate in the Beauce area.

The similarity in landscape between the Eastern Townships and northern New England is unmistakable. Vermont's Green Mountains continue north of the border as the Sutton Mountains which, in turn, are followed by a ridge of low hills in the upper Bécancour basin near Thetford Mines.

The Lower St. Lawrence and the Gaspé Peninsula

To the northeast of the Chaudière River, the Green Mountains-Sutton Mountains belt is known as the Notre-Dame Mountains, whose northern slopes descend to a narrow coastal plain along the lower St. Lawrence River. Shielded by the Chic-Chocs from arctic north winds, this area, once called "Quebec's Medi-

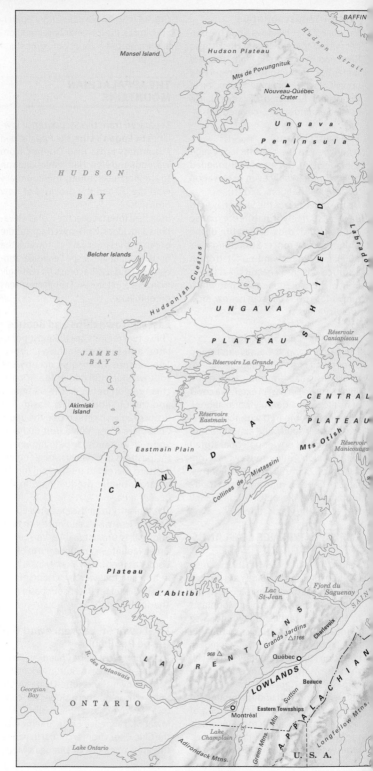

Regional Landscapes

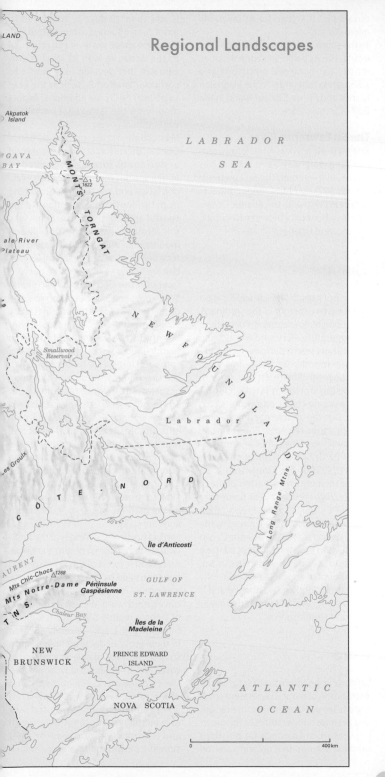

LAND

Akpatok
Island

UNGAVA
BAY

LABRADOR

SEA

MONTS TORNGAT

△ 1622

ale River
Plateau

Smallwood
Reservoir

N E W F O U N D L A N D

Labrador

es Groulx

C Ô T E - N O R D

Long Range Mtns.

Île d'Anticosti

LAURENT

Mts Chic-Chocs △ 1268
Mts Notre-Dame Péninsule
Gaspésienne

GULF OF

TN S.

Chaleur Bay

ST. LAWRENCE

Îles de la
Madeleine

NEW
BRUNSWICK

PRINCE EDWARD
ISLAND

ATLANTIC

OCEAN

NOVA SCOTIA

0   400 km

terranean," is known for its favorable microclimate.

To the south and east of the Gaspé Peninsula, the Appalachian zone includes mostly flat-lying red sandstone and schist strata that underlie the Magdalen Islands and Prince Edward Island in the Gulf of St. Lawrence.

The St. Lawrence River

Known in Mohawk as *Kaniatarowanenneh* ("big waterway") and in French as *fleuve Saint-Laurent*, the St. Lawrence River (1,197km/744mi long) connects the Great Lakes with the Atlantic Ocean. It forms a boundary between New York, Ontario, and Quebec.

Climate

Because of its high latitude and location at the eastern margin of the continent, Quebec undergoes extreme fluctuations in temperature. Very cold winters and surprisingly warm periods during the summer months are the hallmarks of a continental climate. Of course, with increasing northern latitude, summers become cooler and winters turn frigid, but the sizable gap in seasonal temperatures remains. For example, Montreal's average summer temperature is 22°C/72°F, and the winter averages -9°C/16°F. For Kuujjuarapik, an Inuit settlement on the eastern shore of Hudson Bay, the equivalent figures are 11°C/52°F and -23°C/-9°F. Precipitation is abundant and locally reinforced by the nearby open seas of the Atlantic Ocean and Hudson Bay. Annual totals average between 35cm/13in and 110cm/43in. The amount of annual rainfall generally decreases inland and northward and is fairly evenly divided between summer rains and winter snows.

Flora

Latitude is an important factor in the distribution of natural vegetation cover since it largely determines the length and average temperatures of the growing season. In Quebec's far northern reaches, the nominal growing season is less than 40 days as compared to more than 180 days around Montreal. Elevation above sea level and proximity to the ocean as well as local microclimates that develop in response to particular landforms, such as the Lake Saint-Jean basin, are additional factors modifying the latitudinal pattern of vegetational cover.

Most common in the southern portion of Quebec, the mainly broadleaf hardwood or **deciduous forest** is dominated by maple species mixed with beech, hickory, basswood, ash and oak. Stretching from the southern Laurentians to the coastal areas of the Gaspé Peninsula, this forest persists in mostly hilly and mountainous areas. With increasing latitude and altitude it gradually mixes with balsam fir and yellow or white birch.

Covering the Côte-Nord, Abitibi and Saguenay–Lac-Saint-Jean regions, the dense **boreal forest** is dominated by straight-trunked, coniferous (conebearing) trees. Extending broadly in homogeneous stands, these needle-leaf softwood forests are better adapted to the shorter growing season. Common associations include fir stands with white birch or black spruce, lichenspruce woodlands as well as Jack pine and birch-aspen stands. The boreal forest constitutes the largest reserve of wood fibre in Quebec. An ongoing reforestation program, launched by the government of Quebec in the 1980s, aims to protect this valuable resource by the planting of several million saplings annually.

Farther north at the fringes of the highlatitude boreal forest begins the **taiga**. An extensive forest of softwood species, it is controlled by the subarctic climate and grows increasingly sparse as one travels northward. Well-spaced clusters of trees—mainly black spruce, white birch, or tamarack—already stunted in their growth, decrease in height to shrublike forms and give way to ground cover such as lichens and arctic mosses. The tree line marks the northern limit of the taiga. Two factors—low average summer temperatures and lack of available water—limit the growth and reproduction of trees. The brief summer period melts only a shallow layer of soil on top of the solidly frozen permafrost.

The northernmost vegetational zone, the **tundra**, has been called a cold desert. Interspersed by bedrock outcrops and fields of shattered rocks, a thin carpet of grasses, mosses, lichens and flowering herbs clings tenuously to the ground. Widely scattered low shrubs of willow and birch manage to survive only in sheltered pockets. In the tundra, year-round moisture is scarce and summers are too short and cold to support the growth of trees. The ground is perennially frozen and impermeable. Inadequate drainage at the surface creates the tundra's characteristic landscape of bogs, or "muskeg." During the few long summer days, the grassy tundra hastily completes its annual flowering cycle, spectacular in both color and intensity.

Fauna

Considering the immensity of Quebec's landmass, the variety of animal life is relatively poor. Slightly more than 50 species of mammals, such as beaver, deer and bear (brown and polar); 350 bird species, of which only 5 to 7 percent winter in the area; and 120 species of fish have been identified.

From south to north, animal diversity decreases in Quebec: From 50 mammal species in the Ottawa River Valley to some 20 on and around the Ungava Peninsula. In the southern portion of Quebec, herds of white-tailed deer and moose (Laurentians and Chic-Chocs) predominate, contributing to Quebec's reputation as a hunter's paradise. Indeed, Quebec offers 16 wildlife reserves abounding in popular game animals, such as moose, caribou, white-tailed deer and black bear. Birds of prey include the red-tailed hawk, merlin, kestrel and great horned owl. Quebec is on the flyway of migrating Canada and snow geese, and several areas on the St. Lawrence shores are renowned for bird watching in spring and fall.

Farther north the taiga provides habitat to herds of **caribou**, such as the George River herd, which roams the area south of Ungava Bay and numbers 300,000 head. Seven smaller herds are found along the transitional zone between taiga and tundra. The area is punctuated by myriad lakes and waterways teeming with salmon, smelt, pike, and trout. Among animal species indigenous to the rugged tundra are the arctic hare, fox, and polar bear, as well as the Gyrfalcon and Snowy Owl (Quebec's bird animal emblem).

Many species of **marine mammals** travel up the St. Lawrence River on their migratory routes. They include the common seal as well as the beluga, humpback, fin and minke **whales**. Whale watching is a popular attraction, especially in the Saguenay fjord and Côte-Nord regions.

Caribou, Mt. Jacques-Cartier

Parc national de la Gaspésie / Jean-Pierre Huard / Sépaq

HISTORY

Time Line

PRE-COLONIAL PERIOD

BC

c. 20000-
15000 — Earliest human migration into North America from Asia during the last ice age.

c. 5000-
1000 — Nomadic hunters of the Archaic culture occupy most of the continent.

c. 1000 —Development of the Woodland culture: appearance of pottery and agriculture.

AD

c. 1000 —Norse sailors reach the shores of present-day Newfoundland.

c. 1100 — The Thule people, ancestors of the Inuit, migrate into the Ungava Peninsula.

1492 — Christopher Columbus lands on the island of San Salvador in the Caribbean.

NEW FRANCE

1534 — In the Gaspésie Region, **Jacques Cartier** claims Canada in the name of François 1, King of France.

1534-
1608 — The Huron and the Algonquin force the Iroquois out of the St. Lawrence Valley.

1535 — On his second voyage, Cartier travels upstream on the St. Lawrence to Hochelaga, the site of present-day Montreal.

1608 — **Samuel de Champlain** founds **Quebec City**, the first permanent European establishment in North America.

1609-
1633 — French and Hurons form an alliance against the Iroquois and British..

1610 — British navigator **Henry Hudson** discovers the strait and bay that today bear his name, in his quest for the Northwest Passage.

1627 — The Company of One Hundred Associates is founded.

1642 — **Maisonneuve** founds Ville-Marie, later renamed **Montreal. Iroquois Wars** begin.

1648-
1649 — Iroquois destroy Huronia (in present day Southern Ontario) and regain control of the St. Lawrence Valley.

1670 — The **Hudson's Bay Company** is founded, it operates in North America but its headquarters are in London, England.

1673 — Father Marquette and Louis Jolliet explore the Mississippi.

1701 — Montreal Peace (*La Grande Paix de Montréal*) marks the end of the Iroquois Wars.

1730s-
1750s — La Vérendrye family explores the Canadian West.

1744 — Pierre-François-Xavier de Charlevoix publishes *History and General Description of New France.*

1755 — Acadian deportation.

1756 — Beginning of the Seven Years' War, in which Austria, Russia, France and Spain oppose Great Britain and Prussia.

1759 — British defeat the French at the **Battle of the Plains of Abraham** (Quebec City) on September 13. On September 18, Quebec City surrenders to the British.

1760 — Montreal surrenders to the British.

1763 — The **Treaty of Paris** marks the end of the Seven Years' War. New France is ceded to Great Britain.

BRITISH REGIME

1774 — **Quebec Act** recognises the French social system and civil laws and grants the freedom to practise the Roman Catholic religion.

1775-
1776 — American invasion and occupation of Montreal; American defeat in Quebec City.

1783 — American Independence recognized by Great Britain. Americans loyal to the British Crown begin emigrating to Canada and Quebec.

1789 — French Revolution and spreading of new ideas. Counter-revolutionary current after the death of Louis XVI.

1791 — Constitutional Act divides the country into Lower (Quebec) and Upper (Ontario) Canada; each province is granted a legislative assembly.

1806 — *Le Canadien,* first Francophone newspaper, is founded in Montreal.

1812-
1814 — War of 1812; second American invasion; French Canadians and Indians win victory for the British at the Battle of the Châteauguay, under the command of Salaberry.

1837-
1838 — **Patriots' Rebellion** in the Montreal region and the Richelieu Valley. Suspension of the Constitution of 1791.

1841 — **Act of Union** creates the United Canadas.

1845-
1848 — François-Xavier Garneau publishes *History of Canada.* Major wave of Irish immigration.

1852 — Laval University, first Francophone university in North America, founded in Quebec City.

1854 — Seigneurial regime is abolished.

CANADIAN CONFEDERATION

1867 — British North America Act (renamed **Constitution Act, 1867** in 1982) creates the Canadian Confederation.

1870 — Rupert's Land is sold to the Canadian Confederation.

1892 — Construction of the **Château Frontenac** begins in Quebec City.

1900 — Creation of the first cooperative savings and loan company *(caisse populaire)* by Alphonse Desjardins.

1910 — Montreal newspaper *Le Devoir* is founded by Henri Bourassa.

1912 — The Canadian government gives Quebec province a portion of Rupert's Land, thereafter known as Nouveau-Québec.

1918 — Quebec women obtain the right to vote in federal elections; right to vote in provincial affairs is granted in 1940.

1927 — After years of dispute, the territorial limit between Quebec and Labrador is established; Quebec does not officially recognise the border.

1939-1945 —World War II; large wave of immigration from southern Europe.

CONTEMPORARY QUEBEC

1948 — Quebec adopts its provincial flag.

1959 — Opening of the **St. Lawrence Seaway** enabling ships to navigate from the Atlantic to the Great Lakes in the US.

1960 — Government of Prime Minister Jean Lesage heralds the beginning of the **Quiet Revolution** (*Révolution tranquille*).

1967 — World Exposition in Montreal; publication of the Report of the Royal Commission on Bilingualism and Biculturalism in Canada.

1968 — The Parti Québécois is founded.

1969 — Passage of Bill 63, first law promoting the use of the French language in Quebec.

1970 — A hostage-taking by the Quebec Liberation Front (Front de libération du Québec) leads to the October Crisis and the enactment of the War Measures Act.

1973 — Construction of phase 1 of the James Bay project begins.

1976 — **Summer Olympic Games** in Montreal; election of the Parti Québécois, under the leadership of **René Lévesque**, first nationalist-sovereign party to become elected.

1977 — **Bill 101**, the charter on the French language, is passed.

1980 — Referendum on sovereignty is rejected by 60 percent of the voters.

1982 — The Canadian Constitution of 1867 is repatriated from London. The **Constitution Act, 1982** calls for a new constitution. Quebec is the only Canadian province that refuses to sign the new constitution.

1985 — Historic Quebec City becomes the first urban center in North America to be inscribed on UNESCO's World Heritage List.

1987-
1990 — **Meech Lake Accord:** Quebec sets five conditions upon which it will adhere to the Constitution of 1982.

1988 — The socio-cultural region of Nunavik is recognized by the provincial government as homeland of Quebec's Inuit.

1990 — Two provinces (Newfoundland and Manitoba) refuse to sign the Meech Lake Accord by the June 23 deadline. Quebec refuses to sign the 1982 Constitution. Amerindian crisis at Oka.

1992 — Montreal celebrates the 350th anniversary of its foundation.

1993 — The Bloc Québécois becomes the official Opposition in the Canadian House of Commons.

1994 — The Parti Québécois is elected in Quebec, headed by Jacques Parizeau. Lucien Bouchard is elected to replace Parizeau in January 1996.

1995 — A second referendum on Quebec sovereignty is rejected by 50.6 percent of the voters.

1996 — Severe floods devastate the Saguenay region.

1998 — The worst ice storm in the region's history slams into southwestern Quebec, damaging the hydroelectric system and leaving millions without electrical power.

THE NEW MILLENNIUM

2000 — Montreal becomes the home of the first NASDAQ stock exchange satellite market in Canada.

2001 — A nationwide **census** confirmed a population of 30 million in Canada. Federal and Quebec elections renew debate about Quebec sovereignty. Canadian hockey franchise the Montreal Canadiens is sold to an American businessman, but remains in Montreal. Lucien Bouchard resigns as premier and is replaced by Bernard Landry.

2002 — Quebec-born David Pelletier and his ice-skating partner Jamie Salé win gold medals for Canada at the Winter Olympics held in Salt Lake City, Utah.

2003 — A court ruling legalizes same-sex marriage in Quebec. In a general election, the Liberals headed by federalist Jean Charest, defeat the Parti Québécois.

2005 — Bernard Landry resigns as leader of the Parti Québécois, and is replaced by André Boisclair.

2006 — The federal Conservative Party forms a minority government and wins 10 new seats in Quebec.

2007 — The Liberal Party of Quebec barely escapes defeat, and forms a minority provincial government. Official Opposition becomes grassroots, right wing Action Démocratique. Parti Québécois' third place reflects the loss of impetus of the sovereignty option.

2008 — 400th anniversary of the founding of Quebec City. According to the Canadian government, it "reminds us that French is Canada's founding language."

People and Events

EARLY SETTLEMENT

According to recent archaeological excavations and interpretations, the earliest migration of humans into the North American continent occurred some 15,000 or more years ago. The first settlers are believed to have journeyed from Asia, crossing over the land bridge that joined Siberia and Alaska during the glacial period. After a few thousand years, the ice sheet retreated from the central part of present-day Canada, clearing the way for human occupation.

Two principal cultures mark the many centuries separating the initial settlement of central Canada and the arrival of the Europeans in the 11C. The first, known as the "Archaic" culture (5000 to 1000 BC), were nomadic peoples, who relied on hunting and gathering for sustenance. During the subsequent cultural period known as "Woodland" (1000 BC to AD 1500), native peoples adopted a sedentary lifestyle characterized by the production of pottery and the development of agriculture (particularly corn) to complement their diet of fish and game. It is thought that at least three million people inhabited the North American continent immediately prior to European contact.

For centuries after the short-lived Viking settlements on the coast of present-day Newfoundland in AD 1000, Europe appeared to have forgotten about the existence of the North American continent. It wasn't until the 16C that

Arrival of Champlain (1608) by George Agnew Reid

National Archives of Canada, Ottawa (C - 11015)

Quebec's indigenous peoples first came into contact with Europeans—primarily the cod fishermen who had ventured up the St. Lawrence beyond the famous breeding grounds of Newfoundland's Great Banks.

The arrival of European missionaries and fur traders had a profound effect on indigenous cultures, bringing about changes in their lifestyle and political alliances. However, native peoples largely resisted the Church's attempts to convert them to the Catholic faith, as described in Relations, the Jesuits' historic account of their missionary work in New France. In fact, the native cultures already possessed their own elaborate systems of beliefs and customs. Nonetheless, the modification of intertribal political relations, traditional trade routes, devastating wars, zealous colonisation and endemic diseases brought to the New World by Europeans eventually brought about the permanent disruption of native lifestyles.

Jacques Cartier by Théophile Hamel

National Archives of Canada, Ottawa (c – 11226)

NEW FRANCE

In the 15C, European explorers set sail in hopes of finding the route to India. Among these was Christopher Columbus who, in 1492, claimed the island of San Salvador for the Spanish Crown. Although French explorer **Jacques Cartier** (1491–1557) sailed to the New World between 1534 and 1542, France did not establish a firm presence on the North American continent until 1608, when **Samuel de Champlain** (c.1570-1636) founded Quebec City. Shortly after, Europeans began exploring the continent in search of beaver and mink, the mainstay of the lucrative **fur trade** that played a decisive role in Quebec's history.

In the early 17C, the administration and development of the colony was entrusted to private companies such as the Company of One Hundred Associates (Compagnie des Cent-Associés, 1627), composed of merchants and aristocrats intent on colonising New France for commercial gain. However, settlement progressed slowly; by 1663, there were approximately 3,000 inhabitants, fewer than half of whom were born in the New World. The Jesuits' attempts at evangelisation had little success, and the fur trade led to alliances and to the Iroquois Wars. Between 1627 and 1701, the Iroquois nations repeatedly raided Algonquian-speaking Amerindians, notably the Huron, Montagnais and Algonquin, who had allied themselves with the French settlers. Beginning in 1642, the French retaliated by building a series of forts and providing their allies with firearms. However, the attacks continued until 1701, when the Iroquois signed the Montreal Peace Treaty and established their neutrality.

A Royal Colony (1663–1763)

Under the reign of Louis XIV (1643-1715), the administration of New France mirrored that of other French colonies. A governor conducted the colony's military and external affairs; another appointed official ruled over judicial and financial matters and landlords, or *seigneurs,* performed various administrative functions. The seigneurs also enforced the law, erected mills, collected dues (tithes, annuities and grain taxes) and could, at will, subject their tenants to forced labor. Seigneurs, military personnel and religious communities allocated land plots to tenant farmers under a mode of land distribution and occupation known as the **seigneurial**

system. These land plots, known as rangs, formed long, narrow rectangles perpendicular to a body of water or a road. Farmers comprised 80 percent of the population, which stood at 20,000 at the beginning of the 18C and at approximately 70,000 in 1760.

In a truly epic adventure, explorers pushed back the geographical boundaries of New France. Between the 1730s and 40s, the La Vérendryes engaged in an extensive exploration of North American waterways, travelling as far as Manitoba, Saskatchewan, Wyoming, Montana and the Dakotas. They built forts and opened a fur trade route that was used by their successors.

The British Conquest

The traditional rivalry between France and England, exacerbated primarily by conflicting interests in the fur trade, led to recurring wars between New France and the surrounding British colonies, ultimately resulting in the capture of Quebec City in 1629. In 1632 the city returned to the French following the signing of the Treaty of Saint-Germain. The Treaty of Utrecht (1713) brought about a temporary peace that lasted until the Seven Years' War (1756–1763), in which France, Austria, Spain and Russia opposed Great Britain and Prussia. On September 13, 1759, British General Wolfe defeated French General Montcalm on the Plains of Abraham, heralding the end of the French colony. Montreal surrendered to the British on September 8, 1760, and the colony was ceded to England in 1763, by the Treaty of Paris.

THE BRITISH REGIME

Era of Constitutions (1760–1791)

The late 18C is known as the "era of constitutions." The military conquest had placed English Protestants, governed by a constitutional monarchy, in opposition with French Catholics, subjects of an absolute monarchy. The constitution of 1774 (known as the Quebec Act) gave the great majority of Francophones the right to maintain the seigneurial system and French civil laws, and the freedom to practise the Roman Catholic religion.

The inhabitants of the 13 American colonies won their independence from England in 1776, trying in vain to convince Canadians to join them during an invasion that was finally crushed at Quebec City. Loyalists—American citizens faithful to the British Crown—made their way north; many of them settled in the area known as the Eastern Townships.

Quebec remained sympathetic to the French Revolution of 1789 until the regicide of Louis XVI in 1793. British colonial authorities looked unfavorably upon the abolition of monarchy and the execution of its royal representative, and the Catholic Church, witnessing the overthrow of royal and ecclesiastical authority, fostered a counter-revolutionary current through its sermons and editorials. Despite attempts to maintain the status quo, a liberal-minded middle class was gradually taking shape. In 1791 the British parliament gave its North American colonies a new constitution, granting a separate legislative assembly to Quebec (Lower Canada) and Ontario (Upper Canada). This was Quebec's first experience in parliamentary democracy.

From Constitutional Debates to Popular Uprisings (1791–1840)

French Canadians grew accustomed to British institutions and, by the turn of the century, they constituted a majority in the elected assembly, hoping to draw attention to their grievances. Led by **Louis-Joseph Papineau** (1786–1871), the Patriot Party (Parti patriote), also known as the Parti canadien until 1826, was hindered by a British governor and legislative council that frequently defeated bills submitted by the peoples' representatives.

The constitutional impasse and British colonial policies eventually led to several uprisings, known as the **Patriots' Rebellion**, particularly in the region of Montreal (Saint-Denis-sur-Richelieu, Saint-Charles-sur-Richelieu, Saint-Eustache). Various beliefs and convictions were reflected in this rebellion of 1837–38: A democratic ideology that valued the supremacy of the House of Assembly, an anti-British and anti-colonial sentiment based on a belief in the right to self-government, and a movement away from the power held by the seigneurs and the clergy. After the failure of the rebellions, Governor-General Lord Durham was sent to assess the state of the colony; in 1839, he submitted a report recommending the union of the two Canadas, in order to assimilate French Canadians.

The Act of Union (1840–1867)

Passed in 1841, the Act of Union joined Lower and Upper Canada into one province. At the time, Lower Canada's population stood at 750,000 (510,000 French Canadians) and Upper Canada numbered 480,000 inhabitants. Although Upper Canada's debt was far greater, the two public debts were consolidated, and the Legislative Assembly adopted English as the language of the Province of Canada.

By the mid-19C, the extremely high birthrate of the seigneurial era had led to overpopulation in Lower Canada, and large numbers of people moved to new settlements in the Mauricie, Saguenay–Lac-Saint-Jean and Bas-Saint-Laurent regions or to the industrial towns of New England. Although vast new regions were opened to colonisation in Quebec, nearly one million French-Canadians immigrated to the US between 1850 and 1930.

Weakened by its lack of clergy and official recognition, the Catholic Church proved staunchly loyal to the British government from 1763 to 1840, even during the Patriots' Rebellion; it was rewarded for its good faith after 1840, when it received a special legal status that allowed it to retain its assets. As it became more involved in the political scene and forged close ties to the party led by **Louis-Hippolyte Lafontaine** (1807-64), the Church gained control over public education. Working with Upper Canada Reformists, Lafontaine secured the right to a "responsible government" formed by the parliamentary majority.

Although the Union began in a period of renewed political liberalism, it ended with the emergence of an ideological and political conservatism. Frequent political crises finally led to a new political system of government known as Confederation, which French-Canadian Liberals opposed in vain.

CANADIAN CONFEDERATION

Ratified by the British Parliament in 1867, the **British North America Act** (today known as the Constitution Act, 1867) established the Canadian Confederation—a new political entity that included Quebec among its four founding provinces (along with Ontario, Nova Scotia and New Brunswick). The Confederation's **Constitution of 1867** called for a parliamentary system of government and a separation of federal and provincial powers. Education was among the key areas of jurisdiction granted to the provinces. To guarantee the rights of the Protestant minority in Quebec and the Catholic minority elsewhere in Canada, the controversial **Article 93** created a school system divided along religious rather than linguistic lines.

The Constitution used the term French Canada to refer to Francophones living in Quebec, New Brunswick, Ontario and Manitoba. It was during this time, when British imperialism reached its apogee, that **Wilfrid Laurier** (1841–1919) became the first French prime minister of Canada (1896–1911). Among the other important events of the early 1900s was Quebec's opposition to the draft imposed by the federal government. Between 1870 and 1917, Francophone Catholic minorities outside Quebec gradually lost a number of educational and linguistic rights.

A Nationalist Revival

This progressive loss of rights as well as the issue of autonomy, and the threat to the French language stemming from business, publicity and industrialisation, gave rise to two nationalist trends. The first, embodied by **Henri Bourassa** (1868-1952), founder of Montreal's Francophone daily *Le Devoir* (1910), advocated greater autonomy for Canada within the British empire, and greater autonomy for each province within the Confederation. Historian **Lionel Groulx** (1878–1967) promoted a nationalist ideology based on the threefold identity of French Canadians: Catholic, Francophone and rural. Groulx's campaign began just as Quebec's rural culture was weakening and ended as the role of Catholicism in Quebec society was fading.

In Quebec the economic crisis of 1929, coupled with turmoil wrought by World War II, lasted into the 1940s; both these events led to economic and social interventions primarily backed by the federal government. So began an era of federal centralisation vividly opposed by **Maurice Duplessis,** premier of Quebec from 1944 to 1959.

NEW IDENTITY

The Quiet Revolution

In the 1960s there appeared a climate of social and economic change that contrasted sharply with the staunch conservatism of Duplessis's successive governments. Among the events that led to the so-called Quiet Revolution of 1960–66 (*la Révolution tranquille*) were the economic prosperity engendered by the mining industry of the Côte-Nord region, Quebecers' introduction to consumerism through the automobile and television (1952), and the strengthening of the labor movement during the miners' strike (1949) in Asbestos.

The Quebec government launched a series of economic and social programs aimed at gaining economic leverage for Quebec. In 1962 it nationalized its hydroelectric industry (Hydro-Québec was first nationalized in 1944); in 1965 it created the *Caisse de dépôt et placement* to manage the assets of a new pension plan, and it helped promote Francophone business in Quebec. The government also intervened in social and cultural matters by taking over the management of health and social services from the Church, administering public education and creating the Ministry of Cultural Affairs (1961). By taking charge of the educational and cultural sectors, the provincial government was eventually realizing an objective first set by Liberals in the 19C.

A Sovereign State?

The increasing role of the provincial government paralleled the rise of a political nationalist ideology. The issue of Quebec's sovereignty became a hotly debated topic between supporters of a federalism—personified by **Pierre Elliot Trudeau**, prime minister of Canada from (1968 to 1979 and 1980 to 1984—and partisans of Quebec sovereignty—embodied by **René Lévesque**, leader of the Parti Québécois and premier of Quebec from 1976 to 1985. Lévesque (1922–87) transformed what was primarily a cultural nationalism into a political nationalist ideology. Nonetheless, on May 20, 1980, Lévesque's Parti Québécois lost a referendum on Quebec sovereignty when 60 percent of Quebecers voted against separation.

The tension between the provincial and federal governments reached new heights when Quebec declined to sign the new **Canadian Constitution of 1982** and the Charter of Rights and Freedoms. Pierre Elliot Trudeau left politics in 1984 as the Progressive-Conservative party of Quebec-born Brian Mulroney took power in Ottawa.

René Lévesque retired from the political scene in 1985. Six months later, the Parti Québécois was defeated by the Quebec Liberal Party, headed by Robert Bourassa. The Liberal government announced it would sign the 1982 Constitution provided five conditions were met. At a meeting held at Meech Lake, near Ottawa, the Canadian prime minister and the 10 provincial premiers tentatively agreed to these conditions. The **Meech Lake Accord** (April 30, 1987) which provided a special status for Quebec as a "distinct society," had to be ratified by the federal government and all 10 provinces before June 23, 1990. However, a consensus was not reached and the failure of the Meech Lake Accord once again renewed doubts about Quebec's adherence to the Canadian constitution.

No generally acceptable solution to this thorny issue has yet been reached. The narrow failure of a second referendum on Quebec sovereignty, held in October 1995 (50.6 percent of Quebecers voted "no") indicates that the questions of sovereignty and Quebec's relationship with other Canadian provinces will likely continue to dominate the political scene in the years to come.

ART AND CULTURE

Marked by French, British and American influences, set in a nordic climate, Quebec's rich and varied architecture and art constitute a unique cultural heritage within the North American landscape.

Architecture

17C

Due to the ephemeral nature of Amerindian constructions, very little remains from the period preceding the arrival of Europeans. The earliest structures found in Quebec date from the late 17C. Erected by craftsmen and architects imported from France, these simple constructions bear the influence of various regional styles, in particular those of Brittany and Normandy. With a view to defending and protecting the strategic location of both Quebec City and Montreal, the colonial administration encouraged the building of fortifications around the early settlements. The villages that grew inside fortified walls provided a model for the urban centers that subsequently developed. Among fortification vestiges, only the old powder magazine and redoubt of the Quebec Citadel remain as examples of French regime military design.

The dearth of trained craftsmen and tools gave rise to domestic architecture characterized by simplicity of design and

Pierre Ethier/ MICHELIN

Old Sulpician Seminary, Montreal

lack of ornamentation. Illustrating the austerity of these early constructions, the Jacquet House (1699), in Quebec City, was built of rough fieldstone and topped by a steep roof. Toward the end of the century, the principal urban areas were embellished by impressive administrative and religious edifices, erected by the French-born architects **Claude Baillif** and **François de la Joüe**. The Château Saint-Louis and the Quebec Basilica-Cathedral figured among those imposing monuments; unfortunately, neither of the original structures has survived intact. The arrival of religious orders (Ursuline, Augustine and Jesuit) gave rise to an institutional style that reflected the influence of French classicism. Noteworthy buildings from this period are Quebec City's Ursuline monastery, whose interior courtyard is reminiscent of 16C French chateaux, and Montreal's Old Sulpician Seminary. These and other opulent residences, were erected with stone vaulting.

EARLY–MID-18C

Following several devastating fires, such as the one in Quebec City's Lower Town, local administrators established new ordinances that "Canadianized" the architecture. Constructions were adapted to the North American context, giving rise to a vernacular style that later evolved into the "maison québécoise" (previously "maison canadienne"). Strict regulations required the use of slate roofs and stone vaults, while prohibiting decorative elements liable to help spread fire. Erected in 1798, the Calvet House in Montreal exemplifies this common building type by its simple fieldstone walls, firebreaks (the part of the wall extending beyond the roof as a shield against flying sparks), corner consoles, wide chimney stacks, and gabled roof.

Architectural Terms

Apse The rounded or polygonal termination of a church, in which the altar is housed.

Baldachin An ornamental canopy over an altar supported by columns.

Barrel vaulting Continuous arched vault of semicircular cross section.

Bas-relief Low relief. A form of sculpture in which figures or shapes project slightly from the background plane.

Bastion In military architecture, a masonry structure projecting from the outer wall of a fortification.

Battlement The uppermost portion of a fortified wall with alternate solid elements and openings (embrasures or crenels).

Blockhouse In 18C and 19C military architecture, a fortified structure, commonly of wood, with a square floor plan and an overhanging upper floor.

Buttress A masonry structure built against a wall to add support or strength.

Capital Crowning feature of a column or pilaster.

Cornice A molded projection crowning the top of a building or wall.

Curtain wall In modern architecture, a nonbearing exterior wall suspended on the face of a building like a curtain.

Dormer window A small window projecting from a sloped roof.

Embrasures A series of crenels or intervals cut into the top portion of a battlement.

Fanlight A semicircular window over a door or window.

Gable The vertical triangular section of wall closing the end of a double-sloped roof.

Mansard roof A roof with two slopes on all four sides, the lower slope being the steeper of the two (named after the 17C French architect, François Mansart).

Nave The central main body of a church designed to accommodate the congregation.

Pediment Any triangular or semicircular crowning element used over doors, windows or niches.

Pilaster An engaged pier or pillar projecting slightly from a wall surface, generally with base and capital.

Portal A monumental entrance or gate.

Porte-cochere A large covered entrance porch.

Portico A porch or covered walk consisting of a roof supported by columns.

Quoin A cornerstone often distinguished from the adjoining masonry by a special surface treatment.

Redoubt A small free-standing fortification.

Reredos A decorative screen or wall behind an altar sometimes forming part of the retable.

Retable A decorative screen placed above and behind an altar and generally containing a work of art.

Rose window A large circular stained-glass window dissected by stone members or mullions arranged like the spokes of a wheel.

Turret A small tower generally placed at the corner of a building.

The Baillairgé Family

The 18C saw the emergence of this dynasty of prolific architects, painters and sculptors. **Jean Baillairgé** (1726–1805) left France to work on new Canadian projects under the renowned military engineer **Chaussegros de Léry** (1682–1756). Shortly after landing in Quebec, he was selected to draw up plans for several buildings, including the Quebec City cathedral. After studying in France at the Académie Royale de peinture et sculpture, his son, **François** (1759–1830), returned to Quebec City and elaborated designs for the cathedral's interior. **Thomas** Baillairgé (1791–1859), Quebec's preeminent 18C architect, studied sculpture with his father, François, and with the Montreal woodcarver and sculptor Louis-Amable Quévillon (1749–1823), known especially for his interior decoration of the church at Sault-au-Récollet. Thomas contributed to the Quebec cathedral and later supervised the construction of churches throughout the province. Drawing on British architectural trends, Thomas developed an original style, which combined Neoclassical influences and Quebec's mixed architectural heritage. Thomas and his father collaborated on the elaborate interior of the Saint-Joachim church between 1815 and 1825. Son of a cousin of Thomas, **Charles** Baillairgé (1826–1906) was trained as an architect and engineer. He became Quebec City's engineer in 1866, beautifying the city with monumental edifices, such as the main pavilion of Université Laval, new public spaces and imposing staircases.

LATE 18C

Following the British Conquest, the province's urban areas and the villages east of Quebec City along the St. Lawrence River lay in ruins. Though post-French Regime architecture still dominated until 1800, British influence drastically altered the architectural landscape in the early 19C. The Neoclassical style, in particular Palladianism, bore a determining influence on constructions. Transformed into single-family homes, domestic structures of this period, based on the British model, occupied a relatively small area of land, but were built with two or three stories. Massive chimneys rising from a four-sided gently sloped roof replaced the characteristic steeply pitched roof of the French Regime constructions.

The development of commerce and a relatively prosperous economy fostered the growth of new urban areas around nascent industries, such as Sherbrooke and Saint-Hyacinthe. Cities also sprung up around military fortifications (Chambly, Sorel and Vaudreuil). Beginning in the 1780s, resort areas along the banks of the St. Lawrence attracted a wealthy British bourgeoisie, who developed a taste for the "picturesque style" imported from Great Britain

19C

Palladianism continued to dominate the early part of the century. This popular style, inspired by the works of the 16C Italian architect Andrea Palladio, is characterized by austerity and symmetry of design and employs elements from classical antiquity, including pediments, pilasters, Doric and Ionic columns, cornices and quoins. In addition, the structures designed in this style were often faced with a smooth layer of cut stone. The Holy Trinity Anglican Cathedral in Quebec City represents a colonial version of Palladianism. A more resolutely classical style appears about 1830, as exemplified by the large yet elegant Bonsecours Market in Montreal.

The **maison québécoise**, the Quebec equivalent of the rustic English cottage, came into vogue in the 1830s and 40s. Offering a harmonious synthesis between the French heritage and British influence, this type of building is embellished by picturesque ornaments and incorporates amenities such as large windows, balconies, reception rooms and heating systems.

The mid- to late 19C reflects an eclectic mix of more exuberant revival styles, inspired by architectural trends of the past and made possible by new materials and building techniques developed in the 19C. Numerous churches in Quebec City were erected in the

Gothic Revival style popularized by the French architect and restorer Viollet-le-Duc, who is credited with resurrecting the prevailing style of the Middle Ages. Catholic churches were generally based on French Gothic architecture, while Protestant places of worship adopted the British model. Victor Bourgeau's Notre-Dame Basilica in Montreal and the Chalmers-Wesley Church, by John Wells, in Quebec City, exemplify two variants of this style.

Modeled on Italian palaces and villas, the **Renaissance Revival style** was associated with the wealthy British elite and therefore used mainly for commercial buildings. The Ritz-Carlton in Montreal exemplifies this style, characterized by wide cornices, exuberant ornamentation and rustication.

The **Second Empire style**, in fashion during Napoleon III's reign, gained prominence in the 1870s under the Quebec architect **Eugène-Étienne Taché** (1836–1912). In search of a unified architecture for governmental buildings of the new province following the Confederation of 1967, Taché drew on this style for his plans of the Parliament Building in Quebec City. Recognisable by its distinctive double-sloped mansard roof pierced by dormer windows, the style also introduced arched lintel windows, a profusion of columns and wrought-iron roof cresting, as seen in the Shaughnessy House in Montreal.

After creating several works in Gothic Revival, the architect **Victor Bourgeau** (1809–88) became a proponent of the **Baroque Revival style**. His masterpiece, Mary Queen of the World Basilica-Cathedral, a small-scale replica of St. Peter's Basilica in Rome, illustrates the tenets of this style by its massive proportions, enormous dome, and elaborate interior embellished by an imposing baldachin.

While striving to adapt the Second Empire style to the Canadian environment, Eugène-Étienne Taché proposed structures that would reflect the era of New France's discoverers, Cartier and Champlain. Inspired by the French chateaux of the Loire valley, Taché designed monumental edifices, complete with towers and turrets, conical roofs and machicolation. The most famous example of the **Chateau style** remains the Château Frontenac, erected by **Bruce Price** (1843–1903) in 1892.

In the late 19C, another interpretation of Medieval architecture, the **Romanesque Revival**, was mainly used for religious buildings. This style was appropriated by H.H. Richardson, the prominent American architect who later modified it into the Richardsonian Romanesque, characterized by rounded arches and buttresses, squat columns, arcades and deep-set windows. Montreal's Windsor Station is an excellent example of this distinctly North American style.

20C

The turn of the 19C saw a wave of architects turning to the École des Beaux-Arts in Paris for inspiration. The exuberant **Beaux-Arts style,** which employs a classical vocabulary in monumental compositions, became the preferred institutional style and proliferated under the government of Louis-Alexandre Taschereau. Montreal's Museum of Fine Arts, boasting an imposing staircase and portico colonnade, illustrates this style, which relies on monumentality and symmetry. Introduced to the province at a time of economic prosperity, the Beaux-Arts style also symbolized wealth and power. Near the Olympic Stadium in

Place de la Cathédrale, Montreal

Montreal, the Château Dufresne with its elegant coupled columns, balustrades and elaborate ornaments reflects the tastes of the opulent French Canadian bourgeoisie of the day.

The invention of steel-frame constructions heralded the beginning of the first skyscrapers, or buildings with more than 10 storys. Influenced by the Chicago school, these structures reveal a complete break with past architectural trends. New techniques and building materials, such as reinforced concrete, provided architects with innumerable possibilities.

Introduced at the Paris Exposition in 1925, the **Art Deco style** made its appearance in Quebec's large corporation buildings. Hallmarks of the style include vertical lines and geometric ornaments carved on marble, bronze and other expensive building materials. The Price Building in old Quebec City presents a stunning Art Deco ensemble.

After a long period of artistic stagnation, the late 1950s marked the beginning of urban renewal and the growth of modern architecture. Modern architecture embodied practical and functional thinking, developed in the works of Le Corbusier and Gropius. Simple, geometric lines, devoid of ornamentation, typified a style that did not rely on any past tenets of architecture. The influential architect Mies van der Rohe, proponent of the **International style**, made use of glass curtain walls, black metal and reinforced concrete, as seen in the Westmount Square and the Fairmont Queen Elizabeth Hotel. Montreal's Place Ville-Marie, erected by I.M. Pei, and Habitat '67, designed by **Moshe Safdie**, also illustrate these modern trends that changed profoundly the image of Quebec's largest city.

Ecclesiastical architecture experienced a renaissance under **Dom Paul Bellot** (1876–1944), a Benedictine monk, who drew inspiration from Viollet-le-Duc's works and introduced modern church architecture into Quebec. Known as "modern Gothic," his style is best illustrated by the Abbey of Saint-Benoît-du-Lac, in the Eastern Townships, and the St. Joseph's Oratory, in Montreal.

In recent years, **postmodern** currents have presented an eloquent reply to the monotony and anonymity of the architecture of the 1960s. Post-Modernism often incorporates existing structures and uses elements from previous styles, such as pointed arches, fanlights and other embellishments, to produce a harmonious ensemble that blends with its environment. Montreal's La Place de la Cathédrale, Maison Alcan and the Canadian Center for Architecture, by **Peter Rose** and **Phyllis Lambert**, all exemplify this trend.

Art

AMERINDIAN ART

Through the centuries Quebec's Amerindian peoples have developed diverse modes of artistic expression that bear witness to their distinctive lifestyles and beliefs.

Traditional Art

Most Algonquian-speaking Amerindians (namely Abenaki, Algonquin, Cree, Mi'kmaq, Montagnais and Naskapi) are descendants from nomadic peoples who excelled in the art of beadwork (shell, bone, rock or seed) and embroideries (porcupine quills and moose or caribou

Chair Back Panel, Micmac (19C)

hair). Caribou-hide vests and moccasins, and various birchbark objects were often decorated with geometric incisions and drawings. Red, the symbol of continuity and renewal, was the predominant color. Elaborate belts of **wampum** (beads made from shells) feature motifs illustrating the main events in Amerindian history. Wampum was exchanged at peace ceremonies and during the signing of treaties. The smaller, quasi-sedentary, Iroquoian-speaking groups included Hurons, Mohawks, Onondagas and Senecas. As agricultural societies, they formed semipermanent villages and constructed multifamily dwellings known as longhouses; out of their sedentary lifestyle evolved an artistic repertoire free from the constraints of nomadism. Among their most beautiful works are exquisite moosehair embroideries that gradually began incorporating floral motifs under European influence. Huron women were the most adept at this delicate art; the complex techniques they applied with remarkable skill have never been replicated. Also of interest are the wooden masks known as "False Faces" that represented mythological figures associated with traditional healing practices.

The Contemporary Scene

Amerindian art has undergone a profound transformation in the past 10 years. Whereas artists traditionally relied on the use of natural materials such as hide and bark, today they are exploring new media such as canvas, acrylics and charcoal; consequently, new techniques have emerged although inspiration is still drawn from social and cultural traditions. The result is a new, contemporary vision of aboriginal art that keeps alive the memory of the past.

INUIT ART

Art forms developed over centuries have brought no small renown to the inhabitants of North America's arctic regions.

Origins

The earliest known artifacts produced by the Inuit are small stone projectile points attributed to the Pre-Dorset and Dorset cultures, which developed in the first millenium BC. Petroglyphs or rock carvings attributed to these cultures have been found in the steatite hills of Kangiqsujuaq. The Thule people, generally considered to be the ancestors of the present-day Inuit, crafted more refined objects including combs and figurines. Generally small in size, these early artifacts were closely associated with religious beliefs and practices. Beginning in the 19C, many miniature sculptures made of stone, ivory (walrus tusks) and whalebone were traded for staples such as salt and firearms, provided by Europeans. With the decline of traditional lifestyles resulting from increased contact with the non-indigenous peoples, sculpture and other forms of arts and crafts gradually lost their magic or religious significance and provided a new source of income to the Inuit population.

Inuit Art Today

Today the term "Inuit art" evokes images of steatite carvings. Abundant in the northern regions, **steatite** (known as soapstone) is a soft rock ranging from greyish green to brown. Other harder rocks commonly used include green serpentine, argillite, dolomite and quartz. Modern Inuit sculptures, which can reach impressive dimensions, represent local fauna, life in the great northern regions and other arctic themes popular with the public. Other art forms include printmaking, sculpted caribou antlers, rock engravings and tapestries. In recent decades, the art trade has become an

Soapstone Sculpture

FCNQ/drawing by R. Corbeil/MICHELIN

lucrative economic activity for the Inuit population.

In order to prevent the exploitation of Inuit artists by retailers from the south, local **cooperatives** were created in the 1960s and have since been brought together under the umbrella of "la Fédération des Coopératives du Nouveau-Québec," which controls the marketing of artworks. The most renowned centers for Inuit sculpture are the villages of Povungnituk and Inukjuak, located on the shores of Hudson Bay. Salluit and Ivujivik are also well-known artistic communities. Three artists had a profound effect on the development of Inuit sculpture: Joe Talirunili (1893–1976), Alasua Amittuq Davidialuk (1910–1976) and Charlie Sivuarapik (1911–1968). Among the foremost sculptors of the current generation are Joanassie and Peter Ittukalak, from Povungnituk, and Eli Elijassiapik, Lukassie Echaluk and Abraham Pov of Inukjuak.

PAINTING AND SCULPTURE

17C–18C

The arrival of French and British colonists in the early 17C introduced European aesthetics and forms to Quebec's artistic landscape.

Religious Art

Religion was the very fabric of life in New France. Each village had its own catholic church and great pains were taken to decorate its interior. As most canvases were imported from France, very few local votive paintings were executed in this early period. A notable exception to this are the works of Brother Luc (1614–1685), a member of the Récollets order.

In early colonial times, altars, retables, baldachins and statues were all imported from France. The transportation of such large objects proved problematic, however, and craftsmen were eventually trained locally. Sculptures, always made of wood, were carved in relief and gilded. The Baroque style, very much in fashion in France at that time, remained the preferred style until the mid-19C among Quebec sculptors.

The art of church decoration was handed down through generations; certain families became famous for their artistic accomplishments. In the 1650s brothers Jean and Pierre **Levasseur** became the first of a dynasty of sculptors that continued into the 18C with Noël and Pierre-Noël Levasseur. Although they were best known for their religious artwork, they also sculpted ships' figureheads and other naval ornaments.

In the years following the British Conquest (1759), religious art came to a virtual standstill. But in the late 18C, church building resumed at a rapid pace. In Quebec City, the **Baillairgé** family was gaining wide recognition for its wood sculptures; three generations, represented by Jean (1726–1805), François (1759–1830) and Thomas (1791–1859), would perpetuate the tradition.

At the same time, **Philippe Liébert** (1733–1804) was winning acclaim in Montreal, particularly for his decoration of the church at Sault-au-Récollet, which contains sculptures by his student **Louis-Amable Quévillon** (1749–1823). This renowned sculptor and designer developed a distinctive style inspired by Louis XV decoration, with foliage, arabesque and finely adorned vaults. Throughout the early 19C, the so-called Quévillon school embellished the interiors of numerous ecclesiastical edifices throughout Quebec.

Later in the century, a new form of religious statuary made with plaster casts appeared, and eventually led to the decline of traditional wood sculpting. While most artists were turning to new art forms, sculptor **Louis Jobin** (1845–1928) was an exception. In 1881 he created the monumental statue (wood and metal) known as **Notre-Dame-du-Saguenay**, which overlooks the Saguenay from high atop a cliff. In the Church of Saint-Georges-de-Beauce, Jobin's equestrian sculpture of **Saint-Georges** (1912) was the last work created by a traditional wood sculptor. The craft of wood carving has nonetheless survived in certain areas of Quebec, such as Saint-Jean-Port-Joli, but it is above all a popular folk art, with no connection to the religious art that adorns many Quebec churches.

The Montreal Museum of Fine Arts

Still Life with Daisies by Marc-Aurèle de Foy Suzor-Côté

Military Topographic Art

In the period following the Conquest, British army officers were sent to Quebec to paint topographic views of the colony for military purposes. Some of this artwork, inspired by the romantic ideals of late 18C England, is best exemplified by the carefully executed watercolors of officer Thomas Davies (1737–1812) and the equally remarkable works of George Heriot (1766–1844) and James Cockburn (1778–1847).

Late 18C and 19C

Quebec art entered its Golden Age in the late 18C, at a time of economic prosperity. The primarily European-trained artists began producing works focusing on such popular subjects as **landscapes** and, above all, **portraits**, commissioned by an emerging and wealthy bourgeoisie. The work of self-taught painters like Louis Dulongpré (1754–1843), François Beaucourt (1740–94) and **Jean-Baptiste Roy-Audy** (1778-1848) may seem somewhat naive by European standards. The next generation of portraitists were trained in France where they acquired a more classical style. The best known among these is **Antoine Plamondon** (1802–95), who also painted religious themes. Théophile Hamel (1817–70) gained recognition as a leading portraitist of his day. Breaking with the tradition of portraiture, **Joseph Légaré** (1795–1855) created paintings that depicted contemporary events against dramatic backgrounds, such as *L'incendie du quartier Saint-Roch*.

Throughout the 19C, the arrival of European artists had a decisive impact on Quebec painting. Paul Kane (1810–71), born in Ireland, came to Canada as a child. He traveled extensively and perfected his skills as a painter in Europe. His splendid portraits of native peoples are now of great historical interest. Among the painters who developed a marked interest in regional themes is **Cornelius Krieghoff** (1815-72). This Dutch-born painter reproduced superb landscapes as well as scenes of daily life in the Montreal region in unprecedented detail.

By the mid-19C Montreal had evolved into a sophisticated city, prosperous enough to lend financial assistance to an association whose goals were to promote the arts, organize exhibitions and mount a permanent collection. The oldest art gallery in Quebec, the **Art Association of Montreal**, was founded in 1860. It is the former name of the present-day Montreal Museum of Fine Arts.

The late 19C is marked by the emergence of photography. Acclaimed for his portraits and his renditions of the increasingly urban landscape of Montreal, Scottish-born **William Notman** (1826–91) figures among Canada's most prominent photographers.

20C

At the onset of the 20C, the influence of the so-called Paris school was already visible in Quebec art, particularly in the works of Wyatt Eaton (1849–96) and Montreal art professor William Brymner (1855–1925). Their followers include Impressionist-style painters **Marc-Aurèle de Foy Suzor-Côté** (1869–1937), Maurice Cullen (1866–1934), Clarence Gagnon (1881–1942) and Modernist-Fauvist **James Wilson Morrice** (1865–1924).

Although a contemporary of these artists, **Ozias Leduc** (1864–1955), a native of Mont-Saint-Hilaire, stood apart from the rest with his deeply mystical, luminous paintings. His still-lifes and landscapes reveal a spiritual symbolism that goes far beyond their subject, reflecting the long-lived union of art and religion in Quebec. In addition to the frescoes adorning the church of Mont-Saint-Hilaire, Leduc's works can be viewed in the Notre-Dame Basilica in Montreal, and in several public collections.

Sculpture

Through the turn of the 19C, Quebec sculpture lost its exclusively religious character. This was the era of great commemorative monuments. Among the most notable sculptors were artist-architect **Napoléon Bourassa** (1827–1916) and the celebrated **Louis-Philippe Hébert** (1850–1917). Applying the techniques of French Realism to his art, Hébert created, among others, the famous Maisonneuve monument, and the statues of Jeanne Mance and Msgr. Ignace Bourget, all located in Montreal. **Alfred Laliberté** (1878–1953) fashioned sculptures along the fluid lines of Art Nouveau while maintaining an academic approach. One of his best-known works is a monument dedicated to Dollard des Ormeaux. Suzor-Côté, a close friend of Laliberté, used the same Art

Nouveau techniques to create a series of bronzeworks. His *Femmes de Caughnawaga* (Montreal Museum of Fine Arts) showing a group of Amerindian women fighting against the wind is so brilliantly executed that it seems the wind itself has sculpted the silhouettes.

Contemporary Arts Society

In the 1930s Montreal artists began to rebel against the "wild landscape nationalism" of the "Group of Seven," English-Canadian painters, most of them from Toronto, who claimed sole authorship of a typically Canadian style of painting. A staunch critic of the Group, **John Lyman** (1886–1967) attempted to redirect Canadian art according to the precepts of the Paris school of thought. In 1939 he created the Contemporary Arts Society and organized a group known as the Modernists. Its members included André Biéler, **Marc-Aurèle Fortin** (1888–1970), Goodridge Roberts (1904–74), Stanley Cosgrove and **Paul-Émile Borduas** (1905–60).

Automatists and Plasticists

World War II marked a turning point in the evolution of Quebec art. In 1940 **Alfred Pellan** (1906–88) returned to Quebec after an extended stay in France, to exhibit paintings strongly influenced by Picasso and other proponents of Cubism. Paul-Émile Borduas and several fellow artists, including **Jean-Paul Riopelle** (1923–2002), Pierre Gauvreau, Fernand Leduc ,and Jean-Paul Mousseau, founded the group called "**les Automatistes**," whose paintings reflected the goal of Surrealism to transfer onto canvas the creative impulses of the psyche. In 1948, the Automatists published the **Refus Global**, a manifesto whose virulent attacks on the established, fossilized order of Quebec society had a far-reaching impact that went well beyond the artistic milieu.

As a response to the lyricism and spontaneity of the Automatists, Guido Molinari and Claude Tousignant founded the **Plasticist** group (1955), freeing painting from the surrealist idiom through the use of an abstract geometric vocabulary. Form and color were the key elements of their work. However, no single school of thought prevailed over the inspirational and creative effervescence of contemporary art, although several Montreal painters such as Charles Gagnon, Yves Gaucher, Ulysse Comtois and sculptors Armand Vaillancourt, Charles Daudelin and Robert Roussil developed their own highly personal styles.

Current Art Scene in Quebec

The Montreal World Exposition of 1967 renewed interest in public art. Under a provincial law passed in 1978, building constructors must allocate one percent of construction costs for all new public buildings erected in the province to artwork. Sculptors often collaborate with architects to integrate their art into the building design. The most remarkable example of this can be seen in Montreal's subway system. Each station is designed by different architects and incorporates pictorial art and sculptures. The work of Marcelle Ferron, at the Champ de-Mars station in Old Montreal, and Jordi Bonet (1932–1976), at the Pie-IX station near Olympic Stadium, are among the most interesting.

In recent years, Quebec art has evolved alongside major international currents; it has distanced itself from traditional painting while emphasizing more diverse forms and techniques, including "installation," a primarily sculptural idiom that also includes other art forms such as painting and photography. Among its proponents are Betty Goodwin, Barbara Steinman, Geneviève Cadieux, Jocelyne Alloucherie and Dominique Blain. Michel Goulet and Roland Poulin have made important contributions to the field of sculpture. Melvin Charney, an architect and urban planner, has also produced remarkable works; his most important creation is the garden of the celebrated Montreal's Canadian Center for Architecture.

Literature

Throughout the era of exploration and colonization, the literature of New France was limited to travel memoirs (Cartier, Champlain), stories, descriptive writings (Sagard, Charlevoix), and the famous historical missives known as the **Relations**, written by Jesuit missionaries recording their life and work in the New World.

EMERGENCE OF QUEBEC LITERATURE

Two newspapers, *Le Canadien*, founded in 1806 in Quebec City, and *La Minerve*, founded in 1826 in Montreal, were instrumental in the development of French-Canadian literature.

In 1837 the young Philippe Aubert de Gaspé published the first French-Canadian novel, entitled *L'influence d'un livre*, inspired by legends. The first fiction novels were influenced mainly by rural traditions, as evidenced in *The Canadians of Old* (*Les Anciens Canadiens*), written in 1863 by **Philippe Aubert de Gaspé** senior. Nationalist and conservative ideologies were also a source of inspiration as in Pierre Joseph Olivier Chauveau's novel *Charles Guérin* (1846–53). Indeed, Quebec literature was long influenced by a wave of conservative ideology that arose in the 1860s, promoting the moral values and precepts of the Catholic Church.

Historical novels, inspired by **François-Xavier Garneau's** *History of Canada (Histoire du Canada)*, published in the 1840s, became very popular in the mid-1800s, as did the romantic poetry of Octave Crémazie (1827-79). Louis-Honoré Fréchette (1839–1908) published his *Légende d'un peuple* in 1887.

20C

The early 20C was dominated by the nationalist works of writer and historian **Lionel Groulx** (1878–1967), leader of the "Action française", and by the poet Émile Nelligan (1879–1941), who produced his entire work between the ages of 17 and 20, before being confined to a mental asylum. In 1916 French-born **Louis Hémon**'s novel *Maria Chapdelaine*, depicting life in rural Quebec, was published posthumously, and is now translated into eight languages. In 1933 **Claude-Henri Grignon** wrote his celebrated novel *The Woman and the Miser* (*Un homme et son péché*), which have been the core subject of the immensely popular television series and movie, *Séraphin*.

Urbanization and the trauma of World War II resulted in greater introspection among Quebec writers as they questioned the established order. The end of World War II marked the end of the dominance of rural life, which formed the basis of traditional French Canadian society. Novelist **Robert Charbonneau** abandoned his tales of rural life for psychological novels. Quebec poetry was redefined through the works of **Alain Grandbois** (1900–75) and **Hector de Saint-Denys Garneau** (1912–43). **Roger Lemelin**'s *The Town Below (Au Pied de la Pente Douce,* 1944) was the first novel to explore the lifestyle of the urban working class. The theme of city life also permeated the works of **Gabrielle Roy**, such as *The Tin Flute (Bonheur d'occasion),* published in 1945. Roy was born and raised in rural Manitoba (Western Canada), and thus her take on Montreal poor, industrial neighborhoods was particularly poignant.

The Quiet Revolution (*la Révolution tranquille*) of the 1960s reflected Quebecers' growing awareness of their distinct, fragile cultural identity and their reappraisal of traditional values and institutions. The literature of the day faithfully reflected this period of upheaval as writers explored a rich variety of subjects and styles. It is the poets, however, who instilled the most strength and energy into Quebec literature at that time: **Gaston Miron** (1928–96), Gatien Lapointe, Jacques Brault, and Fernand Ouellette. The 1960s witnessed the rise of new novelists to prominence, while already well-known writers became associated with the finest of Quebec letters, among them **Hubert Aquin** (*Hamlet's Twin/Neige noire*), **Marie-Claire Blais** (*A Season in the Life of Emmanuel/Une Saison dans la vie d'Emmanuel*), **Roch Carrier** (*La guerre, yes sir!*), **Réjean Ducharme** (*The Swallower Swallowed/ L'avalée des avalés*), **Jacques Ferron** (*The Juneberry Tree/L'amélanchier*), **Jacques Godbout** (*Knife on the Table/ Le couteau sur la table*), **Anne Hébert** (*Kamouraska and In the Shadow of the Wind/Les fous de Bassan*) and **Yves**

LOUIS HÉMON

MARIA CHAPDELAINE

Récit du Canada français

Précédé de deux préfaces: par M. Emile Boutroux, de l'Académie française, et par M. Louvigny de Montigny, de la Société royale du Canada.

Illustrations originales de Suzor-Côté

Ouvrage honoré d'une souscription du Secrétaire d'État du Canada et du Secrétaire de la province de Québec

MONTRÉAL
J.-A. LeFebvre, éditeur,
LA COMPAGNIE IMPRIMERIE GODIN-MÉNARD LIMITÉE
41, RUE BONSECOURS, 41
1916

Thiery Marcoux/Bibliothèque nationale du Québec

Thériault (*Agaguk*). Also during the 1960s, playwright **Michel Tremblay** made a resounding entrance onto the literary scene with *Les Belles-Sœurs*. In the 1960s and 70s, poet-singer-novelist **Leonard Cohen** (b. 1934, in Montreal) wrote of the sexual revolution and resistance to the Vietnam War. Two of the best-known Anglophone novelists are **Hugh MacLennan** (1907–90) and Montreal-born **Mordecai Richler** (b. 1931), who has won numerous literary prizes including the prestigious Governor General's Performing Arts Awards. Nova Scotia-born MacLennan, a professor at Montreal's McGill University, confronted the issue of Quebec's relationship to the rest of Canada in his *Two Solitudes* (1945). Following the trend of the 1960s, the early 1970s were characterized by a broad diversity of styles, most notably the "psychological" novel. Prominent authors from this extremely prolific period of Quebec literature include Louis Hamelin (*La rage*), Suzanne Jacob (*Laura Laur*), Claude Jasmin (*Mario/La sablière*), Sergio Kokis (*Le pavillon des miroirs*), Marie Laberge (*Julliet*), Robert Lalond (*Le petit aigle à tête blanche*) and Monique Larue (*True Copies/Copies conformes*). In 2002, **Yann Martel** won the coveted Booker Prize for Fiction for his *Life of Pi*.

Theater

The theatrical arts were introduced somewhat late in Quebec: The first permanent French theater companies appeared in the 1880s. But it was only in the late 1940s to early 1950s that the foundations of what has become an enduring theatrical tradition were laid. At that time, an original repertoire and several theatrical institutions gradually took shape, as a generation of actors, trained for the most part with Father Legault's Les Compagnons de Saint-Laurent, paved the way for their successors. Professional theater companies were created: the Théâtre du Rideau Vert (1949), the Théâtre du Nouveau Monde (1951), the Quat'Sous (1954) and the avant-garde Apprentis-Sorciers and Égregore.

Gratien Gélinas created *Tit-Coq* (1948), a play based on a popular character whose deceptively naive demeanor hid a mind capable of astute social criticism. In 1959 Gélinas wrote *Bousille et les justes* while heading the Comédie-Canadienne, a name that reflected the will to create a truly French-Canadian theatrical repertoire. A friend of Jean Anouilh and Arthur Miller, Marcel Dubé staged *Un simple soldat* at the Comédie-Canadienne in 1958; his ability to explore universal themes won him wide recognition. The Compagnie Jean Duceppe was founded by the comedian **Jean Duceppe** (1923–90) in 1973, and garnered an excellent reputation for its contemporary repertoire.

Michel Tremblay, whose plays have had more international exposure than those of any other Quebec playwright, pursued his predecessors' exploration of city life. From *Les Belles-Sœurs* (1968), which is considered a milestone in the development of Quebec theater, to *The Real World?* (*Le vrai monde?*, 1987), Tremblay has created a true human comedy, with a cast of characters who speak the street slang heard in the working class neighborhoods of Quebec City and Montreal.

The strength and originality of Quebec's modern theater lie in the **experimental works** of authors like Jean-Pierre Ronfard (*Vie et mort du roi boiteux*, 1981) at the Théâtre Expérimental de Montréal, and Gilles Maheu at Carbone 14. Playwright Normand Chaurette came on the scene in the 1980s with such pieces as *Provincetown Playhouse and Fragments of a Farewell Letter Read by Geologists* (*Fragments d'une lettre d'adieu lus par des géologues*, 1986); in 1996, his *Le passage de l'Indiana* gained wide acclaim at the Avignon Festival, and garnered a prestigious Governor General's Performing Arts Award. Other renowned names of Quebec theater include Michel Marc Bouchard (*The Orphan Muses/Les muses orphelines*, 1989), René-Daniel Dubois (*Don't Blame the Bedouins/Ne blâmez jamais les Bédouins*, 1985) and Marie Laberge (*Night/L'homme gris*, 1986). In Quebec's Ligue nationale d'improvisation, famous in the French speaking world, actors improvise dialogue in the context of a competitive, rough ice hockey game, by far Quebec's best-loved sport. The widely acclaimed **Cirque du Soleil** (Circus of the Sun) has delighted audiences around the world with its innovative and enchanting blend of traditional circus entertainment, music, theater and dance, embellished with stunning costumes.

Music

The Montreal Symphony Orchestra, conducted by Californian Kent Nagano, is widely acclaimed. Since 1963 the Montreal International Music Competition (Concours international de Montréal) has welcomed young musicians from all over the world. Both the Mount Orford and Lanaudière music camps are vibrant training centers. The Festival de Lanaudière, a summer music festival in Joliette, has earned international recognition.

COMPOSERS, CONDUCTORS AND MUSICIANS

The authors of Canada's national anthem, *Ô Canada,* are two French-Canadians; Adolphe-Basile Routhier (1839–1920) wrote the lyrics and Calixa Lavallée (1842–91) composed the music.

The Orchestre Métropolitain du Grand Montréal at Basilique Notre-Dame

Conductor Wilfrid Pelletier (1896–1982) launched Montreal's dynamic music scene while Claude Champagne (1891–1965), composer of the *Symphonie gaspésienne,* opened the way for numerous other composers. Among the foremost are Alexander Brott (founder of the McGill Chamber Orchestra), Jean Papineau-Couture and Jean Vallerand. The Contemporary Music Society of Quebec (Société de musique contemporaine du Québec), founded in 1966, includes composers such as Serge Garant, Pierre Mercure, Gilles Tremblay and André Prévost.

Pianists Henri Brassard, André Laplante and Louis Lortie have all triumphed in international music competitions, while violinist Angèle Dubeau and pianist Marc-André Hamelin have carved brilliant careers at home as well as abroad. Kenneth Gilbert is known for his research and remarkable renditions of 17C and 18C harpsichord music. Raymond Daveluy, Mireille and Bernard Lagacé are famous for their mastery of the pipe organ. Founded in 1879, the Casavant Frères company of Saint-Hyacinthe has maintained its reputation as one of the world's foremost organ manufacturers.

OPERA

Since the days of Chambly's Emma Lajeunesse (1885–1958), better known as **Albani**, several Quebec voices have been heard in Milan, New York, Paris and London: soprano Pierrette Alarie, contralto **Maureen Forrester** (1930), tenors Raoul Jobin and Leopold Simoneau, bass Joseph Rouleau and baritones Louis and Gino Quilico.

The Montreal Opera has staged several productions each year since its creation in 1980.

TRADITIONAL AND POPULAR MUSIC

Music is the heart and soul of Quebec's oral tradition. From the songs of the "voyageurs" to *Un Canadien errant* (1842), popularized by Nana Mouskouri, Quebec's folk repertoire, inspired by traditional French songs, was part of everyday life.

Félix Leclerc (1914–88) was Quebec's preeminent folk musician. A raconteur and poet, he introduced Quebec culture to France after World War II, leading the way for many other Quebec folk singers or *chansonniers.*

In the late 1950s, several chansonniers and musicians formed a group known as "les Bozos," named after one of Leclerc's songs. They included Raymond Lévesque, Clémence Desrochers, André Gagnon, Claude Léveillé (*Frédéric*)—who worked with Edith Piaf—and Jean-Pierre Ferland (*Je reviens chez nous*). Joining this talented new generation of singers and songwriters was **Gilles Vigneault**, the poet of Natashquan. His song *Gens de mon pays* accompanied the rise to power of the Québécois Party. Pauline Julien and Renée Claude are known today for their renditions of works by Quebec's great folksingers.

The rock music of **Robert Charlebois** reflected a more critical social outlook typical of the 1960s. At that time, large-scale shows and a recording industry heavily influenced by American culture were adding a whole new dimension to Quebec music. The California counter-culture was echoed in the music of very creative groups such as Harmonium and Beau Dommage.

Diane Dufresne created a highly personal and dramatic style that has won her numerous awards at home and in France. She often sang compositions by **Luc Plamondon**, one of the most famous Quebec songwriters. Plamondon founded the Quebec Society of Professional Authors and Composers (Société professionnelle des auteurs et compositeurs du Québec) and worked on the rock opera *Starmania* in 1976. The late Sylvain Lelièvre, whose musical career took shape in the early 1970s, is considered among Quebec's finest singer-songwriters. Richard and Marie-Claire Séguin, the rock group Offenbach, and Claude Dubois also rose to prominence in the 1970s, and Ginette Reno powerful voice made her one of Quebec's most acclaimed pop singers.

Such singers and composers as Richard Desjardins, Luc de Larochelière and Paul Piché appeared on Quebec's musical scene during the 1980s. The 1990s witnessed the phenomenal rise of song-stress **Céline Dion**, whose acclaim today extends worldwide. Other musical stars of note include Laurence Jalbert, Isabelle Boulay, Bruno Pelletier and Garou, who were all celebrated in France as well as in Quebec.

In 2004, Montreal-based anglophone artist Sam Roberts won both Artist and Album of the Year Juno Awards (the annual Canadian music awards) for his *We were born in a flame* recording. His success marked the beginning of an enduring series of English-speaking bands, like Arcade Fire, who find inspiration and creative synergy in Montreal, mainly in the Mile End, the multi-ethnic, western portion of trendy Plateau Mont-Royal.

Cinema

Since 1895 most of the films shown in Quebec were imported from the US. The first feature films were produced in the province between 1944 and the introduction of television in 1952. But the birth of the Quebec film industry really dates back to the 1960s.

Several executive directors and directors of photography were trained at the National Film Board of Canada, a federal institution (1939) based in Montreal since 1956. The NFB has acquired an international reputation for its animation films, especially those of Frédéric Back (two-time Oscar winner), and its documentary tradition, which evolved into a genre known as "cinéma-vérité," a widely recognized trend in the Quebec film industry, best reflected in the works of **Pierre Perrault** (*The Moontrap*, 1963; *Wake up, mes bons amis!*, 1970) and Michel Brault (*Les Ordres*, 1974).

Claude Jutra won international fame for *Mon Oncle Antoine* (1971) and *Kamouraska* (1973), based on a novel by Anne Hébert. Jean Beaudin's movie *J.A. Martin, photographe* (1975) won an award at the Cannes Film Festival.

Denys Arcand reached the European and American public with his films *The Decline of the American Empire* (1986) and *Jesus of Montreal* (1989); the latter was nominated at Cannes and Hollywood. Jean-Claude Lauzon's *Night Zoo* won 13 of the 17 Genies awarded during the Canadian film industry's annual gala awards celebration in 1987. Robert Lepage's 1995 movie *The Confessional (Le confessionnal)* won the Prix Claude-Jutra.

In 2003, Denys Arcand's ultimate recognition came about with *Les invasions barbares* (sequel to *The Decline of the American Empire*). The movie won the foreign film Oscar, as well as two awards in Cannes.

Various movies by Quebecan directors have been very successful, including *Seducing Doctor Lewis* (Jean-François Pouliot) and *C.R.A.Z.Y.* (Jean-Marc Vallée). *See Films in Planning your Trip for a selection of Quebec's films.*

THE PROVINCE TODAY

Government

Quebec's political system derives from the Canadian Constitution of 1867, which defines the jurisdiction of the provincial and federal governments.

Legislative power rests with the unicameral **National Assembly of Québec**, created in 1968 to replace the Legislative Assembly. The 125 members of "l'Assemblée nationale du Québec" are elected by universal suffrage for a maximum of five years (elections are generally held every four years). The members belong to a range of parties reflecting the various political tendencies among the electorate. The **Lieutenant-Governor**, the official representative of the British Crown, joins with the National Assembly to form the **Parliament**.

The government is headed by the party that obtains the most seats in the National Assembly. The leader of this majority party—who is designated the **Premier**—appoints his **Executive Council** from among the National Assembly members. This council, which constitutes the government's **executive branch**, is responsible for introducing bills to the Assembly. Much of the Assembly's work is carried out by parliamentary committees, which review and investigate various matters brought before the legislative body.

Quebec's **judicial branch** is composed of two levels: The lower courts and the Court of Appeal. The first level is made up of the municipal courts, the Quebec Court and the Superior Court. The Quebec Court (1988), comprising the Provincial Court, the Courts of Sessions of the Peace and the Juvenile Court, is responsible for certain civil, criminal and penal issues. Judges serving on the Quebec Court are appointed by the provincial government. Appointed by the federal government, the Superior Court rules on all cases outside the jurisdiction of the other courts and acts as a court of appeal for offences concerning penal law. The federally appointed Court of Appeal is the general appellate court for the entire province.

The Supreme Court of Canada, with nine judges appointed by the federal government, is the highest court in the land and as such can hear appeals on decisions reached by Quebec's Court of Appeal.

THE ELECTORAL SYSTEM

The principle of universal suffrage applies to all citizens 18 years of age and over. The plurality single-member electoral system is based on the concept of territorial representation. Each of the 125 Quebec members of Parliament represents the population of one constituency or "riding." Since 1963, Quebec electoral law stipulates that all parties must file financial statements and sets a limit on expenses, while at the same time providing state contributions for the financing of standard administrative and electoral expenses of parties that obtain a minimum level of electoral success. For the purposes of public administration, Quebec is divided into 17 administrative regions.

FEDERAL GOVERNMENT

Quebecers also elect members to the Canadian House of Commons in Ottawa, and are represented in the Canadian Senate by legislators appointed by the federal government. Representation in Ottawa is usually proportional to a province's population. Currently (2008), Quebec is represented by 75 of the 308 federal members of Parliament and 24 of the 105 senators.

INTERNATIONAL RELATIONS

Under the Canadian Constitution, international relations fall within federal jurisdiction. However, since the 1960s, Quebec has obtained permission to institute Its own foreign delegations and economic development offices and created a Ministry of International Affairs, using the principle of international extension of internal powers, in an effort to fully assume its responsibilities in matters of immigration, foreign loans, the environment and, above all, culture.

With an increasingly prominent role in the entire French-speaking world, including former French colonies in Africa, Quebec has achieved a unique status within the context of Canadian representation at international French-language events. Quebec City hosted the *Second Sommet de la Francophonie* (1987). The eighth summit was held in Moncton, New Brunswick (officially the only bilingual province in Canada) in 1999, attended by 52 government officials and heads of State. Since 1988 Quebec and Canada have both participated in TV5, the international French-language television network. In the 2006 census, nearly seven million Canadians reported French as their mother tongue, second in the world after France.

Economy

Historically, Quebec's abundant natural resources have constituted its primary economic base. These industries are becoming increasingly important and lucrative in a globalized industrial world hungry for finite resources. Although Quebec's vast forests, farmlands and waterways continue to be widely exploited, the province's economy relies heavily on services and manufacturing. Industrial giant Bombardier, a world leader in the manufacturing of public transportation material and business planes, started in Quebec as a snow-mobiles maker. Quebec is also a leader in pharmaceuticals (Apotex Inc.) and a number of knowledge-based industries. However, the rise of China as the world's manufacturing superpower has been devastating traditional manufacturing sectors like textiles and apparel.

THE FUR INDUSTRY

A driving force in the settlement of northern Quebec and a traditional activity of the Amerindian and Inuit populations, trapping has become a somewhat marginal activity at the national level. Nonetheless, Canada remains a major producer and Montreal is the center of its fur industry. Canada is known internationally as the producer of the world's finest furs. Amerindian and Inuit trappers and breeders are now grouped into cooperatives. Quebec trappers harvest mostly beaver, muskrat and marten. Increasingly, furs are produced through "farms" and not trapping.

AGRICULTURE

Until the turn of the 19C, agriculture was the cornerstone of the Quebec economy. Commercial agriculture began in the 1880s with the marketing of milk

Farm near Oka

©Benoît Desjardins

and dairy products. Today agriculture accounts for less than two percent of the gross domestic product.

The principal farming areas developed in the fertile regions bordering the St. Lawrence River (e.g. Bas-Saint-Laurent, Beauce, Gaspé Peninsula). Quebec's agricultural industry is primarily based on animal products (milk, pork, poultry and cattle), large-scale cultivation of cereal products (corn, barley, oats and wheat), as well as vegetable and fruit farming. The main seasonal fruits are apples, strawberries, raspberries and blueberries. However, Quebec is a the forefront of small scale, organic production of fruits and vegetables in North America.

THE FOREST

The exploitation of Quebec's extensive forested lands has generated considerable revenue since the colonial period. In many regions, farmers turned to forestry to supplement their livelihood during the long winter months. Early in Quebec's history, shipbuilding, construction and heating created a great demand for wood on the domestic market as well as in England, where much of Quebec's timber production was exported to supply the wood-hungry British Navy. At the onset of the 20C, new technologies and an increasing demand for newsprint fueled a phenomenal market for **pulp and paper**. Commercial forest land is essential to the regional economy and is located mainly in Abitibi-Témiscamingue, Côte-Nord and Saguenay-Lac-Saint-Jean. Sawmills and workshops generate half the jobs and products in the lumber industry. One-third of Canada's pulp and paper production originates from Quebec, particularly from the Mauricie Region, and Canada remains the world's top producer of newsprint (source FAO, 2005).

FISHERIES

Virtually all of Quebec's major fishing centers are located on the Gaspé Peninsula, the Magdalen Islands and Côte-Nord. In recent years, annual catches brought in by Quebec's fishermen have contributed relatively little to the gross domestic product (approximately $134 million in 2005). Once treated, these catches generate products reaching a value of $305 million.

Ocean catches generally include cod, Greenland halibut, rockfish, mackerel, and herring. The proportion of revenue coming from shellfish (crab, shrimp and lobster) is on the rise, as fish stocks are decreasing.

Inland, most commercial fishing is concentrated to the west of Cape Tourmente and particularly in the region of Lake Saint-Pierre (Yamaska, Maskinongé, Nicolet and Sorel). The main catches are sturgeon, perch and eel, but freshwater fish stocks are also a cause of concern.

MINES

The history of Quebec's mining industry is closely linked to three distinct eras and three regions. Asbestos mining started in the last quarter of the 19C in the Eastern Townships. In the 1920s gold and copper were discovered in the Abitibi region. Finally, after 1945, iron ore was mined in the Côte-Nord region in Fermont and Schefferville (Duplessis region).

Two-thirds of Quebec's mineral production involves metallic minerals (gold, silver, iron, copper, lead, zinc); the other third involves non-metallic (asbestos) and various mineral substances. The Côte-Nord produces nearly half of Quebec's mineral resources. One quarter of the province's minerals and virtually all its gold production emanate from the mines of Abitibi. Quebec is the world's largest exporter of asbestos. Although mining remains the principal activity in several regions, total mining production accounts for less than 2 percent of the gross domestic product.

HYDROELECTRIC POWER

Quebec imports oil and natural gas but produces and exports hydroelectric power. The province's industrialization has been and remains closely linked to its hydroelectric resources which, as early as 1900, provided low-cost energy for the lumber, petrochemical and electro-metallurgic industries, particularly aluminium plants (Alcan, Reynolds). Proponents of economic nationalism soon demanded the nationalization of the province's hydroelectric industry, a step already taken by Ontario at the beginning of the 20C. From the days of the Shawinigan Water and Power Co. (1902) to the creation of **Hydro-Québec** (first nationalization in 1944 to be followed by large-scale nationalizations in 1962–63 on the initiative of René Lévesque, as minister under the government of Jean Lesage), hydroelectricity became a key element of Quebec's economic policy. The first hydroelectric dams on the Manicouagan River reflected the will of Quebecers to take charge of their economy and develop an engineering expertise that is now in demand worldwide.

Quebec electricity is mainly produced by its hydroelectric plants, three quarters of which are owned by Hydro-Québec. There are also a few thermal plants and one nuclear power plant (Gentilly-2,).

The province exports some of its production to other Canadian provinces and to the US. The ambitious James Bay project has sparked great controversy over the environmental and cultural consequences on the northern regions of the province. Yet generally Quebecers are very proud of their hydropower industry and see it as less environmentally damaging than the non-renewable forms of energy.

NEW DIRECTIONS

The Quiet Revolution (*Révolution tranquille*) was characterized by increased Quebec government intervention in education, social affairs and the economy. Viewed in the North American context, Quebec's political economy has distinct characteristics reflected in its nationalization programs (asbestos and hydroelectricity), corporate aid and investment institutions, large-scale infrastructure projects (Expo '67, Montreal subway opening in 1966,

Traffic on the St. Lawrence Seaway between Montreal and Lake Ontario (2007)				
Vessel Transit		**Commodity**	**%**	**tons**
Cargo vessels	4,450	Grains	26.1	10,405,868
Non-cargo/ ballast vessels	803	Mining products	46.8	18,645,539
		Processed products	27	10,761,370
Pleasure craft	2,100	Other products	0.1	43,010
Traffic revenue	**$33,453,092**	**Total cargo**	**100.0**	**39,855,787**

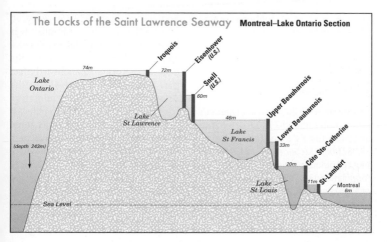

The Locks of the Saint Lawrence Seaway Montreal–Lake Ontario Section

Montreal's 1976 Olympic Games, massive hydropower projects) and linguistic policies that promote the role of Francophones in the commercial, industrial and financial sectors.

Montreal, already the headquarters of several Canadian banks and insurance companies and of the Montreal stock exchange, benefited from these linguistic policies, which enabled more and more Francophones to take part in the city's economy. Even though Montreal's role as Canada's main financial center was eclipsed by Toronto in the 1970s, the Greater Montreal area continued to dominate the provincial economy. The Montreal metropolitan area contains approximately one-half of Quebec's manufacturing companies and jobs.

Although in recent years traditional sectors of the Quebec economy have suffered, and in some places disappeared, owing to increased competition mainly from Asian nations, the province has found new markets for its high-tech expertise in aeronautics, telecommunications and engineering. The **service industry** has been the stronghold of the economy since the 1950s.

Since the establishment of a north-south railway network in 1850, the opening of the **St. Lawrence Seaway** (1959), which enabled ships to sail into the very heart of the US by way of the Great Lakes, and an the completion of an extensive network of expressways, and the North American Free Trade Agreement (1994), the economies of Quebec and the US have become more closely integrated. Some 85 percent of Quebec's foreign exports are bound for the US.

Population and Language

According to the 2008 census, Quebec's population totalled 7,730,612 inhabitants (Canada's population being 33,287,000). Quebec ranks as the second most populous province behind Ontario (population 12,861,940). Almost four out of every five Quebecers reside in urban areas, and the "exode rurale" trend in continuing; cities are growing and rural areas are less and less inhabited.

EARLIEST INHABITANTS

In 2006, 108,425 Quebecers (less than two percent) claimed native ancestry. This includes **Amerindians**, Inuit, and Metis. The largest of the three groups, the Amerindians, are divided into Nine Nations, namely (in descending order of population number) the Mohawk, Cree, Montagnais, Algonquin, Atikamekw, Mi'kmaq, Huron-Wendat, Naskapi, and Abenaki.

Currently, the largest spoken language by aboriginal families in Quebec are the Iroquoian (Mohawk and Huron dialects) and Algonquian (Cree, Montagnais/Naskapi, Mi'kmaq and Abenaki dialects). Today the majority of Quebec's Amerindian population lives in the communities of Pointe-du-Buisson, Mashteuiatsh, Odanak, Lorette and Kahnawake. A large Cree-speaking population (around 11,810) is concentrated in the villages of the James Bay region.

The Inuit, the inhabitants of Quebec's subarctic regions, number approximately 12,000. The province's Inuit population lives primarily in the coastal villages of Nunavik, the vast region occupying Quebec's northernmost territory. Their language is Inuktitut.

NON-INDIGENOUS POPULATION

In the 2006 census, 5,877,660 Quebecers declared that French was their only mother tongue; 575,555 declared that English was their only mother tongue and, interestingly, 939,350 declared that neither French nor English was their mother tongue. Italians, Greeks, and Eastern Europeans represented the largest waves of immigrations in the first part and the mid-20C. However, the Asian, Black and Arabic immigration has been the most sustained in the last few decades. Most immigrants come to and stay in the Montreal area, where they often have family ties and where integration is easier.

Nearly half of Quebec's population resides in Montreal's metropolitan area. Since World War II, and especially between 1965 and 1980, when Quebec's nationalistic fervor was increasing, the

Anglophone population that settled in Quebec City, Montreal and the Eastern Townships during the post-1815 wave of immigration has seen its numbers decline. Montreal's cosmopolitan flavor developed at the turn of the 19C with the arrival of Italian and Eastern European immigrants. After 1945 immigration intensified, originating mainly from Mediterranean countries. International events and internal policies have influenced this trend. In the 1970s southeast Asians, mostly French-speaking Vietnamese (and some Cambodians), emigrated to Quebec in unprecedented numbers, as did Latin Americans (particularly Chileans) in the following decade, all to escape difficult political circumstances. Since the early 1990s, Asians have been the largest immigrant group: 64,566 entered Quebec between 2001 and 2005. By the end of the 1990s, policies to encourage French-speaking immigration resulted in an influx of people from France, Algeria, Morocco and Haiti. During 2005, some 43,400 people immigrated to Quebec, 57 percent of whom had some knowledge of French.

THE LANGUAGE DEBATE

Three factors gave rise to the language controversy that culminated in the 1960s and 1970s: A vivid awareness of the fragility of French culture in North America, which first led Quebecers to perceive and refer to themselves as "Quebecois" rather than "French Canadians"; the first signs of a decrease in fertility (the birth rate declined by 50 percent between 1951 and 1986); and lastly, an acute awareness of the consequences of heavy postwar international immigration (immigrants overwhelmingly integrated into the English minority rather than the French majority).

In Quebec, the language problem became focused on the issue of education. Conscious of the role of schools in the development of cultural identity, the Government of Quebec passed laws (Bill 63 in 1969, Bill 22 in 1974) establishing restrictions on the admission of immigrants into English schools. The pro-sovereignty Parti Québécois, elected for the first time in 1976, passed the landmark **Bill 101** in the following year. Bill 101 is a form of charter defining the status of the French language and regulating its use. In the field of education, current legislation allows children of parents who completed an English elementary school curriculum anywhere in Canada to attend English public elementary and secondary schools. In 1988 the government passed **Bill 178**, amending Bill 101's stipulation that commercial signs appear only in French. The new law required businesses to post French signs outdoors, while allowing the use of bilingual signs indoors, provided that the French language appear more prominently than the other language. The law was further amended in 1993 with the passage of Bill 86 permitting bilingual exterior signage, again under the condition that the French language clearly predominate.

Today, the language debate still exists, but the actual separation of Quebec from Canada appears increasingly improbable. In turn, Quebec seems to have developed a true national identity within the confines of the Canadian Confederation. Anyhow, it is remarkable that the descendants of the 60,000 French-speaking inhabitants of New France, at the time of the British Conquest in 1759, have not only resisted assimilation to the English language in North America, but have developed and nurtured a distinct, vibrant French-speaking culture.

Customs and Traditions

Quebec's customs and traditions reflect the values of a rural people whose everyday life was greatly influenced by the Catholic Church and the rigors imposed by the natural environment. The oral and material heritage of Quebec is permeated with reminders of harsh winters, the era of the *coureurs des bois,* the settlement of forest regions and the predominance of the Church. The Catholic Church long remained the focus of Quebecers' social and cultural life. Although the role of this institution has gradually diminished since the mid-20C, reminders of its once powerful presence are everywhere, in countless churches with silver-colored steeples, tiny processional chapels and wayside crosses.

Industrialization and urbanization have radically transformed the traditional Quebec lifestyle. In the city and countryside, many old customs have given way to the 21C, while others endure.

LEGENDS

The numerous stories, childhood tales, legends and proverbs of Quebec are of French inspiration. Long winter nights were ideal for the telling of fantastic tales. A favorite is the legend of the *chasse galerie* or "wild chase." As winter approached, young men often joined logging camps to supplement their income. Life was harsh in these camps, and the men's dreams sometimes drifted to a wife or girlfriend back home. On New Year's Eve, the devil appeared with a tempting offer: He would take the lovelorn men to their sweethearts in a special canoe capable of travelling through the air at great speed. In exchange, the men would promise to refrain from using swear words during the entire trip lest they be eternally damned. The men stood by their word on the way home, but on the return trip, they would sometimes forget their promise and speak the forbidden words. The flying canoe would come crashing to earth and the souls of the unfortunate passengers plummeted into hell.

The Seasons

The traditions and festivities that have developed over the centuries in the southern part of the province are intimately linked to the four seasons.

Spring – In late March the maple sap starts, heralding the return of spring and the celebrations associated with the making of maple syrup. This sweet "water" was traditionally collected in pails hung on spouts inserted into the trunks of maple trees. The water was then boiled down to the proper consistency, producing maple syrup. This tradition known as sugaring-off is still very much a part of Quebec culture, but the pails have for the most part disappeared; today, maple water is collected in plastic tubing that brings the sap directly to a central evaporator. For the traditional sugaring-off parties, families and friends congregate in large wooden cabins known as sugar shacks, built at the edge of maple groves. Inside, long picnic tables are laden with a variety of hearty dishes and desserts cooked or covered in maple syrup. Hot syrup is also poured over snow to form a taffy-like substance known as *tire d'érable,* which is deftly rolled onto a stick.

Summer – The 24th of June is dedicated to St. John the Baptist, but it is also Quebec's national holiday. As a religious and national holiday, "la Saint-Jean-Baptiste" as it is commonly called, is a major annual event, celebrated throughout the province as a sign of Quebec's cultural and linguistic distinctiveness. Floats, flag parades, bonfires and live shows by some of Quebec's major entertainers are typically part of the celebrations.

Autumn – The hot, humid summer is followed by Quebec's most beautiful season, fall. As the nights grow cooler, maple trees display their autumn finery: vivid reds, rusty oranges and golden yellows. This is the best time to visit the Laurentians and the Eastern Townships. It is also harvest time in apple-growing country. Many orchards are open to the public and resound with the sounds of families and friends who turn apple-picking into a pleasant outing.

Winter – The snow usually starts falling in late November or early December and melts in April. Although the days are cold and short, the winter months are generally very sunny and bright because of the sparkling snow. Quebecers celebrate winter with carnivals, the most famous of which is the **"le Carnaval de Québec,"** (Quebec City Carnival) with its famous parades, giant ice castle and ice sculpting contests. Another traditional winter activity is ice fishing on lakes and rivers.

Another popular tale is the story of Rose Latulippe, the girl who danced with the devil. One night, during a dance, the door opened and a handsome stranger strolled in. Subjugated by his charm, Rose left her usual partner to dance with the newcomer. After several hours of dancing, the exhausted young girl tried to stop but discovered she could not. Her partner continued to whirl and twirl her 'round the dance floor until she thought this hour must surely be her last. Just as she despaired, the village priest appeared. Recognizing the work of the devil, he chased him off with prayers and a few drops of holy water. Poor Rose was exorcized and vowed never again to dance with any other than her appointed beau.

...AND FOLK HEROES

Logger **Louis Cyr** (1863–1912) became a legend in his own time. Weighing over 165kg/364lb, he acquired a reputation as the world's strongest man, by lifting a platform on which 18 people stood, weighing 1,967kg/4,336lb. His record still stands.

Born in the Lake Saint-Jean region, **Alexis Lapointe** owed his nickname "Alexis le trotteur" (Alexis the trotter) to his amazing speed. He could run 240km/149mi in a single day and often raced horses and even trains. It is said that the autopsy performed on him revealed double joints, bones and muscles akin to those of horses.

VERNACULAR OBJECTS

Quebecers' appreciation of beauty and form is reflected in the design and decoration of buildings, furniture and everyday objects. Even the most functional items were decorated with symbols and motifs that are still visible in the countryside: Wooden maple-sugar molds in the shape of hearts and leaves, weather vanes with animal motifs, barn doors and shutters with floral motifs.

From the earliest days of the colony, clothing was designed to protect Quebecers from the bitterly cold winters. Tuques, mittens, woolen scarves and boots are still essential. A hooded coat known as a "canadienne," and fur coats made of fox, raccoon and mink where traditionally popular winter gear. They have been replaced by "technical apparel" made with modern fabrics, often made in Quebec.

CULINARY TRADITION

The Beauce region is famous for syrup, taffy, maple sugar, pie, yogurt, ice cream, and liqueur. The Saguenay-Lac-Saint-Jean region serves heavy but delicious culinary delights such as *cipaille,* a six-layer meat pie with short crust, and *soupe aux gourganne,* a soup made with a type of very large bean. Other traditional dishes include thick stew, known as *ragoût,* and a meat pie called *tourtière.* Fish and all kinds of seafood abound in several regions: Fresh or smoked salmon from the Côte-Nord, lobster from the Magdalen Islands, different fish from the Gaspé Peninsula, shrimp from Matane and winkles from Bas-Saint-Laurent.

For dessert, sugar pie and maple syrup are traditional favorites.

Regional Specialties

Courtesy La Cabane à Sucre Millette

Lac des Seize Îles, Laurentides
Id Port, Montreal
Guillaume Pouliot/Tourisme Laurentides

AMOS

ABITIBI-TÉMISCAMINGUE REGION
POPULATION 12,685

Originally called Harricana after the river that flows through its center, the town was later renamed Amos in honor of Alice Amos, wife of Lomer Gouin, premier of Quebec in the early 1900s. Amos is the cradle of the Abitibi region. The "agriculturalist" movement promoted by French-Canadian religious and political leaders, who painted a return to the land as a panacea for the economic crisis of the 1930s, brought settlers to the area. The Catholic Church played a major role in the development of the region; in addition to providing moral and at times political support, priests acted as social mediators. Agriculture, mining, and forestry remain the region's main industries.

- **Information:** 892 Rte. 111. ☎1-800-670-0499. www.48nord.qc.ca.
- **Orient Yourself:** Amos is located 604km/375mi northwest of Montreal by Rtes. 117 and 111; 56km/35mi north of Val-d'Or by Rte. 111. Daily flights from Montreal to Val-d'Or by Air Canada Jazz. ☎514-393-3333.
- **Don't Miss:** Pageau Refuge, a unique insight into Northern Canada's wildlife.

Sight

Cathédrale Sainte-Thérèse d'Avila (Cathedral of St. Teresa of Avila)

11 Blvd. Mgr-Dudemaine. ⊙Open year-round, daily 9am–5pm. ☎819-732-2110.

Located in the heart of town, this cathedral (1923) is a rare example of the Romano-Byzantine style in North America, the structure features a circular floor plan crowned by a spectacular dome. Noteworthy decorative elements include a 2.75m/9ft painted dove adorning the dome's interior, pink Italian marble, and stained-glass windows imported from France.

An **Art Gallery** showcases and sells artwork and handicrafts from artists and artisans of the Abitibi region. *Centre d'exposition d'Amos, 571 1re Rue.*

Excursions

Pikogan Village

4km/2.5mi north of Amos. Turn left on Rue Principale, left again on 1ère Ave. Ouest and then right on 6e Rue Ouest, which becomes Rte. 109. Continue another 2km/1.2mi to the village, located on the left side of the road.

All the residents of this Algonquin village are originally from the Lake Abitibi region. Founded in 1954, the village is now administered solely by indigenous people, reflecting their desire to reclaim their culture. All the services of a vibrant community exist here, including classes in the Algonquian language at the school. The **church**★ (⊙*open mid-Jun–mid-Aug, Mon–Sat 9am–4.30pm, Sun 1pm–5pm; rest of the year & holidays by appointment only; ☎$4; ☎819-732-3350*) of the St. Catherine's Mission, built in 1968, is reminiscent of a wigwam, an Amerindian architectural form. The church's interior is decorated in the local Amerindian style.

Refuge Pageaus (Pageau Refuge)

8km/5mi east of Amos. Take Rte. 111 East toward Val-d'Or, and turn left on Rang Dix, at Figuery, toward Saint-Maurice (4241 Rang Croteau). ⊙Open Jun, Sat–Sun 1pm–4pm; Jul–Aug, 10am–4pm; Sept–Oct, Sat–Sun 1pm–4pm; Nov–May, Sat 1.30pm tour. ☎$12. ☎819-732-8999. www.refugepageau.ca.

Formerly a trapper, owner Michel Pageau has been an animal lover for over 30 years. Forest rangers and hunters direct him to injured, mistreated or abandoned animals which he then cares for. Once nursed back to health, the animals are set free; those unable to survive in the wild remain at the Refuge. Michel Pageau and its refuge have become synonymous with northern Canada's wildlife. A **zoo** (Kids) with cages tagged with the Algonquian, French, and English names of the animals delights youngsters.

Preissac
*35km/22mi southwest of
Amos by Rte. 395.*
Lost in time, the village of Preissac is nestled in a rural setting on the edge of the Kinojévis River. Next to the bridge over the rapids is a fine spot for a picnic. Just before reaching the Lake Preissac outfitter (*approximately 15km/9.3mi*

from Rte. 117), a lookout point on Rte.95 affords a splendid **view**★ overlooking the lake. Fishing and tourism services, a marina and a campground are located on the shores of the lake.

Le Dispensaire de la Garde
In La Corne, 26km/16mi southeast of Amos on Rte. 111. Open mid-Jun–Sept, daily 9am–5pm. $5. 819-799-2181. *www. dispensairedelagarde.com.*
Experience the history of colonization, the early days of rural clinics, the social role and personal life of nurses in this house. Guides dressed as nurses lead visitors through the multimedia presentation that brings rural medicine to life.

ÎLE D'ANTICOSTI★★
DUPLESSIS
POPULATION 270
MAP: SEE LOCAL MAP ÎLE D'ANTICOSTI

A true ecotourism destination, this island stretches more than 222km/138mi in length and 56km/35mi at its widest point. Pastoral Anticosti Island lies in the estuary of the St. Lawrence River, south of the Mingan Archipelago (Côte-Nord) and northeast of Forillon National Park (Gaspé Peninsula). Mantled with lush coniferous forests and crisscrossed by more than a hundred rivers teeming with Atlantic salmon and trout, Anticosti is a favorite for deer hunters. French industrialist Henri Menier, who purchased the island in 1895, created a private hunters' paradise upon it. Today, some 166,000 white-tailed deer are everywhere—on the streets and even on people's front lawns.
Outside Port-Menier, the only village of the island, the 7943sq km/3067sq mi of Anticosti where divided into outfitting establishments and a Quebec national park. The island is not only a pleasant vacation spot for nature lovers, who can admire a rich variety of birds and wildflowers in a pastoral setting, but also a great place for a coastal tour by sea kayak. Limestone formations laden with fossils provide for fascinating rock collecting. Some fossils dating from the early Paleozoic era (420 to 500 million years ago) are considered by geologists to be unique.

- **Information:** 36 Chemin des Forestiers, Port-Menier. 1-888-463-0808 & 418-962-0808. www.tourismeduplessis.com.
- **Orient Yourself:** There are two means of getting to Anticosti Island. **By air:** from Montreal, Quebec City, Mont-Joli or Havre-Saint-Pierre to Port-Menier, contact SÉPAQ Anticosti 1-800-463-0863. *www.sepaq.com/antocosti.* **By boat:** Relais Nordik, a passenger and supply ship 1-800-463-0860, departures from Rimouski 418-723-8787, Sept-Îles 418 968-4707, Havre-Saint-Pierre. 418 538-3533. www.relaisnordik.com.
- **Don't Miss:** Vauréal Falls and Canyon; while driving, *do* miss the many deer!
- **Organizing Your Time:** When you arrive in Port-Menier, get a schedule of current activities: hiking and sea kayaking are available seasonally. Rent a mountain bicycle or car for day trips. Learn all the excursions available on Anticosti Island while you are there and select the most appropriate according the weather.

Address Book

⚓ *For price ranges, see the Legend on the cover flap.*

WHERE TO RENT A CAR

At **Auberge Port-Menier**. ☎*418-535-0122*. To visit the island, a radio-equipped, four-wheel-drive motor vehicle essential.

Anticosti is an immense, rugged natural territory crossed from west to east by route Henri-Menier, also known as "la route TransAnticostienne", a dirt road to which several secondary roads are connected. A long distance may separate your place of accommodation from the attraction that you wish to visit, whether in or outside the National Park. Be sure to take these distances into account when you plan your outings. Route Henri-Menier is the only road traversing the island from west to east. It is paved between Port-Menier and the airport (7km/4.3mi), but elsewhere has a gravel surface. Dirt roads link Port-Menier to deer hunting and fishing lodges and camps on the Jupiter River.

WHERE TO STAY

SÉPAQ Anticosti organizes vacation packages that include airfare from Mont-Joli (on the Gaspé Peninsula), lodging in cottages, board, and rental of a four-wheel-drive. For example, the NaturExpress packages (2 nights, meals & air transportation from Havre-Saint-Pierre, Quebec City or Montreal) would allow you to stay at **Auberge Port-Menier**, on the seashore. In an air-conditioned mini-bus, a guide will take you to the Vauréal Falls, the Observation Canyon, and the Wilcox shipwreck. You'd discover Baie Sainte-Claire and the ruins of the Château Menier, and you'd visit the Ecomuseum. SÉPAQ packages extend to 14 days.

In addition to vacations organized by SÉPAQ are private outfitters (like *Pourvoirie du lac Geneviève* and its chalets not far from the Port-Menier airport ☎*418-535-0294 & 1-800-463-1777. www.anticostiplg.com*).

Another lodging option is **Hôtel de l'Île**, a basic, friendly accommodation with 10 rooms (**$$**) in Port-Menier, ☎*418-535-0279. www.hoteldelile.ca.tc.*

WHERE TO EAT

Meals are included in most packages sold by private outfitters and SÉPAQ. However, simple and more elaborate dishes are served in Port-Menier hotel restaurants:

$ Hôtel de l'Île – *In the village of Port-Menier.* ☎*418-535-0279.* Casual restaurant serving fast food, pizza and simple meaty dishes. Loads of calories to fuel your discoveries.

$ Auberge Port-Menier – *In the village of Port-Menier.* ☎*418-535-0122.* Seafood, charbroiled steak, pasta, regional specialties. Operated by SÉPAQ.

WHERE TO PITCH A TENT

At Wilcox campground, on the north shore of the island, near Pointe Fortune. *For information*, contact SÉPAQ Anticosti. ☎*1-800-463-0863.*

WHERE TO LEARN

Écomusée d'Anticosti – *In the village of Port-Menier. Late Jun–late Aug, daily 8am–5pm (free admission).* ☎*418-535-0250.* Museum on the history of Anticosti and its natural wonders.

A Bit of History

Archaeological excavations on the island trace the presence of humans here back 3,500 years. The name Anticosti may derive from the Indian word *notiskuan,* meaning "the place where bear are hunted," or it could have originated with Basque or Spanish fishermen who called it *anti costa,* or "before the coast."

Jacques Cartier mentioned the island after his first voyage to New France in 1534, but settlement occurred there only after 1680 when Anticosti was granted to Louis Jolliet in recognition of his discovery of Illinois and his expedition to Hudson Bay. The initial settlement was destroyed by Admiral Phips' fleet in 1690. Anticosti was passed down to Jolliet's three children, and in

Parc national d'Anticosti/ Jean-Pierre Huard/Sépaq

Anticosti Canyon

1763 it was annexed to Newfoundland, which had become a colony of the British Crown according to the terms of the Treaty of Utrecht (1713) (💷 *see Introduction: History*).

During the next century, the island changed owners several times. In 1872 an English enterprise known as the Anticosti Island Company (or Forsyth Company) made an unsuccessful attempt to colonize the island, as did its successor, the Stockwell Company, and others.

The Menier Era: 1895–1926 – French industrialist and heir to a fortune from the chocolate industry, **Henri Menier** set out in the late 19C to find a piece of land that would serve both as an investment property and as a hunting and fishing retreat for himself and his friends. On December 16, 1895, Menier purchased Anticosti Island for $125,000.

To ensure his comfort on visits to Anticosti and entertain his guests, Menier constructed a hunting lodge overlooking the bay between Port-Menier and Baie-Sainte-Claire. The sumptuous mansion, known as the "chateau" by locals, was of Norwegian and Norman inspiration.

Upon Henri Menier's death in 1913, Anticosti was inherited by his brother Gaston Menier who, although appreciative of the island's beauty, was somewhat intolerant of his brother's extravagances. In 1917, due to economic problems in France that weakened the powerful chocolate industry, the Menier family closed down their lumber operation on the island and, in 1926, Anticosti was sold for $6.5 million to the Anticosti Corp., a consolidated venture of three Canadian pulp and paper companies. Over the years, the furnishings of the mansion were sold or transported to company holdings on the mainland. Chateau Menier fell into such disrepair that the structure was considered a hazard, particularly to local children who would wander on the site. Orders were issued to burn it down in 1953.

New Developments – The Anticosti Corp. engaged in forestry activities and brought prosperity to the island for a brief period after the Menier era. In 1974 the Quebec Government acquired Anticosti for the sum of $23.78 million. Citizens were allowed to purchase land and residences in 1983, and a municipal government was established. Most of the island is now part of the Anticosti Reserve, covering 4,575sq km/1,766sq mi.

Port-Menier Area

Port-Menier

The only remaining village on the island, Port-Menier was established at the turn of the 19C as the island's deep-water port. A general store, bank, post office, and laundromat are housed in the village center, and there is a grocery store nearby.

Baie-Sainte-Claire

15km/9.3mi west of Port-Menier. Originally known as English Harbour, the village was renamed by Henri Menier in honor of his mother. The site was first settled in the mid-19C by fishermen from Newfoundland and the Maritimes. The Forsyth Company attempted unsuccessfully to develop the village, and when Martin-Zédé arrived there on behalf of Menier in 1895, he found only 11 families in residence. The village was transformed into a viable planned community, but was eventually abandoned in favor of the new village of Port-Menier. By 1931, Baie-Sainte-Claire lay in ruins. In 1985 a lime kiln was rebuilt to the west of the village site. The original kiln had been used for nine years under Menier, producing slake lime for mortar and whitewash. Laws prohibiting hunting at Baie-Sainte-Claire make it an ideal spot to observe the unafraid **white-tailed deer**, which can sometimes be seen in herds of up to a hundred.

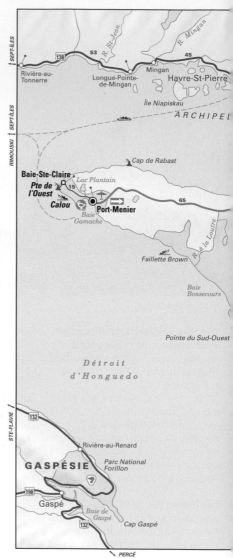

Pointe de l'Ouest (West Point)

1km/.6mi south of Baie-Sainte-Claire. Despite the many lighthouses along the Anticosti shore, shipwrecks were numerous. Since the early 18C, over 200 ships have sunk near the island. Remains of the **Calou**, which shipwrecked in 1982, can be seen from this point.

The first lighthouse built on this site (1858) was one of the most powerful on the St. Lawrence; its light could be seen for 50km/31mi in clear weather.

Tour of the Island

From Port-Menier to Baie de la Tour

169km/105mi.

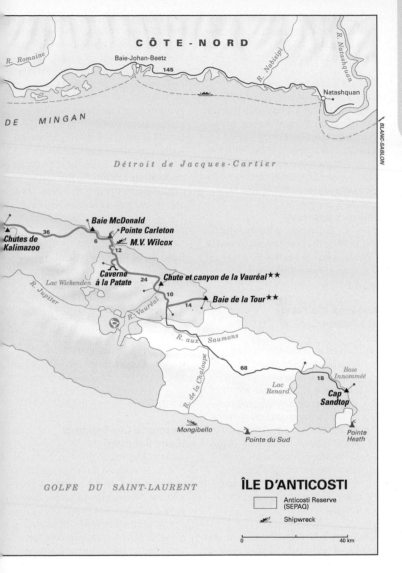

ÎLE D'ANTICOSTI

Anticosti Reserve (SEPAQ)

Shipwreck

0   40 km

Chutes de Kalimazoo (Kalimazoo Falls)
65km/40mi. Access to the falls is 1.7km/1mi from the main road.

▶ *Follow signs to the Kalimazoo Falls. Take the trail on the right down to the stream, cross it, then turn left to get a good view of the falls.*

The falls cascade into a small, clear pond flanked by limestone cliffs.

Baie McDonald (McDonald Bay)
36km/22mi.

This scenic bay with its sandy beach was named for a fisherman from Nova Scotia, Peter McDonald—popularly known as Peter the Hermit—who settled on Anticosti in the late 19C. After some time, his wife returned to Nova Scotia, but the fisherman stayed on, living as a hermit. According to legend, Martin-Zédé coaxed McDonald into coming to Baie-Sainte-Claire when he became ill, but after his recuperation, the feisty old fellow (aged 87) made the trip home, traveling some 120km/74mi through the forests on snowshoes.

Pointe Carleton
6km/3.7mi east of Baie McDonald.
The road passes along sandy beaches offering good views of the sea. The picturesque lighthouse on the point was built in 1918. *Lodging is available here at the Wilcox Campground. For information, contact SÉPAQ Anticosti. ☎1-800-463-0863. (see Planning Your Trip).*

Wilcox Shipwreck
Near Pointe Carleton, at the mouth of La Patate River, the beached hull of the *M.V. Wilcox* lies exposed to the pounding surf. This former minesweeper wrecked here in June 1954.

Caverne à la Patate
(La Patate Cavern) *12km/7.5mi.*

▷ *Turn off the main road approximately 3km/1.8mi beyond the two bridges that cross La Patate River and one of its tributaries. With a four-wheel-drive vehicle, it is possible to continue on the forest road for about 2km/1.2mi. Then, on foot, follow the path indicated by colored ribbons for approximately 1hr to reach the entrance to the cavern. It is advisable to bring along a safety helmet when visiting the cavern.*

Discovered in 1981, the cavern was explored and mapped by a team of geographers the following year. The entrance to the cavern measures 10m/33ft high and about 7m/23ft wide. The total length of the passages is 625m/683.5yd.

Chute et canyon de la Vauréal★★
(Vauréal Falls and Canyon)

▷ *The trail to the waterfall begins 24km/15mi east of La Patate Cavern. To reach the canyon, return to the main road and turn back toward Pointe Carleton. The turn-off is at 1.5km/1mi.*

The Vauréal River was originally called Morsal in honor of a descendant of the Huguenots who arrived on Anticosti in 1847 and spent 45 years near the river. Menier renamed it Vauréal after one of his properties in the Oise region of France.
The one-hour hike along the riverbed to the base of the waterfall offers spectacular scenery. The greyish limestone walls, sometimes patterned with red and green schists, are carved into an undulating pattern by the forces of nature. Along the way, the steep walls are dotted with crevasses and caves. The waterfall plunges 76m/249ft into the canyon.

Baie de la Tour★★ (Tour Bay)

▷ *Turn left off the main road 10km/6.2mi beyond Vauréal Falls. Continue on the secondary road for 14km/8.7mi.*

Limestone cliffs dramatically plummeting into the sea create a breathtaking view from the sandy beach of the bay.

▷ *Return to the main road.*

Detour to Cap Sandtop
(Cape Sandtop)
172km/107mi round-trip. The road ends at Cap Sandtop. A dirt road stretches over this part of the island; in poor weather, deep ruts can sometimes make driving difficult.
The Natiscotec River marks the boundary of the SÉPAQ nature reserve. Low, sparse vegetation characterizes the marshlands found on this part of the island.
The Renard River leads back into the SÉPAQ nature reserve. Renard Bay was once the site of an early settlement, where the Menier family eventually established a lobster-packing plant. A bird sanctuary is nestled in the small inlet between La Chute River and Innommée Bay.

▷ *Return to Port-Menier by the same road.*

BAIE-SAINT-PAUL★★

Baie-Saint-Paul occupies a spectacular **site**★ at the confluence of the Gouffre and St. Lawrence rivers. The community long remained the only settlement between Saint-Joachim and Tadoussac.

Surrounded by rolling green hills, Baie-Saint-Paul has inspired many artists and today boasts more than a dozen art galleries, an exposition hall and an art center, and charming auberges set in traditional *Québécois* houses. During the 1970s, the town was the hub of acrobats, clowns, and jugglers who later founded the **Cirque du Soleil**, a now internationally acclaimed circus troupe.

August brings the annual **Canada Young Painters Symposium** to the Baie-Saint-Paul Arena; artists produce large-scale works of art while the public looks on.

- **Information:** 6 Rue Saint-Jean-Baptiste. ☎418-665-4454. www.tourisme-charlevoix.com.
- **Orient Yourself:** Baie-Saint-Paul lies some 95km/59mi northeast of Quebec City on Rte. 138.
- **Don't Miss:** The stunning view from the visitor information center on Rte 138.
- **Organizing Your Time:** At dawn and at dusk, enjoy the surrounding views, among the best in Canada. Take in the art and the architecture in the town's core during the day. This is a tourist town, so plan to avoid queues in the summer.
- **Especially for Kids:** Introduce children to art through children-specific programs at the Centre d'exposition de Baie-Saint-Paul.
- **Also See:** CÔTE DE CHARLEVOIX, ISLE-AUX- COUDRES.

Sights

Arriving in Baie-Saint-Paul from the south on Rte. 138, enjoy a **view**★★ of the St. Lawrence valley and river.

Stroll the village's narrow streets and admire the old houses of picturesque Rue Saint-Jean-Baptiste. Note in particular nos. 143–145. Wander down Saint-Joseph Street to shop at art and antique boutiques, then go to the wharf and perhaps take a cruise or sea kayaking trip.

Carrefour culturel Paul-Médéric (Paul Médéric Cultural Center)

4 Rue Ambroise-Fafard. Open Tue–Sun 11am–5pm. ∞$4. ☎418-435-3681. This art gallery (1967, Jacques Deblois), built as a commemorative monument to the Canadian Confederation, displays the works of Charlevoix artists. In the weaving and tapestry studios, craftspeople create works using traditional and modern techniques.

Centre d'exposition de Baie-Saint-Paul (Baie-Saint-Paul Art Exhibition Center)

23 Rue Ambroise-Fafard. Open mid-Jun–Aug, Tue & Wed 10am–6pm, Thu–Sun 12pm–8pm; Sept–mid-Jun, Tue–Fri & Sun 11am–5pm, Sat 12pm–6pm. ∞$4. Free on Sat. ☎ 418-435-3681. www.centredexpo-bsp.qc.ca.

Designed by architect Pierre Thibault, the center plays host to traveling exhibits from around the world.

Seen from the wharf on Rue Sainte-Anne, Île-aux-Coudres seems to block the entrance to the bay.

Excursions

Leaving the city by Rte. 362 Est, pause where an overlook provides another **view**★★ of Baie-Saint-Paul, the St. Lawrence and the south shore. Nearby, on the right, the Chemin Vieux Quai reaches the shore, and provides a closer view of Île-aux-Coudres.

BAIE-SAINTE-CATHERINE★

CHARLEVOIX REGION
POPULATION 227
MAP: SEE LOCAL MAP CÔTE DE CHARLEVOIX

This community is set on a low plateau bordering a bay at the mouth of the Saguenay River, on the north shore of the St. Lawrence. In 1609 Samuel de Champlain met the Montagnais chief, Sagamo, at the southern point of the bay. Their meeting led to the alliance against the Iroquois, which was to have grave consequences for New France.

The first settlers arrived in Baie-Sainte-Catherine in 1820, and for many years they logged trees to produce timber destined for the European market. Today whale watching is the major attraction in Baie-Sainte-Catherine as well as in Tadoussac, across the fjord.

- **Information:** 621 Rte. 138. ☎1-800-667-2276.
- ▶ **Orient Yourself:** Baie-Sainte-Catherine is approximately 210km/130mi northeast of Quebec City by Rtes 40 and 138.
- **Don't Miss:** Stop at one of highway lookouts as whales can often be seen from the shore, particularly as you approach the mouth of the Saguenay fjord.
- ⏱ **Organizing Your Time:** The ferry for Tadoussac may be very busy in summer. You can watch whales from the shore... and watch for the best time to go for the ferry, visible from the shore.
- **Especially for Kids:** There is a play area for children to enjoy, while adults watch—and wait—for whales; a sometimes unexciting endeavor for young children.

Sights

Whale-watching cruises★★
Depart from the municipal wharf May–Oct, daily 10am & 1.15pm (late Jun–Labor Day, additional cruise 3.45pm). Round-trip 3hrs. Commentary. Reservations required. ⬢$59. ✗ ♿ 🅿 Croisières AML. ☎ 418-692-1159 and 1-800-563-4643. www.croisieresaml.com.

Cruises offer the opportunity to view whales up close and discover the marine environment of the St. Lawrence via underwater cameras. The marine mammals of the St. Lawrence river include Minke Whale, Fin Whale, Blue Whale, White or Beluga Whale, and Gray Seals.

Centre d'interprétation et d'observation de Pointe-Noire
On Rte. 138, just before the descent to the Saguenay. ⏱Open mid-Jun–Labor Day, daily 9am–6pm; Sept–early Oct, Fri–Sun 9am–5pm.⬢$5.45. ♿🅿☎418-237-4383. www.parkscanada.gc.ca.

Situated on a cape overlooking the mouth of the Saguenay River, the Pointe-Noire observation center affords a fine **panorama** of the St. Lawrence estuary and the cliffs embracing the Saguenay Fjord. The interpretation center (part of the Saguenay-St. Lawrence Marine Park) introduces visitors to this unique natural environment, where salt and fresh water meet.

Excursions

Ferry to Tadoussac
Departs from Quai de l'Anse-au-Portage year-round, 24h/day. One-way 10min. ♿.
This free ferry service is the only means of crossing the deep waters of the Saguenay on Rte. 138. It is an unforgettable trip with the fjord on the left and the majestic St. Lawrence on the right. Whale sightings from the ferry.

BAS-SAINT-LAURENT★★

CHAUDIÈRE-APPALACHES–BAS-SAINT-LAURENT
MAP: SEE LOCAL MAP CÔTE DE CHARLEVOIX

Situated on the south shore of the St. Lawrence River, between Quebec City and the Gaspé Peninsula, the regions of Chaudière-Appalaches and Bas-Saint-Laurent are characterized by fertile plains and plateaux; to the north loom the foothills of the Appalachian Mountains. The peaceful rural landscapes along the shore are divided into long, narrow strips of farmland, laid out perpendicular to the river in the manner of the old seigneurial rang system. To the north, the Laurentian Mountains plunge into the St. Lawrence, creating picturesque scenery.

- **Information:** Tourisme Bas-Saint-Laurent,148 Rue Fraser, Rivière-du-Loup. ☎418-867-1272 & 1-800-563-5268. www.tourismebas-st-laurent.com/www. chaudiereappalaches.com.
- ▶ **Orient Yourself:** Chaudières-Appalaches is across the bridge from Quebec City. It spreads east to just before La Pocatière, where Bas-Saint-Laurent begins, and spreads all the way to Gaspésie.
- **Don't Miss:** Grosse-Île; the Aulnaies Seigneurie in Saint-Roch-des-Aulnaies; the eel interpretation center in Kamouraska.
- **Organizing Your Time:** You can make a circuit following the shoreline of the St. Lawrence River to return to Quebec City by crossing on the ferry at Rivière-du-Loup. The routes described here follow the more interesting secondary roads, but if you need to get farther along more quickly, use the four-lane Rte. 20 (to just beyond Rivière-du-Loup). The sun sets spectacularly on the St. Lawrence River, so plan a rest or meal stop along the river every day at dusk.
- **Especially for Kids:** Parc du Bic is a good place to camp, with a variety of outdoor activities, such as hiking and bird watching.
- **Also See:** KAMOURASKA, RIVIÈRE-DU-LOUP.

Driving Tours

1 From Lévis to Rivière-du-Loup *187km/116mi.*

Lévis★
See Entry Heading.
Outside Lévis, Rte. 132 runs alongside the St. Lawrence, affording views of Quebec City and of the Montmorency Falls on the north shore.

▶ *After 13km/8mi, turn left to Beaumont.*

Beaumont
Built between 1726 and 1733, the **church** of Beaumont is one of the oldest in Quebec (after St. Peter's Church on Île d'Orleans and the votive chapel at Cap-de-la-Madeleine). It was here that the commander of the British troops, General Wolfe, posted a proclamation of British supremacy in 1759. When the villagers removed the proclamation, Wolfe's soldiers attempted to destroy the church by burning it, but the structure survived intact.

The church was enlarged by extending the façade and adding a chapel on the north side, as well as a sacristy. Its simple nave ends in a circular apse. The church interior boasts a magnificent carved wood **décor** fashioned by Étienne Bercier, a craftsman from the Montreal studio of Louis-Amable Quévillon. Crafted between 1809 and 1811, the choir is graced with Louis XV-style panelling and a coffered vault. The finely sculpted tabernacle of the main altar dates from the 18C. Above it hangs a painting by Antoine Plamondon, *The Death of St. Étienne.*

▶ *Continue through the village to rejoin Rte. 132.*

Moulin de Beaumont (Beaumont Mill)

7km/4.3mi beyond the village of Beaumont, turn left. 2 Rte. du Fleuve (Rte. 132). ⏱*Open Jun 24–Aug 24, Tue–Sun 10am–4.30pm; May–Jun 23 & end Aug–end Oct, weekends 10am–4.30pm.* ∞*$7.* ✗ ♿ P ☎*418-833-1867.*

This four-storey mill overlooking the Maillou Falls (chute-à-Maillou) was built in 1821 to card wool for the seigneury. In 1850 it became a grain mill and, later, a sawmill. The mill, restored to operating condition, was reopened in 1967, and local residents furnished the third floor and attic with early French-Canadian pieces. On the premises, visitors can purchase bread made with freshly ground flour.

Behind the mill, a panoramic stairway leads to the base of the cliff, on the shores of the St. Lawrence, where the foundations of the Péan Mill can be seen. This late-18C mill operated for 144 years until 1888. Archaeological excavations have been underway on this site since 1984.

▸ *Return to Rte. 132, continue for 4km/2.5mi and turn left.*

Saint-Michel

Located in the center of the village, the **church** dates from 1858. The **presbytery** (1739), built in the typical Quebec style, is adorned with shutters carved with a fleur-de-lis on the top and a maple leaf on the bottom. In the late 18C, it was bombarded by the British and subsequently renovated.

▸ *Return to Rte. 132.*

This agricultural region is dotted with several houses with brightly colored trim. The road follows the water's edge, offering good views of the St. Lawrence and the islands that make up the Île-aux-Grues Archipelago.

Montmagny

31km/19mi northeast of Saint-Michel.

▸ *After passing the bridge, turn left at the manor.*

This charming city features several noteworthy sights. At the **Musée de l'Accordéon** (Accordion Museum), housed in the historic Manoir Couillard-Dupuis (around 1800), you can see accordions being made, and learn the history of the bellowed instrument (*301 Blvd. Taché Est;* ⏱*open Jun 23–Labor Day, daily 10am–4pm; rest of the year, Mon–Fri 10am–4pm;* ∞*$4;* ♿ P ☎*418-248-7927; http://accordeon.montmagny.com*). At the **Centre éducatif des Migrations**, interactive exhibits on white geese and a multimedia presentation on the Grosse Île quarantine complex are on view (*53 Avenue du Bassin Nord;* ⏱*open Jun 23–Oct 22, daily 10am–5pm;* ∞*$6;* ♿ P ☎*418-248-4565*). At the Snow Goose Festival held in October, you can sample the variety of ways the locals serve up their feathered friends.

Archipel de l'Isle-aux-Grues (Isle-aux-Grues Archipelago)

☛*Guided excursion to the Archipelago departs from Berthier-sur-Mer late Jun–Labor Day, 9.45am; rest of the year, call for hours. Round-trip 6hrs. Commentary. Reservations required.* ∞*$41.* ♿ P *Croisières Lachance* ☎*418-259-2140. www.croisieres lachance.qc.ca.*

Of the 21 islands comprising the archipelago, Grosse-Île, Isle-aux-Grues and Île-aux-Oies are the most important. **Isle-aux-Grues,** the only permanently inhabited island, is 10km/6.2mi long, and is accessible by air (*Air Montmagny, depart from Montmagny Nov–Apr, daily; on demand the rest of the year; reservations required; one-way* ∞*$20;* ♿ P ☎*418-248-3545*) or ferry (*depart from Montmagny Apr–Dec daily; one-way 25min; free, call ahead for schedule;* ♿ P ☎*418-241-5117; www.traversiers. gouv.qc.ca*).

European settlement of Isle-aux-Grues dates from 1679. Today this tranquil haven draws lovers of nature and peace and quiet. Snow geese flock here during the spring and fall. On the southeast tip of the island, outside the village of Saint-Antoine, stands an elegant manor house overlooking the St. Lawrence.

Lieu historique national du Canada de la Grosse-Île-et-le-Mémorial-des-Irlandais★ (Grosse Île and the Irish Memorial National Historic Site of Canada)

🕐Open mid-May–mid-Oct, daily 9am–6pm. ✕ 🅿 ☎418-234-8841. www.parks canada.gc.ca. Ferries to Grosse-Île depart from Berthier-sur-Mer; one-way 30min. Commentary. Reservations required. ☞Visit & ferry $43.50.

The ever-increasing number of European immigrants to Canada prompted the government to establish, in 1832, a quarantine station on Grosse Île to protect the country from the infectious diseases (especially cholera) that were then ravaging Europe. In the first year of operation some 50,000 immigrants first set foot on Canadian soil here. In 1847, thousands of Irish fleeing famine, political repression and typhus arrived. More than 5,000 perished on Grosse Île before ever reaching Quebec City.

The island was divided into three zones. The western part of the island was known as the Hotel Sector. Healthy immigrants were lodged in hotels according to the class of passage they took on the ship coming from Europe. The Village Sector in the middle part of the island housed the employees of the quarantine station and their families. To the east, the Hospital Sector included 21 structures, of which one is still standing.

The quarantine station on Grosse Île closed in 1937, after operating for more than a century. The facility was taken over by Canadian and US military authorities as a research station for biological and chemical warfare. It then became a research center for animal diseases and animal quarantine station. In 1990 it became a national historic site.

A veritable Ellis Island (☞see THE GREEN GUIDE New York City) of Canada, Grosse Île offers the visitor a touching rendezvous with the past. On the island, a guided walk in the Hotel Sector includes a visit to the third-class hotel, the cemetery, the Bay of Cholera, and the monument erected in 1909 in memory of the Irish immigrants buried on the island. Visitors continue aboard a tourist trolley to the Village Sector, to view the chapels for employees and their families. The tour ends at the Hospital Sector.

L'Islet-sur-Mer – 23km/14mi.
🕐See Entry Heading.

Saint-Jean-Port-Joli★ – 13km/8mi.
🕐See Entry Heading.

Saint-Roch-des-Aulnaies
14km/8.7mi.
Located on the south shore of the St. Lawrence, this peaceful community takes its name from the alder trees (aulnes) lining the Férée River. Granted to Nicholas Juchereau de Saint-Denis in 1656, the Aulnaies seigneury is among the oldest in the region. However, the land remained unsettled until the late 17C, owing to Iroquois hostilities. In 1837, the seigneury was sold to Amable Dionne (1781–1852), a wealthy merchant and mayor of Kamouraska for over 30 years, who erected the magnificent manor house for his son, Pascal-Amable.

Completed in 1849, the Gothic Revival **Église Saint-Roch-des-Aulnaies** (3km/1.8mi east of the village entrance on Rte. 132; 🕐open mid-Jul–mid-Aug, daily 10am–5pm; ♿🅿☎418-354-2552) displays several paintings by Joseph Légaré (1795–1855). The carved choir and altar were designed by François Baillairgé. Situated 400m/1,312ft beyond the church, the small fieldstone **processional chapel** was erected in 1792 (🕐open Jun 24–Labor Day, daily 10am–5pm).

Set on a promontory overlooking the junction of two rivers, the **Aulnaies Seigneurie** (3km/1.8mi east of the church on Rte. 132; turn right, go up the hill to the parking area and information booth; 🕐open mid-Jun–Labor Day, daily 9am–6pm; early Jun & rest of Sept–mid-Oct, weekends 10am–4pm; ☞$8.75; ✕🅿☎418-354-2800 & 1-877-354-2800; www.laseigneuriedesaulnaies.qc.ca), a Victorian-era wooden house flanked by two octagonal towers, was completed in 1853, according to a design by the noted architect Charles Baillairgé. Guides dressed in late 19C costumes conduct tours through the house and describe the life of the period. Outside, visitors can enjoy walks through the manicured

Trois Pistoles

gardens and the wooded park as well as visit the adjacent 1842 **gristmill** (moulin banal).

La Pocatière★ – *10km/6.2mi.*
♿*See Entry Heading.*

Rivière-Ouelle
10km/6.2mi.
Originally known as Rivière-Houel in commemoration of one of Samuel de Champlain's officers, the territory was conceded by the Intendant Jean Talon to Jean-Baptiste Deschamps, also known as Boishébert de la Bouteillerie, in 1672.

Saint-Denis-de-la-Bouteillerie
11km/6.8mi.
Located in the center of the village, the **Maison des Chapais** dates back to 1834 (♿*visit by 45min guided tour only, Jun–mid-Oct, daily 9am–5pm;* ⊗*$6;* ⎄ ☎*418-498-2353; www.maison chapais.com*).
Built by Jean-Charles Chapais, one of a signers of the Confederation, the house remained in the Chapais family until 1968.
In 1866 the porch and spiral staircases were added, and the present interior furnishings were bought. The living room furniture dates from the early 19C, while the dining room and bedroom are appointed in the Second Empire style.
The road passes across a wide flood plain, affording expansive views of the Laurentian Mountains across the

St. Lawrence. Perpendicular to the shoreline, eel traps extend into the river.

Kamouraska★ – *10km/6.2mi.*
♿*See Entry Heading.*

Rivière-du-Loup★ – *41km/25mi.*
♿*See Entry Heading.*

2 From Rivière-du-Loup to Sainte-Luce

130km/80mi by Rte. 132.

Cacouna
10km/6.2mi from Rivière-du-Loup.
The seigneury was conceded to Daulier Duparc in 1673, but the first colonists began settlement around 1750. Amerindians named it Kakouna, meaning "land of the porcupine." In the mid-19C, Cacouna became a popular seaside resort, and large hotels and luxurious vacation homes were constructed. Today, only the sumptuous Victorian houses along the water's edge recall the town's heyday.

Église Saint-Georges (St. George Church)
Turn right off Rte. 132 onto Rue de l'Église and continue for 2 blocks. ⊘*Open during masses only.* ♿⎄ ☎*418-862-4338.*
The fieldstone church (1848) was partially reconstructed in 1896. The interior by F.-X. Berlinguet (1852) is richly decorated with carved and gilded detailing,

crystal chandeliers and Italian paintings from the late 19C. The organ dating from 1888 is one of the few remaining works of Eusèbe Brodeur, a predecessor of the Casavant Brothers of Saint-Hyacinthe. Nearby, the Neoclassical **presbytery** was built between 1835 and 1841.

Trois-Pistoles
36km/22mi.
The town derives its name from an old monetary unit used throughout Europe until the late 19C. According to local legend, a small vessel shipwrecked on the coast of Île aux Basques in the early 17C. One of the sailors holding a silver mug lost it in the river and exclaimed: *"Voilà trois pistoles de perdues!"* (There go three pistoles). The seigneury was granted to Denis de Vitré in 1687, but the region was frequented much earlier by Basque fishermen whose presence is confirmed by the remains of ovens on the **Île aux Basques,** located 4km/2.5mi offshore.

Église Notre-Dame-des-Neiges (Church of Our Lady of the Snow)
From the center of town, turn right onto Rue Jean-Rioux. ◷*Open May–mid-Oct, daily 9am–4.30pm.* ◉*$2 (*◕*guided tour).* 🅿️☎*418-851-1391.*
This monumental edifice was constructed in the 1880s according to plans drawn up by David Ouellet. The bell towers and the angular lines of the four façades set this church apart. The ornate interior is the work of Canon Georges

Bouillon, a proponent of the Romano-Byzantine style. Note the abundance of gilding, and the wooden Corinthian columns painted to resemble marble.

▷ *After 29km/18mi turn right for Saint-Fabien, continue for 2km/1.2mi.*

Saint-Fabien
Built in 1888, the octagonal **Adolphe Gagnon barn** (⚟*closed to the public*), located at the center of the village, is the only one of its kind in the Bas-Saint-Laurent region. Blending into the landscape, the almost-round construction conceived by American theorist Orson Squire Fowler, was designed to offer greater wind resistance, eliminate wasted space, and facilitate storage of fodder. According to popular belief, the octagonal form made it impossible for demons to take refuge in the corners of the structure.

Parc national du Bic★ (Bic) Kids
Main entrance at Cap-à-l'Orignal, 6km/3.7mi from center of Saint-Fabien. ◷*Open daily year-round.* ◉*$3.* 🍴♿ 🅿️☎*418-736-5035. www.sepaq.com/pq/bic/en. Nature programs in the summer at the interpretation center (*◷*open Jun–mid-Oct, daily 9am–5pm;* ☎*418-736-5035).*
This 33sq km/13sq mi provincial conservation park was created in 1984 to preserve the plants and wildlife along the southern shoreline of the St. Law-

© Sepaq/Mathieu Dupuis

Hiker at Cap-à-l'orignal in Parc national du Bic

rence River. The park boasts a variety of flora including both deciduous and boreal forests. Gray and Harbor seals are occasionally spotted on the rocky coast in Orignal Bay.

Le Bic
15km/9.3mi from Saint-Fabien.
This small town is renowned for its spectacular **setting**★★ on the shores of the St. Lawrence. According to local legend, when the world was created, the angel responsible for distributing mountains had a surplus at the end of the day while passing over Bic. To lighten his load, he emptied the remaining mountains on this spot.

Rimouski★ – *16km/10mi.*
⚐ *See Entry Heading.*

▶ *After 14km/8.7mi, at the junction with Rte. 298, turn left toward Sainte-Luce and continue for 4km/2.5mi.*

Sainte-Luce
Cottages line the shore in this pleasant summer resort town, which occupies a picturesque site on the St. Lawrence.

BEAUCE★

The name Beauce refers to the area drained by the Chaudière River as it flows from Lake Mégantic, just north of the American border, into the St. Lawrence River. Like its French namesake, a region to the southwest of Paris, "la Beauce" is a vast, flat area of fertile farmlands. The region becomes more mountainous farther south. Throughout this region, visitors will see the greatest concentration of maple groves in Quebec. A popular tradition rich in folklore and special events has developed around the theme of the maple tree and is reflected in regional folk art. During the sugaring-off season in spring, people gather in sugar shacks to sample maple taffy (*tire d'érable*) and take part in the festivities known as sugaring-off parties (*parties de sucre*).

Cascading over numerous falls interspersed with more tranquil areas, the Chaudière River is navigable in only a few places, and its frequent floods often make newspaper headlines. Despite the construction of a dam at Saint-Georges-de-Beauce, the Chaudière may still inundate the villages along its banks in the spring.

The region's inhabitants (*Beaucerons*) are known for their sense of tradition and entrepreneurial spirit.

🛈 **Information:** 13055 Boulevard Lacroix, Saint-Georges. ☎418-227-4642 & 1-877-9BEAUCE. www.destinationbeauce.com.

▶ **Orient Yourself:** Maine's Rte. 201 becomes Rte. 173 at the border and travels northwest toward Quebec City through valleys and forests along the Chaudière River.

☺ **Don't Miss:** The colorful maple forests in the fall and sugar shacks in the early spring.

🕐 **Organizing Your Time:** Most Beauce's attractions are along the Rte. 173 corridor.

Kids **Especially for Kids:** The long covered bridge near Notre-Dame-des-Pins.

A Bit of History

President Kennedy Road (Route du Président Kennedy) – In 1775, twelve years after New France was ceded to England in the Treaty of Paris, an American expeditionary force of 1,100 men led by Col. Benedict Arnold traveled along the Kennebec River to the state of Maine, and from there marched northward along the Chaudière River in an attempt to capture Quebec City.

The 13 American colonies engaged in the fight against British rule hoped to persuade the Canadians to join their cause. A great many soldiers died during the arduous northern trek; the survivors were defeated by troops under the command of Guy Carleton.

Every year some 600,000 Americans en route to Quebec follow this road (Rte. 173), now named for US president John F. Kennedy.

The Gold Rush of 1846 – In the 19C the Beauce region was the El Dorado of Canada. In 1846 a gold nugget the size of a pigeon's egg was discovered on a tributary of the Chaudière, and prospectors poured in to sift the sands of the stream between Notre-Dame-des-Pins and Saint-Simon-les-Mines. By the beginning of the 20C, $1 million worth of gold ore had been extracted. Vestiges of the mining heyday are still visible today.

Driving Tour

From Quebec City to Lac-Mégantic *221km/137mi.*

▶ *Leave Quebec City by Rte. 73 Sud and cross the Pierre-Laporte Bridge continuing south; 1km/.6mi after the bridge, turn off at Exit 130. Follow the signs to Parc de la Chute de la Rivière Chaudière.*

Parc des Chutes-de-la-Chaudière★ (Chaudière River Falls Park)

In Charny. ⏱*Open year-round, daily 8am–9pm.* 🅿*Tourisme Lévis.* ☎*418-838-6026. www.tourismelevis.com.*

Just before it joins the St. Lawrence, the Chaudière River drops over a cliff in spectacular falls, 35m/115ft high and 121m/397ft wide. The Abenaki Indians named these falls asticou, meaning "boiler," because of the kettle-shaped basin at the foot of the cascades. The name chaudière, the French word for "boiler," was subsequently given to the entire river.

Steps descend to a suspension bridge hung across the river. From here, visitors can enjoy exceptional views of the falls, magnificent during the spring run-off.

▶ *Return to Rte. 73 and at Exit 123 take Rte. 175 Sud. At Saint-Lambert, cross the Chaudière River and take Rte. 171 Sud. At Scott (34km/21mi), the road crosses the river again and becomes Rte. 173 Sud.*

Sainte-Marie-de-Beauce
9km/5.6mi from Scott.

One of the oldest communities in the region, Sainte-Marie was part of the seigneury given to **Thomas-Jacques Taschereau** in 1736. Taschereau was a member of an influential family which included Elzéar-Alexandre Taschereau (1820–98), the first Canadian to be made a cardinal in the Roman Catholic Church, and Louis-Alexandre Taschereau (1867–1952), premier of Quebec from 1920 to 1936. Sainte-Marie was also the birthplace of **Marius Barbeau** (1883–1969), writer, ethnomusicologist and founder of the Quebec folklore archives at Laval University, in Quebec City.

Today Sainte-Marie's economy thrives on the baked-goods industry. In 1923 Arcade Vachon and his wife, Rose-Anne Giroux, purchased a bakery in Sainte-Marie and began making the "petits gâteaux Vachon" (snack cakes) that are now famous throughout the province.

Église Sainte-Marie (St. Mary's Church)

⏱*Open year-round, Mon–Sat 8am–8pm, Sun 8am–noon.* ♿🅿☎*418-387-5467.*

The church (1856, Charles Baillairgé) is one of the first Gothic Revival structures built for the Catholic Church in Quebec. The exterior is English in inspiration while the interior is modeled after the work of Viollet-le-Duc. Of a rare harmony in its overall effect, the interior can be compared to the interior of Montreal's Notre-Dame Basilica, designed by Victor Bourgeau.

After 10km/6.2mi, the road passes through **Vallée-Jonction**. Located at a railway junction, this small community overlooks the Chaudière River. Route 112 to Thetford Mines crosses the river at this point.

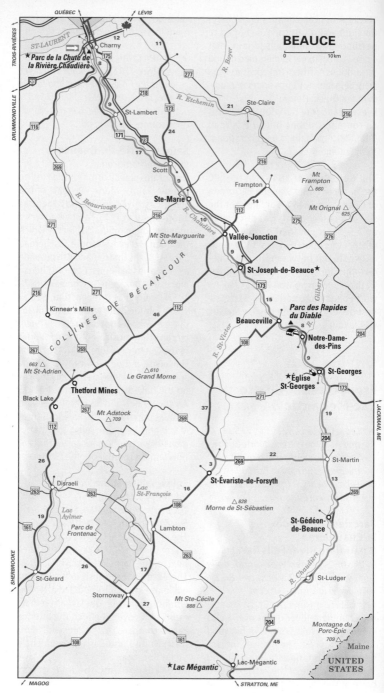

BEAUCE

▸ *Turn off Rte. 173 and enter Saint-Joseph-de-Beauce.*

Saint-Joseph-de-Beauce★
9km/5.6mi from Vallée-Jonction.
Set in the valley of the Chaudière River, this former seigneury was conceded

to Joseph Fleury de la Gorgendière, a wealthy Quebec merchant, in 1737.

Town center

Intersection of Rue Sainte-Christine and Ave. du Palais.

Designed by F.-X. Berlinguet, **Église Saint-Joseph** (St. Joseph's Church) features a narrow façade surmounted by a tall steeple. Its interior was completed in 1876 by J.F. Peachy. Facing the church, a large brick **presbytery** (1892, G.-É. Tanguay) evokes the design of small 16C French chateaux. The former **convent** (1889, J.F. Peachy) and **orphanage** (1908) are in the Second Empire style. Behind the church stands the **Lambert School** (1911, Lorenzo Auger), a functional edifice enlarged in 1947 and again in 1995. The institutional ensemble is completed by the **courthouse-prison**, a Neoclassical structure erected between 1857 and 1862. To the rear, a post-Modern addition blends harmoniously with the original structure.

▶ *Continue on Ave. du Palais which rejoins Rte. 173 south of the town center.*

Beauceville

15km/9.3mi.

Built on the steep slopes of the Chaudière River valley, this community was the birthplace of the poet **William Chapman** (1850–1917), emulator and rival of Louis Fréchette.

Across the river stands the **Église Saint-François d'Assise** (Church of St. Francis of Assisi); of note in its interior are the main altar and angel statues (○*open during services only*).

Parc des Rapides du Diable (Devil's Rapids Park)

3km/1.8mi south of town.

The park is strewn with paths leading to the Chaudière River and the "devil's rapids" that tumble over the rocky riverbed. The foundations of a mill used to extract gold from quartz rock during the gold rush are still visible.

▶ *Turn off Rte. 173 and head toward Notre-Dame-des-Pins.*

Notre-Dame-des-Pins

8km/5mi from Beauceville.

In the mid-19C gold prospectors gathered here before embarking on their journey along the Gilbert River to Saint-Simon-les-Mines.

Covered bridge

Turn right on 1ʳᵉ Ave., just before the modern bridge.

The 154.5m/507ft covered bridge across the Chaudière River is the longest in the province. First built in 1927, it was carried away by ice during the winter of 1928. Rebuilt in 1929 with three central piers, the bridge remained in use until 1969 when it was closed to vehicular traffic (*picnic area near bridge*).

▶ *Continue south; turn off Rte. 173 at Saint-Georges exit.*

Saint-Georges-de-Beauce

9km/5.6mi.

The industrial capital of the Beauce region was originally named Sartigan, meaning "changing river," by the indigenous Abenaki villagers. In 1807 a German settler by the name of **George Pozer** bought the land and gave the town its present name. Saint-Georges experienced some growth after the American invasion of 1775, but its greatest economic expansion followed the opening of the Kennebec Route to New England in 1830. In 1967 the Sartigan dam was erected to control the capricious flow of the Chaudière River.

Église Saint-Georges★ (St. George's Church)

On 1ʳᵉ Ave. in Saint-Georges-Ouest, across the river. ○*Open early Jun–late Aug. Mon–Fri 10am–noon & 1pm–4pm, Sun 1pm–4pm; Sat and rest of the year by appointment.* ○*Closed major holidays.* ▣ ☏*418-228-2558.*

This beautiful church (1902, David Ouellet), with its monumental cut stone façade, dominates the west bank of the Chaudière. Three spires, one 75m/246ft tall, rise above the edifice. The present church replaces a previous stone building (1862) and an earlier wood structure (1831). Before the entrance stands a copy of Louis Jobin's masterpiece, *St. George*

MICHELIN

Église Saint-Georges

Slaying the Dragon. The original (1912), an enormous wooden sculpture sheathed in bronze and gilded, is displayed nearby at the Centre culturel Marie-Fitzbach on the second floor.

The ornate **interior** of this three-story church features tiered balconies embellished with painted and gilded woodwork. The altar is surmounted by a broad canopy with St. George at its summit.

▶ *An optional excursion is a short drive west to Saint-Évariste-de-Forsyth.*

Saint-Évariste-de-Forsyth
44km/27mi by Rtes. 173, 204, 269 and 108.
Perched on a hill, this community affords lovely views of the surrounding countryside.

▶ *Return to Rte. 204.*

Saint-Gédéon-de-Beauce
38km/24mi.
The countryside opens onto Lake Mégantic, source of the Chaudière River, and the surrounding mountains.

Lac Mégantic★ – *45km/28mi.* ⚐ *See Entry Heading.*

BEAUHARNOIS

MONTÉRÉGIE REGION
POPULATION 12,041

This industrial suburb of Montreal, part of the municipality of Beauharnois-Salaberry, was founded in 1819, and named for the **Marquis de Beauharnois** (1671–1749), 15th governor of New France, who was granted a seigneury in this area. Today the small city is the site of a major power plant and a canal that diverts ships on the St. Lawrence Seaway around the rapids connecting Lakes Saint-François and Saint-Louis.

🛈 **Information:** ☎450-377-7676 & 1-800-378-7648. www.tourisme-suroit.qc.ca.
▶ **Orient Yourself:** Beauharnois is located 40km/25mi southwest of Montreal by the Mercier Bridge and Rte. 132. Rte. 201 at Salaberry-de-Valleyfield crosses the St. Lawrence River and connects to Autoroute 20.
🚲 **Don't Miss:** Beauharnois Power Plant.
🧒 **Especially for Kids:** The Beauharnois Power Plant is exciting and educational for older kids; all ages will enjoy weekend activities at Pointe-du-Buisson Archaeological Park.
⚐ **Also See:** BEAUHARNOIS CANAL.

A Bit of History

Construction of the power plant by the Beauharnois Light, Heat and Power Co. began in 1929, but was not completed until 1948. In 1953 and 1961, the canal was widened and the power station enlarged, making the Beauharnois power plant the largest hydroelectric plant in Canada at the time.

The present **Beauharnois Canal** was completed in 1932. Water is diverted from the original channel of the St. Lawrence into the canal by a system of dams and control works near Coteau-du-Lac. It is nearly 25km/16mi long by 1km/.6mi wide and 9m/29ft deep, and has two locks.

Sights

Centrale de Beauharnois★★ (Beauharnois Power Plant)

This enormous hydropower plant is among the most productive in Quebec, with a generating capacity of 1,645,810 kilowatts. With a total length of 864m/2,834ft, it is also one of the longest in the world. Its run-of-the-river dam uses neither reservoir nor falls to control or speed the water flow. Instead, the station harnesses the powerful flow of the St. Lawrence River, notably the 24m/79ft drop between Lakes Saint-François and Saint-Louis. Water passes through the canal at a rate of 3km/1.8mi per hour or 8 million liters/2.1 million gal per second. During the long winter, Quebec consumes all the power generated; for the remainder of the year, excess capacity is transmitted to Ontario and the US by 735,000-volt power lines.

Visit

Visit by free guided tour (90min) only, reservations required, May 21–Labor Day, daily 9.30am, 11.15am, 1pm, 2.45pm. ⏱ 🅿 ☎ 1-800-365-5229. www.hydro quebec.com.

In the interpretation center (located in Melocheville, across the canal), a permanent exhibit provides an excellent introduction to the site. On the tour, visitors will see the enormous **alternator hall** (864m/2,833ft long), where electric vehicles or tricycles are used by staff to check the turbines. Each of the 36 turbines weighs over 100 tons, is 4m/13ft high and 6m/20ft in diameter; their installed capacity, or optimal output, is 1,645,810 kilowatts. The tour also includes a visit to the **control room**, where computers monitor operations and regulate output. The rooftop of the plant affords a spectacular view of the intricate network of power lines extending in all directions. Montreal and the St. Lawrence are visible in the distance.

Beauharnois Locks

2km/1.2mi west of the power plant by Rte. 132 Ouest. 🅿 Parking area next to the lock.

From this vantage point near the power plant, visitors can view the lower of the two Beauharnois locks. It enables vessels to bypass the power plant by raising them 12.5m/41ft. The upper lock, located 3.2km/2mi upstream, provides an additional 12.5m/41ft lift to the level of the Beauharnois Canal. The lock system is best viewed from the parking area.

Parc archéologique de la Pointe-du-Buisson★ (Pointe-du-Buisson Archaeological Park) 🧒

Melocheville, 5km/3mi west of lock by Rte. 132. ⏱ Open mid-May–Labor Day Tue–Fri 10am–5pm, weekends 10am–6pm; rest of Sept–mid-Oct, weekends only noon–5pm. 🎫 $5. ♿ 🅿 ☎ 450-429-7857; www.point edubuisson.com.

This pleasant, wooded peninsula protruding into the St. Lawrence is popular with fishing enthusiasts in search of sturgeon, brill and eels in the rapids. Remains of human life dating back to 5000 BC have been found here, making this peninsula an important archaeological site.

The park offers various educational activities, as well as guided tours. In the summer season, visitors can watch archaeologists in action. Two **interpretation centers** display the recovered artifacts and re-create the different eras of human activity at Pointe-du-Buisson.

Paths lead through the park, providing good views of the rapids. Note the **Potsdam sandstone**, the oldest sedimentary rock in the Montreal area, exposed by river erosion.

Excursion

Lieu historique national du Canada de la Bataille-de-la-Châteauguay★
(Battle of the Châteauguay National Historic Site)

On Rte. 138 between Howick and Ormstown, 24km/15mi southwest of Beauharnois.

The Châteauguay River valley, located southwest of Montreal, is a peaceful stretch of rural communities. However, for a short time during the War of 1812, it became the setting of an important battle, a turning point in the United States failed attempt to invade Canada.

On October 26, 1813, 300 Canadian troops (French-Canadians and a few dozen Mohawk Indians from nearby Kanawake) under the command of Lieu-tenant-Col. **Charles-Michel de Sala-berry** (1778–1829) met an American army of 2,000 soldiers led by Major-Gen. Wade Hampton. Salaberry managed to outwit the larger force by playing on the Americans' lack of familiarity with the territory, and succeeded in repelling the attack.

Visit

🕐 *Open mid-May–late Aug, Wed–Sun 10am–5pm, Sept–mid-Oct, Sat–Sun 10am–5pm.* ✎*$4.* ♿ 🅿 ☎*450-829-2003. www.pc.gc.ca.*

An interpretation center stands beside the Châteauguay River, adjacent to the battle site. A model shows the positions of US and Canadian forces llustrate the hardships of army life in the early 19C.

CÔTE DE BEAUPRÉ★★

QUEBEC CITY REGION

MAP: SEE LOCAL MAP CÔTE DE BEAUPRÉ

The Beaupré Coast is a narrow stretch of land nestled between the Canadian Shield and the St. Lawrence River, east of Quebec City. It extends from the Mont-morency Falls to the massif of Cape Tourmente (660m/2,165ft). The name of the region derives from an exclamation made by Jacques Cartier who, noting the meadowland alongside the river, said *"Quel beau pré!"* (What a fine meadow!). The Beaupré Coast, dotted with numerous villages established during the French Regime, is renowned for the popular shrine at Sainte-Anne-de-Beaupré and the resort area of Mont Sainte-Anne.

- 🛈 **Information:** ☎1-877-783-1608. www.cotedebeaupre.com /www.quebecregion.com.
- ▶ **Orient Yourself:** The Beaupré Coast is accessible from Quebec City by Rte. 440, which becomes Rte. 40 and then Rte. 138. If time allows, visitors are advised to take the much more interesting Rte. 360 (Ave. Royale) from Beauport.
- 🅿 **Parking:** Avenue Royale is often very narrow and street parking is limited: Use designated lots near attractions.
- 🚫 **Don't Miss:** Montmorency Falls; the drive along Avenue Royale; Cape Tourmente National Wildlife Reserve; skiing at Mont-Sainte-Anne.
- 🕐 **Organizing Your Time:** Although not a long drive, a full day on the Beaupré Coast is a day well spent. To visit both Montmorency Falls and Cape Tourmente, plan to use the faster Rte. 360 one way and the scenic Avenue Royale the other.
- **Especially for Kids:** A family package (✎*$27.50*) provides access to the Montmorency Falls Park for a full day, and includes parking and unlimited use of the cable-car.

A Bit of History

The seigneury of Beaupré was among the largest in New France, stretching from the Montmorency River to Baie-Saint-Paul. Champlain established his first farm here in 1626; it was destroyed by the notorious adventurers, the Kirke Brothers, in 1629. Settlers began working this fertile land in the 1630s and founded the first rural parishes in New France. Beaupré's seigneur from 1668 through 1680 was François de Laval, the first Bishop of Quebec City. Msgr. de Laval was responsible for planning the King's Highway (Chemin du Roy), which ran from Quebec City to Saint-Joachim and is known today as the Avenue Royale. After Msgr. de Laval's death, the seigneury remained in the hands of the Quebec Seminary until the end of the seigneurial regime in 1854.

From Quebec City to Cap-Tourmente 48km/30mi.

▸ *From Quebec City, take Rte. 440 east to Exit 24, then Ave. d'Estimauville to Rte. 360 (also called Ave. Royale as far as Beaupré); turn right and continue 3km/1.8mi.*

Beauport

This community, the oldest settlement on the Beaupré Coast, is now a suburb of Quebec City. The first settlers arrived in 1634 and named the village after a medieval abbey on the north coast of Brittany.

Bourg du Fargy★

In the heart of Beauport stands an impressive group of buildings known as the Bourg du Fargy. The **Maison Bellanger-Girardin** (*600 Ave. Royale*) is typical of the residential architecture found throughout the Beaupré Coast. Its elongated form is the result of two distinct construction stages (1722 and 1735); its steep roof is characteristic of the heavy beam framework popular in the late 17C. Restored in 1983, the house is now used to display the work of local artists. Also situated in this neighborhood are a number of attractive Victorian houses.

Note the **Beauport Convent** (1866, F.-X. Berlinguet) with its mansard roof topped by a large statue of the Virgin Mary. The **Église Notre-Dame-de-la-Nativité** (Church of Our Lady of the Nativity), originally designed by Charles Baillairgé, was built in 1849. Twice destroyed by fire, the church was subsequently rebuilt within the same walls. Only its two tow-

ering spires were not replaced after the fire of 1916. The stone **presbytery** (1903) stands nearby.

The road continues along an escarpment overlooking the Île d'Orléans.

Parc de la Chute-Montmorency★★ (Montmorency Falls Park) Kids

5km/3mi. ◷ Open year-round, daily 8.15am–9pm. ♿ 🅿 ($8.75/car). ☎418-663-3330. www.sepaq.com/ct/pcm/en.

Before emptying into the St. Lawrence, the Montmorency River cascades over a cliff in spectacular falls 83m/272ft high (30m/98ft higher than Niagara Falls). Named by Samuel de Champlain for Charles, Duc de Montmorency, who was Viceroy of New France from 1620 through 1625, the falls have long been a major attraction. In the winter months, the spray creates a great cone of ice known as a sugarloaf, which sometimes exceeds 30m/98ft in height. Before the last ice age, the Montmorency Falls emptied directly into the St. Lawrence River. They are now about 450m/1,476ft away from the river and mark the edge of the Canadian Shield.

With its enormous energy potential and its excellent location near the St. Lawrence, the site proved ideal for a powerful commercial empire that grew up here during the 19C. In 1811 a sawmill was established at the foot of the falls, an enterprise that by mid-century had

Parc de la Chute-Montmorency/ Steve Deschênes/ Sépaq

Chute Montmorency

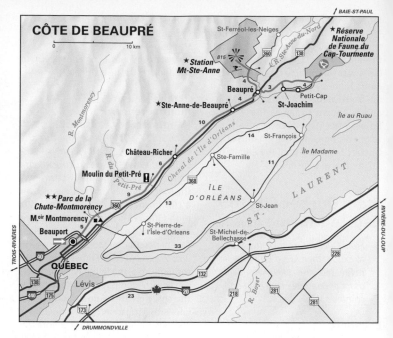

CÔTE DE BEAUPRÉ

become the most important of its kind in British North America. Under the direction of Peter Patterson and subsequently his son-in-law George Benson Hall, the company grew and diversified, but did not survive an economic crisis that eventually weakened the demand for lumber. In 1884 a power plant was established here, the first in the world to transmit hydroelectric power over long distances (11.7km/7mi). A second power plant began service in 1895, and in 1905 a cotton mill was built at the foot of the cliff. Only a few traces remain today of these nearly two centuries of intense industrial activity.

Manoir de Montmorency (Montmorency Manor)

This elegant house with terraces overlooking the Montmorency Falls has changed hands several times and undergone numerous modifications over the years. It was built in 1780 as a vacation home for Frederick Haldimand, governor-general of British North America. From 1791 to 1794, it was inhabited by Edward, Duke of Kent, and his morganatic wife. Peter Patterson and his descendants made their home here. At the turn of the century it was renovated

as a popular luxury hotel known as "Kent House." Destroyed by fire in May 1993, the structure was rebuilt along its original architectural lines. Today Montmorency Manor houses a restaurant and reception rooms in addition to a **visitor center**★ (◷ open Jun–Sept, daily, 8.30am–8pm; closes earlier the rest of the year weekends only; ☓ ♿ 🅿 ✉ 418-663-3330) presenting the area's historic, economic, and human heritage.

Upper Lookout

From the Montmorency Manor, a footpath traces the flank of the cliff leading to the bridge above the falls. From here, a spectacular **view**★★ embraces the furious waters tumbling over the cliff. The silhouette of the Île d'Orléans is visible in the distance. The footpath continues on the other side to a smaller bridge over a side crevice; from here you can see the sites of the power plant and the former cotton mill, with the towers of Quebec City and the Château Frontenac looming in the distance. Farther along, note the traces of a redoubt built here in 1759 by the British general, Wolfe, during his siege of Quebec. Helped by their Amerindian allies, the French militia overtook this redoubt using combat techniques developed by the indigenous population.

Lower Lookout

A panoramic stairway dotted with numerous lookout points leads to the bottom of the falls, allowing superb, closeup **views** of the powerful waters (waterproof gear is advised to protect from the spray). Over time, the falls have carved out a large cauldron at their base, creating an immense, powerful whirlpool. The force of these turbulent waters (an average 35,000 liters/9,248gal per second) was harnessed in 1885 to activate sawmills and provide electricity for Quebec City. A **cable-car** returns visitors to the upper level (⊘*open late Apr–late Oct, daily 8.30am;* ⊘*rest of the year, call for hours;* ⊘*$8.50;* ☎*418-663-3330*).

▷ *Return to Rte. 360.*

Observe the high-tension power lines strung on large pylons, which carry electricity from the Manic-5 power station to Montreal, across the St. Lawrence. Past this point the road takes on a more rural character.

Moulin du Petit-Pré (Mill)

9km/5.6mi from Montmorency Manor. This large three-story stone mill, located just beyond the Petit-Pré River, was built in 1695 by the Quebec Seminary to supplement its income and to supply the needs of Quebec City merchants; it was therefore the first "industrial" mill in New France. The mill was destroyed during the Conquest and rebuilt in 1764. It remained in operation until 1955. The **Beaupré Coast Interpretation Center** (⊘*open mid-May–mid-Oct, daily 9.30am–4.30pm; rest of the year, Mon–Fri 10am–4.30pm;* ⊘*$6;* ♿🅿☎*418-824-3677*), housed in the mill loft, provides information on the geology, history, and socio-economic development of the region. Displays include photographs, documents, sketches, games, and videos.

Château-Richer

6km/3.7mi.
First settled in 1640, this community was named after a priory in France. The Église La-Visitation-de-Notre-Dame (Church of the Visitation of Our Lady, 1866) dominates the village from high on the cliff above the river. From the church, **views** of the coast reach as far as Cap-Tourmente. A quarry carved out of the cliff is visible to the north of the town. In the 18C and 19C, limestone from Château-Richer was often used in the construction of buildings in Quebec City. Regular in form and light gray in color, the stone from this quarry replaced the darker limestone of Beauport by the early 19C.

On Avenue Royale, large bread ovens stand next to some of the older homes; the ovens were often built separately from the houses because of the danger of fire. One is still in use, and visitors can purchase freshly baked bread.

▷ *Rte. 360 gradually descends to river level as it approaches Sainte-Anne.*

Sainte-Anne-de-Beaupré★
10km/6.2mi. ♿*See Entry Heading.*

Beaupré
4km/2.5mi.
Located on the Sainte-Anne-du-Nord River, just before it joins the St. Lawrence, Beaupré was part of the town of Sainte-Anne-de-Beaupré until 1927. Now it is a separate community, dominated by its pulp mill.

Station Mont-Sainte-Anne★
4km/2.5mi. ♿*See Entry Heading.*

▷ *Return to Beaupré (4km/2.5mi) and take Ave. Royale to Saint-Joachim. Turn right onto Rue de l'Église.*

Saint-Joachim *3km/1.8mi from Beaupré.* ♿*See Entry Heading.*

Réserve nationale de faune du Cap-Tourmente★ (Cape Tourmente National Wildlife Reserve)
4km/2.5mi. ⊘*Open mid-Apr–early Nov, daily 8.30am–5pm; early Jan–mid-Apr weekends 8.30am–4pm.* ⊘*$6.* 🍴♿🅿☎*418-827-4591. www.captourmente.com.*

Cap Tourmente was named for the stormy winds that sweep through the St. Lawrence River valley east of Île d'Orléans. The wildlife reserve is a haven for more than 290 species of birds. In April, May, and October, thousands of Greater Snow Geese invade this massif overlooking the St. Lawrence during their spring and winter migrations, and thousands of visitors gather to see them. The huge birds are a magnificent sight as they rise from the river or descend upon the neighboring mudflats in a white flurry of beating wings and raucous cries. The bulrushes that proliferate on the marshy edges of the St. Lawrence provide the sustenance required for the enormous distance the geese must travel between their winter home on the coast of Virginia and their summer nesting grounds north of the arctic circle, on Baffin Island.

The snow geese are a protected species that can be hunted only by special permit. Displays and films can be seen in the **interpretation center** situated 1.5km/1mi from the entrance (⊙open *May–Oct, daily 9am–4.45pm; Apr and Nov weekends only*).

At the entrance to the reserve stands **La Petite-Ferme** (little farm), built on the spot where Samuel de Champlain established, in 1626, the first farm of New France.

Nearby, le **Vignoble Domaine du Royarnois** (*146 Chemin du Cap-Tourmente,* ☎*418-827-4465*) is a fine example of the Quebec City area wineries flourishing in microclimates. It features a lovely house dating 300 years.

BOUCHERVILLE

MONTÉRÉGIE REGION
POPULATION 39,062
MAP: SEE LOCAL MAP MONTREAL

Boucherville is one of Quebec's oldest communities. In 1667, the seigneury featuring beautiful islands was granted to **Pierre Boucher**, governor of Trois-Rivières. Boucher and the first settlers arrived the following year. For almost three centuries Boucherville developed, first, as an agricultural community, and later as a resort town. The opening of the Louis-Hippolyte Lafontaine Tunnel under the St. Lawrence in 1967 transformed Boucherville into an industrial and residential suburb of Montreal. Yet it has kept a historical core and beautiful parks. Boucherville is the birthplace of Louis-Hippolyte Lafontaine (1807–64), prime minister of the United Canadas, 1842–1843 and 1848–1851.

- ⓘ **Information:** ☎450-466-4666. www.tourisme-monteregie.qc.ca.
- ▶ **Orient Yourself:** Boucherville is on the South Shore of the St. Lawrence River opposite Montréal-Est, and bordering the large Montreal suburb of Longueuil.
- ⊙ **Don't Miss:** Parc national des Îles-de-Boucherville.
- ⊙ **Organizing Your Time:** Beware of the tunnel to Montreal, not a swift, pleasant drive at peak hours. The tunnel is the main link to the Boucherville islands.
- Kids **Especially for Kids:** Deer watching on Boucherville Islands.
- ⓒ **Also See:** Église de la Sainte-Famille, affording a view of the islands.

Sights

Boulevard Marie-Victorin, the city's main thoroughfare, is lined with beautiful 19C houses, several of which belonged to descendants of the city's founder. Note the mid-18C manor house at no. 470, built for François-Pierre Boucher de Boucherville, and the 19C brick structure at no. 486, built for Charles-Eugène Boucher, premier of Quebec from 1874 to 1878 and from 1891 to 1892.

Maison Louis-Hippolyte-Lafontaine (Louis-Hippolyte Lafontaine House)

314 Blvd. Marie-Victorin, near exit 18 of Rte 132. ◷*Open Jul–mid-Aug, Thu–Sun 1.30pm–5.30pm; rest of the year, Thu, Sat, Sun only, same hours.* 🅿 ☎*450-449-8347.*

Located in a park near the St. Lawrence, this dwelling belonged to the father-in-law of Louis-Hippolyte Lafontaine. Constructed in 1766 and rebuilt after the fire of 1843, the house was moved from Boucherville's historic center to its present site in 1964. The house is a fine example of New France home architecture. It is now a small Boucherville heritage museum.

Lafontaine lived here from 1813 through 1822, before undertaking his law studies in Montreal. The highlights of his career are displayed. Lafontaine is generally considered to be the main proponent of "responsible government," a term used to designate a government empowered by a locally elected assembly rather than the British Crown. Such form of government was essential to ease the tensions between Canadians and their British rulers.

Église de la Sainte-Famille★ (Church of the Holy Family)

560 Blvd. Marie-Victorin. ◷*Open year-round, Mon–Sat 9am–4.30pm, Sun 8am–noon.* ♿🅿☎*450-655-9024.*

This church (1801) rises above a small square also occupied by a cultural center and a nursing home. It was designed by the parish priest, Father Pierre Conefroy, who supervised the construction. His efficient and cost-effective management of the project became codified as the "Conefroy plan specifications" (*plan-devis Conefroy*), which were thereafter adopted as a blueprint for the construction of churches throughout the province. Father Conefroy adopted the Latin cross floor plan to provide much-needed space for rural parish churches, which had experienced somewhat of a population explosion in the late 18C. In recognition of his successful endeavor, Father Conefroy was named vicar-general of the diocese and supervised all church construction in Quebec.

The original interior décor, commissioned from the studio of Louis-Amable Quévillon, was destroyed in the fire of 1843. Renovated by Louis-Thomas Berlinguet, the architectural treatment is typical of the style of Thomas Baillairgé. The Louis XV paneling exemplifies Berlinguet's attention to detail and ornamentation. The main altar and side altars, designed by Quévillon, survived the fire of 1843. The massive Baroque **tabernacle**, is a major work dating from the French Regime.

Across the street, a monument to Pierre Boucher commands a view of the Boucherville islands and Montréal-Est. The neighboring streets, especially Rue de la Perrière and Rue Saint-Charles, are lined with 19C houses.

Parc national des Îles-de-Boucherville (Boucherville Islands National Park)   Kids

Rte 25 (Exit 1 on Charron Island), also small ferries (pedestrians, bicycles) from Boucherville and Longueuil in summer ☎*514-493-1967*≈*$3.50 (return fare).*
◷*Open year-round, daily 8am–dusk.* ≈*$3.50 (family rate $7). Bicycle & canoe rentals mid-May–Oct.* ✗🅿☎*450-928-5088 & 1-800-665-6527. www.parcs quebec.com.*

Five islands form a popular Quebec national park. From the information center on Sainte-Marguerite Island, a passenger ferry and footbridges provide access to the other islands. Bike paths (27km/17mi), hiking trails (27km/17mi), and canoe circuits lace the islands, affording pleasant **views** of Montreal across the river. Hundreds of deer roam freely, with no predator in sight.

CAP-DE-LA-MADELEINE

MAURICIE REGION
POPULATION OF TROIS-RIVIÈRES 126,603
MAP: SEE LOCAL MAP VALLÉE DU SAINT-LAURENT

Cap-de-la-Madeleine is on the north shore of the St. Lawrence, east of the St. Maurice River. "Le Cap" is a borough of the city of Trois-Rivières (&see TROIS-RIVIÈRES), but it has a distinct history and identity. Founded in 1635 by the Jesuit Father Jacques Buteux, who was later killed by the Iroquois, Cap-de-la-Madeleine is a renowned Marian pilgrimage site, and has been since the 19C when French-Canadians formed one the most intensely Roman Catholic peoples in the world.

- **Information:** ☎819-375-1122. www.tourismetroisrivieres.com.
- ▶ **Orient Yourself:** Cap-de-la-Madeleine is located 150km/93mi northeast of Montreal by Rtes. 40 and 755 (Exit 10).
- ☺ **Don't Miss:** The basilica and pilgrimage destination at Shrine of Notre-Dame-du-Cap.
- ⊙ **Organizing Your Time:** The shrine is a large site with lots to see. Leave enough time to enjoy the adjoining gardens and the views of the St. Lawrence River.

A Bit of History

The Miracles – In the mid-17C, a wooden chapel to Mary Magdalene was erected on this site by European settlers. A stone church did not appear until 1717, when a community was established here. **Father Luc Désilets**, who arrived in the mid-19C, renewed the ministry and by 1878, a larger church was required to accommodate the growing congregation. Father Désilets planned to bring stones for the new church across the St. Lawrence over an ice bridge. But unusually mild weather left the river free of ice, prompting Father Désilets to vow to preserve the existing 18C church in exchange for a miracle that would allow the stone to be transported across the river. On March 16, 1879, the temperature dropped and ice appeared on the river, remaining just long enough for the parishioners to bring the stones across. After the last load had arrived, the now-famous "Bridge of Rosaries" (*pont des Chapelets*) promptly broke up.
Regarding the ice bridge as a miracle from Our Lady of the Rosary, Father Désilets kept his vow and preserved the old church, adorning the interior with a statue of the Virgin, donated by a parishioner. On the night of the consecration in June of 1888, the priest, along with Father Frédéric Jansoone and Pierre

LaCroix, an afflicted pilgrim, witnessed a second miracle, when the eyes of the statue of the Virgin appeared to open in their presence.

Pilgrimage Center – Although public pilgrimages to the church began as early as 1883, news of the second miracle brought worshippers flocking to Cap-de-la-Madeleine. Specially constructed steamship quays and railroad lines facilitated access to the shrine, and in the 1950s, a new basilica was built to receive growing numbers of pilgrims. Today, thousands of people make the pilgrimage annually. The Oblate fathers have administered the shrine since 1902.

Sight

Sanctuaire Notre-Dame-du-Cap★★

- ▶ *On Rue Notre-Dame, east of town; follow signs.*

Basilique Notre-Dame-du-Rosaire (Our Lady of the Rosary Basilica)

⊙*Open May–mid Oct, daily 8am–9pm (Aug 10pm). Pilgrimages May 1–Oct 8; rest of the year, daily 8am–5pm.* ♿ P ☎819-374-2441. www.sanctuaire-ndc.ca.

This lovely octagonal basilica was designed by Adrien Dufresne, a student of Dom Paul Bellot (1876–1944), a Benedictine monk. Construction began in 1955, and the basilica was inaugurated in 1964. The conical central tower surmounting the structure is 78m/256ft tall, and a 7m/23ft stone statue of the Madonna adorns the façade. The weighty exterior hides an interior appointed in blue and gold, the colors of the Virgin. The basilica can accommodate 1,800 people, all of whom can enjoy an unobstructed view of the main altar. The Casavant organ, built in Saint-Hyacinthe in 1963–65, has 75 stops and more than 5,500 pipes. The altar is of Italian marble.

Begin to the left of the main entrance. The basilica's interior is renowned for its remarkable **stained-glass windows**. Jan Tillemans (1915–80), a Dutch Oblate father, fashioned the windows in the medieval tradition between 1956 and 1964. Each bay contains five lancets and a rose window nearly 8m/26ft in diameter. The first rose window, to the left of the main entrance, depicts the shields of the Canadian provinces, while the lancets represent the patron saints of Canada. The second window, in delicate hues of white and green, portrays Christ triumphant on the cross in the center and scenes from his life in the lancet panels. The third window, depicting the Mysteries of the Rosary, is colored primarily in blues and reds. The window to the right of the altar presents the prophets and evangelists in bright greens and blues, and the fifth window provides a multicolored glance at some of Canada's pioneers. The sixth window tells the story of Our Lady of the Cape.

The Small Shrine and Park
Same hours as basilica.
Beside the basilica stands the original stone church (1717), now a votive chapel. Along with the church of St. Peter's (Île d'Orléans), this chapel shares the distinction of being among the oldest shrines in Quebec. The miraculous statue stands above the altar of painted and gilt wood. In 1973 a modern annex was added to the church, incorporating some of the stones transported across the ice bridge

Sanctuaire Notre-Dame-du-Cap

Detail of Window 1, Sanctuaire Notre-Dame-du-Rosaire

in 1879. The small shrine is set in a park overlooking the river. The Stations of the Cross wind their way through the southern half of the park, ending before replicas of the Crucifixion and the tomb of Jesus in Jerusalem. In another section, the Mysteries of the Rosary are embodied in 15 bronze sculptures produced in France (1910). A small lake and the Bridge of Rosaries (pont des Chapelets) commemorate the ice bridge of 1879.

Address Book

For price ranges, see the Legend on the cover flap.

WHERE TO STAY

$$ Hotel-Motel Penn-Mass
303 Blvd. Sainte-Madeleine. ☎819-379-8877 & 1-800-847-6277. *www.penn-mass.com. 37 rooms.* Near the Notre-Dame-du-Cap Shrine, large, comfortable rooms. The Penn-Mass attracts English-speaking pilgrims.

$$ Gîte du Chemin-du-Roy B&B
382 Rue Notre-Dame Est. ☎819-374-7997. *www.gitescanada.com/duroy382.* Lavish rooms in Victorian house on the river. Fabulous rooms provide outstanding value.

CARILLON

LAURENTIANS REGION
POPULATION OF ST-ANDRÉ-D'ARGENTEUIL 2,889

Located on the Ottawa River close to the treacherous Long-Sault rapids, the historic village of Carillon was named after Philippe Carrion de Fresnay, a French officer who ventured here to trade furs in 1671. In 1682 Carillon was incorporated into the Argenteuil seigneury granted to Charles-Joseph d'Ailleboust, and remained a trading post throughout the turbulent fur trading times.

In the 19C Carillon became a military settlement protecting the canal system built to circumvent the rapids. More recently, Hydro-Québec built a power plant harnessing the rapids. In 1999, Carillon became a borough of the regional municipality of St-André-d'Argenteuil.

- **Information:** ☎1-800-561-6673. www.laurentians.com & www.argenteuil.qc.ca.
- ▶ **Orient Yourself:** Carillon is located on Rte. 344, approximately 70km/43mi west of Montreal by Rte. 40 (Exit 2). It can also be reached by the Pointe-Fortune ferry, on the Ontario border.
- **Don't Miss:** During boating season, the lift lock is operated at Carillon.
- ⏱ **Organizing Your Time:** Experience old and new aspects this important waterway: visit the Argenteuil Museum in the old barracks building, then take a tour of the hydropower station.
- **Especially for Kids:** The hydropower station tour and the lift lock.

A Bit of History

Dollard des Ormeaux – The town's renown is linked to a legendary act of bravery that took place at Carillon in 1660. From the time it was founded in 1642, Montreal lived under constant threat of attack by the Iroquois. In May 1660, Adam Dollard des Ormeaux (1635–60) intervened to save the very existence of the tiny settlement located east of Carillon. With the help of 40 Hurons, he and 17 other French-Canadian men held 300 Iroquois warriors at bay for a full week. Dollard and his companions sacrificed their lives, but their heroism so impressed the Iroquois that they gave up their attack on Montreal. The following month, the first furs reached Montreal safely, marking the beginning of a thriving trade. Ever since, Dollard des Ormeaux has been celebrated as the saviour of the young colony.

Centrale hydro-électrique de Carillon

Guillaume Pouliot/Tourisme Laurentides

Sights

Musée régional d'Argenteuil (Argenteuil Regional Museum)
On Rte. 344: 44 Rte. du Lonng-Sault. ⏱*Open 10.30am–5pm early Mar–mid-Jun, Mon–Fri; mid-Jun–mid-Sept, Tue–Sun; mid-Sept–mid-Oct, Wed–Sun; mid-Oct–mid-Dec, Tue–Fri.* ⚹*$4.* 🅿 ☎*450-537-3861.* This lovely stone structure was completed as a military barracks in 1837 and was used to protect the canal. During the Patriots' Rebellion (1837–38), it accommodated 100 British soldiers and officers. It was later converted into a hotel.

Since 1938 it has housed a museum dedicated to local history. Exhibits are devoted to Dollard des Ormeaux and Sir John Abbott (1821–1893), member of parliament for Argenteuil County and prime minister of Canada from 1892 to 1893. Many 18C and 19C musical instruments, clocks, and French and Canadian furniture on display were donated by community members.

Centrale hydro-électrique de Carillon (Carillon Power Station)

Entrance on Rte. 344 in Carillon. Visit by guided tour (1hr 15min) only, mid-May–Jun 24, Mon–Fri 9am–3pm; Jun 24–Labor Day, Wed–Sun 9.30am–3.30pm. ☎800-365-5229. www.hydroquebec.com.

Built between 1959 and 1964 at the foot of the Long-Sault rapids, this power station is a run-of-the-river plant with an installed capacity of 654,500kw. Its 14 turbines harness the flow of the Ottawa River, estimated at 2,000cu m/ 7,842cu ft per second. The plant and its spillway span the entire river. The guided tour of the plant includes a short film (*15min*) and a visit to the turbine chamber, the control room and the roof, from which the reservoir and power lines can be seen.

Lieu historique national du Canada du Canal-de-Carillon (Carillon Canal National Historic Site of Canada)

Open mid-May–early Oct daily 8am–8pm. $1.45. ☎450-447-4888. www.parkscanada.gc.ca.

This 60m/197ft-long navigation **lock** replaced seven older ones. It provides the greatest single lift (nearly 20m/66ft) of any conventional lock in Canada. Navigation to Ottawa upstream from this lock is unimpeded. The stone building of the **Maison du collecteur** (toll house) was built in 1843 for the toll collector, who levied the tolls on barges and other vessels using the canal system. Beside it, parts of the former 19C canal and lock system still remain.

Parc Carillon (Carillon Park)

Entrance just upstream from the power plant.

Extending about 3km/1.8mi along the shores of the reservoir, this park provides picnic spots. Near the dam stands a **monument** to Dollard des Ormeaux and his comrades. Jacques Folch-Ribas fashioned the 18 granite monoliths (8m/26ft high) to commemorate the battle fought by the gallant defenders.

CHAMBLY ★

MONTÉRÉGIE REGION
POPULATION 20,332
MAP: SEE VALLÉE DU RICHELIEU

A residential suburb of Montreal, the city of Chambly occupies a splendid natural site on the western shore of the Chambly Basin. Formed by the widening of the Richelieu River just below significant rapids, the basin is often dotted with sailboats. Fort-Chambly is a rare example of large French military fortifications in North America.

- **Information:** 1900 Ave. de Bourgogne (near Fort Chambly). ☎450-466-4666 & 1-866-469-0069. www.tourisme-monteregie.qc.ca.
- **Orient Yourself:** Chambly is 30km/18.6mi east of Montreal by Rte. 10 (Exit 22).
- **Parking:** Street parking; parking lots (fee) near attractions.
- **Don't Miss:** Fort Chambly National Historic Site; the Richelieu River rapids.
- **Organizing Your Time:** Check times for the current daily activities and special events at Fort Chambly. Plan to arrive early during summer to park and give yourself time to enjoy the walking and cycling paths along the basin and upper part of the canal.
- **Especially for Kids:** Educational programs and activities at Fort Chambly.
- **Also See:** VALLÉE DU RICHELIEU.

A Bit of History

In 1665 Captain **Jacques de Chambly** was ordered to build a fort here to defend the route to Montreal against raids by the Iroquois. For services rendered to the colony, he was granted the seigneury in 1672. Today the town still bears his name.

The river rapids were harnessed early in the 19C to activate seven mills including carding, sawing, and fulling mills. In 1843 the Chambly Canal was completed, facilitating navigation and trade between Canada and the US. Strings of barges pulled alongside the shore by horses were traditionally used to transport wood and other raw materials south to the New England states. During this period Chambly enjoyed great commercial prosperity. Today the city still attracts some light industry.

Artists and Heroes – Chambly's beautiful setting has long attracted artists. The Impressionist painter **Maurice Cullen** (1866–1934) lived here, as did his stepson **Robert Pilot** (1898–1967). Chambly is also the birthplace of Emma Lajeunesse (1847–1930). Better known by her stage-name, **Albani**, Lajeunesse was an internationally acclaimed opera singer and one of the greatest sopranos of her generation. The city's most illustrious native son is Charles-Michel de Salaberry (1778–1829), hero of the Battle of the Châteauguay.

Sights

▶ *Start at city hall at the corner of Rue Bourgogne and Rue de Salaberry.*

The Charles-Michel de Salaberry **memorial**, erected in 1881 in front of Chambly's city hall, is one of the first historical bronzes created by the great sculptor, Louis-Philippe Hébert. Just north on Rue Martel, in front of St. Joseph's Church (1784), stands the sculptor's last known work: A statue of Father Pierre-Marie Mignault, parish priest of St. Joseph's for 40 years.

▶ *Follow Rue Bourgogne east to reach the Chambly Canal.*

Lieu historique national du Canada du Canal-de-Chambly (Chambly Canal National Historic Site of Canada)

Near the marina. ⓟ*Parking available across the bridge on Rue Bourgogne.* ◷*Open daily, mid-May–mid-Oct, hours vary.* ⚒⚙☎*450-447-4888 & 1-888-773-8888. www.pc.gc.ca/canalchambly.*
Completed in 1843, this historic canal runs about 19km/11.8mi, from Saint-Jean-sur-Richelieu to the Chambly Basin, skirting numerous rapids in the Richelieu River. Its nine locks (eight of which are operated manually) raise passing vessels over 24m/79ft. At the turn of the 19C, the canal was a busy commercial waterway used by more than 4,000 crafts annually. Today although the canal has lost its economic importance, it is still used for boating and other recreational activities.

Parks Canada owns the canal and manages, with the Friends of the Canal, an information office that displays photo exhibits. Some of the locks' original mechanisms still exist, and visitors can observe locksmen operating the cranks that open and close the sluice gates. A bicycle path follows the banks of the canal to Saint-Jean-sur-Richelieu.

▶ *Continue along Rue Bourgogne to Rue du Fort.*

Lieu historique national du Canada du Fort-Chambly★★ (Fort Chambly National Historic Site of Canada)

2 Rue de Richelieu, where the rapids reach the basin. ◷*Open Apr–mid-May & Sept–Oct, Wed–Sun 10am–5pm; mid-May–early Jun, daily 9am–5pm; mid-Jun–early Sept, daily 10am–6pm.* ☞*$5.70.* ⚙ⓟ☎*450-658-1585. www.pc.gc.ca/fortchambly.*
Located in a magnificent park where the river widens to form the Chambly Basin, this fort has been restored to its 18C appearance. Vestiges of the original stone structure, conceived by military engineer Josué Boisberthelot de Beaucours, can still be seen. Fort Chambly

is the only remaining fortified complex in Quebec dating back to the French Regime. Erected between 1709 and 1711 during the Anglo-French wars, the stone fort replaced an earlier wooden structure erected by Jacques de Chambly in 1665, to defend the Richelieu rapids on the crucial trade route between Montreal and Albany, New York. The new fort was laid out in a square with bastions at each corner, and with the main entrance located on the western flank. Several buildings with dormer windows overlook the inner courtyard. A chapel topped by a mansard roof and small steeple faces the main entrance. Located inside the fort, an **interpretation center** features displays on the history of Fort Chambly and its occupants under the French Regime, and a description of the restoration project. Slide shows and dioramas re-create life at the fort and in the surrounding region.

Fort Chambly NHS

MICHELIN

Corps de Garde (Guard House)
On Rue Richelieu near the fort.
Also accessible through the park.
After the Conquest, British officials established extensive military installations in Chambly. During the War of 1812, the fort was garrisoned with as many as 6,000 men and enlarged to accommodate the infantry, cavalry, and artillery. Several expeditions launched against the Patriots in 1837–38 originated from Chambly. The fort and military camp were abandoned when the garrison departed in 1851.

The façade of the stone guardhouse (1814) features an imposing pediment supported by columns, exemplifying the Palladian style adopted by the military throughout the British colonies. The house contains displays on the period of occupation by the British garrison (1760–1851) and on the development of the city.

Église Saint-Stephen (St. Stephen's Church)
2004 Rue Bourgogne.
This fieldstone edifice built in 1820 to serve as the garrison church was modeled after the Catholic churches of the period. The liturgical furnishings and the sombre décor, however, distinguish the

interior as a Protestant place of worship. The cemetery contains several interesting funeral monuments, among them one belonging to the Yule family, former seigneurs of Chambly.

▶ *Continue along Rue Richelieu to the junction with Rte. 112.*

Rue Richelieu★
Several attractive houses line this street, a former portage route established along the rapids in 1665.

Address Book

🖝 *For price ranges, see the Legend on the cover flap.*

WHERE TO STAY
$$ A la Claire Fontaine B&B
2130 Ave. de Bourgogne.
☎450-447-7940 & 1-866-447-5888.
www.alaclairefontaine.ca. 4 rooms.
A well-appointed house near the Fort. Elegant and very comfortable rooms, one has a heated floor.

WHERE TO EAT
$$ Fourquet Fourchette
1887 Ave. de Bourgogne. ☎450-447-6370 & 1-888-447-6370. *www.fourquet-fourchette.com.* An innovative restaurant combining New France and Amerindian recipes with local craft beers. By Fort Chambly.

Near the guardhouse at no. 12 stands the **Maison Beattie**, a brick structure (1875) that now serves as the Chambly Tourist Office and the Historical Society of the Chambly Seigneury (Société d'histoire de la Seigneurie de Chambly).

The first section of Rue Richelieu, from the guardhouse to Rue des Voltigeurs, passes through the former military domain. Buildings erected by the British army were transformed into residences at the end of the 19C. At n°. 10 stands a former barracks (1814). The stone house at n°. 14 was once the commandant's residence. From Rue des Voltigeurs to Rue Saint-Jacques, the second section of Rue Richelieu crosses the former seigneurial domain, where several military officers settled in comfortable residences.

The **Manoir de Salaberry**, at n°. 18, was constructed in 1814 for Charles-Michel de Salaberry, who lived here until his death in 1829. With its pediment and two-story portico, the residence is one of the finest examples of Palladian-inspired architecture in Quebec.

At n°. 27 stands a monumental stone house built in 1816 for the merchant John Yule, brother of seigneur William Yule. The house at n°. 26, built in 1920, was once the studio of the noted painter Maurice Cullen.

Rue Richelieu stretches alongside the **Parc des Rapides**, providing **views** of the tumultuous Chambly rapids and the Chambly dam. On this site stood the Willett wool factories and mills; powered by the river current, they were the source of Chambly's prosperity throughout the 19C.

▶ *From the Parc des Rapides, go back to Fort Chambly and reach Avenue de Bourgogne, Chambly's main street. Turn right on de Bourgogne and enjoy views of the Basin and the canal before turning right again at Rue Martel (after 1km/.6mi). The junction is at City Hall. Rue Martel and the ajoining Parc Martel afford spendid views of the Basin, Fort Chambly, and Mont-Saint-Hilaire.*

CÔTE DE CHARLEVOIX★★★

CHARLEVOIX REGION
MAP: SEE CÔTE DE CHARLEVOIX

The Charlevoix Coast is one of Canada's loveliest regions, its rugged landscape marked by mountains sweeping down into the mighty St. Lawrence River. In this area, the river actually becomes an arm of the sea and is called "la mer" (the sea), and its wide banks are referred to as "la côte" (the coast), suggesting that this large body of saltwater is no longer a river. The pristine coast affords good views of the river, and the opposite shore is visible on clear days. Designated a UNESCO World Biosphere Reserve in 1989, the region is also a mecca for art and nature lovers attracted by its natural beauty, maritime past, and old-time resort tradition.

🛈 **Information:** ☎1-800-667-2276. www.tourisme-charlevoix.com.

▶ **Orient Yourself:** Charlevoix is accessible by Rtes. 40 and 138, northeast of Quebec City. Rte. 138 traverses the region, which starts at the border of Cape Tourmente, about 40km/25mi from Quebec City. Rte. 362 also connects Baie-Saint-Paul to La Malbaie–Pointe-au-Pic.

🚗 **Don't Miss:** Scenic Rte. 362; Baie-Saint-Paul and its art galleries; the understated, yet moving Musée maritime de Charlevoix.

🕐 **Organizing Your Time:** Stop at the information center on Rte. 138 just before entering Baie-Saint-Paul for a superb view of the region and to get current details about local events. Visit Baie-Saint-Paul, then follow Rte. 362 along the coast. If you have the time, take the ferry from Saint-Joseph-de-la-Rive to explore Isle- aux-Coudres before continuing along the coast to Malbaie.

Kids **Especially for Kids:** Activities at the spectacular Canyon Sainte-Anne and Sept-Chutes dam; whale-watching near the Saguenay Fjord.

A Bit of History

The first settlers moved into the Charlevoix region toward the end of the 17C. They were predominantly lumberjacks and navigators, since the coast did not lend itself to agriculture. Some remote communities remained inaccessible by road until the mid-20C. Charlevoix is named for Pierre-François-Xavier de Charlevoix (1682–1761), a Jesuit historian who wrote the noted *History and General Description of New France* (*Histoire et description générale de la Nouvelle-France*).

Charlevoix Schooners – Until the late 1960s, small schooners, called *goélettes*, sailed the St. Lawrence transporting provisions and wood destined for the Charlevoix Coast, the Côte-Nord, Bas-Saint-Laurent, and the Gaspésie. More than 300 of these vessels, known locally as *voitures d'eau* (literally "water cars"), were built in Charlevoix. The small vessels were originally equipped with sails, and later with motors. Today their hulls lie abandoned along the shore.

Visitors stopping along the clifftop roads of this region can often hear the rumbling of powerful motors from freighters passing in the distance on the St. Lawrence River. These freighters gradually replaced the traditional schooners.

A Choice Resort – As early as the 1760s, visitors flocked to Charlevoix, attracted by the beauty of its landscapes. After the Conquest, two Scottish officers, Capt. John Nairn and Lieutenant Malcolm Fraser, received the former seigneury of La Malbaie–Pointe-Au-Pic from military governor Gen. James Murray (1721–1794), and named it Murray Bay. In the mid-19C, Charlevoix became a popular resort area. City dwellers began refurbishing traditional residences and later constructed elegant summer homes. Canada Steamship Lines brought many wealthy tourists to the region aboard their luxurious cruise ships and built the enormous Manoir Richelieu Hotel in 1899. Reconstructed in 1929 after a fire, the hotel is the sole survivor among the grand hostelries of the period. The great white boats (*bateaux blancs*) discontinued their visits in the 1960s, when the opening of the Côte-Nord road marked the end of an era. Today numerous inns welcome tourists.

Artists' Haunt – Charlevoix has long attracted and inspired painters, poets, and writers. Its villages and panoramas are immortalized in the works of such well-known Canadian artists as Clarence Gagnon, Marc-Aurèle Fortin, René Richard, Jean-Paul Lemieux, and A.Y. Jackson. Baie-Saint-Paul, especially, is known as an artists' haunt, as are Port-au-Persil and Les Éboulements. Among the writers and poets who have lived here are Laure Conan and Gabrielle Roy.

Driving Tour

From Beaupré to Baie-Sainte-Catherine

220km/136mi.

▸ *Leave Beaupré on Rte. 138. After 4km/ 2.5mi, turn left, following signs.*

Canyon Sainte-Anne★★ Kids
🕐*Open Jun 24–Labor Day, daily 9am– 5.45pm; May–Jun 23 & early Sept–Oct, daily 9am–4.45pm.* ⟨$11. ✕ ♿ 🅿 *206 Rte 138 Est.* ☎*418-827-4057. www.canyon ste-anne.qc.ca.*
This splendid wilderness setting affords visitors the opportunity to observe the sedimentary rock marking the beginning of the St. Lawrence Plain juxtaposed against the granitic gneiss that forms the Canadian Shield. At this point, the Sainte-Anne-du-Nord River drops in a steep and narrow waterfall, plunging 74m/243ft into a mass of foam and whirlpools. Interpretative panels dot the paths leading through the woods to the river and falls; three footbridges span the river, allowing excellent views. A third footpath leads to the bottom of the canyon.

▸ *Rejoin Rte. 138; after 15km/9.3mi turn left on Rte. 360 for Saint-Ferréol-les-Neiges. Continue for 10km/6.2mi, following signs.*

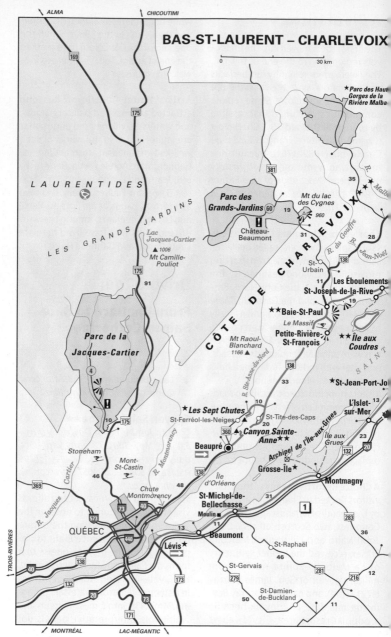

BAS-ST-LAURENT – CHARLEVOIX

Les Sept-Chutes★ (Seven Falls)

Kids ⏱ *Open late Jun–late Aug, daily 9am–5.45pm; late May–Jun 22 & Aug 21–mid-Oct, daily 10am–4.30pm.* $11. 🅿 *4520 Ave. Royale.* ☎ *418-826-3139. www.septchutes.com.*

Between 1912 and 1916, a dam and generating station were built here, where the Sainte-Anne-du-Nord River cascades over seven separate falls. The generators remained in operation until 1984; in 1999 they were restarted.

Today a pleasant park, the site affords lovely views of the falls, as well as the opportunity to discover a part of Quebec's natural and industrial heritage. The

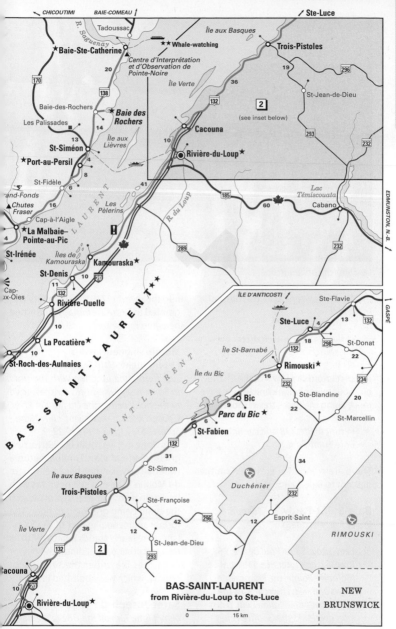

dam above the falls and the wooden aqueduct that carried water to the turbines are still standing. The **generating station**, one of the oldest of its type in Quebec, is open to the public (*visitors must descend 325 steps to reach the station*). An interpretation center recounts the history of the hydroelectric facility.

▶ *Return to Rte. 138. After 30km/18.6mi turn right to Petite-Rivière-Saint-François and continue for 10km/6.2mi.*

Petite-Rivière-Saint-François
The road descends steeply through the forest to a small community located

Les Éboulements landscape

on the St. Lawrence, at the base of a great cliff.

▶ *In the village, turn left after the church.*

The pier affords a **view**★ of the Charlevoix mountains plunging into the St. Lawrence along the rock-strewn shores.

▶ *Return to Rte. 138 and continue to Baie-Saint-Paul.*

There are wonderful **views**★★ on the descent to Baie-Saint-Paul.

Baie-Saint-Paul★★ – *13km/8mi.*
See Entry Heading.

▶ *Leave Baie-Saint-Paul by Rte. 362. Rte. 362, and later Rte. 138 from La Malbaie–Pointe-au-Pic, provide views of the St. Lawrence. As the road leaves Baie-Saint-Paul, a rest stop overlooks the Gouffre valley and the Île aux Coudres.*

Les Éboulements
19km/11.8mi.
This community, perched on the mountain's edge 300m/948ft above the St. Lawrence, takes its name from the series of landslides (**éboulements**) that followed a violent earthquake in 1663, propelling half the mountainside into the river. In 1710 the seigneury was granted to Pierre Tremblay who settled here and built a mill.

Moulin seigneurial des Éboulements (Old Stone Mill)
Just before the junction with the road to Saint-Joseph-de-la-Rive. Access road to the right, before the Du Moulin River. ◷*Open late Jun–early Sept, daily 10am–5pm.* ◉*$3.* ✗ 🅿 ☎*418-635-2239.*
This stone mill was built in 1790 for Seigneur Jean-François Tremblay atop a waterfall on what then became "Rivière du Moulin." The mill still operates with its original equipment. Visitors watch the grain being ground into flour. The former seigneurial manor of the Sales-Laterrière family stands nearby. With its mill and other outbuildings, the manor illustrates life under the seigneurial regime, which was abolished in 1854.

Saint-Joseph-de-la-Rive
3km/1.8mi. Turn off Rte. 362 to the right toward Saint-Joseph-de-la-Rive and follow a very steep descent to the St. Lawrence.
Sandwiched between the St. Lawrence and the mountains, the community offers lovely views of Île aux Coudres and the river. It was one of the main shipbuilding centers for the traditional Charlevoix schooners, many of which lie scattered along the village shore.

The ferry to Isle-aux-Coudres leaves from this town.

Take time to tour the schooners at the **Musée maritime de Charlevoix** (*305 Rue de l'Église;* ⊙*open mid-May–late Jun & Labor Day–mid-Oct, Mon–Fri 9am–4pm, weekends 11am–4pm; late Jun–Labor Day, daily 9am–5pm;* ✆*$5;* ☎*418-635-1131; www.musee-maritime-charlevoix.com*) for a taste of Charlevoix's maritime past. At the **Papeterie Saint-Gilles** (*304 Rue Félix-Antoine-Savard;* ⊙*open year round;* ☎*418-635-2430; www.papeteriesaintgilles.com;* ✆*$3*), an old paper workshop founded by priest and writer Félix-Antoine Savard, guides explain how 17C paper was made.

Isle-aux-Coudres★★

Ferry service (free): Depart from Saint-Joseph-de-la-Rive Apr–Oct, daily 7.30am–11.30pm every hour; rest of the year, daily 7.30am–11.30pm (Jan–Feb 11pm) every 2hrs. Société des traversiers du Québec. ♿☎*1-877-787-7483. www.traversiers.gouv.qc.ca.* ♿*See Entry Heading for description.*

▶ *Return to Saint-Joseph-de-la-Rive and Rte. 362 to Les Éboulements and continue toward Saint-Irénée.*

Along this stretch, the St. Lawrence can often be spotted. Take the unpaved Cap-aux-Oies road for 1km/.6mi and stop at the bottom of the steep hill for a **panorama** of the cape and the south shore of the St. Lawrence. As it sweeps down to river level, Rte. 62 again reveals spectacular **views**.

Saint-Irénée

15km/9.3mi from Les Éboulements.
Saint-Irénée was the birthplace of lawyer and poet **Adolphe-Basile Routhier** (1839–1920), who wrote the French lyrics to the Canadian national anthem. Rodolphe Forget (1861–1919), who built the railway that follows the north shore of the St. Lawrence, had a summer home here. Known as **Le Domaine Forget**, this estate is set in a lovely area overlooking the river. Today it is devoted to the performing arts; concerts are given throughout the summer.

The road passes through or nearby La Malbaie–Pointe-au-Pic and Cap-à-l'Aigle. Small protestant churches can be seen along the way.

La Malbaie–Pointe-au-Pic★
– *14km/8.7mi.* ♿*See Entry Heading.*

▶ *Rejoin Rte. 138.*

The road leads up the mountainside to Saint-Fidèle, providing a view of the Îles de Kamouraska (a Quebec nature reserve), and then descends to river level.

▶ *6km/3.7mi after Saint-Fidèle, turn right for Port-au-Persil.*

Port-au-Persil★
30km/18.6mi from La Malbaie–Pointe-au-Pic.
This cove on the St. Lawrence has long been a favorite with artists. Beside the old quay, a tiny Anglican church and a cascade add a picturesque note.

Saint-Siméon
4km/2.5mi.
This town is the location of the large ferry (*65min*) that crosses the St. Lawrence to Rivière-du-Loup.
Ferry service on the N.M. Trans-Saint-Laurent (capacity 100 cars, 399 passengers): Depart from Saint-Siméon daily year-round, one to five crossings a day depending on the time of year. ✆*$37.70 (vehicle), $13.60 (passenger).* ♿☎*418-638-2856 & 514) 989-4425. www.traverserdl.com.*
This crossing is spectacular. In winter, the ship knocks ice floating on the river.

Baie des Rochers★
17km/10.5mi.
An unpaved road (*about 3km/1.8mi*) leads to this lovely deserted bay, dominated by an old wharf. A small island close by is reachable at low tide.

▶ *Return to Rte. 138.*

The St. Lawrence comes into view again near Baie-Sainte-Catherine.

Baie-Sainte-Catherine★ – *23km/14mi.* ♿*See Entry Heading.*

CHIBOUGAMAU

BAIE JAMES REGION
POPULATION 7,563

The Chibougamau region, a vast expanse of lakes and forests, is bordered by Lakes Mistassini, Chibougamau, and Aux Dorés. The name Chibougamau is derived from the Cree word *shabogamaw,* meaning "lake traversed by a river." The indigenous population in this region consisted of nomadic hunters and gatherers who separated into small multifamily groups for the long winter and reassembled into large bands at various strategic meeting places during the summer. Today half the town's inhabitants are Francophones of European descent and half are Cree, who live mostly around lakes and rivers, drawing their livelihood primarily from the immense boreal forest that is divided into familial hunting territories.

- **Information:** 512 Rte. 167 Sud. ☎418-748-7276 & 418-748-6060. www.tourismebaiejames.com.
- ▶ **Orient Yourself:** Chibougamau is located 700km/434mi north of Montreal by Rtes. 40, 55, 155, and 167 (starting at Lake Saint-Jean). *One daily flight departs from Montreal on Air Creebec ☎800-567-6567; for schedules www.aircreebec.ca.*
- **Don't Miss:** The Albanel-Mistassini-and-Waconichi Lakes Wildlife Reserve for a real wilderness camping experience.
- **Organizing Your Time:** Allow at least 10 hours to drive from Montreal to Chibougamau via Lac St-Jean on Rte. 167, or 13 hours via Mont-Laurier on Rte. 117. If you intend to camp or fish, be sure to make your reservations before you leave.
- **Especially for Kids:** Outdoor activities, such as canoeing, are available everywhere.

A Bit of History

Lake Chibougamau was situated along the northern route traveled by early European explorers. Among these were Des Groseillers (1618–96) and Radisson (1636–1710), followed closely by Father Charles Albanel (1616–96). Trading posts gave way to the mining town of Chibougamau, built in the midst of the boreal forest on a sandy plain near Gilman Lake, 15km/9mi north of Lake Chibougamau.

Traces of ore were first discovered in the 1840s. Several companies in the mining industry saw the area's great mineral wealth. Prospectors, mining engineers, promoters, and geologists flooded into the area. It was not until 1950, with the completion of a 240km/149mi winter road between Saint-Félicien and Chibougamau, that mining companies established themselves here permanently.

The first copper, zinc, and gold mine opened in 1951 on the site of Chapais, 44km/27mi from Chibougamau.

Today Chibougamau harbors mainly miners and forest workers. Several sawmills and working mines remain. Prospecting continues mainly within the Lake Aux Dorés complex. Both copper and gold are mined in this area. Once the extracted rock has passed through the local concentrators, it is shipped by train to Chapais and then on to the Noranda smelter in Rouyn-Noranda.

Sight

Église Saint-Marcel (St. Marcel's Church)

This striking building was constructed during the 1960s. The roof, with its openwork center, is composed of two concrete shells thrust upward in opposing curves; the resulting design evokes the form of a fish, an ancient Christian symbol.

Excursion

Réserve faunique des Lacs-Albanel-Mistassini-et-Waconichi (Albanel-Mistassini-and-Waconichi Lakes Wildlife Reserve)

🕐*Reserve open Jun–Labor Day, daily 7am–7pm. The entrance is located 3km/1.8mi from Chibougamau on Rte. 167. Administrative offices open Mon–Fri 8.30am–5pm;* 🕐*closed major holidays.* ⚠️📞*1-800-665-6527 & 418-748-7748. www.sepaq.com.* ⚠️*Wilderness camping (reservations* 📞*418-890-6527) is limited to 14 consecutive days. All waste must be packed out. Self-guided overnight canoe trips: One-month advance notice is required. Rowboats may be rented by reservation only; no guide services available.*

This immense expanse of wilderness, stretching over 16,400sq km/6,332sq mi, is covered with forests of black spruce and fir. A multitude of lakes, including Lake Mistassini—the largest lake in the province (2,019sq km/780sq mi)—make this a haven for fishing enthusiasts.

Waconichi Reserve

Named after the hills to the west of Lake Waconichi that protect Amerindian encampments from the frosty northwest winds, the reserve includes a tourist complex with fishing facilities. Recently built log cabins (*27km/16.8mi from Chalco checkpoint; reservations required* 📞*1-800-665-6527*) are located on a lovely **site**★.

Mistassini

From the Chalco checkpoint, drive 67km/41.6mi on Rte. 167 and turn left toward Mistassini (Baie-du-Poste); continue for 16km/10mi.

Mistassini is located on the old fur trading route leading to Fort Rupert (Waskaganish), on Hudson Bay. A Cree community, known as the Mistassini, already inhabited the area in 1640. The Hudson's Bay Company (HBC) maintained a trading post at Fort Rupert for 100 years, but competition from the Northwest Company eventually forced the HBC to move inland.

In order to intercept the furs before they arrived at Fort Rupert, the French established their own trading post in Mistassini in 1674, after Father Charles

Albanel's visit to the area. The first trading post at Neoskweskau, on the Eastmain River, was moved to the north of Lake Mistassini in 1800 and to the south of the lake, where Mistassini is now located, in 1835.

Excursion

From Chibougamau to Val-d'Or

About 413km/250mi southwest on Rtes. 167, 113 and 117.

Chapais

44km/27mi from Chibougamau by Rtes. 167 and 113.

The town was named in honour of the politician and historian Sir Thomas Chapais. The first major ore deposit in the Chibougamau-Chapais region was discovered on this site in 1929, by Leo Springner. In 1989, the Chapais sawmill was awarded a prize as the largest lumber producer in Eastern Canada. A new thermal mill converts wood residue into electric energy.

Waswanipi

93km/58mi.

Like Mistassini, Waswanipi has been designated as an Indian and wildlife reserve. Many Cree who live in this area are employed in the mines at Desmaraisville and Miquelon, south of Waswanipi; others work on reforestation projects in the region.

Lebel-sur-Quévillon

120km/74mi from Waswanipi, 213km/132mi from Chapais.

In 1965 the shores of Lake Quévillon, fed by the Bell River, were still pristine wilderness. Since then, a small, vibrant community has developed.

Located at the edge of town on Blvd. Quévillon is a municipal campground and beach with water sport equipment rental and charted walking trails.

Senneterre
84km/52mi.

Located at the town's three entry points, three sculptures, representing the forestry and railway industries and the Canadian armed forces, serve as reminders of a difficult but glorious past, while instilling hope for the future of this dynamic little forestry community.

Lac Faillon
45km/28mi east of Senneterre, on access road N-806.

Lake Faillon offers visitors a lovely setting enhanced by the unspoiled beauty of the Mégiscane River. Recreational activities on the lake include swimming, boating, canoeing, and fishing.

Val-d'Or★ – *67km/41mi by Rtes. 113 and 117.* ⛵ *See Entry Heading.*

CHICOUTIMI★
SAGUENAY–LAC-SAINT-JEAN REGION
POPULATION OF SAGUENAY 146,332
MAP: SEE FJORD DU SAGUENAY

Located at the confluence of the Saguenay, Chicoutimi, and Du Moulin rivers, the Chicoutimi is the core district of the City of Saguenay (created in 2002 by the merger of the cities of Chicoutimi, Jonquière, La Baie, Laterrière, and some adjacent townships). Chicoutimi is also the economic, cultural, and administrative center of the Saguenay region as well as its episcopal seat. The University of Quebec maintains a campus here.

Chicoutimi was the site of a major fur trading post as early as 1676, but it was not founded as a community until 1842, when Métis trader Peter McLeod built a sawmill at the foot of waterfalls on the Du Moulin River. This event marked the beginning of the area's important forestry industry. Chicoutimi draws its name from the Montagnais word *eshko-timiou,* meaning "to the edge of deep waters."

From Chicoutimi the visitor can behold a fine view★ of the rounded cliffs flanking the Saguenay River on its descent toward the St. Lawrence. The Saguenay can be crossed by car on the Dubuc Bridge (*pont Dubuc*), or on foot or by bicycle via the Sainte-Anne footbridge.

Every February, Chicoutimi celebrates its **Carnaval-Souvenir**, during which the inhabitants dress in furs and period costume, and re-create winter activities of a bygone era.

- **Information:** 295 Rue Racine Est. ☎418-698-3167 & 1-800-463-6565. www.bleuvacances.ca.
- **Orient Yourself:** Chicoutimi is located 200km/124mi northwest of Quebec City by the scenic Rte. 175.
- **Don't Miss:** Cruise the Saguenay Fjord on La Marjolaine.
- **Organizing Your Time:** The Marjolaine cruises on the fjord will take 6–7 hours (*8.30am–3.45pm, 12.30pm–6.30pm*). There is free parking at the dock.
- **Especially for Kids:** Village de la sécurité (Safety Village).

Sights

Scenic Cruises★★
Depart from dock at bottom of Rue Lafontaine Jun–Sept, daily 8.30am & 12.30pm. Duration 4.5hrs. Bilingual commentary. Return to Chicoutimi by bus. ☜Starting at $45. 🍴 🅿 *Croisières Marjolaine Inc. ☎418-543-7630. www. croisieremarjolaine.com*

Cruises on the majestic Saguenay fjord are among the most spectacular and popular excursions in Quebec. The boats descend the river to the lovely village of Sainte-Rose-du-Nord; stop below the rocky promontory known as the Tableau (150m/492ft high); pass by Saint-Basile-du-Tableau, one of the smallest villages in Quebec; and enter Eternity Bay (Baie Éternité), dominated by the towering peaks of Cape Eternity and Cape Trinity. The highlight of the cruise is the dramatic arrival at the foot of **Cap Trinité**. Set in this wild and rocky setting is a gigantic statue of the Virgin. The three ledges for which the cape was named are clearly visible from the boat; sometimes, rock climbers can be seen here.

On the return trip, the views of Ha! Ha! Bay and of Chicoutimi itself are equally pleasant.

Croix de Sainte-Anne★ (St. Anne's Cross)

On north side of the Saguenay, 3km/1.8mi from the Dubuc Bridge. Turn left on Rue Saint-Albert, right on Rue Roussel, and left on Rue de la Croix.

Located high above the Saguenay, the terrace offers a wonderful **view** of Chicoutimi and the area. The present 18m/59ft-high cross (1922) is the third to stand on this site. The first one was constructed in 1863 to guide the ferries sailing up the river and prevent accidents. The second cross (1872) was erected in gratitude for the protection accorded the city during the Great Fire of 1870, which devastated much of the land around the Lake Saint-Jean and the Saguenay River. Below this viewpoint one can see the lovely façade of Église Sainte-Anne (St. Anne's Church, 1901). The Jacques Cartier lookout (*intersection of Rue Jacques Cartier Est and Blvd. Talbot*) and the Beauregard lookout (*east of the Jacques Cartier lookout, near the statue of Our Lady of the Saguenay*) also afford excellent views of the Saguenay.

La pulperie de Chicoutimi, Centre d'Interprétation★ (Chicoutimi Pulp Mill Interpretation Center)

300 Rue Dubuc. ○*Open Jun 24–early-Sept, daily 9am–6pm; Jan–Jun, Wed–Sun* *10am–4pm.* ⬲*$9.* ⬥ ℗ ☏*418-698-3100 & 1-800-698-3100. www.pulperie.com.*

This former pulp and paper mill, standing on a picturesque **site**★★ at the mouth of the Chicoutimi River, was one of the most important industrial complexes in Quebec. The mill was founded in 1896 by the Chicoutimi Pulp and Paper Co., Canada's largest producer of pulp by 1910. In 1920 the company employed over 2,000 people in its four mills and mechanical workshop. The mill closed after the Crash of 1929.

Near the entrance at the top of the gorge stands Building 1921. This enormous former workshop of pink granite today serves primarily as an **interpretation center**.

Farther down, along the river, stand the remains of two paper mills, dating from 1898 and 1912. Part of the enormous conduit that brought water down to power the mills still exists. Steps lead up the river to a hillock overlooking the entire installation of the mill. The water tower is still functioning. Architect René P. LeMay (1870–1915) designed several of these buildings using local stone instead of the brick traditionally used in industrial constructions. The choice of stone as a building material contributes to the charm of the site.

Maison Arthur-Villeneuve (Arthur Villeneuve House)

In Building 1921.

Beginning in 1994 local efforts to highlight the region's heritage resulted in the relocation to this site of the home of painter Arthur Villeneuve, formerly located at 669 Rue Taché Ouest. Villeneuve (1905–1990) worked for many years as a barber while painting in his

Chicoutimi Pulp Mill

André Ellefsen

spare time. A deeply religious man, he gave up his shop in 1957 and dedicated the rest of his life to painting after hearing a sermon on the use of one's talents. The fame of this local folk painter has spread far beyond his simple home. Villeneuve decorated his house with colorful (and sometimes terrifying) murals.

Cathédrale Saint-François-Xavier (Cathedral of St. Francis Xavier)

Rue Racine at Rue Bégin. ◯Open year-round, daily 8am–11.30am, 1.30pm–4pm. ☎418-549-3212.

The twin square towers flanking the stone facade of the cathedral (1915) overlook the city of Chicoutimi. The cathedral was rebuilt after a fire in 1919. Inside, note the sculpture of Christ by Médard Bourgault, the pulpit and

Bishop's throne by Lauréat Vallières and the organ manufactured by the Casavant Brothers of Saint-Hyacinthe.

Le Relais du Village de la sécurité (Safety Village)   Kids

200 Rue Pinel. On north side of Saguenay River, 4km/2.5mi from bridge. Turn right on Rue Pasteur, right on Rue Saint-Gérard, and left on Rue Pinel. ◯Open Jun–Labor Day, daily 9.30am–5.30pm; mid-May–mid-Jun & Sept, call for hours. ◉$6. ⚒ ♿ P ☎418-545-6925.

Developed primarily to increase young people's awareness of security issues, this scale-model village offers activities and attractions, including train rides and miniature motorized cars. Other attractions simulate an auto crash and a house fire, while a 30m/98.4ft-high weather tower offers a fine **view** of the region.

CÔTE-NORD ★

MANICOUAGAN REGION

MAP: SEE CÔTE-NORD

The Côte-Nord, or North Shore, extends from the mouth of the Saguenay River north to the Labrador border. The Upper North Shore, the southernmost region, stretches from Tadoussac to Sept-Îles, and the Middle North Shore from Sept-Îles to Havre-Saint-Pierre. The Lower North Shore, so named because it is the closest to the ocean, encompasses the area between Havre-Saint-Pierre and Blanc-Sablon; in this vast expanse of taiga, the majority of towns and villages can only be reached by plane or boat.

The Inuit and Montagnais have inhabited the area for thousands of years, and the Montagnais, living in seven reserves scattered along the coast, still form a major part of the population. In the second half of the 15C, Basque fishermen came to this region to hunt whales. Fishing remained the primary industry until the 1920s, when pulp mill companies began exploiting the forest resources, thus creating an important forestry industry. In the 1950s, the discovery of rich mineral deposits, primarily iron ore, prompted another surge of economic growth, as did the harnessing of the Manicouagan and Outardes rivers for hydroelectricity in the early 1960s.

- 🛈 **Information:** 197 Rue des Pionniers, Tadoussac. ☎418-235-4744 & 1-888-463-5319. www.tourismemanicouagan.com.
- ▷ **Orient Yourself:** Rte. 138 traverses the Côte-Nord from Tadoussac to Natashquan. Most of the Lower North Shore is accessible only by boat or plane.
- ☺ **Don't Miss:** Manic-5 dam, Mingan National Park Islands.
- ◔ **Organizing Your Time:** From Tadoussac, Natashquan is 800km/500mi on Rte. 138. Unless you continue with your vehicle on board the M/V Nordik Express to Labrador and Newfoundland, you will need to retrace your route to return. From Baie-Comeau take a day trip (6hr there and back) along the Manicouagan River to the Manic-5 Daniel Johnson Dam. From Baie-Comeau, allow 3.5 hours to drive to Sept-Îles. Plan to spend a day at the Mingan Archipelago (about 2.5 hours' drive farther east).
- ⚓ **Also See:** ARCHIPEL DE MINGAN.

Driving Tours

①From Tadoussac to Sept-Îles
450km/279mi by Rte. 138.

Tadoussac★★ –
See Entry Heading.

Grandes-Bergeronnes
26km/16mi from Tadoussac; drive through Petites-Bergeronnes.
Named Bergeronnettes (wagtails) by Samuel de Champlain in 1603, after he spotted a flock of these yellow, long-tailed birds, the region had already been frequented by Basque fishermen and Montagnais long before. The first European settlers arrived in 1844 and erected a flour mill in Petites-Bergeronnes and a sawmill in Grandes-Bergeronnes.
Today **whale watching** is the main attraction. Favorable ecological conditions in the area produce an abundance of plankton, which in turn attracts belugas and blue whales to these waters. It is possible to observe them at sea or from the shore at Cap-de-Bon-Désir.

Archeo-Topo Interpretation Center
498 Rue de la Mer. Open mid-May–Jun & Sept–mid-Oct, daily 9am–5pm, Jul–Aug, daily 8am–8pm. $4.50. 418-232-6286; www.archeotopo.qc.ca
Archaeological exhibits here focus on the excavations carried out in the Grandes-Bergeronnes region, which have uncovered traces of human occupation dating back 5,500 years.

Cap-de-Bon-Désir Nature Interpretation and Observation Center
6km/3.7mi east of Grandes-Bergeronnes. Open mid-Jun–Labor Day, daily 8am–8pm; Labor Day–early Oct, daily 9am–5pm. $7. 418-232-6751.
Part of the Parc marin du Saguenay–Saint-Laurent (Saguenay–Saint-Laurent Marine Park), the center provides various activities and information to introduce visitors to regional history and the underwater environment of the estuary. Whales and other marine mammals are often visible from the observation tower (*binoculars available for rent*).

Les Escoumins
13km/8mi.
Basque fishermen established this small community in the late 15C, naming it Esquemin. Now known as Les Escoumins, the charming town offers ideal spots for whale watching and is noteworthy for its fishing and scuba diving. When crossing over the Escoumins River, visitors can see an unusual construction to the left: It is a **salmon ladder** designed to help the salmon as they swim upstream to spawn in the waters where they were born.

Baie-Comeau
160km/99mi.
Named for Napoléon-Alexandre Comeau, a trapper, geologist, and naturalist from the Côte-Nord, the city of 25,554 inhabitants traces its industrial beginnings to Col. Robert McCormick (1880–1955) and his establishment of the Quebec North Shore Paper Co. in 1936. Today the company, known as the Quebec and Ontario Paper Co., is one of the region's foremost employers.
Constructed of multicolored granite stones and reminiscent of the works of the 20C French modernist, Auguste Perret, **Cathédrale Saint-Jean-Eudes** (*open during masses only, Wed & Fri–Sat 7.15pm, Sun 10am; 418-589-2370*) overlooks the mouth of the Manicouagan River. Situated in the Marquette sector to the east, **Amélie Quarter** boasts fine homes built in the 1930s. On Rue Cabot stands **Le Manoir Hotel,** rebuilt in the French Colonial style. **Église Sainte-Amélie** (*37 Ave. Marquette; open Mon–Fri 9am–6pm; 418-296-5578*) is dedicated to the memory of Amélie McCormick, wife of the town's founder and benefactor. The **frescoes★** adorning the interior are the work of Italian artist Guido Nincheri and were restored in 1996.

Excursion to the Manic-Outardes Complex
430km/267mi round-trip from Baie-Comeau. See Entry Heading.

Godbout
54km/33.5mi from Baie-Comeau.
The village occupies a beautiful **site★** in the bay between Pointe-des-Monts

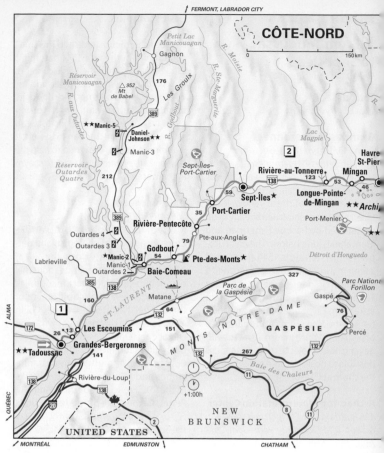

Cape and the mouth of the Godbout River. The village and the river were named after the pilot and navigator, Nicolas Godbout, who settled on Île d'Orléans in 1670. A ferry connects the village to Matane, on the south shore.

Musée Amérindien et Inuit de Godbout (Amerindian and Inuit Museum)

Facing the port, 2km/1.2mi south of Rte. 138. ○*Open late Jun–late Sept daily 9am–10pm.* ∞*$5.* ⌂ ✕ P *134 Chemin Pascal-Comeau.* ☎*418-568-7306. www. vitrine.net/godbout.*

Directors Cécile and Claude Grenier have created a warm and intimate museum exhibiting a fine collection of Amerindian arts and Inuit sculptures, mostly from the Northwest Territories. Splendid photographs of arctic animals by Fred Bruemmer are hung through-

out the museum. An authentic Algonquin bark canoe is suspended in the pottery workshop.

▶ *Continue on Rte. 138 for 29km/18mi, turn right on Route du Vieux Phare and continue for 12km/7.4mi.*

Phare de Pointe-des-Monts★ (Pointe-des-Monts Lighthouse)

○*Open mid-Jun–mid-Sept, daily 9am–5pm.* ∞*$8.* ⌂ ✕ P ☎*418-939-2400.* Access by a narrow, winding road off Rte. 138.

Built in 1830, the 28m/91.8ft lighthouse stands at the point where the St. Lawrence River widens into a gulf. For 150 years the lighthouse served as a home for the lightkeepers and their families. Today the interior houses a small museum that re-creates the lives and duties of the various keepers; also

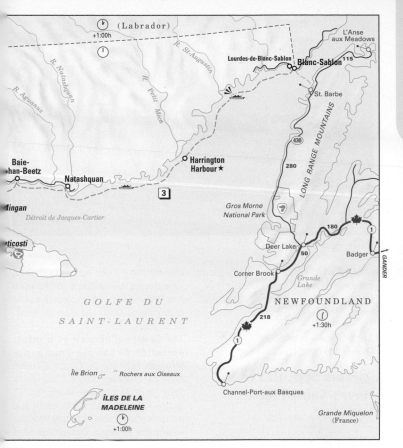

on display are items salvaged from area shipwrecks. Activities organized here include trout and salmon fishing, deep-sea fishing, scuba diving, whale- and seal-watching, and excursions to observe and photograph local fauna, including black bears, ospreys and gannets. A small inn and several vacation cottages are located on the site.

▶ *Return to Rte. 138.*

Between Pointe-aux-Anglais and Rivière-Pentecôte, the road passes beside beautiful sandy beaches.

Rivière-Pentecôte
79km/49mi from Godbout.
The village and nearby river were named in the 16C by Jacques Cartier, when he stayed here on Whitsunday (*Pentecôte*). Rivière-Pentecôte was the birthplace of

the North Shore's first newspaper, *L'Écho du Labrador,* founded in 1903 by Joseph Laizé, a Eudist missionary.
From the tourist information center overlooking the village, the **view**★ of the church and the tiny oratory of St. Anne, perched on a cape, is very picturesque.

Port-Cartier
35km/21.7mi.
Owing to its deepwater port, this industrial and commercial town has become a major center for transshipping minerals and cereals in Canada. The town lies on the banks of the Rochers and Dominique rivers, at the point where they empty into the St. Lawrence. The two islands situated at the mouth of the rivers are devoted to recreational use, including swimming, camping and sport fishing (the region is known for its salmon).

Rivière-Pentecôte

Located on Île Patterson is the Taiga, a botanical garden of native plants. On Île McCormick, a café-theatre exhibits the work of local artists.

Sept-Îles★ – *59km/37mi.*
⟳ *See Entry Heading.*

②From Sept-Îles to Havre-Saint-Pierre

222km/138mi by Rte. 138.

Rivière-au-Tonnerre
123km/76.4mi from Sept-Îles.
This pleasant fishing village takes its name from the thunderous rush of nearby waterfalls. Dominating the town center is the **Église Saint-Hippolyte** (*Church of St. Hippolyte* ⟳*open Jun 24– early Sept, daily 8am–5pm;* ☎*418-465-2842*). Construction of the church began in 1905, according to plans designed by the parish priest. More than 300 church members each gave three months of work and two cords of wood per winter for its completion (one cord equals about 3.5cu m/13.7cu ft). The numerous carvings on the vault were done by a parishioner using only a penknife.

Longue-Pointe-de-Mingan
53km/33mi.
Set on a narrow strip of land jutting out into the Gulf of St. Lawrence, Longue-Pointe is considered the gateway to the Mingan Archipelago. An Ameri-

can military base was established here during World War II. Visitors can catch glimpses of the islands of the archipelago from the Rue du Bord-de-la-Mer.

The **Centre d'accueil et d'inter-prétation de Longue-Pointe -de-Mingan** (*625 Rue du Centre;* ⟳*open mid-Jun–end Aug, daily 8.30am–6pm; Sept–mid-Oct, 9am–6pm;* ✆ *$7;* ⟳☐☎*418-949-2126*) is a research and interpretation center providing information on the various activities organized by the Mingan Archipelago National Park Reserve, including educational programs and tourist excursions. Presented here are the natural history of the region and marine mammals of the Gulf of St. Lawrence. Visitors can also make arrangements for **whale watching cruises** (*depart from Longue-Pointe-de-Mingan mid-Jun–mid-Oct daily at 7.30am; round-trip 6–8hrs; commentary; reservations required;* ✆*$105;* ⟳☐*Station de recherche des Îles Mingan;* ☎*418-949-2845*).

Mingan
10km/6.2mi.
Of Basque origin, the name of this Montagnais reserve, created in 1963, means "strip of land." A trading post and fishing village during the French Regime, Mingan boasts one of the most productive fishing ports along the coast. The Montagnais operate a fish packing plant and marketing company known

as Les Crustacés de Mingan. At the village entrance, on Rte. 138, the **Musée montagnais** (Montagnais Museum) exhibits tools, household items, and photos illustrating the heritage of the Montagnais (○ *open late Jun–mid-Aug, daily 9am–6pm;* Ⓟ ☎418-949-2234).

Montagnais Church★

15, Rue Nashipetimit. ○*Open year-round, daily 8am–7pm.* ☎418-949-2272.
Located near the cultural center, the church was built in 1918 by Jack Maloney, the legendary Jack "Monoloy" of Gilles Vigneault's song, *Les bouleaux de la rivière Mingan* (The Silver Birches of the Mingan River). In 1972 the church was remodeled in the Montagnais style: The pulpit is decorated with caribou antlers; the Stations of the Cross are painted on skins stretched across frames of birch branches; the baptismal font is hollowed out of a maple trunk; and the tabernacle is in the form of a wigwam.

Havre-Saint-Pierre

36km/22mi.
This industrial town was first settled in 1857 by Acadian fishermen from the Magdalen Islands. The town's economy was based on marine resources until 1948, when the mining company, QIT-Fer et Titane (Quebec Iron and Titanium), began exploiting the world's largest known ilmenite deposits (naturally occurring iron and titanium oxides), discovered around Lakes Tio and Allard, 43km/26.7mi north of town.

Centre d'accueil et d'interprétation de la réserve du Parc national de de l'Archipel-de-Mingan (Information and Interpretation Center of the Mingan Archipelago National Park Reserve)

1010 Promenade des Anciens. ○*Open mid-Jun–early Sept, daily 8.30am–6pm.* 🚹Ⓟ☎418-538-3285 & 1-888-773-8888 or 418-538-3331 (off season). www.pc.gc.ca.
The center displays photographs of flora and fauna found in the Mingan Archipelago and provides information on organized activities on the islands.

▶ *Continue to Rue de la Berge and turn right.*

Masison de la culture Roland-Jomphe (Roland-Jomphe Cultural Center)

957 Rue de la Berge. ○ *Open mid-Jun–early Sept, daily 9am–9pm.* ☜ *$2.* 🚹☎418-538-2450.
In the former Clarke Trading Co. store (1926–63). The interior has been refurbished to appear as it would have been in the 1940s, and displays recall the cultural heritage of the village and its economic evolution. The center also presents films and lectures on regional themes.

Excursions from Havre-Saint-Pierre

Archipel de Mingan★★ –
🏛 *See Entry Heading.*

Île d'Anticosti★★ –
🏛 *See Entry Heading.*

▷ *Natashquan marks the end of Rte. 138. The Lower North Shore is not linked to the rest of Quebec by road beyond that point. A boat trip from Havre-Saint-Pierre to Blanc-Sablon is described below. However, Baie Johan Beetz is not accessible by commercial vessels. Visitors may choose to drive to Natashquan and begin the boat trip there (details below).*

③From Havre-Saint-Pierre to Blanc-Sablon

The Basse Côte-Nord (Lower North Shore) marks the eastern extremity of Quebec. The area is bordered by Labrador to the north; the island of Newfoundland lies to the southeast. Many villages along the Lower North Shore are former trading and fishing posts that date back to the French Regime. Yet of the 16 communities established within the 358km/222.4mi expanse between Kegasha and Blanc-Sablon, 12 are predominantly English-speaking (inhabited by descendants of fishermen from Newfoundland and the English Channel Island of Jersey), three are French-speaking and one is Montagnais.
Relais Nordik, Inc. operates a weekly **boat trip**★ between Havre-Saint-Pierre

Address Book for Havre-Saint-Pierre

⚭ For price ranges, see the Legend on the cover flap.

WHERE TO STAY

$$–$$$ Hôtel-Motel du Havre – *970 Blvd de l'Escale.* ☎418-538-2800 & 1-888-797-2800. *38 rooms.* Prices include a continental breakfast. Havre-Saint-Pierre largest hotel. It is a reliable, clean, comfortable option. The staff is warm and helpful. Despite being near the main road (Rte. 138), it is far enough away from it to be pleasantly quiet.

WHERE TO EAT

$$ La Promenade – *1197 Promenade-des-Anciens.* ☎418-538-263. **Seafood.** This Promenade-des-Anciens is no Promenade-des-Anglais, but rather a pristine beach. La Promenade is a casual restaurant where proper seafood is taken seriously. It is an excellent place to enjoy the local fruits de mer with a pleasant view on the origin of the aquatic protein. Reasonable prices for the seafood, and a non seafood menu that is very affordable.

and Blanc-Sablon aboard the *Nordik Express.* It is possible to purchase a ticket for passage only, but the plan including cabin and meals is recommended. The boat stops in most of the coastal villages and at Anticosti Island (*⊙departs from Havre-Saint-Pierre mid-Apr–mid-Jan, Wed 11.15pm, arrives at Blanc-Sablon Fri 7pm; round-trip including cabin & meals ∞from $225/person/night for superior cabins; reservations required for passage & vehicle transport 30 days in advance for Anticosti, 4 months in advance for passengers/vehicles going east of Natashquan;* ⊡*Relais Nordik, Inc.* ☎418-723-8787 & 1-800-463-0680; www.relaisnordik.com.*

Baie-Johan-Beetz

Accessible by Rte. 138, not by boat trip. This small village bears the name of Johan Beetz, a Belgian aristocrat who emigrated to Canada in 1897. He first established a trade in luxury furs. Later on, he became a successful breeder of fur-bearing animals and attained international recognition for his breeding methods and scientific publications. His **house** (1899) is set on a rocky promontory overlooking the bay (*⊙open Jun 24–Aug 21, daily 10am–12.30pm, 1.30pm–4pm;* ∞*$5;* ⬟*guided tours;* ⊡☎*418-648-0557*). An accomplished artist, Beetz decorated several doors and walls of his home with his paintings of flowers and animals.

Baie-Johan-Beetz

Christine Boulez/ MICHELIN

Natashquan
Rte. 138.

An atmosphere of calm and tranquillity permeates this fishing village, birthplace of the noted poet and singer, Gilles Vigneault. Natashquan was colonized by Acadians from the Magdalen Islands in 1855. On a sandy point jutting out into the St. Lawrence, weathered fishing sheds (*galets*) are remnants of a bygone era. The name Natashquan signifies in Montagnais "the place where they hunt bear." Since 1952 the nearby village of Pointe-Parent has been a Montagnais community.

▶ *Rte. 138 ends at Natashquan. Passage from Natashquan to Blanc-Sablon is possible aboard the Nordik Express (departs from Natashquan Apr–mid-Jan, Thu 8am; round-trip including cabin & meals ☞$349–$589/person; reservations required for passage & vehicle transport 30 days in advance; P Relais Nordik, Inc. ☎418-723-8787; www.relaisnordik.com).*

Harrington Harbor★
13hrs 45min from Natashquan.
Better to disembark on the return journey to Natasquan, as the ferry calls at 5pm and not midnight!

Brightly painted houses welcome the Nordik Express in Harrington Harbor. The charming fishing village is on a small island; its port makes it one of the most accessible villages on the journey to Blanc-Sablon. Wide wooden sidewalks and bridges connect the rocky terraces dotted with picturesque houses and shops. The large grey building dominating the village was the first hospital of the region and is now a home for the elderly. Nearby, the **craft shop** offers a fine selection of handmade sweaters, parkas and hooked rugs, as well as Montagnais moccasins and mittens.
In the afternoon of the second day, passengers aboard the Nordik Express can enjoy spectacular **views**★ as the ship meanders by rocky islands speckled with lichens and moss, and skirts towering cliffs on which conifers form patterns of deep green.

©Pierrette Guertin/iStockphoto

Harrington Harbor

Blanc-Sablon
21hrs 45min from Harrington Harbor.
Blanc-Sablon is situated 1.5km/1mi from the Quebec-Labrador border. The area around the Blanc-Sablon River is the site of key archaeological digs, revealing an Amerindian settlement dating back 7,200 years.

Lourdes-de-Blanc-Sablon
5km/3mi by road.
Just west of Blanc-Sablon, the largest village of the region boasts an airport and a hospital. In the church, **Musée Scheffer** (*Scheffer Museum;* ⊙ *open year-round daily 9am–7pm;* ♿ P ☎ *418-461-2000*) is dedicated to Msgr. Scheffer (1903–66), first Bishop of Labrador from 1946 until his death.

Ferry to St. Barbe, Newfoundland
Departs mid-Apr–mid-Jan (subject to change due to weather and ice conditions). One-way 1hr 30min. Reservations advisable mid-Jun–Oct. ☞*$11.25/person; $22.75/car. M/V Apollo operated by Labrador Marine.* ☎*1-866-535-2567 & 709-535-0810. www.labradormarine.com.*
Ferry crossings connect Blanc-Sablon to Sainte-Barbe, Newfoundland, located 139km/86mi south of l'Anse-aux-Meadows (☝*consult THE GREEN GUIDE Canada*), site of the oldest known European settlement in North America. Iron work and other artifacts excavated from the site are Norse in origin and were dated back to approximately AD 1000.

Lieu historique national du Canada de COTEAU-DU-LAC★

A National Historic Site of Canada, Coteau-du-Lac is located on the northern bank of the St. Lawrence River at the point where it leaves Lake Saint-François. The history of this community is closely linked to the presence of turbulent rapids nearby. Over the years, various canal systems were constructed to avoid the rapids and facilitate navigation. The problem was finally resolved by the construction of the St. Lawrence Seaway (&see INTRODUCTION).

- **Information:** Tourisme Suroît, 1155 Blvd. Mgr-Langlois, Salaberry de-Valley-fied. ☎450-377-7676 & 1-800-378-7648, www.tourisme-suroit.qc.ca.
- **Orient Yourself:** Coteau-du-Lac is located approximately 40km/25mi southwest of Montreal via Rte. 20 (Exit 17) or Rte. 338.
- **Parking:** On site.
- **Especially for Kids:** Educational programs ranging from two hours to full-day activities (see website for current programming and fees).

Visit

Open mid-May–late Aug, Wed–Sun 10am–5pm; late Aug–early Oct, Sat–Sun 10am–5pm. $4. ☎450-763-5631. www.pc.gc.ca.

Vestiges of one of the first canal lock systems in North America are located on a pleasant **site**. Visitors get an idea of how pioneers lived and solved the difficulties of trade and transportation on the St. Lawrence River.

Until the early 20C, the rapids were most treacherous between Montreal and Kingston. The construction of the **Beauharnois canal** and hydroelectric plant in the 1920s necessitated a system of dams and waterworks to divert water into the hydroelectric station. The river level thus dropped 2.5m/8ft, and the rapids lost much of their force.

Conquering the Rapids – When traveling downriver, the indigenous people who first settled the area "portaged" their canoes around the most dangerous parts of the rapids. Fur trade, however, brought crowds of trappers with heavier canoes and more goods to transport. In 1750 the French at Coteau-du-Lac solved the problem by building a *rigolet* canal, actually a stone dike, to facilitate passage to the Great Lakes. The remains of this dike are still visible from the park's walkways.

After the American Revolution (second-half of 18C), the British army established outposts along the St. Lawrence River and the Great Lakes. The *rigolet* canal proved too small for their large boats, so the British built a new **canal** in 1779. Approximately 300m/984ft long and 2.5m/8ft deep, the canal incorporated three locks which raised boats 2.7m/9ft. It remained in service until 1845, when the first Beauharnois canal opened. A boardwalk runs through the old, now dry canal.

Archeology findings – Archaeological excavations have uncovered various parts of the warehouses and military barracks built during the American Revolution and the War of 1812.

Octagonal Blockhaus – Built during the War of 1812, this unusual eight-sided blockhouse was burned down in 1837 to prevent its falling into the hands of the Patriots. The log exterior and stone foundations were rebuilt by Parks Canada in 1967. The interior includes a ground floor and an overhanging upper floor. The walls are pierced by gun embrasures. Inside, informative displays describe the transport of goods on the canal.

ISLE-AUX-COUDRES★★

CHARLEVOIX REGION
POPULATION 1,304
MAP: SEE BAS-ST-LAURENT – CHARLEVOIX

This enchanting island off the coast of Charlevoix occupies an exceptional **site** overlooking Baie-Saint-Paul. The small island, 11km/6.8mi long by 5km/3mi across at its widest point, retains its rural peace and charm to the delight of tourists who visit in the summer months. Île aux Coudres was named by Jacques Cartier in 1535 for the hazel trees (*coudriers*) that once grew there in abundance. The first European settlers arrived in 1728. In addition to farming, they hunted the beluga whale, which they named *marsouin* (white porpoise), for oil. For a long time, the island was part of a seigneury owned by the Quebec City Seminary. Until the 1950s, the island housed several shipbuilding centers that manufactured the sail and motor schooners used for coastal navigation and for hunting the beluga. The centers also constructed heavy canoes that allowed the inhabitants to reach the mainland shores even in winter, when the waterways were frozen. It was here in the 1960s that Pierre Perrault, from the National Film Board of Canada, filmed his renowned documentaries on the beluga whale hunt and the Charlevoix *voitures d'eau*.

- **Information:** ☎1-800-667-2276. www.tourisme-charlevoix.com.
- **Orient Yourself:** Isle-aux-Coudres is about 120km/74.5mi northeast of Quebec City by Rtes. 138 and 362. *The ferry from Saint-Joseph-de-la-Rive docks at the town of Isle-aux-Coudres and departs Apr–Oct daily 7.30am–11.30pm every hour; rest of the year daily 7.30am–11.30pm (Jan–Feb 11pm) every 2hrs.* ♿ *Société des traversiers du Québec* ☎1-877-787-7483. www.traversiers.gouv.qc.ca.
- **Don't Miss:** A soothing stroll along the water's edge.
- **Organizing Your Time:** From the ferry dock, turn right to circumnavigate the island. Stop at the Schooner Museum, then the Mill before continuing your circuit along the river side. Stop for the view at Pointe-du-Bout-d'en-Bas before returning to the ferry.
- **Especially for Kids:** The Schooner Museum.
- **Also See:** CÔTE DE CHARLEVOIX.

Crossing the river in winter

Today Isle-aux-Coudres is linked to the mainland year-round by ferry. Before this link was established, however, crossing the icy St. Lawrence in the winter months required special skills acquired over many years of practice. The crossing was achieved by a combination of canoeing through the unfrozen waters and getting out of the canoe to pull it over the changing ice floes. This ability to navigate the icy waters is demonstrated each February during a dangerous, spectacular, and quite famous canoe race at the **Quebec Winter Carnival** (*see Calendar of Events*). It is one of the highlights of the Winter Carnival.

Visit

Visitors can make a **tour** of the island by car or on bicycle (*ca. 26km/16mi*). Beached schooners, remnants of a past age, can be seen in several places. The site of Pointe du Bout d'en Bas, at the northern edge of the island, provides a picturesque **view**★ of the lush green landscape of the village of Les Éboulements.

Musée Les Voitures d'Eau★ (Schooner Museum)

In Isle-aux-Coudres village. Open mid-Jun–early-Sept, daily 9.30am–6.30pm; mid-May–early Jun & mid-Sept–mid-Oct, weekends 10am–5pm. $3. ☎418-438-2208.

Tourisme Charlevoix/J.-F. Bergeron, Enviro Foto

Seacape at sunset

Devoted to the schooners known as voitures d'eau, literally "water cars," this maritime museum presents displays and photographs of a mode of transportation which, until the 1960s and the development of a road system, was a way of life for the islanders. The schooner *Mont-Saint-Louis,* built in 1939 and in service for 35 years, can be boarded.

Église Saint-Louis (Church of St. Louis)

In Isle-aux-Coudres. ⏱*Open year-round, daily 8am–6pm.* ♿ 🅿 ☏*418-438-2442.* Built in 1885, this church boasts a charming interior décor and an altar sculpted by Louis Jobin. The statues of St. Louis and St. Flavien were carved by François Baillairgé between 1804 and 1810. The care with which the clothing and the anatomy of the statues were executed reflects the great talent of this eminent artist. Note the two **processional chapels** (*about 200m/656ft before and after the church*), built by volunteers in 1837.

Les moulins de l'Isle-aux-Coudres★ (Isle-aux-Coudres Mills)

In Isle-aux-Coudres. ⏱*Open Jun 24–mid-Aug, daily 9am–6.30pm; late May–Jun 23 & mid-Aug–mid-Oct, daily 10am–5pm.* ☚*$8.* 🅿☏*418-438-2184.*

A stone windmill (1836) stands next to a water mill (1825) on this site beside the Rouge River. The two mills, built by Thomas and Alexis Tremblay respectively, operated until 1948. Restored by the Quebec government, they provide a rare opportunity to compare the two different mechanisms. An **interpretation center** in the former miller's house explains their history. Visitors can also buy wheat flour ground by millstones. Farm equipment dating from the turn of the century is on display outside the mills.

Cidrerie et Verger Pedneault, Pomology Economuseum

In Isle-aux-Coudres. ⏱*Open late Jun–early Sept, daily 8am–8pm; early Sept–Oct and May–Jun, 8am–6pm; Nov–Apr, 9am–5pm.* ♿ 🅿 ☏ *418-438-2365. www.charlevoix.net/vergerpedneault.* ☚*No charge.*

The orchard of Verger Pedneault produces several types and flavors of cider, including ice cider, a product that has become a symbol of Quebec and Canada, and is exported around the world. The family-run business also produces jam, honey, cider vinegar, and butter. Visitors can witness the making of apple and plum ciders, pick their own fruits, and of course, taste the ciders!

DRUMMONDVILLE

CENTRE-DU-QUÉBEC REGION
POPULATION 68,091

Drummondville was founded by British authorities after the War of 1812 as a military outpost on the Saint-François River. Frederick George Heriot, a Scottish officer, established a settlement here in 1815, naming it after the British governor Sir Gordon Drummond. At Heriot's death in 1843, the community was well established, operating several riverside mills, factories, and stores. The nearby falls were later harnessed for hydroelectricity.

Today Drummondville is an important industrial center, producing textiles and other manufactured goods. Every July, the Mondial des cultures de Drummondville is celebrated throughout the city.

- **Information:** 1350 Rue Michaud. ☎819-233-4636 & 1-888-233-4676. www.centreduquebec.com.
- ▶ **Orient Yourself:** Drummondville is 110km/68mi east of Montreal by Rte. 20 (Exit 177). It is a logical stop between Montreal and Quebec City.
- **Don't Miss:** The historic Village Québécois d'Antan.
- **Organizing Your Time:** Allow 3–4 hours to tour the Village Québécois d'Antan in Drummondville. Drive to the Ulverton Woolen Mills and return via Asbestos.
- **Especially for Kids:** Horse and buggy rides at the Ulverton Woolen Mill.

Sight

Village Québécois d'Antan★ (Québécois Village of Old)

1425 Rue Montplaisir, Rte. 20 (Exit 181). Open Jun–Labor Day daily 10am–6pm. Sept Fri–Sun only. $18. P ☎819-478-1441 & 1-877-710-0267. www.village quebecois.com

Knowledge of French is essential for understanding the guides, signs, and brochures. English-speaking visitors are advised to tour the village with someone who can act as an interpreter. Tours in English (large groups only) can be arranged in advance.

This village re-creates life in the region between 1810 and 1910. Some 70 authentic period buildings have been brought from their original sites to this wooded terrain near the Saint-François River. Each dwelling, shop and barn is "inhabited" by a guide in period costume who welcomes visitors and explains the

Le Village Québécois d'Antan

M. Frédéric Côté/Le Village Québécois d'Antan Inc.

lifestyle of the former occupants. The structures exemplify a broad variety of architectural styles, from the log cabins of the first settlers through the maison québécoise with its cantilevered roof, to the mansard-roofed dwellings introduced by the Loyalists after the American Revolution.

Note in particular the village **church**, a reconstruction of Drummondville's Church of St. Frederick (1822); the stained-glass windows (1950) by Guido Nincheri were created for the Chapel of Mont-Saint-Antoine in Montreal, and brought to the village in 1984. The neighboring presbytery (1833) is an excellent example of the *maison québécoise*. The Townships school (1892) is divided into two rooms, one for boys and one for girls. Visitors can tour the homes of the apothecary, the shoemaker, and the notary, as well as the forge, the carding and sawmills, and the farm (1895) with its stables for horses and oxen.

A covered bridge (1868) from Stanbridge spans a small stream. In the operator's home (1910), early telephones and an 1876 switchboard are exhibited. Visitors can buy bread made as it was in the 1870s, eat meals typical of the period, and have their photographs taken in period costumes.

Excursions

Musée populaire de la photographie

217 Brock (downtown, in the basement of Église Saint-Frédéric). ◷*Open year-round, Wed–Sun 1pm–5pm.* ⊚*$5.* ╳ 🅿 ☎*819-474-5782.*

The Musée populaire de la photographie displays the techniques and esthetics of the photographic art. Cameras and images from every era of the history of photography convey a sense of wonder toward the convergence of arts and science into photography.

Moulin à laine d'Ulverton (Ulverton Woolen Mills)   Kids

About 30km/18.6mi south by Rte. 143; turn right at Ulverton. Also accessible from Rte. 55 (Halte du Moulin exit). ◷*Open mid-Jun–mid-Sept, Wed–Sun 10am–5pm;*

mid-May–mid-Jun, Sun 10am–5pm, mid-Sept–mid-Oct, weekends 10am–5pm. ⊚*$7.* 🅿 ☎*819-826-3157. www.moulin.ca.*

The large shingled structure of this former carding mill rises above the Ulverton River, a tributary of the Saint-François River. Built by William Dunkerley in 1849, it changed hands several times. The mill fell into decay after 1949 but was renovated in the early 1980s. The operation of early 20C carding and spinning machines is demonstrated inside the mill.

Asbestos

Asbestos is situated 60km/37mi southeast of Drummondville by Rtes. 143, 116 and 255; 170km/105.6mi east of Montreal by Rtes. 20, 55 and 116; 60km/37mi north of Sherbrooke by Rtes. 143 and 249.

Asbestos grew and prospered around a gigantic, crater-like open-pit asbestos mine, the second largest in the world. It is currently 335m/1,099ft deep, approximately 2km/1.2mi across, and yields 650 tons of fiber annually. The deposits extend to a depth of more than 1,450m/4,756ft. The complex process of separating the fiber from the rock is carried out in the 12-story mill. Over 100 different types of asbestos, graded according to their temperature resistance, are produced here. Visitors watch the mining from a lookout.

Musée minéralogique et d'histoire minière d'Asbestos (Mining History Museum)

341 Blvd. Saint-Luc, off Rte. 255. Follow signs. ◷*Open Jun 24–late Aug, Wed–Sun 11am–5pm; rest of the year by reservation.* ⊚*$4.* ♿ 🅿 ☎*819-879-6444 or 819-879-5308.*

At this museum, numerous samples of asbestos and ore-bearing rocks are displayed, alongside information on the history of the Jeffrey Mine and the entire Asbestos region. A film (*20min*) explains the blasting, drilling and crushing methods used to extract asbestos fiber from the rock.

CANTONS DE L'EST★★
CANTONS DE L'EST REGION

Contrary to their name, the Eastern Townships (also called *Estrie* in French) occupy the southwest part of Quebec along the US border. The area was named in the 18C because of its location east of Montreal.

The Townships, as they are generally called in English, are situated in a mountainous region of the Appalachian chain, which extends from Alabama to Newfoundland. In the Townships, tree-covered hills rising to nearly 1,000m/3,280ft are interspersed with deep valleys and lakes. The region is popular with Montrealers attracted by leisure activities, including water sports in the summertime and skiing during the winter.

- **Information:** ☎1-800-355-5755. www.easterntownships.org.
- ▶ **Orient Yourself:** Cowansville is about 80km/50mi southeast of Montreal by Rtes. 10 and 139. Sherbrooke is 150km/93mi east of Montreal by Rtes. 10 and 112.
- **Don't Miss:** Historical museums in Missisquoi and Brome County; Coaticook Gorge Park; pretty Loyalist towns like North Hatley.
- **Organizing Your Time:** If you allow a full day for each of the two loops described here, you'll have the time to enjoy the many scenic stops and the interesting museums along the way.
- **Kids** **Especially for Kids:** The Coaticook Gorge park offers great lookout views and has lots of room for children to run.

A Bit of History

After the American Revolution (1775–83), the uninhabited land along the border to the southeast and southwest of Montreal was surveyed by the British authorities and plots were granted to Loyalists who had left the US after the war. These first settlers were mainly from New England, and the towns and villages they established reflect this heritage. After 1850, however, increasing numbers of French-speaking people moved into the region; today its population is mostly Francophone.

Driving Tours

1 Round Trip from Cowansville *159km/98.7mi.*

Cowansville
Located on the south arm of the South Yamaska River, Cowansville is today a small industrial center. This predominantly Francophone community was founded by Loyalists in 1802, and named for its first postmaster, Peter Cowan. Numerous Victorian houses line Rue Principale and Rue Sud in the residential area. The Bromont ski center is located nearby.

▶ *Follow Rue Sud (becomes Rte. 202 after crossing the Rte. 104 bypass) to Dunham.*

Dunham
10km/6.2mi.
One of the first Loyalist settlements, Dunham was established in 1796 on land granted to Thomas Dunn, a British administrator. The village is known for its vineyards. Its charm is enhanced by three steepled churches (Roman Catholic, Anglican and United) and several stone houses.

▶ *Continue west on Rte. 202 to Stanbridge East (10km/6.2mi).*

The road between Dunham and Stanbridge East is often called the **Wine Route** (Route des vins) because it crosses a region in Quebec where the climate is favorable to the cultivation of grapes. Elsewhere, the climate is too harsh.

Farm west of Brome

Musée de Missisquoi★ (Missisquoi Museum)

In Stanbridge East, on Rte 202. ⏱Open late May–Thanksgiving Day, daily 10am–5pm. ♿$5. 🅿 ☎450-248-3153. www. museemissisquoi.ca

Three buildings make up the rural museum created by the Missisquoi Historical Society. The main edifice is a three-story brick **mill** built by Zébulon Cornell, a Vermont native, in 1832 to replace an earlier stone structure on the picturesque Brochets River (Pike River). The mill closed in 1963 and was converted into a museum. Rooms on the main floor re-create life in the 19C, and the displays on the upper floor illustrate various activities and handicrafts of the era. Visitors can see the original water wheel, still turning in the river current. To the east (*20 River St.*), **Hodge's General Store** is stocked with goods and provisions from the period, thus preserving its 19C charm. **Bill's Barn** (*River St., near the Rte. 202 intersection*) displays traditional farm machinery.

▸ *Take Rte. 237 southeast to Frelighsburg.*

Frelighsburg
10km/6.2mi.
A gristmill was established in 1794 on this enchanting site in the Brochets River valley, near Mt. Pinacle. A small community soon developed and was later named for Abram Freligh, a physi-cian who moved here from New York in 1800. Today Frelighsburg is best known for its apple orchards.

▸ *Turn left on Rue Principale (Rte. 213). After 2km/1.2mi turn right on Rue Selby, continue for 4km/2.5mi and turn right on Rue Dymond (proceed cautiously on gravel roads), which becomes Rue Jordan after 3km/1.8mi. Continue for 10km/6.2mi; turn left on Rte. 139 to Sutton and continue 2km/1.2mi.*

The road passes to the north of **Le Pinacle** (675m/2,214ft), providing fine **views**★ of the Sutton valley.

Sutton★
21km/13mi.
Mt. Sutton (972m/3,188ft) towers over this lovely winter resort, especially popular with skiing enthusiasts. The first settlers arrived in 1795 and constructed a foundry in the valley. In 1871 a new railway opened the area to vacationers. Today numerous arts and crafts studios and shops enhance the town's charm.

▸ *Drive south on Rte. 139 for 2km/1.2mi, turn left on Rue Brookfall and immediately right on Chemin Scenic. After 11km/6.8mi, turn left on Rte. 105A and left again on Rte. 243 to Mansonville (24km/15mi).*

The road offers several entrancing **views**★ of the Sutton area, then follows the valley of the Missisquoi River. The Jay Mountains in Vermont are visible to the south.

Mansonville
37km/23mi.

This community in the Missisquoi River valley is named for its first settler, Robert Manson, who moved from Vermont in 1803 and built a gristmill and a sawmill. The town has a New England-style village green and also claims one of the few remaining round barns in Quebec (*visible from Main St. across from the Church of St. Cajétan*). The circular structure was conceived by the Shakers, a religious sect of the Quakers; its purpose was to keep the devil from haunting any corner.

Mount Owl's Head
12km/7mi, through Vale Perkins.

This mountain (751m/2,463ft) was named after Chief Owl, an Abenaki Indian. According to legend, his profile could be seen on the mountain after his death. Today Owl's Head is a popular ski resort. The path leading to the top (*climb of about 1hr*) affords spectacular **views**★★ of Lake Memphrémagog.

▶ *Return to Mansonville. Take Rte. 243 to South Bolton (13km/8mi).*

Detour to Saint-Benoît-du-Lac★
26km/16mi round-trip from South Bolton. Take Rte. 245 to Bolton-Center (5km/3mi), and turn right toward Austin. Turn right again on Fisher Rd., following signs. ⟳ *See Entry Heading.*

▶ *Return to South Bolton.*

Lac-Brome★ (Knowlton)
14km/8.6mi from South Bolton.

Part of the municipality of Lac-Brome, the community of Knowlton enjoys a pleasant setting on Lake Brome. Founded by New England settlers in the early 19C, the town was named for Paul Knowlton, who built the community gristmill and a general store in 1834. Many of the brick and stone buildings are housed by boutiques, art galleries and antique shops. Just to the south lies the community of Brome, home of the **Brome Agricultural Fair**, the largest annual agricultural event in the area.

Musée historique du comté de Brome★ (Brome County Museum)
130 Rue Lakeside (Rte. 243). ⏱ *Open mid-May–mid-Sept, Mon–Sat 10am–4.30pm, Sun 11am–4.30pm.* ⟳$5. ☎450-243-6782.

This museum comprises several period buildings. The old Knowlton "Academy" (1854) offers the chance to see a schoolroom of yesteryear.

The Martin Annex houses military exhibits including a **Fokker DVII,** a German World War I fighter plane acquired for the museum by Senator G. G. Foster, a Knowlton resident. In the courthouse (1854), a renovated reception room evokes the solemn atmosphere of a turn-of-the-century court. A re-created general store occupies the Fire Hall (1904).

▶ *Return to Cowansville (20km/12mi) by Rte. 104.*

② Round Trip from Sherbrooke *153km/95mi.*

▶ *Leave Sherbrooke and take Rte. 143 to Lennoxville.*

Lennoxville
5km/3mi.

British Loyalists founded Lennoxville in 1794, naming the town for Charles Lennox, Duke of Richmond, who became governor-in-chief of British North America in 1818. The town is located at the junction of the Massawippi and Saint-François Rivers, a site formerly occupied by the Abenaki and later by French missionaries. Lennoxville is home to an agricultural research center.

Bishop's University

An educational and cultural center, this small yet prestigious English institution (1843) features Medieval-style buildings. Nearby is **St. Mark's Chapel**, a Gothic Revival edifice adorned with luminous stained-glass windows and richly carved woodwork. The benches on each side face each other across the center aisle.

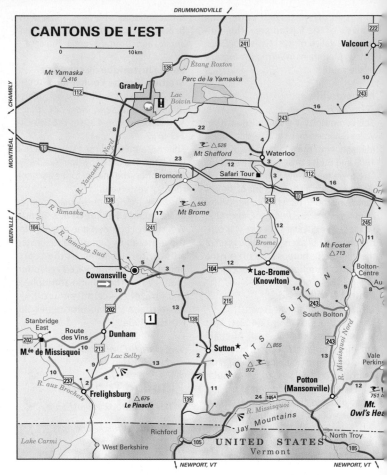

CANTONS DE L'EST

> *Continue south on Rte. 143 for 3km/1.8mi, then turn left on Rte. 147 to Compton.*

Compton

17km/10.5mi.

This quiet village was the birthplace of **Louis-Stephen Saint-Laurent** (1882–1973), 12th prime minister of Canada. The eldest of seven children born to a French Canadian storekeeper and an Irish schoolteacher, Saint-Laurent studied law at Laval University. He went into private practice and soon gained recognition for his eloquence in both English and French. At the age of 60, after a long and successful career as a lawyer, Saint-Laurent decided to enter politics. He was asked by Prime Minister Mackenzie King to serve as his Quebec lieutenant during

World War II, and succeeded Mr. King as head of the Liberal Party in 1948. An ardent Canadian nationalist, "Uncle Louis," as he was fondly called, fought to establish a distinct Canadian identity during his years as prime minister (1948–57).

Lieu historique national du Canada Louis-S.-St-Laurent★(Louis S. St. Laurent National Historic Site of Canada)

On Rue Principale (Rte. 147) in Compton. *Open mid-May–Sept, daily 10am–5pm.* *$4. 819-835-5448. www.pc.gc.ca/ st-laurent.*

The authentically re-created general store of J.B.M. Saint-Laurent, the prime minister's father, is stocked with replicas of the goods sold here at the turn

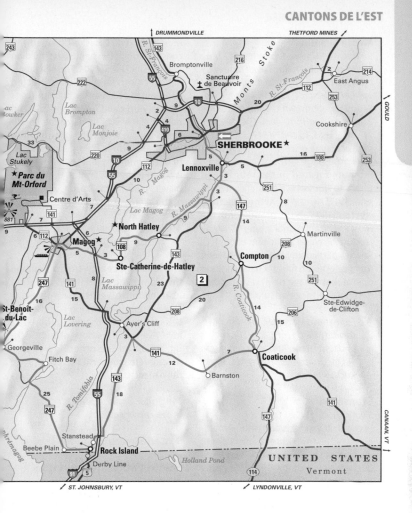

of the 19C. During its heyday, the general store served as a place for locals to visit and exchange ideas; politics were a frequent topic of discussion. Visitors can use headphones to eavesdrop on simulated conversations around the pot-bellied stove. A **multimedia biography** (*20min*) presents the highlights of Saint-Laurent's life and career. Also open to visitors is the simple clapboard house full of mementoes of the Saint-Laurent family, who lived in it until 1969.

Coaticook
14km/9mi.

This town on the Coaticook River takes its name from the Abenaki word *koa-tikeku,* meaning "river of the land of pines." The first settler, Richard Baldwin, recognized the economic potential of harnessing the falls. Today Coaticook is a small industrial town and the center of a thriving dairy industry.

Parc de la Gorge de Coaticook★ [Kids]
Access from Rte. 147 at northern edge of town. ○*Open lateJun–Labor Day, daily 9am–7pm; rest of the year daily 10am–5pm.*⊛*$7.* ╳ P ☎*819-849-2331. www.gorgedecoaticook.qc.ca.*

The Coaticook River is enclosed by a narrow, rocky, 1km/.6mi gorge whose sides rise to 50m/165ft, then turns at a sharp angle and tumbles over several sets of falls. Skiing or hiking allows for beautiful discoveries along the several kilometers of scenic pathway. An impressive suspended footbridge (169m/554ft) affords a nice **view** of the gorge.

Musée Beaulne

96 Rue de l'Union. From Rte. 141 (Rue Main), turn left on Rue Lovell at railway tracks, left again on Rue Norton, then right on Rue de l'Union. ○Open mid-May–mid-Sept, Mon–Sun 10am–5pm; rest of the year, Mon–Sun 1pm–4pm. ○Closed Dec 21–Jan 5. ○$5. P ☎819-849-6560. www. museebeaulne.qc.ca.

Take a passage through time at this museum located in the refurbished **Château Norton**★, a magnificent mansion (1912) owned by **Arthur Osmond Norton** (1845–1919), proprietor of the most important manufacturer of railway jacks in the world at the turn of the 19C. Rooms, particularly the Victorian living room (adorned in fine oak panelling) and dining room, have been restored and decorated with period furniture.

▸ *From the town center, take Rte. 141 toward Magog for 19km/11.8mi and turn left on Rte. 143. Continue 18km/11mi, crossing over Rte. 55 to Rock Island.*

Stanstead

37km/23mi.

Located on a rocky island in the Tomifobia River, this town (three former villages in one: Stanstead Plain, Rock Island, and Beebe Plain) overlooks the picturesque river valley.

⊚ *The Tomifobia River marks the Canadian-American border. Vehicles crossing the bridge must proceed through US Customs (on the right) before continuing into Vermont or returning to Canada.*

Opéra et bibliothèque Haskell (Haskell Library and Opera House)

Heading south on Rte. 143, turn left onto Cordeau St. immediately after the bridge beyond Canadian Customs. Turn left and park on Rue Church P. The entrance to the building is on the US side, but you do not have to clear US Customs to enter the Vermont library. ↝Visit by guided tour (30min) only: May–end Oct, Tue–Sat 10am–5pm (Thu 8pm). ○Closed major holidays. ○$3. ☎819-876-2471. www. haskellopera.org.

Martha Stewart Haskell funded the construction of this handsome building between 1901 and 1904. The half-stone, half-brick turreted building, erected in memory of Haskell's husband, sits squarely on the Canadian-American border; the line of demarcation is indicated on the floor. The ground floor serves as a public library for residents of both countries and the upper floor is occupied by a delightful theatre. The players perform in Canada, while most of the audience sits in the US.

▸ *Take Rte. 247 through Beebe Plain and Georgeville to Magog.*

The road veers eastward through the tiny community of Fitch Bay before heading northwest to Georgeville, a small, English-speaking community. Upon leaving Georgeville, there is a lovely view of the abbey of Saint-Benoît-du-Lac on the other side of Lake Memphrémagog, and of Mt. Orford in the distance.

Magog★ – *41km/25.4mi.*
Ⓖ*See Entry Heading.*

▸ *Leave Magog on Rte. 108.*

Sainte-Catherine-de-Hatley

8km/5mi.

Situated atop a hill in the center of town, the Sanctuaire Saint-Christophe (Sanctuary of St. Christopher) affords expansive **views** of Lake Magog and Mt. Orford.

North Hatley★

9km/5.6mi.

North Hatley (named for an English village near Cambridge) occupies a lovely **site** on the northern bank of Lake Massawippi where the river of the same name leaves the lake. A drive along the lakeshore provides glimpses of attractive homes and inns.

▸ *Return to Sherbrooke (11km/6.8mi) by Rte. 143.*

Parc national du Canada FORILLON★★

GASPÉSIE REGION
MAP: SEE GASPÉSIE

Created in 1970, Forillon National Park of Canada is located on the eastern tip of the Gaspé Peninsula, where the Gulf of St. Lawrence meets the Bay of Gaspé. The majestic, remarkably diverse landscape (245sq km/95sq mi), created largely by erosive forces, includes limestone cliffs towering over the sea; mountains of spruce, fir, poplar, and cedar; wildflower meadows; and pebbly beaches tucked away in coves. Visitors can observe black bears, beavers, fox, moose, and porcupines; seagulls, cormorants, kittiwakes, and guillemots; seals and occasionally whales. In addition, the park provides a great variety of recreational activities.

- **Information:** ☎418-368-5505 & 1-888-773-8888. www.pc.gc.ca/forillon.
- **Orient Yourself:** The park is located 899km/557mi northeast of Quebec City on Rte. 132, between the towns of Rivière-au-Renard and Gaspé.
- **Don't Miss:** The vertical cliffs, plunging into the sea.
- **Organizing Your Time:** Stay on Rte. 132 along the St. Lawrence River shoreline to the Cap-des-Rosiers entrance to the park and site of the tallest lighthouse in Canada. Stop at the interpretation center for the indoor exhibits or outdoor activities before crossing through the park to visit Grande-Grave. The park has 367 semi-serviced campgrounds, and is a better choice for camping than closer to the popular Percé Rock—but you will need to reserve ahead during summer.
- **Especially for Kids:** A great place for sea kayaking to watch seals.
- **Also See:** GASPÉ, PERCÉ.

Visit

Open year-round, daily. $6.90 ($5.20 Labor Day–Jun 25) ⚠ 🅿.

Interpretation Center

Near Cap-des-Rosiers in the northern sector (Secteur nord) of the park. Open early–late Jun and late Aug–mid-Oct, daily 10am–5pm; Jun 25–Aug 20, daily 9am–6pm. ☎418-368-5505.

An informative exhibit describes the history of fishing in the region and the interrelation between land and sea. Aquariums (Kids) house many examples of marine life. Visitors can also see films about the flora, fauna and geology of the park. Pleasure cruises depart from the dock near the center. Experienced sea kayakers can rent kayaks in the park and paddle on their own. Non-experienced kayakers can join a guided tour where they should be able to (nature willing) watch harbor and grey whales.

Cap Bon Ami

3km/1.8mi south of the interpretation center by a secondary road.

From the picnic lookout and along the walkway leading to the beach, **views**★★ of the sea and the limestone cliffs of Cap Bon Ami are magnificent.

- *Return to Rte. 132, and follow signs leading to the southern sector of the park. At the junction with the secondary road, turn left.*

ACTIVITIES

More than 40km/24.8mi of trails are maintained for hiking, and visitors can enjoy swimming, scuba diving, fishing, biking, and horseback riding. Campgrounds are located in the park at Des-Rosiers, Cap Bon Ami and Petit-Gaspé, and there are numerous picnic areas.

Anse-Blanchette, Parc national Forillon

Grande-Grave★

16.5km/10mi from the interpretation center.

A thriving fishing community from the 19C to the mid-20C, this small village was inhabited by settlers from the Channel Islands of Jersey and Guernsey. Today several buildings have been restored to reflect the style of the 1920s. The first floor of the **Hyman & Sons Store** is stocked with goods that would have been found in a general store at that time. On the second floor, an exhibit describes the activities of fishermen and their families throughout the year. The Blanchette house is the residential component of the Grande-Grave historic site.

Nearby, in **Anse-Blanchette**, stands the brightly painted house that belonged to Xavier Blanchette in the late 19C. The interior and outbuildings, including the *chafauds*, or racks for drying fish, re-create the life of a self-sufficient fisherman.

▶ *Continue on secondary road to Anse-Saint-Georges and Anse-aux-Sauvages.*

Cap Gaspé★

8km/5mi round-trip on foot from Anse-aux-Sauvages.

This pleasant walk through newly forested lands that were cleared at the turn of the 19C to build homes for fishermen offers **views**★ of the Bay of Gaspé and the Île Bonaventure, an island famous for its bird reserve where millions of shore birds can be seen.

▶ *Return to Rte. 132.*

On the way back to Rte. 132, the road skirts the southern sector of the park, site of a Protestant church, an amphitheater, a campground, and a recreational and tourist center.

Fort-Péninsule

8km/5mi. The blockhouse built here during World War II served as a complement to the naval base at Sandy Beach, on the south shore of the Bay of Gaspé. It was built by the Canadian government to prevent German submarines from entering the St. Lawrence.

Penouille

1km/.6mi.

The sandy shores and taiga of this peninsula provide a sharp contrast to the immense limestone capes and boreal forests found in the rest of the park. Penouille, an old Basque word meaning "peninsula," is the site of many organized activities in summer. The Penouille **beach** is the most popular one in the park.

GASPÉ★

GASPÉSIE REGION
POPULATION 14,929
MAP: SEE GASPÉSIE

On July 24, 1534, the Breton explorer Jacques Cartier set foot on this site and took possession of the land in the name of François I, King of France. Located on a hillside where the York River empties into the Bay of Gaspé, the city is now the administrative and commercial center of the peninsula. The name Gaspé is derived from the Mi'kmaq word gespec, meaning "limits of the land."

- ℹ **Information:** ☎418-368-6335 & 1-800-463-0323. www.tourismegaspe.org.
- ▶ **Orient Yourself:** Gaspé is located 738km/458.6mi northeast of Quebec City by Rte. 132.
- 🅿 **Parking:** In the summer, parking can be scarce on main street (Rue de la Reine), go nearby to Place Jacques-Cartier where there is ample, free parking.
- 🚫 **Don't Miss:** Musée de la Gaspésie.
- 🕐 **Organizing Your Time:** Stop at the ship-shaped Musée de la Gaspésie to learn about the region's history, and be sure to go out on the balcony for the view. If you plan to drive farther east along the coast, explore Gaspé in the morning to give the tourist buses time to leave Percé Rock.
- ♿ **Also See:** GASPÉSIE, PERCÉ.

Sights

Musée de la Gaspésie★ (Museum of the Gaspé Peninsula)

80 Blvd. Gaspé (Rte. 132). ⏰Open Jun 24– early Oct, daily 9am–5pm. Early-Oct–Jun 23, Tue–Fri 1pm–5pm.☜$7. ♿🅿 ☎418-368-1534.

This regional museum is dedicated to the preservation of Gaspésian culture and ethnological heritage. It highlights historical events and regional geography. Set on Jacques-Cartier Point, the museum offers good **views**★ of the Bay of Gaspé and the Forillon peninsula.

Jacques-Cartier Monument

In the park next to the museum, six cast-iron steles form a monument (1984) commemorating the discovery of Canada and the first encounter between Cartier and the native population. The dolmen-shaped steles, adorned with bas-reliefs illustrating Cartier's arrival in the New World on one side and excerpts of texts written by Cartier and Father Le Clercq on the other, are the work of Jean-Julien and Gil Bourgault-Legros of Saint-Jean-Port-Joli.

▶ *From the museum, turn left onto Blvd. Gaspé in the direction of the town center. At the traffic light, turn right onto Rue Adams, continue for two blocks and turn left onto Rue Jacques-Cartier; the cathedral is on the left.*

Cathédrale du Christ-Roi★ (Christ the King Cathedral)

⏰*Open year-round, daily 8.30am–4pm. ♿🅿 ☎418-368-5541.*

The cathedral's unusual lines and cedar exterior blend in the environment. In the strikingly simple interior, sunlight filters past massive beams creating a warm glow on the wooden sheathing. A stained-glass window and a bronze portray a triumphant Christ. The fresco, donated by France in 1934, illustrates Cartier's arrival in the New World. Beside the cathedral stands the **Croix de Gaspé** (Gaspé Cross), also known as the Jacques-Cartier Cross. The 9.6m/31.5ft cross was carved in a single block of granite from a quarry near Quebec City. It was unveiled during the 1934 celebrations.

GASPÉSIE★★★

GASPÉSIE REGION

The Gaspé peninsula, commonly known as the "la Gaspésie" in French, is bounded by New Brunswick and the Baie des Chaleurs to the south, the Gulf of St. Lawrence to the east, and the St. Lawrence River to the north. Tiny fishing villages nestled in coves dot the wild, rocky, and sea-battered northern coast of the peninsula, culminating in the breathtaking beauty of Forillon and Percé. In the Chaleur Bay area to the south, agriculture, fishery, and forestry form the backbone of economic activity, but the scenic wonders of both coasts have made tourism the region's principal source of revenue, and windmills now generate an ever increasing amount of electricity. The spectacular scenery is complemented by the charm of the peninsula's simple lifestyle. Except for a few towns and villages, the interior of the peninsula is a dense wilderness of mountains and forests.

- **Information:** ☎1-800-463-0323. www.tourisme-gaspesie.com.
- ▶ **Orient Yourself:** From Quebec City, Matane is 400km/250mi. Rte. 132 follows the coast around the peninsula, and Rte. 299 crosses the Chic-choc Mountains.
- **Don't Miss:** Windmills at Cap-Chat, Forillon Park, Percé Rock, Bonaventure Island. Be sure to spend some time at the Jardins de Métis.
- 🕘 **Organizing Your Time:** Allow a day for each of the sections proposed below to take you around the Gaspé peninsula.
- **Kids Especially for Kids:** Count fish swimming through the salmon ladder in Matane.

Driving Tours

1 From Sainte-Flavie to Parc de la Gaspésie

167km/104mi on Rte. 132.

Sainte-Flavie

This agricultural village and resort town is the gateway to the Gaspé Peninsula. Sainte-Flavie is renowned for its beautiful sunsets.

Centre d'art Marcel Gagnon

564 Route de la Mer. ⊙Open May–late Sept, daily 7.30am–9pm. ✕ & 🅿 ☎418-775-2829; www.centredart.net.
The main attraction in this small arts center is The Great Gathering (Le grand rassemblement), contemporary artist Marcel Gagnon's composite sculpture of more than 80 figures emerging from the St. Lawrence River. A permanent exhibit of the artist's paintings and smaller sculptures occupies the interior, and visitors can witness Gagnon himself at work in his studio.

Parc de la rivière Mitis★ (Mitis River Park)

900 Route de la Mer. ⊙Open late Jun–Labor Day, daily 9am–5pm. ☜$5. ✕ & 🅿 ☎418-775-2969.
In this park, an "eco-tourism site," park trails are lined with displays on nature and its preservation. Magnificent landscapes of the St. Lawrence and Mitis Rivers make the visit as enjoyable as it is informative. Nature exhibits in the reception center (Kids) enable visitors to appreciate and understand the vast and complex ecosystem around them.

Jardins de Métis★★ (Reford Gardens) – *9km/5.6mi.* 🕮 *See Entry Heading.*

Matane

55km/34mi.
The community of Matane is renowned for its salmon fishing and shrimp production. In the town center, behind the city hall, a 44m/144ft **fish ladder**★ (*passe migratoire*) built on the **Mathieu-d'Amours Dam** enables salmon to travel upstream (*visitors can view the salmon passing by through porthole windows;* 🕘 *open mid-Jun–Labor Day,*

Address Book

For price ranges, see the Legend on the cover flap.
Other area accommodations and restaurants are listed under Percé and Parc de la Gaspésie.

WHERE TO STAY

$$ *Centre d'art Marcel Gagnon – 564 Route de la Mer, Sainte-Flavie.* b418-775-2829; www.centredart.net. Closed Oct–Mar. 10 rooms. Simple and clean describe the comfortable rooms on the upper floor of the art center. Breakfast is served in view of Marcel Gagnon's composite sculpture, Le grand rassemblement (The Great Gathering).

WHERE TO EAT

$$ *Chez Pierre – 96 Boul. Perron Ouest, Tourrelle.* b418-763-7446. **Seafood**. For a proper introduction to Gaspésie's bounty of the sea, try Chez Pierre's dégustation poissons a survey of delights including snow crab, marinated turbot and home-made smoked salmon. There is also a speciality, *la tulipe en pâte aux fruits de mer* (flower shaped seafood pastry). Reasonable prices, efficient service, and a nice view of the water complement the gastronomic experience. The is a small restaurant with a warm, intimate feel.

---

daily 7.30am–9.30pm; call for hours in September; $3. ☎418-562-7006).

Cap-Chat

70km/43.5mi. To see the wind turbine, turn right 3km/1.8mi west of Cap-Chat bridge.

Towering above the landscape at 110m/361ft, the vertical-axis **wind turbine**★, named Éole, is the largest of its kind in the world (visit by guided tour only (1hr): late Jun–late Sept, daily 9am–5pm; $10; ☎418-786-5719; www.eolecapchat.com). A rotor with two curved blades turns wind power into electricity. Éole, a joint project of the National Research Council and Hydro-Québec, has been in full automatic operation since 1988. Guides describe the turbine mechanism and discuss low impact energy sources.

Cap-Chat Rock

From Rte. 132, turn left 2km/1.2mi west of village. Follow gravel road for .5km/.3mi. The village drew its name from this rock thought to resemble a sitting cat (chat). Nearby, a lighthouse dating from 1871 serves as the starting point for several nature trails.

Parc de la Gaspésie★ (Gaspésie Park)

33km/20.5mi. After 16km/10mi, take Rte. 299 from Sainte-Anne-des-Monts. See Entry Heading.

Grande-Valleé

MICHELIN

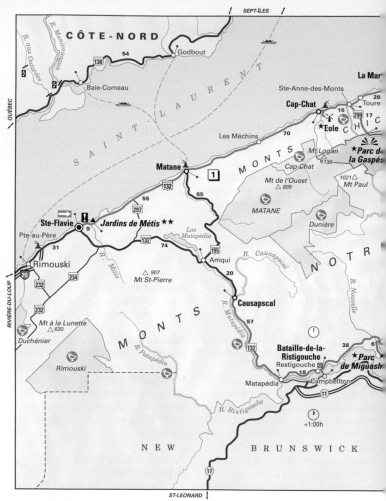

②From Parc de La Gaspésie to Gaspé

259km/161mi.

▶ *Return to Sainte-Anne-des-Monts and continue on Rte. 132 to La Martre.*

La Martre

26km/16mi.

From this little village perched atop a promontory, the **view** encompasses the surrounding capes and the ocean. The top of the red octagonal lighthouse (*phare*) provides a spectacular **view**. The adjoining **Musée des phares** houses exhibits dating from the 18C (🕐 *open*

early Jun–late Sept, daily 9am–5pm; 🎫$3; ✗ ♿ 🅿 ☎418-288-5698).

Scenic Route from La Martre to Rivière-au-Renard★★

153km/95mi.

Rte. 132 hugs the coastline, up and over rocky cliffs, affording splendid views of hills, valleys, picturesque fishing villages, and the ocean. In the region of **Mont-Saint-Pierre**, shale cliffs rim the bay, and just east of **Sainte-Madeleine-de-la-Rivière-Madeleine**, the lighthouse and surrounding buildings grace the lush, green hills. From the hilltop, before arriving at **Grande-Vallée**, the view of the village and its bay is lovely. In the town center stands a covered bridge

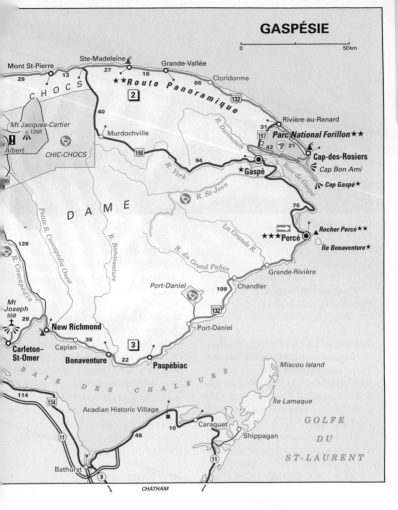

GASPÉSIE

dating from 1923. Past the fishing village of **Rivière-au-Renard**, at the northern tip of Forillon National Park, expansive views sweep across fields to the Gulf of St. Lawrence.

Cap-des-Rosiers

21km/13mi from Rivière-au-Renard.
This village, named for the abundance of wild roses Jacques Cartier found when he arrived here in the 16C, has witnessed numerous shipwrecks off its rocky coast. The **lighthouse** (*37m/121ft*) is the tallest in Canada (☛ *visit by guided tour (30min)only: mid-Jun–Sept, daily 10am–7pm;* ☞*$2.50;* ☎*418-892-5577*).

Parc national du Canada Forillon★★ – ☛*See Entry Heading.*

Gaspé★ – *42km/26mi from Cap-des-Rosiers.* ☛*See Entry Heading.*

③ From Percé to Causapscal *337km/209.4mi.*

Percé★★★
76km/47mi from Gaspé.
☛*See Entry Heading.*

▶ Take Rte. 132 through Grande-Rivière, Chandler and Port-Daniel to Paspébiac.

Cap-des-Rosiers

Paspébiac
109km/67.7mi.
In 1767 Charles Robin, from the Island of Jersey, chose this location to establish the headquarters of his cod fishing empire, the Charles Robin Company (CRC).

Site historique du Banc-de-Pêche-de-Paspébiac (Banc-de-Pêche-de-Paspébiac Historic Site)
Turn left off Rte. 132 onto Route du Banc and continue to the waterfront. ⏱*Open mid-Jun–Sept, daily 9am–5pm.* ✆*$5.50.* ✕&🅿☎*418-752-6229.*
To ensure the success of his exports of dried, salted cod (known as "Gaspé Cure") to Europe, Charles Robin created an entire town, complete with a naval yard, blacksmiths, carpenters, and a company store. Eleven buildings erected by the CRC around 1783 were restored after a fire in 1964. Visitors can visit buildings and view live demonstrations of traditional activities like net-mending and barge-building.

West of Paspébiac extends the pleasant coastal region of the **Chaleur Bay**. This scenic body of water, which also washes the northern shores of New Brunswick, was discovered by Jacques Cartier in 1534. The area's moderate climate (*chaleur* means warmth) attracts visitors who enjoy water sports.

Bonaventure
22km/13.6mi.
The village, which takes its name from a ship that sailed into the Chaleur Bay in 1591, is well known for its salmon river. There is nice beach here. Bonaventure exudes a colorful Acadian ambiance and spirit.

Musée acadien du Québec (Quebec Acadian Museum)
In the center of Bonaventure, east of the church on Rte. 132. ⏱*Jun 24–Labor Day, daily 9am–6pm; rest of the year, Mon–Fri 9am–4.30pm, weekends 1pm–4.30pm.* ✆*$7.* ✕&🅿☎*418-534-4000.*
The museum exhibits antiques and old photographs, and an audiovisual presentation recalling the Acadians' contribution to Quebec's culture.

New Richmond
35km/21.7mi.
A Loyalist stronghold, the town boasts several charming residential areas that still maintain a late 19C Anglo-Saxon flavor.

Village Gaspésien de l'héritage Britannique (Gaspesian British Heritage Village)
351 Blvd. Perron Ouest. ⏱*Open mid-Jun–mid-Sept, daily 9am–5pm.* ✆*$10.* ✕&🅿☎*418-392-4487.*
Relive the bicentennial history of descendants form the British Isles in the Gaspé Peninsula. The 24 buildings making up this reconstructed village came from the communities surrounding Chaleur Bay. The **Harvey House** exemplifies the Colonial Revival style popular in the US at the end of the 19C. Other dwellings

Pull on your boots, grab your fishing tackle and take to Quebec's pristine waters for a fly-fishing experience! Fly-fishing requires proper equipment and casting technique, but it can become an enjoyable activity and even some people's passion. Fishing with artificial flies dates as far back as AD 1 when they were used to simulate insects too delicate to use as natural bait.

Select your flies, rod, reel, and fly line based on the fishing conditions. Make sure your reel has a reliable drag and carries enough backing if your destination includes one of Quebec's many famous Atlantic salmon rivers. Required gear includes boots or waders, a vest, hat, insect repellent, warm clothing, raingear, and polarizing sunglasses. Serious anglers study characteristics of rivers and streams, understand effects of weather and tides, and know how these variables relate to fly-fishing and fish behavior in differ-

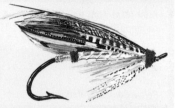

ent seasons. Local sporting goods stores can help outfit you with the appropriate gear and provide information about fishing permits. For additional information, contact Quebec's ministry of Développement durable, Environnement et Parcs: ☎1-800-561-1616 (*English message follows the French message*) or www. mddep.gouv.qc.ca.

R Corbel/ MICHELIN

dating from the late 17C through the early 20C reveal architectural styles typical of their respective periods. The visit ends at the lighthouse overlooking Cascapédia Bay.

Carleton-sur-Mer
28km/17.4mi.
Founded by Acadians between 1756 and 1760, the village was originally called Tracadièche, derived from the Amerindian word *tracadigash* meaning "the place where there are many heron." In the late 18C, Loyalists renamed the settlement in honour of Governor General Guy Carleton, later known as Lord Dorchester. Nestled between mountains and the sea, Carleton's scenic location has contributed to its great success as a seaside resort.

Footpaths along Éperlan Creek (Sentiers de l'Éperlan)

A network of trails follows Éperlan Creek past several waterfalls, revealing splendid mountain scenery, and leads to the back of Mt. Saint-Joseph.

Mont Saint-Joseph

By car from the town center, take Rue de la Montagne 6km/4mi to the summit.

From the top of Mt. Saint-Joseph at an altitude of 558m/1,830ft, the **panorama**★★ spans the Chaleur Bay, from Bonaventure to the Miguasha Peninsula, and extends south to New Brunswick. Inside the stone **Oratory of Our Lady** (Oratoire Notre-Dame, 1924), note the mosaic above the altar and the stained-glass windows (*open mid-Jun–early Sept, daily 9am–7pm; rest of Sept and Oct, daily 9am–5pm. $4; ⊁ ⅋ ◻ @418-364-2256*).

▸ *After 18km/11mi, turn left and continue 6km/3.7mi.*

Parc de Miguasha★ –
See Entry Heading.

▸ *Rejoin Rte. 132 and continue 38km/23.6mi.*

Lieu historique national de la Bataille-de-la-Ristigouche (Battle of the Ristigouche National Historic Site)

In Pointe-à-la-Croix. Open early Jun–Thanksgiving Day, daily 9am–5pm. $4. ⅋ ◻ @418-7885676. www.pc.gc.ca/ristigouche.

France's last naval attempt to save its North American colony from British control was thwarted in the estuary of the Ristigouche River in July 1760. Two merchant ships, protected by a frigate, were to deliver troops, and ammunition to Quebec City, capital of New France. Upon reaching the Gulf of St. Lawrence, the French learned that five British warships had arrived ahead of them. To avoid battle, French commander La Giraudais moved his fleet at the head of Chaleur Bay, on the Ristigouche River

estuary, hoping that the larger British ships would be unable to go in shallower waters. Acadians and Micmac Indians helped the French set up batteries to block the river channel. After days of battle, the British managed to force the French to abandon their ships.

Interpretation center

In the reception area, the giant anchor and part of the hull recovered from frigate *Le Machault* are on display. An animated film (*15min*) recounts the battle. In the exhibit halls, scenes depict life on board, using many objects recovered from the wreckage, including personal items such as belt buckles, pipes, tobacco boxes, candle snuffers, and clothing, as well as tools used to repair wood on board and tighten masts. The contents of the holds include fabric, clothing for troops, and trade goods ranging from nails to combs. Earthenware, Chinese porcelain, and other luxury merchandise are also on display.

Detour to New Brunswick

An interprovincial bridge links Restigouche with Campbellton, New Brunswick Rte. 11 leads to the Acadian Historic Village (Village historique acadien) located 10km/6.2mi west of Caraquet, and to the Marine Center at Shippagan. For descriptions, consult THE GREEN GUIDE Canada.

Continue on Rte. 132 through the Valley of the Matapédia in landscapes of quaint villages, rolling forest, covered hills, and the ever-present Matapédia River, famous for salmon fishing.

Causapscal

75km/46.6mi.

Set at the confluence of the Causapscal and Matapédia rivers, this town of 2,556 is a great departure point for salmon fishing expeditions. At the **Site historique Matamajaw** (*53C Rue Saint-Jacques; open Jun–Sept, daily 9am–5pm; $5. @418-756-5999*), relive the lifestyle of High Society fishing enthusiasts at the Matamajaw Salmon Club. In its specially designed channel, observe Atlantic salmon in their natural habitat.

PARC DE LA GASPÉSIE ★

GASPÉSIE REGION
MAP: SEE GASPÉSIE

In the heart of the Gaspé Peninsula between the St. Lawrence River and Chaleur Bay lies an 802sq km/309sq mi area devoted to the conservation of plant and animal life native to Quebec. *Le Parc national de la Gaspésie* is the only place in this province where woodland caribou, moose, and white-tailed deer coexist. A "sea of mountains," with 25 summits over 1,000m/3,280.8ft, this Quebec national park includes a section the spectacular Chic-Chocs massif, at the far north end of the Appalachian range.

- **Information:** ☎1-866-727-2427. www.sepaq.com.
- ▶ **Orient Yourself:** The park is located 516km/320.6mi northeast of Quebec City by Rte. 132. From Sainte-Anne-des-Monts, take Rte. 299 south for 17km/10.5mi to the entrance of the park. The interpretation center is 21km/13mi inside the park limits. From New Richmond, take Rte. 299 north for 99km/61.5mi to the interpretation center.
- **Don't Miss:** Seeing caribous: Nowhere else can you admire these nordic mammals in southern Quebec.
- **Organizing Your Time:** The interpretation center has information about current activities in the park. Guided tours and seasonal equipment rentals can be arranged at the center. It's always chillier and windy on the mountain tops, don't forget to dress for it
- **Especially for Kids:** The park has an extensive network of trails, many of which are interpreted and easy for children.

Visit

Open daily year-round. $3.50. ☎418-763-7494. www.sepaq.com. Three sectors of the park are devoted to recreational activities. In the **Mont-Albert Sector,** a hike (🥾) to the mountaintop (1,151m/3,775ft) reveals a 13sq km/8sq mi plateau strewn with vegetation characteristic of the northern tundra. In the **Lake Cascapédia Sector,** the ridges of the Chic-Chocs massif offer spectacular **views**★★ of the Appalachians and the St. Lawrence Valley to the north, and the Sainte-Anne River valley to the east. Mt. Jacques-Cartier (1,268m/4,159ft) is found in the **Galène Sector.** Its windy dome, home to caribou and arctic-alpine flora, affords an

Address Book

For price ranges, see the Legend on the cover flap.

WHERE TO STAY
PARC DE LA GASPÉSIE

$$$ Gîte du Mont-Albert – *Route du Parc, Sainte-Anne-des-Monts.* ☎418-763-2288 or 866-727-2427. www.sepaq.com. *48 rooms, 19 chalets.* Located within the Parc de la Gaspésie, this charming inn provides a comfortable base for enjoying the park's seasonal activities. Efficient service and clean and cozy rooms—all with views of Mont-Albert—makes this a good place for a romantic weekend getaway or the annual family vacation.

ACTIVITIES
Hiking and nature programs are especially popular activities in the park. Visitors can also enjoy salmon fishing, trout fishing, canoeing, mountain biking and picnicking. For cross-country ski enthusiasts, day and overnight ski trips are organized from mid-December until mid-April in various sectors of the park (there are some 15 mountain shelters within park boundaries).

expansive **view**★★ of the McGerrigle Mountains.

Centre d'interprétation (Park's Welcome and Information Center)

🕐 *Open mid-May–mid-Oct, daily 8am–8pm; late Dec–mid-Apr, daily 8.30am–4.30pm.* 🎿*Hiking and camping equipment rental and sales.* △ ✕ ♿ 🅿 ☎*1-866-727-2427.*

A permanent exhibit provides an intro duction to the fascinating landscape found in the park and to the plant (arctic-alpine) and animals, especially caribou, that thrive on its mountaintops. During the summer months, naturalists answer questions at the summit of Mt. Jacques-Cartier and Mt. Albert. In the evening, lectures, slide shows, plays, and films on themes related to the park are presented at the center.

GATINEAU★

OUTAOUAIS REGION
POPULATION 243,998
MAP: SEE PARC DE LA GATINEAU

Facing Ottawa across the wide waters of the Ottawa River, Gatineau is the Quebec section of the National Capital Region (NCC). The core district of Gatineau is Hull, where you will find the Canadian Museum of Civilization, Canada's most popular museum. Gatineau is Quebec third largest urban area, behind Montreal and Quebec City. However, beautiful natural settings are never very far in Gatineau. You will observe that the contrast between French-speaking Gatineau and mainly English-speaking Ottawa is striking.

- ℹ **Information:** ☎103 Rue Laurier. ☎819-778-2222 & 1-800-265-7822. www.outaouais-tourism.org/www.gatineau.ca.
- ▶ **Orient Yourself:** Five bridges cross the Ottawa River, linking Gatineau and Ottawa. From east to west they are: The Macdonald-Cartier, Interprovincial (also names Alexandra), Du Portage, des Chaudières, and Champlain bridges. Boulevard Maisonneuve, connected to the Du Portage Bridge, leads to the Gatineau Highway (Autoroute 5).
- 🅿 **Parking:** Metered street parking is available; city and private lots (☞*fee*).
- ⊘ **Don't Miss:** Canadian Museum of Civilization, Gatineau Park. Also make time to see the Maison du Citoyen, a remarkable city hall building.
- 🕐 **Organizing Your Time:** Plan to spend most of a day at the Canadian Museum of Civilization: you can take a break outside on the grounds along the waterfront and enjoy the best view of Canada's Parliament Buildings across the Ottawa River. Plan to enjoy some hiking or cycling in Gatineau Park.
- 🧒 **Especially for Kids:** The Children's Museum within the Canadian Museum of Civilization can keep kids busy for hours.

A Bit of History

Hull was founded by Loyalist settler **Philemon Wright** in 1800, some 26 years prior to the establishment of Bytown (Ottawa) across the river. Wright built a mill beside the Chaudière Falls and named his community Hull after the Yorkshire town from which his parents had emigrated. Logging activities develo── ped quickly at the small farming set-

tlement, made possible by the region's abundance of red and white pine trees, which were well suited for shipbuilding. Wright and his fellow settlers rafted the long, straight trunks down the river to Montreal and from there to Quebec City, where they sold them to the British Navy, thus beginning an industry that continued throughout the 19C.

In 1851 another American, **Ezra Butler Eddy**, arrived in Hull. He started a

nespin business and a match fac-
y that acquired national fame; "Eddy
.es" are still sold all over the continent.
:ddy's pulp mill dominates part of the
Gatineau waterfront. Gatineau's downtown economy is now focused on two
large federal government complexes
(Place du Portage and Les Terrasses de
la Chaudière).

Not unlike Ottawa, Gatineau has laid out
bike paths along the river. Not far from
here, gamblers head for the enormous
(23,400sq m/251,878sq ft) avant-garde
structure on the banks of Lake Leamy
that houses the **Casino du Lac-Leamy**.
The Jacques Cartier Park (*off Rue Laurier*) affords particularly good **views**★
of Ottawa on the opposite bank of the
Ottawa River, including Parliament Hill,
the Fairmont Château Laurier, and the
National Gallery of Canada (⚑ *see THE
GREEN GUIDE Canada*).

Canadian Museum
of Civilization★★★

Directly across the Ottawa River from
Parliament Hill stand the remarkable
buildings of the Canadian Museum of
Civilization. The museum is dedicated
to the history of Canada since the arrival
of the Vikings, and to the art and traditions of indigenous peoples and
various ethnic groups who have established themselves in Canada throughout
the centuries.

Through its impressive collection of five
million artifacts and the use of innovative and interactive displays, dioramas,
and high-tech projection systems, the
museum seeks to promote intercultural
understanding among the 275 different
peoples who call Canada home and to
preserve their cultural heritage.

Architecture

The two museum buildings represent
architect Douglas Cardinal's breathtaking vision of the Canadian landscape.
Using computer-assisted design techniques, Cardinal was able to create the
sweeping curves that evoke the emergence of the North American continent
and its subsequent molding by the
wind, water and glaciers. Fossil impres-
sions are visible in the Tyndall limestone
sheathing the exterior walls.

The building to the left of the main
entrance, the **Canadian Shield Wing**,
houses storage space, administrative
offices and laboratories for conservation
and restoration. On the right, the vast
Glacier Wing (16 500sq m/19 734sq yd)
contains the museum's exhibit halls. Some
3 300sq m/3 947sq yd of space is reserved
for temporary exhibits organized by the
museum or other institutions; the remainder houses permanent exhibits.

Visit

*100 Rue Laurier, between Interprovin-
cial Bridge and Rue Victoria.* ⏱ *Open
Jul–Labor Day, daily 9am–6pm (Thu–Fri*

Canadian Museum of Civilization

9pm); May–Jun & rest of Sept–mid-Oct, daily 9am–6pm (Thu 9pm); rest of the year, Tue–Sun 9am–5pm (Thu 9pm). $10 (free Thu 4pm–9pm). ☒♿🅿 ($8). ☎819-776-7000 & 1-800-555-5621. www. civilization.ca

IMAX Cinema
Main level. Features change periodically; films are shown alternately in English and French. Tickets available at main entrance booth or through Ticketmaster ☎613-755-1111. Advance purchase recommended. $10. Films and screening times information ☎819-776-7010.

Two seven-story IMAX screen (10 times the size of a conventional movie screen), provide unparalleled viewing opportunities for a maximum of 295 spectators (*latecomers not admitted*). The seats in the steeply inclined auditorium tilt backward for greater viewing ease and comfort. IMAX is a Canadian technology; there are 300 IMAX theaters in 40 countries.

Canadian Children's Museum [Kids]
Main level. This delightful place for "hands on" learning encourages children to discover the world by participating in activities they enjoy, either individually or aided by supervisors. Near the museum entrance, the **Kaleidoscope** features temporary exhibits specially created for children. In the **Crossroads** area, children can climb aboard a Pakistani bus for an imaginary trip to eight different countries, and the **Grand Adventure** offers a superlative opportunity to get to know other countries and cultures by way of the International Village, a veritable microcosm of the planet Earth. Here, kids can embark on

several exciting adventures, includir. trip across the desert with a mysterio pyramid looming in the background. costume room, puppet theatre, toys and games section and an art studio complete the indoor activities. Weather permitting, **Adventure World,** an enclosed outdoor exhibition park, invites visitors to climb on a real tugboat, play a life-size game of chess, or get into the cockpit of a Cessna 150.

Canadian Postal Museum
Main level. The postal history of Canada and other countries is delightfully presented via a multimedia theater, an art gallery, and thematic exhibits. The varied collection of some 25,000 objects, 200,000 stamps, and 5,000 works of art includes clay tablets (2043 BC) from Mesopotamia; cancellation markings; Valentine's Day cards; and a broad assortment of mail boxes.

Grand Hall
Lower level. This immense elliptical space houses the museum's stunning masterpiece exposition presenting the rich cultural and artistic heritage of the Amerindian peoples of Canada's west coast. Looking down across the wide expanse of the hall, visitors will see the façades of six chieftains' houses, symbolizing a traditional Amerindian village erected between the coastal rain forests (represented here by an enormous mural photograph) and the Pacific Ocean (evoked by a smoothly polished gray granite floor). Built on-site by native artisans using their ancestral techniques, each façade reveals the particularities of a distinct culture: Coast Salish, Nuu-chah-Nulth (Nootka), Kwakwaka'wakw (Kwakiutl), Nuxalk, Haida, and Tshimshian. Most of the arti-

facts incorporated into the façades date from the second half of the 19C. Majestic totem poles (some original) illustrate the artistic talent of the Pacific Coast peoples. Worth noting is the openwork Wakas pole (1893); this 12m/39ft masterpiece stood in Vancouver's Stanley Park for 60 years. Floor-to-ceiling windows on the left open onto the Ottawa River and Parliament Hill, flooding the hall with natural light.

First Peoples Hall

Lower level. Dedicated mainly to the arts and cultures of Canada's indigenous populations as well as their long history and their role in present-day society, this hall presents the richness and diversity of the First Nations through a wide variety of permanent and temporary exhibits. Comprising some 10,000 paintings, carvings, sculptures, photographs, and diverse craft objects, the permanent collection of contemporary indigenous art—shown on a rotating basis—features works by established artists (Norval Morrisseau, Bill Reid, Alex Janvier, Kenojuak Ashevak, Pudlo Pudlat, Jessie Oonark) as well as rising talents (Edward Poitras, Shelley Niro, Arthur Renwick, David Ruben Piqtoukun, Toonoo Sharky, James Ungalaq).

Canada Hall

Upper level. A 17m/56ft vaulted ceiling surmounts this enormous exposition hall, in which reconstructed buildings and artifacts illustrate one thousand years of Canadian history and heritage. Some of the objects on display are authentic, while others are re-creations. Along a meandering passage through time, visitors witness the arrival of the Vikings in Newfoundland around the year 1000, and discover the life of the early European adventurers who fished the waters of the North Atlantic long before the great voyages of exploration. Early Acadian settlements and 18C farms and villages of the St. Lawrence Valley evoke the history of New France. Another scene explains how fur and timber trading encouraged westward movement, symbolized by a tent and a Conestoga wagon. An Ontario street scene depicts the development of commerce and communication during the second half of the

Drawing by R. Corbel/MICHELIN

Inuit Ublumi (1974) Sculpture by Pierre Karlik

19C. The small turn-of-the-century Prairies railway station and a full-size grain elevator evoke the settlement of western Canada and the development of the rail system between 1870 and 1914. The journey through time ends with the era of industrialization (a working-class neighborhood in Winnipeg; a west coast fish cannery; and the Northwest Territory's Wildcat Café) and effects of modernization on daily life and traditional values during the 20C.

Additional Sight

Maison du Citoyen (City Hall)

25 Rue Laurier between Rue Victoria and Rue Hôtel-de-Ville. ◷ *Open Jun 24–Labor Day, Mon–Fri 8.30am–4pm; rest of the year, 9am–4pm.* ◉ *$10.* ♿ 🅿 ☎ *819-595-2002.*
Gatineau's city hall is called "la Maison du Citoyen" (Citizen's House) to reflect a will to open the doors to a beautiful, brightly lit brick structure (1980) encompassing an art gallery, the city library, a performance hall, conference rooms and office space, all of which are set around a large glassed-in atrium called the **Agora**.
The Hall of Nations displays objects of art given by numerous countries throughout the years.
Outside the building is a pleasant park used as a skating rink in winter. La Maison du Citoyen is connected to a conference center (Palais des Congrès), a hotel, and a shopping center by enclosed passageways.

Parc de la GATINEAU★★

OUTAOUAIS REGION

Covering 356sq km/137sq mi of lovely rolling hills interspersed with lakes, Gatineau Park lies nestled between the valleys of the Ottawa and Gatineau rivers. This enchanting place is named after the French fur trader from Trois-Rivières, **Nicolas Gatineau**, who disappeared in 1683 during a trip up the river that now bears his name. Gatineau is also the namesake of the community, located at the junction of both rivers, and of the surrounding range of hills, part of which is included in the park. William Lyon Mackenzie King, tenth prime minister of Canada, helped create Gatineau Park in 1938. Formerly part of an Algonquin and Iroquois territory, the park is now administered by the National Capital Commission. Within its boundaries lie several federal government buildings, notably the prime minister's summer residence on Lac Mousseau (Harrington Lake); and the Willson House, the official meeting center on Meech Lake, where negotiations on the controversial Meech Lake Accord took place in 1987.

- **Information:** 33 Chemin Scott, Old Chelsea. ☎819-827-2020 & 1-800-465-1867. www.canadascapital.gc.ca/gatineau.
- **Orient Yourself:** The park can be accessed from Gatineau, Old Chelsea, or Wakefield.
- **Parking:** In designated lots at beaches and trails, $8.90 daily park pass.
- **Organizing Your Time:** During summer, drive up the Champlain Parkway to the Champlain Lookout to view the Ottawa Valley. On the way back, stop at the Mackenzie King Estate for afternoon tea.
- **Especially for Kids:** During summer, take the kids for a swim at one of the six supervised beaches.

Visit

Park open daily year-round. Parkways closed from first snowfall until early May. Visitor center open all year daily 9am–5pm. closed Christmas. $8.90/car. ☎819-827-2020. www.canadas capital.gc.ca/gatineau.

Scenic Parkway

51km/31.6mi round-trip from Gatineau on Rte. 148; start on the Gatineau Parkway.
This beautiful drive skirts high walls of pink granite rock, then winds its way through the dense hardwood forests of the Gatineau Hills. Rounded by glaciers, these hills end in an abrupt slope, the Eardley escarpment, which demarcates the Canadian Shield. Several viewpoints afford superb views of the Ottawa River valley with its productive farms and sparkling lakes.

Belvédère Champlain★★ (Champlain Lookout)

6km/3.7mi round-trip from the intersection of the Champlain Parkway and the Lac Fortune Parkway.
The edge of the Eardley escarpment, at an altitude of 335m/1,098ft, offers a superb **panorama** of the Ottawa valley, where the Canadian Shield meets the St. Lawrence Lowlands. Below the lookout, a nature trail is dotted with eight observation stations, where various hardwood trees and other vegetation in the park are identified for visitors.

Domaine Mackenzie-King★ (Mackenzie King Estate)

3km/1.8mi round-trip from the Gatineau Parkway; take Kingsmere Rd. Open mid-May–mid-Oct, daily 10am–6pm. ☎819-827-2020.
At the heart of Gatineau Park lies the estate of the man who held power in Canada for a total of 22 years. **William Lyon Mackenzie King** was Canada's prime minister from 1921 to 1930 and 1935 to

DOMAINE MACKENZIE KING

1 Boathouse   4 Garage   7 Garage
2 Guest cottage   5 The Farm   8 Forge
3 Ice house   6 Garden   9 Arc de Triomphe

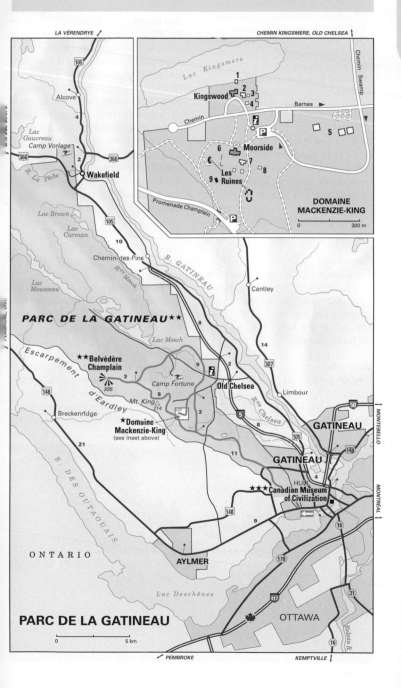

PARC DE LA GATINEAU

ACTIVITIES

The scenic drive that runs throughout the park is particularly beautiful in October, when the trees sport fall's splendid colors. In summer, visitors can enjoy a wide variety of activities including cycling, hiking, swimming, boating, fishing, and camping. In the winter months, the park becomes a skier's paradise, offering 190km/118mi of trails for cross-country skiing and downhill ski centers at Camp Fortune and Vorlage.

1948. During these years, he retreated to the park to escape the pressures of power. When he died in 1950, he left his personal estate of 231ha/5701 acres to the Canadian people. The estate comprises several houses and is criss-crossed by walks landscaped by Mr. King himself.

Kingswood

This rustic cottage was the first summer home built by Mr. King in 1903. He enlarged the house in 1924 and continued to live here until 1928. A pleasant walk to the lake offers a view of the **boathouse (1)**.

Moorside

This attractive clapboard house was purchased by Mackenzie King in 1924, and he lived here from 1928 to 1943. The upper-floor rooms have remained intact;

the ground floor now houses a delightful tea and lunch room. In the former **garage (4)**, an audio-visual presentation (*15min*) explains the life and career of former Prime Minister King.

The Ruins

Mr. King salvaged pillars, stones and other architectural features from buildings slated for demolition and had them installed on his estate as a means of landscaping his property. A few sections of the former Parliament Building, destroyed by fire in 1916, can be found, as well as some stones from the British Parliament bombed in 1941.

A third house, **The Farm (5)**, where King lived from 1943 until his death, is now the official residence of the Speaker of the House of Commons (⊶ *closed to the public*).

Excursions

Old Chelsea

▷ *From Gatineau, take Rte. 5 north for 8km/5mi to Exit 12 (Old Chelsea/ Gatineau Park); turn west (left) onto Chemin Old Chelsea.*

By the early 19C this tranquil village was a stopping place for lumbermen travelling into backcountry forests. Settlers recognized that picturesque Chelsea Creek could provide power for saw- and gristmills, and the hamlet grew, eventu-

Domaine Mackenzie-King

Old Chelsea Charmers

Neighboring Gatineau Park, Old Chelsea serves as a supply base for the recreational needs and creature comforts of park users as well as Old Chelseans. **Greg Christie's** (*148 Chemin Old Chelsea;* ☎*1-800-345-4734*) has been renting bikes, skis, and other outdoor equipment to area visitors for years, while **Gerry and Isobel's Restaurant/Boutique** (*14 Chemin Scott;* ☎*819-827-4341*) serves delicious homemade fare to hungry hikers, bikers, leaflookers and such, amid a wonderful assortment of local books, artwork, and other wares. Next door is the **Galerie Old Chelsea** (☎*819-827-4945*), a co-op that displays and sells the works of many local artists. Restaurants include the illustrious **Les Fougères** (*783 Rte. 105;* ☎*819-827-8942*), where the hands-on chef-proprietors at this dining spot favored by Ottawa residents offer locally smoked fish (*from* **La Boucanerie Chelsea Smokehouse**, *just south of the restaurant;* ☎*819-827-1925*) and other specialties. Try the fish of the day or the confit de canard (roasted, salted duck), a Quebec favorite.

ally becoming a service center. By the 1870s, four hotels—all owned by Irishmen—prospered as well-frequented watering holes. Old Chelsea is home to Gatineau Park's **information center** as well as shops, art galleries, cozy restaurants, and rental stores catering to outdoor enthusiasts. New England pioneers, attracted to the areas timber and agriculture, are buried in the **Old Protestant Burying Ground**. Look for the grave of Asa Meech, minister, doctor, teacher, and farmer, for whom nearby Meech Lake (of the Meech Lake Accord) is named. Genealogists especially, will enjoy St. Stephen's Church and cemetery, where headstones date from the 1700s.

Wakefield

From Old Chelsea, take Rte. 5 north for 10km/6.2mi, then continue on Rte. 105 to Wakefield for another 10km/6.2mi. From Gatineau, take Rte. 5 and Rte. 105 for 32km/19.8mi.

Wakefield occupies a beautiful site on the banks of the wide Gatineau River. In the early 19C, the first British settlers arrived from Britain and named the village after a town in Yorkshire, England.

Wakefield is extremely attractive, with its picturesque setting, its old covered bridge spanning the Gatineau River, and the recently restored **Maclaren Mill**, named after an early family in the region. The village also provides an access point to Gatineau Park at Lac Philippe and a famous bungee jump.

Lester B. Pearson is buried at the MacLaren Cemetery in Wakefield. An outstanding diplomat, Pearson received the 1957 Nobel Peace Prize for helping to resolve the Suez Crisis. The United Nations Emergency Force he had proposed became the first of many worldwide peacekeeping assignments in which Canadian troops would serve.

The village has a somewhat bohemian nature to it, and boasts a number of small cafés, pubs, and galleries. Many artists live in the surrounding mountains and valleys, including Celtic jeweler and painter Tiffany Teske. A weekly regional newspaper, the Low Down to Hull and Back News, (a play on the Gatineau River communities from Low downstream to Hull) is also published in the village.

GATINEAU-CHELSEA-WAKEFIELD STEAM TRAIN

165 Rue Deveault. ☎*819-778-7246. www.steamtrain.ca.*
Take a 64km/39.7mi ride on one of the oldest steam trains still in operation in Canada—built in 1907. On a half-day trip from Gatineau you will follow the winding path of the Gatineau River to picturesque Wakefield. Tour guides and musicians accompany you on the delightful journey. Opt for the Sunset Dinner Train to enjoy fine French cuisine served in the old-time dining car.

GRANBY

EASTERN TOWNSHIPS REGION
POPULATION 58,390
MAP: SEE CANTONS DE L'EST

Settled by Loyalists in the early 19C, Granby was named for John Manners, Marquis of Granby, commander of British forces in North America in 1766. The rubber and tobacco factories that developed here on the banks of the Yamaska Nord River soon transformed the town into an industrial center. The wealth generated from this development is evidenced by the large and gracious Victorian houses along Rues Elgin, Dufferin, and Mountain. Palmer Cox (1840–1924), whose famous elf stories for children were inspired by Scottish folklore, is a native of Granby. Today the nearby Yamaska Park, as well as the ski centers at Bromont and Mt. Shefford, draw outdoor enthusiasts to the community.

- **Information:** 111 Rue Denison Est (Place de la Gare). ☎450-372-7056 & 1-800-567-7273. www.easterntownships.org.
- ▶ **Orient Yourself:** Granby is located 80km/49.7mi east of Montreal by Rtes.10 (Exit 68), 139, or 112.
- ◷ **Organizing Your Time:** The Granby Zoo is the area's key attraction, and worth a full day visit.
- **Especially for Kids:** The waterpark at the Granby Zoo.

Sights

Jardin zoologique de Granby★ (Granby Zoo)   Kids

Entrance and parking on Blvd. Bouchard (Rte. 139), at the corner of Rue Saint-Hubert. ◷*Open early-Jun–late Jun, daily 10am–5pm; late Jun–late Aug, 10am–7pm; hours vary in fall and winter, call ahead.* $26.49. ✕ & ☐ ☎1-877-472-6299. www.zoodegranby.com

This popular zoo features more than 1,000 animals from all over the world. In addition to indigenous species and African mammals, the zoo boasts a nocturnal animals' cave, Bear Mountain, and Cats Pavilion. Of particular interest is the Reptile House, featuring turtles, iguanas, rattlesnakes, and anacondas. The heated wave pool is the largest of its kind in Quebec.

Centre d'interprétation de la nature du lac Boivin (Lake Boivin Nature Interpretation Center)

700 Rue Drummond. Turn left on Rue Drummond from Rue Principale. ◷*Open year-round weekdays 8.30am–4.30pm, weekends 9am–5pm.* & ☐ ☎450-375-3861.

Set on the shores of Lac Boivin, this nature center offers visitors a choice of four short trails through the marshland surrounding the lake. From the observation tower, visitors can admire **views** of Mt. Brome and Mt. Shefford.

Excursion

Waterloo

19km/11.8mi east on Rte. 112.

The town was named Waterloo to commemorate Wellington's victory over Napoleon. A hill there resembles the one in the Belgian Waterloo. Visitors with a taste for adventure should not miss the **Safari Aventure Loowak** (*5km/3mi south of town by Rte. 241, at 475 Chemin Horizon*), with its exciting treasure hunts and daring "missions" (✏*visit by 1hr 30min guided tour only, year-round daily 10am–5pm;* $10; *reservations required;* ☐ ☎450-539-0501; www.safariloowak.qc.ca). Insects, plants and minerals are on view in the Loowak Museum.

PARC DES GRANDS-JARDINS

CHARLEVOIX REGION
MAP: SEE BAS-SAINT-LAURENT – CHARLEVOIX

Just over an hour's drive from Quebec City, and reflective of the province's northern regions, lies Grands-Jardins (literally "great gardens"), a Quebec National Park. Clear blue lakes surrounded by forests of black spruce and a ground cover of lichen (cladonie), on which caribou feed in winter, are typical of the taiga found in subarctic climates. The park was created in 1981 to preserve the caribou's habitat. As many as 4,000 caribou roamed the land at the beginning of the century, but by the 1920s they were already extinct as a result of over-hunting. Between 1969 and 1972 some 80 caribou were reintroduced to the area; today the population has increased to between 100 and 125 caribou.

▪ **Information:** ☏418-439-1227 & 1-800-665-6527. www.ParcsQuebec.com.

▸ **Orient Yourself:** Parc des Grands-Jardins is located 133km/83mi northeast of Quebec City. Take Rte. 138 to Baie-Saint-Paul (91km/56mi) and then continue on Rte. 138 for another 11km/7mi to the junction with Rte. 381 Nord. Take Rte. 381 past Saint-Urbain (4.5km/3mi) and continue an additional 18km/11mi to the reception center of the park at Thomas-Fortin. *Overnight accommodations available in the park include camping (wilderness or with facilities), cottages, and huts. For more information, call Château-Beaumont interpretation center ☏418-846-2218.*

🕐 **Organizing Your Time:** Be fully prepared for winter and back-country activities in the park: this is true wilderness and there are few facilities. Campsites are available near day hiking trails; check current conditions with the visitor centers.

Visit

🕐*Open late May–early Oct for camping, cycling, and canoeing; year-round for hiking; self-registration kiosks at trail entrances or when visitor centers are closed.* ⬡$3.50. △ 🅿 ☏1-800-665-6527. www.parcsquebec.com

Secteur du Mont du lac des Cygnes (Sector of Lac des Cygnes Mountain)

1.5km/1mi from the Thomas-Fortin Reception Center.
A 2.7km/1.7mi hiking trail leads to a viewpoint where visitors can admire a striking **panorama**★★ of the St. Lawrence River and the Charlevoix valley, with its scattered lakes and villages. On the climb to the summit (980m/3,214ft), hikers encounter three distinct types of vegetation. Mountain vegetation is characterized by forests of silver birch, poplar and pine. In the subalpine environment, taiga dominates, while tundra prevails in the alpine region.

ACTIVITIES

The Château-Beaumont interpretation center organizes hikes (*departures at 10am and 1.30pm*) led by naturalists. Several hiking trails wind their way across the taiga zone; for information, contact the *Thomas-Fortin Reception Center* ☏418-846-2218. Canoe rentals available.

▸ *Continue on Rte. 381 for approximately 18km/11mi. A reception center marks the main entrance to the park.*

Château-Beaumont Interpretation Centre

🕐*Open mid-Jun–mid-Oct, daily 9am–6pm.* ♿🅿 ☏418-439-1227.
Exhibits here showcase the park and its unique natural environment. The center also serves as the point of departure for various nature activities and excursions.

Canoeing in Jacques-Cartier National Park

Parc de la JACQUES-CARTIER★

QUEBEC CITY REGION
MAP: SEE BAS-SAINT-LAURENT – CHARLEVOIX

Located in the highlands of the Laurentian Mountains, Jacques-Cartier National Park covers an area of 670sq km/259sq mi. The coniferous boreal forest extending from Quebec across to Alaska reaches its southernmost point here, on the rolling mountaintops of the massif, which ends in an abrupt 600m/1,968ft drop to the Jacques-Cartier River. Here, the coniferous forest gives way to deciduous vegetation. Extensive logging of the plateau disrupted the fragile environmental equilibrium, causing the disappearance of caribou and salmon, two species well adapted to the harsh climate of the region. The park was created in 1981 in an effort to better monitor logging operations and preserve the area's magnificent natural heritage.

- **Information:** ☎1-877-844-2358.www.jacques-cartier.com.
- **Orient Yourself:** Parc de la Jacques-Cartier is located 40km/24.8mi north of Quebec City on Rte. 175.
- **Don't Miss:** The chance to see a nearly pristine Canadian forest near Quebec's provincial capital.
- **Organizing Your Time:** The park is easily accessible for day trips from Quebec City. In the best conditions, its a 20min drive. The park has more than 100km/62mi of hiking trails and a network of bicycling trails in summer, and 55km/34mi of backcountry skiing and snowshoeing trails during winter.
- **Especially for Kids:** Enquire at the visitor center about renting a canoe for the calm water excursion, or dogsledding in the winter.

Visit

Open mid-Dec–mid-Mar & mid-May ... daily. Call for hours. ⬧$3.50. △✗ ... 18-848-3169. www.sepaq.com.

Centre d'accueil et d'interprétation (Welcome and Interpretation Center)

Turn left off Rte. 175 from Quebec City at la Vallée secteur entrance. Continue

ACTIVITIES

In summer, visitors can enjoy canoe-ing and kayaking on the turbulent Jacques-Cartier River (26km/16mi). More than 100km/62mi of hiking trails, laid out along 15 nature walks, meander through the forest and along the river. Four mountain-bike trails cover more than 50km/31mi of the park over former logging and gravel roads. There are 100 campsites and group camping facili-ties. Kayaks and canoes can be rented at the interpretation center. Fishing permits can be purchased here as well. In winter, the park is open to cross-country skiers (*information in off season* ☎418-528-8787).

10km/6.2mi into the park. Maps of the park and activity information are available at the welcome center (🕐closed during winter season).

A permanent exhibit on the Laurentian Massif and an audio-visual presentation on the geographical formations found in the area provide explanations of the geological forces that shaped the park's spectacular landscapes.

The road into the park begins to the left of the interpretation center and follows the Jacques-Cartier River behind the center. After crossing the river, the road surface changes from asphalt to gravel.

The trail known as **Sentier des Loups** (*10km/6.2mi round-trip*) offers splendid **views**★★ of the entire Jacques-Cartier River valley.

BAIE JAMES★

BAIE-JAMES REGION

Covering an area of 350,000sq km/135,135sq mi between the 49th and 55th parallels, the James Bay territory makes up 20 percent of Quebec's total land area. A wilderness of innumerable lakes, mighty rivers, and coniferous forests of spindly black spruce and gray pine, the region is home to some 40 species of animals including caribou, moose, black bear, beaver, lynx, beluga whales, and seals, and a multitude of waterfowl and fish.

🛈 **Information:** ☎1-888-748-8140. www.tourismebaiejames.com.

▶ **Orient Yourself:** Radisson (La Grande) is located 1,448km/899.7mi northwest of Montreal and 625km/388mi north of Matagami by the James Bay Rd. At the information booth located 6km/3.7mi north of Matagami, visitors can make reservations for guided tours of the power plants. At 381km/236.7mi, there is a 24hr gas station with a mechanic on duty during regular working hours, and a snack cafeteria. Flights are available between Montreal, Quebec City, Val-d'Or, and Radisson on Air Inuit, Air Wemindji, and Air Creebec. Accommo-dations (camping, hotel rooms, studio apartments) are available in Radisson.

⊛ **Don't Miss:** Robert Bourassa Generating Facility and La Grande-1 Power Plant.

🕐 **Organizing Your Time:** From Matagami, the only service station is 381km/236.7mi farther north, so stock up and make your reservations for the tour of the power plants. Allow a full 4hrs for the tour of the massive generat-ing facilities near Radisson. Take the paved road west to just past Chisasibi to look out onto James Bay before returning south. While it is possible to drive 582km/361.6mi east from Km 544 along the Trans-Taiga road to Quebec's service center at Brisay, it is a very remote gravel road with towns or services.

Kids **Especially for Kids:** Robert Bouraasa Power Plant.

A Bit of History

Cree Population – The Crees of Quebec are part of the large Algonquian linguistic family. Their spoken language is Cree. In 1997 the sedentary population numbered approximately 12,000 people, living in nine villages: Whapmagoostui (Kuujjuarapik–Poste-de-la-Baleine), Chisasibi, Wemindji, Eastmain and Waskaganish, on the east coast of James Bay and Hudson Bay; and Nemaska, Mistassini, Oujé-Bougoumou and Waswanipi, farther inland. Native to the northern forests, the Crees have hunted (moose, caribou, beaver, and geese) and fished in the region for thousands of years. In 1950 the federal government became more involved in the region, establishing a compulsory English-language educational system. Since the mid-1970s, the Crees have exercised a strong degree of autonomy, governing their own school system, health, and social services as well as housing and economic development programs. Each community is administered by a local band council. The Crees have established numerous organizations and companies, such as Air Creebec.

James Bay and Northern Quebec Agreement (Convention de la baie James et du Nord québécois) – In 1971 the provincial government passed a law to develop Quebec's northern territory and created corporations to oversee the developmental, technical, and financial aspects of the Hydro-Québec project. The energy project immediately raised legal questions regarding native rights not taken into account by the provincial government. The Inuit and Cree nations obtained an injunction and eventually entered into negotiations with the federal and provincial governments and three corporations to resolve the issue of territorial claims. On November 11, 1975, all parties, including the Grand Council of the Crees of Quebec and the Northern Quebec Inuit Assn., signed the James Bay and Northern Quebec Agreement. It was the first modern-day settlement of native claims in Canada. Under the agreement, the Inuit and Cree yielded certain claims and rights.

In return, they were awarded exclusive hunting, fishing, and trapping rights in designated areas; ownership of certain lands (16 percent of the claimed terri-

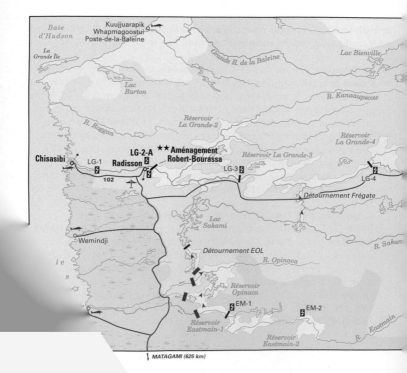

y); the creation of aboriginal coun-
...s to oversee community and regional
affairs and to participate in decisions
concerning the various phases of the
James Bay project; and financial compensation. In addition, programs for
health care, education, and economic
development were implemented.

James Bay Energy Project –
Envisioned to exploit the vast hydroelectric potential of Quebec's remote
northern reaches, this ambitious
long-term project originally called for
the construction of 19 power plants
grouped in three distinct complexes: La
Grande, Grande-Baleine (Great Whale),
and Nottaway-Broadback-Rupert. To
this day, only the **La Grande complex**
is nearing completion. The first phase
of the project extended from May 1973
to December 1985, at a cost of almost
$14 billion, and led to the construction
of 2.000km/1,242.7mi of roads linking
the area with the south, five airports,
and five working camps.
This colossal undertaking required the
construction of 215 earth-and-rockfill
dams and dikes, displacing enormous

ACTIVITIES

The Mandow Agency (☎819-855-
3373) offers a variety of activities,
including guided tours of the village.
James Bay is located 15km/9.3mi
from the center of Chisasibi. To
reach the shores of James Bay, leave
the center, turn right and continue
straight toward the La Grande River
for 2km/1.2mi. Turn left and follow
the road for another 2km/1.2mi. At
the fork, turn left and continue for
11km/6.8mi.

amounts of gravel, rock, and sand—
enough, in fact, to construct the Great
Pyramid of Cheops 80 times over!
The three power plants house a total of
37 generator sets and have a combined
capacity of 10,282 megawatts (1 mega-
watt=1 000 000 watts). During the second phase of the project, between 1988
and 1996, construction of La Grande-1,
La Grande-2-A, La Forge-1, La Forge-2
and Brisay were completed, bringing
the total capacity of the La Grande complex to over 16,000 megawatts—more
than half the electricity produced in
Quebec. Agreements in 2002 and 2004
effectively ended legal battles between
the Cree and the Quebec government,
ostensibly ensuring the eventual completion of Eastmain-1 (currently under
construction), Eastmain-1A, and Sarcelle
and promising a combined total capacity of over 17,000 megawatts.

La Grande

Radisson

Of the five temporary villages established during the construction of the La
Grande complex, Radisson is the only
one that remains as a permanent settlement. It is located on the south shore
of the La Grande River, just west of the
Matagami Road and 5km/3mi west of
the Robert Bourassa power plant. Th
hub of the village is the Pierre Radis
community center; it houses sho
post office and recreational fa
including a gymnasium and
ming pool. Living quarters fo
ees of Hydro-Québec, and

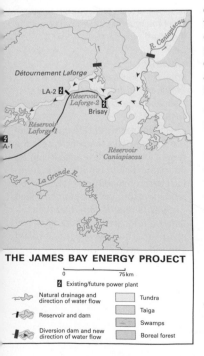

THE JAMES BAY ENERGY PROJECT

0 ———— 75 km

⚡ Existing/future power plant

Natural drainage and direction of water flow

Reservoir and dam

Diversion dam and new direction of water flow

Tundra
Taiga
Swamps
Boreal forest

Spillway, Robert Bourassa Generating Facility

Hydro-Québec

connected to the center by enclosed passageways.

Aménagement Robert-Bourassa★★ (Robert Bourassa Generating Facility)

Visit by guided tour (3.5hr) only, mid-Jun–Labor Day, daily at 1pm (2pm Tue) in French (English tours available on request); rest of the year, Mon & Fri 8.30am, Wed 1pm. Reservations required 48hrs in advance. ✕ ♿ 🅿 ☎ *Hydro-Québec in Radisson 1-800-291-8486.*

The guided tour includes a documentary on the construction and operation of the complex, explanations on the production of electricity, and a visit to the power plant. The most powerful hydroelectric facility in Quebec, the Robert Bourassa power plant has an installed capacity of 5,328,000 kilowatts. The reservoir covers an area of 2,835sq km/1,094sq mi and is contained by one dam and 31 dikes.

Spillway

Used to release excess water accumulated in the reservoir during exceptionally strong floods, the spillway is extended in a "**giant's staircase**★" made up of 10 steps, each 10m/33ft high and 122m/400ft wide. Carved out of rock, it is a visible testimony to the feats of engineering achieved at the La Grande complex.

Robert Bourassa Power Plant

The Centrale Robert-Bourassa is located 137m/450ft underground in an immense granite cavern, .5km/.3mi in length, equipped with 16 generator sets. It is the largest underground power plant in the world and the most productive power plant in North America.

The **La Grande-1** power plant, situated an hour's drive west of Radisson, is a more conventional river dam. *⏱Buses bring visitors to LG-1 Wed–Mon at 8am (except Tue) from mid-Jun–Labor Day. Reserve 48hrs in advance.*

Excursions from Radisson

Circuit de visite de l'Aménagement Robert-Bourassa (Driving tour of the Robert-Bourassa Generating Facility)

Depart from the Hydro-Québec information center in Radisson, which provides maps and information about the tour.

This pleasant drive, dotted with informative panels, winds for some 30km/18.6mi around the dikes of the Robert Bourassa reservoir and offers scenic views of the surrounding area.

Chisasibi

From Radisson, head south on the Matagami Rd. for 20km/12.4mi. Turn right and continue on the asphalt road for 82km/51mi.

The hydroelectric development of the territory caused a sharp increase in the flow of the La Grande River as it empties into James Bay. In 1981 the Crees residing in the community of Fort George, on an island at the river's mouth, demanded (by way of referendum) that their village be relocated to a site 8km/5mi upstream. The new village was called Chisasibi, meaning "Great River."

JOLIETTE★

LANAUDIÈRE REGION
POPULATION 19,044
MAP: SEE LANAUDIÈRE

Set on the banks of the Assomption River, the industrial and commercial center of Joliette is the capital of the beautiful and mountainous Lanaudière region. An important artistic and cultural center, it is also the seat of a Roman Catholic bishopric and home to several Catholic orders.

- **Information:** 500 Rue Dollard. ☎450-759-5013 & 1-800-363-1775. www.lanaudiere.ca.
- **Orient Yourself:** Joliette is about 75km/46.6mi north of Montreal by Rtes. 40 and 31.
- **Don't Miss:** The Joliette Art Museum, The Joliette Cathedral and its works by Ozias Leduc. Also try and get to the Lanaudière International music Festival.
- **Organizing Your Time:** If you can be in Joliette during the international music festival, plan a visit to the art museum around the concert schedule.
- Kids **Especially for Kids:** The longest skating track in Quebec during winter.

A Bit of History

In 1828 the notary **Barthélemy Joliette**, a descendant of the famed explorer Louis Jolliet who mapped the Mississippi River with Jacques Marquette in 1673, built a mill on the banks of the Assomption River. First known as L'Industrie, the town was given its present name at its incorporation in 1863. Joliette and his wife, Marie-Charlotte de Lanaudière, were the town's first benefactors, providing land for the church and a college.

The town gained a reputation as a cultural center through the efforts of various religious orders, especially the Viatorian clerics. A member of this order, **Father Wilfrid Corbeil** (1893-1979), played a key role in developing the arts. One of his greatest achievements was the creation of the Joliette Art Gallery. The town's prestigious music festival was the brainchild of Father Fernand Lindsay.

Festival de Lanaudière (Lanaudière Festival)

From early June to early August, musicians and singers from all over the world perform classical and popular music concerts during the largest international music festival in Canada (*see Calendar of Events*). Performances are held at various churches throughout the city and in neighboring villages, as well as at a mod-

Festival international de Lanaudière

Address Book

For price ranges, see the Legend on the cover flap.

WHERE TO STAY

$$$ Hôtel Château au Joliette – *450 Rue St-Thomas.* ☎*450-752-2525 & 1-800-361-0572.* *www.chateaujoliette.com.* Large, comfortable rooms in Joliette's signature hotel. Conveniently located as you enter Joliette, "le Château" is near the city center.

WHERE TO EAT

$$–$$$ Restaurant Canard Noir *–153 Rue St-Charles-Borromée Nord.* ☎*450-755-2429.* *www.canardnoir.com.* The Launaudière region produces duck, venison, bison, and various cheeses celebrated by nearby Montreal gourmets. Le Canard Noir offers a large selection of Quebec specialities, even at lunch. Ice cider and a variety of Quebec liqueurs will finish off your meal nicely.

ern open-air amphitheater set in a charming, wooded site. Blessed with excellent acoustics, the covered amphitheater can accommodate more than 10,000 concertgoers. There are 2,000 reserved seats and large surrounding grassy slopes. ☎ *450-759-4343 & 1-800-561-4343.* *www.lanaudiere.org.*

Sights

Musée d'art de Joliette★ (Joliette Art Museum)

145 Rue Wilfrid-Corbeil. Open Jul–Aug, *Tue–Sun 11am–5pm; rest of the year, Wed–Sun 11am–5pm.* Closed major *holidays.* $8. ☎*450-756-0311.* *www.musee.joliette.org* The Joliette Art Museum is one of the finest in Quebec. This regional museum maintains a collection of more than 8,000 works. It is housed in a stark structure designed in the International style. In addition to permanent exhibits, the museum mounts temporary exhibits of contemporary art.

Lower Level

A diverse selection of paintings (Marc-Aurèle Fortin, Paul-Émile Borduas, and others) relates the evolution of Canadian visual arts from 1885 to the present.

und Floor

llery, devoted to religious art, con-utiful Québécois and European works from the Middle Ages e 1960s, including a finely ooden pulpit from Saint-ière-du-Loup (c. 1840)

and several altars, notably one from the village of Champlain (in the Mauricie region) attributed to François Normand. Also on view here are several 15C wooden sculptures.

Second Floor

On exhibit are works from the permanent collection dating from the 15C to the 21C, including those of Canadian artists such as Alfred Pellan and Jean-Paul Riopelle, as well as international artists Henry Moore, Arman, Segal and others.

The "**Pit**" **spring** is situated near the museum, in Renaud Park, on the corner of Rue De Lanaudière and Rue Saint-Charles-Borromée. Residents and visitors alike can taste and bottle the sulphurous waters of this spring discovered in 1881 by Pierre Laforest, better known by his nickname "Pit." A statue of Barthélemy Joliette stands nearby.

Cathédrale de Joliette

2 Rue Saint-Charles-Borromée Nord. Open year-round, Mon–Fri 11.30am–*3.30pm, Sat 2pm–5pm, Sun 10am–noon.* Closed major holidays. ☎*450-753-7596.* Built between 1888 and 1892, this spacious church is dedicated to the 16C Italian prelate Charles Borromeo, who played a major role in the clergy reforms enacted at the Council of Trent (1545–63). The church became a cathedral in 1904. Its architects adopted the Romano-Byzantine architectural style. The tall central spire can be seen from various points throughout the city. The stained-glass windows designed in 1912 by Henri Perdriau depict episodes from ne Old Testament. Also worth noting are the Stations of the Cross, by Georges Delfosse (1869–1939) and the painting of St. Charles Borromeo by Antoine Plamondon, which hangs above the altar. Adorning the vault spanning the structure, 23 works by Ozias Leduc tell the story of the life of Jesus and the mysteries of the Rosary.

In winter, behind the cathedral, a 4.5km/2.8mi section of the Assomption River is cleared to form Quebec's longest Kids **skating rink** on a river. It is a lively and popular local attraction.

Résidence Saint-Viateur (Viatorian Clerics House)

Beside the cathedral stands the old Joliette novitiate, a remarkable group of buildings dominated by a massive tower. This modern take on the Norman abbey of Saint-Georges de Boscherville (13C) was built between 1939 and 1941 under the supervision of Father Wilfrid Corbeil. The complex includes the residence and the infirmary for the Clerics of Saint Viator, a religious order founded in Lyon, France by Father Louis-Marie Querbes, in 1831.

Chapel★

○*Open year-round daily 9am–4.30pm. Reservations required.* ☎450-756-4568.
The harmonious interior was decorated between 1940 and 1945 by Marius Plamondon of Quebec City. He designed the **stained-glass windows** and also carved the Stations of the Cross and the Old Testament figures at the ends of the pews. The sculpture on the altar depicts Isaac's sacrifice. The chapel has retained all its original furnishings.

Maison Antoine-Lacombe (Antoine Lacombe House)

Located in the municipality of Saint-Charles-Borromée, 2km/1.2mi north of the center of Joliette; take Rue Saint-Charles-Borromée (which becomes Rue de la Visitation) to the corner of Rue Davignon.
○*Open year-round, Thu–Sat 1pm–5pm.* ☎*450-755-1113; www.maisonantoine lacombe.com.*
This charming stone residence was built in 1847 and renovated in 1968. It now belongs to the municipality and serves as a cultural center, hosting art exhibits, conferences and concerts. Adjoining gardens allow for a most pleasant outings in refined surroundings.

JONQUIÈRE

SAGUENAY–LAC-SAINT-JEAN REGION
VILLE DE SAGUENAY POPULATION 146,332
MAP: SEE FJORD DU SAGUENAY

This major industrial center located south of the Saguenay River was formed in 1975 by the merger of three municipalities: Jonquière, Arvida (named for its founder, philanthropist Arthur Vining Davis), and Kénogami. Then, in 2002, a new city—Ville de Saguenay—was formed by the merger of the cities of Chicoutimi, Jonquière, La Baie, and Laterrière, and some adjacent townships.

The original town of Jonquière was founded in 1847 by Marguerite Belley and her sons, who moved here from the Charlevoix region. They named the new community after the Marquis of Jonquière, governor of New France from 1749 to 1752. Two major industrial concerns were established in the early 20C: the Price Paper Co. at Kénogami in 1912, and the Alcan aluminum smelter at Arvida in 1926. Until the 2004 closing of much of the Arvida facilities, it had been largest producer of aluminum in the western world.

Information: 2665 Blvd du Royaume. ☎418-698-3167 & 1-800-463-6 www.bleuvacances.ca.

▶ **Orient Yourself:** Jonquière is 200km/124mi north of Quebec City Rtes. 175 and 170.

Don't Miss: The view from Mont-Fortin, the aluminum bridge

Enjoy the Outdoors

Take some time out to fish for speckled trout, rent a boat, or simply relax at the **Parc et Promenade de la Rivière-aux-Sables** (*2230 Rue de la Rivière-aux-Sables*). Located in the oldest part of the city, the park and promenade offer a playground, marketplace, and public square—delightful places to be outside and enjoy the fresh air.

Sights

Église Notre-Dame-de-Fatima★ (Church of Our Lady of Fatima)

3635 Rue Notre-Dame. Access from Blvd. du Royaume at the corner of Rue de Mont-fort. ○*Open year-round, daily 9am–5pm.* ♿🅿☎*418-542-5678.*
Known as the "teepee," this modern church (1963) rises more than 25m/82ft above the surrounding area. It is shaped like a white concrete pyramid, split vertically. Two stained-glass windows by Guy Barbeau lend a striking luminosity to the interior; the windows rise the full height of the building, joining the two halves of the pyramid.

Mont Jacob

Access from Rue Saint-Dominique by Rue du Vieux-Pont.
Mont Jacob dominates the western part of Jonquière and affords a superb **view** of the region. At its summit, the **Centre national d'exposition** (○*open Jul–Aug, daily 10am–6pm; rest of the year, weekdays 9am–5pm, weekends noon–5pm;* ○*closed Dec 24–26 & Dec 31–Jan 2;* ♿🅿☎*418-546-2177*) serves as the setting for cultural activities and events celebrating the city's history, art, and architecture.

Mont Fortin★

Access from Blvd. du Saguenay by ...Desjardins.
...mmit is accessible by car when the ...en. The view from this mountain, ...a ski center in winter, encom-...panorama of the entire area. ...bridge and Shipshaw dam ...e direction, while Kéno-

gami and Jonquière, indicated by the spire of the Church of Our Lady of Fatima, are visible in the other.

Pont d'aluminium★ (Aluminum Bridge)

Access from Blvd. du Saguenay by Rte. du Pont.
This 150m/492ft bridge weighs less than 164 tons, a third of what a comparable steel structure would weigh. Spanning the rocky gorge of the Saguenay, it was built by Alcan in 1948 to demonstrate the properties of aluminum. Remarkably, it requires no maintenance and has never been repaired.

Centre d'histoire Sir-William-Price (Sir William Price Heritage Center)

○*Open late Jun–Labor Day, daily 9am–5pm (rest of the year, visits on request). $6.* ♿🅿☎*418-695-7278. www.sirwilliam price.com.*
A young man of Welsh descent, William Price emigrated to the Saguenay region and became rich by supplying Canadian wood to the British Navy during the Napoleonic Wars and the ensuing Continental Blockade. Price and the industrial endeavors of his descendants are synonymous with the economic destiny of the region. The hour spent in this center will be one of the most interesting and enlightening of your trip. The Price Heritage Center is located inside a lovely Anglican chapel dating from 1912. In addition, guided tours (🚶 *Tue, Thu, Sat at 1pm*) of the large Abitibi-Consolidated paper mill will introduce you to modern paper-making processes.

Église Sainte-Thérèse-de-l'Enfant-Jésus

2811 Blvd. Saguenay (corner of Rue Mel-lon, in the traffic circle). ○*Open mid-Jun–mid-Aug, Tue–Sat 12.30pm–7.30pm.* 🅿☎*418-548-4066.*
This pretty, smallish catholic church is classified as a historic monument. The Église Sainte-Thérèse-de-l'Enfant-Jésus was built in 135 days in 1927–1928. The church incorporates several outstanding decoration features and works of art, like stained glassed windows and bronze doors.

KAHNAWAKE

MONTÉRÉGIE REGION
POPULATION 8,500
MAP: SEE MONTREAL

This Mohawk reservation of Kahnawake, also called Caughnawaga, is situated on the southern shore of the St. Lawrence River, near Montreal. The word 'Kahnawake' means "above the rapids" in the Mohawk language.

In 1668 Jesuit missionaries founded the Saint-François-Xavier Mission in La Prairie, which intended to convert the local native population to Catholicism. In 1717 the mission was moved to its current site in Kahnawake. Known for their amazing lack of vertigo, the Mohawks of Kahnawake have gained renown throughout North America for their expertise in tall construction projects, including skyscrapers. They often work on sites in the major cities of Canada and the US.

- **Information:** ☎450-466-4666 & 1-866-469-0069. www.kahnawake.com/ www.tourisme-monteregie.qc.ca.
- **Orient Yourself:** The Kahnawake reservation is located 10km/6.2mi southwest of Montreal by the Honoré-Mercier Bridge (Rte. 138). Take the first exit after crossing the bridge. The surface area of the reserve is approximately 5,059 hectares/12,501 acres.
- **Organizing Your Time:** The Kahnawake reservation is located just across the busy Mercier Bridge. Beware rush-hour traffic to and from Montreal.

Visit

Church and shrine

Open Jun–Sept, Mon–Fri 9am–5pm, weekends 10am–5pm; rest of the year Mon–Fri 9am–5pm. Contribution requested; $3 for a guided tour (⟶). ☎450-632-6030. www.ourkateri.com.

Built by the Jesuit priest, Félix Martin, the church contains the tomb and relics of Kateri Tekakwitha, *Lily of the Mohawks*, who was beatified by John Paul II. Inside, the small **museum** features displays on the young woman and the Mohawk way of life.

5 Nations Iroquois Site

Open year-round, daily 9am–5pm; guided tours by appointment in fall and winter. $10 (including guided tour). ☎450-632-6030. www.5nations.qc.ca.

The 5 Nations Iroquois Site provides a guided tour of an Amerindian 'long house' and an account of Iroquois myths and legends (by appointment only in fall and winter). This can be your chance to partake in traditional ritual dancing of North American Indians. The site includes a large Indian arts and crafts store.

Kateri Tekakwitha

Born in 1656 in Auriesville (in present-day New York State) of an Iroquois father and an Algonquin mother, Kateri Tekakwitha was orphaned at the age of four by a smallpox epidemic (a "European disease" unknown to Indians) that killed h parents and left her nearly blind. She was adopted by her uncle and named Te witha, meaning "one who moves with hesitation." In 1676 she was baptized Jesuits and named for St. Catherine of Siena (Kateri). Ill-treated in New fled to the Mission of Saint-François-Xavier in 1677 and died three ye the age of 24. At the tricentennial of her death in 1980, she became t of Amerindian origin to be beatified by the Roman Catholic Church

KAMOURASKA★

BAS-SAINT-LAURENT
POPULATION 701
MAP: SEE CÔTE DE CHARLEVOIX

The seigneury of Kamouraska (which means "where rushes grow by the water's edge" in the Algonquian language) was granted to Olivier Morel de la Durantaye in 1674 by Louis de Buade, Comte de Frontenac, governor of New France. The first settlers arrived the following year and by the 18C, Kamouraska was one of the largest communities in the Bas-Saint-Laurent (Lower St. Lawrence) region. Since the 19C grain, potato, and dairy farming have constituted the town's principal economic activity.

The term "**Kamouraska roof**" refers to the curved overhanging eaves, a local architectural feature of many of the houses throughout the region. The design, which first appeared on several public buildings (including the church at Saint-Jean-Port-Joli), seems to add height to the ground floor, which otherwise appears crushed by the heavy roof.

- **Information:** ☎418-867-3015 & 1-800-563-5268. www.kamouraska.com.
- ▶ **Orient Yourself:** Kamouraska is located 163km/101mi northeast of Quebec City by Rte.73 (Pierre-Laporte Bridge) and Rte. 20 (Exit 465).
- **Don't Miss:** Kamouraska Salt and Marsh Ecological Center.
- **Organizing Your Time:** Make sure to admire the sunset on the St. Lawrence River.

Sights

Musée régional de Kamouraska (Kamouraska Regional Museum)

69 Ave. Morel (Place de l'Église). Behind the church in the town center. ○*Open Jun–Thanksgiving, 9am–5pm; Thanksgiving–* *Dec 21, Tue–Fri 9am–5pm, Sat–Sun 1pm–4.30pm.* ⊛*$5.* ✕ P ☎*418-492-9783.*

The edifice containing the museum was built as a convent in 1851. Devoted to the cultural history of the Kamouraska region, the museum displays household items and furniture typical of the homes and lifestyles of the early European set-

© Guy Dagenais

s. Farm implements and craftsmen's ~ols illustrate the working conditions of the community's forefathers. A large collection of fishing tackle and models demonstrating eel fishing techniques emphasizes the crucial role the St. Lawrence played in the lives of local residents. The museum also houses an altar, carved in 1737 by François-Noël Levasseur for Kamouraska's second church (1727). The genealogy of the region is also explored.

Berceau de Kamouraska (Old Kamouraska)
3km/1.8mi east of town center, Rte. 132. The former heart of the village, now known as the "Kamouraska Cradle," was the location of the first two churches of the community (1709 and 1727) and the cemetery where 1,300 pioneers are buried. A simple, open-air chapel commemorates the spot.

Halte écologique des battures de Saint-André-de-Kamouraska (Kamouraska Salt and Marsh Ecological Center)
9km/5.6mi east of Old Kamouraska, 3km/1.8mi west of Saint-André; located

> ### How Do You fEEL?
> At the **Site d'Interprétation de l'Anguille de Kamouraska** (*205 Ave. Morel;* ☎*418-492-3935*), take a guided tour and discover the secrets of traditional eel fishing. End the experience by sampling a smoked version of the snakelike fish.

near the rest area on Rte. 132. ⏱*Open Jun 24–Labor Day, daily 8am–9pm; early May–Jun 23 & rest of Sept–late Oct, daily 10am–6pm.* ⬧*$3.* ⚠ ✗ 🅿 ☎*418-493-2604. www.sebka.ca.*
The interpretation center is designed to stimulate interest in and respect for the marsh and river ecozystems. Experienced guides lead organized activities related to ecological themes, including plant and animal life in the marsh, beluga whales, peregrine falcons, and other birds. A trail (6km/3.7mi) leads to the salt marsh (*batture* in French), and on to a rocky promontory equipped with scenic belvederes and bird-watching stations.

LA BAIE
SAGUENAY–LAC-SAINT-JEAN REGION
POPULATION OF VILLE DE SAGUENAY146,332
MAP: SEE FJORD DU SAGUENAY

This industrial center occupies a magnificent **site**★ on an inlet of the Saguenay Fjord, popularly known as Baie des Ha! Ha!. According to local legend, the bay was originally named after Rue des Ha! Ha!, a one-way street in 17C Paris. Another story has it that early explorers of the area, mistaking the bay for a river, sailed up it as though it would lead them inland, and named it for the cries of laughter that erupted once they had discovered their folly. In the summer months, the region's history is brought to life through the pageantry of **La fabuleuse histoire d'un royaume** (The Fabulous Story of a Kingdom, as Saguenay is said to be "a kingdom"). You can also catch a glimpse of salmon swimming upstream at the passe migratoire (fish ladder) on the Rivière-à-Mars located in the middle of the city.

🛈 **Information:** 3205 Boul. de la Grande-Baie Sud. ☎418-698-3167 & 1-800-463-6565. www.bleuvacances.ca/www.saguenay.worldweb.com/LaBaie.

▶ **Orient Yourself:** La Baie is 212km/131.7mi north of Quebec City by Rtes.17* and 170. It is 20km/12.4mi southeast of Chicoutimi by Rte. 372.

⏱ **Organizing Your Time:** Visit the Fjord Museum, then stop at the tourism next door to get information about current seasonal activities.

Kids **Especially for Kids:** The Site de la Nouvelle-France.

La Pyramide des Ha! Ha!

Don't miss **La Pyramide des Ha! Ha! at the Parc des Ha! Ha!** (*Rue Monseigneur-Dufour;* ☎*418-697-5077*). Conceived by the artist Jean-Jules Soucy, this 21m/69ft-high aluminum pyramid with a 24m/78.7ft base is covered with some 3,000 red and white triangular traffic yield signs and serves as a stage and an observation point.

A Bit of History

Arriving in 1838, the first settlers were members of a group called the **Society of Twenty-One** (Société des Vingt-et-Un), whose aim was to settle the Saguenay–Lac-Saint-Jean region. They created three villages at the site of present-day La Baie: Bagotville, Port-Alfred, and Grande-Baie. La Baie was formed by the merger of these communities in 1976. Then, in February 2002, La Baie was merged with the cities of Chicoutimi, Jonquière, and Laterrière to create a new city named Ville de Saguenay.

La Baie quickly grew into a forestry center and today boasts a large pulp mill. The city's greatest asset, however, is its extensive port, which serves the large bulk carriers transporting bauxite from the Caribbean and South America to supply the aluminum smelters in the region.

Address Book

🖖 *For price ranges, see the Legend on the cover flap.*

WHERE TO STAY

$$ Auberge de la Grande-Baie – *4715 Blvd de la Grande-Baie.* ☎*418-544-9334. www.aubergegb.com.* ✗♿🅿*41 rooms.* Very pleasant, just outside town. Good dining, too.

$$$$ Auberge des 21 – *621 Rue Mars.*☎*418-697-2121. www.aubergedes21.com.* ✗♿🅿*30 rooms.* ⚑**French**. Excellent, lavish auberge. **Le Doyen** restaurant is one of the most renowned "tables régionales" ...ebec.

Sights

Scenic drive

Just before Rte. 372 begins its descent to the Mars River in Ha! Ha! Bay, a lookout provides an excellent **view**★★ of the bay. On clear days, the panorama can extend some 48km/29.8mi. Farther on, Rte. 372 joins Rte. 170, which skirts the bay and offers several lovely vistas along a 12km/7.4mi stretch.

Parc Mars (Mars Park)

At the junction of Rte. 170 (Rue Bagot) and Rte. 372 (Blvd. Saint-Jean-Baptiste), continue on Rue Bagot and turn left on Rue Mars.

This waterfront park offers superb **views**★ of the bay and its surrounding hills, as well as of the impressive shipping facilities. About 200,000 tons of newsprint and lumber and more than 3 million tons of bauxite pass through the port annually.

Musée du Fjord (Fjord Museum)

3346 Blvd. de la Grande-Baie Sud (Rte. 170). ◷*Open late Jun–Labor Day, daily 9am–6pm; rest of the year, Tue–Fri 9am–4.30pm, weekends 1pm–5pm.* ☞*$10.* ♿🅿☎*418-697-5077. www.museedufjord.com*

This museum offers science, history, and art exhibits relating to the Saguenay region, the province of Quebec, and Canada.

Excursion

Saint-Félix-d'Otis

43km/26.7mi east of La Baie.

In summer, the **Site de la Nouvelle-France** (*370 Vieux Chemin;* 🧒◷*open early Jun–mid-Aug, Tue–Sun; mid–end Aug, Thu–Sun;* ⚑*guided tours (1.5hr) 9.30am, 3.30pm;* ☞*$15; children $7;* ☎*418-544-8027; www.sitenouvellefrance.com*) invites visitors to relive history in the reconstructed buildings of the French Regime. A small Huron village, a Montagnais camp, and an Old French country house and its *dépendances* (small farm) allow you to experience the customs and habits of the Amerindians and the first settlers.

LA MALBAIE★

CHARLEVOIX REGION
POPULATION 9,121
MAP: SEE CÔTE DE CHARLEVOIX

La Malbaie enjoys a beautiful **site**★ on the north shore of the St. Lawrence at the mouth of the Malbaie River. The three districts of La Malbaie hug the shores of the bay: Pointe-au-Pic, Cap-à-l'Aigle and Rivière-Malbaie. A golf course is laid out along an escarpment at the south entrance to Pointe-au-Pic. Winter activities include skiing at the Mont-Grand-Fonds center nearby.

- **Information:** 495 Blvd. de Comporté. ☎418-665-4454 & 1-800-667-2276. www.charlevoixtourisme.com.
- **Orient Yourself:** La Malbaie–Pointe-au-Pic is about 140km/87mi northeast of Quebec City by Rte. 138. The latter forms Blvd. de Comporté, which becomes Rue Principale in Pointe-au-Pic.
- **Don't Miss:** Pointe-au-Pic, craddle of Canada's tourism industry, or the Charlevoix Casino housed in the stately Fairmont Le Manoir Richelieu, overlooking the river.
- **Organizing Your Time:** The best way to see the Hautes-Gorges-de-la-rivière-Malbaie is from the water: The summer dusk cruise offers the most interesting light, calmest water, and best time to see animals.
- **Especially for Kids:** A trip to Fraser Falls.

A Bit of History

Samuel Champlain dubbed this place *malle baye* (bad bay) in 1608, when he anchored his ships here only to discover, the following day, that they had run aground. After the Conquest, the land surrounding the bay was granted to two Scots, Malcolm Fraser and John Nairn. They called it **Murray Bay** in honor of General James Murray, chief administrator of the colony, and welcomed many visitors to the area. The most famous of the hotels that gradually replaced the hospitality of the local seigneurs is the **Richelieu Manor** (*Manoir Richelieu; access by Rte. 362 and Chemin des Falaises*), a vast, picturesque,

Hautes-Gorges-de-la-rivière-Malbaie Provincial Park

Château-style edifice overlooking the St. Lawrence. Near the hotel, which was rebuilt in 1929 after a fire, stands a second building (1930) housing the **Charlevoix Casino**.

Sights

Vacation Villas

Most of the villas and summer residences on the two hillsides surrounding La Malbaie were built between 1880 and 1945. The influence of the "Shingle" style of architecture popular along the Atlantic Coast of the US can be seen in the cedar-shingled dwellings. Vacationers visiting the region for hunting and fishing came to appreciate the rustic character of the sober interiors and simple furnishings that local architect, Jean-Charles Warren (1868–1929) designed. Warren erected about 60 of these grand villas, initiating a "Laurentian" style that integrated buildings into their surroundings by using local materials and positioning the structure to take the fullest advantage of the magnificent scenery.

Musée de Charlevoix (Charlevoix Museum)

10 Chemin du Havre. ⏱Open Jun–late Sept, 9am–5pm; rest of the year, Mon–Fri 10am–5pm, weekends 1pm–5pm. ➤$5. ♿🅿☎418-665-4411. www.museed echarlevoix.qc.ca.

Paintings, sculptures and textiles in the permanent collection provide an understanding of local Charlevoix art, heritage, and history. The museum also presents changing exhibits on various themes. The rotunda affords an impressive view of the surroundings.

Excursions

Chutes Fraser (Fraser Falls)　Kids

In Rivière-Malbaie, about 3km/1.8mi. After the bridge over the Malbaie River, turn left and take Chemin de la Vallée for 1.5km/1mi, then turn right following signs for the campground. ⏱Open mid-May–mid-Oct, daily 8am–10pm. ➤$5. ⚠✗🅿☎418-665-2151. www.campingchutesfraser.com.

These falls on the Comporté River are set in a pleasant area. The river drops about 30m/98.4ft forming a lacelike pattern across the rocky ledges. In the spring, or after a rainfall, the Fraser Falls can be spectacular.

Parc provincial des Hautes-Gorges-de-la-rivière-Malbaie★ (Provincial Park of the High Gorges of the Malbaie River)

Take Rte. 138 and turn left toward Saint-Aimé-des-Lacs. Continue 35km/21.7mi. ⏱Park open year-round. Visitor Center open late May–mid-Oct, daily 7am–9pm. ⚠✗🅿☎800-665-6527 or 418-439-1227. www.sepaq.com.

The mountains in this spectacular park rise more than 1,000m/3,280ft, dominating the high gorges of the Malbaie River and the valley of the Martres River. A **cruise** leads to the steep-sided gorges of the Malbaie River (departs from the wharf at the end of the dirt road mid-Jun–mid-Oct, 11am, 1pm, 2.45pm; Jun 23–Labor Day, additional 4.30pm & 6.30pm cruises; round-trip 1hr 30min; commentary; ♿reservations required; ➤$34; ♿🅿☎418-439-1227; www.sepaq.com).

LA POCATIÈRE★

Birthplace of agricultural education in Canada, La Pocatière is situated on a terrace above the coastal plain. Various research is carried out here, particularly in agroalimentary studies, continuing the city's vocation as an educational center. The industrial sector is dominated by the Bombardier factory, renowned for its world famous snowmobiles and rail transportation equipment.

- **Information:** ☎418-856-5040 &1-888-856-5040. www.bas-saint-laurent.gouv.qc.ca/www.basstlaurent-travelguide.com.
- ▶ **Orient Yourself:** La Pocatière is 131km/81.4mi northeast of Quebec City by Rte.73 (Pierre-Laporte Bridge) and Rte. 20 (Exit 439).
- **Don't Miss:** Musée François-Pilote or Seigneurie des Aulnaies in Saint-Roch-des-Aulnaies.
- **Especially for Kids:** The Lumberjack life exhibit at Musée François-Pilote.

Sight

Musée François-Pilote★ (François Pilote Museum)

10km/6.2mi east of Saint-Roch-des-Aulnaies, turn right off Rte. 132. At the top of the hill, turn right and immediately turn right again into the parking lot of the Collège de Sainte-Anne. The museum is situated behind the school. Entrance on the second floor. ©*Open May–Sept, Mon–Sat 9am–noon, 1pm–5pm, Sun 1pm–5pm; rest of the year, Mon–Fri 9am–noon, 1pm–5pm, Sun 1pm–5pm.* ⊚*$4.* ▯ ☎418-856-3145.

This museum of Quebec ethnology centers on rural life in the province at the turn of the 19C. The museum is named after François Pilote, who founded the first permanent school of agriculture in Canada in 1859.

Yesteryear

First floor. The exhibit covers the history of maple sugar-making, with a reconstructed sap house; a vast collection of vehicles, including sleighs, horse-drawn buggies, and motorcars; trade implements used by lumberjacks, carpenters, blacksmiths, shoemakers, and weavers; and numerous farm tools. A second exhibit on coastal navigation from the mid-18C through the mid-19C contains model ships and nautical instruments.

At that time, goods were transported by small schooners called *goélettes.*

Natural Sciences

Second floor. Experience the history of the evolution of agriculture from the time of Champlain, to the future. In the adjoining rooms, Canadian mammals, seashells, firearms, and religious objects are on display.

Family Life

Third floor. Three rooms (living room, dining room, and bedroom) re-create the comforts of an upper class family in the 1920s, while a variety of household items in seven rooms reflect the lifestyle of a farming family in Quebec around 1900. A rural schoolroom, a general and a jewelry store, and professional offices of a country doctor, a dentist, and a notary complete the exhibit.

Education

Fourth floor. This floor features a presentation on the history of agricultural education in Quebec and education in general. It includes exhibits on breeding, aviculture, biology, and zoology as well as chemistry, physics, astronomy and fisheries. Also on view is a soil laboratory and the magnificent Tanguay collection of 400 mounted birds, in some 200 different species, native to Quebec.

LA PRAIRIE

MONTÉRÉGIE REGION
POPULATION 21,609
MAP: SEE MONTREAL

Located on the southern shore of the St. Lawrence, this community is today a residential suburb of Montreal. In 1647 the seigneury of "La Prairie de la Magdelaine" was granted to Jesuit missionaries eager to convert the local Amerindians. However, the Iroquois wars delayed colonization for over 20 years. The first settlers protected themselves by erecting a wooden palisade around their settlement. In 1691 they were attacked by British forces from New England led by John Schuyler, a commander from Albany. The settlers won the battle, which left over 100 soldiers dead on both sides.

Iroquois hostilities ended with the Great Peace of Montreal treaty in 1701, and the area enjoyed a period of rapid development during the first half of the 18C. After the Conquest, English merchants developed transportation and travel routes. In 1836, rivers and roads were supplemented by Canada's first railway, built by the Champlain and St. Lawrence Railroad Co., which ran from La Prairie to Saint-Jean-sur-Richelieu (☞ *see ST-JEAN-SUR-RICHELIEU*). The railroad company's major shareholder was the famous financier and brewer, John Molson. Several brickyards, still ranking among the largest in Canada, were established in the 1890s.

▯ **Information:** ☎1-866-469-0069. www.ville.tourisme-monteregie.qc.ca.
▸ **Orient Yourself:** La Prairie is 18.4km/11.4mi southeast of Montreal by the Champlain Bridge and Rte. 15 Sud (Exit 46). To reach the old section, take Rue de Salaberry to Blvd. Taschereau (Rte. 134), turn left (north) as far as Chemin Saint-Jean (Rte. 104) and turn left again.

Vieux-La Prairie (Old Town)

The devastating fires of 1846 and 1901 destroyed most of the old buildings in the historic district known as Vieux-La Prairie. A few interesting buildings remain, most built of sandstone and reminiscent of the beginnings of English Classicism (*no. 120 Chemin de Saint-Jean and no. 166 Rue Saint-Georges*). At least two buildings (*no. 115 and 150 Chemin de Saint-Jean*) illustrate the urban architectural style developed in New France. Most of the remaining buildings in the historic district are wood structures, typically found in the suburbs of Montreal at the beginning of the 19C (*nos. 34, 238 and 240 Rue Saint-Ignace*).

...se de la Nativité (Church of ...irth of the Virgin Mary)

... Saint-Jean. ⏲ Open year-round, ...–5pm; for additional hours, call ▯ ☎450-659-1133.

The church (1841) dominates the old village, locally called Vieux-Fort (old fort). The monumental Neoclassical façade, topped by a slender spire, has become the symbol of La Prairie. Two sets of colonnades and a domed bell tower recall Montreal's old Catholic cathedral. The interior, inspired by the Church of Saint Martin-in-the-Fields, displays Neoclassical symmetry.

Musée du Vieux-Marché (Old Market Museum)

249 Rue Sainte-Marie. ⏲*Open Jun–lat-Aug, Mon–Fri 9am–5pm, weekends 11am–5pm; rest of the year, Tue, Wed, Fri 9am–5pm.* ♿ ⓟ ☎*450-659-1393.*
Originally a market, this brick structure (1863) also served as a police and fire station. The building houses the Historical Society of La Prairie de la Magdelaine, proud to display the city's archives and exhibits tracing the history of the old town in the **Musée du Vieux-Marché**.

Réserve faunique
LA VÉRENDRYE

OUTAOUAIS–ABITIBI REGION

Named for Pierre Gaultier de Varennes, **Sieur de la Vérendrye**, the famed explorer of the Rocky Mountains, this reserve (13,615sq km/5,257sq mi) was created in 1939 and is a favorite with nature lovers in search of adventure or tranquillity. The many lakes and watercourses that feed the Outaouais and Gatineau Rivers provide a habitat for more than 150 species of birds, and fish such as pike, walleye, bass, lake trout, and speckled trout. A variety of mammals, notably moose, bear, deer, beaver, and fox, roam the vast coniferous forests covering the territory.

Information: ☎819-438-2017 & 1-800-665-6527. www.sepaq.com.

Orient Yourself: The reserve is about 300km/186.4mi northwest of Montreal by Rte. 15 and Rte. 117. Its northern entrance is 54km/33.5mi from Val-d'Or. There are campsites, cabins, and a lodge for visitors inside park limits.

Organizing Your Time: The Réserve faunique de la Vérendrye is situated between the Abitibi and Laurentians regions, so it makes sense to plan a trip to the park as you drive from one region to another.

Visit

Registration centers open late May–Oct, daily 8am–4pm. △ ¾ ♿ 🅿 ☎819-438-2017. www.sepaq.com.

Route 117
The main road traversing the reserve (*180km/111.8mi*) affords pleasant views of the many rivers and lakes found throughout the park. **Lake Jean-Péré** is one of the park's main attractions and the starting point for various canoe excursions. The route passes by the Cabonga Reservoir and the Dozois Reservoir, controlling the flow of the Gatineau and Outaouais rivers respectively, before crossing the dam that straddles the latter river.

ACTIVITIES
Approximately 800km/497mi of canoe circuits are available, complete with wilderness campsites and portage routes. The most popular place to begin is Lake Jean-Péré, which offers some relatively easy excursions for beginners. Canoes and small fishing boats are available for rent.

© Deschênes/ Sépaq

Summer fun in Réserve faunique La Vérendrye

LAC-BOUCHETTE

SAGUENAY–LAC-SAINT-JEAN
POPULATION 1,332
MAP: SEE SAINT-JEAN

This small community nestled between La Tuque and Lake Saint-Jean was founded in 1890. It is named in honour of Joseph Bouchette, an engineer and land surveyor who mapped this area in 1820.

🛈 **Information:** ☎1-800-253-8387. www.bleuvacances.ca.

▶ **Orient Yourself:** Lac-Bouchette is 218km/135.4mi north of Quebec City, and 25km/15mi south of Chambord on Lake Saint-Jean by Rte. 155.

◈ **Don't Miss:** St. Anthony's Hermitage.

🕐 **Organizing Your Time:** Lac Bouchette is a pleasant stop between Trois-Rivières and Lac Saint-Jean. Route 155 winds constantly; there are literally hundreds of curves on that road, and a constant flow of large, heavy trucks. So drive carefully and prepare for the fact that this not an expressway.

Pilgrimage Center – Lac-Bouchette is most famous for its shrine founded in 1907 by the abbot **Elzéar Delamarre** (1854–1925), Superior of the Chicoutimi Seminary. Father Delamarre spent his summers in the region, eventually building a summer retreat and a chapel near Lake Bouchette. In 1916 he discovered a natural grotto resembling the Massabielle grotto at Lourdes, France. Before his death, many pilgrims had made the trek to the grotto. Today this former summer retreat is owned by the Capuchin Brothers, and is visited by more than 200,000 faithful every year.

Sight

Ermitage Saint-Antoine★ (St. Anthony's Hermitage)

2km/1.2mi west of Rte. 155 across Lakes Ouiatchouan and Bouchette. 🕐*Open year-round daily 7.30am–11pm.* ⚠✕♿ 🅿☎*418-348-6344. www.st-antoine.org* The red brick monastery of the Capuchin Brothers, built in 1924, dominates the site.

First chapel
The first chapel built by Father Delamarre in 1907 was dedicated to St. Anthony of Padua. After discovering a grotto similar to the one in Lourdes, Delamarre expanded the chapel and dedicated it to Our Lady of Lourdes. This later chapel has a Gothic Revival interior, embellished with arches and fan vaulting. The earlier chapel, now a side aisle, contains the tomb of Father Delamarre. The walls of the modest chapel are decorated with a group of 23 **paintings**★ representing the life and miracles of St. Anthony, executed between 1908 and 1920 by Charles Huot (1855–1930).

Marian chapel
Built in 1950, this modern chapel resembles a grotto. The stained-glass windows (1971) were designed by Guy Bruneau. The large one at the back represents Bernadette Soubirous kneeling before Our Lady of Lourdes.

Chapel grounds
Steps lead from the Marian Chapel to the grotto discovered by Father Delamarre in 1916. Nearby stand an open-air chapel overlooking the lake, and a copy of the Holy Steps of Rome; a path leads up the hillside to the 14 Stations of the Cross, sculpted in stone.

LACHINE

MONTREAL REGION
POPULATION OF MONTREAL 1,620,693
MAP: SEE MONTREAL

Today a part of the Pôle des rapides tourism district of Montreal, Lachine has a rich history that is closely linked to the development of the French colony and to the commercial and industrial evolution of the province. In 1667 Robert Cavelier de La Salle was granted a seigneury by the Sulpicians at the point where the St. Lawrence empties into Lake Saint-Louis. As La Salle was forever in search of the elusive "passage" to the East, his seigneury was facetiously nicknamed 'La Chine' (French for China).

Lachine soon became an outpost for the city of Ville-Marie, the original French name of Montreal (The Amerindian name of Montreal was Hochelaga). On August 4, 1689, the community was the site of a brutal massacre. About 1,500 Iroquois attacked and burned the village to the ground, killing over 200 people. Another 100 were taken prisoner. The massacre is thought to have been an act of revenge for the execution of several Iroquois chiefs that had been ordered by the governor of the colony two years earlier.

Lachine became a borough of the city of Montreal in January 2006.

- **Information:** ☎514-364-4490 & 1-877-266-5687. www.poledesrapides.com.
- **Orient Yourself:** Lachine is about 19km/11.8mi southwest of downtown Montreal by Rue Wellington and Blvd. LaSalle. The borough can also be reached by Rte. 20 Ouest. Visitors can take a bicycle on the metro from Montreal (weekends only), disembark at ⏱*Lionel-Groulx,* and ride along the canal.
- **Parking:** Metered street parking (🚗*watch days and times*); parking lots (👓*fees*).
- **Organizing Your Time:** Consider cycling along the Lachine canal: The cycle path runs along the full length of the old canal, with lots of places to stop to eat and green spaces to enjoy. Have lunch at the Lac Saint-Louis end, and explore the canal interpretation center and fur trade historical site. During summer there are frequent guided tours and special activities at the site.
- **Especially for Kids:** A jet boat excursion on the Lachine Rapids.

Sights

Lachine Rapids and Canal★

Beyond Lake Saint-Louis, the level of the St. Lawrence drops 2m/6.5ft over a distance of 2km/1.2mi. In 1603, from the top of Mt. Royal, Champlain had noted the existence of "the most impetuous rapids one is likely to see."These impressive rapids presented a considerable obstacle to the various explorers wishing to travel up river.

As early as 1680, Dollier de Casson, superior of the Saint-Sulpice seminary, proposed the construction of a canal to bypass the rapids. The project was not undertaken, however, until 1821. Completed in 1824, the 13.6km/8.5mi channel linked Lake Saint-Louis and the Port of Montreal; seven locks raised ships a total of 14m/49ft. The canal was enlarged twice, from 1843 to 1849 and from 1873 to 1884. It remained the only passage around the rapids until the opening of the St. Lawrence Seaway in 1959.

No longer used for travel, the canal today forms a recreational corridor about 15km/9.3mi long. A pleasant bike path borders the old docks of Montreal and Verdun and connects the Old Port to Lachine. In winter it becomes a trail for cross-country skiers.

The rapids are visible from the Boulevard LaSalle in the borough of LaSalle. Jet boats departing from the Old Port in Montreal offer heart-pounding **excursions**★★ (Kids) down this tumultuous stretch of the river.

Musée de Lachine (Lachine Museum)

On Blvd. LaSalle, turn left before crossing the canal. Angringon; bus 110. ⏰*Open late Apr–mid-Dec, Wed–Sun 11.30am–4.30pm.* 🅿 ☎514-634-3478.

This museum is set around an old stone house built from 1669–1685 by Charles Le Moyne and Jacques Le Ber, two of the first merchants to settle in Lachine. The house is now known as the Maison Le Ber-Le Moyne. Displays of period furniture and tools complement the exhibits on historical themes and handicrafts. An adjacent modern structure, called Benoît-Verdickt Pavillon, houses furniture dating from the 1850s to the present, as well as traveling contemporary art exhibits.

Outside the museum, the church in Kahnawake can be seen across the lake.

Parc René-Lévesque (René Lévesque Park)

From Blvd. LaSalle, turn left onto Chemin du Canal.

Formerly called Grande-Jetée, this park is situated on a peninsula jutting out into Lake Saint-Louis. The peninsula was built up on land reclaimed from the river between 1873 and 1884 to shelter the third entrance to the Lachine Canal. The park was renamed after René Lévesque (1922–1987), premier of Quebec from 1976 through 1985. Foot and cycle paths lead to the tip of the peninsula past 12 pieces of contemporary sculpture created for various symposia held every two years in the borough's parks. Note in particular Georges Dyens' work, *Les forces vives du Québec* (Quebec's Vital Forces), unveiled in 1988 to honor Lévesque.

The park affords views of the St. Lawrence as it leaves Lake Saint-Louis, of the borough of Lachine and, downstream, of the bridges spanning the river. A ferry operates between the tip of the peninsula and Saint Louis Park in summer.

Centre d'interprétation du canal de Lachine (Lachine Canal Interpretation Center)

711 Blvd. Saint-Joseph, on Monk Island, at end of 7ᵉ Ave. in Lachine. ⏻*Angrigngon, then bus 195.* ⏰*Site open daily sunrise–10pm; call for special activity times.* ♿🅿☎514-283-6054. www.pc.gc.ca/canalLachine.

The Pavillon Monk (1974), a small stone building serving as an interpretation center, exhibits photographs on the construction and history of the canal. In the canal's heyday, 15,000 ships a year passed through the locks, carrying wheat and wood. In the second half of the 19C, entrepreneurs eager to exploit the region's hydraulic power created the largest concentration of industry in Canada along its banks: Nail factories, flour mills, sawmills, and others.

Lachine Rapids Tours LTD

...g the Rapids: Jet Boat Excursion on Rapides de Lachine

Fur Trade at Lachine National Historic Site of Canada★

1255 Blvd. Saint-Joseph, across from 12ᵉ Ave. and from the Sainte-Anne College. Angrignon, then Bus 195 West. Open Apr–mid-Oct, daily 10am–12.30, 1pm–5pm (6pm weekends); mid-Oct–Nov, Wed–Sun 9.30am–noon, 12.30pm–5pm. $4. ✕ ♿ P ☎514-637-7433. www.pc.gc.ca/lhn-nhs/qc/lachine/default.asp.

This stone warehouse, used to store furs and trade goods from 1803 through 1859, contains an interesting and evocative display on Montreal's fur trade. Strolling among bundles of fur and boxes of merchandise, visitors can identify the different stages of the industry's history. On display are maps of the fur country showing the trading posts of both the North West Company and the Hudson's Bay Company. Before the North West Company merged with the Hudson's Bay in 1821, nearly 80 percent of the furs exported to Europe passed through Lachine.

Promenade Père-Marquette (Father Marquette Walk)

Main access on Blvd. Saint-Joseph, across from 18ᵉ Ave.

The walk along Lake Saint-Louis was named for Father Jacques Marquette (1637–1675), who discovered the Mississippi River with Louis Jolliet in 1673. It affords views of the Couvent des Sœurs de Sainte-Anne (Sisters of St. Anne Convent), who run the Sainte-Anne College (1861), across from the warehouse, and of the Église des Saints-Anges-Gardiens (Church of the Guardian Angels), erected in 1919.

Les Berges cycle path is a linear park that stretches for 21km/13mi along he banks of the St. Lawrence River. Bicycles are not the only way to enjoy nice views of the wide river and the Lachine Rapids: The Les Berges path is also open to rollerblades and walking shoes. In wintertime, try cross-country skiing here. Rest areas and heritage sites will provide relaxation and education to your outing.

LANAUDIÈRE

LANAUDIÈRE REGION
POPULATION 429,053
MAP: SEE LANAUDIÈRE

Located on the southern edge of the Canadian Shield, the Lanaudière region forms a corridor of fertile plains extending from the St. Lawrence in the south to Lake Taureau in the north, and from the Laurentians in the west to the Mauricie region in the east. One of the earliest areas to be colonized by the French, the region (one of Quebec's 17 administrative regions) takes its name from Marie-Charlotte de Lanaudière, daughter of the seigneur de Lavaltrie and wife of Barthélemy Joliette, who built several mills in the area and financed the construction of the first railway in the mid-19C.

The Lanaudière region provides a wealth of outdoor activities, from boating and hiking in summer to skiing and snowmobiling in winter. The international music festival of Lanaudière (see Calendar of Events), in Joliette, and the region agricultural exhibition in Berthierville attract visitors from far and wide.

- **Information:** ☎1-800-363-2788. www.lanaudiere.ca.
- ▶ **Orient Yourself:** The Lanaudière region extends northwest from th Lawrence River, from Montreal east to Berthierville, all the way to tian mountains (Lanaudière comprises a large part of Mont Tre
- **Don't Miss:** Sir Wilfrid Laurier National Historic Site.
- **Organizing Your Time:** Avoid driving from Montreal to La traffic periods. Make time to visit the Old Terrebonne wh
- **Especially for Kids:** Seven Falls of Saint-Zénon

Driving Tour

Circuit From Terrebonne
314km/195mi.

Terrebonne★ – See Entry Heading.

▷ *Take Rte. 125 to Rte. 25 and exit onto Rte. 640. At Exit 22 Est take Rte. 138 Est.*

Repentigny
23km/14.2mi.
Set on the banks of the St. Lawrence River at the confluence of the Prairies and Assomption rivers, this community of 76,237 inhabitants is named after Pierre Le Gardeur de Repentigny, who was granted the seigneury in 1647.
The strikingly modern **Église Notre-Dame-des-Champs**★ (*187 Blvd. Iberville; turn left from Rue Notre-Dame;* ○*open year-round, Mon–Thu 8.30am–9.30am, Fri 3pm–4.30pm, Sat 4.30pm–5pm, Sun 10am–noon;* ☎*450-654-5732*) was conceived in 1963 by Roger d'Astous, a former student of Frank Lloyd Wright. The building's curved walls resemble a tent, enclosing a harmonious interior space lit from a row of windows that punctuate the upper portions of the walls. A modern clock tower stands beside the covered walkway leading to the church. **Église de la Purification** (*Rue Notre-Dame between Rue Hôtel-de-Ville and Rue Brien;* ○*open Jun–mid-Aug, Mon–Fri 9am–4.30pm; rest of the year by appointment only;* �&☎*450-581-2484*), with its twin towers, was built in 1723 during the French Regime.

▷ *Take Rte. 138 (Chemin du Roy) towards the northeast and continue 1km/.6mi after the junction with Rte. 158.*

road hugs the St. Lawrence shore, ...ing numerous views of the wide ...estic river.

...es Cuthbert
...hapel)
...Open Jun–Labor Day,
P ☎*450-836-7336.*
...ier.org.

In 1765, Scottish-born James Cuthbert, aide-de-camp to General Wolfe, purchased the seigneury of Berthier. Cuthbert's wife, Catherine, is buried in this chapel, which he constructed in 1786 to perpetuate her memory. Dedicated to St. Andrew, the chapel served as the first Presbyterian place of worship for the area, and remained in use until 1856. It is the oldest Protestant chapel in Quebec.

▷ *Return to the junction and continue on Rte. 158 towards Joliette (westbound).*

Joliette★ – See Entry Heading.
27km/16.7mi.

▷ *From Saint-Charles-Borromée, continue north along Rue de la Visitation (Rte. 343) and turn right on Rte. 348, which follows the Assomption River (through Sainte-Mélanie) until the junction with Rte. 131 (28km/17.4mi). Continue on Rte. 131 towards Sainte-Émélie-de-l'Énergie (29km/18mi).*

As the countryside becomes more mountainous, Route 131 enters the narrow **Noire River valley**★. The road crisscrosses the dark and shallow river, punctuated with splendid cascades.

Sept-Chutes de Saint-Zénon★ (Seven Falls of Saint-Zénon)
20km/12.4mi from Sainte-Émélie-de-l'Énergie. In Parc régional des Sept-Chutes, 4031 Chemin Brassard Sud (Rte. 131). ○*Open May–Nov, daily 9am–5pm.* ☎*$5.* P☎*450-884-0484 & 1-800-264-5441. www.matawinie.org.*
Only one of the cascades, the "Bridal Veil" (Voile de la mariée), is accessible. Though spectacular during the spring thaw, the 60m/197ft-high cascade dries up in summer.
Sturdy wooden steps lead to the top of the falls and continue to Lake Guy. From there, the trail meanders through birch trees and moss-covered rocks to hidden cascades and, a little farther, vast and peaceful Lake Rémi (*15min from Lake Guy*). Across the lake, an impressive cliff rises abruptly out of the water.

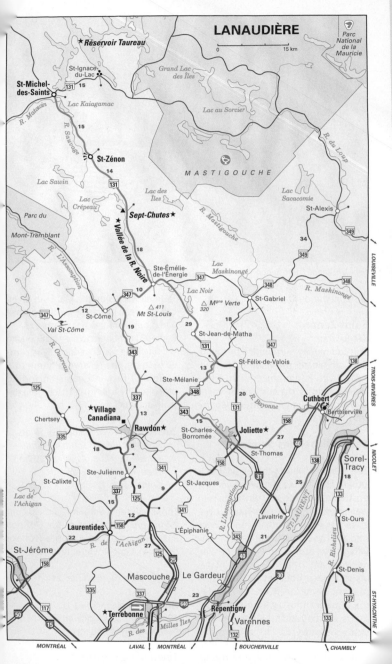

LANAUDIÈRE

Parc National de la Mauricie

★ Réservoir Taureau

0   15 km

St-Ignace-du-Lac

St-Michel-des-Saints 131 15

Lac Kaiagamac

Grand Lac des Îles

Lac au Sorcier

R. Matawin

R. Sauvage

15 St-Zénon 131

14

R. du Loup

Lac Sawin

Lac Crépeau 131

MASTIGOUCHE

Lac des Îles

Lac Sacacomie

Parc du Mont-Tremblant

R. L'Assomption

▲ Sept-Chutes ★

Vallée de la R. Noire

18

R. Mastigouche

St-Alexis 349

Ste-Émélie-de-l'Énergie 347

Lac Maskinongé

34

349

348 348

R. Maskinongé

LOUISEVILLE

347 10

Lac Noir

Mᵍⁿᵉ Verte 320

St-Gabriel

12 St-Côme

▲ 411 Mt St-Louis

Val St-Côme

19

29

18

347

R. Ouareau

343

St-Jean-de-Matha 131

St-Félix-de-Valois 347

138

TROIS-RIVIÈRES

125

★ Village Canadiana

337 13

Rawdon ★

13

Ste-Mélanie 348

343

20

R. Bayonne

131

Cuthbert

Berthierville

158

Chertsey 335

5

St-Charles-Borromée

15

Joliette ★ 27

158

NICOLET

18 Ste-Julienne

5

341

St-Thomas 158

40

138

Sorel-Tracy 18

St-Calixte

337 9

125 9

St-Jacques 341

31

25

133

Lac de l'Achigan

15

12

L'Assomption

St-Ours

Laurentides 158

22

R. de l'Achigan 27

125 25

L'Épiphanie

343

Lavaltrie

21

ST-LAURENT

R. Richelieu

12

St-Denis

St-Jérôme 158

Mascouche 335 337

Le Gardeur

23

40

30

137

★ Terrebonne

640

Repentigny

Varennes

133

50 117 15

R. des Milles Îles

132

ST-HYACINTHE

MONTRÉAL   LAVAL │ MONTRÉAL /   │ BOUCHERVILLE   \ CHAMBLY

Those eager to embark on a longer hike should return to Lake Guy and follow the Mont Brassard circuit, which leads the visitor to a lookout, at an altitude of 150m/492ft, offering a wonderful **view**★ of the U-shaped valley of the Noire River to the south. The trail continues through a lush fore[st] birch and pine trees. Before reachi[ng] steep descent to the cascades, th[e] Brassard belvedere offers an [...] **view** of Lake Rémi and the [...] to the west.

Sept-Chutes de Saint-Zénon

▶ *Continue on Rte. 131 Nord.*

Saint-Zénon
14km/8.7mi.
This community, surrounded by mountains, dominates the valley of the Sauvage River. Beside the church, a fine **view** extends to the north of the valley known as the Nymph's Corridor (*Coulée des nymphes*).

Saint-Michel-des-Saints
15km/9.3mi.
The village of Saint-Michel-des-Saints is situated beside the Matawin River, just upstream from the spot where its wild waters empty into the calm Taureau Reservoir. Founded by Father Léandre Brassard and two colleagues in 1862, the tiny village was at that time 80km/49.7mi north of any other inhabited place. Msgr. Ignace Bourget bestowed its present name on it in 1883. Today the lumber industry, tourism, water sports, hunting and fishing support the local economy.

éservoir Taureau★ (Lake Taureau)
ed Lac Toro by native Attikamek, this
reservoir has a circumference of
700km/435mi. It was created in
control water flow in the Saint-
er and supply the power sta-
igan. The dam creating the
he former location of the

Taureau Rapids on the Matawin River. Lake Taureau has many sandy beaches and is popular for water sports.
Route 131 continues to the Mastigouche Wildlife Reserve. Covering 1,574sq km/607.7sq mi, the reserve is home to a variety of fish and game, including brook trout. Hunting and fishing are the main activities.

▶ *Return to Saint-Michel-des-Saints and take Rte. 131 south to Sainte-Émélie-de-l'Énergie (47km/29.2mi), then Rte. 347 west towards Saint-Côme.*

The ski center at Val Saint-Côme (*12km/7.4mi from intersection of Rtes. 347 and 343*), with more than 20 slopes, is one of the area's largest winter resorts.

▶ *Continue south on Rte. 343.*

Rawdon★
89km/55.3mi south of Saint-Michel.
See Entry Heading.

Town of Laurentides
25km/15.5mi by Rte. 337.
Also known as Saint-Lin-des-Laurentides, this small industrial and commercial town was the birthplace of Sir Wilfrid Laurier (1841-1919), lawyer, politician and prime minister of Canada from 1896 to 1911.

Lieu historique national du Canada de Sir-Wilfrid-Laurier (Sir Wilfrid Laurier National Historic Site of Canada)

Corner of 12e Ave. (Rte. 158) and Rte. 337. ⟶Visit by guided tour (1hr) only; early May–mid-Jun, Mon–Fri 9am–5pm; May–mid-Jun, Mon–Fri 9am–5pm; mid-Jun–Labor Day, daily 9am–5pm. ⟜$4. ♿🅿☎450-439-3702 & 1-800-463-6769. www.pc.gc.ca/laurier.

The interpretation center here exhibits displays on the former prime minister's life and the important role he played in Canadian politics. The simple brick house adjacent to the center is furnished to reflect life around 1850, when Laurier was a boy. And when Laurier's father was the mayor of Saint-Lin-des-Laurentides.

Seventh prime minister of Canada, Wilfrid Laurier is a key figure in Canadian history. He was the first French Canadian prime minister, and he his considered the father of a modern, bilingual, autonomous Canada that is playing a role in international affairs. Laurier encouraged immigration and the development of Western Canada.

LAURENTIDES★★

LAURENTIANS REGION
MAP: SEE LAURENTIDES

The Laurentian Mountains (the "Laurentians") extend across the province of Quebec from east to west. Formed more than one billion years ago in the Precambrian era, they are among the oldest mountains in the world and form part of the Canadian Shield, a vast plateau in the shape of a horseshoe which nearly encircles Hudson Bay. The range of low, rounded mountains rises to a maximum altitude of 968m/3,175ft at Mont Tremblant. To Montrealers, the Laurentians are a haven for recreational retreats; on weekends, city dwellers rush northward on Highway 15 to enjoy this vast summer and winter playground.

- **Information:** Maison du tourisme des Laurentides at the Porte du Nord, Exit 51 from Autoroute 15 Nord. ☎1-800-561-6673. www.laurentians.com.
- **Orient Yourself:** The Laurentides region extends north from the Ottawa River and Laval. Autoroute 15 takes you north from Montreal into the Laurentian Mountains, then becomes Rte. 117 extending northwest to Mont-Laurier. Rte. 344 follows the Ottawa River west towards Gatineau and Ottawa.
- **Organizing Your Time:** The roads going north can be very busy on weekends—especially during winter, but also during the fall colors. Mont Tremblant has become a very popular, all-season resort, and offers a wide range of activities for all ages and abilities.
- **Especially for Kids:** A stroll in the Parc linéaire du P'tit Train du nord.

A Bit of History

Few people inhabited this area before the arrival of the legendary **Father Antoine Labelle** (1833–1891). Deputy-minister of agriculture and colonization, Father Labelle devoted his entire life to persuading his fellow French Canadians to settle in the wilderness. He traveled by canoe and on foot to select sites for new settlements and was responsible for the establishment of more than 20 parishes in the Laurentians. Today many of these communities still bear the names of their parish saints, particularly in the area just north of Montreal. Thus the name **Valley of the Saints** has be given to the area beside the Nord where Saint-Jérôme, Saint-S Sainte-Adèle, and Sainte-A located.

Despite Father Labelle's e lish agriculture, farmi unprofitable in the ever, a new sourc during the 20C.

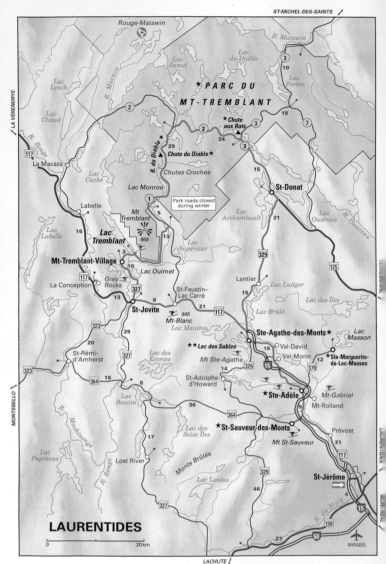

ST-MICHEL-DES-SAINTS

Rouge-Matawin

R. Matawin

Lac
du Diable

Lac
Jamet

Lac
Forbes

★ P A R C D U
MT - T R E M B L A N T

Lac
Lynch

Lac
Chaud

R. Macaza

2

★ Chute
aux Rats ▲

2

24

3

15

7

3

117

R. Rouge

LA VÉRENDRYE

29 ▲ ▲ Chute du Diable ★

R. du Diable

15

3

La Macaza

Chutes Croches

Lac
Caché

Lac Monroe

1

Park roads closed
during winter

St-Donat

Labelle

Lac
Labelle

16

Lac
Tremblant

Mt
Tremblant

968

5

13

Lac
Supérieur

Lac
Archambault

21

Lac
Ouareau

R. Ouareau

Mt-Tremblant-Village

3

10

Lac Ouimet

329

125

La Conception

Gray
Rocks

327

117

13

9

St-Faustin~
Lac Carré

Lantier

Lac Ludger

15

Lac des Îles

St-Jovite

21

117

Lac Brûlé

945
Mt-Blanc

Lac Manitou

Ste-Agathe-des-Monts ★

Lac
Masson

323

25

Lac des
Écorces

★★ Lac des Sables

18

Val-David

12

St-Rémi-
d'Amherst

327

Mt Ste-Agathe

329

Val-Morin

370

Ste-Marguerite-
du-Lac-Masson ★

20

323

364

15

8

St-Adolphe-
d'Howard

14

15

Ste-Adèle ★

Mt-Gabriel

Lac
Beavin

36

364

9

Mt-Rolland

Lost River

17

Lac des
Seize Îles

★ St-Sauveur-des-Monts

Prévost

Lac
Papineau

R. Rouge

Monts Brûlés

Mt St-Sauveur

21

117

Lac Louisa

329

St-Jérôme

46

4

15

LAURENTIDES

0   20 km

R. du Nord

158

27

50

LACHUTE

MIRABEL

MONTEBELLO

R. Mackinongé

LAURENTIDES

MONTREAL

population of Montreal began to retreat to the Laurentians in search of recreational activities.

...day boaters, swimmers, and anglers ...the many lakes of the region. The ...ding hills are the domain of the ...rseback riders and golfers. In ...veral renowned theaters ...rs to visitors. During the ...mountains display a ...re-red, orange, and

gold foliage. In winter, the area attracts downhill and cross-country skiers and offers a wide range of après-ski activities. The Laurentians have the highest concentration of alpine ski centers in North America. Small chalets and luxurious homes are nestled in the mountains and along lakesides. The region's principal resorts cater to an international clientele.

Driving Tour

From Saint-Jérôme to Saint-Donat *177km/110mi.*

Saint-Jérôme
51km/31.6mi from Montreal by Rte. 15 (Exit 43, Rue de Martigny Est).
Founded in 1830, this city grew rapidly, primarily through the efforts of Father Labelle. Known as the "Gateway to the Laurentians," it is an important administrative center located on a pleasant site beside Nord River (the St.-Anne du Nord River).

Cathédrale Saint-Jérome
355 Place du Curé-Labelle. Opens 30min before every mass; call for times. Contribution requested. ☎450-432-9741.
The long spires of this imposing stone church (1900) tower above the community of Saint-Jérôme. The rounded forms of its portico and pinnacles, and the monumental treatment of the décor are hallmarks of the Romano-Byzantine style. Inside, note the stained glass by D.A. Beaulieu of Montreal.
Across from the cathedral, a bronze **statue** of Father Labelle, by Alfred Laliberté, stands in a pleasant square. The former courthouse (palais de justice), on the north side of the square, has been converted into an exhibition center focusing on contemporary visual arts.

The Jackrabbit
The community of Prévost was for many years the home of **Hermann Johannsen**, better known by his sobriquet "Jackrabbit." This intrepid sportsman almost single-handedly introduced cross-country skiing to the Laurentians, laying out many trails by himself, including the famous Maple Leaf Trail that ran from Prévost to Mont Tremblant.

Promenade
Located between Rue de Martigny and Rue Saint-Joseph, this walk (*610m/667yd*) is lined with descriptive panels that recount the history of this community. The walkway also affords views of the Nord River.

▶ *From the center of Saint-Jérôme, take Rue de Martigny Est to Rte. 117 (Blvd. Labelle) and continue north.*

Traveling north, ski centers come into view from the highway. In 1932 the first ski tow was established in this vicinity. Skiers paid five cents to be hauled up the hill by a system of pulleys, rope and tackle, powered by an automobile engine.

▶ *Continue on Rte. 117 for 5km/3mi, then turn left on Rte. 364 and continue for 2km/1.2mi.*

Parc Linéaire le P'tit Train du Nord
Access – *Rte. 15 and/or Rte. 117 from St-Jérôme or any of the 23 towns and villages that lie along the park.* Open Dec–Apr for cross-country skiing and snowmobiling. $5/daily in winter (free in summer); May–Oct for hiking and cycling. ☎450-224-7007 & 1-800-561-6673. www.laurentians.com.

For over 70 years the railway line P'tit Train du Nord brought nature lovers to the many fine parks and resorts of the Laurentians. Today hikers, cyclists, cross-country skiers, and even snowmobilers cherish the recently developed "linear park" for its 200km/124.3mi of maintained pathways. Val-David and Mont Tremblant are the most popular of the 23 village access points. Former train stations now operate as trail service centers offering information booths, cafés, bicycle rer restrooms and showers. The hard-packed trail and low grade (two perce average) allow all levels of outdoor enthusiasts to enjoy the fields, fore and rivers of the Laurentian wilderness. Day-trippers favor the St.-Fa Carré–Mont Tremblant section for a picnic lunch and swim at the mu at the Old Mont Tremblant Village, while other visitors prefer week with overnight stays at the quaint B&Bs located close to the pa

Address Book

⌖*For price ranges, see the Legend on the cover flap.*

WHERE TO STAY

$$$$ Fairmont Tremblant – *3045 Chemin de la Chapelle, Mont Tremblant.* ✗⌖🅿🛏📶 ☎819-681-7000 or 1-800-441-1414. www.fairmont.ca. 314 rooms. Reigning above Mont Tremblant Village, this resort hotel remains in character with the re-created 18C atmosphere of its surroundings. Its château-like exterior and rustic pine and stone interior recall the early days of New France. Costumed employees show you to the rooms that echo country charm with pine furnishings and plaid drapes and bedspreads. Just outside the hotel, you'll have immediate access to the ski slopes. The Fairmont Tremblant fine-dining restaurant, **Loup-Garou ($$$)**, incorporates regional ingredients such as venison and maple syrup.

WHERE TO EAT

$ Cabane à sucre Millette – *1357 Rue St-Faustin, Saint-Faustin–Lac Carré.* ♿☎819-688-2101. www.millette.ca. **Québécois**. For a truly authentic Québécois experience, don't miss a meal at the Millette family's "sugar shack." Syrup-making implements like *outils à marquer le bois* (tree-marking tools) decorate the rustic wood-panelled interior. After touring the syrup-making facilities, enjoy folk music while you savor copious servings of traditional favorites such as *soupe aux pois des Laurentides* (Laurentian pea soup); *jambon fumé au sirop d'érable* (maple-syrup smoked ham); *saucisses dans le sirop d'érable* (sausages in maple syrup); and *crêpes au sucre à la crème chaude* (crêpes with warm maple sugar)

$$$$ Restaurant La Forge – *Place St-Bernard, Mont Tremblant Resort.* ☎819-681-4900. **Regional Canadian**. Encircled by evergreens, this inviting restaurant is located at the base of the ski lifts. Leather chairs and decorative iron tools help create its warm, yet sophisticated ambience. The circular bar stocks some 250 wines and a number of single-malt scotches. The open kitchen prepares regional dishes like Boileau deer tournedos with morello cherries and peppercorns, or rack of Quebec piglet served with Oka cider and golden Sainte-Julie honey.

Saint-Sauveur-des-Monts★

Nestled in the mountains, this charming and lively village boasts a variety of restaurants, fashion stores and handicraft shops, cafés, bars and discos, most of which are located along the busy main street (*Rue Principale*), near the church of Saint-Sauveur (1903).
Saint-Sauveur is the oldest Laurentian resort, having welcomed visitors since 1930. The **Mont-Saint-Sauveur** ski center is one of the largest in the Laurentians, boasting more than 25 ski lifts within 3km/1.8mi of the community.

⋯lon 70

⋯e Principale, turn left on Ave.
⋯is and continue 1km/.6mi to
⋯uveur. At the foot of

⋯ veritable wooden pal-
⋯ter Rose of Montreal,
⋯77. A monumental

façade topped by two massive chimneys characterizes the internationally acclaimed building, credited with introducing the post-Modern style to Quebec.

▷ *Return to Rte. 117.*

Route 117 continues its course through the mountains. The Rouge River offers sports enthusiasts exciting whitewater rafting opportunities as it flows past several communities.

Sainte-Adèle★

9km/5.6mi.
Nestled in the Laurentian Mountains, this community occupies a lovely **site**★ surrounding the small Lake Sainte-Adèle. In 1834 Augustin-Norbert Morin (1803-1865), lawyer and politician, founded this village named for his wife, Adèle. Today the community is dominated by

e vast and luxurious resort hotel, **Hôtel Le Chantecler** (☎1-888-916-1616; www.lechantecler.com). Sainte-Adèle boasts two downhill ski centers, Côtes 40–80 and Chantecler, where the Canadian ski team trains regularly. Popular with artists and writers, the village features numerous restaurants and charming country inns.

Mont-Saint-Sauveur

Sainte-Marguerite-du-Lac-Masson★
From center of Sainte-Adèle, take Rte. 370 to the right. About 24km/15mi round-trip.
After 4km/2.5mi, the road crosses the Nord River and passes the Alpine Inn, an imposing log structure built in 1934, in the rustic style. Several lakes can be glimpsed before the road reaches Sainte-Marguerite-du-Lac-Masson, a quiet village on **Lake Masson**. A narrow road circles the lake, offering panoramas of the area.

Many more ski centers can be seen, their ski trails cutting swathes of green down the mountainsides in summer. Route 117 passes through Val-Morin and Val-David, known for their summer theatre and resort hotels.

Sainte-Agathe-des-Monts★
– 18km/11mi.   *See Entry Heading.*

Over the next 21km/13mi, the road criss-crosses the former route of the famed "P'tit train du nord" (little train of the north), immortalized in a song by Félix Leclerc. This popular shuttle made the trip (in the years prior to the establishment of ski areas) between Montreal and the Laurentians throughout the winter, serving the region's agricultural communities. The service was eventually superseded by the automobile, and the tracks have been removed.

To the south of Saint-Faustin, the **Mont Blanc** (945m/3,100ft) ski center is visible.

Saint-Jovite
30km/18.6mi.
This small tourist center of fairly recent vintage is located in the valley of the Diable River. Visitors will find many restaurants, antique stores and handicraft shops.

▷ *From Rue Ouimet turn right on Rue Limoges (Rte. 327).*

The lovely **Lac Ouimet** (6km/3.7mi) is encircled by hills, with the long ridge of Mont Tremblant visible to the north. Overlooking the lake is the Gray Rocks resort hotel, with its ski slopes, golf course, and sailing facilities.

▷ *Continue northward on Rte. 327.*

Claude-Henri Grignon

A native of Sainte-Adèle, the writer and journalist Claude-Henri Grignon (1894–1976) published his famous novel *Un Homme et son péché* (published as *The Woman and the Miser* in English) in 1933. Set in Sainte-Adèle and centered on the miserly **Séraphin Poudrier**, the novel takes the reader back to the days when the so-called *Pays d'en Haut* (the highlands) were being settled. It won the Prix Anathase David in 1935 and was subsequently adapted for radio, television, and film. Grignon's masterpiece, written in the realist-naturalist style, remains a classic in Quebec literature.

Mont-Tremblant Village

4km/2.5mi. Lake Mercier marks the entrance to the village. The road continues toward Lake Tremblant (3km/1.8mi) and the Mont Tremblant ski center (www.tremblant.com).

Located on the shores of Lake Tremblant, the resort of Mont Tremblant will delight visitors in all seasons with its beauty and wide range of activities. The village is renowned for its fine restaurants.

Lac Tremblant (Lake Tremblant)

A pleasant **cruise** (70min) sails over Lake Tremblant *(12km/7.5mi from Quai Fédéral: Call or see website for times; commentary; $18; Croisières Mont Tremblant; 819-425-1045; www.croisierestremblant.com).* Near the boat dock, a tributary of the Diable River, known simply as Décharge-du-Lac, leaves the lake in a display of falls and whirlpools. Luxurious homes line the lake shores, while the imposing Mont Tremblant looms to the east. At the beginning of the 20C, this was a logging area with no roads. The northern end of the lake is still inaccessible by car; residents reach their homes by boat in summer and snowmobile in the winter months. The lake is famous for its fish (landlocked salmon, trout, muskie) and its clean waters. It offers several beaches and water sports. At the Mont Tremblant ski station, the great ridge of the mountain dominates the resort community at its base. The tiny Roman Catholic church with a prominent red roof is a replica of the church built in Saint-Laurent, on th Île d'Orléans, in the early 18C.

In summer, the peak of Mont Tremblant (968m/3,175ft) can be reached by chairlift. On clear days, the peak offers a magnificent **view**★.

Parc du Mont Tremblant★

From Lake Tremblant, follow the Chemin Duplessis (follow sign for Lac Supérieur) for 13km/8mi to the junction with the road from Saint-Faustin. The entrance to the park is 5km/3mi north of the junction. In the summer season when all roads in the park are open, exit at the Saint-Donat entrance and continue to Saint-Donat. Off season, visitors must return to the Lac Supérieur (Saint-Faustin) entrance.

The road follows the **Diable River**★ from the Mont Tremblant ski center to the Croches Falls.

Saint-Donat

10km/6.2mi from park entrance.

The resort of Saint-Donat lies in the Lanaudière region at an elevation of 472m/1,548ft and is surrounded by mountains. It is set on the shores of Lake Archambault, but stretches as far as Lake Ouareau to the east.

▸ *Continue on Rte. 329 Sud to Sainte-Agathe-des-Monts.*

Just outside Saint-Donat, the road affords beautiful views of Lake Archambault.

cling in the Parc Linéaire le P'tit Train du Nord

LAVAL

LAVAL REGION
POPULATION 368,709
MAP: SEE MONTREAL

In the 17C the Jesuits gave the name **Île Jésus** to this large island just to the north of Montreal. The first parish, Saint-François-de-Sales, was created in 1702 and the fertile land was quickly settled.

A master sculptor and principal designer of church interiors in Quebec in the early 19C, **Louis-Amable Quévillon** (1749–1823) was born and lived in the small parish of Saint-Vincent-de-Paul. With the help of apprentices, friends, and associates, he created what historians labeled the "Quévillon school."

In the 20C the advent of the automobile, together with the building of bridges and highways, rapidly changed Île Jésus, transforming it into the main industrial and residential suburb of Montreal. In 1965 the 14 municipalities on the island merged and selected their new name in honour of Msgr. Laval, former seigneur of Île Jésus. Today Laval is the most populous city in Quebec after Montreal.

- **Information:** ☎450-682-5522 & 1-877-465-2825. www.tourismelaval.com.
- ▶ **Orient Yourself:** The island of Laval is located 12km/7.4mi north of downtown Montreal. Laval is now easily accessible by three subway stations, and is actually closer to the Montreal airport than downtown Montreal.
- **P** **Parking:** Metered street parking (but watch days and times); parking lots (fees).
- ⏱ **Organizing Your Time:** Drive to the west end of the island to visit the Économusée de la Fleur, then follow Rte. 440 back to the Cosmodôme. The parks and old village along the Rivière Mille-Îles on Boulevard Ste-Rose make a pleasant place to take kids to unwind.
- **Kids** **Especially for Kids:** The Cosmodôme (enquire about the Space Camp).
- **Also See:** MUSÉE ARMAND-FRAPPIER.

Sights

Cosmodôme★★

2150 Autoroute des Laurentides (Chomedey). From Montreal, take Rte. 15 (Exit 9) and follow signs.

The Cosmodôme opened in 1994 with a mission to "promote the study and practice of space science and technology." A ¾-scale replica of an Ariane rocket stands in front of the ultramodern complex, making it easy to spot from afar.

Space Science Center

⏱ *Open late Jun–Labor Day, daily 10am–5pm; rest of the year, Tue–Sun 10am–5pm.* ⏱ *Closed Jan 1 & Dec 25.* ☞*$11.50.* ✗ ♿ P ☎*450-978-3600. www.cosmodome.org.*

Interactive consoles, mural panels, scale models, large-scale replicas, simulators, and videos make for a fascinating, hands-on visit to Canada's only museum devoted

to the history and exploration of space. A path through the exhibits traverses six different thematic sections, introducing visitors to the wonders of the universe. In the first section, a multimedia show (*20min*) traces the history of human space exploration. In the second section, various scientific instruments of yesteryear bring home the incredible technological strides achieved in human knowledge of the universe. The third section focuses on telecommunications, from prehistory to the present. Earth is next—the importance of water, continental drift, undersea mountains, and other aspects of our planet are examined. Don't miss the magnificent mural representation of the continents as viewed from space. The fifth section boasts two themes: teledetection and its various roles, ranging from meteorology to espionage; and human exploration of the moon. On view here is a space rock donated by NASA. The las

Address Book

🛏 *For price ranges, see the Legend on the cover flap.*

WHERE TO STAY

$$$–$$$$ Hôtel Sheraton Laval – *2440 Autoroute des Laurentides.* ☎*450-687-2440. www.sheraton-laval. com.*✕🅿🛁 Spa. *241 rooms.* Large, reliable, very comfortable hotel near the Cosmodôme, plenty of shopping and several Laval attractions. Excellent restaurant. Convenient access to Montreal's airport and downtown core. In-hotel spa (☎*450-682-3365 & 1-866-263-7477; www.amerispa.ca).*

WHERE TO EAT

$$$ Restaurant Derrière les fagots – *166 Blvd. Sainte-Rose (in the Sainte-Rose borough, in the northern section of Laval).* ☎*450-622-2522. www.derrierelesfagots.ca.* At the core of Laval's most historic district, inside a *maison canadienne* (French Canadian house of old), lies one of Quebec's best restaurants. *Derrière les fagots* (a French expression meaning the best wines in a restaurant are often hidden from view) proves that the best restaurants are often away from the downtown locations. Original, fresh, regionally-inspired French cooking in a cozy, warm setting.

---

section offers the chance to explore the solar system; note in particular a holographic image of the Hubble space telescope surrounded by meteor fragments. The final exhibit ("Are We Alone?") details historic efforts to communicate across the universe.

Space Camp Canada   Kids

🎧*Reservations required. For information* ☎*450-978-3600.* Modeled after similar programs in the US, the camp offers an array of space-oriented educational activities for kids and adults. Programs of varying length, some necessitating overnight stays and all run by specially trained counselors, initiate campers to the life and work of real astronauts through workshops, exercises, training programs and mission simulations.

Complexe Culturel André-Benjamin Papineau (André-Benjamin Papineau Cultural Center)

5475 Blvd. Saint-Martin Ouest (borough of Chomedey). Leave Hwy 13 at Exit 15 and follow the signs to Maison Papineau. 🕐*Open early Mar–early Dec, Tue–Sun 1pm–5pm.* ♿🅿☎*450-688-6558.* This stone house, with its steep roof and high chimneys, was built between 1818 and 1832 by André Papineau. Its most famous resident was his son, André-

Benjamin, cousin of Louis-Joseph, fellow Patriot who took part in the 1837 rebellion, politician and mayor of Saint-Martin (one of Laval's boroughs). The beautiful ancestral fieldstone home was moved to this spot when Highway 13 was constructed. The house now functions as a cultural center and art gallery presenting visual arts.

Musée Armand-Frappier (Armand-Frappier Museum)

In the borough of Chomedey. 531 Blvd. des Prairies. 🕐*Open year-round, Mon–Fri 10am–5pm, Sat–Sun upon reservation.* 🎟*$6.* ☎ *450-686-5641. www.musee-afrappier.qc.ca.* The mission of the Armand Frappier Museum is to generate and nurture a broad interest in biosciences and biotechnologies. No matter how old you are, you will be engaged by the museum's wide array of programs and activities. Discover the universe of micro-organisms through a visit of the MicroZoo exhibit, animated activities, scientific camps, initiation to laboratory work, conferences on bioscience-related current event topics, the universe of the infinitesimally small is within your reach. Armand Frappier is a well known Quebec scientist, and Laval is a center of biosciences and biotechnologies.

LÉVIS★

CHAUDIÈRE-APPALACHES REGION
POPULATION 129,521
MAP: SEE QUEBEC CITY

The city of Lévis is located on the southern shore of the St. Lawrence, opposite Quebec City. In 1759 British General Wolfe built a redoubt on these rocky cliffs, from which he planned to bombard the capital of New France. Initially called Aubigny, the community was renamed in 1861 for François-Gaston, Duc de Lévis, who defeated the British at Sainte-Foy in 1760.

During the 19C, Lévis became a center for timber exports to England. In 1828 the Davie Shipbuilding Co., from the neighboring city of Lauzon, established the first shipbuilding center in Canada here. With the arrival of the railway in 1861, Lévis became a major business center. Today the city is noted for its port, wood-related industries, and as the birthplace and headquarters of the Desjardins cooperative savings and loan company (*Caisse populaire Desjardins*). Lévis and Lauzon were incorporated in 1990.

- **Information:** ☎418-838-6026 & 1-888-831-4411. www.tourismelevis.com/ www.chaudiereappalaches.com.
- **Orient Yourself:** A ferry connects Lévis to Quebec City, located just across the river. Lévis is located 252km/156.5mi east of Montreal by Rte. 20 (Exit 325).
- **Parking:** Metered street parking (⊘*watch days and times*); parking lots (⊜*fees*).
- **Don't Miss:** The unforgettable ride on the Quebec City ferry.
- **Organizing Your Time:** From Quebec City, take the ferry across the river, then go to the Lévis Forts National Historic Site of Canada or Lévis Terrace for the views down the St. Lawrence river and take the ferry back towards Quebec City.

A Bit of History

Alphonse Desjardins – On December 6 1900, Alphonse Desjardins (1854–1920), a journalist and stenographer in the House of Commons, founded the first cooperative savings and loan company (*Caisse populaire*) in North America. This people's bank, based on a European concept and adapted to local conditions, sought to bring economic independence to French Canadians, thus slowing their exodus to the US. With his wife, Dorimène, Desjardins ran the first "caisse pop" from his home in Lévis and went on to open 184 branches throughout the province. Towards the end of his life, requests for federation with the *Caisse populaire Desjardins* were coming in from French Canadians living in other provinces, and from French Canadians who formed 'Little Canadas' in large New England cities like Manchester (New Hampshire). Although Desjardins laid the basic groundwork, the *Caisse populaire centrale* was not united until 1932, some 12 years after his death. Today the **Desjardins Cooperative Movement** (Mouvement Desjardins), with headquarters in Lévis, includes more than 1,300 caisses populaires and over 5 million members. It is the largest financial institution in Quebec, and it is actively marketing its services in English Canada.

Sights

Terrasse de Lévis (Lévis Terrace)

- *From Rte. 132, take Rue Côte-du-Passage, bear left on Rue Desjardins, and turn left on Rue William-Tremblay.*

Built during the Depression, this terrace was inaugurated in 1939 by George VI and Queen Elizabeth I. Located high above the river, it offers an excelle view★★ of the older areas of Lévis and Quebec City, with the Citadel, Château Frontenac and port. The view extends to Mont Sainte-Anne in the east, and as far as the Quebec City Bridge in the west.

Carré Déziel

In the heart of old Lévis, Déziel Square is surrounded by several interesting buildings, including the imposing Église Notre-Dame-de-la-Victoire (Church of Our Lady of Victory), erected in 1851. At the center of the square stands a **monument** to Joseph-David Déziel sculpted by Louis-Philippe Hébert. Déziel (1806–82) was the first parish priest and the superior of the Lévis College, which he founded in 1851. Today he is considered to be the founder of Lévis.

Maison Alphonse-Desjardins★ (Alphonse-Desjardins House)

8 Ave. Mont-Marie at corner of Rue Guenette. Visit by guided tour (45min) only, year-round, Mon–Fri 10am–noon, 1pm–4.30pm, weekends noon–5pm. Closed Jan 1–2 & Dec 24–26 & 31. ☎418-835-2090. www.desjardins.com.

Built between 1882 and 1884 in the Gothic Revival style, this small, white clapboard house was the home of Alphonse and Dorimène Desjardins for more than 40 years. The house was restored in 1982 by the Mouvement Desjardins as a tribute to its founder. Displays of artifacts describe Desjardins' life and the beginning of the coopera-

Société historique A. Desjardins

lphonse Desjardins

tive movement. Desjardins' office ar other rooms have been refurbished t reflect the period (1906) when the *Caisse Populaire de Lévis* had its head office in the house.

Lieu historique national du Canada des Forts-de-Lévis★ (Lévis Forts National Historic Site of Canada)

2km/1.2mi by Rte. 132 Est and Chemin du Gouvernement. Open early May–late Aug, daily 10am–5pm, Sept weekends 1pm–4pm. $4. ☎418-835-5182 & 1-888-773-8888. www.pc.gc.ca/levis.

The fort n°. 1 (1865–72) stands opposite Quebec City, atop Point Lévy, the highest point on the south shore. It is the sole vestige of three such forts built to protect the city from possible American attack during the American Civil War, and from the **Fenian Raids**. The Fenians were members of a secret, New York-based Irish society fighting to liberate Ireland from British domination and occupy British North America, or the Dominion of Canada. The fort was never completely garrisoned, and was nearly abandoned after the Treaty of Washington in 1871.

Shaped like an irregular pentagon, the fort is composed of a series of massive earthen ramparts with a tall embankment protecting the casemates, ditches and vaulted tunnels leading to the caponiers (stone and brick structures armed with small cannons). Its design marks the transition between two styles of fortification: the classical system, which involved enclosing protected areas with contiguous walls; and the mid-19C system of erecting a series of detached forts. Overlooking the river, the fort offers splendid **views**★ of the Montmorency Falls Park and Île d'Orléans.

Excursions

Ferry to Quebec City★

Departs from dock in Lévis (accessible on foot, with a bicycle, or by car) year-round daily 6am–2am, every 30min daytime, every hour in the evening; more frequent sailings in high season. $3/adult, $3/

cle, $6/car. & *Société des traversi-*
...s du Québec. ☎1-877-787-7483. *www.*
...raversiers.gouv.qc.ca.
This ferry, in operation since 1812, offers
fine **views** of the old capital, its port
installations and harbor, and is by far the
most scenic way to arrive in Quebec City.

It is a simple 10min ferry ride, and yet it
will be a great memory.

Bas-Saint-Laurent★★ –
 See Entry Heading.

Beauce★ – *See Entry Heading.*

L'ISLET-SUR-MER

CHAUDIÈRE-APPALACHES REGIONN
POPULATION 3,876
MAP: SEE CÔTE DE CHARLEVOIX

Built along the banks of the St. Lawrence, L'Islet-sur-Mer originally consisted of
two seigneuries conceded to the Couillard and Bélanger families by Frontenac in
1677. Since the 18C, the community's economy has thrived on maritime activity.
Through the years, the village's native sons have taken to the sea as captains,
pilots, sailors, or fishermen.

- **Information:** Tourism L'Islet. ☎1-800-278-3555. www.chaudiereappalaches.com.
- **Orient Yourself:** L'Islet-sur-Mer is 92km/57mi east of Quebec City by Rte. 73 (Pierre-Laporte Bridge) and Rte. 20 (Exit 400, Rte. 285), between Cap-Saint-Ignace and Saint-Jean-Port-Joli.
- **Organizing Your Time:** The Maritime Museum of Quebec has demonstrations of boat-building and two-day boat-building workshops. Be sure to allow time to explore the well-planned park along the river.
- **Especially for Kids:** Take the guided tour of the Bras d'Or hydrofoil at the Maritime Museum of Quebec.

Sights

Église Notre-Dame de Bonsecours★ (Church of Our Lady of Perpetual Help)

Open Jun 24–Labor Day, Mon–Sat 9am–4pm, Sun noon–4pm. & ☎418-247-5103.
The fieldstone church was built in 1768
and enlarged in 1884, when the façade
was refurbished and twin steeples
added. The statues in the niches of the
façade, representing St. John the Baptist
on the left and St. Francis of Assisi on the
right, are the work of Amable Charron,
who also designed the cornices of the
interior. The main altar was fashioned
by François Baillairgé and the tabernacle by Noël Levasseur. Six paintings
by Antoine Plamondon grace the walls.
The Stations of the Cross were carved in
1945 by Médard Bourgault, a native of
Saint-Jean-Port-Joli.

Musée Maritime du Québec (Maritime Museum of Quebec)

200m/656ft beyond church, 55 Chemin des Pionniers Est. *Open Thanksgiving Day–end May, Mon–Fri 10am–4pm upon reservation; end May–Jun 24 and Labor Day–Thanksgiving, daily until 5pm.* $9; extra charge for hydrofoil ride. & ☎418-247-5001. www.mmq.qc.ca.
Dedicated to the memory of Capt.
Joseph-Elzéar Bernier (1852–1934), a
native of L'Islet-sur-Mer who was a navigator and a pioneer of arctic exploration,
the museum focuses on the maritime
history of the St. Lawrence River.
The collection includes elaborate models
of different ships, in addition to numerous objects recovered from the 191*
wreck of the *Empress of Ireland.* Behir
the museum, visitors can board the *Er*
Lapointe, an icebreaker built in 194
the fleet of the Canadian Coast
The other vessel, the *Bras d'Or 40*

Gold), is a hydrofoil used by the Canadian Navy between 1968 and 1972.

Another permanent exhibition is "la chalouperie." A "chaloupe" is a rowing boat, and various models of every era show slices of maritime life in Quebec. The permanent exhibition gets rearranged, updated and upgraded from time to time.

Spectacular temporary exhibitions portray specific aspects of life on the sea and significant achievements in sailing, fishing and dealing with the challenges of living by and from the sea.

LONGUEUIL

MONTÉRÉGIE REGION
POPULATION 231,969
MAP: SEE MONTREAL

Located on the south shore of the St. Lawrence, Longueuil was part of the seigneury granted to **Charles Le Moyne** in 1657. Between 1685 and 1690, Le Moyne built a massive stone fort that would serve as an outer defence to protect Montreal against the Iroquois and named it Longueuil after his birthplace in Normandy, France. The fort was demolished in 1810. Le Moyne fathered 12 sons, several of whom were famous in their own rights. He left his seigneury to his eldest son Charles, who was granted a patent of nobility by Louis XIV. Among his other sons were the explorer **Pierre Le Moyne d'Iberville**, who helped Pierre de Troyes defeat the English at James Bay in 1686 and became governor of the conquered trading posts. His son **Jean-Baptiste Le Moyne de Bienville** founded New Orleans in 1718.

Today Longueuil has become an industrial suburb of Montreal and is home to manufacturing plants for aircraft parts, textiles, furniture, and toys.

🛈 **Information:** 205 Chemin de Chambly. ☎450-670-7293. www.tourisme-monteregie.qc.ca.

▶ **Orient Yourself:** Longueuil is 9.3km/5.7mi southeast of Montreal by the Jacques-Cartier Bridge. It can also be reached by metro and, from mid-May to early October, by a water shuttle connecting Old Montreal to the Longueuil marina and bike path system (☎514-281-8000; www.navettesmaritimes.com).

🅿 **Parking:** Metered and not always easy to find in Old Longueuil.

🕐 **Organizing Your Time:** Crossing the Jacques-Cartier bridge at weekends is easier and there is more to see and do in Old Longueuil then.

Sights

Cathédrale Saint-Antoine-de-Padoue (St. Anthony of Padua Cathedral)

On the corner of Rue Saint-Charles and Chemin de Chambly. 🕐*Open year-round, daily 9am–noon, 1pm–5pm.* 🕐*Closed major holidays.* ☎450-674-1549.

imposing stone church (1885–1887) its single steeple and dome is actu- "co-cathedral" for the diocese of ean–Longueuil along with the in Saint-Jean-Sur-Richelieu.

It stands on the former site of Le Moyne's fort. The ornate interior has three naves, and features paintings by the noted artist Jean-Baptiste Roy Audy.

From the end of the Chemin de Chambly, the tower of Montreal's Olympic Stadium is visible.

Maison Rollin-Brais (Rollin-Brais House)

205 Chemin de Chambly.
Built between 1794 and 1801, this stone house with its shingle roof and high

Follow the Paths to the Islands

Behind the Maison André-Lamarre (*255 Chemin de Chambly*), four footbridges cross Route 132 and lead to a network of bike paths along the St. Lawrence. At the eastern end of this network, a ferry crosses to Charron Island and the Boucherville Islands Park *(departs from the marina mid-Jun–Aug Mon, Thu–Sun 10am–5pm every hour; mid-May–mid-Jun & Sept–mid-Oct weekends 10am–5pm; 5min; $3.50 round-trip; Croisières Navark ☎514-871-8356).*

chimneys originally served as a forge, but was later transformed into an inn.

Vieux Longueuil (Old Longueuil)

A number of historic houses, most of them made of stone, line Rue Saint-Charles Est, the core of Old Longueuil. The **Couvent de Longueuil** (*n°. 70*) was originally built in 1769, and a convent wing was added in 1844. The **Maison Daniel-Poirier** (*n°. 100*) dates from 1749.

The **Maison André-Lamarre** (*n°. 255*), built in 1740, is Longueuil's oldest home. The original pitched gable was replaced by a mansard roof in 1895. Today the house is the headquarters of the Longueuil historical society.

Take time to enjoy the relaxed, sophisticated ambiance of Old Longueuil.

LOUISEVILLE

MAURICIE REGION
POPULATION 7,433
MAP: SEE MAURICIE

In 1665 Charles de Jay, Sieur de Mannereuil, built a wooden fort on this site. At the end of the 19C, the village was named after Princess Louise, daughter of Queen Victoria and wife of the Marquis of Lorne, governor-general of Canada from 1878 through 1883. Today Louiseville is a pleasant agricultural community.

- **Information:** ☎819-228-2744. www.tourismemauricie.com.
- **Orient Yourself:** Louiseville is 106km/65.8mi northeast of Montreal by Rte. 40 (Exit 166) and Rte. 138, which forms the main street.
- **Don't Miss:** Église Notre-Dame-de-Padoue
- **Organizing Your Time:** Louiseville is a pleasant stop between Montreal and Trois-Rivières.

Sights

Église Saint-Antoine-de-Padoue (Church of St. Anthony of Padua)

On Rte. 138 in center of town. ◔*Open year-round, daily 9am–3pm.* ☎819-228-2739.

This imposing church with its twin steeples was built between 1917 and 1921. The interior is decorated with frescoes and mosaics. Blocks of colored marble create a lovely contrast between the warm beige walls and columns and the cool incandescence of the rose and blue marble sheathing the apse. The frescoes on each side of the choir (*The Nativity* on the left and *The Annunciation* on the right) are by Father Antonio Cianci and Olga Storaci Caron, respectively.

Parc des Chutes Sainte-Ursule (Sainte-Ursule Falls Park)

11km/7mi by Rte. 348 and a small well-road. ◔*Open year-round, daily 9* $7. ☎819-228-3555 & 6160.www.chutes-ste-ursule.c

Trout Festival, in a town!

Only in Canada can you find a fishing festival right in a middle of a town! Thousands of people gather in Saint-Alexis-des-Monts (population 3 118) to catch numerous truites mouchetées, the most beautiful and delicious of the Canadian trout species. It is a true family event, with fishing lessons, country music shows, draws, and a fishing tournament where tens of thousands of dollars are up for grabs. Saint-Alexis-des-Monts is 30km/20mi northeast of Louiseville by Rte. 349. *Annually, 10 days at end Jun.* ☜*Participation fee $20. www.festivaldelatruitemouchetee.com.*

The Maskinongé River drops 70m/230ft at this point where the Canadian Shield abruptly meets the St. Lawrence Lowlands. In 1663 an earthquake changed the course of the river to cut through this rocky gorge of gneiss and pink gran-ite. Trails follow the river as it tumbles through the gorge, leading to the site of a 19C paper mill; only its foundations remain. An observation tower offers views of the entire series of seven falls.

ÎLES DE LA MADELEINE★★

ÎLES DE LA MADELEINE
POPULATION 12,560
MAP: SEE ÎLES DE LA MADELEINE

This isolated and windswept outpost of Quebec lies in the middle of the Gulf of St. Lawrence, closer to Cape Breton (Nova Scotia) and Prince Edward Island than to the Gaspé Peninsula. Of the eight islands and numerous islets that make up the archipelago, six are linked by a series of sandy isthmuses, forming a hook-shaped mass about 72km/44.7mi long, stretching southwest to northeast. The islands offer a wealth of outdoor activities to the visitor, ranging from sightseeing to swimming and hiking.

- **Information:** 128, Chemin Principal (near the ferry). ☎418-986-2245 & 1-877-624-4437. www.tourismeilesdelamadeleine.com.
- ▶ **Orient Yourself:** The Magdalen Islands—Îles de la Madeleine in French—are 920km/571.6mi northeast of Montreal and 250km/155.3mi southeast of Gaspé in the Gulf of St. Lawrence. Regular ferries run from Prince Edward Island 100km/62mi to the south, and a cruise ship designed to hold vehicles connects the islands to Gaspé and the St. Lawrence River through to Montreal.
- **Don't Miss:** The rock formations at the headlands of the beach near Cape Trou; the Maritime Museum on Havre Aubert Island; the view from Entry Island.
- **Organizing Your Time:** Rent a car near the port at Cap-aux-Meules, if you did not bring your own on the ferry, and you can drive the full length of the archipelago. As you drive south to Havre Aubert Island, stop along the long beach and watch the kite surfers. The road northwest to the eastern islands travels along another long sand dune, but continue to the Grand Échouerie Beach where you'll find the water surprisingly pleasant for swimming in the summer. Before you leave, be sure to take the ferry across to Entry Island, hike up the easy trail to the peak for a view of the full archipelago.
- **ially for Kids:** Grand Échouerie Beach; the Island Aquarium in e on Havre Aubert Island.
  GROSSE-ÎLE.

A Bit of History

Discovery – During the 15C, the Magdalen Islands were a frequent stopping point for Basque and Breton fishermen in search of fish, seals, walruses, and whales. The archipelago was officially discovered in 1534 by Jacques Cartier during the first of his three expeditions in the Gulf of St. Lawrence. Cartier landed first at Rocher aux Oiseaux (Bird Rock), then at Île Brion, due north of the islands, which he described in the ship's log as "the best land we have yet seen. A single acre of this soil is worth more than all of Newfoundland. We found it full of beautiful trees, prairies, fields of wild wheat, and flowering pea plants as varied and as lovely as anything I have seen in Brittany, and appearing to have been planted with much labor."

In the decades following Cartier's discovery, the islands were inhabited sporadically by Mi'kmaq Indians and by French explorers and fur traders. The archipelago is thought to have been named for Madeleine Fontaine, wife of **François Doublet**, the nobleman who colonized the territory in the name of the French Crown in 1663.

The Acadian Deportation – The archipelago was not permanently inhabited until after 1755, when it became a refuge for French colonists who had settled Acadia (now the west coast of Nova Scotia). An area of territorial dispute between Britain and France from 1604 through 1710, Acadia was ceded to Britain in 1713 under the Treaty of Utrecht, which ended the Spanish Succession War in Europe.

When the Acadian settlers refused to swear an oath of unconditional allegiance to Great Britain, the governor of Nova Scotia, Charles Lawrence, issued a **Deportation Order** (August 1755), which forcibly expelled the Acadians to the American colonies. Several hundred escaped, fleeing to the Magdalen Islands and France's other remaining colonies, the islands of Saint-Pierre and Miquelon, off the southern coast of Newfoundland (consult THE GREEN GUIDE Canada).

In accordance with the terms of the Treaty of Paris (1763), the Magdalen Islands were ceded to Britain, while France retained control of Saint-Pierre and Miquelon. In the wake of the French Revolution, the Acadian refugees on these two islands joined their compatriots on the Magdalen Islands, preferring the British monarchy to the new French republic. These former Acadians are the ancestors of many of the islands' present population, known as *Madelinots*.

After the Conquest, the British government annexed the Magdalen Islands to Newfoundland but they soon became a seigneury of the Province of Quebec under the Quebec Act of 1774. King George III granted seigneurial title to Admiral Isaac Coffin in 1798 as a reward for his services to the British Empire, and the Coffins retained control of the islands for the next century. The hardships they exercised on their Acadian tenants forced many of the settlers into exile, this time to the north shore of the St. Lawrence. It was not until 1895 that the Acadians settlers obtained the rights to the land that they had painstakingly cleared and developed.

Economy – Traditionally the Acadians were skilled fishermen and farmers. Fishing and agriculture were supplemented by logging operations in the 19C, which accounts for the bare hills found on the islands of Entrée and Havre aux Maisons. Today, fishing and tourism are the chief economic activities. The islands, actually the visible part of a vast undersea plateau, are surrounded by shoals which are a natural breeding ground for lobster, snow crab, scallops and other shellfish. Cod, haddock, flounder, mackerel, and ocean perch are also found. These fish are processed at the Madelipêche plant near the port at Cap-aux-Meules and transported to the mainland for sale. Another economic activity is salt mining on Dune du Nord. The salt is used to de-ice Quebec roads in wintertime.

Magdalen Islands Today

Architecture – The Magdalen Islands have developed distinctive building types, although even the oldest constructions date back to only 1850. The earliest known type of structure is the

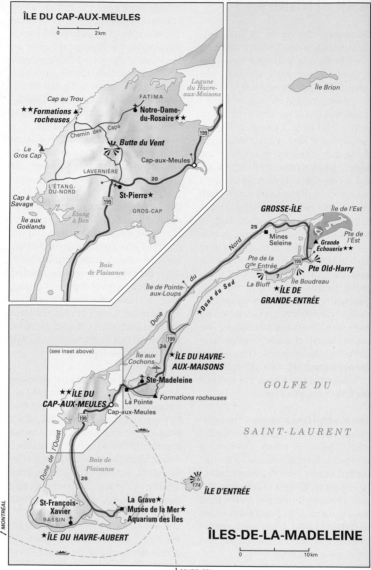

ÎLE DU CAP-AUX-MEULES

0   2 km

Lagune du Havre-aux-Maisons

FATIMA

Cap au Trou

★★ Formations rocheuses

✠ Notre-Dame-du-Rosaire ★★

Chemin des Caps

Le Gros Cap

✠ Butte du Vent

Cap-aux-Meules

LAVERNIÈRE

L'ÉTANG-DU-NORD

199

St-Pierre ★

20

Cap à Savage

Île aux Goélands

Étang à Ben

GROS-CAP

Île Brion

Baie de Plaisance

GROSSE-ÎLE

Île de l'Est

25

Mines Seleine

Nord

Pte de l'Est

▲ Grande Échouerie ★★

199

Pte de la Gde Entrée

Pte Old-Harry

Île de Pointe-aux-Loups

Dune du Sud

La Bluff

Île Boudreau

★ ÎLE DE GRANDE-ENTRÉE

Dune du

Dune

199

24

Île aux Cochons

★ ÎLE DU HAVRE-AUX-MAISONS

(see inset above)

✠ Ste-Madeleine

★★ ÎLE DU CAP-AUX-MEULES

La Pointe

Cap-aux-Meules

Formations rocheuses

GOLFE DU

199

SAINT-LAURENT

Dune de l'Ouest

Baie de Plaisance

26

174

ÎLE D'ENTRÉE

St-François-Xavier

BASSIN

La Grave ★

✠ Musée de la Mer ★

Aquarium des Îles

★ ÎLE DU HAVRE-AUBERT

ÎLES-DE-LA-MADELEINE

0   10 km

MONTRÉAL

SOURIS, P.E.I.

fisherman's cottage with adjoining subsistence farm. These cottages consist of a small, single-story building with two rooms on the ground floor and a small room in the attic. Larger houses were built after 1900, with four rooms on each floor. Many traditional homes feature mansard roofs, adopted from the presbyteries and convents that appeared on the islands about 1875.

The large wooden churches at Bassin, La Vernière and Grande Entrée are designed in the style of Catholic churches in the Maritime Provinces (such as Church Point), while numerous Protestant churches bear witness to an active Anglophone community. In the 1960s several new parishes were created on the islands, resulting in an unusually large number of contemporary religious churches in this part of Quebec.

Landscape – The Magdalen Islands' most striking features are without ques-

Cliffs on Île du Cap aux Meules

tion the **rock formations** cut into the land by the pounding sea. In places, the red sandstone cliffs have been sculpted into arches, tunnels, caves, and defiant promontories topped by emerald-green grass. Expansive white beaches stretch away to meet the blue sea, the whole lot forming a multicolored seascape, at the same time savage and serene.

Vegetation – Tall trees on the island are rare: Those that escaped the 19C lumbermen's axes have been twisted into unique, tortured shapes by the winds. Wildflowers abound in spring and summer. The **pitcher plant**, a carnivorous plant found in peat bogs, captures insects by drowning them in fluid secreted in its pitcher-shaped leaves. In freshwater marshes, the **multicolored iris** grows in colonies that are sometimes quite dense. Erosion is controlled by **dune hay** (*ammophile*), with its expansive root system, and moss, covering the dunes.

Wildlife – The archipelago's location in the middle of the Gulf of St. Lawrence makes it an ideal resting spot for migratory birds. Many species nest here year-round, including the Atlantic Puffin, the Northern Gannet and the endangered Piping Plover. The rare Snowy Owl (Quebec's bird emblem) is indigenous to the islands. Grey, Common, and Greenland seals can also be found on many deserted beaches and islets.

Île du Cap-aux-Meules★★ (Cap aux Meules Island)

The largest of the islands, this is the archipelago's commercial and administrative center. Its three separate municipal districts (Cap-aux-Meules, Fatima, and Étang-du-Nord) are connected by scenic drives through the forested hills and along the coast. The island was named for the millstones, or *meules,* found on the cape overlooking the port.

The quaint **port** at Cap-aux-Meules is the archipelago's lively gateway. Evenings are a good time for a stroll to observe a variety of boats and trawlers, some dry-docked for repairs, others being readied for the next day's fishing.

▶ *Take Rte. 199 (Chemin Principal) west to La Vernière. In La Vernière, Rte. 199 intersects with Chemin de l'Église.*

Butte-du-Vent (Vent Hillock)

The Chemin de l'Église leads up into the hills toward the butte du Vent (*turn left on Chemin Cormier and immediately right on Chemin des Arsène; caution is advised on the unpaved roads; four-wheel-drive vehicle strongly recommended*). This is the highest point on the island, affording extensive **views**★★ of the entire archipelago and Plaisance Bay.

Address Book

VISITOR INFORMATION

GETTING THERE

The **Tourism Association** (Association Touristique des Îles-de-la-Madeleine) information office (*128 Chemin Principal, at the corner of Chemin Débarcadère, Cap-aux-Meules (adjoining the ferry parking)*; ☎418-986-2245; www.tour-ismeilesdelamadeleine.com) provides literature and information about guided tours of the islands, scenic cruises, outdoor activities, restaurants, and accommodations.

Several private operators offer tours of the island (by van or boat) varying in length from several hours to a full day. To watch seals and view the cliff formations, scenic cruises are highly recommended. For close-up views of the cliffs and wildlife, hike along one of the trails around the islands (*for information, contact the Club Vacances Les Îles center on Grande Entrée Island ☎418-985-2833 & 1-888-537-4537; www.clubiles.qc.ca*).

TIME

The Magdalen Islands are on Atlantic time, which is one hour ahead of Eastern time (rest of Quebec).

ACCESS

By air: Daily service between Montreal, Quebec City, Gaspé and Havre aux Maisons Island on Air Canada Jazz with connections for all Air Canada and Star Alliance destinations (☎1-888-247-2262; www.aircanada.com); and service between Montreal, Quebec City, Bonaventure (Gaspésie) and Havre aux Maisons Island on local airline Pascan Aviation Inc. (☎418-877-8777 and 1-888-313-8777; www.pascan.com).

By car/boat: From Montreal, take Rte. 20 to Rivière-du-Loup, then Rte. 185 to Edmunston, New Brunswick (NB), and

Rte. 2 to Moncton (NB). From there, take Rte. 15, then Rte. 16 to Cape Tourmentine (NB), and cross the toll bridge (*10min*) linking New Brunswick to Prince Edward Island (PEI). From Borden, take Rte. 1 to Charlottetown (PEI), then Rte. 2 to Souris (PEI) for the ferry to Cap-aux-Meules. *Ferry from Souris–Cap-aux-Meules (5hrs): Tue–Sun service Apr–Jun & Sept; daily service Jul–Aug, Sun–Tue–Thu–Sat Oct–Nov; Tue–Fri–Sat Dec–Jan. One-way $44/person, additional $82/vehicle. Reservations required, imperatively in summer.* ✗ 🚻 🅿 *CTMA Traversier Ltd. Cap-aux-Meules ☎1-888-986-3278. www.ctma.ca.*

The cruise ship *Vacancier* departs weekly from Montreal to Cap-aux-Meules (*2 days; one-way double occupancy $556-$705, meals included; reservations required*). For schedules, contact CTMA in Cap-aux-Meules (☎418-986-3278) or in Montreal (☎514-937-7656).

WHERE TO STAY

Inns, hotels, motels, and B&Bs are concentrated on the islands of Cap aux Meules, Havre aux Maisons and Havre Aubert. In addition, many residents offer B&B accommodation, as well as rooms, cottages and houses for rent. It is advisable to reserve lodging well in advance for a stay during the peak tourism months of July and August. Contact the Tourism Association.

WHERE TO EAT

Eating is one of the best things about the Magdalen Islands. Lobster is very affordable in season (early May to early July). Snow crab, scallops and highly delicious fish are cooked as regional specialties like *pot-en-pot* or as part of French classics like *bouillabaisse*.

▶ *Return to Chemin de l'Église, turn left on Chemin des Huet, then right on Chemin des Caps to the municipality of Fatima.*

Église Notre-Dame-du-Rosaire★★ (Church of Our Lady of the Rosary)
709 Chemin Les Caps, in Fatima. 🕐*Open year-round, daily 8am–5pm.* ☎ *418-986-2685.*

A lovely example of contemporary religious architecture, the church celebrates the archipelago's maritime way of life.

From the outside the building resembles a scallop shell; the interior abounds in nautical symbolism, including porthole windows, an altar and pulpit evoking a breakwater, and recessed Stations of the Cross scattered across the wall in a wave pattern. The church's design, by Jean-Claude Leclerc, is reminiscent of the Ronchamps chapel in eastern France by the renowned 20C architect Le Corbusier.

▸ *Return south on Chemin des Caps. Turn right on Chemin de la Belle-Anse and drive to the coast.*

Formations rocheuses★★ (Rock formations)

Visitors can walk northward along the coast from Chemin de la Belle-Anse to **Cap-au-Trou** (Cape Trou) to see some of the most dramatic formations on the archipelago. Here the sea has bitten savagely into the red sandstone, leaving deep fissures and jutting promontories. In places where the arches have collapsed, only solitary columns of stone withstand the force of the sea. (*Note: the cliffs can be unstable; avoid the edges and use caution when walking in this area*).

▸ *Continue south on Chemin de la Belle-Anse; turn right on Chemin des Caps, then right on Chemin de l'Étang-du-Nord.*

Other impressive rock formations can be found along the coast near Étang-du-Nord, where a small, lively port provides a haven for numerous fishing trawlers. A stroll along rugged **Cap-à-Savage** (Cape Savage) is highlighted by good views of Cap aux Meules' western coast and of tiny **Île-aux-Goélands** (Goélands Island), named for the large gulls (*goélands* in French) that flock there.

▸ *Return to Cap-aux-Meules.*

Île du Havre-Aubert★ (Havre Aubert Island)

The gently rolling hills of the southernmost island in the archipelago are the setting for some of the prettiest examples of local domestic architecture. The community of Havre-Aubert is the center of the islands' cultural life.

La Grave★
Northeast of Havre-Aubert.
This historic site takes its name from the words "la grave" in reference to the meeting place where merchants came to buy the fishermen's salted and dried products. Here, some 15 grey-shingled buildings line the road that skirts a small bay and leads out to Cape Grindley. This historic site includes stores, an ironworks, two **chafauds** (sheds where cod was dried and prepared) and several warehouses. Abandoned by the fishing industry, the buildings now house artisans' boutiques, where craftspeople create and sell objects made from local materials such as sand, alabaster, and sealskin.

Aquarium des Îles (Aquarium of the Islands) Kids
🕒 *Open Jun–Aug, daily 10am–6pm; Sept, daily 10am–5pm.* ✆*$4.* ♿ 🅿 ☎*418-937-2277.*
Tanks of fish native to the archipelago surround a large, open pool where visitors can handle the fish. On the upper floors, a gallery features displays which explain and demonstrate the methods of fish preservation and processing (drying, smoking, and canning) that enable Madelinot fishermen to export their products.

Musée de la Mer★ (Museum of the Sea)
Cape Gridley, adjacent to La Grave. 🕒*Open late Jun–Labor Day, Mon–Fri 9am–6pm, weekends 10am–6pm; rest of the year, call for hours.* ✆*$5.* ♿ 🅿 ☎*418-937-5711. www.tourismeilesdelamadeleine.com/musee.*
Here, displays of boats, navigational instruments and diverse artifacts acquaint visitors with the maritime history and culture of the Magdalen Islands. The exhibit also covers fishing methods and presents the story of the "ponchon," a mail barrel that was the only means of communication during February of 1910, when a severed telegraph cable

resulted in the archipelago's complete isolation from the mainland.

▶ *From La Grave, return to the center of the island via Rte. 199, bearing left at Chemin du Bassin.*

The scenic drive through the community of Bassin and along Anse-à-la-Cabane winds past colorful houses typical of the islands. Many structures feature mansard-style roofs; others have verandas and balconies, with finely crafted posts and railings and intricately carved corbels.

Église Saint-Francois-Xavier (St. Francis-Xavier Church)

In Bassin. ◐Open year-round, daily. ♿🅿 ☎418-937-5580.
This large wooden church was built in 1939, in the Romanesque Revival style. The presbytery (1876), topped by multiple mansard roofs, is the best example of Second Empire architecture on the islands.

Île du Havre-aux-Maisons★ (Havre aux Maisons Island)

One of the loveliest islands of the archipelago, Havre aux Maisons has retained its rural charm, with its scattered houses, winding roads, farmland and **baraques**—small buildings with sliding roofs designed to shelter hay. Several scenic drives skirt the coastline, affording charming views.

▶ *At Havre aux Maisons Island, turn left at Chemin du Cap-Rouge, and again at Chemin des Cyrs for views of Petite Bay, Cochons Island and La Pointe.*

At **La Pointe**, small wharves buzz with activity. Lobster is sold live or cooked, and visitors can watch clams being cleaned and prepared.

▶ *Return to Rte. 199 and continue to Chemin Central.*

Église de Sainte-Madeleine (Saint Magdalen Church)

25 Chemin Central. ◐Open year-round. ♿☎418-969-2212.
Built in 1969, the structure features great upward curves that unite the church and the presbytery around a central entrance. The nave, lit by a windowed wall, is in the form of an amphitheater. Its low ceiling confers a sense of intimacy to the vast space.

▶ *Return to Rte. 199 and turn left on Chemin de la Pointe-Basse.*

The drive to the harbor at Pointe-Basse, along the Chemin du Quai (on the right), passes by a complex of abandoned fumoirs, large wooden smokehouses filled with rods on which the fish were hung during the smoking process.

▶ *Return to Chemin de la Pointe-Basse.*

The road offers views of this island's **rock formations,** which are concentrated around Anse-à-Firmin and Cape Alright. At **Dune du Sud**★, visitors will find a superb, wide beach and relatively calm currents.

▶ *Continue on Chemin de la Pointe-Basse which runs along the coast and becomes Chemin des Échoueries before rejoining Rte. 199.*

Eastern Islands

The easternmost islands of the archipelago are connected to the others by **Dune du Nord**, a narrow ridge. North of the dune is a government-operated **salt mine** (mines Seleines), which produces salt used to de-ice Quebec's roads in winter.

Municipality of Grosse-Île

The smallest of the contiguous islands is inhabited mainly by English-speaking descendants of Scottish tenant farmers who arrived in the early 18C, having been forced off the lands they tended in their native Scotland, as a result of the development of sheep-rearing. It is

Islands Arts and Crafts

The Magdalen Islands are home to a number of artists' studios and crafts work-shops open to the public. Island artists and artisans use local materials such as wood, sand, shells, stones, and even algae to fashion a variety of items for sale. Here's a selection of studios and galleries:

Île du Cap-aux-Meules

Boutique Art Tendance – *715 ch. Principal, Cap-aux-Meules.* ☎418-986-5111. Alabaster stone, sand, glass and wood objects; paintings accented with algae; greeting cards incorporating sand; shell brooches; and stained-glass works.

Galerie-boutique Le Flâneur – *1944 ch. de l'Étang-du-Nord.* ☎418-986-6526. Art gallery with tea room. Watercolors and other paintings, as well as crafted dolls. A selection of teas and desserts.

Île du Havre-Aubert

Atelier d'art La Baraque – *489 ch. du Bassin, Havre-Aubert.* ☎418-937-5678. Objects crafted from local alabaster stone; sculptures; watercolors and other paintings; and decorative sweaters.

La Banquise du Golfe – *998 Rte. 199, La Grave, Havre-Aubert.* ☎418-937-5209. Hand-knit clothing designed in Canada; watercolors and acrylic paintings; pottery made by Magdalen Islanders; and solid-brass objects.

Émerance – *949 Rte. 199, La Grave, Havre-Aubert.* ☎418-937-9058. Locally crafted jewelry: One-of-a-kind creations and wearables fashioned from precious metals.

Les Artisans du sable – *907 Rte. 199, La Grave, Havre-Aubert.* ☎418-937-2917. A remarkable boutique featuring sand-made sculptures, big and small, in the sandy universe that is the Magdalens. You can watch the sculptures being made.

Île du Havre-aux-Maisons

La Méduse – *638 Rte. 199 ch. de la Carrière, Havre-aux-Maisons.* ☎418-969-4681; *www.meduse.qc.ca.* Blown-glass objects and small sculptures. Artists may be seen at work in this glass-art studio.

here that the traditional lifestyle based on fishing and agriculture has changed the least.

Grosse-Île (population 531) is governed by municipal administration distinct from the rest of the Îles de la Madeleine municipality.

East Point National Wildlife Reserve

🕐*Open Jun 24–Aug. Information on the reserve: the Canadian Wildlife Service* ☎1-800-463-4311.

Bordered to the southeast by a vast beach, this 1,440ha/3,557 acre area offers an excellent introduction to the world of sand dunes: their wildlife (seals, migratory birds), their flora (dune hay) and their glorious topography (beaches, marshes).

Plage de la Grande-Échouerie★★ (Grand Échouerie Beach)

This seemingly endless expanse of sand that stretches out and around the east-ernmost point of the wildlife reserve is considered the archipelago's loveliest beach. The term *échouerie* refers to the rocky ledges where walruses bask in the sun.

Île de la Grande-Entrée★

Lobster fishing formed the basis for settlement of this small stretch of land, which was colonized in 1870.

Pointe Old-Harry (Old Harry Point)

Grand Échouerie Beach leads to this point, now a small harbor protected by a typical Madelinot jetty made of dolosses, or anchor-shaped cement blocks. Walrus hunting, which began in the 17C, brought the first European settlers to the islands. The walruses were slaughtered and processed at Old Harry.

Route 199 runs the length of the island, ending at the small fishing port of Grande Entrée, where docks and fishing boats are painted in bright colors.

Coastal hiking trails

These trails afford some of the archipelago's most impressive **views**★★★ of jagged cliffs and jutting promontories, tidal pools and vast beaches, twisted trees and colorful wildflowers. From the parking lot at the end of Chemin des Pealey, hikers in search of vast panoramas can explore La Bluff and Boudreau Island, for vistas extending as far as Pointe-de-l'Est (East Point).

Île d'Entrée (Entry Island)

Ferry from Cap-aux-Meules harbor May–Dec, Mon–Sat 8am & 3pm crossings. Reservations recommended in summer. $22; G.G.R. Cyr Transport Inc. 418-937-7172 or contact the Tourism Association office.

The only inhabited island that remains detached from the others, this outpost is home to approximately 200 English-speaking residents. Its smooth, treeless hills are laced with trails from which hikers can view fascinating rock formations and wildlife, especially the cormorant, a long-necked seabird.

From Big Hill, the highest peak in the islands (174m/571ft), the **view** embraces the entire archipelago.

MAGOG★

EASTERN TOWNSHIPS REGION
POPULATION 23,880
MAP: SEE CANTONS DE L'EST

This community on the shores of beautiful Lake Memphrémagog was originally named Décharge du Lac (the "outlet"), because of its location at the source of the Magog River. In 1888 the town adopted the name Magog, a shortened version of the Abenaki word Memphrémagog, meaning "large expanse of water." The first settler was Loyalist Ralph Merry who arrived in 1799. Today Magog is a textile manufacturing center and a popular resort, spawned by its lakeside location and the proximity of Mt. Orford Park.

- **Information:** Memphrémagog Tourism Office, 55 Rue Cabana (access by Rte. 112). 819-843-2744 & 1-800-267-2744. www.cantonsdelest.com.
- ▶ **Orient Yourself:** Magog is 120km/74.5mi east of Montreal by Rte. 10 (Exits 115 or 118) and 25km/15.5mi southwest of Sherbrooke by Rte. 112, which becomes Rue Principale.
- **Don't Miss:** Enjoy quiet contemplation or a retreat at the Benedictine Abbey.
- **Organizing Your Time:** Take the cruise—then the sunset at the Abbey.
- **Especially for Kids:** Labyrinthe Memphremagog.
- **Also See:** PARC DU MONT-ORFORD★.

Sights

Parc de la Pointe-Merry★ (Pointe-Merry Park)

Just south of Rue Principale (Rte. 112). This pleasant green space affords splendid **views**★ of the northern end of the lake, which stretches over 50km/31mi,

crossing the border into Vermont. The wooded peaks of Mt. Orford and Owl's Head are visible from the lake.

Scenic Cruises★

Three types of cruises depart from Quai Magog Jun 24–Labor Day, daily 10am–6pm, mid-May–Jun 23 & rest of Sept–mid-

Oct, weekends noon–2pm. Reservations advised for the round-trips of 1hr 25min (☞$23) and 2 ½ hours (☞$28.00). Reservations required for the 7hr round-trip cruise to Newport Vermont (☞$86.27). All prices include taxes. Commentary. ✕ ♿ 🅿 *Croisiéres Memphrémagog Inc.* ☎*819-843-8068. www.croisiere-mem phremagog.com.*

The cruise leads passengers to some of the loveliest areas of Lake Memphrémagog.

Excursions

Abbaye de Saint-Benoît-du-Lac★ (Saint-Benoît-du-Lac Abbey)

20km/12.4mi. Leave Magog on Rte. 112 Ouest; turn left after 5km/3mi. 🕐*Open year-round, daily 5am–9pm. Reservations for visits (or for accommodation) must be made by telephone but only at specified times (to respect the monks' prayer schedules): Daily 8.15am–10.45am; 1.15pm–4.45pm; 5.40–6.20 pm; 7.05pm–7.35pm (also Thu 7.35pm–7.50pm).* ♿ 🅿 ☎*819-843-4080. www.st-benoit-du-lac.com.*

Saint-Benoît-du-Lac Abbey

Tourisme Cantons-de-l'Est/Sylvain Majeau

The drive to Saint-Benoît-du-Lac, whose only inhabitants are the monks of the Benedictine abbey, offers lovely glimpses of Lake Memphrémagog. The abbey (1912) was founded by members of the Saint-Wandrille-de-Fontenelle abbey in Normandy, who were exiled to Belgium after being banned from France in the early 20C. The monks founded a novitiate on the site in 1924, and Saint-Benoît-du-Lac was elevated to the rank of abbey in 1952. The monastery complex, surmounted by an impressive bell tower, occupies a magnificent **site★★**, striking for its peace, serenity and sheer beauty. Most of the structures were designed in 1938 by French Benedictine monk, **Dom Paul Bellot** (1876–1944), who lies buried in the abbey cemetery. The buildings were completed and blessed on July 11, 1941. Montreal architect Dan S. Hanganu conceived the plans for the abbey church, consecrated on December 4, 1994.

Visitors can attend vespers in the oratory and listen to Gregorian chants at daily services. St. Benedict taught his monks to practise hospitality, so adults can stay at the abbey (☞$40) either for a short visit or retreat: men can remain onsite, while women stay at nearby Saint Scholastica's Villa. The prayer-life of the monks must be respected, although you can request a meeting with a monk. The monks produce cider, as well as two well-known cheeses, L'Ermite and Mont-Saint-Benoît, which are sold in a small shop on the premises.

Parc du Mont-Orford★ (Mt. Orford Park) –
🅟*See Entry Heading.*

Labyrinthe Memphrémagog

1.5km/1mi. west of downtown Magog near Rte. 112, on Chemin Plage des Cantons. 🕐*Open daily May–mid-Oct, 10am–dusk.*☞*$10.* ♿ 🅿 ☎*819-868-4188. www.cantonsdelest.com/labyrinthemem phremagog.*

Children and adults can spend almost two hours solving riddles and finding the middle of the giant maze on foot or with in-line skates (rentals available). Canoes, kayaks and sailboats can also be rented for a ride on the splendid adjoining Mempremagog Lake.

COMPLEXE MANIC-OUTARDES

MANICOUAGAN REGION
MAP: SEE CÔTE NORD

Today the combined capacity of Manic's eight power plants is 6,821 megawatts (1 megawatt = 1,000,000 watts). A network of 735,000-volt power lines (the first of this type used for commercial purposes) transports electricity from the plants to major cities. The three power plants comprising the **Outardes Complex** (⊶ *closed to the public*) are fed by a 652sq km/252sq mi reservoir established 93km/58mi upstream from the confluence of the Outardes and St. Lawrence rivers. Most of the dams and dikes of the Outardes complex are earth-and-rockfill constructions made of material found near the sites.

- **Information:** Hydro-Québec 1-866-LA-MANIC (☎1-866-526-2642) & Tourisme Manicouagan (1-888-463-5319). www.tourismemanicouagan.com.
- **Orient Yourself:** Manic-5 is located 214km/133mi north of Baie-Comeau on Rte. 389, a paved but winding road known as "Chemin de la Manic." Manic-2 is 21km/14mi north of Baie-Comeau by the same route. Rte. 389 is partially paved beyond Manic-5 but it continues to Fermont (345km/214.3mi from Manic-5) and Wabush (390km/242.3mi).
  A campground with gas station and snack bar is located near Manic-2; a restaurant and gas station are located near Manic-3; a motel (☺reservations required) with restaurant and gas station is situated 3km/1.8mi from Manic-5. Accommodations are also available in Baie-Comeau (for additional information check: www.tourismecote-nord.com).
- **Don't Miss:** The waters above the Manic-5 dam form an enormous ring visible from space: The lakes were created when a giant meteor hit Earth some 200 million years ago.
- **Organizing Your Time:** Manic-5 is 212km/131.7mi north of Baie-Comeau on Highway 389, and the drive along the river valley alone is worth the visit. However, it is not an easy drive, with lots of sharp curves and large trucks. A shuttle service makes things easier (*late Jun–Aug, daily, departs from L'Orange Bleue restaurant in Baie-Comeau at 7.30am, returns at 5pm; ⊜$45 including breakfast at L'Orange Bleue, 905 Rue Boissé; ☎418-589-8877*).

A Bit of History

Begun in 1959, the mammoth undertaking of harnessing the energy of the Manicouagan and Outardes rivers took 20 years to complete. The project led to the development of new technologies that surpassed any previous engineering feats and established several world records. The completion of the seven power plants involved the mobilization of thousands of men and women and the transportation of tons of material into the vast forest wilderness of the Manicouagan region.

Beneath the site chosen for the construction of the main dam at Manic-3, permeable alluvial deposits threatened to allow water seepage into the projected structure. To prevent such seepage, engineers sank a double concrete wall 131m/429.8ft into the earth's surface, creating the world's largest waterproof shield.

Visit

Manic-2★

⊶*Visit by guided tour (1hr 30min) only, Jun 24–Labor Day, daily 9.30am, 11.30am, 1.30pm & 3.30pm; rest of the year, by appointment (7 days in advance) only. (Visitors 18 years and older must show official photo ID before entering facility).* ☎1-866-526-2642. www.hydroquebec.com/visit/cote_nord/manic-2.html.
Guides describe the Manic-Outardes dams and explain how electricity is produced and transmitted to consumers. Scale models complement the talk.

Daniel Johnson Dam at Manic-5

Operating since the mid-1960s, Manic-2 was the first power plant of the Manic-Outardes Complex to produce electricity. The giant concrete wall is 94m/308.4ft high and 692m/2,270ft long and is one of the largest hollow-joint gravity dams in the world. Because of its tremendous weight, a gravity dam can withstand the enormous pressure exerted by the water trapped in its reservoir. The power plant, located at the base of the dam, has a head of 70m/229.6ft. The facility's eight turbine-alternators can generate up to 1,015,200kwh.

Manic-5★★

Measuring 214m/702ft in height and 1,314m/4,307ft in length, the spectacular **Daniel Johnson Dam**★★ is the largest arch-and-buttress dam in the world. The dam was completed in 1968 after seven years of construction, and is named for the former prime minister of Quebec, Daniel Johnson, who died on the site of the complex on the morning of its inauguration. The dam regulates the water supply to all the power stations of the Manicouagan complex.

With the construction of the dam, two semicircular lakes—the Manicouagan and the Mouchalagane—were united into an immense ring of water encircling an island. The diameter of the reservoir is 65km/40.3mi. A study of the reservoir led geophysicists to theorize that the natural depression of the lakes may

have been created by a meteorite that crashed to earth some 200 million years ago. The depression is comparable with a moon crater, and rock found at the site is similar to samples of moon rock brought back to earth by astronauts. The Manic-5 power plant is located approximately 1km/.6mi downstream from the dam. Its head is 150m/492ft high, and its turbines are capable of producing 1,528,000kwh.

Visit

✎Visit by guided tour (1hr 5min) only: Jun 24–Labor Day daily 9.30am, 11.30am, 1.30pm & 3.30pm. (Visitors 18 years and older must show official photo id before entering facility.) ⊡ ☎1-866-526-2642. http://www.hydroquebec.com/visit/cote_nord/manic-5.html.

Guides present an overview of the dam. Then visitors board a bus that takes them to the base of the massive arches and across the top of the dam overlooking the countryside and the Manicouagan River.

Manic-5 PA

This underground power plant began production in 1989 with four generator sets. The initials "PA" stand for *puissance additionnelle* (additional power) because this new facility provides supplementary power to Manic-5 during peak periods. The total energy potential of the two Manic-5 power plants is 2,592 megawatts.

MAURICIE★

MAURICIE REGION
MAP: SEE MAURICIE

The Mauricie region encompasses the valley of the Saint-Maurice River, which flows southward for 560km/348mi, from the Gouin Reservoir in the northern part of central Quebec to the St. Lawrence River. The Saint-Maurice River was named after Maurice Poulin de la Fontaine, who explored the waterway in 1668. Capital of the Mauricie, Trois-Rivières is the major industrial center of the region.

- ▤ **Information:** ☎1-800-567-7603. www.tourismemauricie.com.
- ▶ **Orient Yourself:** The valley of the Saint-Maurice River extends from Trois-Rivières north to La Tuque, along Rtes. 55 and 155.
- ⊘ **Don't Miss:** Tranquil, clear waters plus night-time constellations at Normand Lake at Saint-Maurice Wildlife Reserve.
- ⊙ **Organizing Your Time:** Shop for supplies before visiting Saint-Maurice Wildlife Reserve, as you're only allowed out of the reserve for an hour before another charge is applied for re-entry.
- Kids **Especially for Kids:** At the Forges-of-Saint-Maurice, kids can handle authentic artifacts and tools as well as compare dress worn in the 18C, when the forge was in its heyday.

A Bit of History

The valley of the Saint-Maurice River has been an important industrial region since the 18C. Rich veins of iron ore were first mined here in 1730, and forestry has dominated the regional economy since 1850. In the late 19C, hydroelectric plants were established in Grand-Mère, Shawinigan and La Gabelle. Their energy supply, together with the invention of floating booms (chains of logs enclosing free-floating logs), led entrepreneurs to establish pulp mills between 1890 and 1900. Chemical plants later opened in Grand-Mère and Shawinigan, and eventually, a major aluminum plant was built in Shawinigan.

Driving Tour

From Trois-Rivières to La Tuque *170km/105.6mi.*

- ▶ *Leave Trois-Rivières by Boulevard des Forges.*

Lieu historique national du Canada des Forges-du-Saint-Maurice★★ (The Forges-of-Saint-Maurice National Historic Site of Canada) Kids

13km/8mi. ⊙*Open mid-May–Labor Day, daily 9.30am–5.30pm; rest of Sept–mid-Oct, daily 9.30am–4.30pm.* ⊚*$4.* ⟁ ▣ ☎*819-378-5116. www.pc.gc.ca/forges.*

The ironworks on the banks of the Saint-Maurice River operated 150 years (1729–1883) and engendered Canada's first industrial community. By special warrant of King Louis XV, François Poulin de Francheville established the first blast furnace in 1730 as part of an initiative to exploit the natural resources of New France. At its productive zenith, the furnace was capable of reducing 19 tons of raw ore per day to four tons of liquid cast iron. Iron was smelted here until 1883. Today this national historic site commemorates the inception of Canada's massive iron and steel industry.

The Grande Maison (1737), which housed managers' offices, a store, and living quarters, today serves as the park's reception center. Displays on the ground floor explain the economic and social conditions in Canada during the early years of the forge's operation. Objects

Address Book

For price ranges, see the Legend on the cover flap.

WHERE TO STAY AND EAT

$$$ Hôtel Sacacomie – *4000 Rang Sacacomie, St-Alexis-des-Monts.*
✕ ♿ 🅿 Spa 🖶 *819-265-4444 & 1-888-265-4414. www.sacacomie.com. 110 rooms.*
The famous, almost mythical Hôtel Sacacomie sits in the pristine Mastigouche wildlife reserve above a tranquil lake. The building is constructed of logs and comfortable rooms boast wood paneling. It is a Canadian dream come true! This year-round resort offers a wealth of outdoor recreational activities, including hiking, fishing and ice fishing, skating, snowmobiling, canoeing, kayaking, mountain biking, horseback riding, and cross-country skiing, dogsledding, and forest excursions.

The **restaurant ($$$)** serves some of the best of Quebec specialties, like Lanaudière duck and foie gras, Kamouraska lamb, bison and deer venison, a delicious assortment of Quebec cheeses, and the local pride: Speckled trout from Saint-Alexis (*see Saint-Alexis-des-Monts Trout Festival under LOUISEVILLE*). Sugar pie with crème fraîche completes this tasty, calorific hymn to the new Québécois gastronomy.

produced at the forge, which included guns and ammunition, cooking pots, wheel hubs, horseshoes, and cast-iron bedsteads, are on view in the basement. On the upper floor, a "sound and light" narration uses a scale model of the forge village as it appeared around 1845. From the Grande Maison, a path leads to the vestiges of the **blast furnace**. The shape of the structures comprising the ironworks has been re-created by a three-dimensional metal structure. At the blast furnace (*haut fourneau*), an excellent interpretation center explains the smelting process in layman's terms; particularly interesting is reconstructed hydraulic machinery of the type used during the 18C. Other displays present the sources and types of ore, and a small, furnished cabin illustrates the life led by forge workers and their families during the late 18C.

A pleasant path leads down to the Saint-Maurice River; along the way, other vestiges are visible, including the **upper forge** (*forge haute*), the finerystack of the **lower forge** (*forge basse*), and the **mill** (*moulin*). On the river's shore, a spring known as the **Devil's Fountain** (*Fontaine du Diable*) is a source of natural gas.

▸ *Continue northward on Blvd. des Forges and take Rte. 55 (Exit 196).*

Shawinigan
23km/14.3mi (Exit 217 South).
This community was formerly referred to as "la ville de l'électricité" (the city of electricity) because it generated all the power needed to supply Montreal. The name Shawinigan comes from the Algonquian word *ashawenikan,* meaning "portage on the crest."
In 1852 a water slide was built to transport logs around the various falls on the Saint-Maurice River. In 1899 the falls were harnessed for their hydroelectric power; this in turn led to the construction of pulp mills, chemical plants and an aluminum smelter.

▸ *From town, take Rte. 157 Sud across the bridge to Shawinigan-Sud and follow signs for the "parc des chutes de Shawinigan" and Shawinigan-Sud.*

La Cité de l'énergie
1000 Ave. Melville. 🕐 *Open mid-Jun–Labor Day, daily 10am–6pm (last admission at 3pm for a complete visit); early Jun–mid-Jun & early Sept–mid-Oct, Tue–Sun 10am–5pm (last admission at 2pm for a complete visit).* 🔖*$16.* ♿🅿🖶*819-536-4992 & 1-866-900-2483. www.citedelenergie.com.*
Constructed next to the Shawinigan Falls, the City of Energy enlightens visitors to the key role hydroelectric

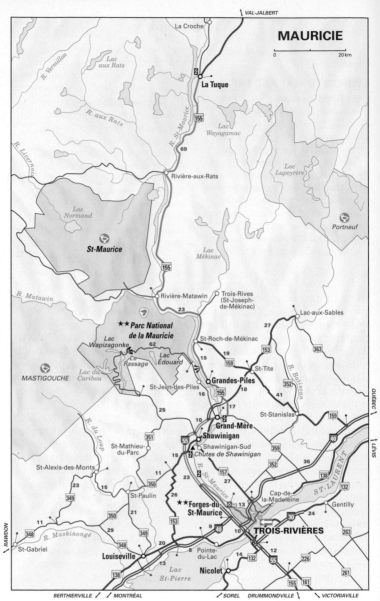

power plays in the history of Quebec. A science center complete with interactive displays and multimedia presentation, observation tower and two hydroelectric power plants brings to life the innovations and inventions of the hydroelectric industry.

Although the rocky beds of the **chutes de Shawinigan** (Shawinigan Falls) are scenic throughout the year, the falls are most impressive during the spring run-off or after heavy rainfall.

▶ *Return to Rte. 55.*

Grand-Mère
10km/6.2mi (Exit 223).
In 1890 a hydroelectric power station was built here and pulp mills were constructed shortly afterwards. The

town was named after a giant rock that protruded from the middle of the river, resembling the head of an old woman (*Grand-Mère* means "grandmother"). To make room for the Hydro-Québec dam in 1916, the rock (rocher de Grand-Mère) was relocated, piece by piece, to a tiny park in the center of town (corner of 5e Avenue and 1re Rue).

▶ *Leave Grand-Mère by the bridge over the Saint-Maurice River and take Rte. 155.*

Grandes-Piles
17km/10.5mi.
Founded in 1885 as a transfer point for lumber boats, this community is perched on a cliff overlooking the river. The municipality was named for the pile-shaped rocks located in the waterfall south of the village.

Musée et village du Bûcheron★ (Lumberman's Museum & Village)
On Rte. 155 in Grandes-Piles. ⏱*Open mid-May–mid-Oct, daily 9.30am–6pm.* ☞*$13.* ✕👤🅿☎*819-538-7895 & 1-877-338-7895.* *www.museedubucheronlespiles.com.*
Some 20 buildings and a collection of more than 5,000 objects re-create a typical Québécois logging village during the early 20C. The rough, axe-hewn timber structures evoke the rudimentary living conditions of the men for whom the cutting and transportation of wood was a way of life. In each of the buildings, objects and furnishings highlight the living conditions of loggers, fire watchmen and storage guards. Visitors can enjoy a snack in the restored cook's house and visit the sawmill, forge, lumbermen's quarters and stables.

▶ *Continue on Rte. 155.*

Between Grandes-Piles and Saint-Roch-de-Mékinac, the drive affords lovely **views**★ of the powerful Saint-Maurice River and the rocky cliffs on the opposite shore. In spring, osprey (*balbuzard*), large fish-eating hawks, nest here and visitors can often see them circling above the river.

▶ *Continue to Rivière-Matawin (38km/23.6mi).*

Detour to the Réserve faunique du Saint-Maurice (Saint-Maurice Wildlife Reserve)
Accessible only by bridge across the Saint-Maurice River (☞round-trip toll: $12/car, cash only). A welcome center (2km/1.2mi from Rivière-Matawin) provides maps and information for various activities (camping, fishing, hunting, canoe-camping, nature study, dogsledding, hiking; for lodging, call ☎819-646-5687). ♿Note: you can leave the reserve for a maximum of one hour (and not be charged re-entry fee) if you leave your ticket at the gatehouse. ⏱*Open mid-May–mid-Sept, Mon–Fri 7.30am–9.30pm, weekends 8am–4pm; late Sept–Nov, Mon–Fri 8am–4.30pm, weekends 7.30am–9.30pm (♿certain roads may be closed in winter; call in advance).* ✕👤🅿☎*819-646-5687.* *www.sepaq.com.*
This vast wilderness of forests, lakes, and streams is a haven for fishermen and canoeists. Numerous campgrounds are scattered around Lake Normand, famous for its clear waters and long, sandy beaches.
The 22km/13.6mi **Pioneers Circuit**, a canoeing and camping route, runs through the hills and woods of the reserve. Other sights include waterfalls (the Dunbar waterfall is most spectacular), rock formations (including the "boat-rock," shaped like a boat), and a nature trail through the boreal forest.

La Tuque
69km/42.8mi.
A former fur trading post, La Tuque, like many other towns in this region, owes its existence to vast forested areas and a powerful waterfall. It boasts a pulp and paper mill and a hydroelectric plant (1909). Its name is derived from a hill shaped like the popular woollen hat known as a *tuque*.
La Tuque is the birthplace of singer-composer **Félix Leclerc** (1914–88), who became the first Quebec songwriter to acquire international fame. His songs praise the beauty of the forests and rivers of Quebec, with special emphasis on the St. Lawrence River.

Parc national du Canada de la MAURICIE★★

MAURICIE REGION
MAP: SEE MAURICIE

Established in 1970 with a view to preserving a representative slice of the Laurentian Mountains, Mauricie National Park comprises 536sq km/207sq mi in a transition area between the deciduous woods of the south and the boreal forest. Maples and conifers thickly cover rounded hills rising some 350m/1,148ft and interspersed with numerous rivers and lakes. For 5,000 years, the region's rich natural resources have attracted indigenous peoples, trappers, loggers, raftsmen, fishermen and hunters. Before being designated a national park, it was one of the largest private hunting and fishing grounds in North America.

- **Information:** ☎1-800-567-7603. www.tourismemauricie.com.
- ▶ **Orient Yourself:** Mauricie National Park is located some 70km/43.5mi north of Trois-Rivières by Rte. 55. Its two principal entrances are the west entrance near Saint-Mathieu (exit 217) and the east entrance near Saint-Jean-des-Piles (Exit 226; follow the signs). West entrance and reception center (☎819-538-3232) ⊙open early May–mid-Oct. East entrance open year-round. Accommodations limited to camping, although the Wabénaki and Andrew lodges (⊙open year-round) provide dormitory-style lodging. ⊙Reservations required for the lodges ☎819-537-4555. Camping and overnight hiking reservations ☎1-877-737-3738 or 819-538-3232.
- ⊙ **Don't Miss:** 3D slide show, Mystic Laurentians at the St-Jean-des-Piles Visitor Reception Center.
- ⊙ **Organizing Your Time:** Viewing wildlife is best at dawn or dusk and on La Cache Trail (1km/.6mi return trip) find a hidden observatory that enables you to see them better. The Parc de la Mauricie is one the best places in Canada to admire the fall colors season.
- **Especially for Kids:** On Saturdays, naturalists present educational games, props, talks about wildlife such as the Eastern Wolf, and the Wood Turtle.

Visit

⊙Park open year-round. Visitor centers at the Saint-Jean-des-Piles and Saint-Mathieu entrances offer information, entrance permits and canoe rentals and interpretative displays; open early–mid-May–Labor Day, daily 7am–10pm; early Sept–mid-Oct, daily 9am–4.30pm (Fri 10pm); Saint-Jean-des-Piles visitor center is open year-round for winter activities daily 8.30am–5pm. ☞$7.80. ⚠ ✗ ♿ Ⓟ ☎1-877-737-3783 or 819-538-3232. www.pc.gc.ca/mauricie.

ACTIVITIES

Canoeing and canoe-camping are among the best ways of exploring the park (canoes and security equipment can be hired on site). Several trails with rudimentary campsites run through the backcountry. Some circuits require difficult and extensive portaging over relatively rough terrain, and canoeing lessons are strongly recommended. Visitors can swim, hike, and fish for speckled and lake trout.

Scenic Drive

62km/38.5mi between the two park entrances.

This wonderful drive meanders through the pink metamorphic rocks of the Canadian Shield. The road follows the long, finger-shaped **Lac Wapizagonke** over 16km/10mi, providing several viewpoints of cliffs and sandy beaches. The observation deck at Le Passage (30km/18.6mi) affords a superb view. The road leads to **Lac Édouard**, a narrow stretch of water surrounded by a natural beach, then descends to the eastern entrance of the park, offering pleasant views of the Saint-Maurice River.

LAC MÉGANTIC★
EASTERN TOWNSHIPS REGION
MAP: SEE LAC MÉGANTIC

Situated in the southeast corner of Quebec, this lovely lake covers 26sq km/10sq mi and reaches depths of 75m/246ft. Located near the American border, its southern end is surrounded by the Blanches Mountains. From Lake Mégantic, the Chaudière River flows northward across the southern part of the province to join the St. Lawrence near Quebec City.

Discovered by Father Druillettes in 1646, the lake region was settled by the Abenaki in 1700. They called it *Namesokanjik,* meaning "place where fish abound." Formerly a logging center, Lake Mégantic is now a haven for fishermen and vacationers.

- **Information:** ☎1-800-355-5755. www.easterntownships.org.
- **Orient Yourself:** Lake Mégantic is located 190km/118mi southeast of Quebec City by Rte. 73 and Rtes. 173 and 204. The municipality of Lac-Mégantic lies at the junction of Rtes. 204 and 161.
- **Don't Miss:** Mont Mégantic ASTROlab and the observatory's telescope—the most powerful in Canada. The view from Mont Joseph is also one not to miss.
- **Organizing Your Time:** Arrive early enough in the afternoon to tour the ASTROlab so you can view the sky at night, hopefully on a clear evening. The Perseids, in early August, are the shooting-star/meteor shower "season"—a truly spectacular astronomical phenomenon.
- **Especially for Kids:** At Mont Megantic, in the daytime visit the ASTROlab and don't miss children's workshops (summer only) on the history of the universe. At night, participate in star observation.

Visit

Lac-Mégantic

This municipality (population 5,949) is located on the northern shores of Lake Mégantic, where it empties into the Chaudière River. It was founded in 1885 by Scottish settlers who left their architectural signature in the numerous redbrick buildings along the main street. Today the town is a small industrial and commercial center. A pleasant park beside the lake (*behind the courthouse*) provides good views of the mountains, notably the peak of Mt. Mégantic to the west.

The **Église Sainte-Agnès** (Church of St. Agnes) houses a lovely **stained-glass window**, depicting the Jesse Tree, created in 1849 for the Church of the Immaculate Conception, located in London's Mayfair district (UK) (◔*open year-round, 9.30am–noon, 1.30pm–4.30pm;* ☎819-583-0370).

Excursion to Mont-Mégantic
59km/36.6mi.

▶ *Leave Lac-Mégantic by Rte. 161.*

The road rises above the lake, overlooking the Blanches Mountains to the south. At Woburn (27km/16.7mi), turn right on Rte. 212 and continue for 18km/11mi. The road reaches Notre-Dame-des-Bois, the village with the highest altitude (549m/1,801ft) in the province.

▶ *In Notre-Dame-des-Bois, turn right following signs to ASTROlab and Parc National du Mont Mégantic Park. Mont Mégantic is 13km/8mi. (☎819-888-2941; www.sepaq.com).*

Mont Mégantic

At the base of Mont Mégantic's peak (1,100m/3,608ft) find the **ASTROlab**, an astronomy activity center open in the day and in the evening, which houses a high-definition multimedia room. There are two observatories

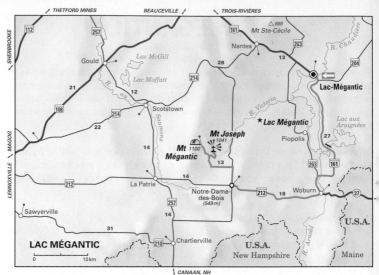

on the summit which you can visit during guided day or evening tours. Mont Mégantic's telescope is the largest in eastern North America, measuring 1.6m/5.2ft in diameter and weighing approximately 26 tons. A second, public telescope is of professional calibre (61cm/24in). Popular night-time astronomy evenings allow visitors to observe stars and constellations through it (when visibility permits). Reservations are required for tours of the summit, but not to visit the ASTROlab at the mountain's base. *Call or check website to select from many different tours available from late May–early Oct, reservations required; $11–$22 (fee does not include $3.50 park entry); 819-888-2941; www.sepaq.com).*

▶ *Return 3km/1.8mi and turn left, following a rough road that climbs steeply for 1km/.6mi up Mont Joseph.*

Mont Joseph

Father Corriveault of Notre-Dame-des-Bois constructed the small sanctuary here in 1883 after the village inhabitants were miraculously saved from devastating tornadoes after praying to St. Joseph. The summit affords a stunning **view**★★ of the surrounding mountainous region.

ASTROlab

JARDINS DE MÉTIS★★
(Reford Gardens)

GASPÉSIE REGION
MAP: SEE GASPÉSIE

In 1886 Lord Mount Stephen (1829–1921), president and founder of the Canadian Pacific Railway Company, purchased this tract of land at the confluence of the Métis and Saint Lawrence rivers from the Seigneur of Grand-Métis, Archibald Ferguson. The land was to be Stephen's salmon fishing retreat, but he spent very little time at Grand-Métis, and in 1918 he gave the land to his niece, Elsie Stephen Reford. From 1926 through 1959, Mrs. Reford gradually transformed the estate into magnificent gardens. Over 3,000 varieties of flowers and ornamental plants, including many rare species, flourish in six distinct gardens that rank among the loveliest in the world.

- **Information:** ☎1-800-463-0323. www.tourisme-gaspesie.com.
- **Orient Yourself:** The gardens (Jardins de Métis) are located in Grand-Métis, 350km/217.5mi east of Quebec City. They are accessible by Rtes. 73 (Pierre-Laporte Bridge in Quebec City) and 20 to Rivière-du-Loup (198km/123mi) and Rte. 132 to Grand-Métis (152km/94.4mi).
- **Don't Miss:** The International Garden Festival at the Reford Gardens. Musical brunches held Sundays, June through September feature regional players and cuisine. There are also garden lectures given by experts (check schedule), tastings (*every Thursday from 5pm–7pm*), as well as literary events (in French only).
- **Organizing Your Time:** A visit to the Gardens can take a half day, and the Park walk can last up to three hours, so garden enthusiasts should allocate at least a day here. Save time for the Mitis River Park walk by the gardens. Naturalist guides available.
- **Especially for Kids:** Check family activities at the garden's International Garden Festival (usually late June to beginning of October).

Visit

Open Jun, daily 8.30am–6pm; Jul–Aug, daily 8.30am–8pm; Sept–mid-Oct, daily 8.30am–6pm. $14 (free for children 13 and under). ☎418-775-2221. www.jardinsmetis.com.

Entrance Garden
This floral massif displays the brilliant colors of annual flowers from early June through early October. Perennials such as peonies, lupins and daylilies bloom earlier in the season. Peeking among the spruce trees bordering this colorful array of flowers are forget-me-nots and horsetails. Tuberous begonias flower near the rock garden from mid-summer until fall.

Les Rocailles (Rock Garden)
On a slope beside a meandering stream lies a small alpine garden of saxifrage, spiraea, phlox, and alpine pinks. In the center bed is the rare **Bock willow**, a small shrub of Chinese origin introduced by Mrs. Reford. Nine types of ferns including the ostrich fern, the Canadian maidenhair fern and the interrupted fern can be found here.

Rhododendron Garden
The spectacular floral display of rhododendrons in early summer is followed by the blooming of roses, which continues until the first frost. A favorable microclimate and careful maintenance (soil enrichment, acidity testing, winter protection) account for the beauty of this garden, which also includes red Japanese maples and the pride of the gardens, the **blue poppy** (*meconopsis betonicifolia*). The floral emblem of the gardens, the blue poppy is native to the alpine prairies of the Himalayas and was introduced by Mrs. Reford, who painstakingly adapted it to her gardens. This rare and beautiful flower blooms from mid-June through mid-July.

Jardins de Métis

Allée royale (The Long Walkway)

A tribute to the English garden, this walkway, lined with annuals, perennials and shrubs, is designed so that at least one species is in flower throughout the season. From the end of July until mid-August, blooming delphiniums attract a multitude of ruby-throated hummingbirds.

Villa Reford (Estevan Lodge)

To the left of the Long Walkway, the sumptuous Victorian residence—called Estevan Lodge by Mrs. Reford—overlooks the gardens. Built by her uncle in 1887 as a fishing retreat, the house was enlarged as a summer home for the Refords in 1927. The first floor of the villa now houses a restaurant, snack bar, and handicrafts boutique. A garden shop is located in the adjacent coach house.

In the **museum**, located on the upper floors, visitors can see the Refords' sitting room overlooking the bay, their apartments, the darkroom, and the attic. On the other side of the attic, furnished rooms re-create several aspects of daily life on the estate.

At the end of the well-maintained lawn leading from the villa to Mitis Bay, a low wall constructed along the waterside promontory is bordered by poplars and conifers that protect the gardens from harsh winter winds.

Jardin des pommetiers (Crab Apple Garden)

A stroll along the woods leads to this garden's beautiful flower beds, arranged in patterns of sweeping curves accented by crabapple trees and patches of lawn and ground cover.

Jardin des primevères (Primula Glade)

The conifer with drooping branches at the entrance is a **False Sawara cypress** imported from Japan by Mrs. Reford. In spring, different varieties of primrose burst into bloom.

Sous-bois (Woodland Garden)

The remaining land of the estate is a wooded area containing shrubs and other plants native to Quebec.

International Garden Festival   Kids

International as well as provincial designers create avant-garde, experimental designs in landscape architecture and the visual arts at the Reford Gardens. Dates alter annually but generally they are late June to beginning of October. See www.jardinsmetis.com/english/festival/concepteurs.htm for more information.

PARC DE MIGUASHA★

GASPÉSIE REGION
MAP: SEE GASPÉSIE

Miguasha is a Quebec national conservation park, where visitors are introduced to the fascinating world of fossils through exhibits and on-site observation of the cliff in the company of researchers and park personnel. In 1999 the park was designated a UNESCO World Heritage Site.

ℹ Information: ☎1-800-463-0323. www.tourisme-gaspesie.org.

▶ **Orient Yourself:** The Parc national de Miguasha is located 242km/150.3mi southeast of Rimouski by Rte. 132, and 294km/182.6mi southwest of Gaspé, near Chaleur Bay and the New Brunswick border.

😊 **Don't Miss:** Walk down to the beach to look for fossils.

Especially for Kids: Virtual deep sea dive into ancient tropical oceans—an animated film "Dive Into the Origins," shown daily on a giant screen.

Geological Notes

On the north shore of the Ristigouche River, in Chaleur Bay, lies an escarpment containing fossils embedded in sedimentary rock since the Upper Devonian Period (370 million years ago). The site of Miguasha was once probably a tropical lagoon fed by several rivers and surrounded by lush plant life. The shifting of sands and deposit of sediments gradually buried aquatic and plant life layer by layer. Over millions of years, the sediments became rock, and the embedded life forms were preserved as fossils.

Two geological formations are visible at Miguasha: The Fleurant conglomerate, consisting mainly of sandstone (at the base); and the grayish Escuminac formation (at the top). The latter consists mostly of silt, sandstone and argillaceous schist, and measures only 8km/5mi long by 1km/.6mi wide.

The storehouse of paleontological information contained in this cliff was first discovered in 1842, although scientific study here did not begin until 1880. Soon afterwards, the site gained popularity with European geologists, who collected and removed many of the fossils. In the 1970s, as part of a move to protect the fossil deposits from unauthorized removal, the provincial government purchased portions of the cliff.

Parc national de Miguasha

©François Rivard/ATRG

Visit

🕐 *Open early Jan–end May, Mon–Fri 8.30am–4.30pm; Jun–Aug, daily 9am–6pm; Sept–mid-Oct, daily 9am–5pm.* 🍴$11.75. ✗ ♿ 🅿 📞418-794-2475 & 1-800-665-6527. www.sepaq.com/pq/mig/en.

Musée d'histoire naturelle (Natural History Museum)

Fossils on display represent ferns, invertebrates and 20 groups of fish from the Upper Devonian Period. Among the outstanding finds of the Miguashan fossils is *Eusthenopteron foordi*, which resembles the earliest known amphibian, *Ichthyostega*. Fossils found in Greenland indicate that this amphibian may have lived some 20 million years after the Miguashan fish.

Amphitheatre   Kids

Showings of a 2D/3D animation Dive Into the Origins is a first in North America, depicting marine creatures from long ago coming back to life in tropical oceans. A collaboration between computer graphics designers and paleontologists brings ancient seas back to life.

Laboratory

Guides explain methods of disengaging fossils from the host rock. With the use of microscopes, visitors can examine fossil samples.

Cliff Walk

A short walk down to the cliff offers a firsthand look at the sedimentary strata. Guides help visitors to locate fossils. A 1.9km/1mi hiking trail surrounds the site. 🙂*Note: it is forbidden to remove fossils from the park.*

ARCHIPEL DE MINGAN★★

DUPLESSIS REGION

MAP: SEE CÔTE NORD

The Mingan Archipelago is made up of approximately 40 islands lying in the Gulf of St. Lawrence, north of Anticosti Island. The string of islands measures 95km/59mi in length. The Mingan Archipelago National Park Reserve of Canada, created in 1984, extends from Longue-Pointe to Baie-Johan-Beetz, on the Côte-Nord.

The sedimentary rocks of the Mingan Archipelago were formed by the accumulation of limestone deposits at the edge of the Canadian Shield some 500 million years ago. The weight of glaciers, constant freezing and thawing, and the relentless pounding of the sea caused fissures to form. Over time these fissures eroded, slowly creating the string of islands and their characteristic monoliths.

- **Information:** 📞1-888-773-8888. www.pc.gc.ca/mingan & www.tourismeduplessis.com.
- ▶ **Orient Yourself:** Access from Havre-Saint-Pierre or Mingan by boat. Havre-Saint-Pierre is located 855km/530mi northeast of Quebec City and 214km/133mi northeast of Sept-Îles. 🚗*Motorized vehicles are forbidden on the archipelago.*
- **Don't Miss:** Cruising or kayaking around the islands.
- 🕐 **Organizing Your Time:** Cruises take 3hr 30min, so plan your time accordingly if you also want to scuba dive, sea kayak or snorkel.
- **Also See:** HAVRE-SAINT-PIERRE.

Geographical Notes

Monoliths – These spectacular rock formations were wrought by the elements over millennia. Because all the monoliths are approximately the same height (from 5m/16.4ft to 10m/32.8ft), it is believed they were once part of the same rock. The monoliths are nicknamed "flower pots" (*pots de fleurs*) in reference to the vegetation sprouting from their tops. Over the years, the residents of the area have come to recognize familiar shapes in the forms created by nature, and have

The monoliths in the Mingan Archipelago National Park Reserve

given the monoliths whimsical names such as "Bonne Femme" (Matron) and "Tête d'Indien" (Indian Head).

Flora – The icy Labrador Current, distinctive soil deposits, high humidity, and a powerful sea all contribute to the islands' unique bioclimate. Approximately half the land on the islands is covered with coniferous forest, but exceptional ecological conditions have fostered a diverse collection of plants, including ferns, orchids, mosses, and lichens, some of which are normally found only in arctic or alpine climates. Some 40 plants growing on the islands are extremely rare. The most notable is the **Mingan thistle** (*chardon*), not known to be found anywhere else in eastern Canada; it was discovered in 1924 by Brother Marie Victorin, the founder of Montreal's Botanical Gardens.

Fauna – Of the many sea birds living in the archipelago, probably the most endearing one to residents and visitors alike is the cute **Atlantic puffin** (*macareux*), whose red, yellow and blue beak and bright orange feet have earned it the nickname "sea parrot" (*perroquet de mer*). Other birds to look for are the Common Eider, the Black Guillemot, and the Common and Arctic tern. Three types of seals are found in the waters around the islands: The Grey Seal, the Harp Seal and the Harbor Seal. The Fin Whale can sometimes be spotted.

A Bit of History

Early human occupation – Dictated by various needs, the Montagnais Amerindians (also called Innus), Basque, French, British, Acadians, and Canadians came to occupy the Mingan Islands occasionally or on a permanent basis, to make use of its natural resources, to practice a form of commerce, to take shelter and to reinvent themselves through permanent residence or tourism. Human occupation of the Mingan Archipelago goes back at least 2,000 years—long time before Jacques Cartier. The first inhabitants, groups of Amerindians, were attracted by the plentiful marine resources of this part of the Gulf of St. Lawrence and amongst other things gathered molluscs, fished salmon and hunted seals. In the 15C and 16C centuries, the Basque fished for cod and hunted whales in the Mingan archipelago. The Basque left signs of their activities on Île-Nue-de-Mingan and Île-du-Havre-de-Mingan, which contain the remains of stone ovens used to melt whale fat.

Montagnais, French, and English – Before the Europeans gradually took over their land, the Montagnais occupied an immense territory reaching from the Duplessis (Côte-Nord) to the Saguenay–Lac-Saint-Jean regions. The epoch of the French seigneurs and concessionnaires resulted in the setting up of a fur trading post on Île-du-Havre-de-Mingan. The fur trade with the Montagnais continued under British rule, while the French seigneuries were handed over to British merchant traders—in this case to those of the Hudson Bay Company (HBC). The HBC obtained a monopolistic commercial status in the area and made sure that there would be no human settlement on the coast shore or in the archipelago.

Settlements on the coast shore – Around 1850, when the HBC lost its monopoly, villages began to spring up along the coast. New settlers came from Jersey, from French Canada, and from Acadia. The Mingan archipelago islands were used by these newcomers for hunting, food gathering, and for shelter. In the process, many boats were sunk in the area, which led to the construction of two lighthouses in the archipelago, the first in 1888, on Île-aux-Perroquets, the second in 1915, on Petite-Île-au-Marteau. Human occupation of the archipelago at this time was marked by a number of attempts at permanent settlements, as well as fox breeding on Île-du-Havre and the setting up of a commercial shellfish trade on Île Saint-Charles. Finally, since the foundation of these villages, the Mingan Archipelago has been increasingly used as a tourist resort.

A road for development – The North Shore of the St. Lawrence River is still very new in terms of major developments. No paved road reached Sept-Îles before 1960, and Natashquan was only reachable by air or sea until 1996. Route 138 reached Havre-Saint-Pierre in 1976. That highway allowed for the significant development of the economy of the Duplessis region. Of course, Route 138 was not built in order to bring tourists to admire the Mingan archipelago, yet without the road, very few tourists could enjoy the monoliths, flora, and fauna that make the Mingan Archipelago National Park so precious and popular today.

Visit

🕐 *Park open mid-Jun–late Aug (few services, including access to the islands, are available before and after that time period).* ☜*$5.80.* ⚠ *(mid-May–mid-Oct)* ☜*$15.85. www.pc.gc.ca/mingan.*

Nature Information Centers

Parks Canada operates two information centers in the Mingan Archipelago National Park Reserve: One at Longue-Pointe-de-Mingan and the other at Havre-Saint-Pierre. Open from early June through early September, the centers organise workshops on plants, wildlife, geology, and geomorphology, as well as films, lectures, and special exhibits on island-related themes. Visitors interested in organized interpretation programs, wilderness camping, scuba diving and kayaking in the reserve must register at one of the centers.

☜Guided **walking tours** (3hrs) allow to explore Grosse-Île-au-Marteau. Evening walks at Petite-Île-au-Marteau are truly special. The guides conduct the tours in French, but tours in English are available on request.

Sea Cruises★

To fully appreciate the natural wonders of the Mingan Archipelago, visitors should tour the islands by boat. Cruises departing from Havre-Saint-Pierre specialize in geological interpretation; visitors disembark on Niapiskau Island for a closer look at the monoliths (*depart from the Havre-Saint-Pierre marina, mid-Jun–Labor Day, daily 8am, noon & 3.45pm; round-trip 3hrs 15min; commentary (French only); reservations suggested;* ☜*$40;* ♿🅿*La Relève Jomphe Inc.;* ☎*418-538-2865 & 1-866-538-2865; www.croisierejomphe.com*).

Cruises leaving from Mingan offer views of the "flower pots," and concentrate on sighting marine life and sea birds (*depart from the Parks Canada wharf mid-Jun–early Sept, daily 7.30am & 1pm; round-trip 5hrs; commentary by naturalists (mainly in French);* ⊙*reservations required;* ☜*$70;* ♿🅿*Randonnée des Îles Ltée.* ☎*418-949-2307 & 1-866-949-2307*).

The Mingan Islands Cetecean Interpretation Center in Longue-Pointe-de-Mingan (☎*418-949-2845; www.rorqual.com*) schedules some combined **whale watching and scientific research expeditions** that leave from the same Havre-Saint-Pierre dock.

PARC DU MONT-ORFORD★

EASTERN TOWNSHIPS REGION

MAP: SEE CANTONS DE L'EST

Parc du Mont-Orford, a Quebec national park, covers an area of 58sq km/ 23sq mi in the Appalachian Mountains of Quebec. Mt. Chauve (600m/1,968ft) towers to the northeast, while Mt. Orford (881m/2,890ft), a well-known ski center, dominates the southwest horizon.

- **Information:** ☎1-800-355-5755. www.easterntownships.com.
- ▶ **Orient Yourself:** The western entrance of the park (116km/72mi east of Montreal) is reached by Rte. 10 (Exit 115) and Rte. 141 North. The latter loops through the southern section of the park and exits by its eastern entrance, reaching the town of Cherry River and connecting with Exit 118 of Rte. 10. The park is 7km/4.3mi northwest of downtown Magog.
- **Don't Miss:** Panorama of the region's mountains and watersheds from the summit of Mont Orford.
- **Organizing Your Time:** Plant walks, hikes, water-based activities abound: You could spend a few hours or an entire day here. There is a supervised beach at Lake Fraser. In winter, Mont Orford is a popular ski resort.

Visit

In Magog-Orford, 3321 Chemin du Parc (Rte 141). *Park open year-round, daily. Interpretation Center open year-round, daily 8am–4.30pm (extended hours seasonally).* $3.50. (mid-May–mid-Oct) ($5/vehicle) ☎819-843-9855 & 1-800-665-6527. www.parcquebec.com.

Mont Orford (Mount Orford)
On Rte. 141, 1km/.6mi from western park entrance. Access by chairlift or on foot.

From the top of the chairlift, splendid **views**★ extend over Lake Memphrémagog and the surrounding mountains. The summit (short walk around television tower) offers a **panorama**★★ north to the St. Lawrence Valley, west to the Monteregian hills, south to Lake Memphrémagog and east to the Appalachian Mountains.

Lac Stukely (Lake Stukely)
Turn left off Rte. 141, 4km/2.5mi from western entrance, and follow secondary road for 6km/3.7mi.

Snowshoeing in Parc du Mont-Orford

Parc national du Mont-Orford/Jean-Pierre Huard/Sépaq

ACTIVITIES

The park includes lakes for sailing and swimming; hiking trails through forests of sugar maple, birch, fir, and pine; downhill and cross-country skiing and ice-skating in winter; a golf course; an arts center (below) and several beaches, picnic areas, and campgrounds.

This pretty lake is reached after a pleasant drive beside the Cerises (Cherry) River and Cerises Pond. Stukely Lake is bordered by sandy beaches and features several rocky islets.

Centre d'arts Orford (Orford Arts Centre)

On Rte. 141, 1km/.6mi from eastern entrance or 1km/.6mi from road leading to Lake Stukely. ◐*Open mid-Jun–mid-Aug, daily 8am–10pm;* ☞*guided tour of the sculpture garden* ☜*$5; rest of the year, main building open Mon–Fri 9am-4.30pm, no guided tours.* ✗ ⓟ ☎*819-843-9871 & 1-800-567-6155. www.arts-orford.org.*

The Orford Arts Centre, founded in 1951, enjoys a fine reputation for its courses in musical training. The 500-seat concert hall (salle Gilles-Lefevre), in the shape of an amphitheater, is located on a lovely wooded site. The Man and Music pavilion of Montreal's Expo '67 is a special part of the music school complex. A theater, several residences, and **outdoor sculptures** are scattered among maple and birch woods. The celebrated center draws artists from around the world to its **Orford Arts Centre Summer Festival**, from mid-June to mid-August annually (◐ *see Calendar of Events*).

Musée international d'art naïf (International Museum of Naïve Art)

In Magog-Orford near Rte. 10 (Exit 115 or 118), at 81 Rue Desjardins, in the Center culturel de Magog. ◐*Open Jul–Aug, daily 11am–5pm; Sept–Jun, Wed–Sun 1pm–5pm or by appointment.* ☜*No charge.* ✗ ⓟ ☎*819-843-2099. www.museedart naif.com.*

Some 350 artists from 30 countries have contributed to the permanent collection of the only museum in Canada solely dedicated to naïve art.

Naïve painting has been particularly well developed in Quebec since the 1930s. It is a colorful genre of painting, where the light is diffused from all directions, and where the artist lets emotions direct the creative process. It is often original and inspiring.

PARC DU MONT-SAINT-BRUNO

MONTÉRÉGIE REGION
MAP: SEE VALLÉE DU RICHELIEU

One of the best-known Monteregian hills, Mont Saint-Bruno rises 218m/712ft above the surrounding plain. The public park, created in 1985, covers a 5.9sq km/2.3sq mi section of the mountain. This Quebec national park is part of the former seigneury of Montarville, granted in 1710 to Pierre Boucher by the Sieur de Vaudreuil, governor of New France. Mills were developed to harness the waterways of the mountain, and apple trees were planted in the sandy soil. Today more than 850 apple trees remain. In 1829 part of the seigneury was sold to François-Pierre Bruneau, a Montreal lawyer whose name (with modified spelling) was subsequently given to the mountain.

- 🛈 **Information:** ☎1-866-469-0069. www.tourisme-monteregie.qc.ca.
- ▶ **Orient Yourself:** Mt. Saint-Bruno Park is about 20km/12.4mi east of Montreal by Rte. 20 (Exit 102) or Rte. 30 (Exit 121). It is situated near the pretty suburban municipality of Saint-Bruno-de-Montarville.
- 🕐 **Organizing Your Time:** This popular park is less than an hour's drive from downtown Montreal, and is a great "natural oasis."

SEASONAL ACTIVITIES

Mont Saint-Bruno is popular with walkers, hikers, and mountain bikers during the summer. In late September and October, a walk in the fall colors is a must. The small mountain provides the closest downhill skiing from Montreal, so winter is actually the season when the park is the most frequented and the only time when there is a permanent food service on site. Most of the year, the canteen opens only on weekends.

APPLE PICKING

Beautiful, crisp and succulent apples are ripe for the picking in the Mont Saint-Bruno park's orchard. The apple orchard produces several varieties popular in Canada, such as Empire, Sunrise, Honeycrisp, Macintosh, Cortland, Lobo, Golden Russet and Delicious. A free shuttle service is provided between the park's parking lot and the orchard. Information ☎450-653-7544.

Visit

Open year-round, daily 8am–dusk. $3.50. ☎ 450-653-7544. www.sepaq.com.

From the parking lot, a pleasant trail leads past the former site of the Mont-Saint-Gabriel College, through woods of red oak and maple, to two lakes: Lake Moulin and Lake Seigneurial. Beside the former stands an old stone **mill** dating from 1761, the only survivor of the numerous mills that once harnessed these waters. It nows serves as a nature interpretation center. Beside it and along the lake shore, apple trees recall the era of the Montarville seigneury.

Longer trails lead to the three other lakes of the park: Lake Bouleaux, Lake Tortue, and Lake Atocas (an Amerindian word meaning "cranberry").

STATION MONT-SAINTE-ANNE★

QUEBEC CITY REGION

MAP: SEE CÔTE DE BEAUPRÉ

Created in 1969 as a sports center for the city of Quebec, this provincial park covers the broad slopes of Mt. Sainte-Anne as well as part of the Jean-Larose River valley. An internationally known downhill skiing center that has hosted several World Cup races, the park boasts abundant snowfall, especially on the north side of the mountain.

Ski areas include more than 200km/124mi of cross-country trails and over 50 downhill runs (vertical drop: 625m/2 060ft). At night the trails are lit over quite some distance, creating a magical effect.

- **Information:** ☎1-877-783-1608. www.quebecregion.com.
- **Orient Yourself:** Mt. Sainte-Anne is about 40km/24.8mi northeast of Quebec City by Rte. 440 and Rtes. 138 and 360.
- **Don't Miss:** Whatever the season, head to the summit by gondola to view the panorama with view of Île d'Orléans. Cycling enthusiasts should take in Velirium; the June mountain biking festival features astounding stunts and races during three weekends of activities. In winter, there is an excellent snow sport school for boarders or skiers of all ages and abilities.
- **Organizing Your Time:** Avoid driving during rush hour to and from Québec City.

Visit

Park open daily during winter ski season Nov–late Apr, and in summer season late May–mid-Oct. Camping fee $26 (no service site) to $39 (full service site). ☎418-827-4561 & 1-888-827-4579. www.mont-sainte-anne.com.

ACTIVITIES

Cross-country skiing, downhill skiing, snowboarding, dogsledding, hiking, mountain biking, horseback riding, golf, paragliding, and mountain climbing, depending on the season.

Panorama★★

Access to the summit (15min) by gondola late Jun–mid-Oct, daily 10am–4.30pm. Round-trip 30min. ☞*$16.* 🕐*Ski hours and chairlift fees Nov–Apr, Mon–Fri 9am–10pm, weekends 8.30am–10pm.* ☞*$58/day or $43/half-day (call for ski packages); mountain bike package and rentals available.* ✕ ♿ 🅿

The summit of Mont Sainte-Anne affords an outstanding view of the mighty St. Lawrence River. To the south, the Beaupré Coast, punctuated by the twin spires of Sainte-Anne-de-Beaupré's Basilica, is visible, as well as Île d'Orléans and Quebec City. To the east of Île d'Orléans, the St. Lawrence reaches a width of 10km/6.2mi and separates two distinct landscapes: The Laurentian Shield (Beaupré Coast) and the Appalachians, on the south shore. The Laurentian Mountains rise on the horizon to the north.

Chutes Jean-Larose (Jean-Larose Falls)

From ski center, walk eastward about 700m/2,296ft to a charted path.

Before joining the Sainte-Anne River, the Jean-Larose River drops about 68m/223ft in a steep, narrow canyon, creating a series of falls, one of which is 33m/108.2ft high. The rock has been carved away by the water, and the falls, hidden in the trees, are very picturesque. The path descends steeply (*397 steps*), providing several good viewpoints.

PARC DU MONT-TREMBLANT★

LAURENTIANS REGION

MAP: SEE LAURENTIDES

Designated a forest reserve as early as 1894, Mont Tremblant is Quebec's oldest provincial park. The recreational wonderland, covering 1,500sq km/930sq mi, abounds in lakes and rivers, notably the Diable and Assomption rivers, with their tumultuous rapids and waterfalls. Mountains rise to an altitude of over 931m/3,063ft. Long winding roads and trails beckon hikers, especially in the fall when the bright red foliage of the maple trees blends with the soft yellow hues of the birches. The park has a rich and diverse fauna (moose, black bear, and beaver), and a multitude of birds, including the Great Blue Heron and the Bald Eagle.

- 🄸 **Information:** ☎1-800-561-6673. www.laurentians.com.
- ▶ **Orient Yourself:** Mont Tremblant Park is located about 140km/87mi north of Montreal. There are three main entrances: From Saint-Donat (Rtes. 15 and 329); from Saint-Faustin (Rtes. 15 and 117); and from Saint-Côme (Rtes. 25 and 343). Sections of the access roads are unpaved. *Campsites and shelters are available in the park; for reservations* ☎819-688-2281.
- ☺ **Don't Miss:** Waterfalls in the Cachée (Hidden) Sector of the park.
- 🕐 **Organizing Your Time:** Canoeing and canoe-camping is superb on some of the 400 lakes and six rivers, with the Diable (Devil) or Assomption rivers being the most popular. Factor time for this when planning your trip.
- 🄺🄸🄳🅂 **Especially for Kids:** Le Diable sector is perfect for family outings.

A Bit of History

"Trembling Mountain" – According to one legend, the Algonquin named the mountain Manitonga Soutana (Mountain of Spirits) because of the trembling caused by the streams tumbling down its sides. According to another Amerindian version, the name Manitou Ewitschi Saga (Mountain of the Fearsome Manitou) was

Parc national du Mont-Tremblant/Jean-Pierre Huard/Sepaq

Aerial view of Parc du Mont-Tremblant

chosen, in reference to the nature god who made the mountain tremble when man came and interfered with it.

Visit

🕐*Park open mid-May–Sept, daily 7am–9pm; Oct–Apr, daily 9am–4pm. Sections of the park's roads are closed during winter.* ⚆*$3.50.* ⛺ 🍴 ♿ 🅿 ☎*819-688-2281. www.parcsquebec.com.*

▶ *From the Lac Supérieur entrance, take Park Road no. 1.*

This picturesque route follows the **Diable River★**, from the Mont Tremblant ski area to the Croches Falls.

Lac Monroe (Lake Monroe)
11km/6.8mi from entrance.
This large and attractive lake has many facilities for visitors, including a beach, canoe and bicycle rentals, hiking trails, and campsites. The road follows the shoreline for several kilometers, offering good views. On the other side of the road, a nature trail (*2.7km/1.7mi*) leads to Femmes Lake. Lake Lauzon is located a bit farther on.

▶ *Continue on Park Road no. 1.*

Chute du Diable★ (Devil's Falls)
8km/5mi from Lake Monroe. Park and follow the trail on foot for 800m/2 624ft.
The dark waters of Diable River drop steeply in a forceful fall and suddenly change course, leaving a mass of shattered rocks at the base of the falls.

▶ *10km/6.2mi after the waterfall, the road turns away from Diable River. Head east towards Saint-Donat and Chute-aux-Rats on Park Road nº. 2 and continue over 24km/15mi.*

Address Book

PARK ACTIVITIES

Summer: canoe-camping, sailing, nature interpretation, fishing, swimming, hiking, horseback riding, and mountain biking. Guided excursions mid-May–mid-Oct; *for reservations* ☎*819-688-2336.* Winter: Snowshoeing and snowmobiling, cross-country and downhill skiing at Tremblant resort.

🕯*For price ranges, see cover flap.*

WHERE TO STAY

$$$–$$$$ Fairmont Tremblant (☎*819-681-7000 & 1-800-257-7544; www.fairmont.com*) is a magnificent hotel aiming at emulating the natural beauty of its mountainous, forested surroundings. Located near Mont Tremblant, the region's most picturesque village, it is an all-star proposition.

Dogsledding, Saunas and, Snow

With hiking trails, bike paths, golf courses, and plenty of organized events, the Mont Tremblant area is a cornucopia of recreational choices in summer. Opportunities for exercise don't wane much in winter either. Diversions include **La Source Aquaclub** (☎1-888-857-8001), an indoor pool with waterfalls, and dogsledding (☎819-687-2005) with **Alaskan Expédition**. For experienced skiers, the nearby **Le Scandinave** with an amazing setting (☎1-888-537-2263; *www.scandinave.com*) offers a different spa experience in a woodsy outdoor setting along Rivière du Diable. During winter, the idea is to slowly raise your body temperature in a repeating cycle of heat, cold and rest while getting up the nerve to jump into the hole cut into the frozen river! The Finnish sauna, Jacuzzi, and Norwegian steam baths are joined by outdoor heated sidewalks. Compared with the river—which fewer than a quarter of visitors brave—the bracing Nordic waterfall seems tame. Swedish massages are offered here, too.

Chute-aux-Rats★

The Pembina River plunges 18m/59ft over a layered cliff, and at the end of the Chute-aux-Rats hiking trail (🚶) is one of the prettiest falls in the Lanaudière region. Picnic tables are located in the swimming area and a wooden stairway scales the side of the mountain, following the falls to the top.

▷ *Continue on Park Road no. 3 to the exit (5km/3mi).*

MONTEBELLO

OUTAOUAIS REGION

POPULATION 1,080

This community on the north shore of the Ottawa River, between Gatineau and Montreal, was the home of **Louis-Joseph Papineau** (1786–1871), member of Parliament, president of the Legislative Assembly, eloquent speaker, and leader of the Patriots. Since 1930, Montebello is best known for being the location of a famous hotel made of logs that has hosted numerous international conferences: *Le Château Montebello*.

- 🛈 **Information:** ☎1-800-265-7822. www.outaouais-tourism.ca.
- ▷ **Orient Yourself:** Montebello is 130km/80.7mi west of Montreal and 70km/43.5mi east of Gatineau by Rte. 148.
- 🚗 **Don't Miss:** In winter, curling rink at Le Château Montebello; in summer, horseback riding along woodland trails. Also, visit Fairmont Le Château Montebello's sister property, Kenauk, a wilderness north of the main hotel featuring cedar housekeeping cabins on remote lakes.
- 🕐 **Organizing Your Time:** Le Château is an hour's drive east of Ottawa-Gatineau; an hour-and-a-half west of Montreal. Kenauk cabins are accessed by long, winding gravel roads—their ensured remoteness is well worth the drive.
- 🧒 **Especially for Kids:** Many family activities include those around Canadian Thanksgiving (2nd Monday in October), Christmas, and the "sugaring off" maple syrup season, in March, when maple sap is converted to various sweets.

A Bit of History

In 1674, Msgr. de Laval was granted the seigneury known as Petite-Nation, then inhabited by Algonquins. The notary, Joseph Papineau, father of Louis-Joseph, purchased the seigneury in 1801 and established the first settlement. In 1845, upon returning from eight years of exile after the failed Rebellion, Louis-Joseph built a manor on the land, naming it after a friend, the **Duke of Montebello**, son

Château Montebello

Manoir-Papineau

of one of Napoleon's generals. In 1878 the community that had developed around the manor also took this name. Montebello was also home to Papineau's son-in-law, artist and architect Napoléon Bourassa (1827–1916), and his illustrious grandson, Henri Bourassa (1868–1952), politician and founder of Montreal's most intellectual French-language daily newspaper *Le Devoir*.

Sights

Fairmont Le Château Montebello★

Entrance off Rte. 148, 392 Rue Notre-Dame.

This enormous octagonal wood structure is the largest log building in the world. With its six radiating wings, it stands on the banks of the Ottawa River on the former Papineau estate. It was built in 1930 in 90 days by the Montreal architect, Harold Lawson, for the exclusive Seigniory Club. Ten thousand red cedar logs from British Columbia were used in the construction.

Today an exclusive hotel, the Fairmont Le Château Montebello (☎1-800-257-7544 *(reservations); www.fairmont.com*) has hosted many international events. The hall boasts one the largest fireplaces in the world.

Lieu historique national du Canada du Manoir-Papineau★ (Papineau Manor National Historic Site of Canada)

🐾 *Visit by guided tour (45min) only, mid-May–Aug, daily 10am–5pm. Sept–mid-Oct weekends only.* ☜*$7.80.* ☎*819-423-6965. www.pc.gc.ca/papineau.*

The manor was built between 1848 and 1850 by Louis-Joseph Papineau. It is an extraordinary structure with castlelike towers.

The main floor of the manor was recently restored to reflect the period of the Papineau family's residence. A fireproof library built in a four-story tower once held Papineau's volumes. Visitors can see the funeral chapel where Louis-Joseph Papineau was laid to rest, the estate's original granary and several outbuildings, as part of a self-guided tour of the estate.

MONTREAL★★★

CITY POPULATION 1,620,693 (METROPOLITAN AREA 3,620,693)

Located on the largest island of the Hochelaga Archipelago in the waters of the mighty St. Lawrence River some 1,600km/1,000mi from the Atlantic Ocean, the cosmopolitan city of Montreal offers the visitor a wealth of attractions. Owing to its key position at the head of a vast inland waterway connecting the Great Lakes, the city is Canada's foremost port as well as a leading industrial, commercial, and cultural center. The second largest city in Canada after Toronto (which surpassed Montreal in the mid-1970s), Montreal is home to the world's largest Francophone population after that of Paris, and displays a vibrant, distinctive French culture. The city's Anglophone community, concentrated primarily in the western part of the Island, also possesses a unique, interesting, blended character. Montreal has the distinction of being the Canadian urban center with the highest proportions of bilingual (English and French) and trilingual (usually English, French, and mother tongue of an immigrant) speakers.

Old World cultures mesh in the North American setting and Nordic climate of Montreal, creating a fascinating vitality with an international flair. The city's numerous and varied ethnic groups sometimes make it seem like a miniature mosaic of the world.

- **Information:** ☎514-873-2015 & 1-877-266-5687. www.tourisme-montreal.org.
- ▶ **Orient Yourself:** Montreal is 533km/331mi north of New York City, 509km/316mi northeast of Toronto, and 200km/124mi east of Ottawa. Montreal is a hub for air traffic into Eastern Canada, and is connected by rail and expressways to Ottawa, Toronto, and New York City.
- **Parking:** Street parking is permitted but there are many restrictions, particularly during festivals and winter snow removal. Note carefully the complicated posted signs for times and days of the week—fines are swift and costly. City and private parking lots are usually the best option for visits more than an hour long.
- **Don't Miss:** Old Montreal, Downtown Montreal, the Olympic Stadium area, the view of Montreal from Mont Royal, Plateau Mont-Royal, Rue Saint-Laurent.
- **Organizing Your Time:** Montreal is served by an efficient but crowded public transit system, and many attractions are within walking distance of a Metro station. The Montreal Museums Pass ($45) is available at participating museums and tourist info centers; it provides admission to 31 museums over three days during a three-week period. You can easily spend a full day visiting the Olympic Stadium area sights. If you drive there, park near the Botanical Gardens for lower-priced parking, then take the free animated mini-train to the Insectarium. The Biodome and Stadium are a short walk across Rue Sherbrooke. Plateau Mont-Royal and Rue Saint-Laurent are neighborhoods that come alive at night and on weekends.
- **Especially for Kids:** Insectarium, iSci at the Old Port, La Ronde.

Geographical Notes

Lying at the confluence of the Ottawa and St. Lawrence rivers, the island of Montreal measures 50km/31mi in length and 17km/10.5mi at its widest point. The island is connected to the mainland by a tunnel and fifteen road bridges, five of which span the St. Lawrence.

Since 2006, the City of Montreal has been divided into nineteen boroughs, occupying most of the Montreal Island, which is dominated by a 233m/764ft hill, known as **Mont Royal**. Nicknamed "the Mountain," Mt. Royal is one of the Monteregian Hills, a series of eight peaks in the St. Lawrence valley.

Montréal Old Port

A Bit of History

Montreal Island was inhabited by Mohawks of the Iroquois nation long before Europeans set foot in North America. In 1535, **Jacques Cartier** landed on the island while searching for gold and a route to the Orient, and encountered the Mohawk village of **Hochelaga** at the foot of the mountain. Legend has it that Cartier, having climbed the mountain, was so taken by the view before him that he exclaimed "It's a royal mountain!" (*C'est un mont réal!*). According to respected historian Gustave Lanctot, however, Montreal was named by Cartier in honor of Cardinal de Medici, bishop of the Sicilian town of Monreale.

When **Samuel de Champlain**, the "Father of New France," sailed up the river from his newly established settlement of Kebec (Quebec City) in 1611, Hochelaga had ceased to exist. Champlain considered founding a new community on the Île Sainte-Hélène, but his project never materialized.

The City of Mary – The 17C was a period of zealous evangelization on the island. The Roman Catholic Church, hoping to regain the ground lost during the Protestant Reformation, viewed colonization as a means of spreading the faith. During this period, two Frenchmen decided to establish a mission on Montreal Island: **Jérôme Le Royer de la Dauversière**

and **Jean-Jacques Olier**. The latter had founded the Sulpician Order in Paris in 1641. They raised money and chose **Paul de Chomedey, Sieur de Maisonneuve** to lead their mission, which they called **Ville-Marie** (City of Mary).

Maisonneuve and about 40 companions crossed the Atlantic in 1641. After wintering in Quebec City, they arrived on the island in May 1642. Despite their high-minded ideals, the Catholic missionaries ultimately came into conflict with the peoples they had hoped to convert. The hostilities continued until peace with the Iroquois was established by an historic treaty (named *Grande paix de Montréal*) in 1701.

18C – After the failure of evangelization initiatives, Ville-Marie (soon renamed Montreal) began to grow as a center of the fur trade. Explorers set off across the Great Lakes and their attendant waterways, returning loaded with pelts. The furs were prized in Europe, where they were transformed into luxurious apparel, mainly hats. The fur trade became Montreal's principal commercial activity, one strong enough to spawn other businesses and farms all over the island. By the time of the **British Conquest**, the city of Montreal was firmly established. After the surrender of Quebec City in 1759, British troops commanded by Gen. Jeffery Amherst marched on Montreal. In 1760 Chevalier de Lévis prepared a gallant defence of

233

the city, but Montreal's governor, Marquis de Vaudreuil, ordered him to surrender without a fight.

Following the Conquest of Canada, most of the French nobility returned to France. The first English-speaking people to settle in the city were Scots, attracted by the fur trade.

In 1775–76, Montreal was again occupied. American troops under General Richard Montgomery invaded the city in an attempt to persuade Montrealers to join the thirteen colonies in revolt against the British Crown. During the seven-month occupation, many leading Americans, including **Benjamin Franklin**, visited Montreal. Early in 1776, the occupying troops departed for Quebec City, where they were defeated by the British Army. After the American Revolution, an influx of Loyalists from the US swelled Montreal's Anglophone population.

19C – The fur trade in Montreal reached its heyday in the late 18C and early 19C. Trading posts, where the local indigenous population brought furs to exchange for a wide range of goods, were established all over northern Canada. The furs were subsequently transported to Montreal by canoe. The **North West Company**, a partnership between some of the great figures in Montreal history, including Fraser, Frobisher, Mackenzie, McGill, McGillivray, McTavish, and Thompson, was created in 1783. These men and others founded the **Beaver Club**, an association of important, prosperous fur traders who had wintered in the Northwest.

In 1821 the merger of the North West Company with its rival, the **Hudson's Bay Company (HBC)**, marked the decline of Montreal's dominance in the fur trade. The HBC exported its furs to Europe via Hudson Bay, bypassing Montreal. Fortunes had nonetheless been made in Montreal, and the profits were invested in other sectors of activity as the 19C progressed.

Even though Montreal did not participate in the American Revolution, the city and its region were the center of revolts against British rule in 1837 and 1838. The colony was administered by a Crown-appointed governor and his council. The assembly elected by the Canadian people lacked the power to enforce its decisions. Many leading French-Canadians, among them **Louis-Joseph Papineau** and **George-Étienne Cartier**, raised their voices in protest. The motivations behind the **Rébellion des Patriotes** were not lost on the vastly outnumbered British, who subsequently granted full representative government to French Canada. After several years of exile, Papineau briefly returned to politics before retiring to Montebello; Cartier went on to become a great Quebec politician and one of the Fathers of Canadian Confederation (1967).

An Expanding Economy – About 1820, Montreal's economy experienced a conversion to commerce and import-export activities. The Anglophone business community established St. James Street (today renamed Rue Saint-Jacques) as a financial center, and founded the Bank of Montreal (1817) and the Board of Trade (1822), institutions whose investment activities promoted development in the city and throughout Quebec and Canada. Today, Rue Saint-Jacques is home to the Montreal Stock Exchange as well as the city's dominant financial and banking institutions.

After 1815 the Anglophone community's economy was fueled by additional British immigrants, coming mainly from Ireland. In the 1860s Montreal experienced an influx of rural French-Canadians, who restored its Francophone character. About 1840, the enlargement of the **Lachine canal**, which had enabled vessels to circumvent the Lachine rapids since its completion in 1824, spurred further industrialization. A new system of canals, on the St. Lawrence River as far as the Great Lakes and on the Richelieu River as far as New York via Lake Champlain and the Hudson River, opened new commercial axes, which were quickly supplemented by railroad lines. The first short-line railroad (1836) linked La Prairie to Saint-Jean-sur-Richelieu.

Montreal rapidly became the headquarters of financing, construction, employment, and maintenance for the rail system. The opening of the Victoria bridge in 1859 brought rail traffic across the river, establishing a continuous, north–south railroad link between Montreal and Vermont.

Montreal's **port** grew with the construction, in the 1880s, of the Canadian Pacific railway line linking the nation's Atlantic and Pacific coasts. Development of the Prairie provinces created new markets for Montreal: Inland grain made its way by rail to the port's storage silos before being exported across the Atlantic, and products manufactured in the city were transported west in wagons.

20C – The period of growth that followed World War I came to an abrupt halt during the Great Depression. Lack of funds lead to widespread unemployment, and the skeletal outlines of unfinished projects marked the cityscape. The post-World War II years brought renewed prosperity and dynamism to the city. Under the leadership of Mayor Jean Drapeau, the downtown and eastern areas of Montreal underwent a major modernization. Since the 1960s, Montreal has emerged as an international city, hosting several important international events: The most successful World Fair of the 20C, **Expo '67**, which marked the centennial of Canada's Confederation; the 1976 summer **Olympic Games** and in 1980 and 2000, the renowned flower exhibition, the **International Floralies**.

However, during the 1970s, several companies relocated their headquarters to Toronto, and Montreal was relegated to the status of second-largest metropolis in Canada. Since the mid-1990s, Montreal has regained its economic dynamism of old and remains a major center of Francophone culture.

Le Métro de Montréal – *Metro map.* Inaugurated in 1966 in time for Expo '67, the four lines of the metro now extend over 71km/44mi with 68 stations. It was designed according to the Parisian Métro "tire on rail" technology and is completely underground to remain unperturbed during winter storms. In places the tunnel is close to the surface, but sinks to a maximum of 55m/180ft as it passes under the St. Lawrence River to Longueuil. The décor of each metro station was conceived by a different architect, in relation to its surroundings, and enhanced by so many works of art that "le Métro" is, in itself, a tourist attraction. Some of the more noteworthy stations in the system include Place-des-Arts, Peel, Place-Saint-Henri, Outremont, Acadie, du Collège, and de la Concorde. In some stations, like McGill, Berri-UQAM, and Bonaventure, the voyager exits the train to find himself in a bustling subterranean city center.

Ville souterraine – *Ville Souterraine map.*
Temperatures in Montreal change dramatically from season to season, but pedestrians can move throughout most of the business district without exposure to climactic extremes via the "the underground city." Montreal's pedestrian city began in the 1960s with the construction of the landmark skyscraper, **Place Ville-Marie**. Particularly remarkable for the spaciousness of its corridors and for its aesthetically "landscaped" atmosphere, the system connects the principal downtown hotels and office buildings; major department stores; hundreds of boutiques; several cinemas; numerous restaurants; two railway stations; the bus terminal; the city's major cultural center, **Place des Arts**; and two major convention centers, **Place**

CineRobotheque, a truly Canadian film experience

Nine thousand award-winning films and short feature films from the celebrated National Film Board (NFB) of Canada collection can be accessed via a touch screen at the CineRobotheque. Alone or with a friend, you sit in a private viewing booth from which you select what you want to see. Pay $3 per hour, and 65 years of Canadian film making is yours. NFB CineRobotheque. *Open Tue–Sun noon–9pm.* 514-496-6887. www.nfb.ca/cinerobotheque.

Address Book

For price ranges, see the Legend on the cover flap.

GETTING THERE

By Air – **Montréal-Pierre Elliott Trudeau International Airport** in Dorval: 22km/13.6mi (*approximately 30min*) from downtown by shuttle bus (*$13*) or taxi (*$40*); free shuttle minibuses to Dorval hotels; airport departure tax $10. Information: *514-394-7377 & 1-800-465-1213 or www.admtl.com.*

By Train – **VIA Rail Canada** Central Station (Gare centrale): *895 Rue de la Gauchetière Ouest* (Bonaventure). *Information & reservations: 514-989-2626 & 1-888-842-7245 or www.viarail.ca.*

By Bus – Montreal Bus Central Station (Orléans Express, Canada Coach, Greyhound, Vermont Transit, etc.): *505 Blvd. de Maisonneuve Est* (Berri-UQAM). *Information: 514-842-2281 or www.orleansexpress.com and www.greyhound.ca.*

GETTING AROUND

Métro & Bus – Local métro and bus service are provided by Société de Transport de Montréal (STM) (*514-288-6287; www.stm.info*). The métro generally operates from 5.30am–1am (*lines 1, 2 & 4*) or 12.15am (*line 5*). Each metro line is designated by a number and a color; the direction is indicated by the name of the station at the end of the line in that direction. Métro tickets (which may also be used on buses) are available at metro stations and may be purchased individually (*$2.75*), or in a booklet (*lisière*) of six (*$12*). Tourist passes (*cartes touristiques*) are also available (*$9/day or $17/3 days*). *Lost and found: 514-786-4636.*

Car Rental – Major rental car companies are located at the airport, and throughout the city: Avis (Namur) *514-387-2847;* Budget (train station) *514-866-7675;* Discount (Guy) *514-932-3312;* Hertz (train station) *514-938-1717;* and Thrifty (bus terminal) *514-845-5954.*

Taxis – Co-op *514-725-9885;* Pontiac *514-931-6666* (providing tours); Allante Limousine *514-643-0262.*

VISITOR INFORMATION

Tourist Information – Main Infotouriste office: *1255 Rue Peel* (Peel). *Open early Sept–late-Jun, daily 9am–6pm; late-Jun–Labor Day 8.30am–7.30pm, rest of the year daily 9am–6pm.* *514-873-2015 & 1-877-266-5687. www.tourism-montreal.org.*

Accommodations – Staff at Infotouriste office will make hotel reservations for you, in person or on the phone. *For specific listings of hotels, see below.*

Montreal Daily Newspapers – English: *The Gazette.* French: *Le Journal de Montréal, Le Devoir, La Presse.*

Post Office – Postal facilities are located in pharmacies throughout the city, look for the *Canada Post* sign. Main post office at *1250 Rue Université, corner of Rue Cathcart* (McGill) *514-344-8822 or 1-800-267-1177. www.canadapost.ca.*

CURRENCY EXCHANGE OFFICES

Montréal-Pierre Elliott Trudeau International Airport – ICE Currency Exchange (counters in Arrivals & Departures buildings, open daily) *514-828-0061.*

Currency Exchange – Corporation d'échange Canada, *1257 Rue Peel* (Peel) *514-866-0227* (adjoining the main Infotouriste office).

USEFUL NUMBERS

Police–Ambulance–Fire (emergency calls only): *911*
Telephone Area Code: *514*
Directory Assistance *411*
Tourisme Québec *514-873-2015*
Canadian Automobile Association (CAA/AAA) *514-861-7575*
Road conditions *1-888-355-0511*
Weather (24hrs/day) *514-283-4006*
Shoppers Drug Mart/Pharmaprix Pharmacy, 901 Rue Sainte-Catherine Est (corner of Rue Saint-André, Berri-UQAM), open until midnight every day *514-842-4915.*

WHERE TO STAY

$ HI-Montreal Youth Hostel – *1030 Rue Mackay.* *514-843-3317 or 1-866-843-3317. www.hostellingmontreal.com. 243 beds.* Organized into private rooms and small dorms that accommodate between four and ten people, this Hostelling International youth hostel sits a few minutes from downtown and the train station.

$$$ Auberge de la Fontaine – *1301 Rue Rachel Est.* ☎*514-597-0166 or 800-597-0597. www.aubergedelafontaine.com. 21 rooms.* A 19C Victorian mansion, Auberge de la Fontaine sits in a residential area of the Plateau Mont-Royal district facing beautiful La Fontaine Park. Colorful contemporary rooms, concierge service, access to the kitchen for snacks and beverages, and a generous breakfast buffet served each morning in the sunny dining room make for a restful stay outside the frenzy of downtown.

$$$ Château Versailles – *1659 Rue Sherbrooke Ouest.* ☎*514-933-8111 or 1-888-933-8111. www.versailleshotels.com. 65 rooms.* Composed of four interconnected 19C Victorian town houses and a modern tower annex across the street, this former pension is prized for its price, personal service and convenient location in the museum district.

$$$ Fairmont The Queen Elizabeth – *900 Blvd. René-Lévesque Ouest.* ☎*514-861-3511 or 1-800-441-1414. www.fairmont.ca. 1 039 rooms (including 100 suites).* The cavernous Queen Elizabeth's convenient location above Montreal's Underground City and the railway station makes it a favorite with touring celebrities, such as John Lennon and Yoko Ono, who recorded Give Peace a Chance here in 1969 during their "bed-in" in suite 1742. Besides incorporating a large health club, a beauty salon and a shopping arcade, the hotel boasts the **Beaver Club ($$$$)**, known for its fine French cuisine and remarkable history.

$$$ Hôtel de l'Institut – *3535 Rue St-Denis.* ☎*514-282-5120 & 1-800-361-5111. www.ithq.qc.ca/en/hotel. 42 rooms.* Occupying the top floors of the modern bunker-like structure that houses the Institut de Tourisme et d'Hôtellerie du Québec, the hotel offers comfortable, modern rooms and the impeccable service you would expect from closely supervised students of the art of hospitality. A few steps away lie some of the trendiest places in Montreal—the

Auberge de la Fontaine
©Auberge de la Fontaine

Plateau Mont-Royal district and the Quartier Latin.

$$$$ Hostellerie Pierre du Calvet – *405 Rue Bonsecours.* ☎*514-282-1725 & 1-866-544-1725. www.pierreducalvet.ca. 10 rooms.* ♿ *See Maison Pierre du Calvet.)* Step back in time at the oldest home open to public accommodation within the walled city of Montreal. Former home of French merchant, Pierre du Calvet, the 18C structure has been restored as an elegant European house chockablock with family heirlooms, antiques and Oriental rugs. Romantic rooms exude Old World ambience with original stone walls, fireplaces and four-poster canopy beds. Enjoy breakfast in the airy, plant-filled Victorian greenhouse. Dinner is served nightly to the public in the main **dining room ($$$)**.

$$$$ Hôtel Le Germain – *2050 Rue Mansfield.* ☎*514-849-2050 or 1-877-333-2050. www.hotelboutique.com. 101 rooms.* This office-building-cum-boutique hotel oozes refined luxury. Asian minimalism prevails in the light-filled loft-like rooms, done in earth tones with dark wood furnishings handcrafted by local artisans. Sumptuous bedding and upscale amenities make these some of the most sought-after rooms in the city.

$$$$ Hôtel Place d'Armes – *701 Côte de la Place d'Armes.* ☎*514-842-1887 or 1-888-450-1887. www.hotelplacedarmes.com. 48 rooms.* This charming boutique hotel is strategically located on Place

237

d'Armes in the center of the ecclesiastic and financial district of Old Montreal. Calming colors and rich mahogany furnishings characterize the elegant rooms; amenities include bathrobes, down comforters, whirlpool baths, and Internet access for business travelers. Large windows afford splendid views of Chinatown, downtown Montreal and the Notre-Dame basilica.

WHERE TO EAT

$ Beauty's – *93 Ave. Mont-Royal Ouest.* ☎*514-849-8883.* **American**. If breakfast or brunch is your thing, come wait in line with *les gens branchés* (everyone who is anyone) at this 1950s-style diner. Bagels, smoked salmon, and blueberry pancakes are the main attractions at this crowded eatery in the Plateau Mont-Royal district.

$ Le Commensal – *1204 Ave McGill College, at Rue Ste-Catherine.* ☎*514-871-1480. www.commensal.com.* **Vegeterian buffet**. Arguably the tastiest vegetarian restaurant in the western world! This downtown address of Le Commensal, the ultimate québécois-végé experience, proves that vegetarian food can be matched with an appealing dining room. You can eat simple salads or indulge in creamy dishes and sweet maple syrup desserts.

$$ Le Piton de la Fournaise – *835 Rue Duluth Est. Dinner only. Closed Mon.* ☎*514-526-3936.* **Réunion/Creole**. Upon entering this vibrant restaurant, you'll feel as if you've stepped off the boat at Île de la Réunion right in the middle of the Indian Ocean. The cuisine blends Indian, African and French influences and the décor highlights arts and crafts from the island. Just listening to the staff speak Creole is a treat in itself.

BYOW – Bring your own wine. Restaurants that don't have a liquor license can allow patrons to bring in their own favorite vintages. Most BYOW (*apportez votre vin*) eateries are located in the Plateau Mont-Royal district and the Quartier Latin.

Table d'hôte – These fixed-price meals typically include a three-course menu consisting of a starter, main dish, and dessert.

$$ Restaurant Daou – *519 Rue Faillon Est.* ☎*514-276-8310.* **Lebanese**. The lively ambience here, occasionally with belly dancers, complements Middle Eastern specialties such as tabbouleh and kibbeh, making you feel as if you've just stepped into a big, joyous Lebanese wedding party. The décor is ordinary, but expect good food for a good price.

$$ Stash Cafe – *200 Rue Saint-Paul Ouest.* ☎*514-845-6611; www.stashcafe. com.* **Polish.** Montrealers as well as tourists are drawn to this Polish restaurant for its welcoming ambience. Break here for a slice of cake with coffee, or sample savory traditional dishes such as sausages and cabbage rolls.

$$$ La Marée – *404 Place Jacques-Cartier.* ☎*514-861-9794.* **Seafood**. Situated in one of the most-trafficked sections of the city lies Montreal's best bet for seafood. Enjoy favorites such as *escalope de saumon au ragoût de pineau des charentes* (grilled salmon in a sauce flavored with *pineau des charentes* liqueur) or *poêle de homard à la tomate et basilic* (lobster sautéed in tomato, butter and fresh basil).

$$$ Moishes – *3961 Blvd. St-Laurent.* ♿☎*514-845-3509. www.moishes.ca.* **North American**. A Montreal institution for over 60 years, this steak house is justifiably renowned for its house-aged, charcoal-grilled steaks, which are even better when paired with a selection from Moishes' fine wine list. The courteous and efficient waitstaff serve up favorite accompaniments like pickled salmon and broiled peppers.

$$$ Le Petit Moulinsart – *139 Rue Saint-Paul Ouest.* ☎*514-843-7432. www.lepetitmoulinsart.com.* **Belgian**. A warm welcome and attractive décor make visitors feel right at home in this charming restaurant. Images of Tintin (a Belgian comic character) on the walls and menu only increase its appeal. Relax and partake of succulent mussels or a fabulous crème brûlée.

$$$ Restaurant Julien – *1191 Rue Union.* ☎*514-871-1581.* **French**.Be careful not to overlook the side streets when looking for fine dining. Hidden away from the main boulevards, this elegant restaurant well deserves its years-long reputation for unfailingly high standards in both dining room and kitchen. Prepare to enjoy fine cuisine in a polished setting, either inside or, in summer, out on the lovely terrace.

$$$$ Toqué! – *900 Place Jean-Paul-Riopelle. Dinner only. Closed Sun & Mon.* ☎*514-499-2084. www.restaurant-toque. com.* **French**. Located in the Old Montreal district, Montrealers and international food critics alike consider this restaurant one of the finest in the city. Chef Normand Laprise's contemporary French cuisine, artfully presented using the freshest—and often unusual (milkweed buds, fiddlehead ferns)—local produce is the reason why. Signature dishes served by the professional waitstaff include *gigot d'agneau de Rimouski et son jus fumé au thym* (leg of lamb in its own juices scented with thyme), and *poêlée de mousserons* (sautéed St. George's mushrooms).

SHOPPING AND DINING

Below are some of the venues the city offers:

Underground City – A large number of boutiques, movie theaters and malls in the are connected with the métro. Opening hours for stores: Mon–Fri 9.30am–6pm (Thu & Fri 9pm; in summer, Mon–Fri 9pm), Sat 10am–5pm; most stores are also open Sunday, noon–5pm:

Complexe Desjardins, *150 Rue Sainte-Catherine Ouest* (◐Place-des-Arts or Place-d'Armes) ☎514-281-1870, extension 2266.

Eaton Center, *705 Rue Sainte-Catherine Ouest* (◐McGill) ☎*514-288-3708.*

Place Montréal Trust, *1500 McGill College Ave.* (◐McGill or Peel) ☎*514-843-8000.*

Place Ville-Marie, *1 place Ville-Marie* (◐Bonaventure or McGill) ☎*514-866-6666.*

Promenades de la Cathédrale, *625 Rue Sainte-Catherine Ouest* (◐McGill) ☎*514-845-8230*, extension 215.

A variety of boutiques, clothing stores, antique shops, art galleries and fashionable restaurants can be found along Sainte-Catherine, Sherbrooke, Peel, Crescent and de la Montagne streets. Galleries, gift shops offering aboriginal art, cafés and restaurants in Old Montreal. Along Rue Saint-Denis are elegant fashion boutiques, art studios, cafés and restaurants. Ethnic groceries and restaurants, franchise stores, nightclubs and discotheques can be found along Blvd. Saint-Laurent.

ENTERTAINMENT

For current entertainment schedules and addresses of principal theaters and concert halls, consult the free cultural newspapers *Mirror* and *Hour* (English), *Ici* and *Voir* (French), or review the arts and entertainment supplements in local newspapers (Friday and Saturday editions). Tickets for major entertainment or sports events may be purchased at the venue or through the following offices: **Admission** ☎*514-790-1245 & 1-800-361-4595, www. admission.com;* **Telspec** ☎*514-790-1111 & 1-800-848-1594, www.tel-spec.com.* Most major credit cards accepted. For information and schedules on arts, music, movies, sports and recreation, check *www.montrealplus.ca.*

SPORTS

Montreal is home to several professional sports organizations. **Ice hockey:** Montreal Canadiens (National Hockey League), season from Oct–Mar at the Bell Center (◐Lucien-L'Allier) ☎*514-989-2841.* **Canadian football:** Montreal Alouettes (Canadian Football League), season from mid-Jun–early Nov at Percival Molson Stadium (◐McGill) ☎*514-871-2255.* **Soccer:** Montreal Impact (United Soccer League), season from Apr to Sept, at Saputo Stadium (◐Pie-IX and Viau) ☎*514-328-3668.*

Horse races: year-round at Blue Bonnets Hippodrome (◐Namur) ☎*514-739-2741.*

Recreational Activities – Guided bicycle tours or in-line skating (summer): Vélo Aventure Montréal ☎*514-847-0666.* Year-round skating ($5.75) and rentals at Atrium Le1000, *1000 Rue de la Gauchetière* (◐Bonaventure) ☎*514-395-0555.* IMAX Cinemas in Old Montreal (at the Montreal Science Center) ☎*514-496-4724.* Casino de Montréal (◐Jean-Drapeau) ☎*514-392-2746, www.casino-de-montreal.com.*

Bonaventure and **Palais des Congrès**. (In Quebec, the French word *place* commonly designates large interior spaces and commercial centers.)

Vieux-Montréal★★★ (Old Montreal)

The term "Old Montreal" refers to the section of the city formerly surrounded by fortifications. The imposing stone walls (5.4m/17.7ft high and 1m/3.3ft thick) were built early in the 18C and removed a century later. They contained the area today bounded by Rue McGill to the west, Rue Berri to the east, Rue de la Commune beside the river to the south and a line between Rues Saint-Jacques and Saint-Antoine to the north.

During the 18C and 19C, the city gradually expanded beyond the old walls. Montrealers built their houses farther from the river, and businesses were established in what became the downtown area. Warehouses sprang up where homes and gardens had previously flourished and the older Montreal fell into decline. By the 1960s, however, interest in Old Montreal revived. The surviving 18C homes were renovated and the warehouses were transformed into apartment and office buildings. Shops and restaurants opened, signaling the renewal of the area.

Since the mid 1990s, residential (condos) and commercial investments (several hotels) have been made to the tune of hundreds of millions of dollars, while authorities ensure that the historic, architectural, and cultural nature of the area is respected. As a result, Old Montreal has become an attractive place to live and work, as well as a major tourist attraction.

Horse-drawn carriages (calèches) depart from Rue Notre-Dame, Place d'Armes, Rue de la Commune and Place Jacques-Cartier, enabling visitors to discover Old Montreal in the manner of bygone eras.

Walking Tours

[1] Old Montreal

2.2km/1.4mi.
Montreal town map.
Square-Victoria.

Rue Saint-Jacques★
Once the "Wall Street of Canada" until the 1970s, Rue Saint-Jacques is lined with a homogeneous ensemble of 19C and early 20C buildings and still retains much of its former grandeur. Note in particular the **Canada Life Assurance Building** (*nº. 275*), Montreal's first steel-framework skyscraper (1895), and the **CIBC Building** (*Canadian Imperial Bank of Commerce, nº. 265;* open year-round Mon–Fri 9.30am–4pm;), whose façade is adorned with fluted Corinthian columns. The bank features a monumental interior **banking hall.** The decline of Rue Saint-Jacques was accelerated during the mid-1970s when several major financial institutions moved their headquarters to the downtown area or to Toronto. Today, however, the street is experiencing a revival, with several significant new constructions and the conversion of older buildings. The street was named by Dollier de Casson in 1672 after Jean-Jacques Olier, the founder of the Sulpician Order.

Visible to the west is the black, 47-story **Tour de la Bourse★** (Stock Exchange Tower, *nº. 800 Square Victoria*), home to the Montréal Exchange (open year-round, Mon–Fri 8.30am–4.30pm; closed major holidays; 514-871-2424; www.m-x.ca).

Banque Royale du Canada★ (Royal Bank of Canada)
360 Rue Saint-Jacques. Open year-round, Mon–Fri 10am–4pm. Closed major holidays. 514-874-2959.
This building (1928) was the first erected in Montreal after the 1924 modification of zoning regulations authorizing the construction of buildings of more than 10 stories on the condition that setbacks be incorporated into their design. Inspired by the "Setback Law" of New York, the new regulation left more latitude to architects, who were thereafter restricted more by the laws

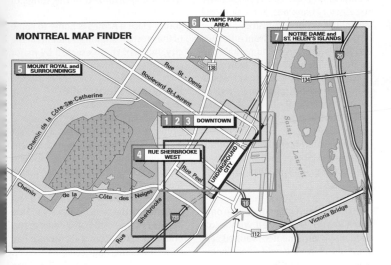

MONTREAL MAP FINDER

5 MOUNT ROYAL and SURROUNDINGS

6 OLYMPIC PARK AREA

7 NOTRE DAME and ST. HELEN'S ISLANDS

1 2 3 DOWNTOWN

4 RUE SHERBROOKE WEST

UNDERGROUND CITY

Rue St - Denis

Boulevard St-Laurent

Chemin de la Côte-Ste-Catherine

Chemin de la Côte - des - Neiges

Rue Sherbrooke

Rue Peel

Saint Laurent

Victoria Bridge

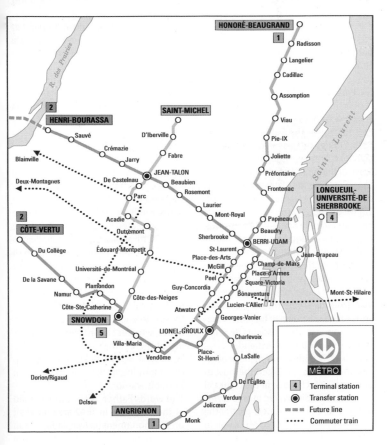

HONORÉ-BEAUGRAND
1
Radisson
Langelier
Cadillac
Assomption
Viau
Pie-IX
Joliette
Préfontaine
Frontenac

SAINT-MICHEL
D'Iberville
Fabre
JEAN-TALON
Beaubien
Rosemont
Laurier
Mont-Royal
Sherbrooke
St-Laurent
Place-des-Arts
McGill
Peel
Guy-Concordia
Atwater

2
HENRI-BOURASSA
Sauvé
Crémazie
Jarry
De Castelnau
Parc
Acadie
Outremont
Édouard-Montpetit
Université-de-Montréal
Plamondon
Côte-des-Neiges
Côte-Ste-Catherine

Blainville
Deux-Montagnes

2
CÔTE-VERTU
Du Collège
De la Savane
Namur

SNOWDON
5
Villa-Maria
Vendôme

LIONEL-GROULX
Place-St-Henri

R. des Prairies

Saint Laurent

Papineau
Beaudry
BERRI-UQAM
Champ-de-Mars
Place-d'Armes
Square-Victoria
Bonaventure
Lucien-L'Allier
Georges-Vanier

LONGUEUIL-UNIVERSITÉ-DE-SHERBROOKE
4
Jean-Drapeau
Mont-St-Hilaire

Charlevoix
LaSalle
De l'Église
Verdun
Jolicœur

ANGRIGNON
1
Monk

Dorion/Rigaud
Delson

MÉTRO

4 Terminal station
● Transfer station
- - - Future line
···· Commuter train

241

of engineering than by city regulations. The 23-story bank was, at the time, the tallest building in the British Empire. The bottom tier—of Renaissance Revival design—is a severe, monumental composition influenced by the Teatro San Carlo in Naples. The entire tower, whose traditional roof has long dominated the skyline of Montreal's financial district, is best viewed from the opposite side of Rue Saint-Jacques. The bank's headquarters were located here until the 1962 completion of the Royal Bank of Canada Tower at Place Ville-Marie.

Interior

The bronze main entry doors open onto a vast vestibule adorned with a coffered, richly ornamented, vaulted ceiling. A blue, pink and gold color scheme enlivens the ground floor, from which four arched doorways give access to the wings and elevators. A magnificent marble staircase leads to the immense **banking hall,** which is 45m/148ft long, 14m/46ft wide and 14m/46ft tall.

▶ *Walk eastward on Rue Saint-Jacques.*

Place d'Armes★

As superior of the Sulpician Order in 1670, Dollier de Casson devised a city plan for Montreal, outlining new streets north of Rue Saint-Paul and a large open square in the center, later to become the site of the Notre Dame Basilica. According to legend, Casson's central square occupied the site of the 1644 battle during which Maisonneuve killed the local Indian chief, causing 200 of the chief's followers to flee the settlement. The Place d'Armes, as the square has been called since 1723, traditionally served as drill grounds where troops presented arms to the sovereign or his representative, in this case, the Messieurs de Saint-Sulpice, seigneurs of the island.

In 1775-1776, during the American occupation, vandals mutilated the bust of George III, which stood at the center of the square. Rediscovered in an old well on the site, the bust is now part of the collection of the McCord Museum. In 1832 the square was the site of an electoral riot against the Tories, led by the legendary Patriot **Jos Montferrand,**

who is immortalized in the songs of Gilles Vigneault.

Today, Place d'Armes is home to some of the most prestigious buildings in the city, many of them erected by major companies and financial institutions.

Banque de Montréal★ (Bank of Montreal)

119 Rue Saint-Jacques.

Dominating the north side of the vast square, Montreal's main branch of Canada's oldest bank presents an imposing façade, evoking the Pantheon in Rome. Along with the Bonsecours market, the edifice (1847) is one of Montreal's finest examples of the Neoclassical style. Step inside to see the elaborate interior redecorated in 1905. From the entrance hall under the dome, huge columns of green granite lead into the massive **banking hall** with its beautiful coffered ceiling. The bank's small **museum** (*turn left at entrance and go through revolving doors;* ◷*open year-round, Mon–Fri 10am–4pm;* ◷*closed major holidays;* ☎*514-877-6810*) features displays showcasing the bank's history, bank notes of different denominations and a collection of whimsical money boxes.

Maisonneuve Monument★ (1)

The monument in the center of the square honors the founder of Montreal, Paul de Chomedey, **Sieur de Maisonneuve** (1612–76). A masterpiece by Louis-Philippe Hébert, the sculpture was completed in 1895 to celebrate the city's 250th anniversary. Maisonneuve is depicted brandishing the standard of France, while grouped below him are some of the prominent figures of Montreal's history: Jeanne Mance, founder of Montreal's General Hospital; Lambert Closse, defender of the fort, and his dog Pilote, who first heard and gave warning of the enemy's approach; Charles Le Moyne, with a sickle and a gun to represent life in the colonies; and an Iroquois warrior.

The words Father Vimont proclaimed at the first mass in 1642 are engraved on the monument (in translation): "You are the grain of mustard seed which will germinate, grow, and multiply all over this country."

New York Life Insurance Building

511 Place d'Armes.

Sheathed in red sandstone, this eight-story edifice (1888) was Montreal's first skyscraper. A synthesis of Romanesque and Renaissance Revival styles, the structure features corner towers, arched-lancet windows and rough-hewn stone. Although at the time steel was beginning to be widely used as a means of interior support in architectural construction, this building's floor weight is borne by its walls.

Aldred Building

507 Place d'Armes.

The form and ornamentation of this Art Deco skyscraper (1930) were inspired by New York City's Rockefeller Center, then under construction.

Basilique Notre-Dame★★★ (Notre Dame Basilica)

🕐*Open year-round, weekdays 8am–4.30pm, Sat 8am–4pm, Sun 12.30pm–4pm(noon when there is a wedding).* ☞*$5 (including 20min guided tour* 👟*).* ♿ ☎*514-842-2925; www.basiliquenddm.org.*

The twin towers of Montreal's most famous religious edifice rise over 69m/226ft on the southern edge of Place d'Armes. At the time of the basilica's construction, they dominated the entire city but have since been overshadowed by the taller structures housing Montreal's financial institutions.

Rulers of Montreal Island, the **Sulpician** seigneurs long opposed the division of their territory into small parishes administered by the bishop of Quebec. To impede such a division, and a lessening of their power, the Sulpicians decided to erect this church, large enough to accommodate the entire community at worship (seating capacity of 2,800). Despite the Sulpicians' efforts, the Diocese of Montreal was established in 1830 and the island subsequently divided into parishes.

The basilica, Quebec's first major building in the Gothic Revival style, was designed by James O'Donnell (1774–1829), an Irish architect from New York, who supervised its construction from 1824 through 1829. A Catholic convert,

Basilique Notre-Dame

O'Donnell is buried in the basilica's basement crypt. John Ostell finished the towers in 1843 according to the original plans. Lack of funds halted progress on the interior until after 1870, when it was finally completed under the direction of Victor Bourgeau.

Notre Dame is Montreal's first large-scale limestone edifice. Its construction required the opening of new quarries, and stonecutters had to be hired and trained to work the stone, thus leading to its widespread application as a sheathing material. The three Baccirini statues adorning the façade were purchased in Italy and represent the Virgin Mary, St. Joseph and St. John the Baptist. The east tower, named Temperance, contains a ten-bell carillon while the west tower, known as Perseverance, houses "Jean-Baptiste," a magnificent, 10,900kg/24,030lb brass bell, cast in London and rung only on special occasions.

Interior

The church's central nave is flanked by two side aisles surmounted by deep-set double galleries. Without deviating from this basic plan, Victor Bourgeau reappointed and enriched the interior décor between 1872 and 1880, embellishing it with the sculptures, wainscoting and giltwork typical of provincial religious

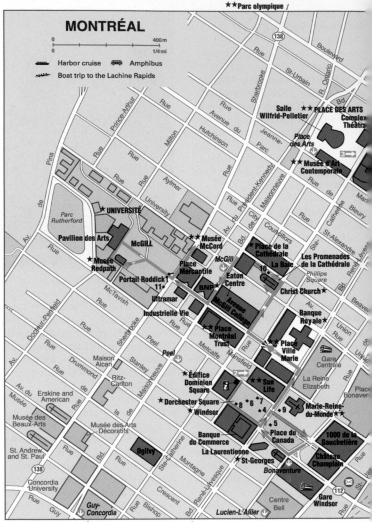

MONTRÉAL

Harbor cruise — Amphibus
Boat trip to the Lachine Rapids

★★ Parc olympique

★★ PLACE DES ARTS
Salle Wilfrid-Pelletier
Complexe Théâtra
★★ Musée d'Art Contemporain
★ UNIVERSITÉ
Pavilion des Arts
McGILL
★★ Musée McCord
★ Musée Redpath
Place Mercantile
Portail Roddick
Ultramar
Industrielle Vie
BNP
Eaton Centre
Avenue McGill College
★ Place de la Cathédrale
Les Promenades de la Cathédrale
La Baie
Christ Church ★
Banque Royale ★
★★ Place Montréal Trust
Place Ville Marie
Gare Centrale
★ Édifice Dominion Square
★ Dorchester Square
★ Windsor
Sun Life
La Reine Elizabeth
Place Bonaven
Marie-Reine-du-Monde ★★
Maison Alcan
Ritz-Carlton
Musée des Beaux-Arts
Musée des Arts Décoratifs
St. Andrew and St. Paul
Banque du Commerce
La Laurentienne
★ St-Georges
Ogilvy
Place du Canada
1000 de la Gauchetière
Château Champlain
Concordia University
Guy-Concordia
Lucien-L'Allier
Centre Bell
Gare Windsor
Parc Rutherford

★ Centre canadien d'Architecture

architecture. Notre Dame's Gothic Revival style is distinguishable from that of non-Catholic churches by the interior furnishings and ornamentation, inspired by the French Gothic style.

The magnificent interior is a veritable gallery of religious art in hand-carved white pine, painted and gilded with 22-carat gold. The nave, measuring 68m/223ft long, 21m/69ft wide and 25m/82ft high, follows the natural slope of the terrain from the entrance to the altar, and the interior space is illuminated by three rose windows piercing the polychromed vaulted ceiling. Designed by Bourgeau and carved by

Henri Bouriché, the altar and **reredos** incorporate white-oak statues, which stand out against the background's soft blue hues. The massive black-walnut **pulpit** was designed by Henri Bouriché; note especially Louis-Philippe Hébert's statues of Ezekiel and Jeremiah at its base. The **stained-glass windows** of the lower level were designed by Jean-Baptiste Lagacé and produced at the Chigot studio in Limoges, France. Commissioned at the basilica's 1929 centenary and installed in 1931, the windows depict scenes from the history of Montreal.

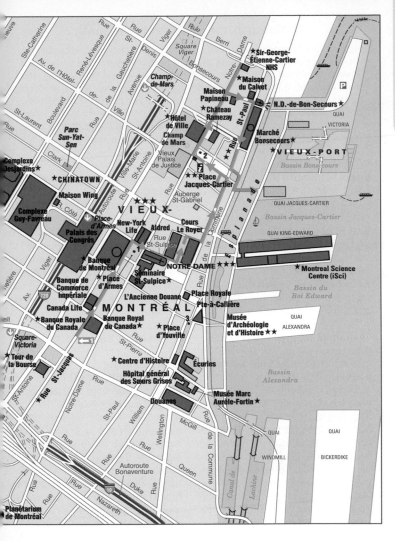

The massive **organ**, one of the world's largest, was produced in 1887 by Casavant Brothers of Saint-Hyacinthe, and has 7,000 pipes, 97 stops, four manual keyboards and a pedal-board. To the right of the entrance, note the baptistry, decorated by Ozias Leduc in 1927. Because of its excellent acoustics, Notre Dame is frequently the setting for organ recitals and Montreal Symphony Orchestra concerts.

Our Lady of the Sacred Heart Chapel (Chapelle Notre-Dame du Sacré-Cœur)
Entrance behind the choir.

Added to the church in 1891, the original chapel was intended mainly for intimate celebrations and weddings. It was completely destroyed by arson in 1978 and reconsecrated in 1982. Its ornamentation combines elements from the original chapel with contemporary additions. The vault is of steel sheathed in linden wood, and side skylights permit daylight to filter into the interior. Dominating the whole is an impressive **bronze reredos**, the work of Charles Daudelin. Measuring 17m/55.7ft high by 6m/19.6ft wide and weighing 20 tons, its 32 panels were cast in England and represent a mortal's difficult journey to heaven.

In Montreal, the Sun Rises in the South

Travelers accustomed to determining their geographical orientation by the position of the sun will have to make an adjustment in Montreal. The St. Lawrence River is considered to flow from west to east, a correct assumption for the most part. However, as it approaches the downtown area, the river makes an abrupt northward swing, and thus flows almost due north as it passes the city. Montreal streets at right angles to the St. Lawrence are thereby considered to be oriented north-south (when actually they extend east–west), and streets parallel to the river are designated east–west (though in reality they run north–south).

Vieux Séminaire de Saint-Sulpice★ (Old Sulpician Seminary)

130 Rue Notre-Dame Ouest.
Located next to the Notre Dame Basilica, the freestone building is the oldest structure in Montreal. It was built in 1685 as a residence and training center by **Dollier de Casson** (1636–1701), Superior of the Messieurs de Saint-Sulpice and Montreal's first historian.

The Sulpician Order

Founded in Paris by Jean-Jacques Olier in 1641, the Sulpician Order was firmly established in Montreal by 1657. In 1663 the Compagnie de Saint-Sulpice acquired the mission of Ville-Marie, including its land titles and seigneurial power, from the Société de Notre-Dame. As seigneurs of the island, the Sulpicians exercised great authority over the population and were responsible for the construction of Notre Dame Basilica. The seminary also served as the administrative center of Ville-Marie. Today the seminary building continues to serve as a residence for the Sulpicians.

A Classical Building

Like numerous other structures in Montreal, the architecture of the seminary bears traits of 17C French classicism. Its palatial, U-shaped plan was adopted by all of the island's religious orders.
The main building, topped by a mansard roof, was enlarged in 1704 and 1712, under the direction of the Sulpician Vachon de Belmont (1654–1732). Two lateral wings around a court of honor were constructed during this period, along with staircase turrets at the juncture of the main buildings. The seminary building conceals from view the main garden which, until the 19C, overlooked the St. Lawrence River.
The façade **clock,** created in Paris, was installed in 1701. Its face was engraved by Paul Labrosse and gilded by the Sisters of the Congregation. Believed to be the oldest public timepiece in North America, the clock's original movement was fabricated entirely of wood. It was replaced by an electric mechanism in 1966.

▶ *Walk down Rue Saint-Sulpice.*

Cours Le Royer (Le Royer Courtyard)

Bounded by Rues Saint-Dizier, de Brésoles, Le Royer, and Saint-Paul.
After 1861, a series of warehouses designed by Victor Bourgeau was constructed on the former site of the Montreal General Hospital. These buildings were renovated into housing units during the 1980s in a large-scale project that began the movement to transform Old Montreal into a residential area. The structures, designed in the protorationalist style, overlook a charming courtyard, dotted with flower-filled planters.

▶ *Follow Rue Saint-Dizier to Rue Saint-Paul and turn left.*

Rue Saint-Paul★★

Along with Rue Notre-Dame, this narrow street is one of the oldest in Montreal. Its curves and dips are explained by its origins as a footpath along the riverbanks between the fort and the hospital. In 1672, Dollier de Casson straightened the street somewhat in his formal plan of the city, and named it in honor of Paul de Chomedey, Sieur de Maisonneuve.

Lovely, well-proportioned 19C buildings presently line Rue Saint-Paul. The section between Boulevard Saint-Laurent and Place Jacques-Cartier incorporates former warehouses, now transformed into shops and artists' studios.

Located in the former International Center of Design (n° 85), Montreal's center for arts and new technologies, the Cité des Arts et des Nouvelles Technologies de Montréal, now serves as a conference center.

Take a short detour to admire the Auberge Saint-Gabriel (*n° 426 Rue Saint-Gabriel*), built in 1754 and today renovated as a restaurant.

Place Jacques-Cartier

Tony Tremblay/iStockphoto

Place Jacques-Cartier★★

With its outdoor cafés, street performers and flower vendors, this cobblestone square is lively all summer, especially in the evenings. The public square was created in 1847 by the city council and named for the famous explorer who, according to tradition, docked his ship at its foot in 1535. During the early 18C, the Marquis de Vaudreuil erected his chateau on the spot now covered with blooming parterres; the building was destroyed by fire in 1803. A bustling fruit, vegetable and flower market operated on the square for over 40 years, until the construction of the Bonsecours Market.

The numerous early 19C buildings surrounding Place Jacques-Cartier today house mainly restaurants. Montreal's City Hall stands on the north side of the square, and the Old Port is accessible from its southern end.

A statue of **Horatio Nelson** (**2**) crowns a 15m/49ft column at the top of the square. Erected in 1809, this monument was the first to honor Nelson (1758–1805), who defeated French and Spanish forces at the battle of Trafalgar in 1805 (a similar, more renowned monument in London's Trafalgar Square dates from 1842).

The **Old Montreal tourist information center** located at the west corner of Place Jacques-Cartier and Rue Notre-Dame (*open Apr–mid-May, daily 9am–5pm; mid-May–late Sept, daily 9am–7pm; rest of the year, Wed–Sun 9am–5pm; 514-874-1696; www.vieux.montreal.qc.ca*) occupies the former site of

the Silver Dollar Saloon. Named for the 300 American silver dollars embedded in the floor, the saloon attracted clients who "walked on top of a fortune."

A tiny side street off Place Jacques-Cartier, **Rue Saint-Amable** is renowned for the artists who, during the summer, show and sell works depicting Montreal and the quarter. The street is named for the wife of Jacques Viger, first mayor of Montreal.

Hôtel de Ville ★ (City Hall)

275 Rue Notre-Dame Est. Main hall open Mon–Fri 10am–4pm; guided tour (1hr) late Jun–mid-Aug, by reservation. Closed major holidays. 514-872-3355.

The first important building in Quebec to adopt the Second Empire style was originally built in the 1870s. After a fire in 1922, the building was reconstructed by Joseph-Omer Marchand, who preserved the original walls but added a story.

General Charles de Gaulle delivered his famous "Vive le Québec... vive le Québec libre!" speech in 1967 from the balcony overlooking the main entrance. Just inside the main door stand two sculptures, recast from the original bronze works, *The Sower and Woman with Bucket*, by Alfred Laliberté. The elegant **main hall** (*hall d'honneur*) is 31m/101.7ft long by 12m/39.3ft wide and features a marbled floor and walls, and a huge bronze chandelier weighing over one ton. The **Council Chamber** can be visited if there is no session in progress (*access from the door under the clock*). Its stained-glass windows represent various aspects of city life during the 1920s.

Walk to the back of City Hall for a beautiful view of downtown Montreal. Excavation of the **Champ de Mars**, now a vast expanse of lawn, has revealed the base of a section of the old stone fortification wall.

Musée du Château Ramezay★

280 Rue Notre-Dame Est. ◷*Open Jun–mid-Oct, daily 10am–6pm; rest of the year, Tue–Sun 10am–4.30pm.* ◷*Closed Jan 1–2 & Dec 25–26.* ⊛*$8.* ✗ ♿ ☎*514-861-3708. www.chateauramezay.qc.ca.*

Across from the City Hall stands one of Montreal's loveliest examples of early 18C domestic architecture (1705). Constructed for Claude de Ramezay (1659–1724), 11th governor of Montreal during the French Regime, the building underwent numerous transformations, always emerging relatively unchanged in appearance but for the tower, which was added in the early 20C. The building's walls are formed of stone fragments and topped with a lead-covered copper roof pierced by dormers. In 1745, Ramezay's heirs sold the house to the **West India Company**, and master builder Paul Tessier (also known as Lavigne) was hired to reconstruct it in 1756. The original structure was doubled in size, allowing for the addition of an "apartment," imposing vaults and firebreak walls.

The house became known as a "chateau" after the Conquest, when British governors resided in it from 1764 through 1849. For seven months in 1775–1776, during the American occupation, it served as the headquarters of Richard Montgomery's army. Benjamin Franklin lodged here during this period while on a diplomatic mission. In 1929, the chateau was one of the first three buildings to be classified as a historic monument of Quebec, along with Quebec City's Church of Our Lady of the Victories and Sillery's Jesuit House.

The Château Ramezay, restored and transformed into a museum in 1895, presents Montreal's economic, political, and social history. Several rooms on the main level house long-term temporary exhibits using objects drawn from the permanent collection, including furniture, paintings, newspapers, letters, costumes and manuscripts. Note especially the room embellished with hand-carved mahogany paneling. Produced in 1725 in Nantes, France, for the headquarters of the West India Company, this remarkable woodwork is attributed to the French architect, Germain Boffrand (1667–1754), a proponent of the Louis-XV style. Shipped to Montreal for display in the French pavilion during Expo '67, the **paneling** was ultimately presented to the Château Ramezay because of the latter's connection with the company.

The basement, with its huge vaults, houses the museum's permanent exhibits, a series of rooms designed to resemble a common room. Other displays here present traditional arts and crafts and furniture.

▶ *Continue east on Rue Notre-Dame to its intersection with Rue Berri.*

Lieu historique national du Canada de Sir-George-Étienne-Cartier★ (Sir George-Étienne Cartier National Historic Site of Canada)

458 Rue Notre-Dame Est. ◷ *Open Jun–Aug, daily 10am–6pm; Apr–May & Sept–late Dec, Wed–Sun 10am–noon, 1pm–5pm.* ⊛*$4.* ♿ ☎*514-283-2282. www.pc.gc.ca/cartier.*

This limestone, mansard-roofed building consists of two houses linked by a covered passage that today serves as a reception area. From 1848 through 1872, the structure was the sometime home and legal office of the renowned statesman, **George-Étienne Cartier** (1814–1873). An influential member of the Sir John A. Macdonald cabinet until

---

Address Book

MUSIC AND AMBIENCE

When in the city for the evening, be sure to stop by **Les Deux Pierrots** (*104 Rue Saint-Paul Est;* ☎*514-861-1270*). A veritable Montreal institution, this nightclub is the perfect place to expose your ears to traditional Quebec music in a most convivial setting.

his death, Cartier was a prominent figure in Canadian politics during the 19C.

The visit begins on the ground floor of the building's eastern section, where colorful signs, mannequins and panels introduce visitors to 19C Montreal society. The second level illustrates Cartier's life and work, highlighting his role as one of the proponents of Canada's railway development, and as a Father of Canadian Confederation.

The meticulously restored western half sends visitors backward in time to the Victorian era. Period furnishings and recorded voices evoke the rather pampered lifestyle of upper class Montrealers during the late 19C.

▸ *Return to Rue Bonsecours and turn left.*

Maison Papineau (Papineau House) *440 Rue Bonsecours.*

This large edifice was erected in 1785 by Jean-Baptist Cérat, also known as Coquillard. With its steeply pitched roof pierced by two rows of dormer windows and carriage door leading to a rear courtyard, the structure represents a typical French Regime house. During a reconstruction in 1831, the original stone walls were covered in wood, sculpted and painted to resemble limestone. This modification lent a Neoclassical appearance to the traditional-style structure. The house was owned by six generations of the Papineau family, including **Louis-Joseph Papineau** (1786–1871), leader of the Patriot party, who lived in it periodically between 1814 and 1837.

The charming **view** down Rue Bonsecours to the little church of Our Lady of Good Help is one of the most photographed perspectives in the city.

Maison Pierre du Calvet★ (Pierre du Calvet House)

401 Rue Bonsecours at corner of Rue Saint-Paul Est.

Constructed in 1725 on a lot belonging to French Protestant merchant, Pierre du Calvet, this structure is Montreal's finest existing example of a traditional urban residence. Typical elements include unadorned fieldstone walls, firebreaks (the part of the wall extending beyond

the roof as a shield against flying sparks), corner consoles, tall chimneys incorporated into large gables, and a pitched roof unrelieved by dormers. The third level, with three small windows, evokes the mansard roofs introduced by the Loyalists. The interior, today renovated as an inn with a public dining room, features beamed woodwork characteristic of the 18C.

Pierre du Calvet (1735–1786), who came to Montreal in 1758, was the house's most infamous resident. He offered his services to the British in 1760 and to the Americans in 1775. These shifts in allegiance endeared him to no one, and he was imprisoned for treason in 1780. After his release in 1784, he set sail for London to appeal this punishment. His ship was wrecked on the return voyage and he was drowned.

Musée Marguerite-Bourgeoys & Chapelle Notre-Dame-de-Bon-Secours★

🕒*Open May–Oct, Tue–Sun 10am–5.30pm; Mar–Apr & Nov–mid-Jan, Tue–Sun 11am–3.30pm.* ⬤*$6.* ☎*514-282-8670. www.marguerite-bourgeoys.com.*

A former school next to the chapel as well as the tower and crypt house a museum dedicated to the life and work of **Marguerite Bourgeoys** (1620–1700). This legendary woman arrived in Ville-Marie with Maisonneuve in 1653, opened the first school and founded the first non-cloistered religious community of women on the continent, the **Congregation of Notre Dame**. For many years, Sister Bourgeoys sheltered the **Filles du Roy** (the "King's wards"), young women who came from France

---

PLACE JEAN-PAUL-RIOPELLE

🚇*Square-Victoria.* Just west of the new wing of the Montreal Convention Center, between Ave. Viger and Rue Saint-Antoine, this small square reflects the new, bolder Montreal urban landscape. It pays tribute to a courageous Quebec artist, Jean-Paul Riopelle (1923–2002), with one of his sculptures, *La Joute*. It is circled at night with fire, showing Riopelle's vision of life.

with dowries provided by Louis XIV to marry the first settlers. A special feature of the museum is its collection of charming figurines, dressed in regional and period costume and displayed in 58 scenes that relate the extraordinary life of this famed Montreal nun. Marguerite Bourgeoys was canonized in 1982. The small **Chapelle Notre-Dame-de-Bon-Secours** is distinguished by its copper steeple, and by a 9m/29.5ft statue of the Virgin with arms outstretched toward the river, created by Philippe Laperle. Commissioned by Marguerite Bourgeoys in 1657, and dedicated in 1678, the original stone chapel burned to the ground in 1754. The present structure dates from the mid-18C.

The façade and interior decoration were added in the late 19C. The tower was constructed over the apse between 1892 and 1894 to house the statue of the Virgin. Also added at this time were an "aerial chapel" and an observatory accessible from the tower (climb of 100 steps). From here, the **panorama**★ extends over the St. Lawrence River, St. Helen's Island, the Jacques-Cartier Bridge, and the Old Port.

The chapel, nicknamed "the Sailors' Church," was hung with small carved ships offered to the Virgin by devout seamen. Some of these votive offerings can still be seen today in the chapel. The oak statue of the Virgin, located in the chapel to the left of the altar, is the focus of special devotion, having been recovered intact after fire and theft. Beneath the nave of the chapel, the foundation walls of the original building have been uncovered, along with the traces of a wood palisade and indications of the Amerindian presence here as early as 400 BC.

▶ *Walk west on the Rue Saint-Paul Est.*

Marché Bonsecours★ (Bonsecours Market)

350 Rue Saint-Paul Est. 🕒*Champ-de-Mars.* 🕐*Open mid-Jun–Labor Day, Mon–Sat 10am–9pm, Sun 10am–6pm; Labor Day–Dec & Apr–late Jun, daily 10am–6pm (Thu & Fri to 9pm), Jan–Mar, daily 10am–6pm.* ☎514-872-7730. *www.marchebonsecours.qc.ca.*

Originally constructed to house Montreal's first interior market, this building (1845) occupies the former site of the Intendant's Palace, destroyed in 1796. With its 163m/534.7ft freestone façade and lofty dome, the elegantly ornamented structure is best viewed from the riverside. The ground-floor merchant stalls were accessible from the outside through large bays. After fire destroyed the Parliament Buildings in 1849, the market became the seat of the Legislature of the United Canadas. From 1852 through 1878, it served as the City Hall, and is now leased for 15 charming shops and craft boutiques, and exhibitions.

Le Village

Montreal has a fantastic (inexpensive, happy) clubbing scene (mainly downtown and on Rue Saint-Laurent, north of Rue Sherbrooke), but what is most unusually pleasant about it is Le Village, the gay community area (métro Beaudry, on Rue Sainte-Catherine, east of the downtown core). Le Village is colorful, fun, arty, and non threatening. The shops and restaurants possess a special flair. At night, on warm summer nights, the neighborhood explodes with energy, music, and more. The Cabaret Mado (*1115 Rue Catherine Est, corner of Rue Amherst,* ☎514-525-7566) drag queen show is so famous that it just about reaches tourist attraction status.

Vieux-Port Esplanade

Pierre Ethier/ MICHELIN

▶ *Continue west on Rue Saint-Paul Est to the foot of Place Jacques-Cartier. Turn left, cross Rue de la Commune and enter the Old Port area.*

Vieux-Port★ (Old Port)

🕐 *Place-d'Armes or Champ-de-Mars.*

In Montreal's early years, barges and canoes were hauled by hand onto the muddy St. Lawrence banks. In the mid 18C, several wooden quays were built on the site of the present port. These were replaced in 1830 by stone piers, loading ramps and a breakwater, constructed by the newly created Harbor Commission. Concrete piers, steel sheds, docks, jetties and a huge grain elevator (demolished in 1978) were erected in 1898. During the 1920s Montreal had become the largest grain port on the continent, with a traffic volume second only to the port of New York, even though at the time, ice forced an annual shutdown of several months.

Today, much of the maritime traffic bypasses Montreal on the St. Lawrence Seaway, and the port's principal activities center on the handling of shipping containers. The older section of the port has been converted into a park featuring cultural and recreational activities during the summer months.

Esplanade

Entrances at Rue Berri, Place Jacques-Cartier, Blvd. Saint-Laurent, and Rue McGill.
With its sunny, breeze-swept spaces and paths for walking, skating or biking, this immense waterfront park comes alive during fine weather, especially during the summer months. The esplanade boasts excellent **views**★ of the city and river, boat trips, bike rentals, and **iSci**—the Montreal Interactive Science Center (*see below*). **Tram tours** allow visitors to discover the entire esplanade and the history of the Old Port (*depart from Jacques-Cartier pier year-round, daily; ☜$5; ☎514-496-7678; www.quays oftheoldport.com*).

Montreal Science Center ★ Kids

Quai King Edward at Blvd. St. Laurent and Rue de la Commune.
Major **Interactive Science Exhibitions** change periodically (*open mid-Jun–early Sept, Mon–Fri 9.30am–5pm, Sat–Sun 10am–5pm; rest of the year daily 10am–6pm; ☜$12; children $9*). ✕ & 🅿 ☎514-496-4724; www.isci.ca) allows spectators to control the action of the adventure by voting on interactive screens, and the **IMAX cinema** (*open Apr–mid-Sept, daily 10am–9.15pm (Fri–Sat to 10.15pm); rest of the year, daily 10am–9.15pm (Mon to 4.15pm); reservations advised; ☜$12*) continues to thrill viewers with its 3D sensations.

At the eastern end of the Quai de l'Horloge, note the **Tour de l'Horloge** (Clock Tower). Completed in 1922, the 45m/148ft tower honors the sailors who perished during World War I. You can climb the 192 steps to the top for a nice panorama of the city (*donation requested*).

Jet Boat Trips on the Lachine Rapids★★ (Expéditions dans les rapides de Lachine)

Champ-de-Mars. Depart from Quai de l'Horloge May–Aug, daily 10am–6pm; Sept–mid-Oct, 10am–4pm. Round-trip 1hr. Commentary. Reservations required. $60. ($12) Lachine Rapids Tours/ Saute-Moutons: 514-284-9607. www. jetboatingmontreal.com

On the wettest, most exciting ride in Montreal, passengers embark upriver to the ferocious Lachine Rapids in unique "jet boats." These specially designed vessels repeatedly mount and descend the tumultuous rapids. Despite the protective clothing provided, passengers can anticipate a thorough soaking. The **views**★★ of Montreal and the surrounding areas are spectacular, particularly if the excursion occurs around sunset.

Harbor Cruises★ (Croisières du port de Montréal)

Depart from Quai King Edward May–Oct, daily 11.30am, 2pm & 4pm; round-trip 1hr 30min; commentary; reservations required; starting at $25. Dancing & dinner cruises available; depart at 7pm; round-trip 4hrs; commentary; reservations required; starting at $40 (plus price of meal). ($9) Croisières AML: 1-800-563-4643 or www.croisieresaml.com

Cruises of various lengths offer visitors a unusual perspective of Montreal from the river. The port installations, bridges, islands, the St. Lawrence Seaway, and the Olympic Stadium are among the highlights.

Amphitours

Depart from the corner of Blvd. Saint-Laurent & Rue de la Commune Jun–Sept, daily 10am–10pm every hour; May & Oct, daily noon, 2pm & 4pm. Round-trip 70min. Commentary. Reservations advised in high season. $32. ($10). 514-849-5181; www.montreal-amphibus-tour.com.

The "Kamada," a specially designed amphibious bus, tours part of Old Montreal before descending into the St. Lawrence River for a cruise around the Cité du Havre.

Place d'Youville Area★

Square-Victoria. Map Montréal.

The St. Pierre River ran along this square to join the St. Lawrence at Pointe-à-Callière, until it was channeled underground in the 19C. The square was named after **Marguerite d'Youville**, who founded the Grey Nuns in 1737.

In 1849 it was the site of the Colonial Legislature created after the Patriots' Rebellion of 1837 with representatives from Lower Canada (Quebec) and Upper Canada (Ontario). Tories burned the building to the ground to show their objection to a law compensating anyone whose land had been damaged during the Rebellions (including rebels). The Legislature moved briefly to Bonsecours Market and then left for Kingston, Quebec, and finally Ottawa, it would never again meet in Montreal.

The buildings surrounding the pleasant square represent different epochs in the city's history, from the 17C Grey Nuns hospital to the 19C warehouses and the immense, Beaux-Arts style **Édifice des Douanes** (Customs House), erected between 1912 and 1936. Today, numerous residences are undergoing renovations, adding to the charm of this up-and-coming area.

Pointe-à-Callière, Montreal Museum of Archeology and History★★

Montreal was born on this small triangle of land, where the St. Pierre River joined the St. Lawrence, in May 1642. The spot had already been cleared in 1611 by Samuel de Champlain, who deemed it an excellent location for a harbor. Thirty-one years later, Maisonneuve established the settlement of Ville-Marie on the site, surrounding it with a wooden stockade.

A 10m/32.8ft **obelisk** (3), *Les Pionniers*, commemorates Maisonneuve's landing. Callière Point is named for Louis-Hector de Callière, Governor of Montreal from 1684 to 1698, whose home formerly occupied the site.

350 Place Royale. Open late Jun–Labor Day, Mon–Fri 10am–6pm, weekends 11am–6pm; rest of the year, Tue–Fri 10am–5pm, weekends 11am–5pm. Closed major holidays. ⊕*$13.* ✗ ♿☎*514-872-9150. www.pacmuseum.qc.ca.*

Opened in 1992, this museum complex brings alive the fascinating history of Montreal from its very beginnings here at Callière Point.

In the striking, contemporary Éperon Building, visitors can view a wonder-fully absorbing multimedia presentation (*16min*) on the evolution of Montreal. Temporary exhibits are mounted on the second floor, and from the third floor belvedere, a lovely **view**★ extends over the Old Port Esplanade.

An underground passage leads from the Éperon Building to the **archeological crypt** located directly beneath Place Royale. Artifacts on display here bear witness to Montreal's many centuries of human occupation. In the crypt, visi-tors can see the actual vestiges of early Montreal, foundations and even walls of structures uncovered in the course of archeological excavations. Scale mod-els of the city illustrate its appearance during various periods, and interac-tive monitors allow visitors to interact with the images of some of Montreal's early inhabitants.

The underground passage ends at the **Old Customs House** (1838, John Ostell). Above ground, the edifice's Neoclassi-cal façade dominates the Place Royale. Today transformed into an interpretation center, the dignified building houses exhibits on the history of Montreal as a center of trade and commerce.

Place Royale

In 1645, Maisonneuve erected his dwell-ing on this square, originally known as the Place d'Armes. By 1706, it had become the public market place, the popular setting for official announce-ments by the town crier, criminal pun-ishments including whippings and hangings, and occasional duels. The square was officially named Place Royale in 1892.

Centre d'histoire de Montréal★ (Montreal History Center)

335 Place d'Youville. 🕐*Open late Jan–Apr & mid-Sept–early Dec, Wed–Sun 10am–5pm, May–mid-Sept Tue–Sun 10am–5pm.*

⊕*$4.50.* ♿☎*514-872-3207. www.ville. montreal.qc.ca/chm.*

Restored in 1981, this redbrick edifice (1903), a former fire station, features ele-ments of Dutch baroque architecture: An elegantly gabled roof, an imposing dormer and sculpted ornamentation. The rear tower was used to hang the water hoses to dry, and stone arches at the front provided access for firefight-ing vehicles.

Today the building houses a delight-ful interpretation center dedicated to Montreal's history from 1535 to the pres-ent. Audio tracks, murals and original objects illustrate the economic, social and urban trends that influenced the city's colorful past.

Écuries d'Youville (Youville Stables)

298–300 Place d'Youville.
Enclosing a pleasant garden courtyard, these low stone structures (1828) were built as warehouses for the Grey Nuns, and later used to store grain. The com-plex never actually served as a shelter for animals; however, it is thought that its present name derives from 19C sta-bles that were located nearby. Restored in 1967, the complex currently houses offices and a restaurant, and the sur-rounding buildings have been renovated as condominiums. Enter the courtyard through the central carriage door.

Hôpital général des Sœurs Grises (Grey Nuns' Hospital)

Bounded by Rue Saint-Pierre, Rue d'Youville, Rue Normand and Place d'Youville.

In 1680, the Sulpicians ceded the marshland near the St. Pierre River to François Charron de la Barre and his brothers, who constructed a hospital on the site in 1694. In 1747, Marguerite d'Youville and the Grey Nuns assumed direction of the hospital, rebuilding it after it was largely destroyed by fire in 1765.

In 1871, due to frequent flooding of the site and increased activity in the adjacent port, the Grey Nuns left the area for a quieter location to the west of the center. Their chapel on Rue Saint-Pierre was demolished, the street was extended to the river, and warehouses were erected.

In 1980, the convent building was renovated to house a novitiate and the general administration offices for the Grey Nuns. The oldest section of the convent can be seen from Rue Normand.

②From Dorchester Square to Mcgill University★★

2.4km/1.5mi. Map Montréal. 🔽*Peel.*

▶ *Begin the walking tour at Dorchester Square.*

This walk through the commercial heart of present-day Montreal leads past some of the city's landmark skyscrapers. The highrises along Avenue McGill College illustrate the diverging tendencies that mark the post-Modern movement.

Dorchester Square★
Surrounded by a group of remarkable buildings, this pleasant green square has long been considered the heart of the city, though more recent skyscrapers have stolen some of the limelight. Formerly known as Dominion Square, it was renamed in 1988 to commemorate Lord Dorchester, Governor of British North America from 1768 through 1778 and from 1786 through 1795. Situated outside city limits prior to 1855, the area originally served as a cemetery, especially for the many victims of the 1832 cholera epidemic. The cemetery was eventually moved to Mt. Royal, and the second bishop of Montreal, **Msgr. Ignace Bourget** (1799–1885), decided

to erect a cathedral on the site, much to the chagrin of his parishioners, residents of the old town who objected to having to walk so far to church.

The square contains several notable memorials, including a statue of **Sir Wilfrid Laurier** (4) by Émile Brunet. Laurier (1841–1919) was the first French-Canadian prime minister of Canada; his famous words carved on the pedestal read (in translation): "The governing motive of my life has been to harmonize the different elements which compose our country." The monument to Laurier faces one of **Sir John A. Macdonald** (5) across the street in Place du Canada. The monument to **Lord Strathcona's Canadian Horse Regiment** (6), honoring the Canadians killed in the Boer War (1899–1901), is the work of George Hill, who also sculpted the nearby lion commemorating **Queen Victoria's Jubilee** (7). The statue of **Robert Burns** (8) was erected by devotees of the renowned Scottish poet (1759-96).

Dominion Square Building★
On northern side of Dorchester Square between Rue Peel and Rue Metcalfe. This imposing Renaissance Revival structure (1929) evokes the grandeur of 15C Florentine palaces. Reputed to be the "largest commercial building in Canada," the edifice displayed several features considered innovative for the time: An underground parking area and two-level shopping mall, and the first wooden escalators to appear in Montreal. Also considered novel was the fact that the building housed both offices and boutiques.

The **Infotouriste** office is located on the ground floor (entrance on Rue du Square-Dorchester) between Rue Peel and Rue Metcalfe (🕐*open late Jun–Labor Day, daily 8.30am–7.30pm; rest of the year, daily 9am–6pm; closed Jan 1 & Dec 25;* ♿ 🅿 ☎*514-873-2015 & 1-877-266-5687*). Visitors will find every tourist service imaginable here, including an information desk, guided tours (☎) of the city, a bookstore, currency exchange, accommodation reservations, car rentals, phones and Internet access.

The Windsor★
1170 Rue Peel.

Today one of Montreal's most distinctive office buildings, the Windsor Hotel was inaugurated in 1878 with a ball honoring the Marquis de Lorne (then governor-general) and his wife Louise, daughter of Queen Victoria. Seriously damaged by fire in 1906 and destroyed in 1957, the structure's main wing was replaced by the Bank of Commerce. The hotel continued to operate in the remaining wing until 1981. The stone and brick façade is topped by a mansard roof pierced with dormers and œil-de-bœuf windows. The renovation of the hotel interior into office space preserved the Adamesque décor of the ground floor, exemplified in the sumptuous ballroom.

Sun Life Building★★
1155 Rue Metcalfe.

This magnificent Beaux-Arts edifice (1913), constructed of steel sheathed in white granite and adorned with colossal colonnades on its four façades, occupies the entire east side of Dorchester Square. Headquarters of the Sun Life Insurance Company, the building could accommodate 2,500 employees and was touted as the "tallest building in the British Empire." Its construction and subsequent expansions (1923–1933) contributed to Montreal's status as Canada's most important financial city during those years. During World War II, the British government stored its Treasury bonds and gold reserves in this building. Today it houses the Sun Life administrative headquarters and other prestigious insurance and brokerage firms.

▶ *Cross Blvd. René-Lévesque and continue down Rue Peel.*

Place du Canada
Several high rises tower over this green plaza, facing Dorchester Square. The elongated **Banque de Commerce** (Bank of Commerce, 1962) presents an unusual contrast between the slate window frames and the glass and stainless steel façade. Across the street rises the post-Modern, copper and glass **La Laurentienne** (Laurentian Building, 1986). Popularly known as the "cheese-grater," the **Marriott Château Champlain Hotel** stands on the south side of the square. The slender building (1967), marked by convex, half-moon windows, bears the influence of Frank Lloyd Wright, mentor of architect Roger d'Astous. The prevailing architectural tastes of the 1990s are reflected in the **1000 de la Gauchetière** office building dominating the southeast corner of the square; it is Montreal's tallest structure at 205m/672ft.

St. George's Anglican Church★
Entrance on Rue de la Gauchetière. ⏱Open year-round, Tue–Sun 9am–4pm. ♿☎514-866-7113. www.st-georges.org.

Erected in 1870, this charming Gothic Revival church is the oldest building on Place du Canada. The well-proportioned interior features a striking double hammer-beam vaulted **ceiling** of red pine and spruce. Of special interest are the oak reredos with its delicate open tracery, the choir stalls and the chancel screens. The side screens and sculptures, also of oak, were produced by the Casavant Company of Saint-Hyacinthe, who installed the organ in 1896.

Gare Windsor (Windsor Station)
Corner of Rue Peel and Rue de la Gauchetière.

Designed by Bruce Price, famed architect of Quebec City's Château Frontenac, this distinctive railway station (1889) is one of Montreal's finest examples of the Richardsonian Romanesque style, characterized by towers, crenelations, turrets and round arches. The station was created to house the administrative center of Canadian Pacific Railways, and now serves as the terminus of the suburban transit network.

▶ *Return to Blvd. René-Lévesque and continue east.*

Basilique-Cathédrale Marie-Reine-du-Monde★★ (Mary Queen of the World Basilica-Cathedral)
Main entrance on Blvd. René-Lévesque, at Rue de la Cathédrale. ⏱Open year-round, Mon–Fri 7am–6pm, Sat 7.30am–6pm, Sun 8.30am–7.30pm. ♿☎514-866-1661.

Designed by Victor Bourgeau, this monumental edifice is distinguished by large Greek columns, ornate decoration and a row of statues lining the cornice. After a fire destroyed the St. James Cathedral (Cathédrale Saint-Jacques) located on the east side of Montreal, Msgr. Ignace Bourget decided to erect a new cathedral in the west quarter to reinforce the importance of the Catholic Church in this Anglophone, Protestant district. A proponent of papal supremacy, the bishop of Montreal selected as a model St. Peter's in Rome, the mother church of Roman Catholicism. The scale of this Baroque Revival replica was reduced to one-third the size of the 16C Italian basilica.

The church was consecrated in 1894. Originally dedicated to St. James the Major, the structure was recognized as a minor basilica in 1919 and adopted its present name in 1955.

Alphonse Longpré (1881–1938) carved the cornice figures, representing patron saints from parishes comprising the Montreal diocese in 1890. The copper dome was added in 1886; its original iron cross was replaced by an aluminium version in 1958. The **statue** (9) of Msgr. Bourget, standing to the right of the cathedral, is the work of Louis-Philippe Hébert. The bishop also appears on the statue's pedestal in the company of the architect of the cathedral, Victor Bourgeau.

Interior

In the entrance vestibule hang the portraits of all the bishops of Montreal, among them the late Msgr. Paul Grégoire, appointed Cardinal in 1989. Cast in copper covered with gold leaf, the magnificent **baldachin** (1900) by Victor Vincent dominates the nave; it replicates the 16C masterpiece that Italian sculptor Bernini created for St. Peter's Basilica. The interior is decorated with large paintings by Georges Delfosse representing episodes in the history of Canada, including the martyrdoms of the Jesuit priest Jean de Brébeuf and Gabriel Lalement; and the drowning of Nicolas Viel, the first Canadian martyr, and Ahuntsic, his Amerindian disciple. In the chapel behind the altar stands a delicate statue of the Virgin by Sylvia Daoust, the renowned 20C Canadian sculptress.

Located on the left side of the nave, a **mortuary chapel** (1933) contains the tombs of several archbishops and bishops. The Italian marble walls and floor are embellished with beautiful mosaics. In the center, note Msgr. Bourget's mausoleum, executed in Rome. Above the altar in the back of the chapel, a magnificent bronze bas-relief represents St. Peter's of Rome.

▷ *Cross Blvd. René-Lévesque and continue east.*

Montreal's largest hotel, Fairmont The Queen Elizabeth (1958), occupies the block of Boulevard René-Lévesque between Rue Mansfield and Rue Université. The Central train station (Gare Centrale), terminus for VIA Rail and Amtrak trains, is located beneath the hotel.

Place Ville-Marie★★

Corner of Ave. McGill College & Rue Cathcart.

Centerpiece of Underground City before its development around the McGill metro station, Place Ville-Marie initiated the rebirth of Montreal's downtown and has become the forerunner of many such developments across the country. Inspired by New York City's Rockefeller Center (⌖consult THE GREEN GUIDE New York City). Place Ville-Marie is one of the few landmark buildings symbolizing Montreal.

The **Banque Royale Tower**★ (1962; I.M. Pei, Affleck and Assocs) dominates the complex. The cruciform structure, sheathed in aluminium, boasts 3,534sq m/38,000sq ft of office space on each of its 42 stories.

The Banque Royale and the three other buildings making up the complex enclose a concrete esplanade that is especially lively in summertime. From this raised vantage point, an unparalleled **vista**★ extends to the north of the city, down Avenue McGill College to the McGill University campus, dominated by the bulk of Mt. Royal. Gerald Gladstone's bronze fountain, entitled *Female Landscape* (1972), stands in the foreground. From the shopping center beneath the esplanade, large skylights afford intriguing views of the surrounding towers. *Access to Underground City (◷ open during business hours) via glass pavilions in front of the Banque Royale Tower.*

▶ *From Place Ville-Marie, proceed northward on Ave. McGill College.*

Extending from Place Ville-Marie to the gates of McGill University, **Avenue McGill College** has become a showplace for post-Modern architecture. Planned in 1857 as a prolongation of the main campus axis toward the downtown area, the avenue is now home to several important architectural projects initiated during the 1980s and 1990s. The avenue is beautifully lit during the Christmas season, and it displays outdoor photo exhibitions year round.

Place Montréal Trust★★
1500 Ave. McGill College.
This enormous edifice (1989) of rose marble blocks partitioned by sheets of pastel blue glass occupies the entire left side of the block between Rue Sainte-Catherine and Boulevard de Maisonneuve. Conceived by the architects **E. Zeidler**, **E. Argun**, and **P. Rose**, the tower's bold design features a cylinder encased in a square base. The glass-walled **atrium** rises five floors from the metro level; a panoramic elevator permits visitors to admire the three-tiered central bronze fountain. With more than a hundred boutiques, a restaurant and numerous exotic food vendors, the atrium is a popular lunchtime spot.

▶ *Walk east on Rue Sainte-Catherine.*

Place Montréal Trust

Lili Thériault/MICHELIN

Montreal's main retail artery, **Rue Sainte-Catherine** is lined with such major department stores as **Ogilvy** and **La Baie**; huge commercial centers, including the upscale Faubourg Sainte-Catherine; and numerous boutiques and restaurants. After business hours, this thoroughfare is transformed into a lively nightspot, abounding in bars and clubs.

Montreal Eaton Center
677 Rue Sainte-Catherine Ouest.
Well-known commercial outlet (175 fashion-oriented shops) in the original Eaton store building (1925)—acquired by Timothy Eaton and enlarged to nine floors in 1930.

Christ Church Cathedral★
Entrance from Rue Sainte-Catherine between Rue University and Ave. Union.
◷ Open year-round, daily 8am–6pm.

Address Book

HIDDEN JEWELS

An unassuming location in the middle of a business district belies the culinary riches put forth at **Le Grand Comptoir** (*1225 Square Phillips;* ☎514-393-3295), where classic bistro dishes like *ris de veau* (calf's sweetbread) and *bavette à l'échalotte* (flank steak with shallots) are easy on both palate and wallet. Looking for a quick, tasty meal, especially in the wee hours? Try the famous smoked-meat sandwiches at **Dunn's** (*1249 Rue Metcalfe, just south of Rue Sainte-Catherine;* ☎514-395-1927), which has been serving up traditional deli fare since 1927. The large, typically North American restaurant is lined up with dining booths and cheery waiters.

&☎514-843-6577, ext. 371. www.montreal.
anglican.org/cathedral.

Distinguished by its triple portico, this lovely structure (1859) reflects the Gothic Revival style. The limestone edifice, topped by a slender central spire, was erected as Montreal's second Anglican cathedral, after the first one burned down in 1856. During the 1980s, the base of the church was discovered to be sinking. In response, the Anglican Church of Canada leased the land to a development company, which saved the church from destruction by shoring up the foundations and constructing an underground commercial complex beneath it.

Before entering, note the **monument** (**10**) (*to the right of the church*) dedicated to Francis Fulford (1803–1868), the Anglican bishop at the time of the cathedral's construction.

A pointed arched nave and ogive windows decorated with trefoil and quatrefoil elements distinguish the interior. The chancel features a beautifully carved stone **reredos**. The William Morris studio of London, England, produced many of the magnificent stained-glass windows. Note the organ below the rose window at the south end: Of North German inspiration, it was built in 1980 by Karl Wilhelm of Mont-Saint-Hilaire. *Organ recitals are regularly held in the cathedral.*

▶ *Enter Les Promenades de la Cathédrale by the doors on either side of the cathedral's main entrance.*

Les Promenades de la Cathédrale

Linking Eaton Center and La Baie department store, this shopping center (1988) is the result of one of Montreal's most spectacular feats of engineering. Excavation and construction occurred beneath the church over a period of several months, during which the structure's weight was borne only by slim pylons. Ogive ornamentation in the underground concourses is a reminder of the presence of the religious monument above.

▶ *Ascend to the street level "cloister," an attractive park located between the cathedral and La Place de la Cathédrale.*

La Place de la Cathédrale★
600 Blvd. de Maisonneuve Ouest.

Postmodern in design, this distinctive, 34-story office tower (1988; Webb, Zerafa, Menkès and Houdsen) reveals the influence of the adjacent cathedral, as much by its pointed arched entrances, colonnades and deep embrasures as by its pitched roof and tall, arched windows. A prominent landmark among Montreal's downtown skyscrapers, the building is sheathed in copper-colored reflecting glass. Step into the navelike **foyer** for the sight of Christ Church Cathedral and its steeple through the five-story curvilinear glass wall.

▶ *Exit to Blvd. de Maisonneuve and walk west to Ave. McGill College.*

Tours de la Banque Nationale de Paris/Banque Laurentienne★ (National Bank of Paris (BNP)/ Laurentian Bank Towers)
1981 Ave. McGill College.

Completed in 1981, the sprawling, twin-towered structure is designed in a play of angles and shapes. The metallic-blue glass exterior of the office complex camouflages the actual number of stories within (16 and 20 stories) and reflects the neighboring buildings. Its jagged, abstract form surrounds a small forecourt highlighted by La foule illuminée, a fiberglass group sculpture by the French artist, Raymond Masson. The "blue building," as it is called by many Montrealers, symbolizes the economic growth experienced by the city during the early 1980s.

Tour l'Industrielle Vie (Industrial Life Tower)
2000 Ave. McGill College.

This granite-clad tower (1986) features a rather conventional exterior enlivened by post-Modern ornamentation. The huge fanlight window at its entrance is repeated at the top of the building.

On the sidewalk, note the delightful bronze **sculpture**, *"Le banc du secret"* by Léa Vivot, of two children on a bench. The work bears numerous bilingual inscriptions, poems and sentiments, all anonymous but for one: "Montreal, a secret to share," signed Jean Doré, former mayor of Montreal.

Maison Ultramar (Ultramar Building)

2200 Ave. McGill College.
This edifice (1990) successfully integrates the former University Club (*892 Rue Sherbrooke*) and the Molson House (*2047 Rue Mansfield*). The building's recessed entranceway surmounted by a rounded glass façade displays the architect's skillful handling of a corner lot.

Place Mercantile

Across from the Ultramar Building; entrance at 770 Rue Sherbrooke Ouest.
This aluminum and glass complex (1982) incorporates, on the Rue Sherbrooke side, the façades of a row of greystones dating from 1872. One of these, Strathcona Hall (1904), was sold by McGill University with the stipulation that the hall be preserved. It collapsed during construction of Place Mercantile, but was entirely rebuilt. Today the building houses the offices of Cacades Inc., Cascades Etcan Inc., and Etcan International Inc.

▶ *Turn right on Rue Sherbrooke.*

McCord Museum★★

690 Rue Sherbrooke Ouest. ◷*Open year-round, Tue–Fri 10am–6pm, weekends 10am–5pm (Jul–Sept, Mon 10am–5pm).* ◉*$12.* ✗ ♿ ☎*514-398-7100. www.mccord-museum.qc.ca.*
Founded in 1921, the McCord figures prominently among Canada's foremost historical museums.
With a view to founding a museum dedicated to Canada's social history, David Ross McCord (1844–1930) donated his extensive personal collections to McGill University in 1919. Today the museum's holdings include over 100,000 artifacts and more than 750,000 historic photos, offering insight into various facets of Canadian history from the settlement of the Amerindians to the present.

Building

In 1968, the museum moved its collections to this sober structure of grey limestone, originally a social center for McGill University students. Erected in 1906 by Percy E. Nobbs, the edifice is highlighted by an elaborate portal flanked by Tuscan pilasters. An extension (1992) has been added to the south of the structure, permitting additional exhibit space, conservation laboratories, a library and various amenities. The new building's façade reflects the elegant style of the original structure. Galleries on two floors showcase the museum's permanent and temporary exhibits.

Collections

A magnificent Haida façade pole of Queen Charlotte Islands (British Columbia) red cedar in the stairwell leads to the second floor. This level houses the permanent exhibit "Simply Montréal: Glimpses of a Unique City," which offers an enlightening look at life in Montreal from the 17C to the present. The unusual variety of objects draws from the museum's holdings of Amerindian art, decorative art (metalware and jewelry, furniture, basketry, glassware, ceramics), sporting equipment, and toys. Also illustrating the Canadian lifestyle are examples from the museum's extensive costumes and textiles collection as well as selections from the **Notman Photographic Archives**. This outstanding collection of negatives and photographs, 400,000 of which were shot by master photographer, William Notman (1826–1891), portrays historical figures, events and Canadian sites over a 78-year period and constitutes a comprehensive chronicle of Canadian life in the 19C and early 20C.

▶ *Cross Rue Sherbrooke to main entrance of the campus.*

McGill University★

End of Ave. McGill College. ☎*514-398-4455. www.mcgill.ca.*
Graced with an attractive downtown campus on the slopes of Mt. Royal, Canada's oldest university originated when its benefactor, the Scottish fur trader James McGill (1744–1813), bequeathed

Address Book

HOUSE OF JAZZ

2060 Rue Aylmer. ☎514-842-8656.
Jazz lovers in the mood for excellent
live music and a laid-back ambience should keep this famed local
hangout in mind when planning an
evening on the town. Stop in for a set
or two and sample tasty barbecued
chicken or ribs, either inside or on
the outdoor terrace in fine weather.

Burnside, his country estate, and
£10,000 for the foundation of an English-speaking university. Granted a Royal
Charter by George IV in 1821, McGill's
first classes (in medicine) were held in
1829, following the incorporation of
the Montreal Medical Institute. In the
years since, the university has witnessed
enormous growth and today claims an
enrollment of over 30,000 students at
the 32ha/79 acre downtown campus
and at the Macdonald College campus
located at Sainte-Anne-de-Bellevue, in
the West Island.

Campus

Enter the campus by the Greek Revival
Portail Roddick (Roddick Gate, 1924),
erected in memory of Sir Thomas
Roddick, dean of the Medical School;
embedded in the gate is a clock, the

McGill University

*Students in front of the Redpath Museum,
McGill University*

gift of Lady Roddick in honor of her husband's extreme punctuality. The more
than 70 buildings located on the university's downtown campus reflect a wide
variety of architectural styles. Ornate
façades, towers and turrets embellish
early 19C limestone structures. Executed
in an eclectic 19C style, they contrast
with the unadorned concrete of more
recent buildings. To the west of the
main avenue, note the beautiful stone
fountain (1930), attributed to Gertrude
Vanderbilt Whitney.

Arts Building

At the end of the main avenue. The central
and east sections of the campus' oldest
structure were designed by John Ostell
between 1839 and 1843. The west pavilion (Molson Hall) and the wings linking
the three sections date from between
1861 and 1880. The Doric portico and
interior were rebuilt in 1924, in the austere Neoclassical style. From the steps
of the portico there is a good **view** of
downtown through the trees of the
campus. The tomb of the university's
founder, James McGill, stands in front
of the building.

Redpath Museum of Natural History ★

To the west of Arts Building. ◷*Open
Mon–Fri 9am–5pm, Sun 1pm–5pm.*
◷*Closed public holidays.* ⓟ ☎514-398-
4086, ext. 4092. www.mcgill.ca/redpath.
This building (1882) was the first in Canada designed to hold a natural history
museum. Its generous benefactor was
Peter Redpath, a wealthy industrialist
and founder of the nation's first sugar
refinery. The building's eclectic Greek
and Renaissance façade evokes an
antique temple.
Inside, visitors can see an incredible
array of treasures, including Egyptian
mummies and the skeleton of an Albertosaurus. The first floor houses offices
and classrooms, as well as a selection
of objects drawn from the museum's
zoology, paleontology and mineral
collections. The upper floors re-create
the charming, studious atmosphere
of Victorian-era museums, and house
an amazing number of invertebrate
and vertebrate fossils, minerals and

other zoological artifacts, as well as Egyptian antiquities.

▸ *Exit the campus by the Roddick Gate and turn right.*

Located on the edge of campus bordering Rue Sherbrooke, just west of the Roddick Gate, a **plaque** (**11**) commemorates the Indian village of Hochelaga which (as was supposed in the 19C) stood on this spot at the time of Jacques Cartier's arrival in 1535.

Additional Sight

Planétarium de Montréal

1000 Rue Saint-Jacques. ◔*Bonaventure.* ◷*Open late Jun–Labor Day, Mon 12.30pm–5pm, Tue–Thu 9.30am–5pm, Fri also 7pm–9.30pm, weekends 12.30pm–4.30pm, 7pm–9.30pm; rest of the year, Tue–Thu 9.30am–5pm, Fri also 6.45pm–9.30pm, weekends 10am–5pm, 6.45pm–9.30pm. Call for show times.* ⌾*$8.* ♿🅿☎*514-872-4530. www.planetarium.montreal.qc.cu.*

Each year, visitors can take in superb multimedia shows (50min, some in French, some in English) presented in the planetarium's 385-seat **Star Theater**, where a German-made Zeiss V projector utilizes 150 separate projectors to create the image of the starry sky on the theater's immense, hemispheric dome. Temporary and permanent exhibits offer an introduction to the natural phenomena of our universe, and provide updates on recent astronomical events.

③ From Place des Arts to Chinatown★

Map Montréal. ◔*Place des Arts.*

Long neglected by the city's leaders, this area experienced a renaissance during and after the French counterculture movement of the 1960s. The decision to erect the modern Place des Arts Complex in the eastern part of the city, made by the municipal administration under mayor Jean Drapeau, reflected a growing interest in Francophone culture and marked the beginning of a series of investments in the then somewhat abandoned French sector of Montreal. The inception of Place des Arts engendered other major projects such as the Desjardins Complex, the University of Quebec at Montreal, the Olympic Stadium, the Guy-Favreau Complex and the Convention Center.

▸ *Begin at Place des Arts. This walk takes the visitor through a section of the Underground City.*

Place des Arts★★

North side of Rue Sainte-Catherine between Rue Jeanne-Mance and Rue Saint-Urbain. ◷*Open year-round, daily.* 🍴🅿⌾*$9. Ticket Office Mon–Sat noon–8.30pm.* ☎*514-842-2112 & 1-866-842-2112. www.pda.qc.ca*

Montreal's premier cultural complex for the visual and performing arts consists of three structures bordering a central square. The imposing concert hall (1963) is flanked by a theater building (1967) and the Montreal Contemporary Art Museum (1992). The buildings are situated around a vast esplanade where lively crowds gather during fine weather. Several annual festivals and events take place here, among them the International Jazz Festival, held in the area near the intersection of Rues Jeanne-Mance and Sainte-Catherine.

The building and its hall

Highlighted by an elliptical façade of windows and slim concrete columns, the building is home to the prestigious Orchestre symphonique de Montréal, the Grands Ballets Canadiens, and l'Opéra de Montréal. The main auditorium (salle Wilfrid-Pelletier) has a seating capacity of 2,982. The interior central hall, called the Piano Nobile, features works of art by renowned Canadian artists: Flamboyant tapestries by Robert Lapalme and Micheline Beauchemin, an imposing sculpture by Anne Kahane, and Louis Archambault's brass-leaf *Anges radieux* (Radiant Angels), which dominates the hall's main staircase. On the lower level, note the aluminium mural by Julien Hébert, ceramic panels by Jordi Bonnet, a marble swan by Hans Schleech and a sculpture by the Inuit

UNDERGROUND CITY

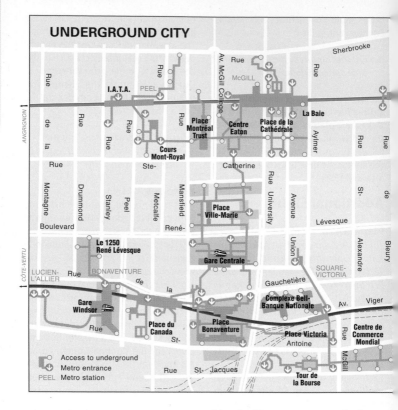

Access to underground
Metro entrance
PEEL Metro station

artist Innukpuk. Jean-Paul Riopelle's *La Bolduc* and a painting by Fernand Toupin also decorate the hall.

Complexe Théâtral (Theater Building)

The complex's theaters are housed in this imposing building situated on the corner of Rues Sainte-Catherine and Saint-Urbain. The Jean-Duceppe Theater is designed exclusively for plays and musicals. Directly above it is the Maisonneuve Theatre, of Italian inspiration. These "stacked" performance spaces are separated by an ingenious system of springs which acts as a floating floor for the Maisonneuve, above, or as a suspended ceiling for the Jean-Duceppe, below. A complete soundproofing system permits separate productions to occur in the two theaters simultaneously. The Studio Theater, a smaller and more intimate space, is located on the metro level.

Musée d'art contemporain de Montréal★★ (Contemporary Art Museum)

185 Rue Sainte-Catherine Ouest. ◑*Open mid-Jun–mid-Sept, daily 11am–6pm (Wed 9pm); rest of the year closed Mon except major holidays.* ◉*$8.* ♿ ₽ ☎*514-847-6226; www.macm.org.*

Rising to the west of the Place des Arts, this imposing edifice houses spacious, well-lit galleries display works selected from the permanent collection of more than 5,000 paintings, sculptures, prints, drawings, photographs and large-scale installations. More than 60 percent of the pieces are by Quebec artists, enabling the museum to showcase major trends in Quebec contemporary art with the work of Paul-Émile Borduas, Jean-Paul Riopelle, Guido Molinari, Claude Tousignant, Alfred Pellan, Ulysses Comtois and Armand Vaillancourt. International contemporary artists are also represented. A **sculpture garden** is accessible from the second floor (◑*closed in winter*); from here extends a view of the Place

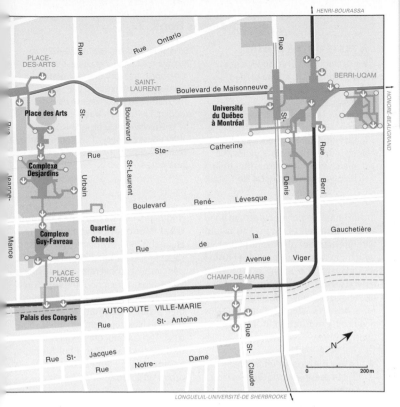

HENRI-BOURASSA

PLACE-DES-ARTS

Rue Ontario

Rue

BERRI-UQAM

SAINT-LAURENT

Boulevard de Maisonneuve

HONORÉ-BEAUGRAND

Place des Arts

St-

Boulevard

Université du Québec à Montréal

St-

Rue

Denis

Rue

Berri

Complexe Desjardins

Rue

Ste-

Catherine

Urbain

St-Laurent

Boulevard

René-

Lévesque

Jeanne-

Complexe Guy-Favreau

Quartier Chinois

Gauchetière

Mance

Rue

de

la

PLACE-D'ARMES

Avenue

Viger

CHAMP-DE-MARS

Rue

St-

Claude

Palais des Congrès

AUTOROUTE VILLE-MARIE

Rue

St- Antoine

Rue

St-

—N—

Rue St-

Jacques

Rue

Notre-

Dame

0   200 m

LONGUEUIL-UNIVERSITÉ-DE-SHERBROOKE

des Arts. Situated in the public space between by the Place des Arts complex and the Contemporary Art Museum is the **Cinquième Salle** (the 'fifth auditorium'), a smaller, multipurpose theater space.

▸ *Take the underground passageway leading to the Desjardins Complex.*

Complexe Desjardins★
South side of Rue Sainte-Catherine between Rues Jeanne-Mance and Saint-Urbain.
Opened in 1976, this complex appears heavy and austere from the outside. The vast interior plaza, better suited to the Montreal climate than an outdoor plaza, consists of four towers embrac-

Nat Gorry/Musée d'art contemporain de Montréal

Musée d'art contemporain de Montréal on the Place des Arts

Address Book

A TASTE OF THE EXOTIC

While Montreal's Chinatown is not large, it boasts a plethora of food shops and restaurants. To build your appetite, wander the shelves at **Kim Phat** (*1059 Blvd. Saint-Laurent*), stocked with an extraordinary variety of exotic foodstuffs: bamboo shoots, jackfruit, dried seaweed, Oriental candies and fragrant spices. Step across the street to simply appointed **Cristal No 1** (*1068 Blvd. Saint-Laurent; ☎514-875-4275*) to sample the famed Vietnamese *soupe tonkinoise*, a savory blend of broth, noodles and thinly sliced beef meat. The restrained yet attractive dining room at **Le Pavillon Nanpic** (*75A Rue de la Gauchetière Ouest; ☎514-395-8106*) offers a variety of Cantonese and Szechuan dishes; try the tasty General Tao chicken.

ing an immense polygonal atrium lined with three levels of shops. This layout is reminiscent of an amphitheater, in which passersby are both spectators and players. The atrium is the site of exhibits and popular cultural activities, like television shows, in contrast to the Place des Arts, which during the 1970s acquired a reputation as a symbol of elitist culture.

▶ *Follow the passage under Blvd. René-Lévesque to the Guy-Favreau Complex.*

Complexe Guy-Favreau

200 Blvd. René-Lévesque.
Completed in 1984, this complex was named for **Guy Favreau** (1917–67), a lawyer, politician, public prosecutor and minister of justice in prime minister John Diefenbaker's Cabinet (1957–63). Consisting of six interconnected structures, it contains Montreal's federal administration offices (including the all important passport office) and numerous apartments, as well as a mall. The redbrick exterior complements the handsome stainless steel and brick interior atrium. Exhibits are regularly organized in the main hall and in the mall. Offering a respite from the downtown bustle, the tranquil exterior **garden** is dotted with fountains and sculptures.

▶ *Exit on Rue de la Gauchetière for Chinatown.*

The massive concrete and glass construction (1983) that forms a bridge over the Ville-Marie Expressway is the original **Palais des Congrès de Montréal** (Montreal Convention Center). Erected in 1983, this mammoth building, capable of accommodating up to 10,000 people, hosts conventions, trade shows and exhibits throughout the year. A new wing opened in 2002, with a multicolored glass exterior that has become one of the architectural symbols of 21C Montreal. The colorful glass wall is in front of the new Place Jean-Paul-Riopelle, another fresh element in Montreal's urban landscape.

Chinatown★ (Quartier chinois)

Along Rue de la Gauchetière between Rue Jeanne-Mance and Blvd. Saint-Laurent, and on cross streets.
Montreal's Chinatown developed during the 1860s, with the arrival of immigrants fleeing the working conditions on the railroads and in the gold mines of the American West. Originally grouped in ghettos as a means of self-defense against official ostracism, the Chinese population in the area declined in the 1950s. Persons of Asian descent now reside throughout the city; primarily retirees and newly arrived immigrants live in Chinatown. On Sundays, however, many families gather in the area, and all shops are open.

Restricted to and frequently jammed with pedestrians, these few blocks of Rues de la Gauchetière and Saint-Laurent have become the social hub of Montreal's Far Eastern community, with numerous Chinese and Vietnamese restaurants and grocery stores. Two large Chinese-style arches (1963) span Rue de la Gauchetière, and a series of bronze medallions on the ground represent Chinese virtues. Murals along Rue Saint-Urbain depict Oriental legends such as that of the Monkey King. On Rue Clark, a small park is dedicated to **Sun-Yat-Sen** (1866–1925), "Father of the Republic and Founder of Modern China."

Erected in 1826, the **Maison Wing** (Wing House, 1009 Rue Côté), one of the oldest houses in the neighborhood, is now a bakery supplying fortune cookies for restaurants throughout the city.

④Rue Sherbrooke Ouest★★

2.3km/1.4mi. Map Rue Sherbrooke Ouest. ⚫Peel.

Begin the walking tour at the corner of Rue Sherbrooke Ouest and Rue Peel. All addresses are on Rue Sherbrooke Ouest, unless otherwise indicated.

One of the city's busiest and most prestigious downtown arteries, Rue Sherbrooke combines a bustling retail sector with some of Montreal's choicest residences. Flamboyant Victorian, Gothic and Romanesque-style structures combine with less decorative 1950s office buildings to form the city's most architecturally heterogeneous district. Rue Sherbrooke marks the southern border of the historic **Mille Carré Doré** (Golden Square Mile), bound on the other sides by Avenue des Pins, Rue Université and the junction of Rue Guy and Chemin de la Côte-des-Neiges (approximately 2.6sq km/1sq mi).

Originally part of the Sulpician seigneury, the area fell into the hands of English and Scottish fur traders after the

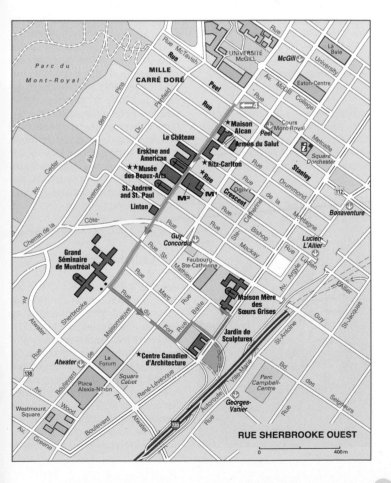

RUE SHERBROOKE OUEST

British Conquest. Successful landowners such as James McGill built country estates near the renowned orchards on the slopes of Mt. Royal, followed in 1885 by an affluent bourgeoisie reaping the benefits of the newly completed Canadian Pacific Railway. At the turn of the 20C, the residents of the Golden Square Mile held seventy percent of Canada's wealth. To the west of the Golden Square Mile lies the town of **Westmount**, a charming residential enclave.

Rue Peel

This elegant street was named for Sir Robert Peel (1788–1850), the British prime minister who founded the Conservative Party (the Tories) and facilitated England's transition to the industrial era by promoting various economic and financial legislation. Peel also created the London police force, nicknamed "Bobbies" in his honor. To the north, Rue Peel is lined with lovely mansions, many belonging to McGill University.

▶ *Return to and continue on Rue Sherbrooke Ouest.*

Rue Stanley was named for the former Canadian governor general who donated the famous Stanley Cup, trophy of the National Hockey League's renowned championship.

Ritz Carlton Hotel

Maison Alcan★

Nº. 1188; main entrance at 2200 Rue Stanley.

The headquarters of Alcan Limited, a major producer of aluminium, features an innovative amalgamation of old and new. Designers of the structure (1983) successfully followed preservation regulations by integrating into its façade the five 19C buildings on the south side of Rue Sherbrooke between Rues Stanley and Drummond.

At the far left, the **Atholstan House** (*nº. 1172*) was commissioned by Lord Atholstan (1848–1938), famed philanthropist and founder of the now-defunct Montreal Star. Constructed in 1895 in the Beaux-Arts style then associated with the wealthy elite, the limestone building features an Adamesque interior and presently houses the offices of Alcan's president.

A superbglass-roofed **atrium** links the five structures to the Davis Building, a modern aluminum-sheathed edifice located at the rear. Worth noting here are several works of art, including colorful textile panels, Inuit steatite sculptures, and *Paolo et Francesca,* a 1985 sculpture by Esther Wertheimer.

Stroll down the pleasant pedestrian walkway linking Rues Stanley and Drummond behind the Maison Alcan building to see the massive, gray **Armée du Salut** (Salvation Army Citadel, *2050 Rue Stanley*), erected in 1884 in the style of an Ionic temple.

▶ *Return to Rue Sherbrooke Ouest.*

Ritz-Carlton Hotel★

Nº. 1228.

Montréal's last surviving grand old hotel, the Ritz-Carlton conjures up nostalgic thoughts of the Roaring Twenties. The elegant structure (1912) features a Renaissance Revival façade of limestone embellished with terra-cotta ornamentation, and a wrought-iron canopy illuminated by superb lamps. The western section of the building was added in 1956; note especially the decorative panels surmounting the windows. The richly decorated lobby and the hotel's reception rooms are replete with marble, bronze, leather and rich wood paneling.

Numerous members of royalty and chiefs of state—among them Charles de Gaulle—have stayed at the hotel. Elizabeth Taylor and Richard Burton were married here in 1964, and the hotel remains a favorite stopping point for celebrities today.

▶ *Walk on Rue Sherbrooke until you reach Rue Crescent.*

Rue Crescent
The two blocks of this street between Rues Sherbrooke and Sainte-Catherine are lined with charming Victorian structures, today occupied by fashionable boutiques, art galleries, fine fabric shops, nightclubs, and restaurants. During the summer months, many of these restaurants open balconies and terraces, adding to the area's lively ambience.

Musée des Arts decoratifs de Montréal★ (Montreal Museum of Decorative Arts) (M¹)
2200 Rue Crescent. Admission included in entrance fee to Montreal Museum of Fine Arts below; same hours and phone number. www.mmfa.qc.ca
Formerly located at the Château Dufresne, the international design collections of this museum were moved in 1997 to an exhibition space adjacent to the new wing of the Montreal Museum of Fine Arts. The latter institution began administering the collection in 2000; a glassed-in passage allows access between the two museums. Conceived by the famed architect Frank Gehry (designer of the Guggenheim Museum in Bilbao, Spain), the galleries house furnishings, ceramics, glass and metal sculptures, jewellery, textiles and graphic arts drawn from a splendid collection numbering more than 4,000 objects. Covering the 20C, with particular emphasis on the period from 1965 to the present, the holdings trace the major trends in decorative arts from Art Nouveau to post-Modernism.

Address Book

À LES JARDINS DU RITZ
1228 Rue Sherbrooke Ouest. ☎514-842-4212. Located behind the luxurious Ritz-Carlton Hotel, this lovely terrace—with its peaceful duck pond—seems far from the bustle of downtown Montreal. Stop here for high tea, served in the traditional English fashion with scones, finger sandwiches and petits-fours accompanied by thick Devonshire cream and delicious assorted jams.

Musée des Beaux-Arts de Montréal★★ (Montreal Museum of Fine Arts)
N°. 1380. ◔*Open year-round, Tue–Fri 11am, Wed 11am–9pm, Sat–Sun 10am–5pm.* ◕*Closed Jan 1 & Dec 25.* ⬦*$15.* ✕&☎*514-285-2000. www.mmfa.qc.ca.*
Located in the center of the Golden Square Mile, this 140-year-old institution ranks among Canada's finest museums. The encyclopedic permanent collection comprises over 30,000 objects, ranging from Old Masters to contemporary Canadian art.

The strengths of the collection lie in the areas of Canadian and Inuit art, prints and drawings, decorative arts ranging from archaic Chinese bronzes to 20C glassware, and the world's largest collection of Japanese incense boxes (over 3,000 pieces).

The Buildings
First established in 1860 as the Art Association of Montreal, the museum moved into the current North Pavilion (also known as the Michael and Renata Hornstein Pavilion) half a century later, with a collection of 467 works of art. Replete with a majestic staircase, a portico colonnade of white Vermont marble, and solid, massive doors, the 1912 edifice exemplifies the Beaux-Arts style commonly employed in museum constructions of the period.

Enlarged twice, in 1939 and 1977, the museum underwent a third major expansion, onto the south side of Rue Sherbrooke in 1991 with the addition of the South Pavilion (**M²**)—also known

Address Book

RUE CRESCENT REVELRY

Fans of car racing, especially Formula One, will revel in the atmosphere of **Formule 1 Emporium** (*2070-B Rue Crescent ☎514-284-3799; www.f1emporium.ca*). Here, in this small shop, race team memorabilia and clothing share space with a selection of small-scale, die-cast replicas of notable competition and passenger cars. Ferrari merchandise is a specialty. One street over from Crescent, meat on skewers and gyrating dancers are the order of the day at **le Milsa** (*1445 Rue Bishop; ☎514-985-0777*), which specializes in traditional Brazilian barbecue. Servers come to your table and carve off slices of beef or turkey or lamb.

the New Sherbrooke apartment complex (1905), the site's former occupant. The large windows and skylights afford expansive views of the city. Facing Rue Bishop, a set of five large vaulted galleries, devoted to temporary exhibits, opens onto a skylit interior.

Due to the museum's extensive program of long-term temporary exhibits, certain galleries may be closed and specific works of art may be displayed in locations other than those indicated here. For information, inquire at the reception desk.

Michael and Renata Hornstein Pavilion

North side of Rue Sherbrooke.

This magnificent structure is largely devoted to the display of **Canadian Art** and Decorative Art. On the second floor, paintings, sculpture, furniture and decorative arts cover the sweep of Canadian art from the 18C through 1945. Works on view may include sculptures by Louis Archambault and Robert Roussil, and paintings by Antoine Plamondon and Cornelius Krieghoff. Visitors may also find paintings by Paul Kane (1810–71) and Suzor-Côté (1869–1937), as well as canvases by the Group of Seven and works of Montreal artists James Wilson Morrice (1865–1924), Ozias Leduc (1864–1955) and Alfred Laliberté (1878–1953). The museum possesses stunning examples

as the Jean-Noël Desmarais Pavilion. A series of underground galleries connects the two pavilions. The new annex, which provided much-needed additional space, is the work of the architect **Moshe Safdie**, renowned for such prestigious commissions as Habitat, Ottawa's National Gallery of Canada, and Quebec City's Museum of Civilization. Adorned with a monumental entry portal, the building incorporates the Renaissance Revival brick façade of

Ice Hockey

A winter preoccupation for more than 100 years, hockey is truly Canada's national game. And the enthusiasm isn't limited to televised games of the major leagues either: more than 580,000 young Canadians in some 25 000 teams participate in organized minor hockey tournaments. Community rinks are ubiquitous.

Derived from the French *hoquet* ("shepherd's crook") for the shape of the stick, hockey originated from variations of stick and ball games brought to Canada by English soldiers in the 1850s. In 1875, Montreal student J.G. Creighton formalized rules and replaced the ball for a flat disk (puck) to give better control on ice.

The fast and often rough play made the sport appealing to spectators. The game spread quickly as rivalry among college amateur teams intensified. Professional teams soon followed. Formed in 1917, the National Hockey League has added US teams over the years and now consists of 30 teams, with only six in Canada. A trophy donated by Governor General Lord Stanley in 1893 is still awarded to the league's winning team in the Stanley Cup championships held each June. The original silver cup is on display in Toronto's Hockey Hall of Fame (*see THE GREEN GUIDE Canada*). The *Montreal Canadiens* won the Stanley Cup a record 24 times.

African Art Gallery, Jean-Noël Desmarais Pavilion, Musée des beaux-arts de Montréal

of 18C–20C Quebec **sacred silverware**, featuring pieces by François Ranvoyzé (1739–1819). Of particular interest on the first floor is the museum's collection of Amerindian and Inuit art.

Galleries of Ancient Cultures

The underground galleries linking the Hornstein Pavilion to the Jean-Noël Desmarais Pavilion house African and Oceanic art featuring sculpted masks and other striking ritual objects, while the Asiatic art section houses porcelains, funerary objects of Chinese antiquity and sculptures from India and Pakistan. The **Islamic art** section offers a large number of ceramics, from Persian pieces of the Sassanian period (3C–7C AD) to Hispano-Moresque wares.

Jean-Noël Desmarais Pavilion

The new building on the south side of Rue Sherbrooke.

The fourth floor is devoted exclusively to **European art** from the Middle Ages to the 19C. Polychromed wood sculptures, triptychs, frescoes and stained-glass windows beautifully illustrate the artistic richness of the medieval era. Renaissance art includes the superb Judith and Didon by Andrea Mantegna, and Flemish artists are represented by Peter Brueghel the Younger's *Return from the Inn*, as well as *Portrait of a Young Man* by Hans Memling. European art of the 17C and 18C includes masterpieces by Rembrandt (*Portrait of a Young Woman, around 1665*), El Greco, Ruysdael, Canaletto and Gainsborough (*Portrait of Mrs. George Drummond*). The 19C section features painters of the Barbizon school, Impressionists and post-Impressionists. Two additional galleries present the museum's impressive collection of prints and drawings, including several works by Albrecht Dürer. *For conservation purposes, prints and drawings are occasionally removed from view.*

The Collections

The **Canadian art** collection is outstanding. You can trace the course of Canadian history from the struggling colony of 17C France to the present day through decorative arts, paintings and sculptures. Traditional furniture and religious and domestic silverware by silversmiths such as Paul Lambert, Samuel Payne and François Ranvoyzé can be found next to early portraits of the bourgeoisie by Jean-Baptiste Roy-Audy and Paul Kane's paintings of Amerindians. Landscapes range from vistas of the Canadian shield by members of the famous Group of Seven to a large collection of paintings by James Wilson Morrice.

The steady progress of Canadian painting into modernism can be traced through major works by Paul-Émile Borduas and the Automatistes, such as the landmark *Black Star* (1957) and Jean-Paul Riopelle's vibrant *Austria* (1954).

Since 2007, a gallery space is devoted to painter Marc-Aurèle Fortin. From the body of work that established his reputation there are two signature canvases: His famous tall trees in Sainte-Rose and a Charlevoix landscape.

Of course, the museum has a rich collection of **European art**. It features paintings, sculptures and objects from the Middle Ages to the present day.

Most of the works in the 19C collection were gifts or bequests from prominent Montreal families and reflect their preference for painters of the Barbizon School such as Corot and Daubigny. A magnificent Daumier (*Nymphs Pursued by Satyrs*), and the striking Tissot painting *October* are included with Impressionist and Post-Impressionist works by Renoir, Sisley, Pissarro, Monet and Cézanne. The collection of early 20C art counts major artists such as Pablo Picasso, Henri Matisse, Lyonel Feininger, Georges Rouault, Salvador Dalí and Otto Dix, and a fine collection of small bronzes.

The **Ancient cultures** collection of antiquities spans most of the entire Ancient world with objects from Africa, Oceania, Central and South America, as well as China, Korea, Japan and India. It also reveals Islamic art, including a 13C bowl inlaid with silver.

The **Mediterranean archeology** collection has expanded contains Greek, Roman, Egyptian and Anatolian series of objects. Several aspects of the Central and East Mediterranean cultures are well represented.

The **decorative arts** section of the museum displays a spectacular design collection in the new **Liliane and David M. Stewart Pavilion** (2001). In total, 700 decorative arts objects covering six centuries of design are presented.

The museum's rich collection of **20C** art and international and Canadian **contemporary art** (since 1960) features works by Picasso, Sam Francis, Christian Boltansky, Alexander Calder, Gerhard Richter, Rebecca Horn and other artists, as well as works by renowned Canadian contemporary artists Jean-Paul Riopelle, Paul-Émile Borduas, Betty Goodwin, and Geneviève Cadieux. The magic realism

of Canadian Alex Colville's *Church and Horse* is also featured.

Church of St. Andrew and St. Paul

N°. 1431. ◷*Open year-round, Mon–Fri 9am–4pm.* ♿☎*514-842-3431.www.stand rewstpaul.com*

Erected in 1932, this Gothic cathedral-like edifice is home to the Black Watch (Royal Highland) Regiment of Canada. Constructed of steel and reinforced concrete sheathed in Indiana limestone, the Presbyterian church features an immense stained-glass window above the main altar, commemorating the victims of World War I. The church also boasts the largest organ in Montreal and a fifty member choir. The first two windows in the left nave were designed by **Edwin Burne-Jones** of the William Morris Studio, an early practitioner of the Arts and Crafts style.

At the northwest corner with Rue Simpson stands the ornate, Beaux-Arts **Linton** apartment complex (*n°. 1509*), one of the largest buildings of its type at the time of its construction (1907). Its brick exterior is lavishly embellished with terracotta ornamentation.

Across the street, an attractive row of grey town houses (*n°s. 1400–1460*) contain some of Montreal's most prestigious art galleries. At n°. 1460, the **Guilde canadienne des métiers d'art** (Canadian Guild of Crafts), a gallery and shop, houses a superb collection of **Inuit sculpture** and Amerindian art (◷*open year-round, Tue–Fri 10am–6pm, Sat 10am–5pm;* ☎*514-849-6091; www. canadianguild.com*).

Grand séminaire de Montréal (Sulpician Seminary)

N°. 2065 at junction with Rue du Fort.

Two **towers** with "pepper-box" roofs mark the former site of a small fort constructed by the Sulpicians in 1685 to protect their mission and its Amerindian converts. The fort was constructed in stone with four towers and a defending wall to protect the chapel, the priests' residence and a barn. The two north towers were destroyed in 1854 to make room for the construction of the seminary (1857). The remaining towers are, along with the Sulpician Seminary on Rue Notre-Dame, among the oldest structures on the island of Montreal. Now restored, the towers are supplemented by a small outdoor panel display illustrating the history of the fort and of the Sulpician congregation.

Inside the main building, the striking seminary **chapel**★ was designed by Joseph-Omer Marchand in 1904 and completed in 1907 (○open year-round, daily 9am–4.30pm; ♿️📷☎514-935-1169; www.gsdm.qc.ca). The monumental interior features a large nave reminiscent of early Christian architecture, spanned by cedar beam vaulting. Note the mosaics adorning the floor, the exquisitely carved oak stalls facing each other in the manner of collegiate chapels, and, in the portico, Descente de la croix, an enormous painting by Napoléon Bourrassa. In 1991 the chapel acquired its superb Guilbault-Thérien organ, manufactured in the classical French tradition of the 18C.

▶ Follow Rue du Fort to its intersection with Rue Baile.

Centre Canadien d'Architecture★ (Canadian Center for Architecture)

1920 Rue Baile. ○Open year-round, Wed–Sun 10am–5pm (Thu 9pm). ○Closed Jan 1 & Dec 25. ≈$10. ♿️📷☎514-939-7026. www.cca.qc.ca.

The brainchild of **Phyllis Lambert**—architect, noted preservationist and heiress to the Seagram fortune—this center was inaugurated in 1989. Lambert collaborated with Canadian architect Peter Rose to restore **Shaughnessy House** (1874), a Second Empire mansion, and to incorporate it into a new construction. A comprehensive reference and research facility, the center also features temporary exhibits, a conservation laboratory and a bookstore.

Trenton limestone, black granite, maple paneling and flooring and aluminum fittings grace the interior of the main building. Located on the first floor, seven galleries display temporary exhibits on architectural themes. Also open to

the public are the Shaughnessy House reception rooms and the delightful **conservatory** and **tea room**, restored to 19C splendor and furnished with works of contemporary design.

Jardin de sculptures (sculpture garden)

Located across Boulevard René-Lévesque, this unusual outdoor space designed by architect Melvin Charney was conceived as a tribute to the buildings of the neighborhood and to the architectural heritage of the Western world. Among the pieces on display in the esplanade overlooking a maze of highways are ten raised sculptures, or "allegorical columns," depicting various architectural elements.

Maison mère des Sœurs Grises

North side of Blvd. René-Lévesque between Rue Guy and Rue Saint-Mathieu. Entrance for visitors at 1185 Rue Saint-Mathieu. 📷. � The interior of the convent is not open to the public. ⚐ The chapel and certain rooms can be visited during the guided tour of the Marguerite d'Youville Centre. Designed in the Neoclassical style, this elegant building (1869–1903) housed the Grey Nuns after their departure from Old Montreal in 1871. The plan is typical of 19C convent architecture. To highlight the chapel at the center of the building, the architect Victor Bourgeau adopted the Romanesque style of medieval French abbeys. The slender steeple, one of the tallest in the city, was added in 1890.

In 1737 Marie-Marguerite Dufrost de Lajemmerais (1701–71), widow of François d'Youville, founded a lay order to care for the old, poor and sick in Mon-

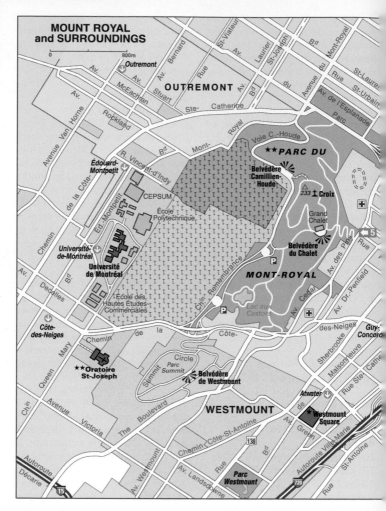

MOUNT ROYAL and SURROUNDINGS

treal. Officially recognized by Louis XIV as the Sisters of Charity in 1753, the members are now known as the Grey Nuns. Marguerite d'Youville's lifetime of service was recognized when she was beatified in 1959 and canonized a saint by Pope John Paul II in December 1990.

5 Mont-Royal and Surroundings★★ *Map Mount Royal and Surroundings.*

Nicknamed "the Mountain," Mt. Royal rises some 233m/764.4ft over the center of downtown Montreal. Residents and out-of-town visitors alike flock to Mt. Royal Park, a popular leisure spot

located on the highest of the mountain's three peaks.

Historically an Anglophone district, the town of **Westmount** (founded 1874), situated on the western flank of Mt. Royal overlooking downtown and the St. Lawrence River, is one of Montreal's choicest residential areas. Westmount's steeply sloping streets are bordered with imposing 19C mansions of brick and stone interspersed with modern residences surrounded by manicured gardens. From the **Westmount Belvedere** (*between n°s. 18 and 36 Summit Circle*), the **view**★ plunges over the rooftops of lovely residences to the three towers of **Westmount Square**★ (*corner of Rue Sainte-Catherine and Ave.*

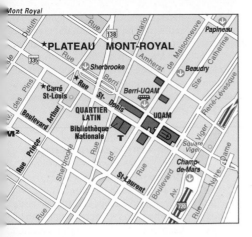

Mont Royal

★PLATEAU MONT-ROYAL

Green), designed by Mies van der Rohe in 1966. The glass and black metal towers house elegant apartments, offices, and shops. The Victoria Bridge is visible in the distance. The community of **Outremont**, founded in 1875 on the mountain's eastern flank, is the enclave of Montreal's Francophone bourgeoisie and is Westmount's counterpart for beautiful homes, private mansions and green lawns and parks. Two cemeteries are located on Mt. Royal, in addition to several reservoirs for drinking water, and the Canadian Broadcasting Corporation/Radio-Canada transmission tower (1963).

Parc du Mont-Royal★★ (Mt. Royal Park)

Access on **foot:** *30min climb from downtown. Walk to top of Rue Peel at Ave. des Pins and take the path with small flights of steps to a steep flight of 204 steps.* **By car:** *Drive up Voie Camillien-Houde or Chemin Remembrance to the parking areas.* **By metro:** ◔*Mont-Royal, and bus 11.* ◷*Open year-round, daily 6am–midnight.* ✕ ♿ 🅿 ☏ *514-843-8240. www. lemontroyal.qc.ca.*

A jewel in Montreal's crown, the city's premier urban park opened to the public in 1876. Planned by the preeminent American landscape architect **Frederick Law Olmsted** (1822–1903), creator of New York City's Central Park, Mt. Royal Park exemplifies the naturalistic manner of garden design popular in the late 19C.

At the time of the park's inception, a $1 million investment was required to appropriate the land. Today the prop-

Aerial view of Mont-Royal

©Benoît Desjardins

erty bears some 60,000 trees, 650 species of plants and flowers, and is home to a proliferation of wildlife including grey squirrels, chipmunks and birds.

The park also features a lake, two excellent lookout points, a chalet/welcome center, an illuminated cross and numerous paths winding through the forest.

Belvédère du Chalet (Chalet Lookout)

From the parking lot, take the footpath to the chalet (7min).

The splendid **view**★★★ from the front of the small chalet here encompasses the bustling downtown. Below the lookout lies the campus of McGill University, notably the distinctive, cylindrical form of the McIntyre Medical Sciences Building. The downtown skyscrapers are prominent, especially the IBM Marathon Building, Bank of Commerce Tower, 1000 de la Gauchetière, the cruciform structure of Place Ville-Marie and Place de la Cathédrale, with its double-sloped roof and copper-colored exterior. From this vantage point, the St. Lawrence River appears as a silver ribbon stretching away to the distance, and looming on the horizon are the shadowy Monteregian Hills, notably the imposing mass of Mt. Saint-Hilaire.

Croix du Mont-Royal (Cross)

Accessible on foot from the chalet.

The 36.6m/120ft metal structure on the summit of Mt. Royal commemorates an episode in Montreal's early history. In December 1642, Sieur de Maisonneuve, founder of Ville-Marie (Montreal), took an oath to carry a cross up the mountain if the settlement were saved from a flood, expected to occur on Christmas Day. The fortress was spared, and Maisonneuve kept his promise on January 6, 1643, erecting a wooden cross at the summit. Today's metal cross dates from 1924. Illuminated at night, it is visible from as far away as 100km/62mi.

Belvédère Camillien-Houde (Camillien Houde Lookout)

Accessible by car on the Voie Camillien-Houde.

From this popular vantage point, the **view**★★ of eastern Montreal is domi-

nated by the Olympic Stadium. To the south, several of the Monteregian Hills are visible. The foothills of the Laurentian Mountains rise to the north. Camillien Houde (1889–1958), the namesake of the viewpoint, served as Montreal's mayor for several nonconsecutive terms between 1928 and 1954.

Université de Montréal

Entrance on Blvd. Édouard-Montpetit at its intersection with Ave. Louis-Colin. ◐*Université de Montréal.*

Created in 1878 as a branch of Laval University in Quebec City, the university became an independent institution by papal decree in 1919. Originally located on Rue Saint-Denis in what is currently the UQAM area, the university moved to its present site in 1942.

Construction of the main pavilion began in 1928, but was interrupted by the Great Depression in 1930 and not resumed until 1941. Designed by Ernest Cormier, the building consists of a central section topped by a lofty tower, with perpendicular wings branching toward the front. Replete with stylized ornamentation, geometric surfaces and setbacks, this striking edifice exemplifies the Art Deco Style. The central hall and the large auditorium have retained their original Art Deco interiors. With an enrollment of nearly 60,000 students, the university is the largest Francophone university in the world outside Paris. Its 13 departments are supplemented by the École Polytechnique (*northeast of main building*) and the École des Hautes Études Commerciales (*Ave. Decelles*).

Oratoire Saint-Joseph★★ (St. Joseph's Oratory)

Entrance on Chemin Queen Mary. ◐*Côte-des-Neiges.* ◷*Open year-round, daily 7am–10pm.* ✕ ♿ 🅿 ☏ 514-733-8211. www.saint-joseph.org

Set on the northwest slope of Mt. Royal, this renowned Roman Catholic shrine is visited yearly by millions of pilgrims. Its enormous dome dominates northern Montreal.

Brother André

Alfred Bessette (1845–1937) entered the Congregation of Holy Cross in 1870 and

Oratoire Saint-Joseph

Pierre Ethier/MICHELIN

took the name Brother André. During 40 years as a doorkeeper at Notre-Dame College (*across from the Oratory*), he preached the healing power of devotion to St. Joseph. In 1904 he erected a small chapel on the path which led from the college to Mt. Royal. Many afflicted people who came to pray with him left the chapel cured, abandoning their crutches, canes and wheelchairs as testament to their recovery, and spreading the lay brother's reputation as a healer. By the early 20C, the crowds of pilgrims had grown to such proportions that the present basilica was planned to receive them.

The Basilica★

Towering 154m/505ft over the city, this colossal temple is surmounted by an octagonal, copper-clad dome. Built of reinforced concrete sheathed in granite, the basilica is 104m/341ft long, 64m/210ft wide and 112m/367ft high. Rising 44.5m/146ft above the roof of the basilica, the dome has a diameter of 38m/125ft. The cross crowning the structure is 8m/26ft high.

Construction of the huge building began in 1924, but was interrupted by lack of funds, the economic depression and technical difficulties. In 1936 the renowned Benedictine monk-architect, **Dom Paul Bellot**, was called upon to act as chief architect of the oratory. He selected concrete rather

than granite for the construction of the dome, and revised the interior plans in a modern style. The monument was completed in 1967.

The visitor is struck by the immensity and austerity of the basilica's **interior**. Henri Charlier carved the stone main altar, the crucifix and the tall wooden carvings of the apostles (*in the transept*); the stained-glass windows were designed by Marius Plamondon. Roger Prévost executed the bronze grilles and Roger de Villiers the life-size Stations of the Cross statues (*around the nave*). The altar in the Chapel of the Blessed Sacrament (*behind the choir*) is the work of Jean-Charles Charuest, and the mosaic of the life of St. Joseph was produced at the Labouret Studio in Paris. *During the summer, organ recitals are held here on Wednesday evenings at 8pm (☎514-337-4622).*

Within the main edifice are a **votive chapel** enshrining the remains of Brother André; a 56-bell **carillon**, originally cast in Paris for installation on the Eiffel Tower; the **crypt**, where daily masses are held; and the **Musée du Frère André** (Brother André Museum; same hours as the Oratory), displaying a collection of photographs and mementos tracing the friar's history. The **chapelle du Frère André** (Brother André's **original chapel**) is located outside the main structure. The **Stations of the Cross★** statues built into the hillside were designed by Louis Parent and executed in Indiana buff stone by the Italian sculptor, Ercolo Barbieri, in 1960.

Outside the basilica, the wide terrace affords a superb**view** of northern Montreal and of the Laurentian Mountains rising on the horizon.

Plateau Mont-Royal★
🚇*Sherbrooke and Mont-Royal.*

Musée des Hospitalières de l'Hôtel-Dieu de Montréal (Hospitallers Museum)
201 Ave. des Pins Ouest. Entrance at Rue Saint-Urbain and Ave. des Pins. 🕐*Open mid-Jun–mid-Oct, Tue–Fri 10am–5pm, weekends 1pm–5pm; rest of the year, Wed–Sun 1pm–5pm.* 🕐*Closed Dec 25.* ⛛*$6.* ♿☎*514-849-2919. www.museedes hospitalieres.qc.ca.*

Housed in a former chaplain's residence (1925), this museum traces the history of the Hospitallers of St. Joseph (a religious order devoted to caring for the sick) and their role in the development of Montreal. In addition to temporary exhibits, the museum displays a selection of some 400 objects (historic documents, medical instruments, sacred art) drawn from its permanent collection of more than 19,000 artifacts.

A massive oak staircase (17C) from the Hôtel-Dieu hospital in La Flèche, France, dominates the entrance hall of the museum's new addition (1992). The ground floor presents the history of Montreal and of the Hospitaller order, and boasts a magnificent gold-leafed retable (1777) sculpted by Philippe Liébert. Exhibits here illustrate the cloistered life of the Hospitaller nuns from the 19C and the early 20C. Displays on the second floor focus on the Hospitallers' nursing vocation. A fine collection of historic medical instruments offers an excellent glimpse at the evolution of medical techniques. The visit ends with a video presentation (*15min*) about the Hospitaller order throughout the world.

Boulevard Saint-Laurent
This lively thoroughfare is the starting point for numbering of east-west streets. Traditionally, it represented the linguistic border between the Anglophone west and the Francophone east, although this limit is not as clear as before. Established in 1672 during the formal planning of the city, and extended to the Prairies River, near Sault-au-Récollet, the artery long formed Montreal's principal passageway, hence its nickname "the Main." After a devastating fire in 1852, the road was extended to the city's new limit at Mile End; it became a boulevard in 1905. For more than a century, the Main has welcomed immigrants who have in various ways affected its development. Chinese immigrants settled in the southern section during the 19C, while Jewish merchants arriving around 1880 concentrated in the northern section as far as Rue Sainte-Catherine and established a textile industry (now largely defunct). Greek immigrants moved into the area during the early 20C, but left the Main after 1940 to relocate on Avenue du Parc. More recently, Slavs, Portuguese and Latin Americans have settled in the area.

Although its popularity diminished somewhat between 1960 and 1980, the boulevard now attracts a diverse crowd to its shops and restaurants (many of which are unchanged since the 1940s) and to the newer cafés and "in" boutiques. A wide range of specialty stores manifests the area's ethnic diversity, and its sidewalk sales remain very popular.

Rue Prince-Arthur
From Blvd. Saint-Laurent, east to Saint-Louis Square.
This small pedestrian street, named for Prince Arthur, third son of Queen Victoria and governor-general of Canada from 1911 to 1916, was a popular center of the counterculture movement during the 1960s. Today the area is home to Italian and Greek restaurants, and is populated in fine weather by musicians, magicians, acrobats, portrait painters, and other street performers.

Carré Saint-Louis★ (Saint-Louis Square)
Rue Saint-Denis between Rue Sherbrooke and Ave. des Pins.
Named for Emmanuel and Jean-Baptiste Saint-Louis, two eminent local businessmen, this picturesque, tree-shaded square is surrounded by lovely Victorian

Pierre Étnier/MICHELIN

Carré Saint-Louis (Plateau Mount-Royal)

structures distinguished by their whimsical rooflines and gables. The district became a select neighborhood during the late 19C, when the Francophone bourgeoisie began moving to the area, attracted by its tranquil atmosphere. Long popular with Quebec artists and poets (Louis Fréchette, Émile Nelligan and, more recently, Gaston Miron lived here), the square was the center of the nationalist movement during the 1970s. Although the fleur-de-lys is still in evidence, today the square is more likely to resound with American folk songs than with separatist chants. It is still considered a Francophone bastion for Quebec writers, musicians, filmmakers and actors.

Rue Saint-Denis★

This avenue is lined with attractive town houses, today occupied by restaurants, art galleries and fashionable stores. Named after Denis-Benjamin Viger, an affluent landowner during the mid-19C, the street was frequented by wealthy Francophones who erected charming Victorian homes. The area became known as Montreal's **Quartier Latin** (Latin Quarter) when several institutions of higher education were established here during the early 20C. The polytechnical institute opened in 1905, followed by the École des Hautes Études Commerciales (*Viger Square*) and the Université de Montréal. The **Saint-Denis Theatre** (**T**) (Théâtre Saint-Denis) was erected

Address Book

LA RUE SAINT-DENIS

The bakery-café **La Brioche Lyonnaise** (*1593 Rue Saint-Denis;* ☎514-842-7017) is absolutely charming, with its stone walls and lace curtains. Light meals, melt-in-your-mouth croissants, and sumptuous pastries. The **Café Cherrier** (*3635 Rue Saint-Denis;* ☎514-843-4308) serves up tasty meals from breakfast to dinner; take a seat out on the terrace in fine weather and watch the crowds pass by. Stop by the elegant showroom of renowned florist/horticulturist **Marcel Proulx** (*3835 Rue Saint-Denis;* ☎514-849-1344) to admire glorious

dried arrangements, rare flowers, and beautiful pieces of decorative art. Enduringly chic, **L'Express** (*3927 Rue Saint-Denis;* ☎514-845-5333) is one of the most popular bistros in Montreal; its relentlessly high standards are apparent in the outstanding wine list, faultless service and consistently excellent cuisine. Tucked away in a tiny shop swathed in rose-colored fabric, **Confiserie Louise Décarie** (*4424 Rue Saint-Denis;* ☎514-499-3445) sells delectable treats such as chocolates, English toffee, and Italian nougat, all wrapped in beautiful packages.

Address Book

TRADITIONAL...

Schwartz's (*3895 Blvd. Saint-Laurent;* ☎*514-842-4813*) is a true Montreal institution. Don't go for the service, or for the décor. Do go for the delicious smoked-meat sandwiches, which have won this old-time delicatessen a devoted following. And stand ready to queue up...

...OR TRENDY

There's always a crowd at **Shed Café** (*3515 Blvd. Saint-Laurent;* ☎*514-842-0220*), where a hip clientele devours pizzas, salads, panini, sandwiches and sinful desserts, all in a most original setting (don't miss the ceiling and the light fixtures).

during this period, followed in 1912 by the Saint-Sulpice Building (*nº. 1700*), now home to the **Bibliothèque nationale de Québec** or **BNQ** (National Library of Quebec). The houses were divided into smaller apartments to accommodate the many students attending these institutions.

The area's economic stability suffered when the Université de Montréal moved to its present campus on the north slope of Mt. Royal, and the street only regained its original vibrancy during the 1960s. Cafés, intimate restaurants, small boutiques and bookshops proliferated, drawing a young crowd back to the area.

Today, the Rue Saint-Denis is a favorite with Montrealers and tourists alike. Known as the "restaurant strip," the section between Rue Sainte-Catherine and Rue Duluth is extremely popular during the summer months, when tables and chairs spill out onto the street.

Université du Québec à Montréal (University of Quebec at Montreal)

Traversed by Rue Saint-Denis, the main section of campus extends between Blvd. René-Lévesque and Blvd. de Maisonneuve. Founded in 1969, this university (known as UQAM) is housed in a series of contemporary brick buildings integrated

with older structures. One of these occupies the former site of Église Saint-Jacques (St. James Church), designed in the Gothic Revival style by John Ostell in 1852. All that remain of the church today are the façade of the south transept facing Rue Sainte-Catherine and the bell tower on Rue Saint-Denis. This spire, which was added to the church about 1880, is the tallest in Montreal at 98m/321ft. With an ever-increasing enrollment of over 40,000 students, the institution is undergoing major expansion, and now occupies some of the buildings that formerly housed the polytechnical institute. A second campus between Place des Arts and Rue Sherbrooke houses an enormous complex for the study of the sciences.

6 Olympic Park Area★★★ *Map Quartier due Parc Olympique.*

Situated in the heart of Montreal's growing East End, this vast, recreational area is dominated by the striking silhouette of the Olympic Stadium.

A Bit of History

In 1883, leading French Canadian businessmen established the community of Maisonneuve 10km/6.2mi outside downtown Montreal in an attempt to rival the Anglophone economic domination of the city. After 1896, Maisonneuve experienced a significant economic boom, becoming a major center for the manufacture of shoes, textiles, baked goods and candy. A shipbuilding industry also took root. To emphasize its prosperity, the city launched a program of aesthetic and structural development based on the tenets of the American "City Beautiful" movement, building the immense **Maisonneuve Park**, grand boulevards and prestigious buildings, including Château Dufresne. However, the exorbitant cost of development, combined with the postwar recession, gradually drove Maisonneuve into bankruptcy; by 1918, the government of Quebec decreed that the city be annexed by Montreal.

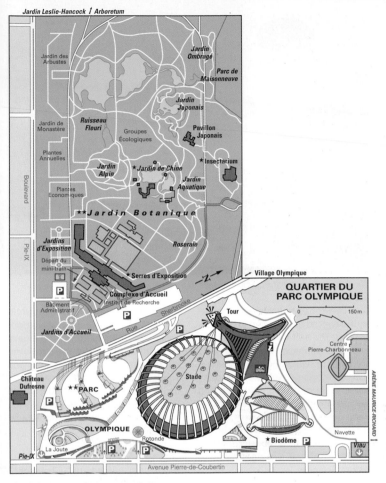

Jardin Leslie-Hancock / Arboretum

Jardin des
Arbustes

Jardin
Ombragé

Parc de
Maisonneuve

Jardin de
Monastère

Ruisseau
Fleuri

Jardin
Japonais

Groupes
Écologiques

Pavillon
Japonais

Plantes
Annuelles

Jardin
Alpin

★Jardin de Chine

★Insectarium

Jardin
Aquatique

Plantes
Économiques

Boulevard

Pie-IX

★★Jardin Botanique

Jardins
d'Exposition

Roseraie

Départ du
mini-train

★ Serres d'Exposition

Village Olympique

QUARTIER DU
PARC OLYMPIQUE

0   150 m

Complexe d'Accueil

Bâtiment
Administratif

Institut de Recherche

Sherbrooke

Tour

Centre
Pierre-Charbonneau

Jardins d'Accueil

Rue

Château
Dufresne

★★PARC

Stade

ARÈNE MAURICE-RICHARD

OLYMPIQUE

Rotonde

★ Biodôme

Navette

Pie-IX

La Joute

Viau

Avenue Pierre-de-Coubertin

Covering 204ha/504 acres, the Maison-neuve Park today encompasses the **Botanical Garden**, an extensive bike trail, a picnic ground, and a snack bar. Families flock here during the summer to enjoy walks and picnics in this pleas-ant, natural setting. During the winter, sports enthusiasts can partake of the five cross-country ski trails lacing the park, and skate on the floodlit ice rink. Situ-ated across from the Botanical Garden on Rue Sherbrooke, the **Olympic Park** has contributed greatly to the economic boom experienced by Eastern Montreal in the past decade.

Parc olympique★★
(Olympic Park)

🕐*Viau or Pie-IX, or by car (entrance to the parking lot from 3200 Rue Viau). Informa-tion desk and ticket office at base of tower. Shuttle service (free) to and from the park, the Montreal Botanical Garden and the Biodôme.*

To accommodate the 1976 summer Olympic Games, a gigantic sports complex covering 55ha/136 acres was erected at the heart of Montreal's East End, in the former City of Maisonneuve. The city's most controversial public proj-ect, the Olympic complex is nonetheless a stunning architectural achievement, and is particularly beautiful at night. The various constructions present a harmo-nious synthesis of form and function,

The Tower and Stadium, Parc Olympique

their lines evoking movement and activity in a concrete monument to the glory of sport. The park includes the stadium and tower complex; a sports center with six pools for swimming, diving and recreation; a concrete esplanade stretching above the largest underground parking garage in Canada; the Pierre Charbonneau Center and the Maurice Richard Arena, both built in 1954. Long idle, the former velodrome has been converted into the Biodôme, a living museum of natural sciences.

History of the Project – Excavation work in the park was begun in 1973, but only the stadium, velodrome, aquatic complex and Olympic Village were completed in time for the 1976 Games. Tremendously expensive ($1.2 billion), the park installations remained incomplete for many years. A series of technical difficulties delayed construction of the stadium tower until 1979. When it was discovered the tower would be too heavy if erected as planned, a moratorium was imposed for four years. Completion of the tower and the roof in 1987 was followed by a series of innovations and adaptations destined to turn the park into a profitable venture. Although the stadium still faces financial difficulties, it has made valiant efforts to remain relevant.

Created in 1975, a government organization, the *Régie des installations olympiques* (RIO), has been in charge of completing, managing and transforming the complex as a recreational and tourist center. The park hosts sports and cultural events. In 2008, the Saputo Stadium opened just south of Rue Sherbrooke. It is the home of the popular "Montreal Impact" soccer team.

Olympic Stadium

Visit by guided tour (30min) only, year-round, daily. English and French tours from 10am in spring & summer; bilingual tours from 11am in fall & winter. **Closed early Jan–Feb.** $8. (($12). 514-252-4737. www.rio.gouv.qc.ca.

The tour of the park installations does not include ascent to the top of the tower. Conceived by the French architect Roger Taillibert, the concrete structure consists of 34 enormous cantilevered ribs crowned by a structural ring containing lighting and ventilation systems. The stadium is dominated by the world's tallest inclined **tower**. From the top of the tower, 26 suspension cables descend to the roof, made of Kevlar, an ultra-thin synthetic fiber with the strength of steel. At the time of its construction, it was the largest mobile roof in the world. When the cables were retracted by means of the 46 winches anchored at the tower's base, the entire roof was hoisted into a niche at the summit of the tower. The stadium could then be closed by redeploying the roof like a parachute over the opening. Despite its strong material, the roof has been subject to deterioration and tears owing to the city's harsh weather conditions, and it is not retractable anymore.

With a seating capacity of 55,147, the gigantic interior space is large enough (18,950sq m/203,763sq ft) to accommodate Rome's Colosseum. Spectators seated in the terraces enjoy an unobstructed view of the playing surface. Intended as a complex for sporting events, the stadium also hosts rock concerts, operatic productions, conventions and religious meetings during summer. The stadium was the setting for the Mass delivered by Pope John Paul II during his 1984 visit to Montreal.

A good perspective of the stadium's exterior can be seen from the footbridge leading from the Pie-IX metro station to the esplanade; in the foreground is La Joute, a bronze sculpture-fountain by the Quebec artist Jean-Paul Riopelle.

Tower Observatory

Open mid-Jun–early Sept, daily 9am–7pm; rest of the year, daily 9am–5pm. Closed mid-Jan–mid-Feb. $13 for the elevator ride. ($12). 514-252-4737 & 1-877-997-0919. www.rio.gouv.qc.ca.
Completed in 1987, the 175m/574ft tower is composed of two parts: The lower concrete base bears the brunt of the weight, acting as the tower's center of gravity. The steel upper section hovers over the stadium at a 45° angle. The tower belongs to the prestigious World Federation of Great Towers. The spine of the stadium's tower can be mounted by a **funicular** elevator that travels up 266m/872ft of rails in two minutes. Though the angle of the climb ranges from 23° to 63.7°, a gyroscope-controlled levelling system ensures that the cabin, which can hold up to 76 people, is always horizontal. The view during the ascent is spectacular: It encompasses the stadium and Montreal's East End. From the observation deck, the panoramic **view**★★★ can extend as far as 80km/49.7mi, weather permitting. Three

large skylights offer a breathtaking vertical view of the stadium. The windows lining the three sides of the triangular deck command expansive views of downtown Montreal, the Laurentian Mountains to the north and the Monteregian Hills to the south. The Botanical Garden is visible directly to the north. Below the observation deck, a hands-on interpretation center presents exhibits revolving around different themes: The park's conception and history, the technological innovations involved in its construction, and the materials used.

Biodôme★

Open Jun 24–Labor Day, daily 9am–6pm; rest of the year, daily 9am–5pm. $16. ($7). 514-868-3000. www.museumsnature.ca. *Shuttle service (free) to and from the Biodôme, Olympic Park and the Botanical Garden.*
Constructed as a velodrome for the Olympic cycling events, this imaginative **building**★ resembles a cyclist's racing helmet. Its vast, scalloped roof spans 160m/526ft and is supported by four "feet." The ceiling's six ribs are composed of 144 jointed sections, each one weighing between 50 and 100 tons. These six arches are linked by transverse bands, forming a trellis to support the skylights, which admit natural light to the interior.

Lack of interest in indoor cycling led to the velodrome's conversion into the Biodome, an innovative museum of environmental and natural sciences. The museum, which opened its doors in 1992, re-creates the habitats of four "ecosystems." Equipped with sophisticated climatic regulators, the habitats support thousands of plants and animals indigenous to the ecosystem. Luxuriant vegetation and a variety of wildlife characterize the torrid **Tropical Forest,** inspired by the Amazonian jungle. Lynx, beaver, and otter frolic in the **Laurentian Forest**, domain of maple trees, pines birches and spruce. Austere granite cliffs rise above the **St. Lawrence Marine Ecosystem**, where visitors can contemplate many types of fish and marine invertebrates. The frozen banks of the **Polar World** harbor penguins and other water birds, illustrating the rigors of life in the arctic and antarctic regions. In the discovery room, visitors can observe the mechanisms by which plants and animals adapt to cold, heat, drought, or darkness. An "environment place" offering films and video completes the installation.

Village olympique
(Olympic Village)

On north side of Rue Sherbrooke, east of Rue Viau.

Nicknamed "the Olympic Pyramids," these twin 19-story buildings (1976) were constructed to house 11,000 athletes for the Olympic Games. Inspired by the complex at Baie-des-Anges in southern France, their exterior galleries and walkways are ill-suited to Montreal's cold winters. The buildings now contain a residential complex.

Jardin botanique de Montréal★★ (Montreal Botanical Garden)

4101 Rue Sherbrooke Est. ◔*Pie-IX.* ◷*Open mid-May–Oct, daily 9am–6pm; Nov–mid-May, Tue–Sun 9am–5pm.* ✍*$16 (including guided tours* ☞☜*).* ✕♿▯*($8).* ☎*514-872-1400. www.museumsnature. ca. Shuttle service (free) to and from the Biodome, Olympic Park and the Botanical Garden.*

Covering 75ha/185 acres, the Montreal Botanical Garden is located across from the Olympic Park and the Biodôme. Ranked among the world's finest horticultural facilities, the garden was founded in 1931 by Brother Marie-Victorin (1885–1944). The garden contains more than 21,000 species from all over the world including 10,000 trees, 1,500 types of orchids and an extensive collection of bonsais. Since 1939, the Research Institute on Plant Biology has been housed in the Art Deco-style Administration Building. Not far from the building lies the **reception garden**, which displays vividly colored annual flowers from April through October. Nearby, the **reception center** leads to the Molson introduction greenhouse, where visitors can get a first glimpse into the plant kingdom before exploring the ten greenhouses and some 30

thematic gardens that make up the Botanical Garden.

Serres d'exposition★ (Conservatories)

A stroll through the garden's ten magnificent exhibition greenhouses leads through reproduced botanical environments from around the world. From the Main Greenhouse, where temporary exhibits change seasonally, continue on to the Chinese Greenhouse, also known as the Jardin céleste. Here you'll find the wonderful **Wu Collection** of *penjings*, given to the Botanical Garden in 1984 by Wu Yee-Sun, a Hong Kong banker who mastered the art of penjing, or "landscape in a pot." Following is a re-created Mexican hacienda, its courtyard and walls covered by cacti and succulent plants. Plants from arid regions occupy the next greenhouse, and the next features over 100 species of begonia and gesneriads. Tropical flora occupies two greenhouses, one devoted to rainforest vegetation, the other to **tropical economic plants** destined for exportation, such as banana, cocoa, coffee, teak, mahogany, palm, mango and bamboo. Orchids and aroids flourish in the last conservatory.

Jardin de Chine★ (Chinese Garden)

Opened in 1991, this enchanting landscape is a replica of a typical Ming dynasty (14–17C) garden from southern China, near the Yangtze River. The largest Chinese garden in the world outside China, it emphasizes natural appearance. Architect Le Wei Zhong skillfully combined two key elements of Chinese gardens, mountains and water, to encourage contemplation.

The seven pavilions, with their steeply curving grey roofs, were prefabricated in Shanghai and assembled on site by Chinese workers. The ornate main pavilion—also called the "Friendship Pavilion"—hosts temporary exhibits to provide the visitor an opportunity to explore the philosophy, art and customs of another world. The large terrace affords sweeping views over the lakes and gardens. Across the lake rises a jagged rock mountain (9m/29.5ft), replete with a stone stairway, cave and tumbling waterfall. Another structure houses a fabulous collection of *penjings*.

Jardin japonais (Japanese Garden)

Designed by the Japanese landscape architect, Ken Nakajima, this 2.5ha/6.2 acre garden (1988) presents a wonderful juxtaposition of water, boulders and plants—including a pond and a waterfall—in the traditional Oriental style, creating an atmosphere of peace and harmony that attracts visitors year-round. The unusual green rocks are peridotites from the Eastern Townships. Exhibit spaces in the **Japanese pavilion** (1989), styled as a traditional Japanese family home, offer visitors a glimpse into Japanese artistic and cultural expression. The pavilion complex includes a Zen garden, composed of raked pebbles and stones considered conducive to meditation. The Japanese garden also features a garden of **bonsais** cultivated according to the Japanese tradition (*on view seasonally*).

The Botanical Garden offers a wealth of other points of interest to delight and enchant plant lovers. The lovely, seasonal **Exhibition Garden** (arranged in traditional French patterns) features shrubs, plants of Quebec, toxic plants, medicinal plants, trial vegetables and hardy perennials. In the **Rose Garden**, visitors can admire over 10,000 specimens planted among the trees and shrubs. Ornamental plants indigenous to aquatic environments, such as lotuses, water lilies and water hyacinths, grow in the **Marsh and Bog Garden**'s 110 pools. In the **Shade Garden**, 1,000 species of primulas and begonias are shaded beneath lime, maple and ash trees; and the **Flowery Brook** features irises, peonies, asters and other flowers arranged in a traditional English garden.

Not to be missed are the **Alpine Garden**, with plants from the world's major mountain ranges displayed in a rock garden setting; the **Leslie Hancock Garden** of azaleas and rhododendrons; the **Arboretum**, which covers more than half of the total area with over 10,000 specimens of about 3,000 different species; and the interesting **First**

Nations Garden, opened in 2001, which incorporates native activities involving plants and trees.

Montréal Insectarium [Kids]

North side of Rue Sherbrooke in the Botanical Garden. ⏰*Open Jan–mid-May, Tue–Sun 9am–5pm; mid-May–Aug until 6pm; Sept–Oct until 9pm. www.museumsnature.ca.*

Built in the shape of a giant bug, this unusual and fascinating museum (1990) displays a vast selection of insects from all over the world (approximately 150,000 specimens). Most of the insects on exhibit are preserved, although a many living specimens can be observed (including a beehive). The collections are presented as thematic exhibits that highlight the fascinating world of entomology and the role insects play in our environment. The insectarium also features a fine collection of monarch butterflies.

Musée du Château Dufresne

Southwest corner of Rue Sherbrooke and Blvd. Pie-IX; entrance on Blvd. Pie-IX. 🚇*Pie-IX.* ⏰*Open year-round, Thu–Sun 10am–5pm.* 💰*$7.* ♿☎*514-259-9201. www.chateaudufresne.com.*

The Château Dufresne was constructed between 1915 and 1918 for two eminent figures of the French Canadian bourgeoisie—the brothers Oscar (a shoe industrialist) and Marius (architect and civil engineer) Dufresne. The symmetrical façade, with eight monumental Ionic columns and a dentiled cornice surmounted by a balustraded terrace, illustrates the tenets of the Beaux-Arts style in vogue at the time of construction. One of the most luxurious homes in the city of Maisonneuve, the reinforced concrete building reflected the grandiose aspirations that eventually led the city into bankruptcy and its subsequent annexation to Montreal.

Interior

Two identical wings, one for each brother, contained a total of 44 rooms decorated with mahogany paneling, ornamentation and furnishings evoking the lifestyle of Montreal's moneyed class in the 1920s and 1930s. An innovation of the period, many of the decorative elements were prefabricated, ordered from catalogues.

The **rooms of Marius Dufresne** (*west side*), are characterized by abundant use of oak and Neoclassical woodwork. Mahogany paneling, Italian marble and French wall coverings characterize the **rooms of Oscar Dufresne** (*east side*), which feature delicately tinted **mural panels**★ by Guido Nincheri (1885–1973) in the parlor. Coffered ceilings, mahogany embellished with gilded foliage, Renaissance-style mural wall coverings; each room here reveals perfection in its myriad details.

⑦Île Ste-Hélène, Île Notre-Dame

Île Sainte-Hélène★ (St. Helen's Island)

Map Îles Ste-Hélène Notre-Dame.

By car: *Take either Jacques-Cartier Bridge or Concorde Bridge.* **By metro:** Ⓜ*Jean-Drapeau.*

In 1611, Samuel de Champlain named the small island in the St. Lawrence, east of the main island of Montreal, after his wife, **Hélène Boulé**. Prior to 1665, when it became part of the Longueuil seigneury, the island served as a strategic defense point for the Amerindians in their battle against European invasion. After Canadian Confederation in 1867, the island became the property of the federal government until the city purchased it as a park early in the 20C. In 1967, Île Sainte-Hélène was extended to cover 138ha/341 acres, in order to host a major World's Fair, Expo '67, along with neighboring Île Notre-Dame. Together, these islands form the **Parc Jean-Drapeau**.

Today, most of the island is a public park, popular with Montrealers for cross-country skiing in winter, and swimming in the outdoor pools in summer. The road skirting the west side of the island provides excellent **views**★ of the city skyline and port installations.

Stewart Museum (Old Fort)

🕐*Open late May–mid-Oct, daily 10am–5pm; rest of the year, Wed–Mon 10am–5pm.* ⏳🚫*$10.* 🍴 🅿 ☎*514-861-6701. www.stewart-museum.org.*

St. Helen's Island was sold in 1818 to the British government, which subsequently erected a citadel. Today the fort houses the **Musée David M. Stewart**★ (David M. Stewart Museum), devoted to the history of European settlement in Quebec. The museum presents displays on the early discoverers and first settlers, their explorations across the continent, the British Conquest, the effects of the American Revolution, the War of 1812 and the Patriots' Rebellion. Note also the wonderful collection of maps and globes, ship models, kitchen utensils, weapons and navigation instruments and many archival documents.

Biosphère and a view of Montréal skyline from Parc Jean-Drapeau

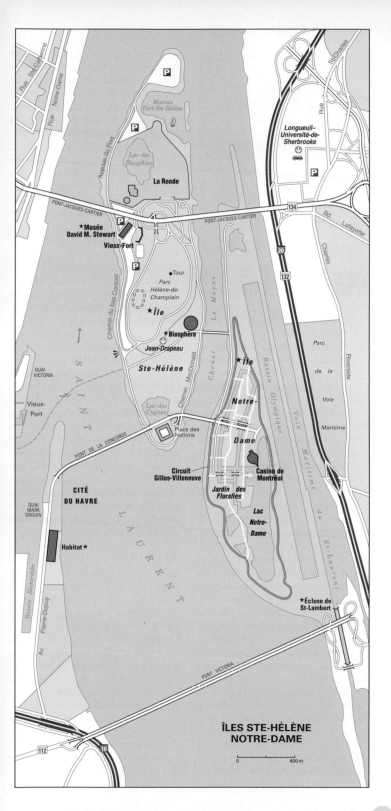

ÎLES STE-HÉLÈNE
NOTRE-DAME

0   400 m

The Goliath, La Ronde

©La Ronde

view★ of Longueuil, the Victoria Bridge and downtown Montreal through the dome's skeleton of interconnecting tubes. The Biosphère also presents temporary exhibits and houses a documentation center for environment-related publications and information.

La Ronde
🕙 *Open mid-May–mid-Jun, daily 10am–8pm; mid-Jun–early Sept, daily 10am–10.30pm; early Sept–late Sept, daily noon–7pm; Oct, Sat noon–9pm, Sun noon–8pm (ticket office closes 1hr before closing time).* ✺*$37.* ⚥ ♿ 🅿 ☎*514-397-2000. www.laronde.com.*

Montreal's major amusement park enjoys a wonderful site at the east end of St. Helen's Island. During summer, the park hosts the International Fireworks Competition.

Environment Canada's Biosphère★
🕙*Open Jun–Oct, daily 10am–6pm; rest of the year, Tue–Fri noon–6pm, weekends 10am–6pm.* 🕙*Closed Jan 1, Dec 25–26.* ✺*$9.50.* ⚥ ♿ 🅿 *($10/summer).* ☎*514-283-5000. www.biosphere.ec.gc.ca.*

This geodesic dome designed by Buckminister Fuller for Expo '67 reveals the form the future was expected to take in the 1960s. Erected to house the US pavilion for the fair, the immense structure (76.2m/250ft in diameter) was originally covered with an acrylic sheath that was destroyed by fire in 1976. Since 1995 the Biosphère has housed Canada's first museum devoted specifically to the conservation of water and the ecosystems of the St. Lawrence River and the Great Lakes. In the **Water Delights Hall** (*1st floor*), interactive consoles and hands-on exhibits highlight the nature of water and the crucial role it plays in the survival of living things. In **Connexions Hall** (*2nd floor*), visitors can view a multimedia presentation (*25min*), then participate in discussions designed to increase awareness of the fragility of our natural environment. The **Visions Hall** (*top floor*) affords glorious views of the St. Lawrence via telescopes; monitors simulate a helicopter flight over the river. From this level, step out to the exterior belvedere for a futuristic

Île Notre-Dame★ (Notre Dame Island)
By car: *Bonaventure Highway and Concord Bridge.* **By public transportation:** *Free bus service from the Jean-Drapeau metro station.* An artificial construction, Notre Dame Island was created for the St. Lawrence Seaway in 1959. Enlarged for Expo '67 with landfill excavated from the metro, the island now extends over 116ha/286 acres. In 1978, a Formula 1 racetrack, the **Gilles Villeneuve Circuit**, was built for the Grand Prix Player's du Canada. It now hosts the Formula 1 race, le **Grand Prix du Canada**: The biggest sporting event in Quebec.

The Expo '67 French Pavilion, formerly known as the Palais de la Civilization, is the island's most prominent edifice. Designed by the French architect Jean Faugeron, the striking structure adorned with aluminium spikes today houses the **Casino de Montréal**.

In summer, **Lac Notre-Dame** (*west side of the island*), lined by a 600m/1,968ft beach, welcomes sailing enthusiasts, swimmers, and windsurfers.

Les Jardins des Floralies (*floral garden*, 🕙*open year-round daily 6.30am–midnight;* ⚥ ♿ 🅿 *($10)* ☎*514-872-6120; www.parcjeandrapeau.com*) features superbgardens created for the International Floralies of 1980 and 2000.

Cité du Havre

Constructed to protect the port, this peninsula links the city to St. Helen's Island via the Concorde Bridge. Among the structures remaining from Expo '67 is **Habitat**★, a futuristic, modular apartment complex, which launched the international career of the architect **Moshe Safdie,** also known for the National Gallery in Ottawa and the Museum of Civilization in Quebec City.

Excursions on the Island

The West End★★

Map Montréal and Environs.

This shoreline drive offers visitors a pleasant break from the bustle of Montreal city. Beginning on the southwestern outskirts of the City of Montreal, a **panoramic road**★ leads to the western tip of the island. The meandering lakeshore drive hugs the St. Lawrence River and Lac Saint-Louis shores and borders affluent residential districts interspersed with numerous parks, equipped with picnic spots and playgrounds. First named Boulevard LaSalle, in LaSalle, the street becomes Boulevard Saint-Joseph, in Lachine, then Chemin du Bord-du-Lac (or Chemin Lakeshore) between Dorval and Sainte-Anne-de-Bellevue.

Maison Saint-Gabriel★ (Saint-Gabriel House)

2146 Place Dublin, in the borough of Pointe-Saint-Charles, 4km/2.5mi from downtown Montreal by Rue Wellington. Turn left at Parc Marguerite-Bourgeoys, and follow signs. ◷*Open Jun 24–Labor Day Tue–Sun 11am–6pm, mid-Apr–mid-Jun & early Sept–mid-Dec, Tue–Sun 1pm–5pm.* ◉*$8.* ☐ ☎*514-935-8136. www.maisonsaint-gabriel.qc.ca.*

In 1668 **Marguerite Bourgeoys** built a house here to care for the filles du roy, the King's wards. Destroyed by fire in 1693, the structure was rebuilt five years later on the old foundations. Restored in 1965 and today considered one of the oldest structures on Montreal Island, the house serves as a historical museum.

Located on the ground floor, the community and reception rooms contain much of the original 18C furniture, and present displays on Marguerite Bourgeoys and her order. Domestic equipment and utensils are on display in the kitchen. A dormitory and the bedroom of one of the *filles du roy* can be seen on the upper floors. Still joined by the original wooden pegs (1698), the rafters and beams of the attic attest to the house's solid construction.

▸ *Return to Rue Wellington and continue to Blvd. LaSalle.*

LaSalle

5km/3mi.
Named for Robert Cavelier de La Salle (1643–1687), this community was formerly part of Lachine, but became independent in 1912. At the end of 6th Avenue, take the path across the old hydro dam (1895) to enjoy superb **views**★ of the Lachine Rapids. Offshore lies Île aux Hérons, an island designated as a nature reserve to protect herons. The long-necked wading birds fish in the rapids and can often be spotted along both banks of the river.

Boulevard LaSalle passes under the double span of the Honoré-Mercier Bridge before entering Lachine. Opened in 1934, the bridge was named for Mercier, premier of Quebec from 1887 to 1891.

Lachine – *7.5km/5mi.*
⌖ *See Entry Heading.*

West of Lachine, the communities on Montreal Island are collectively known as the **West Island**. Lined with opulent residences boasting their private boat docks, yacht clubs and lush parks, the "island's" communities are home to most of Montreal's English-speaking residents. The first suburb, **Dorval** (4.5km/2.7mi), was named for Jean-Baptiste Bouchard, a native of Orval, France, who acquired land here in 1691. Today, Dorval is best known for its international airport.

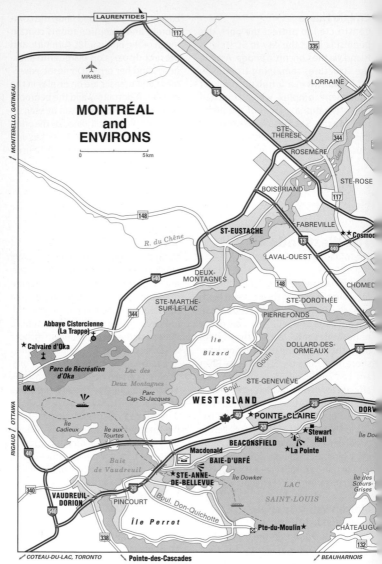

Pointe-Claire★

6km/3.7mi.

This wealthy, traditionally Anglophone suburb on the shore of Lac Saint-Louis was named for the fine and clear (*claire*) **views**★ available from the strip of land that extends into the lake.

Stewart Hall★

On left side of Chemin du Bord-du-Lac (Lakeshore); follow signs. ◷*Pointe-Claire Cultural Center open early May–Labor Day, Mon–Fri 8am–4pm; rest of*

the year, Mon–Fri 8.30am–4.30pm, Sat 9.30am–3.30pm, Sun 1pm–5pm; hours vary slightly for the art gallery and library. ⚐🅿☎*514-630-1220.*

Built in 1915, this copper-roofed stone mansion is a half-scale model of a castle located on the Isle of Mull in Scotland. In 1963 Mr. and Mrs. Walter Stewart purchased the property and donated it to the City of Pointe-Claire as a cultural center. Today the building contains a library, an art gallery with changing displays, and a beautiful wood-pan-

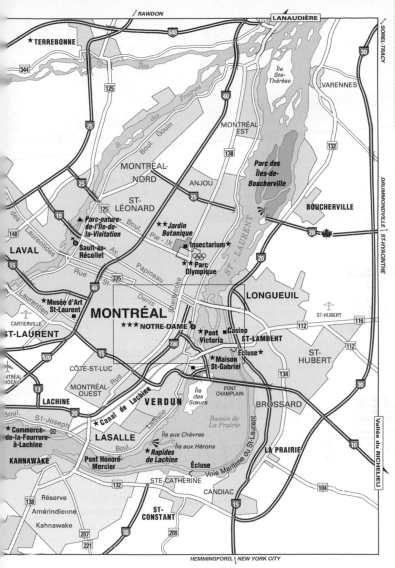

eled reception room. Meetings, plays, concerts, and other activities organized by the Cultural Center are held here. The lovely garden offers magnificent **views**★ of the lake.

La Pointe★

Turn left off Chemin du Bord-du-Lac (Lakeshore) onto Rue Sainte-Anne and park beside the church.

Located at the end of this peninsula jutting into Lac Saint-Louis, the convent (1867) belongs to the Congregation of Our Lady. Behind it, an old stone **windmill** dates from 1709 (*access on foot only*). Once an outer fortification for Montreal, this structure served as a retreat in case of Amerindian attack.

Topped by a single steeple, the Église Saint-Joachim (Church of St. Joachim) was built in 1882. Adjacent to it stands the presbytery with its wraparound porch and distinctive roofline, enlivened by numerous pyramidal forms. The **views** from this site are superb.

MICHELIN

Pointe Claire windmill

After Pointe-Claire, the Chemin du Bord-du-Lac becomes Boulevard Beaconsfield. It traverses the affluent suburb of **Beaconsfield** (*5km/3mi*), named for the British prime minister, Benjamin Disraeli (1804–1880), who was conferred the title of Lord Beaconsfield by Queen Victoria on his retirement.

The road returns to being called Chemin du Bord-du-Lac as it passes through **Baie-d'Urfé** (*6km/3.7mi*), named for François-Saturnin Lascaris d'Urfé, who founded a mission here in 1686.

The garden beside the Baie-d'Urfé Town Hall (*20410 Chemin du Bord-du-Lac*), commands superb **views** of the lake and Île Dowker offshore.

Sainte-Anne-de-Bellevue★
3km/1.8mi.

Located at the western tip of Montreal Island, this community was part of the Bellevue seigneury granted in 1670. Dedicated to St. Anne in 1714, the parish took its present name in 1878.

The main street (*Rue Sainte-Anne*) runs beside the Ottawa River, whose rushing waters join those of the St. Lawrence in Lac Saint-Louis after passing through a lock. Above the lock, the twin spans of Highway 20 and a railway bridge cross to Île Perrot.

Macdonald Campus
Located on Rue Sainte-Anne, at entrance of the community.

In 1907 Sir William Macdonald (1831–1917), Chancellor of McGill University and founder of the Macdonald Tobacco Company, donated 650ha/1,605 acres to the university. Distinctive redbrick buildings were erected on the site, today home to McGill's Faculty of Agriculture and Environmental Sciences.

Especially popular with children, the campus' **experimental farm** (Kids ◷ *open May–Jul, 9am–5pm;* ✗ ♿ 🅿 ☎514-398-7701) features a dairy barn and an animal farm where sheep, goats, pigs, rabbits and other animals thrive. Covering 245ha/600 acres, the Morgan **arboretum** (◷*open daily 9am–4pm;* ✑$5; 🅿 ☎514-398-7811) boasts Canada's most complete collection of indigenous tree species.

▸ *Return on Rue Sainte-Anne and turn left on Blvd. Saint-Pierre. Continue for 2km/1.2mi and take Rte. 40 Est for 20km/12.4mi toward Montreal. Take Exit 62 on Chemin de la Côte-Vertu.*

Saint-Laurent
28km/17mi from Sainte-Anne-de-Bellevue or about 10km/6.2mi north of downtown by Rue Sherbrooke Est (Rte. 138), Rte. 15 Nord and Blvd. Décarie.

This industrial suburb of Montreal was founded about 1687, when the brothers Paul, Michel and Louis Descarie arrived to farm the land they called the Côte Saint-Laurent.

Le Musée des maîtres et artisans du Québec★
On grounds of Cégep Saint-Laurent, at 615 Ave. Sainte-Croix. From Blvd. Décarie, turn right on Rue du Collège. The college is straight ahead at the junction with Ave. Sainte-Croix. ⬇Du Collège. ◷Open Wed–Sun noon–5pm. ✑$5. ♿ 🅿 ☎514-747-7367.

This small museum is located in the Presbyterian Church of St. Andrew and St. Paul (1867), moved from Dorchester Boulevard to this site in 1931. The striking Gothic Revival structure served as a chapel until 1975 when it was converted into a museum. Inside, the intricately carved wooden vault and luminous stained-glass windows can still be seen.

The museum owns an impressive collection of French-Canadian artifacts.

Displayed in exhibits concentrating on particular themes, the objects illustrate such trades as tin smithing, textile fabrication, ceramic making, furniture making, silver and gold smithing and wood sculpting. Of particular interest is the authentic reconstruction of a silversmith's shop. A large collection of religious sculpture and some fine pieces of furniture complement the exhibits. The museum also mounts temporary exhibits on the area's cultural and artistic heritage.

The Northeast

Sault-au-Récollet

Located about 12km/7.4mi north of downtown Montreal by Rue Sherbrooke Est (Rte. 138), Rue Cartier, Rue Rachel and Ave. Papineau.

Today part of the City of Montreal, Sault-au-Récollet is one of the oldest communities on Montreal Island. Set beside rapids on the Prairies River, it was visited by both Jacques Cartier, in 1535, and Samuel de Champlain, in 1615. It was named after a Récollet brother, Nicolas Viel, who drowned in the rapids in 1625 while returning from the Huron country with his Amerindian companion, Ahuntsic. The Sulpicians founded a mission here in 1696, and the parish came into existence in 1736. Sault-au-Récollet was a separate municipality until 1916 when it was annexed by Montreal. Since 1930, the rapids have been harnessed by Hydro-Québec for electricity.

Église de la Visitation-de-la-Bienheureuse-Vierge-Marie★ (Church of the Visitation of the Blessed Virgin Mary)

From Ave. Papineau turn left on Blvd. Henri-Bourassa and left on Rue des Jésuites. ⓊHenri-Bourassa. ⓉOpen year-round, daily 8am–11.30am, 1.30pm–4pm. ⓉClosed Jan 1 & the afternoon of Dec 25. ⓋⓅ☎514-388-4050.

Erected between 1749 and 1752, this edifice is the oldest church on Montreal Island. Its large nave and absence of lateral chapels are in keeping with the style of Récollet churches in New France. The stone **façade** (1850, John Ostell), flanked by two tall towers, was inspired

by the church of Sainte-Geneviève de Pierrefonds (northwest of Montreal), designed a few years earlier by Thomas Baillairgé. Victor Bourgeau later used this same design throughout the region, notably for the Church of St. Rose, in Laval. The elaborate **interior★★** illustrates the aesthetic principles of the Quévillon school. The turquoise and gold vault, adorned with diamond-shaped barrels, is of rare quality; like the sculpted décor in the chancel, it was installed by David Fleury David about 1820. Fashioned by Vincent Chartrand of the Quévillon studio, the magnificent **pulpit★** (1837), with its finely decorated sound reflector, is one of the most beautiful pieces of liturgical furniture sculpted in Quebec. The tabernacle above the main altar is attributed to Philippe Liébert (1732–1804); the main altar and side altars were designed by Louis-Amable Quévillon (1749–1823). The portals (1820) leading to the sacristy are embellished with polychrome bas-reliefs inscribed into Louis XV-style panels.

Parc-nature de l'Île de la Visitation

ⓊHenri-Bourassa. ⓉOpen year-round, daily dawn–dusk. ⓖClosed to vehicles. Reception center open late Apr–mid-Aug, daily 9.30am–6pm; rest of the year, daily 9.30am–4.30pm. ⓧⓋ Ⓟ☞$7. ☎514-280-6733. www.ville.montreal.qc.ca/grandsparcs.

L'île-de-la-Visitation is one of six nature parks operated by the Montreal Urban Community. Its 33ha/82 rolling acres are laced with paths for biking and skiing. Several mills have occupied the strip of land connecting the island to the banks of the Prairies River since the 18C. The last one operated until 1970. Before reaching the island, the attractive, early-19C **Maison du Pressoir** (Cider Press House) can be visited; the original mechanism is exposed, and displays illustrate the cider-making process (Ⓣopen late Apr–late Oct, daily noon–5pm; Ⓥ). Nearby, the **Maison du Meunier** (Miller's House) now hosts local art exhibits (Ⓣopen late Apr–late Oct, daily noon–5pm; ⓋⓅ☞$7. ☎514-850-4222, www.citehistoria.qc.ca).

NICOLET

CENTRE-DU-QUÉBEC REGION
POPULATION 7,827

Set on the banks of the Nicolet River, 3km/1.8mi from its junction with the St. Lawrence, this community is named for one of Samuel de Champlain's companions, **Jean Nicolet** (1598–1642). Settlement began in 1756, when Acadian refugees arrived and established their farms, transforming Nicolet into an agricultural center. A diocese was inaugurated in 1877, and the city is now home to several religious orders. Nicolet is also the site of the Quebec Police Academy. In 1955 a landslide pushed much of the old city into the Nicolet River.

- 🛈 **Information:** 20 Rue Notre-Dame. ☎819-293-6960 and 1-888-816-4007. www.ville.nicolet.qc.ca.
- ▶ **Orient Yourself:** Nicolet is 170km/105mi northeast of Montreal by Rte. 40, Rte. 55 (Laviolette Bridge), and Rte. 132. It is 25km/15.5mi southwest of Trois-Rivières.
- 🐾 **Don't Miss:** Spring migration of snow geese at Centre d'Interprétation de Baie-du-Febvre. Traditional native meal at the Abenaki museum.
- 🕐 **Organizing Your Time:** Rodolphe Duguay House invites artists to set up their easels in the garden every Sat (Jun–Sept) from 10am–5pm; incorporate this into your visit.

Sights

Cathédrale Saint-Jean-Baptiste★★ (Cathedral of St. John the Baptist)

671 Blvd. Louis-Fréchette. ⏰*Open Jun 25–Aug Mon–Sat 9.30am–4.30pm, Sun 12.30pm–4.30pm; rest of the year daily 9.30am–noon & 1pm–4.30pm.* ☎*819-293-5492.*

Distinguished by its detached campanile, this impressive cathedral (1961, Gérard Malouin) resembles a ship's sails. Built of reinforced concrete, it replaces the previous cathedral, which was demolished after a landslide in 1955. The Cassavant organ, which features pipes made by Cavaillé-Coll workshops in France, survived and was integrated into the present cathedral.

Interior

A magnificent **stained-glass window** (50m/164ft wide by 21m/69ft high), the work of Jean-Paul Charland, adorns the façade; surrounding a figure of St. John the Baptist (patron saint of Nicolet), the abstract design bursts into hundreds of colorful prisms as the morning sun shines through. The white oak and hickory nave seats 1,200 people. The

Stations of the Cross are engraved on its stucco walls, beneath portraits of Nicolet's former bishops. The stained-glass window in the apse, by Brother Eric de Taizé, is a stunning representation of the risen Christ.

Ancien collège-séminaire (Old College Seminary)

350 Rue d'Youville.

Religious authorities established the college-seminary in 1803 to encourage young men from urban areas to join the priesthood. The building, designed by Father Jérôme Demers and Thomas Baillairgé, was constructed in 1828; a fire destroyed half of the structure in 1973. The building is now occupied by the Quebec Police Academy.

Musée des religions du monde (Museum of the Religions of the World)

900 Blvd. Louis-Fréchette, just off Rue Notre-Dame in the center of Nicolet. ⏰*Open May–Oct, daily 10am–5pm; rest of the year, Tue–Fri 10am–5pm; weekends 1pm–5pm).* 🎟*$6.* ♿🅿 ☎*819-293-6148. www.museedesreligions.qc.ca.*

Dedicated to the study and preservation of religious heritage, this museum reopened in 1991 in a new, contemporary structure topped by a glass pyramid. On the ground floor, exhibits present various world religions (Buddhism, Christianity, Hinduism, Islam and Judaism) using objects from the permanent collection. In recent years, a special effort has been made by the museum to provide a religious context to major events that shape the world in this era of globalization (massive immigrations, terrorism, etc.)

Temporary thematic exhibits invite reflection on such topics as human spirituality. On the lower level, the Nicolet Seminary Archives are available for research purposes.

The collections of Le Musée des religions du monde consist of over 120,000 objects. Its most important collection includes sanctimonious images, the most comprehensive collection in Canada.

The Musée des religions du monde is not aimed especially at religious people or to people who already follow a defined spiritual path. That is why a promotional slogan of the museum is "Unbelievable!".

Maison Rodolphe-Duguay (Rodolphe-Duguay House)

195 Rang Saint-Alexis. 1km/.6mi by Rte. 132 over the Pierre-Roy Bridge; turn left on Rang Saint-Alexis. Open May–Oct, Tue–Sun 10am–5pm; rest of the year, by appointment only. $3.50 819-293-4103. www.rodolpheduguay.com.

The birthplace and home of artist Rodolphe Duguay (1891–1973) stands on a pleasant site overlooking the Nicolet River. The adjacent studio was added by the artist himself following his return in 1927 from a long sojourn in Paris. In his lifetime, Duguay was best known for his wood engravings, and was a follower of Suzor-Côté. Temporary exhibits present his life and works, and allow a glimpse into the environment in which he worked. Many special activities during summer including poetry readings, Halloween events.

Excursions

Baie-du-Febvre

13km/8mi by Rte. 132.

Nestled along Lac Saint-Pierre lies this small village that serves as the welcome spot for the return of Quebec's snow geese each April. Surrounding fields flooded by the winter's melted snow become shallow lakes that serve as the perfect place for waterfowl who stop for a rest during their annual return home. To get better acquainted with the most important snow goose migration layover in Quebec, visit the **Centre d'Interprétation de Baie-du-Febvre** (*420 Route Marie-Victorin; open Apr–Oct, Tue–Sun 10am–5pm, Nov–Mar, Tue–Thu 10am–5pm. $6; 450-783-6996; www.oies.com*). This center also showcases some of the best animal art by Quebec artists.

Odanak Indian Reserve

25km/15.5mi by Rte. 132. Turn left in Pierreville following signs.

Located on the banks of the Saint-François River, this Abenaki reservation (population 424), known as Arsigontekw, was settled in 1700 by members of the Sokoki and Abenaki communities. The small **church**, the fifth on this site, was entirely decorated by the native population. Note the wooden frieze along the walls, and the statues, especially the one of Kateri Tekakwitha.

Musée des Abénakis (Abenaki Museum)

In former convent beside church, 108 Waban-Aki, Odanak. Open year-round, Mon–Fri 10am–5pm, weekends 1pm–5pm; $8.50. 450-568-2600. www.museedesabenakis.ca.

Temporary and permanent exhibits offer glimpses of the traditional lifestyle of the Abenakis, Odanak history, and the foundation of the Catholic mission. Works by native artists are displayed on a rotating basis.

Workshops are organized where, for a nominal fee, one can learn how to make traditional ornaments.

ÎLE-AUX-NOIX

MONTÉRÉGIE REGION
MAP: SEE VALLÉE DU RICHELIEU

Situated near the US border, this 85ha/210-acre island in the Upper Richelieu was named Île-aux-Noix for the walnut trees (*noix* means "nut") that once flourished on it. As a reward for a brilliant career as a navy captain, Pierre Jacques Payan, Sieur de Noyan, was granted the island seigneury in 1733 by the Marquis de Beauharnois, governor of New France. The first inhabitant of the island was a soldier named Pierre Jourdanet; his rent was fixed at one bag of nuts annually!

🗎 **Information:** ☎1-866-469-0069. www.tourisme-monteregie.qc.ca.

▶ **Orient Yourself:** The island is located 60km/38mi southeast of Montreal by Rtes. 10, 35 and 223, then by ferry service (same hours as Fort Lennox) from Saint-Paul-de-l'Île-aux-Noix. The island is also accessible by boat (4hrs) from Saint-Jean-sur-Richelieu.

⊗ **Don't Miss:** The bastion-type fortress.

🕐 **Organizing Your Time:** Arrange to be there at sundown, and admire the river and the surrounding fort and nature.

Kids Especially for Kids: Weekends in July and August, see *Actions Stations at Fort Lennox 1883,* a theatrical animation during the afternoons.

A Bit of History

Located on a major north–south military and commercial route only a few kilometers (a couple of miles) from the outlet of Lake Champlain, Île aux Noix was first fortified by the French in 1759, during the Seven Years' War; it was captured by the British the following year. The island was occupied in 1775–76 by Americans during the American Revolution. After their departure, the British once again fortified this strategic site. They built a shipyard to establish a fleet that could foil the American warships on Lake Champlain. Shortly thereafter, the British constructed a second, larger military installation named Fort Lennox.

With the American threat temporarily halted, the island was used as a juvenile rehabilitation centre. It was briefly regarrisoned during the Civil War and during the Fenian Revolt, after which it became a holiday resort and then a World War II internment camp. Île aux Noix is now preserved as a national historic site.

Fort Lennox NHS

MICHELIN

Sight

Lieu historique national du Canada du Fort-Lennox★ (Fort Lennox National Historic Site of Canada)

Fort Lennox was erected between 1819 and 1829, at about the same time as the Citadel in Quebec City. It was named for Charles Lennox (1764–1819), Duke of Richmond, governor-in-chief of British North America, who ordered its construction.

The fort was completed just as an improved road system was established along the Richelieu River banks. The roads shifted the military threat from the water to the land, and the fort, no longer strategically positioned, was abandoned by the military for nearly four years. The Trent Affair and the Fenian uprising in the 1860s brought new threats to the British, who re-garrisoned Fort Lennox until 1870.

The bastion-type fortress is typical of 19C military architecture. The fort is surrounded by a wide moat, which forms a five-pointed star around a series of tall earthen ramparts. The corners are protected by bastions that open onto the inner yard. Visitors cross a footbridge and pass under a massive stone archway to enter the main courtyard, which is surrounded by a group of Neoclassical stone structures. The guard house (1823) and officers' quarters (1825–28) are arranged in a symmetrical pattern and are decorated with columns and arches. The soldiers' barracks are also ordered symmetrically around a pedimented pavilion. The fort complex includes two warehouses (1823), a powder magazine (1820) and 17 firing stations, or casemates, located under the ramparts.

Visit

🕐 *Open mid-May–late Jun, Mon–Fri 10am–5pm, weekends 10am–6pm; Jun 24– Labor Day, daily 10am–6pm; rest of Sept– mid-Oct, weekends 10am–6pm.* ⌖$7.85. *(ferry & visit to fort).* ✗ ♿ ☎450-291-5700 & 1-888-773-8888. *www.pc.gc.ca.* The fort occupies a pleasant **site**★ overlooking the Richelieu River. Visitors are led through the principal sections of the fort complex. The building interiors have been restored to re-create life on a British army base in the mid-19C. Among the numerous displays, visitors will see the guardroom with its wood stove and jail; the prison; the soldiers' barracks with hard straw mattresses, uniforms and weapons; the officers' quarters; the brick-lined powder magazine; and the warehouses. The island itself features several relaxing picnic areas.

ÎLE D'ORLÉANS★★

QUÉBEC CITY REGION
POPULATION 6,862

Wedged in the St. Lawrence, within view of Quebec City, this almond-shaped island covers an area of 192sq km/74sq mi. It boasts a varied landscape of maple groves in the north and on the central plateau, oak forests in the southwest, marshes in the centre and sand along the water's edge. Although joined to the mainland by bridge in 1935, the Île d'Orléans still retains the pastoral tranquillity that inspired the 19C artist Horatio Walker and the *chansonnier* (**singer**) Félix Leclerc.

- **Information:** 490 Côte du Pont, Saint-Pierre. ☎418-828-9411 & 1-866-941-9411. www.iledorleans.com/www.quebecregion.com.
- ▶ **Orient Yourself:** Île d'Orléans is located 10km/6.2mi northeast of Quebec City by Rte. 138 or Rte. 40, Exit 325.
- **Don't Miss:** Classical music recitals at Église de Sainte-Pétronille (*call church for details for the summertime events* ☎418-828-1410).
- 🕐 **Organizing Your Time:** The island is surprisingly large and its road is slow. Give yourself time to enjoy the scenery and to make a few pleasant stops.

A Bit of History

Long before the arrival of Europeans, the indigenous population called the island Minigo, meaning "bewitched" in Algonquian, because they considered it to be a land of spirits. When Jacques Cartier came ashore in 1535, the abundance of vines growing on the island prompted him to dub the site the Isle of Bacchus. The following year the name was changed to Île d'Orléans in honor of the son of King François I, the Duke of Orléans. Under the French Regime, the seigneury was laid out in strips of land (rangs) perpendicular to the St. Lawrence, providing optimal access to the waterfront. Today, vast expanses of farmland produce strawberries, raspberries, apples, asparagus, and potatoes. The island is also known for its maple syrup.

Many islanders trace their ancestry back to French colonists who arrived here more than three centuries ago, at a time when the island was more populous than the capital city. In fact, in 1667, the Île d'Orléans claimed a population of 529 while the residents of Quebec City numbered only 448.

Tour of the Island
67km/41.6mi.

▷ *After crossing the bridge to Île d'Orléans (Pont de l'Île), turn right toward Saint-Pétronille. A tourist information center (☎418-828-9411; www.iledorleans.com) is located at*

the intersection of the bridge road and Rte. 368 (it will be on your right when you arrive on the island).

Route 368 runs along the island's 67km/41.6mi circumference, passing through six communities. Driving along the road, visitors will discover splendid scenery and magnificent **views**★★ of the Beaupré Coast and the Bas-Saint-Laurent shoreline. The itinerary along the southern coast, from Sainte-Pétronille to Saint-François, is particularly picturesque. The return trip along the northern side of the island offers scenic views of the Montmorency Falls and Mont Sainte-Anne.

Sainte-Pétronille
5km/3mi from junction of bridge road.
Located on the site of the island's first settlement, this community was conceded in 1649. Hurons sought refuge here in the 1650s after warring with the Iroquois. The small chapel dating from that period has since disappeared. In 1855 a wharf was constructed to load island produce, and a steamship ferry service linked Sainte-Pétronille to Quebec City. This connection led to the development of tourism in the late 19C, and many affluent families erected Victorian-style villas here as summer homes. A three-hole golf course built in 1866 is one of the oldest in North America. The village was known as L'Anse-au-Fort, then as Bout de l'Île (tip of the island) and Village de Beaulieu before acquiring its present name in 1870.

Église de Sainte-Pétronille (Church of Sainte-Pétronille)
Turn left on Chemin de l'Église, then right before the cul-de-sac facing the golf course. ◷*Open late Jun–Labor Day, daily 10am–4.30pm.* ☎*418-828-1410.*
The religious complex includes a convent (1875), a presbytery and a church (1871) designed by J.F. Peachy. The interior was decorated by David Ouellet.

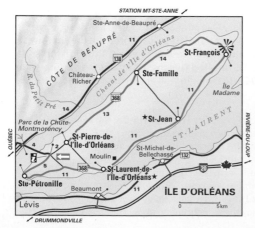

▷ *Continue along Chemin de l'Église, which runs into the Chemin du Bout-de-l'Île. A walkway borders the shoreline. Turn left, then right on Rue du Quai.*

La Goéliche
Rue du Quai.
Known as the Château Bel Air when it was constructed in 1880, and then as Manoir de l'Anse, this imposing Victorian hotel and restaurant stands majestically overlooking the St. Lawrence.

▷ *Return to Rte. 368 and continue to Saint-Laurent.*

Saint-Laurent-de-l'Île-d'Orléans★
11km/6.8mi.
Traditionally the maritime centre of the Île d'Orléans, Saint-Laurent enjoyed a thriving shipbuilding industry in the mid-19C when some 20 family-owned shipyards produced flat-bottom boats, called *chaloupes*. Famous for their clean lines and sturdy construction, these boats remained the primary means of transportation for the islanders until a bridge joined the island to the mainland in 1935. The village still claims the island's only marina, which can accommodate up to 130 boats.

Situated 2km/1.2mi before the town limit of Saint-Laurent, the **Gendreau House** (*n°. 2385 Chemin Royal*), with its steep roof and unusual double row of dormer windows, was erected in 1720. For at least eight generations, it was inhabited by members of the Gendreau family. Next to the marina in the heart of the village, the **Église Saint-Laurent** (St. Lawrence Church, 1860), is topped by a tall, well-proportioned steeple. In the old section of the village, a small processional chapel stands beside the courthouse. Upon leaving town, note the early 18C flour mill, the **Moulin Gosselin** (*left side of road*), which now houses a fine restaurant.

Saint-Jean★
11km/6.8mi.
Founded in 1679 by Msgr. de Laval, this community was home to the island's pilots and navigators. Between 1850 and 1950, the village experienced a period of intense economic growth with the arrival of numerous Charlevoix pilots, who brought with them opportunities for maritime and industrial development. The maritime cemetery commemorates the lives of these seamen, many of whom perished in the course of difficult voyages on the tumultuous waters of the St. Lawrence. Today, the village's residents still pursue the maritime and agricultural activities of their ancestors. Their homes, decorated with nautical adornments, are clustered on the hillsides and along the St. Lawrence shoreline.

Manoir Mauvide-Genest★ (Mauvide-Genest Manor)
Guided tours (45 min) ⊙$8 (self-guided ⊙$8), May–late Jun & early Sept–mid-Oct, weekends and late Jun–Labor Day, daily 10am–5pm. 418-829-2630. www.manoirmauvidegenest.com.
The original house was constructed in 1734 for Jean Mauvide, surgeon to the King and a successful French merchant, and his wife, Marie-Anne Genest, of the Saint-Jean region. By the mid-18C, the wealth accumulated by Mr. Mauvide through his business ventures in the Antilles enabled him to enlarge the rural dwelling into a veritable manor. In 1752, Mr. Mauvide bought half of the Île d'Orléans seigneury. A few years later, when his business failed, he sold the seigneury to his son-in-law. In 1926, Judge J.-Camille Pouliot purchased the manor and undertook its restoration. It is now considered the finest extant example of rural architecture from the French Regime.

The manor contains a museum exhibiting furnishings and objects collected by Judge Pouliot.

Saint-François
11km/6.8mi.
Formerly the seigneury of François Berthelot, the parish was founded in 1679. The community encompasses the eastern extremity of the island as well as the tiny Madame and Ruaux islands. The St. Lawrence changes from fresh to salt water 20km/12.4mi beyond this point. Agriculture, mainly potato crops,

Address Book

⊘For price ranges, see cover flap.

WHERE TO EAT

$ Domaine Steinbach Cidrerie et Relais Gourmand – *2205 Chemin Royal, Saint-Pierre.* ☎*418-828-0000.* *www.domainesteinbach.com.* The food bounty of Île d'Orléans is sold at this domaine: Organic cider and duck confit, and 30 other "produits fermiers" can be enjoyed on a terrace.

$ L'Espace Félix-Leclerc – *682 Chemin Royal, Saint-Pierre.* ☎*418-828-1682.* *www.felixleclerc.com.* Félix Leclerc (1914–1988) is a giant of Quebec song writing. The French-Quebecan spent the end of his life on Île d'Orléans and is buried there. This pavilion pays tribute to Leclerc with a permanent exhibition. Visitors can rest at a café that, at night, becomes an intimate venue for shows.

---

is the primary means of revenue for the villagers.

Ravaged by fire in 1988, the **Église Saint-François** (Church of St. Francis, 1736) was reconstructed on its original foundations in 1992. On the southern side of the church, note the **presbytery** (1867), in the Quebec vernacular style, with a large balcony. A processional chapel marks the town limit. Just outside the village, a lookout tower affords **views**★★ of both banks of the St. Lawrence.

Sainte-Famille
14km/8.7mi.

Msgr. de Laval founded this parish, the oldest on the island, in 1661, and had the first church erected here in 1669. Among the most interesting buildings in the village is the 17C fieldstone farmhouse of Norman inspiration, today occupied by a restaurant specializing in traditional French-Canadian cuisine. A horse and buggy picks up diners from the parking lot on the main road to the house.

Église Sainte-Famille★★ (Holy Family Church)
🕒*Opening times vary; telephone for times.* ♿🅿☎*418-828-2656.*

This tri-steepled edifice is considered the most important church dating from the French Regime. Built between 1743 and 1748, the church was modified in 1807 with the addition of two lateral bell towers. In the Neoclassical **interior** (1921, Thomas Baillairgé), the nave

slopes toward the altar and baldachin. The sculpted vault (1812) by Louis-Bazile David, a student of Quévillon, represents a starry sky. Dating from 1749, the tabernacle of the main altar is the work of the Levasseur family, while the tabernacles of the lateral altars are attributed to Pierre Florent, brother of François. Hanging to the right of the nave is a painting of the Holy Family attributed to Brother Luc, a Récollet painter who visited New France about 1670.

Saint-Pierre-de-l'Île-d'Orléans
13km/8mi.

The parish of Saint-Pierre is distinguished by its two churches. When the parishioners decided to build a new church in 1955, the government acquired the old church, erected between 1715 and 1719, to protect it from demolition.

Old Church★
🕒*Opening times vary; telephone for times.* ♿🅿☎*418-828-9824.*

Damaged during the Conquest, the church was restored and then enlarged in 1775 when the parish priest became auxiliary bishop of Quebec City. The church was again remodelled in the 1830s by Thomas Baillairgé. The interior contains three altars executed by Pierre Émond in 1795 and a sanctuary lamp carved in wood. Note also the box pews, introduced to Quebec by Protestant groups, and, at the front and back of the church, the woodstoves with sheet-metal pipes that heated the nave.

PERCÉ★★★

GASPÉSIE REGION
POPULATION 3,512
MAP: SEE GASPÉSIE

Named for the massive rock pierced (*percé*) by the sea, standing just offshore, this village occupies a magnificent **site** that inspires artists and poets and attracts visitors from all over the world to the Gaspé peninsula. One of Jacques Cartier's landing points in 1534, the area was also frequented by European fishermen in the 16C and 17C. A mission was founded here in 1673, but was destroyed by the British in 1690, to be re-established only after the Conquest. A tiny, isolated fishing village until the advent of tourism at the turn of the 20C, Percé now boasts some of the peninsula's finest restaurants and tourist facilities.

- **Information:** ☎418-782-5448 & 1-800-463-0323. www.perce.info/ www.tourisme-gaspesie.com.
- **Orient Yourself:** Percé is located 750km/466mi northeast of Quebec City and 76km/47mi from Gaspé by Rte. 132.
- **Don't Miss:** Percé Rock.
- **Organizing Your Time:** If you plan to walk out to the rock, confirm the times for the high and low tides: Don't get stranded!
- **Especially for Kids:** Kayaking or canoeing around the Rock.

Sights

Rocher Percé★★ (Percé Rock)

Once attached to the mainland, this mammoth rock wall is 438m/1,437ft long and 88m/289ft high. The limestone block was formed at the bottom of the sea millions of years ago, and contains innumerable fossils. At one time, it may have had up to four holes forming as many archways. One such archway crumbled in 1845, leaving a detached slab called the Obelisk.

Today, only a 30m/98.4ft arch remains. The sculptured limestone is best viewed from **Mont-Joli**★★. The rock is connected to Mont-Joli by a sandbar, exposed at low tide. *Check tide tables at the tourist office. The stairway to the beach and sandbar is accessible from the Mont-Joli parking lot.*

The Coast★★★

The coast along Route 132 offers spectacular **views**★★. Just before entering Percé, a belvedere provides a good view

View of Percé Rock

©JP Huard/ATRG

Address Book

For price ranges, see the Legend on the cover flap.

WHERE TO STAY

$–$$ Auberge au Fil des Saisons – *232 Rte 132 Ouest.* Ⓟ☎*418-782-2666, www.aubergeperce.com. 6 rooms of differeing sizes and configurations.* Outstanding value in this Victorian house facing the Gulf. Cozy rooms decorated smartly with pastel colors. Some rooms with private bathroom, some sharing a bathroom; all rooms have a television as well as a natural view.

$$ Hôtel-motel Fleur de Lys – *248 Rte 132 Ouest.* ☒Ⓟ☎*418-782-5380 & 1-800-399-5380, www.gaspesie.com/fleurdelys. 33 rooms, air conditioning and kitchenettes available.* Families will be happy to settle into a reliable accommodation featuring a heated pool, a playground, and a fire ring. You will enjoy a breathtaking view of the Percé Rock from the hotel, and you can go around town with the hotel's own shuttle service. Direct access to the boardwalk leading to the wharf. Family restaurant and convenience store on site.

$$–$$$ Hôtel La Normandie – *221 Rte. 132 Ouest.* ☒Ⓟ☎*418-782-2112 or 1-800-463-0820. www.normandieperce. com. 45 rooms.* A waterfront hotel in the most traditional sense, the Normandie offers tastefully decorated rooms, most with views of the sea and Percé Rock. Romantic **dining room ($$$)** overlooking the Gulf. An impressive wine list accompanies the table d'hôte menu, which features such favorites as grilled duck breast with orange and green-pepper sauce, and lobster feuilleté with Champagne sauce.

$$–$$$ Manoir de Percé – *212 Rte. 132 Ouest.* ☒Ⓟ☎*418-782-2022 or 1-800-463-0858. www.manoirdeperce.com. 40 air-conditioned rooms.* In the heart of Percé, facing the Rock and Bonaventure Island. Comfortable hotel-motel style accommodation. The **dining room** serves nicely prepared, traditional Gaspesian cooking. Fish and seafood, grilled and regional specialties served family-style. The owners smoke the salmon they serve.

$$$ Auberge au Pirate 1775 – *169 Rte. 132 Ouest. Dinner only.* ☒Ⓟ☎*418-782-5055, www.quebecweb.com/auberge aupirate1775com. 5 rooms in this large B&B.* Wonderfully comfortable rooms, gregarious proprietors, and beautiful views of Percé Rock await you at this Pirate's Inn, coiled into an 18C home. The acclaimed **dining room ($$$)** pleases visitors from far and wide with specialties such as *fondants de chair de crabe en millefeuille* (crabmeat in puff pastry), *brandade de morue et sa compote de tomates fraîches* (brandade of cod with fresh tomato compote), and *le trio du golfe en beurre blanc au vinaigre de framboises* (salmon, scallops and grilled shrimp in raspberry vinegar beurre blanc).

WHERE TO EAT

$$ La Maison du Pêcheur – *155 Place du Quai.* ☎*418-782-5331.* **Québécois**. Located next to the public pier, this Fisherman's House serves breakfast, lunch and dinner. For dinner, choose from delectable bistro classics or Québécois seafood specialties like lobster flavored with maple syrup (the restaurant boasts its own lobster farm) or the mouth-watering, wood-fired pizzas such as La Spéciale du Pêcheur, made with tomato sauce, shrimp, scallops and lobster. Locals favor the seaweed soup. Large dining room and a terrace that is most welcome in the summer.

GETTING TO GASPÉSIE BY TRAIN

The Gaspésie Peninsula is the most interesting remote area reachable by train in Quebec. There are VIA Rail stations in Gaspé, Percé, Carleton, Matapédia, and Mont-Joli.

The so-called *Chaleur* train leaves Montreal at the end of the afternoon and arrives in Gaspésie the next morning. There is a panoramic car (featuring a glass dome) and a bar-lounge car. Sleeper cabins are available, although you can sleep in your seat.

VIA Rail Canada: ☎*1-888-842-7245, www.viarail.ca.*

of Aurore Peak (Pic de l'Aurore). Farther along the road, a path leads up to **Cape Barré**, which affords a commanding view of the cliffs known as **Trois Sœurs** (Three Sisters) to the west, and Percé Rock, Anse du Nord, Mont-Joli, Île Bonaventure and the village, to the east. Leaving Percé, the promontory at **Côte Surprise** offers yet another superb view of Percé Rock, the village and the island.

Mont Sainte-Anne

From Rte. 132, take Ave. de l'Église. Behind the church, a gravel road leads to Mt. Sainte-Anne. A steep but easy trail leads to the summit. Allow 2hrs round-trip.

Rising 320m/1,050ft above Percé, the flat-topped mountain features extraordinary red rock formations that drop off on three sides. Lookouts stationed along the way to the summit provide increasingly expansive **views**★★★ of Percé Rock, the bay, the village and the surrounding area. A statue of St. Anne crowns the mountain summit.

La Grotte (Grotto)

On the return trip from Mt. Sainte-Anne, turn left at Chemin de la Grotte, and continue for 1km/.6mi.

In this scenic grotto, a waterfall cascades into a small pool surrounded by moss and ferns.

La Grande Crevasse★ (Great Crevice)

From the village, take Rte. des Failles up to the Auberge Gargantua (3km/1.8mi). The trail (1hr 30min round-trip) starts behind the inn; ⚠ caution is advised as there is no guardrail.

Passing alongside the west cliff of Mt. Sainte-Anne, the trail offers glimpses of the peaks of the Chic-Choc mountains to the west and the Bay of Gaspé to the north. The Great Crevice (*also visible from Rte. des Failles*) is a deep fissure in the red conglomerate rock which is a part of Mont Blanc, located northwest of Mont Sainte-Anne.

Parc national de l'Île-Bonaventure-et-du-Rocher-Percé★ (Île Bonaventure and Percé Rock National Park)

🕐*Open end May–mid-Oct, daily 9am–5pm. ☜$3.50. ✗ 🅿 $6. ☎418-782-2240. www.sepaq.com*

In summer the Île Bonaventure is home to some 70,000 **gannets** that nest in the ledges and crevices of the 90m/1,259ft cliffs on the east side of the island. This sanctuary is considered the largest colony of gannets in North America. Other seabirds found here are kittiwakes, murres, puffins, razorbills, guillemots, cormorants and gulls.

The **boat trip** to Île Bonaventure takes visitors past Percé Rock and then around the island (*depart from Percé wharf mid-May–mid-Oct, daily 9am–5pm; round-*

©Michel Julien/ATRG

Northern Gannets, Parc national de l'Île-Bonaventure-et-du-Rocher-Percé

trip 1hr 15min with or without stop on island; commentary; 🚍$22; whale watching cruises near island; 🚍$45; Les Bateliers de Percé Inc.; ☎418-782-2974 & 1-877-782-2974). In summer, passengers can disembark on the island to take a closer look at the birds and walk along the nature trails.

Le Chafaud, secteur historique Charles Robin (rue du Quai)

In the Parc national. 🕐*Open Jun–Sept, daily 9am–5pm.* 🗣*Guided tours in English or French at 10am, 11am, 2pm, and 3.30pm.* 🚍*$8.* ♿.

This interpretation enter is a gateway to understanding the historical and natural heritage provided by the wildlife and geological wonders of the Percé area. You will learn why millions upon millions of birds, as well as large marine mammals, come to depend on the nutrient rich waters of the Gulf of Saint-Lawrence.

Exhibits and a documentary will help you to get the most out of a visit of the Parc national de l'Île-Bonaventure-et-du-Rocher-Percé.

Magasin Général Historique Authentique de 1928 (Authentic Historical General Store of 1928)

32 Rue à Bonfils, in the L'Anse-à-Beaufils sector of Percé. 🕐*Open mid-Jun–early Sept, daily 10am–5pm; limited off season schedule.* 🗣*Guided tours in English or French at 10am, 11am, 2pm, and 3.30pm.* 🚍*$9.* ♿ 🅿 ☎*418-782-2225 (off season 418-782-5286).*

The general store was a key institution in early Canada. With the Catholic church and the primary school, the general store completed the trifecta of village essentials in Quebec. And these stores were particularly essential in remote areas like Gaspésie.

This rare, authentically preserved general store features superb antique oak wainscoting. The daily life of the "Gaspésiens" is displayed through objects, tools, and wares.

Guides in period costumes tell stories and anecdotes inspired by the lives of Gaspésie pioneers.

ÎLE PERROT

MONTÉRÉGIE REGION
POPULATION 10,131
MAP: SEE MONTREAL

Located at the confluence of the Ottawa and St. Lawrence rivers, this tranquil island is 11km/6.8mi long by 5km/3mi wide. In 1672 it was granted to **François-Marie Perrot**, governor of Montreal and a captain in the Auvergne Regiment, who had married a niece of Intendant Jean Talon a few years earlier. Perrot used the island's strategic location as a base for illegal trade in liquor and furs with the Amerindians.

It was not until 1703, when Joseph Trottier, Sieur Desruisseaux, acquired the land, that clearing and tilling began. Trottier built a manor house and a windmill (*moulin*) on the estate, known thenceforth as the Domain of Pointe-du-Moulin. Today the island is a pleasant stopover on the route from Montreal to Toronto or Ottawa.

- 🛈 **Information:** Seasonal tourist centre 190 Blvd. Métropolitain. ☎514-453-0855 & 1-866-469-0069. www.tourisme-monteregie.qc.ca. www.ile-perrot.qc.ca.
- ▶ **Orient Yourself:** Île Perrot sits about 45km/28mi west of downtown Montreal by Rte. 20 (Exit 38), between Lakes Saint-Louis and Des Deux-Montagnes.
- 😊 **Don't Miss:** Camping at Parc historique Pointe-du-Moulin during the Perseids meteor showers in August.
- **Kids Especially for Kids:** Kids' days at Parc historique Pointe-du-Moulin include musicians and magicians.

Parc historique de la Pointe-du-Moulin

Visit

Église Sainte-Jeanne-de-Chantal★ (Church of St. Jeanne of Chantal)

Rue de l'Église. Visit by guided tour (30min) only, Jul–Aug. Mon–Fri 10am–5pm, weekends 9am–5pm; rest of the year by appointment only. ☎514-453-2125. Completed in 1786, this little stone church stands on the southern half of the island, in the Village-sur-le-Lac secteur. The view of the church's exterior from the cemetery evokes an image of old and rural Quebec. The elegant interior was decorated between 1812 and 1830 by Joseph Turcaut and Louis-Xavier Leprohon, two sculptors of the Quévillon school. From the church, the **view** over Lake Saint-Louis is splendid.

Parc historique de la Pointe-du-Moulin★ (Pointe-du-Moulin Historic Park) Kids

2500 Blvd. Don-Quichotte. Open mid-May–end Aug, daily 9am–5pm (regularly scheduled guided tours); early Sept–early Oct, weekends noon–5pm. $3 Mon–Fri, $5 weekends. ☎514-453-5936. www.pointedumoulin.com This park, at the eastern end of Île Perrot, covers about 12ha/30 acres and encompasses the location of Joseph Trottier's manor house (now destroyed). The lovely site juts out into the water, offering sweeping **views** of Lake Saint-Louis and of Montreal in the distance. On clear days, the Adirondacks are visible to the southwest. Picnic sites dot the grounds, amid winding paths.

An **interpretation center** (*same hours as the park*) near the park entrance features displays and films (*15min*) tracing the history of the estate, and describing the seigneurial system and traditional 18C farming methods. Activities such as crafts demonstrations, theatrical productions and concerts are offered on weekends in summer.

At the extreme tip of the park stands Trottier's stone **windmill** (c. 1705), which has been rebuilt and is in full working order. The entire upper section of the mill can be revolved with a pole, enabling the broad sails to catch the wind from any direction. On windy summer Sundays, the mechanisms are put into operation, offering an extraordinary view of the ingenious 18C processes involved in harnessing the wind to mill grain. The stone walls are pierced with loopholes, as the mill also served as a fortification in the 18C.

The **miller's house** stands nearby. Built about 1785, it contains displays on traditional family life in New France (cooking and baking, dress, furniture, and architecture)

QUEBEC CITY★★★

POPULATION 491,142 (METROPOLITAN AREA 715,515)
MAP: SEE QUEBEC AND ENVIRONS

Built atop a rocky promontory jutting into the St. Lawrence River, Canada's oldest city has delighted visitors for centuries. Today dominated by the imposing mass of the Château Frontenac, Quebec City has retained its historic character and Old World charm, presenting a mélange of fortifications, narrow cobblestone alleys, and elegant residences, all reflecting the city's traditional role as a military and administrative center. The slender spires of numerous churches dot the skyline, attesting to the French colony's religious origins. Quebec's distinctive French flavor is enhanced by fine restaurants, outdoor cafés and a lively nightlife. In 1985 the city became the first urban center in North America to be inscribed on UNESCO's World Heritage List.

- **Information:** 835 Ave Wilfrid-Laurier. ☎418-641-6290 & 1-877-783-1608. www.quebecregion.com.
- **Orient Yourself:** Quebec City is 500km/310.7mi north of Boston and 230km/143mi northeast of Montreal. The best way to get a sense of the layout of the old city is to stroll the Governor's Walk, a promenade extending along the top of the cliffs behind the Château Frontenac, overlooking the St. Lawrence River.
- **Parking:** Streets are narrow and crowded, so parking is difficult in the older parts of the city. You won't need a car in the Old Quebec City, so don't hire one. If you drive your own car, leave it In a parking lot (enquire at your hotel about free/reduced-cost parking). During winter, pay heed to towing signs, particularly when snow removal is in process.
- **Don't Miss:** Governor's Walk; Château Frontenac (inside and out) and its Sunday brunch buffet, which highlights regional foods; Parliament Building, Museum of Civilization.
- **Organizing Your Time:** The old part of the city is small so plan to explore it on foot. However, be aware that the streets are narrow and many are cobblestoned, so footing can be uneven. The Old City is very hilly and walking can prove exhausting in the summer. The Funicular (⊜$2, in front of Château Frontenac) helps save legwork climbing up the cliff, to and from the Basse-Ville (Lower Town).
- **Especially for Kids:** In winter, don't miss the old-fashioned toboggan run (⊜$2) swooshing down beside the Château Frontenac onto the Governor's Walk (fun for adults, too); girls may particularly enjoy the Economuseum of Dolls; don't forget the Quebec Aquarium.
- **Also See:** ÎLE D'ORLÉANS in summer particularly, MONTMORENCY FALLS, MONT STE. ANNE for skiing or for views of St. Lawrence from a gondola in summer; ice hotel in winter (&see Address Book).

A Bit of History

Craddle of New France – Perched on a promontory at the confluence of the St. Charles and St. Lawrence rivers, Quebec City draws its name from the Algonquian word Kebec, meaning "where the river narrows." In fact, the St. Lawrence is only 1km/.6mi wide at this point. Amerindian hunters and fishermen inhabited the area in the village of Stadacona long before the arrival of Europeans. In 1535,

Jacques Cartier landed on the pristine shores and named the promontory "Cap Diamant" (Cape Diamond) for the precious stones he hoped to find here. Discovering only worthless minerals, Cartier soon abandoned the site.

After an exploratory voyage in 1603, Samuel de Champlain returned to New France in 1608 to establish a fur-trading post at Kebec. Champlain constructed a rudimentary wooden fortress, on the site of the church named Notre-Dame-

Château Frontenac and the Old Town seen from the St. Lawrence River

des-Victoires. The structure, known as the **Habitation**, consisted of two main buildings and served as a fort, trading post and living quarters, and a garden. A second, larger U-shaped fortress was built on the same site in 1624. Champlain also established a fortification on the Cape Diamond heights and named it Château Saint-Louis.

In the 17C, the first settlers arrived in Quebec. Primarily craftsmen and merchants attracted to the profitable fur trade, they erected houses in the Lower Town, which became the center of commercial activity. Seeking protection offered by the fortifications, the colonial government and numerous religious institutions settled in the Upper Town. Reluctant to divide up land plots in the Upper Town, the institutions effectively halted development on Cape Diamond for over a century. The Lower Town remained the main residential and commercial center until the mid-19C.

Strategic Location – Quebec City's location enhanced its development as the political, administrative and military center of New France. Towering 98m/321.5ft above sea level, the Cape Diamond promontory provided the colony with a strategic military location, thereby earning the sobriquet "Gibraltar of America." From this naturally fortified area, the French repelled successive attacks by the Iroquois and by the British. In 1629 the settlement was captured by British conquerors, the **Kirke Brothers**, and retaken by the French in 1632. In 1690, it was besieged unsuccessfully by the British **Admiral Phips**. Hostility between the small French colony and Britain escalated during the 18C, culminating in the Battle of the Plains of Abraham that precipitated the Conquest of 1759. Following the Treaty of Paris in 1763, Quebec City, the former capital of the French colony, assumed a new role as capital of the British dominion.

Economic growth – Situated on the north shore of the St. Lawrence, the town quickly assumed a dominant position as port of entry and exit for ocean-bound vessels carrying goods, travelers and immigrants to North America. During the 18C and 19C, the Old Port became the transit point for trade of raw materials needed by Britain. The loading of fur, cereal and wood cargoes destined for foreign shores, the unloading of goods imported from France, the Antilles, England and Scotland, and a major shipbuilding industry all contributed to the feverish activity along the shores of the St. Lawrence.

Expansion of the lumber trade with Britain, after Napoleon's embargo in the early 19C, enabled Quebec City to maintain a competitive position with

Montreal until the mid-19C. Then the trade in raw timber, superseded by lumber, declined, and Quebec City gradually lost its position as center of production and trade in New France.

Competition from railroad companies located on the south shore of the St. Lawrence increased, and the impact of technological development in ocean-going vessels, enabling them to bypass the city and sail to Montreal, contributed to the city's decline. In addition, the section of the St. Lawrence between the two cities was dredged, allowing larger ships passage. A sudden decrease in demand for wooden ships hastened the demise of the large shipbuilding industry.

To remedy the situation, Quebec City tried to attract various railroad companies, and built the Quebec City bridge to establish a rail link between the northern and southern shores, but all to no avail. After 1850, Montreal became a center of trade, finance, and industry, engendering a westward shift of population and economy. Quebec City experienced a short period of expansion with the footwear industry in the 1920s. However, most jobs today are related to public administration, defence, and the service sector.

Population – Prior to the Conquest, the town's population was made up of French settlers. The influx of British and Irish immigrants in the early 19C led to an increase in the Anglophone population, which numbered 41 percent in 1851, and reached 51 percent by 1861. Following Quebec City's economic decline, the population shift westward decreased the number of Anglophones to 31.5 percent in 1871, and 10 percent in 1921. In 2006, Anglophones accounted for just 1.66 percent of Quebec City's residents, thereby affirming the city's distinct Francophone character.

Quebec City Today – Throughout the centuries, Quebec City has retained its role as a capital city and as a bastion of French culture. The colonial French city is much more in evidence here than in Montreal. In the last three decades, the growth of the provincial government has given the city a new boost, and a

bustling metropolis has developed outside the old walls. In contrast to the modern cities of North America, Quebec City has retained a cachet reminiscent of Old World capitals.

The city's main event is its famous winter **Carnival**. Held in February, this festival attracts thousands of visitors. For ten joyous days, Quebec City bustles with festivities that include a great parade, the construction of a magnificent ice palace, an ice sculpture contest, and canoe races over the partially frozen St. Lawrence. The activities are overseen by an enormous snowman, nicknamed Bonhomme Carnaval.

1 Basse-Ville★★★ (Lower Town)

A Bit of History

The Lower Town began in the early 17C as a fur-trading post, established by Champlain on the area around his "Habitation." In 1636, the year following Champlain's death, the first city plans were drawn up. Between 1650 and 1662, more than 35 parcels of land were conceded to merchants who began constructing shops and residences around the Habitation and its adjoining square, then called the Market Place (*place du marché*). Limited space in the Lower Town inspired the residents to fill in parts of the shore northeast of the square and erect wharves along present-day Rue Saint-Pierre.

In August 1682 a fire devastated the Lower Town. As a result of this disaster, building standards, such as the use of stone rather than wood, were imposed on new constructions, giving rise to the simple stone box construction visible throughout the quarter today.

As commerce, shipbuilding and port activities grew in the 19C, the area occupied by the Lower Town doubled in size. Port activity declined after 1860, severing the economic lifeline of the Lower Town and resulting in progressive deterioration of the buildings in the area over the next century. In 1967 the Quebec Government passed legislation

Address Book

&For price ranges, see the Legend on the cover flap.

PRACTICAL INFORMATION

TELEPHONE AREA CODE: 418

GETTING THERE

By Air – Jean-Lesage International Airport: 16km/10.2mi (approximately 20min) from downtown. No shuttle bus and no other form of public transportation. A taxi costs $30 plus tip. Airport information: ☎418-640-2700 or www.aeroportdequebec.com. Air Canada ☎1-888-247-2262, Westjet ☎1-877-956-6982, Delta Airlines ☎1-800-221-1212.

By Train – Gare du Palais: 450 Rue de la Gare-du-Palais; Gare de Sainte-Foy: 3255 Chemin de la Gare. Information: ☎1-888-842-7245 or www.viarail.ca.

By Bus – Gare du Palais Terminal: 320 Rue Abraham-Martin ☎418-525-3000; Sainte-Foy Terminal: 3001 Chemin des Quatre-Bourgeois. Information: ☎418-650-0087. Orléans Express Coach Lines: ☎1-888-999-3977.

GETTING AROUND

PUBLIC TRANSPORTATION

A local bus service is provided by Réseau de transport de la Capitale (RTQ) (☎418-627-2511; www.rtcquebec.ca). Regular buses operate from 5.30am–1am. Tickets may be purchased in local tobacco shops & newsstands ($2.35) or on board the bus ($2.50, exact change required). Day passes are also available ($6.15/day).

A bus terminal is located in the heart of Old Quebec at Place d'Youville. Several city buses also leave from the Train & Bus Station (Gare du Palais).

Cars – Rental car companies: Avis (at Hilton Hotel) ☎418-523-1075; Budget (in Old Quebec) ☎418-692-3660; Enterprise (at Delta Hotel) ☎418-523-6661; Hertz (in Old Quebec) ☎418-694-1224; Hertz (at the airport) ☎418-871-1571. Streets are narrow and can be congested in the Old Town, Upper and Lower; it is easiest and most pleasant to visit these areas on foot. Visitors may wish to park in one of the city's designated parking areas.

Taxis – Taxis Coop Québec ☎418-525-5191; Taxis Québec ☎418-525-8123; Taxis Coop Sainte-Foy Sillery ☎418-653-7777.

GENERAL INFORMATION

Province of Quebec Tourism – Centre Infotouriste: 12 Rue Sainte-Anne (across from Château Frontenac); open late Jun–Labor Day, daily 8.30am–8.30pm, rest of the year, daily 9am–5pm. **Quebec City Tourism**: 835 Ave Wilfrid-Laurier, near the Parlement (open late Jun–Labor Day, daily 8.30am–8.30pm; rest of Sept–mid-Oct, daily 8.30am–6.30pm; rest of the year, Mon–Sat 9am–5pm except Fri 9am–6pm, Sun 10am–4pm, Closed Dec 25 and Jan 1; ☎418-641-6290 & 1-877-783-1608; www.quebecregion.com).

Lobby, Auberge Saint-Antoine

Auberge Saint-Antoine

Accommodations – &*For specific listings of hotels, see Where to Stay.* Quebec City Tourism (*above*) can provide specific informations about hotels, Bed & Breakfasts, chalets and campgrounds.

Local Press – in English: *The Chronicle-Telegraph* (*weekly*). French: *Le Journal de Québec, Le Soleil.*

Post Office – Open Mon–Fri 8am–7.30pm, Sat 9.30am–5pm. Upper Town Post Office (*near Château Frontenac*): *5 Rue du Fort* ☎*418-694-6102.*

CURRENCY EXCHANGE OFFICES
Caisse populaire Desjardins (Old Quebec) – 19 Rue des Jardins ☎*418-522-6806*

Montreal Currency Exchange – 12 Rue Sainte-Anne ☎*418-694-1014*

Montreal Currency Exchange – *46 Rue du Petit-Champlain* ☎*418-694-0011*

Transchange International – *46 Rue de Buade* ☎*418-694-6906*

USEFUL NUMBERS

POLICE–AMBULANCE–FIRE (EMERGENCY CALLS ONLY) ☎**911**
Directory Assistance ☎411
Health Info daily, 24hrs, answering service provided by registered nurses ☎*418-648-2626*
Brunet Drugstore, *57 Rue Dalhousie* (in the Old Port) ☎*418-694-1262*
Tourisme Québec ☎*1-877-266-5687*
Canadian Automobile Association (CAA/AAA) ☎(member services) *1-800-686-9243* (*emergency road services 24hrs/day*) *1-800-222-4357*
Road conditions ☎*1-888-355-0511*
Weather (24hrs/day) ☎*418-648-7766*
Entertainment – For current entertainment schedules, consult the free tourist publications *Québec Scope and Voilà Québec,* and the weekly cultural newspaper *Voir* (French), or review the arts and entertainment section of the newspapers (weekend editions). Tickets for major entertainment or sports events may be purchased at the venue or through **Billetech** ☎*418-643-8131.*

Sports – Ice Hockey: *Remparts de Québec* (Canadian Hockey League), season Sept–Mar at the Colisée Pepsi: *250 Blvd. Hamel;* ☎*418-691-721; www. remparts.qc.ca.* **Baseball:** Capitales de Québec (Can-Am Baseball League) at Stade Municipal: ☎*418-521-2255;*

www.capitalesdequebec.com. **Harness Racing:** Québec Hippodrôme, Parc ExpoCité ☎*418-524-5283; www.hippo dromedequebec.ca.*

Shopping and Dining – The following streets lend themselves well to strolling, window-shopping, and to discovering a good restaurant: Saint-Jean, Saint-Louis, Saint-Paul and Sainte-Anne, Petit-Champlain quarter, Côte de la Fabrique, Grande-Allée, 3rd Avenue, Cartier, and Maguire.

Quebec City's religious institutions – A $2 guide available from the Corporation du patrimoine et du tourisme religieux de Québec gives information and walking tours of Quebec's religious heritage: ☎*418-694-0665; www. patrimoine-religieux.com.*

WHERE TO STAY

The accommodations listed below have been chosen for their ambience, location or value for money. Prices reflect the cost for a standard double room (two people) in high season (not including any applicable taxes). Room prices may be considerably lower off-season, and many hotels offer discounted weekend rates. The ⊿ *symbol indicates a swimming pool on the premises; the* Spa *symbol indicates the presence of a full-service spa.*

$-$$ Auberge internationale de Québec – *19 Rue Sainte-Ursule.* &☎*418-694-0755 or 1-866-694-0950. www.hostellingquebec.com. 275 beds.* Located within the walls of the Old City, this large, historic hostel is a member of Hostelling International. Open year-round, it offers **dorm-style rooms** accommodating two to eight people, as well as private rooms with or without ensuite bathroom. The **private rooms** provide the best value for money in the walled city. **Family rooms** (for up to five people) with a bathroom are available. Both a cafeteria and kitchen are available on site for hostelers. Common rooms allow for rest and conversations.

$$-$$$ Hôtel Belley – *249 Rue Saint-Paul.* ✗&P☎*418-692-1694 or 1-888-692-1694, www.oricom.ca/belley. 8 rooms.* Old World charm in the form of brick walls and exposed beams, coupled with a great location in the Old Port, make for a comfortable and reasonably priced stay here that is ideal for families or budget conscious couples. **$$$ L'Hôtel du Vieux Québec** – 1190 Rue St-Jean. ✗ & P ☎418-692-1850 or 1-800-361-7787. www.hvq.com. 45 rooms. A good bet for families and student groups, this carefully restored century-old brick hotel in the Latin Quarter boasts lovely rooms with sofas, private baths and mini-refrigerators; some even have kitchenettes. During July-Aug rates include continental breakfast and one-hour orientation on Quebec's culture.

$$$ Monte Cristo restaurant is cozy and very innovative. Member of *The Leading Hotels of the World*.

Simply decorated rooms rest above the **Taverne Belley ($)**, a popular local hangout that serves salads and sandwiches. The hotel also rents apartments across the street for longer stays.

$$$-$$$$ Château Bonne Entente – 3400 Chemin Sainte-Foy, near Rte 540. ✗ & P Spa ☎418-653-5221 or 1-800-463-4390. www.chateaubonneentente. com. 163 rooms. Occupying a landscaped, wooded site convenient to both Old Quebec and the airport, the Château Bonne Entente offers the charms of a country inn while supplying the amenities of a 5-star hotel. Pamper yourself with massages, an outdoor heated whirlpool and other spa services at the Amerispa. Guest rooms boast distinct décor; family suites feature bunk beds and toys for the kids. A new section, *Urbania*, is full of urban chic.

$$$-$$$$ Hôtel Dominion 1912 – 126 Rue Saint-Pierre. & P ☎418-692-2224 or 888-833-5253. www.hoteldominion. com. 60 rooms. Located in a nine-story commercial building constructed in 1912 for Dominion Fish and Fruit, Ltd., this Québécois-owned boutique hotel sits in the heart of the Old Port district. Stained glass and ironwork highlight the exquisitely decorated lobby and reading room. Natural light floods the spacious, high-ceilinged guest rooms through tall windows, and goose-down duvets and pillows wrap guests in comfort. Rate includes a refined continental breakfast.

$$$$-$$$$$ Auberge Saint-Antoine – 8 Rue Saint-Antoine. ✗ & P ☎418-692-2211 or 1-888-692-2211. www.saint-antoine.com. 94 rooms. A renovated 1822 warehouse and an adjoining 1720s English merchant's house are located on one of the city's major archaeological sites. Artifacts from the digs are displayed in the hotel, offering a unique way to learn more about daily life in 17C-19C Quebec. Several rooms and suites—many with the original stone walls and hand-hewn beams—offer stunning views of the St. Lawrence River or the city's fortifications. Member of the *Relais & Châteaux*.

$$$$-$$$$$ Fairmont Le Château Frontenac – 1 Rue des Carrières. & ✗ Spa P ☎418-692-3861 or 1-800-441-1414. www.fairmont.com. 618 rooms. Built in 1892, the regal copper-roofed Château Frontenac towers above Old Quebec as the most enduring symbol of the city. Over the years, this grande dame has hosted the likes of Queen Elizabeth and Sir Winston Churchill. The bustling lobby, lined with elaborate wood paneling, reflects the opulence of those bygone days. Well-appointed rooms vary in size (some are relatively small), shape and view; amenities include a large gym, as well as baby-sitting and limousine service. The hotel's restaurant, **Le Champlain ($$$$)**, serves French/Québécois dishes that celebrate produce from the *terroir* (region). The hotel bar provides great views of the river and a break from the crowds of tourists.

$$$$$ Ice Hotel Quebec – 143 Rue Duchesnay, Pavillion l'Aigle, Saintte-Catherine-de-la-Jacques-Cartier. Open early Jan–late Mar, weather permitting. ✗☎418-875-4522 or 1-877-505-0423. www.icehotel-canada.com. 34 suites. Quebec City hosts the first ice hotel in North America (the second in the world after Jukkasjarvi, Sweden). Fashioned from 10,000 tons of snow and 350 tons of ice, this unique property features an ice chapel (where you can be married or re-exchange vows), two art galleries and a movie theatre. Take the chill off with a cocktail from the **Absolut Bar** before bedding down inside cozy sleeping bags (provided) nestled on deer pelts. One-night accommodations include an Absolut vodka cocktail, a four-course meal in Le Sous-Bois dining room and a buffet breakfast.

Guided tours are available (☞$15 day visit; $13 night visit) if you don't stay overnight.

WHERE TO EAT

The establishments below were selected for their ambience, location and value for money. Prices indicate the average cost of an entrée (main course) and dessert for one person (not including tax, gratuity or beverages). Most restaurants are open daily—except where noted—and accept major credit cards. Call for information regarding hours of operation and reservation policy.

Additional restaurants are listed throughout this guide in the form of Digressions. See Index for a complete listing of eateries described in the text.

$-$$ Portofino Bistro Italiano – *54 Rue Couillard.* P ☎418-692-8888 & 1-866-692-8882. **Italian**. This lively trattoria is located in a home from 1760. You can choose from more than 20 varieties of homemade pasta and 30 different wood-fired pizzas, complimented by a good Italian wine from Portofino's extensive list. You could also sample specialties such as veal scallopini and rack of Quebec lamb. Throw in the noise level of a good time and the flags of popular Italian soccer teams, and even the most reticent in your party will soon be singing "Amore."

$$-$$$ Le Café du Monde – *84 Rue Dalhousie (Old Port).* &☎418-692-4455. **French**. Find delicious staples like *steak-frites* (steak and French fries), *magret de canard* (breast of duck) and *moules* (mussels) in this popular Parisian-style bistro. In addition to the tasty food, a cozy atmosphere and gregarious waiters in white aprons

Café du Monde

make for a pleasant dining experience in a large and lively dining room.

$$$-$$$$ Le Continental – *26 Rue St-Louis.* &☎418-694-9995. *www.restaurantcontinental.com.* **Continental**. One of the oldest restaurants in the city located in an 1845 mansion, this local favorite near Château Frontenac serves up classic specialties such as rack of lamb and duckling à l'orange as well as seafood and steak. Professional service prevails in the dining room, where dark blue walls and wood paneling impart a simple elegance enjoyed by the city's bourgeoisie.

$$$-$$$$ Le Saint-Amour – *48 Rue Sainte-Ursule.* ☎418-694-0667. *www. saint-amour.com.* **French-Québécois**. Dine in casual elegance here in the tile-floored Winter Garden, the Saint-Amour's cheery atrium. *Foie gras de canard du Québec* (Quebec duck foie gras), *saisie de caribou des Inuits aux baies de genièvre* (Inuit caribou steak with juniper berries) and *crème brûlée à la mure* (blackberry crème brûlée) typify the traditional cuisine crafted with a nouvelle twist by chef Jean-Luc Boulay. Treat yourself to the nine-course *menu découverte,* where each dish finds its perfect match from the wide-ranging international wine list.

to support restoration of Place Royale. The archaeological and restoration work began in 1970 and continues today. The Lower Town's commercial vocation still marks the area, as evidenced in the market squares, wharves, and warehouses.

Walking Tour

2.2km/1.4mi.
&Map QUEBEC BASSE-VILLE.

From Dufferin Terrace, take the steep Frontenac stairway to the Lower Town. Follow Côte de la Montagne down the hill to the Casse-Cou stairway on the right descending to Rue du Petit-Champlain. A funicular (cable car) also connects Dufferin Terrace (in front of Château Frontenac) to the Lower Town (in service year-round, daily 7.30am–11.30pm; ⬡*$1.75;* ☎*418-692-1132; www.funiculaire-quebec.com.*

▶ *Begin the tour at Rue du Petit-Champlain.*

Maison Louis-Jolliet (Louis-Jolliet House)

16 Rue du Petit-Champlain.
Completed in 1683 according to plans by the French stonecutter and architect, Claude Baillif, this two-story stone structure was owned by Louis Jolliet, who "discovered" the Mississippi River along with Father Jacques Marquette in 1673. Since 1879 the house served as the lower station for the funicular linking the Upper and Lower towns.

Verrerie La Mailloche★ (Glassblowing studio)

58 Rue Sous-le-Fort, at the intersection of Rue du Petit-Champlain. ⏰*Open mid-Jun–Oct, daily 9am–10pm; rest of the year, 9.30am–5pm. Glassblowers at work Wed–Sun.* ⏰*Closed Jan 1 & Dec 25.* ☎*418-694-0445 & 1-866-694-0445. www.lamailloche.com.*
This studio/museum introduces visitors to the fascinating art of glassblowing. Begin in the studio, where examples of beautiful, richly colored glass are on display. Glassblowers can be seen at work here, carefully extracting molten glass from red-hot ovens and using a variety of tools to shape the formless lumps into vases, carafes, plates, and cups. Panels describe the various stages of the process, and the blowers themselves answer questions quite willingly.
Second-floor galleries display a variety of glassware from different countries, including Italy, France, and England; note also panels recounting the history of glass-making from the third millennium BC.

Rue du Petit-Champlain★

Extending along the foot of the cliff, this cobblestone pedestrian alley was developed in the 1680s. First known as Rue De Meulles, the street was renamed Rue du Petit-Champlain (Little

Champlain Street) when the larger Boulevard Champlain, situated parallel to it along the river, was created during the 19C. The early wooden dwellings along the street were inhabited by craftsmen and Laborers until the 19C, when Irish immigrants who found work associated with the port moved into the district. Much of the neighborhood fell into decay in the early 20C as a result of the economic decline of the port. Recent restoration work carried out by a joint public and private effort has transformed the street into a festive district enlivened by restaurants, boutiques and art galleries. It is deemed the "oldest commercial district in North America."

▶ *At the end of Rue du Petit-Champlain, turn left onto Blvd. Champlain.*

Maison Chevalier★ (Chevalier House)

Corner of Rue du Marché-Champlain and Blvd. Champlain, on Place Royale. ⏰*Open Jun 24–Labor Day, daily 9.30am–5pm; rest of the year, Tue–Sun 10am–5pm (Nov–Apr weekends only).* ☎*418-646-3167 & 1-866-710-8031.*

Address Book

SHOPPING

PETIT-CHAMPLAIN SHOPPING
(*www.quartier-petit-champlain.qc.ca*)
This appealing area boasts all sorts of stores, many specialising in regional fine arts and crafts. Writing home? Try **L'Oiseau du Paradis** (*80 Rue du Petit-Champlain;* ☎*418-692-2679*), where the selection of fine, handmade papers includes cards, tablets, and other writing materials, as well as lamps and masks. Colorful silk scarves and ties are displayed in all their shimmering glory at **La Soierie Huo** (*91 Rue du Petit-Champlain;* ☎*418-692-5920*), where you'll also find scarves of wool and chiffon. **La Dentellière** (*56 Blvd. Champlain;* ☎*418-692-2807*) stocks an impressive selection of imported laces as well as lovely handmade examples by Quebec craftswomen.

Address Book

LE COCHON DINGUE

46 Blvd. René-Lévesque. ☎418-692-2013. www.cochondingue.com. One of Old Quebec's most inviting eateries sports a terrace and an attractive façade of stone pierced by large windows (1911). Friendly service and a relaxed ambience enhance the savory bistro food, especially steak-and-fries (the house specialty), mussels, and tempting desserts. Breakfast is plentiful and delicious.

This three-story stone building occupies the site of the **Cul-de-Sac,** a natural port discovered by Champlain in 1603. The King's shipyards, originally established at the mouth of the St. Charles River, were moved here in 1745, but the basin was filled in during the mid-18C in an effort to enlarge the area of Lower Town.

The imposing structure is composed of three separate buildings. The west wing was built in 1752 for the wealthy merchant and shipowner, Jean-Baptiste Chevalier. The construction was so solid that the walls and foundation withstood bombardment by the British in 1759. However, the house was destroyed by fire and rebuilt in 1762.

Acquired by the Quebec Government in 1956 to serve as part of the Museum of Civilization, the Chevalier House underwent extensive interior renovations, and now features exhibits on traditional Quebec architecture and furniture.

Continue to the corner of Rue du Marché-Champlain and Boulevard Champlain to enjoy the superb **view**★ of the imposing Château Frontenac, looming over the Lower Town.

▶ *Return to the Chevalier House; turn right on Rue Notre-Dame and right on Rue Sous-le-Fort.*

Batterie Royale (Royal Battery)

Rampart at the end of Rue Sous-le-Fort and Rue Saint-Pierre.

Constructed in 1691 at the request of Louis XIV, King of France, this thick, four-sided earthen rampart formed part of the fortifications designed to strengthen Quebec City's defences against the British. Situated at the edge of the river, the battery suffered from the elements and was frequently in need of repair. Destroyed during the Conquest, the defence was not rebuilt. Instead, the British erected two warehouses and a wharf on the site. The royal battery was gradually buried and forgotten until two centuries later, when archaeologists excavating the area unearthed it in 1972. Today this historic rampart has been reconstructed, and replicas of 18C cannons are positioned in 10 of the 11 embrasures; the eleventh was left empty, because any gun set at such an angle, if ever it was fired, would have destroyed buildings along Rue Saint-Pierre. During the summer, interpretive programs here demonstrate the operation of cannons during the French Regime.

▶ *Turn right on Rue Saint-Pierre, then left on Ruelle de la Place, which leads to Place Royale.*

Place Royale★★

This charming cobblestone square occupies the former site of the garden of Champlain's "Habitation." As the town developed around the fortress, a market appeared on the site. The square was known as "place Royale" after the Intendant Champigny erected a bust of Louis XIV on the site in 1686. The area flourished and became the hub of the city's economic activity until the mid-19C, when the port fell into decline.

In 1928 the French Government offered a bronze bust of Louis XIV (**1**) (a copy of Bernini's original 1665 marble sculpture conserved at Versailles) to the City of Quebec as part of that city's program to reaffirm its French heritage. However, through fear of offending the Anglophone population in the city, the monument was not erected until 1948.

Église Notre-Dame-des-Victoires★ (Church of Our Lady of the Victories)

32 Rue Sous-le-Fort. ◷*Open May–mid-Oct, 9.30am–5pm; rest of the year, Mon–Sat 10am–4pm.* ☞*Guided tours in French and English.* ☎418-692-1650 & 418-692-2533.

Place Royale

Built between 1688 and 1723, this stone edifice topped by a single spire stands on the site of Champlain's "Habitation." Built as an auxiliary chapel of Quebec City's main cathedral, it served the congregation of the Lower Town. Like most of the buildings in this part of the city, it was destroyed during the Conquest and rebuilt soon after.

The church was named in thanksgiving for two successful occasions on which Quebec City resisted the sieges of the British. Frescoes adorning the choir recall these victories: One in 1690, during which Admiral Phips' fleet was defeated by the troops of the Count de Frontenac, and the other in 1711, when most of Admiral Walker's fleet was shipwrecked during a storm. The model ship suspended in the nave represents the *Brézé,* a 17C vessel that transported French troops to Quebec.

To the left of the reliquary in the left side chapel hangs a painting of St. Genevieve (1865) by Théophile Hamel. Located above the high altar, the magnificent **retable** (1878, David Ouellet) represents the fortified city.

▸ *Leave Place Royale by Rue Notre-Dame.*

Parc La Cetière (La Cetière Park)

Archaeological excavations undertaken here in 1972 revealed the remains of foundations from structures dating back to 1685. Destroyed during the Conquest, the five stone houses of the block were rebuilt on the same foundations. However, a fire in 1948 and another in 1957 levelled the area. In the scant ruins exposed in the park, it is possible to distinguish an internal partition wall of one dwelling and a chimney base and vent opening of another.

▸ *Take Rue du Porche and turn right on Rue Thibaudeau.*

Place de Paris

To supplement the needs of the Lower Town's growing population, several market places developed near the one on Place Royale (⊘ *opposite left*). Occupying a strategic position near the St. Lawrence, the prosperous Finlay Market (1817) stood on this square until the early 1950s. Today, a contemporary sculpture entitled *Dialogue with History* (**2**) marks the center of the vast, open square. Quebecers have nicknamed it "the colossus of Quebec." A gift from the city of Paris, the sculpture, by the French artist Jean-Pierre Raynaud, was conceived to be viewed in conjunction with the bust of Louis XIV, positioned along the same axis on Place Royale; it represents the dialogue between the present-day population (symbolized by a mass) and the absolute monarch (the

Address Book

BOUTIQUE MÉTIERS D'ART

29 Rue Notre-Dame, on Place Royale.
☎*418-694-0267. www.metiers-d-art.*
qc.ca. Specializing in the work of
Quebec artisans, this little boutique
features a broad selection of art
objects—many of them truly
unique—incorporating an enormous
variety of materials. At the rear of the
gallery you'll find lovely glass sculptures, ceramics, and leaded-glass
windows in vibrant colors.

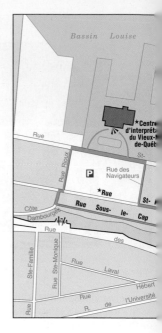

bust). The **Place Royale Interpretation
Center** (*27 Rue Notre-Dame;* 🕐*open Jun
24–Labor Day, daily 9.30am–5pm; rest
of the year, Tue–Sun 10am–5pm;* 🚫*$5;*
🔗☎ *418-646-3167; www.mcq.org*) is
located in the former home (1682) of the
successful merchant, François Hazeur. A
map of New France in 1688 and objects
recovered from archaeological digs
beneath the square bear witness to 400
years of history of this area. Multimedia presentations, exhibits, a discovery
space and guided visits help you relive
the past.

▷ *Leave the square by turning left on
Rue Dalhousie, then turn left on
Côte de la Montagne and right on
Rue Saint-Pierre.*

Rue Saint-Pierre★

During the 19C, this busy thoroughfare developed as Quebec's principal
financial district. Numerous banks and
insurance companies established their
headquarters near or along this street.
Among the noteworthy commercial
buildings that have been preserved
are the **National Bank** (*no 71*), built by
J. F. Peachy in 1862; the former **Molson
Bank** (*no 105*), now occupied by the
local post office; and the **Imperial Bank
of Canada** (*nos 113–115*), which dates
from 1913. Between Rues Saint-Antoine
and Saint-Jacques, note the low porte-
cochere of the Estèbe House, part of
the Museum of Civilization. The former
Hochelaga Bank (*no 132*) stands next to
the **Dominion Building** (*no 126*), Quebec City's first skyscraper. Dominating

the corner of Rues Saint-Paul and Saint-
Pierre, the **Canadian Bank of Commerce** (*139 Rue Saint-Pierre*) exemplifies
the Beaux-Arts style in vogue at the turn
of the century.

▷ *Turn left and continue along
Rue Saint-Paul.*

Rue Saint-Paul★

Built directly on the wharves of the St.
Charles River in 1816, this portion of Rue
Saint-Paul was widened in 1906. At that
time, every building was demolished
and replaced, with the exception of the
old Renaud warehouse (*no 82*), which
had been built in a slightly recessed spot
in 1875. Most of the houses on the south
side of the street date back to 1850 and
have been converted into antique shops,
art galleries and charming restaurants.

▷ *Turn right on Rue des Navigateurs
and left on Rue Saint-André.*

Centre d'interprétation du
Vieux-Port-de-Québec★
(Old Port of Quebec
Interpretation Center)

100 Rue Saint-André on Louise Basin.
🕐*Open early May–Aug, daily 10am–*

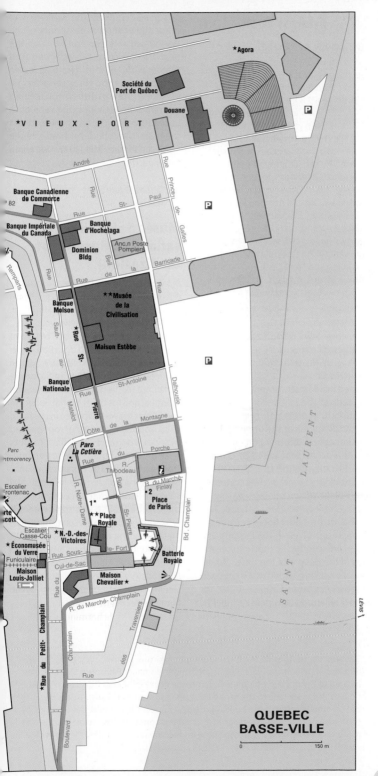

★Agora

Société du
Port de Québec

Douane

★VIEUX-PORT

André

Rue
St-

Paul

Rue
Princesse-
de-
Galles

P

Banque Canadienne
de Commerce

82

Rue

Banque Impériale
du Canada

Banque
d'Hochelaga

Dominion
Bldg

Anc.n Poste
Pompiers

Bell

Barricade

Remparts

Rue

Rue
de

la

Banque
Molson

★★Musée
de la
Civilisation

Sault-

Maison Estèbe

P

★

Rue
Banque
Nationale

Matelot

au

St-

Pierre

St-Antoine

Dalhousie

P

L A U R E N T

Côte
de la
Montagne

Parc
ntmorency

Parc
La Cetière

du

Porche

Rue
Thibodeau

R.

i

R. du Marché-
Finlay

Escalier
rontenac

Rue
Notre-Dame

Rue

1 ■

2
Place
de Paris

St-Pierre

Bd.- Champlain

S A I N T

Escalier
Casse-Cou

cott

★ N.-D.-des-
Victoires

★★Place
Royale

Rue Sous-

le-Fort

★Économusée
du Verre

Batterie
Royale

Funiculaire

Maison
Louis-Jolliet

Cul-de-Sac

Maison
Chevalier ★

★Rue du Petit- Champlain

R. du Marché- Champlain

Champlain

Traversiers

Rue

des

Boulevard

LÉVIS

Address Book

BUILD AN APPETITE...

After a long day of sightseeing, relax over a tasty meal in one of the Lower Town's inviting restaurants. **L'Ardoise** (*71 Rue Saint-Paul; ☎418-694-0213; www.lardoiseresto.com*) bistro will win you over instantly with its cheerful combination of dark woods, wicker chairs and rustic stone. The service is friendly and the food is delicious – try one of the excellent fish dishes. Or, stop in for breakfast. Located near the Museum of Civilization, **L'Échaudé** (*73 Rue Sault-au-Matelot; ☎418-692-1299; www.echaude.com*) serves a tempting variety of beautifully prepared and presented meat, fish and poultry dishes as well as salads. The service is attentive, even when there's a crowd.

5pm; early Sept–mid-Oct, daily 1pm–5pm; rest of the year, by appointment. ✆*$4.* ♿☎*418-648-3300. www.pc.gc.ca/vieuxport*

Housed in a former cement works near the bank of the St. Lawrence, this fascinating interpretation center offers an excellent look at the importance of the timber and shipbuilding industries and the prominent place of Quebec as a port city during the 19C. On the ground floor, a diorama re-creates the bustle of the wharves lining the banks of the St. Charles River during that period. Exhibits on the upper floors describe the processes involved in the logging and shipbuilding industries and explore the lives of the people of the time. Visitors can follow a log of wood as it is chopped in the forest, stored and prepared for export. Mannequins dressed in 19C

costumes represent the workers who made the economic prosperity of the period possible. Several films on the port are shown in the activity room (*atelier d'animation*). The glassed-in terrace on the top floor serves as an excellent **viewpoint** for observing modern port activities; the view onto Lower Town from here is superb. Across the basin, the cylindrical towers of the Stadacona Paper Mill (1927) dominate the waterfront.

▸ *Return to Rue Saint-Paul by Rue Rioux.*

Musée de la civilisation★★ (Museum of Civilization)

Main entrance on 85 Rue Dalhousie. ⏱*Open Jun 24–Labor Day, daily 9am–7pm; rest of the year, Tue–Sun 10am–5pm.* ✆*$10.* ☎*418-643-2158. www.mcq.org.*

Occupying the entire block between Rues Saint-Antoine and de la Barricade, the award-winning structure by the prominent architect, **Moshe Safdie**—acclaimed for his Habitat '67 complex in Montreal and for the National Gallery of Canada in Ottawa—opened in the fall of 1988. Topped by a copper roof pierced by stylized dormers, the edifice consists of two sleek, angular masses of limestone accentuated by a glass campanile. Between the buildings, a monumental staircase leads to a terrace overlooking the **Estèbe House** (Maison Estèbe), a 1752 stone structure preserved and integrated into the museum as a reminder of the bond between past and present. Inside the spacious entrance hall note *La Débâcle,* a massive sculpture representing ice breaking up in spring, by the Montreal artist Astri Reusch.

Rue Sous-le-Cap

Situated at the foot of the Cape Diamant rock, this narrow alley provided the only link between the Place Royale area and the smaller Faubourg Saint-Nicolas, located to the north, until the 19C. Before the development of Rue Saint-Paul, the houses that now face that artery were turned toward Rue Sous-le-Cap. Because the cramped design of the buildings made it impossible to build staircases inside the houses, outside sheds were constructed and connected to the main houses by footbridges spanning the street. These bridges are maintained by the owners.

The museum's stated purpose is to present life and culture in an open and objective manner in order to encourage the visitor to examine his or her own traditions and values with respect to those of other cultures and civilizations. The museum's collection comprises some 240,000 objects and documents in several divisions (costumes and textiles, arts, ethnology). In addition to permanent exhibits illustrating such themes as thought, language, natural resources, the human body and society, the museum organizes eight to ten temporary exhibits throughout the year, some of which are mounted at the **Chevalier House**.

Le Temps des Québécois
(People of Quebec... then and now)

Inspired by the impact of the past on Quebec's society today, this insightful permanent exhibition provides an opportunity for citizens to become reacquainted with their roots and for visitors from outside Quebec to understand the culture of the province. The objects presented evoke, with some nostalgia, the life of the French since their arrival here four centuries ago and their struggles to build a new life in an unknown land. It presents an overview of the events that have shaped Quebec and that helped create what is now clearly a unique society and identity in North America.

Nous, les premières nations
(Encounter with the First Nations)

This emotion-based permanent exhibition documents the history and culture of the First Nations and Inuit people who inhabit Quebec. Inuit art, ceremonial costumes, canoes, Atikamekw- and Algonquin-crafted bark baskets, hunting and fishing implements and Huron and Mi'kmaq ornamental baskets help visitors explore themes such as personal and collective identity and historical and contemporary perspectives on territory, autonomy and traditional ways of life. The visit ends with interviews and legend-telling with members of the First Nations by filmmaker Arthur Lamothe and internet stations for exploring aboriginal sites.

Vieux-Port★ (Old Port)

Access at the corner of Rues Dalhousie and Saint-André.

Covering an area of 33ha/81.5 acres, the port installations are located around the Pointe-à-Carcy where the St. Charles River joins the St. Lawrence. From the settlement of the colony until the mid-19C, the port played a major role in the development of Canada. Imported goods, exported furs and timber, and thousands of immigrants passed through this harbor. Activity declined in the second half of the 19C, and the port fell into disrepair.

In the mid-1980s, a revitalization project financed by the federal government changed the face of the old port with the creation of the **Agora**★ complex, which includes an open-air amphitheater built between the St. Lawrence and the Customs House, and a wide boardwalk along the river. A marina for several hundred pleasure boats complements the former maritime hub.

Édifice de la Douane
(Customs House)

2 Rue Saint-André.

Overlooking the St. Lawrence, the majestic Neoclassical structure (1856–1860) was designed by the English architect, William Thomas. Cut stone masks and masonry dressing ornament the ground floor windows. Fire ravaged the interior of the Customs House in 1864, and again in 1909, destroying the upper level and the dome. The door knocker on the main entrance originally hung on the first English Customs House established in Canada in 1793 in Quebec City. The building was completely restored between 1979 and 1981 and is still occupied by the administrative offices of the Customs Service. Today it is known as one of Quebec's most beautiful buildings and is part of the city's identity.

Société du port de Québec
(Port of Quebec Building)

Rue Saint-André. www.portquebec.ca.

Designed by local architect Thomas R. Peacock, the building (1914) stands on the site where, in 1909, a fire destroyed a grain elevator and also damaged the Customs House.

② Haute-Ville★★★ (Upper Town)

A Bit of History

Originally described as an "inhospitable rock, permanently unfit for habitation," the massive Cap Diamant (named that way because it resembles the shape of a rough diamond) was the site of Champlain's strategic Fort Saint-Louis (1620), built in the center of a staked enclosure. Enlarged in 1629 and renamed **Château Saint-Louis**, the modest wood structure was replaced by a single-story building in 1692. At the request of the Count of Frontenac, it became the official residence of the governor of the colony. Rebuilt after sustaining severe damage during the Conquest, the edifice was razed by fire in 1834.

The Upper Town was not developed until a group of wealthy merchants, the Company of One Hundred Associates (*Compagnie des Cent-Associés*), decided to increase settlement in the colony. The land belonging to a handful of seigneurs was redistributed, and the parcels owned by religious institutions were reduced. The first efforts to urbanize the Upper Town were initiated under Governor Montmagny's administration (1636–48). Though constrained by the hilly topography of the site, as well as the presence of vast lands belonging to institutions, Montmagny planned to erect a large, fortified city. The first houses appeared toward the end of the 17C, near the Place d'Armes and along Rue Saint-Louis. However, the Ursuline, Augustine and Jesuit orders long refused to divide up their land plots, and the military opposed the construction of buildings near fortifications, thus halting any rapid development of the town. By the late 18C, the buildings still reflected the administrative and religious presence in the district.

During the 19C, a new and very elegant residential neighborhood evolved along Rues Saint-Louis, Sainte-Ursule and d'Auteuil, and Avenues Sainte-Geneviève and Saint-Denis, to be surpassed only in 1880, by the Grande Allée, sometimes known as the "Champs Élysées"

of Québec City. Today, the Upper Town forms the heart of Old Quebec (Vieux-Québec), and still functions as the city's administrative center.

Walking Tour
2km/1.2mi. Map HAUTE-VILLE.

▶ *Begin the tour at Place d'Armes.*

Place d'Armes★★
Located outside the confines of the Fort Saint-Louis, the square (1620) originally served as grounds for drill exercises and parades. With the building of the citadel in the early 1900s, Place d'Armes lost its military function and became a public park. Today, this lovely green square is bordered by prestigious buildings. At its center is the **Monument de la Foi** (1) (Monument of Faith), a Gothic Revival sculpture (1916, David Ouellet) standing atop a fountain; it commemorates the third centennial of the arrival of the Récollet missionaries in Quebec. The bas-reliefs represent the arrival, in 1615, of Father Dolbeau, the city's first priest, as well as the missionary work of the Récollets and the first mass celebrated by that order.

Château Frontenac★★
Quebec City's most prominent landmark, the Fairmont Château Frontenac hotel is inextricably linked with the image of the old city. Named after Louis de Buade, Comte de Frontenac, governor of New France (1672–82, 1689–98), the hotel stands on the site of the Château Haldimand, also known as the "Vieux Château." Built in 1786 for Governor Frederick Haldimand, it faced the Château Saint-Louis, which housed the administrative services and reception rooms of the colonial government. In 1880, as part of the numerous beautification projects planned by Lord Dufferin, the idea of building a luxury hotel on the site finally took root.
Bruce Price (1843–1903), who was selected by the Canadian Pacific Railway to design the hotel, found inspiration in the chateau-style architecture that was very much in favor in the city. The American architect adapted an initial

Chateau Frontenac and Terrasse Dufferin

design by Eugène-Étienne Taché. He chose a horseshoe plan and selected copper roofing that contrasted with the brick walls adorned with cut stone. The French château style thus acquired a distinctly Canadian flavor which, up until the 1940s, became the trademark of railway companies and of Canada, a nation whose existence is closely linked to the development of railways from east to west.

Upon its opening in 1893 following completion of the Riverview wing, the hotel was an instant success. The Citadel wing (1899) and the Mont-Carmel wing (1908), bordering the Governor's Garden, were added according to Price's plans. The Rue Saint-Louis wing was annexed a few years later. Between 1920 and 1924, an imposing tower was constructed, reinforcing the hotel's monumental appearance. With the recent addition of the beautifully integrated Claude Pratt wing (1993), the hotel boasts more than 600 rooms.

The hotel's architects adorned the monument with coats of arms and emblems. The coat of arms of the Comte de Frontenac (rooster claws) can be seen above the porte-cochere leading to Rue Saint-Louis. Above the arch overlooking the courtyard is a stone engraved with the Maltese Cross; it is dated 1647 and was taken from Governor Montmagny's

Château Saint-Louis. The interior was rebuilt after a fire in 1926. The entrance and reception halls, the Salon Verchères and the Champlain dining room are eloquent examples of the careful attention brought to the design of this jewel of Canadian architecture.

🔎 *The prominence of Château Frontenac in the city's landscape can best be appreciated from high atop the citadel, from the Marie-Guyart Building observatory, or from the Lévis terrace.*

Address Book

AUX ANCIENS CANADIENS

34 Rue Saint-Louis. ☎418-692-1627. *www.auxancienscanadiens.qc.ca.* Charmingly situated in a historic white house with red trim (1675), this venerable restaurant specializes in local cuisine, offering a delicious introduction to traditional fine dining à la Québécoise. The menu lists classics—pea soup, *tourtière* (meat pie)—and newer favorites such as *feuilleté de saumon* (salmon in puff pastry). For dessert, try maple-syrup pie, or sugar tarts drizzled with cream.

▶ *Continue along Rue Saint-Louis.*

Ancien Palais de Justice★ (Old Courthouse)

12 Rue Saint-Louis.

Now housing the Ministry of Finance, this Second Empire-style building (1887) was erected on the site of the former Récollet convent and church, both destroyed by fire during the late 18C. The façades were fashioned after 16C Loire Valley châteaux. On each side of the main entrance, note the coats of arms of Jacques Cartier and Samuel de Champlain. The capitals, adorned with fleurs de lis, add a distinctly French flair to the imposing edifice.

Maison Maillou★ (Maillou House) (A)

17 Rue Saint-Louis.

Located next to Château Frontenac, this large stone structure now houses the Quebec Chamber of Commerce. Built ca. 1736 by the architect Jean Maillou (1668–1753) as his personal residence, the single-story dwelling was heightened in 1767 and enlarged on its western side in 1799. During the early 19C, the house was occupied by the British army. The metal exterior shutters on the windows date from this period. Carefully restored in 1964, the Maillou house constitutes a fine traditional urban ensemble typical of the 1800s.

At n° 25, the offices of the Consulate General of France occupy the former **Maison Kent** (Kent House) (**B**). Dating back to the 18C, this large white structure adorned with bright blue trim was rebuilt in the 1830s. The Duke of Kent, father of Queen Victoria, is said to have resided here from 1792 to 1794.

Maison Jacquet★ (Jacquet House) (C)

34 Rue Saint-Louis.

Reputedly the oldest house in Quebec City, this small one-story structure, topped by a steep red roof, was erected on land acquired by François Jacquet from the Ursuline Nuns in 1674. Architect François de la Joüe enlarged the original dwelling around 1690, adding a second story. The addition to the side was constructed in 1820. Philippe Aubert de Gaspé lived in the house from 1815 to 1824, giving the house its current name, Maison des Anciens Canadiens (home of the early Canadians), from the title of his 1863 novel. Today a fine restaurant specializing in traditional Quebec cuisine occupies the premises. It is arguably the most authentic place in the province to sample traditional Québécois food

▶ *Turn right onto Rue des Jardins and left onto Rue Donnacona.*

Monastère des Ursulines★ (Ursuline Monastery)

12 Rue Donnacona. 🕐*Open Feb–Sept, Tue–Sat 10am–noon, 1pm–5pm, Sun 1pm–5pm; Oct–Nov, Tue–Sun 1pm–4.30pm.* 👁*$5 (also includes admission to the Ursuline Museum).* ☎*418-694-0694.*

Founded in 1639 by Madame de la Peltrie and Marie Guyart (mère Marie de l'Incarnation), the Ursuline monastery is the oldest educational institution for young women in America and is still in operation today. Begun in 1641, the complex was devastated by fire in 1650 and again in 1686. The Saint-Augustin and Sainte-Famille wings, as well as the kitchen area that links them, were built during a period of reconstruction lasting from 1685 to 1715, and provide the basic outline for the square inner courtyard. The Sainte-Famille wing's steeply pitched roof exemplifies the architectural style dominant under the French Regime. In 1836, the architect Thomas Baillairgé added the Sainte-Angèle wing. Despite several new constructions during the 20C, the imposing grey complex has retained its vast garden and an orchard.

Chapel

Replacing an early 18C structure, the current chapel (1902) is designed in the eclectic style characteristic of religious architecture in Quebec at the turn of 19C. The stair-turret visible at the back of the church is reminiscent of Château-style architecture. It was added in 1889 and survived the demolition of the former chapel.

The interior is composed of two sections: The "exterior chapel," where sat the lay faithful; and the "interior chapel" used by the cloistered nuns. The stunning interior **decoration**★★ was taken from the 18C chapel and beautifully preserved, including the pulpit and sounding board surmounted by a trumpeting angel; the side retable dedicated to the Sacred Heart; and the main retable, a fine example of wood carving executed in the Louis XIV style, in the shape of a triumphal arch. These ornaments, as well as the high altar, were created between 1726 and 1736 under the supervision of the famed Quebec sculptor Pierre-Noël Levasseur. The sculptures are embellished with fine gilding applied by the Ursuline nuns, who maintained a gilding workshop for over two centuries to supply the needs of their order. The sculpted décor found in this chapel is truly unique: Figures of St. Augustine (*left niche*), St. Ursula (*right niche*) and St. Joseph (*upper niche*) represent the epitome of the art of wood carving in Quebec. The vast nuns' choir, with its stalls and galleries, is surmounted by a wooden vault adorned with cupolas. Most of the paintings decorating the chapel were acquired in Paris around 1820 by Abbot Louis-Phillipe Desjardins (1753–1833), formerly the chaplain for the Ursulines. On the right side of the nave hangs *The Parable of the Ten Virgins* by Pietro Da Cortona. On the reverse side of the façade, note the painting by Philippe de Champaigne, *Jesus in the home of Simon the Pharisian*. The nuns' choir features an anonymous work painted in France around 1670, entitled *France bringing Faith to the Hurons of New-France*. Located on the north side, a commemorative chapel houses the

Monastère des Ursulines

Doug Rogers/ MICHELIN

tomb of Marie de l'Incarnation (d. 1672), who was beatified in 1980.

Musée des Ursulines★★ (Ursuline Museum) (M²)

12 Rue Donnacona. ◷*Open May–Sept, Tue–Sat 10am–noon, 1pm–5pm, Sun 1pm–5pm; rest of the year, Tue–Sun 1pm–4.30pm.* ◷*Closed Dec 25.* ◍ *$5 (also includes admission to the Ursuline Monastary).* ☎ *418-694-0694. www. museocapitale.qc.ca.*

Since 1979, this remarkable museum has occupied the former site of the small house belonging to the order's benefactor, Madame de la Peltrie. Representing the occupations and talents of the Ursuline nuns, the collection includes works of art, archival documents, decorative arts, indigenous art and other materials tracing the heritage of the community

Address Book

FEELING HUNGRY?

Restaurants along the Rue Saint-Jean have what it takes to satisfy every taste. The charming **Casse-Crêpe Breton** (*1136 Rue Saint-Jean;* ☎*418-692-0438*) puts forth delicious crepes, both savory and sweet, served with a smile at very affordable prices. Even the most formidable thirst doesn't stand a chance at **Pub Saint-Alexandre** (*1087 Rue Saint-Jean;* ☎*418-694-0015*),

an English pub with live music where an amazing selection of 200 imported beers complement the menu of pasta, salads, sausages and steak-and-fries. Steps away from the Rue Saint-Jean, **Le Petit Coin Latin** (*8 1/2 Rue Sainte-Ursule;* ☎*418-692-2022*) is the perfect spot to enjoy breakfast, a light meal or a peaceful cup of coffee; the staff keep a selection of periodicals on hand for guests to peruse at their leisure.

from 1639 (the Ursulines' arrival in Quebec) to 1759 (the British Conquest).

The historical introduction offered in the first room on the museum's main floor immerses the visitor in that period's social and religious context. The second room, containing cabinets and various personal items, re-creates the living quarters of Madame de la Peltrie. Handicrafts on view here illustrate the social and educational influences that the Ursuline sisters had on the young French girls of the time, and the cultural exchanges that occurred between the nuns and the Amerindians (Marie de l'Incarnation completed the first Iroquois and Algonquian dictionaries).

On the second floor, a room dedicated to monastic life offers a glance at the organization and architecture of the first monastery—an Ursuline's cell, chapel, refectory—through such items as furniture, religious costumes and kitchen utensils. On the same floor, a last room features gilding and glorious **embroideries**, two art forms for which the Ursuline nuns were renowned. Religious art of the Ursulines included in the collection are altar frontals and ecclesiastic vestments from the 17C and 18C, delicately embroidered with gold and silver threads.

▶ *Return to Rue Saint Louis by Rue du Parloir and turn right.*

Across from n° 58, on Rue du Corps-de-Garde, a cannonball is exposed in the roots of a tree. The wall of the Cavalier du Moulin park rises in the background. At n° 72, a plaque attests that General Montgomery's remains were brought here after the failed attack on Quebec City by Americans in 1775–1776.

▶ *Turn left on Rue Sainte-Ursule.*

Église Unie Saint-Pierre (Chalmers-Wesley United Church)

78 Rue Sainte-Ursule. ◷ 🚶 *Open late Jun–late Aug, daily 9am–8pm for guided tours in English and French (on Sunday, English mass at 11.15am and French mass at 9.15am).* ☎418-692-0431.

Two Protestant congregations, one Francophone, the other Anglophone, share this Gothic Revival structure (1853, J. Wells). Staggered buttresses flank the slender steeple. Inside, note the superb stained-glass windows dating from 1909, and the elaborate woodwork adorning the apse and the pews. The early 19C organ was restored in 1985. Concerts are presented on Sundays at 6pm during summer.

Across the street stands the **Sanctuaire de Notre-Dame du Sacré-Cœur** (*n° 71*), built by F. X. Berlinguet in 1910. The sanctuary is a replica of the Gothic chapel dedicated to Our Lady of the Sacred Heart at Issoudun, in France.

▶ *Backtrack on Rue Sainte-Ursule past Rue Saint-Louis.*

On the northwest corner of Rues Saint-Louis and Sainte-Ursule stood the first city hall of Quebec City, founded in 1833. When the present City Hall opened in 1896, combining under one roof the administrative and judicial offices for the city, row houses were erected by David Ouellet along Rue Sainte-Ursule (*n°s. 60–68*), lending the street a picturesque appearance.

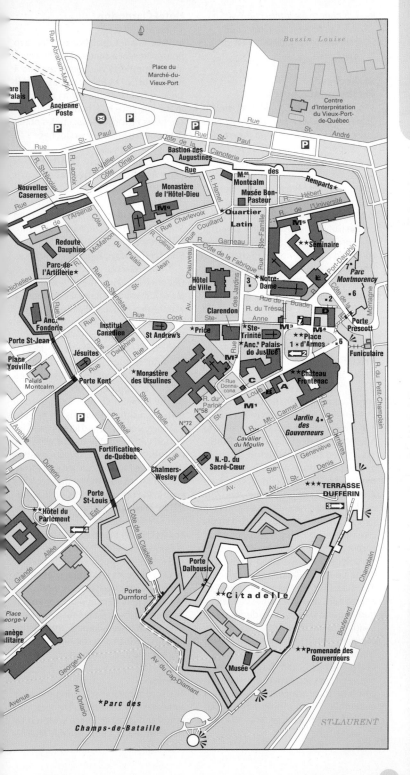

Rue Abraham-Martin

Bassin Louise

Place du
Marché-du-
Vieux-Port

gare
Palais

Ancienne
Poste

Centre
d'Interprétation
du Vieux-Port-
de-Québec

Rue St-Paul

Rue St-André

Rue St-Paul

R. St-Nicolas

R. St-Vallier Est

Côte Dinan

R. Lacroix

Côte de la Canoterie

Bastion des
Augustines

Rue des Remparts ★

Nouvelles
Casernes

Rue de l'Arsenal

Monastère
de l'Hôtel-Dieu

M6

Mme Montcalm

Musée Bon-
Pasteur

★Quartier
Latin

R. de l'Université

M5

★★Séminaire

Redoute
Dauphine

Côte du Palais

Rue McMahon

Rue Charlevoix

R. Collins

R. Couillard

Rue Garneau

Ste-Famille

Rue Ste-Famille

E

Parc-de-
l'Artillerie ★

Rue St-Jean

Chauveau

Côte de la Fabrique

Hôtel
de Ville

3

★Notre-
Dame

Rue de Buade

Rue du Trésor

7 ★ Parc
Montmorency

6

Anc.ne
Fonderie

Rue St-Stanislas

Cook

Av. des Jardins

Clarendon

Ste-Anne

R. du Trésor

Rue Ste-Anne

2

D

Porte
Prescott

Institut
Canadien

St Andrew's

★Price

★Ste-
Trinité

M3

M4

Porte St-Jean

Rue Dauphine

M2

★Anc.n Palais
de Justice

1 ★★Place
d'Armes

2

6

Place
Youville

Jésuites

Porte Kent

★Monastère
des Ursulines

Rue Donnacona

C

Rue St-Louis

B A

★★Château
Frontenac

Funiculaire

R. du Petit-Champlain

Palais
Montcalm

Rue Ste-Ursule

Rue du Parloir

N°58

M1

Mt-Carmel

Jardin
des
Gouverneurs

4

Rue des Carrières

P

N°72

St-

Cavalier
du Moulin

Geneviève

Fortifications-
de-Québec

Rue d'Auteuil

Rue

Chalmers-
Wesley

N.-D. du
Sacré-Cœur

Ste-

Av.

Denis

★★★TERRASSE
DUFFERIN

Dufferin

Porte
St-Louis

★★Hôtel du
Parlement

4

Côte de la Citadelle

3

Grande Allée Est

Porte
Dalhousie

Porte
Durnford

★★Citadelle

Place
George-V

★★Promenade des
Gouverneurs

Manège
Militaire

George-VI

Musée

Av. du Cap-Diamant

Champlain

Boulevard

Avenue

Av. Ontario

★Parc des

Champs-de-Bataille

ST-LAURENT

323

▶ *Continue to the intersection with Rue Sainte-Anne, turn right and continue to the intersection with Rue Cook.*

St. Andrew's Presbyterian Church

5 Rue Cook (Rue Sainte-Anne). ⊘Open Jul–Aug, Mon–Fri 10am–4pm. A bilingual guide shows visitors around the church. On Sundays, English mass at 10.30am. ♿☎ 418-694-1347. www.standrews quebec.ca

Built in 1810 for Presbyterian Scots in Quebec City, the church was enlarged in 1823. Its steeple recalls the one found on the Holy Trinity Anglican Cathedral (♿opposite). Initially, the congregation consisted almost entirely of the Fraser Highlanders, a battalion in General Wolfe's army of 1759. Inside, the ornate main altar faces the former governor's gallery.

▶ *Continue along Rue Sainte-Anne.*

Price Building★

65 Rue Sainte-Anne.

Quebec City's first skyscraper rises conspicuously over the Upper Town. Designed by Montreal architects, Ross and MacDonald, it was built in 1930 to house the head office of Price Brothers, famed for introducing the pulp and paper industry to the Saguenay region. The 16-story building stands on a narrow piece of land some 24m/78ft wide. Its profile resembles a ziggurat, a pyramid with a series of upward steps. Like numerous other North American corporations at that time, Price Brothers selected the Art Deco style, integrating embellishments that reflected its Canadian origin (pinecones, squirrels, aboriginals) and its business activities (lumber and paper). In order that the building blend in with the old city, the company opted for a pavilion roof with copper covering.

In the entrance hall, bas-reliefs and copper doors (entrance and elevator) combine to produce a fine Art Deco ensemble. The building has housed municipal offices since 1984.

Hotel Clarendon

57 Rue Sainte-Anne.

In 1858, Charles Baillairgé erected two houses here for a printer named Desbarats. The property was converted into a hotel in 1875. The following year, an Art Deco entrance pavilion was annexed. In the entrance hall, two large bronze torchères provide rare examples of the Art Nouveau influence in Quebec.

La Cathédrale Holy Trinity★ (The Anglican Cathedral of the Holy Trinity)

31 Rue des Jardins. ⊘Open mid May–mid Oct, Mon–Sat 10am–5pm; rest of year and Sun 10am–2pm. On Sundays, English choral Eucharist at 11am and French mass at 9.30. On Thursdays, English mass at noon. ♿☎418-692-2193.

Designed in 1799 by the army engineers Major Robe and Captain Hall, this edifice was the first Anglican (Episcopal) cathedral to be built outside the British Isles. Completed in 1804, the building is modeled on the Church of St.-Martin-in-the-Fields, in London (England), designed by the architect James Gibbs. Erected on part of a property formerly owned by the Récollet Order, the cathedral features a simple floor plan. The central nave, side aisles and lateral galleries dotted with a double row of windows contribute to the church's innovative design. The façade is turned away from Place d'Armes so that the chancel faces east, in the time-honored Christian tradition. The church steeple, which contains an eight-bell peal, is actually several feet higher than that of the Our Lady of Quebec Basilica. The pitch of the roof had to be raised approximately 3m/10ft in 1816, since its low grade proved too weak to sustain massive snowfall. As a result, the pediment appears somewhat heavier and the great height of the massive church tower seems slightly diminished. A Celtic cross fashioned in AD 542 marks the church entrance.

Interior

The wooden vault spanning the nave simulates stucco coffers. The Ionic columns and pilasters were sculpted by the Montrealer, Louis-Amable Quévillon, who was nearly excommunicated for having participated in the interior decoration of a non-Catholic church. King George III provided the funding for the cathedral, and sent English oak from the Royal Forests of Windsor for the pews. On the left side of the tribune is a royal pew reserved for the British monarch, head of the Church of England, or his/her representative. To the right of the altar, the bishop's chair was carved out of wood from an elm tree that had flourished in the churchyard for some two hundred years. The cathedral treasure, which includes silverware donated by Georges III, is exhibited on special occasions.

To the right of the cathedral stand a large Neoclassical rectory (1841) and a church hall (1890). In summer, the courtyard is a gathering place for artists.

▷ *Return to Rue Sainte-Anne.*

In the quaint pedestrian street of **Rue du Trésor**, artists exhibit sketches and engravings depicting typical scenes of the city.

Ancien Hôtel Union (Former Union Hotel)

Facing the Place d'Armes, the large structure (1805–12) exemplifies Palladian-style architecture, characterized by a simple plan, a massive shape, sash windows, and a low-pitched roof.

Musée du Fort★ (Fort Museum) (M⁴)

10 Rue Sainte-Anne. Open Feb–Mar & Nov, Thu–Sun 11am–4pm; Apr–Oct, daily 10am–5pm. $8. 418-692-2175. http://museedufort.com.

Erected in 1840, this square white building topped by a grey roof was modified in 1898, giving it a whimsical appearance. An excellently narrated sound and light presentation (*30min*) cast upon a large-scale model of Quebec during the 18C traces the city's military and civil history from its foundation in 1608 until the American invasion of 1775-76. The maquette itself provides a unique perspective of the city's distinctive topography.

▷ *Turn left on Rue du Fort and continue to Rue Buade.*

Ancien bureau de poste (Old Post Office) (D)

Entrance on 5 Rue du Fort. Open early Jul–early Oct, Mon–Fri 8am–8pm (Tue & Wed 5.45pm), weekends 9.30am–5pm; rest of the year, Mon–Fri 8am–5.45pm. Closed major holidays. 418-694-6102.

Constructed as the city's main post office in 1873, this edifice presents an imposing façade adorned with Beaux-Arts embellishments. Faced with decorated cut stone, it was enlarged to more than twice its original size in 1914. Above the entrance, a carved bas-relief advertises the Chien d'Or (The Golden Dog), an inn that occupied the site until 1837. The building was renamed the Louis S. St-Laurent Building in honor of the former Canadian prime minister and continues to operate as a working post office. Inside, the Canadian Parks Service presents exhibits on the development of historical and natural sites in Canada.

Monsignor de Laval Monument (2)

In front of the old post office stands a monument to Msgr. François de Montmorency-Laval (1623–1708), first bishop of Quebec. It was erected in 1908, as part of the celebrations marking the bicentennial of his death. Installation of the monument, designed by sculptor Louis-Philippe Hébert, necessitated the demolition of an entire block of eight houses, thus creating an imposing public square.

Rue Buade ends at the **Charles-Baillairgé Stairway** (1893), named in honor of the architect who, after an illustrious career designing buildings, devoted his talents to civil engineering. This cast-iron stairway is one of several Baillairgé designed for the city.

▷ *Descend the stairs and continue up Côte de la Montagne.*

From the foot of the stairs, note the monumental false front of the old post office dominating the Lower Town.

Address Book

MERRY AND BRIGHT

No matter what the season, **La Boutique Noël de Québec** (*47 Rue Buade; ☎418-692-2457*) attracts young and old with its brightly lit trees and myriad decorations, including intriguing strands of lights and an enormous variety of Christmas-tree balls.

Palais archiépiscopal (Archbishop's Palace) (E)

2 Rue Port-Dauphin.
This Neoclassical structure (1847) replaced the first archbishop's residence, erected in the late 17C in Montmorency Park. As part of Lord Dufferin's beautification projects in the late 19C, a false front was erected toward the Côte de la Montagne, making the building visible from the St. Lawrence River. The original façade of the large edifice dominates the main courtyard, leading to the old seminary.

▸ *Return to Rue Buade.*

Facing the Beaux-Arts style presbytery (*16 Rue Buade at the corner of Rue du Fort*), a plaque draws attention to the foundations of a funeral chapel thought to contain the tomb of Samuel de Champlain. There are in fact at least ten theories concerning the possible location of Champlain's tomb!

Basilique-cathédrale Notre-Dame-de-Québec★ (Basilica-Cathedral of Our Lady of Quebec)

🕐 *Open May–mid-Oct, daily 9am–2.30pm; rest of the year, daily 9am–4.15pm.* 🗣 *Guided tours (French and English) plus many events year round: Check calendar on website.* ♿☎*418-694-0665. www.patrimoine-religieux.com.*
Declared a historical monument in 1966, the basilica is the most European of Quebec's churches. Its complex architectural history has yielded an impressive structure that bears witness to the contributions of three generations of Quebec's renowned family of architects.

Early construction

In 1674, following a papal order creating the Diocese of Quebec, the original structure here (1650) was consecrated as a cathedral. Under the direction of François de Laval, who had been appointed Bishop of New France, the building was enlarged and renovated. In 1743, Gaspard Chaussegros de Léry, the royal engineer, enlarged the apse, raised the nave and added to it a clerestory and side aisles by opening arches into the walls of the old nave, leaving thick pillars in place. A new façade was built overlooking the market square, now known as Place de l'Hôtel de Ville. Completed in 1749, the structure was destroyed during the Conquest of 1759.

A Baillairgé Masterpiece

Reconstruction of the church took place between 1768 and 1771 and was modeled on Chaussegros de Léry's work. Jean Baillairgé (1726–1805), the first in the renowned Baillairgé family of joiners, painters, sculptors and architects, rebuilt the south belfry with its two openwork drums surmounted by domes. In 1787, after studying at the Royal Academy of Painting and Sculpture in Paris, his son, François Baillairgé (1759–1830), undertook the task of decorating the interior. He designed the plans for the magnificent baldachin, executed by André Vermare.

François' son, Thomas Baillairgé (1791–1859), continued his father's work and, in 1843, designed the monumental Neoclassical façade whose construction was interrupted two years later when the base of the first of two projected towers showed signs of weakness. Charles Baillairgé (1826–1906), whose father was a cousin of Thomas, designed the plans in 1857 for the brass-plated cast-iron gate that encloses the porch, which enabled him to declare that the building of the monument was indeed a family effort. The church was consecrated as a basilica in 1874 to emphasize its history and status as one of Canada's most important churches.

After the structure was destroyed by fire on December 22, 1922, the city' religious authorities decided to resto it to its original appearance in orde retain the familiar image of "Msgr. de Laval's church." The current monument was reconstructed between 1923 and 1925 from old plans and photographs.

Interior

Recreated after the devastating fire of 1922, the interior evokes the principal features of the 18C cathedral despite the use of concrete, steel, and plaster. Immediately upon entering, the eye is drawn to the light and delicately sweeping baldachin executed by André Vermare. The luminous stained-glass windows of the upper level are French in origin and represent saints, evangelists and archangels. Those of the lower level are German and American and recall important events in the life of the Virgin Mary. The cathedral crypt (*guided tour only; inquire at the reception desk*) houses the sepulchres of Quebec's bishops and of some of the governors of New France. The lamp in the chapel on the right near the entrance to the crypt was a gift from Louis XIV. The Casavant organ of 5,239 pipes is flanked by statues of shepherds, one reading (symbolizing inspiration), and the other playing an instrument (symbolizing improvisation). In 1993, the remains of Msgr. de Laval were interred in a small commemorative chapel (*right side aisle*); a small display to the right of the choir presents his life and works.

Well worth seeing is a 30-minute multimedia "fresco" entitled *Québec Expérience*, which transports the viewer through time to tell the story of the basilica and of Quebec City (*Continuous viewings in English and French, mid-May–mid-Oct, daily 10am–10pm; mid-Oct–mid-May, 10am–5pm; $8; &418-694-4000; tickets available in the cathedral*).

Place de l'Hôtel de Ville

This large open square, designed in conjunction with the cathedral in 1650, became the principal marketplace of the Upper Town in the 18C. Its commercial vocation ended in the late 1880s with the construction of City Hall. Placed in its center, the 1923 **Cardinal Taschereau monument (3)** by André Vermare, is dedicated to the first Canadian cardinal. The bas-reliefs represent the institution

Basilique Notre-Dame-de-Québec

Doug Rogers/MICHELIN

of the Forty Hour Prayer in the diocese (*facing the cathedral*), the career of the Superior of the Quebec Seminary (*facing Rue des Jardins*) and the Cardinal aiding Irish victims of the typhoid epidemic at Grosse-Île, in 1848 (*facing Rue Buade*).

Hôtel de Ville de Québec (Quebec City Hall)

2 Rue des Jardins.

The majestic structure stands on land formerly belonging to the Jesuit Order, who erected a college and church on this site in the very center of Old Quebec, in 1666. The college was demolished in 1877, to be replaced by the City Hall, built in 1896 according to plans by Georges-Émile Tanguay. Stylistically, Tanguay's building presents a curious blend of the Second Empire and French Chateau styles, embellished with Richardsonian Romanesque detailing.

Located north of the basilica, Quebec City's **Quartier Latin**★ (Latin Quarter) is the oldest residential district in the Upper Town. Formerly belonging to the Quebec Seminary, the land was divided up during the late 17C, while the parcelling of other vast properties, belonging to the Ursulines, Jesuits and Augustinian nuns, did not commence until a century later. The narrow streets crisscrossing the quarter are remnants of the passageways that once connected these large holdings. Between 1820 and 1830, the craftsmen who initially populated the district gave way to a French-speaking bourgeoisie, eager to reside in the vicinity of the seminary and its clergy. After World War II, influences from the Parisian existentialist movement gave rise to a bohemian student life in Old Quebec at the same time that Laval University was expanding into the district, occupying dozens of old houses. Though still inhabited by a few longtime residents and families, the neighborhood today caters mainly to students.

Séminaire de Québec★★ (Quebec Seminary)

This influential institution was founded in 1663 by Msgr. de Laval to train and recruit priests destined to work in the newly created parishes of New France. In 1852 the seminary was formally granted a university (Université Laval), Canada's first Francophone higher education institution. In 1950 Laval University moved to a new campus in Sainte-Foy but the university's school of architecture remained here, and today occupies several of the structures in the complex.

Vieux-Séminaire (Old Seminary)

Entrance at 1 Côte de la Fabrique (Welcome Pavilion). ☛*Guided tours of the seminary available in summer (includes admission to the Museum of French America).* ♿ 🅿 *($11/day)* ☎418-692-3891.

The old seminary comprises three sections arranged around an inner court, as is typical of French monastic architecture in the 16C and 17C. The visitor enters by a porte-cochere framed by a portal designed by François Baillairgé and bearing the Seminary's coat of arms. Traditional building crafts were employed in the construction of the three wings, creating a stylistically homogeneous ensemble.

The **Procure Wing** was built between 1678 and 1681 to house the Grand Séminaire; its walls and vaults survived fires in 1701, 1705 and 1865. After the last fire, the building was raised by one stone story. The sundial on the façade bears the inscription *Nos jours passent comme une ombre* ("Our days pass like a shadow"). Within this wing is the marvelous **Msgr. Olivier Briand Chapel**★, noteworthy for the fine wood

Address Book

ⓒ*For price ranges, see the Legend on the cover flap.*

EATING WITH A VIEW

1225 Cours du Général-De Montcalm, in Loews Le Concorde Hotel (between Grande-Allée Avenue and the Plains of Abraham). ☎418-647-2222 & 1-800-463-5256. www.loewshotels.com.
Accessible by a panoramic elevator on the 28th floor of **Loews Le Concorde Hotel** ($$$-$$$$), **L'Astral restaurant** ($$-$$$) tops the list for dining rooms with a great view of the city. Quebec City's only revolving restaurant serves continental cuisine prepared with regional ingredients and affords views of the St. Lawrence, Old Quebec City, Île d'Orléans, Lévis and the Charlevoix Coast. The aerial view is particularly spectacular in winter. In summer, watch the sun set to live piano music (*Tue–Sun evenings*), enjoy a nightcap or discover the popular Sunday brunch (10am–3pm).

BARBECUE

693 Ave. Grande-Allée Est. ☎418-653-1234 *(restaurant and delivery service).* www.st-hubert.com. *At the end of a strip of expensive, somewhat touristy restaurants of the chic Grande-Allée, sits a flagship location of the famous Quebec chain of roast chicken restaurants:*
St-Hubert Barbecue ($-$$). *Here you can say you enjoyed a genuine Quebec food experience at very affordable prices. It is the only family restaurant in the area, but there is also a "trendy bistro" section with a bar. The wood and stone décor is cozy. "Le St-Hubert" on Grande-Allée is a busy place, so don't be surprised if you must queue up, but service is brisk and you should not wait too long. What makes "les rôtisseries St-Hubert" so popular? A tasty, satisfying menu and high, reliable standards. You can have anything on the menu delivered to a hotel room.*

panelling adorning its walls. Executed by the master sculptor Pierre Émond in 1785, the décor exemplifies two distinct styles—Louis XIII and Louis XV. Émond also designed the olive branches framing the engraving of the *Marriage of the Virgin* that dominates the altar piece.

To the right, the **Parloirs Wing** or former Petit Séminaire dates from 1823, as does the **Congregation Wing,** where the porte-cochere is located. The **Congregational Chapel** here, a low-ceilinged shrine devoted to the Virgin Mary, is divided into three naves, separated by two rows of Ionic columns. The main altar, flanked by two similar columns, is surmounted by a gilded **statue**★ of the Virgin, one of the few known wood carvings crafted by the hand of the architect, Thomas Baillairgé.

Musée de l'Amérique Française★ (Museum of French America) (M⁵)

Main entrance at 2 Côte de la Fabrique (Welcome Pavilion). ◯*Open late Jun–Labor Day, daily 9.30am–5pm; rest of the year, Tue–Sun 10am–5pm.* ◯*Closed Dec 25.* ◎*$6.* ♿☎*418-692-2843 1-866-710-8031. www.mcq.org.*

Operated since 1995 as part of the Museum of Civilization, the collections of the Museum of French America encompass objects and works of art reflecting France's rich historic, cultural and social heritage in North America. The museum's holdings include an extensive archive of historical documents; some 195,000 rare books and journals; European paintings from the 15C–19C and Canadian paintings from the 18C–20C; gold- and silverware for religious and domestic use; and extensive collections of textiles, furniture, scientific instruments, stamps and coins, birds and insects as well as botanical, zoological and geological specimens.

The collections are housed in three buildings, of which **Welcome Pavilion** serves as the museum's reception and information center and temporary exhibition space. The second building occupies the seminary's former outer chapel. Erected between 1888 and 1900 according to plans by J. F. Peachy, the chapel features an interior modelled

after the 19C Trinity Church in Paris. The Quebec version, made of galvanized steel painted in trompe-l'oeil, provided better protection against fire. In addition to beautiful pieces of silverware by François Ranvoyzé, Guillaume Loir, Laurent Amiot, and others, the chapel contains one of the most important collections of **relics**★ outside St. Peter's in Rome. The 16 gilded reliquary busts of the apostles were carved by Louis Jobin. The columns around the chapel are adorned with representations of the Seven Sacraments and each lamp symbolizes a gift of the Holy Spirit.

The third structure, the **Jérôme Demers Pavilion**, houses two permanent exhibits. The first, dedicated to the French experience in North America, presents the seven major Francophone communities on the continent: Quebec, Acadia, Louisiana, French Ontario, Métis, and French-American communities in the West and in New England. The second exhibit incorporates the highlights of the seminary's impressive collections to underscore the institution's religious, cultural and educational mission. Temporary thematic exhibits here invite discovery of Quebec by its provincial arts, crafts, folklore and history.

▷ *Leave the museum by Rue de l'Université and turn right on Rue Sainte-Famille. Take Rue Couillard on the left.*

Charming **Rue Couillard** received its name in the 18C, in honor of the sailor, Guillaume Couillard (1591–1663), son-in-law and heir of the lands of Louis Hébert. Its sinuous path leads past the former Hospice de la Miséricorde (n° 14), built between 1878 and 1880 for the Sisters of the Good Shepherd.

Musée Bon-Pasteur (Good Shepherd Museum)

14 Rue Couillard, between Rue Ferland and Rue Saint-Flavien. ◯*Open year-round, Tue–Sun 1pm–5pm.* ◎*$3.* ♿☎*418-694-0243. www.museocapitale.qc.ca.*

This remarkable Gothic Revival structure, with its brick walls pierced by ogive windows, serves as the main building of the **Maison Béthanie**★ (1878, David

Ouellet). The structure formerly housed the Mercy Hospice, a caring institution founded and operated by the Sœurs du Bon-Pasteur (Sisters of the Good Shepherd) as a refuge and halfway house for young women. Today the structure has been renovated as a museum tracing the history of the Good Shepherd community, a lay order founded in 1850 by Marie Fitzbach (later known as Marie-du-Sacré-Cœur). Artifacts, sculptures, furnishings, musical instruments and articles of daily life illustrate the caring and teaching vocations of the sisters, life in the community, and the activities of the order today. Several rooms re-create the atmosphere of common rooms in present-day Good Shepherd convents. Note especially the fine religious art objects crafted by the sisters, including polychromed wood statues and embroidered textiles. A video (*15min*) illustrates the mission of the community in the past and present.

▷ *Turn right on Rue Collins and continue to Rue Charlevoix.*

Monastère de l'Hôtel-Dieu de Québec (Augustine Monastery)

32 Rue Charlevoix.
The founding sisters of the Augustinian Hospitallers of Quebec, Marie Guenet de Saint-Ignace, Marie Forestier de Saint-Bonaventure and Anne Le Cointre de Saint-Bernard, took up residence in 1640 in a makeshift hospital located next to the Jesuit mission, in Sillery. In 1644, upon completion of the monastery, the nuns moved to this site in the old city. The first hospital erected by the nuns was made of wood. In 1695, François de la Joüe enlarged the structure by annexing a stone building; the two structures now form part of the convent and can be clearly seen from the garden. The hospital underwent several expansions during the 19C and 20C, reaching its current capacity in 1960.

Musée des Augustines de l'Hôtel-Dieu de Québec★ (Augustine Museum) (M⁶)

🕐*Open year-round, Tue–Sat 9.30am–noon, 1.30pm–5pm, Sun 1.30pm–5pm.*

🕐*Closed major holidays.* ♿☎418-692-2492. www.museocapitale.qc.ca.
Opened in 1958, the museum presents a collection of objects and artworks tracing the Augustinian nuns' history and heritage in New France. It includes one of the foremost collections of New France-era paintings in Quebec, including portraits of Louis XIV and the Intendant Jean Talon, as well as of the order's benefactors, the Duchesse d'Aiguillon and Cardinal Richelieu; various pieces of furniture, including Louis XIII chairs from the Château Saint-Louis; and a fine collection of surgical implements. From the museum, it is possible to descend to the cellar, where the nuns took shelter during the Conquest (when more than 40,000 cannonballs fell upon Quebec). The relics of the Blessed Catherine-de-Saint-Augustin, a nun who arrived in Quebec in 1648 and was beatified in 1989, are visible in the Catherine-de-Saint-Augustin Center.

Church★

🕐*Same hours as museum.*
To counteract the proliferation of non-Catholic community chapels that appeared in Quebec City with the influx of Protestant Irish immigrants in the early 19C, the Church of Quebec encouraged the nuns to erect a large Catholic church. Designed by Pierre Émond in 1800, under the supervision of Father Jean-Louis Desjardins, the structure features polygonal chapels and an apse, connected to the convent.
The Neoclassical façade (1835) boasts a beautifully sculpted Ionic portal created by Thomas Baillairgé. The small belfry was placed over the façade in 1931.
The sculpted, gilded wood **interior décor** was crafted by Thomas Baillairgé, between 1829 and 1832. Highlights include the high-altar **tabernacle,** a veritable small-scale model of St. Peter's in Rome; the retable, in the shape of a triumphal arch; and the basket-handle wooden vault. The painting above the altar, *The Descent from the Cross*, executed by Antoine Plamondon in 1840, was inspired by Rubens' famous masterpiece which now hangs in the Antwerp Cathedral in Belgium. The church features a collection of paintings confis-

cated from churches in Paris during the Revolution and sent to Quebec in 1817. One of these, *The Vision of Sainte-Thérèse d'Avila,* now hangs in the Notre-Dame-de-Toutes-Grâces chapel.

3 Fortifications★★

In the 17C, Quebec City played a key role in the defense of northeastern French America. As a consequence of the city's strategic location, several fortification projects were undertaken over the years. However, the construction of batteries, redoubts and cavaliers in both the Lower and Upper towns ceased following the signing of the Utrecht Treaty of 1713, which temporarily suspended hostilities between the European factions. During the peace that followed, peripheral forts were the most common means of defense.

The fortification of Quebec City resumed in 1745 in reaction to the capture of Louisbourg, on the island of Cape Breton in present-day Nova Scotia. French military engineer Gaspard Chaussegros de Léry initiated the new fortification project, which was completed by the British after the Conquest of 1759. The British erected a temporary citadel in 1783, then added four circular Martello towers (1805–12), and finally built a new, permanent citadel between 1820 and 1832. The fortifications were faced with red sandstone from a Cap-Rouge quarry.

Following the departure of the British garrison in 1871, local military authorities approved the demolition of certain city gates in order to facilitate passage between the Lower and Upper towns and the Saint-Jean and Saint-Louis faubourgs. Influenced by the historical romantic movement then popular in Europe, **Lord Dufferin**, governor-general of Canada from 1872 to 1878, insisted on the preservation of Quebec's fortifications. In 1875, he submitted a plan for the beautification of Quebec City, which included refurbishing the fortified enceinte, rebuilding the gates to the city and demolishing all the advanced military works that formed a 60m/200ft wide strip along the ramparts, in order to fully expose the complex in the manner of medieval fortifications.

As a result of Lord Dufferin's initiative, visitors can now stroll along the fortification walkways and enjoy panoramic views of the city and surrounding areas.

▸ *From Place d'Armes, follow Rue Saint-Louis to Côte de la Citadelle, turn left and follow the street to its end. Enter through the Durnford gate.*

The Citadel★★

Though the Citadel was built at a time of peace and never used for defensive purposes, its conception dates back to the founding of the city. In 1615, Samuel de Champlain proposed that a citadel be erected on the Cap Diamant heights in order to control access to the hinterlands by way of the St. Lawrence River. Engineer Chaussegros de Léry submitted a similar project in 1716 and, in 1720, he drew the plans of a citadel much like the one that was built a century later, under the supervision of Lieutenant-Colonel Elias Walker Durnford.

The star-shaped plan of the present citadel (1820–52) is typical of Vauban fortifications. Sébastien le Prestre, **marquis de Vauban** (1633–1707), military engineer and marshal of France under Louis XIV, perfected French military architecture by developing advanced works (or outworks) that protected entrances and ramparts from enemy fire. So sophisticated was the Vauban system that the British used it until the beginning of the 19C.

Surrounding the citadel were sloping earthworks known as glacis, which forced the enemy to expose itself to cannon fire from the garrison. Enemy fire, on the other hand, could not reach the stone walls unless it was exceptionally precise. The enceinte is formed of bastions linked together by curtains (straight walls). The bastions were shaped so as to protect the ditches by means of cannon fire, while the tenailles (isolated bastions located in the ditches) protected the curtains and entrances to the citadel.

View from the Citadelle

The Neoclassical **Porte Dalhousie** (Dalhousie Gate, 1830) is the main entrance to the citadel and the site of the changing of the guard ceremony (○*open Jun 24–Labor Day, daily 10am; 35min*) and the retreat (○*open Jul–Aug, Wed–Sat 6pm; 30min*). Paired columns adorn the main façade, creating a monumental effect intended to evoke military might and rigour.

Visit

Visit by guided tour (1hr) only, Apr, 10am–4pm; May–Jun 9am–5pm; Jul–Labor Day, 9am–6pm; Sept, 9am–5pm; Oct, 10am–3pm; Nov–Apr bilingual tour 1.30pm daily. ⊛*$10.* ⟨ P ⟩⊛*418-694-2815 & 1-888-773-8888. www.lacitadelle.qc.ca.*

Some areas of the Citadel are off-limits, as it is still a military base for the Royal 22nd Regiment. Guided tours begin at the powder magazine (1831), which was renovated as a chapel in 1927. The tour then leads to one of the *tenailles*, which formerly housed a prison and today serves as an annex to the Museum of the Royal 22nd Regiment. On view here are many types of arms, military decorations, uniforms and World War I artifacts. From the King's Bastion, visitors can take in a superb **view**★★ of the Château Frontenac and the Upper Town. The tour then leads past the Cap-Diamant redoubt (1693); the residence of the governor-general, partly destroyed by fire in

1976 and subsequently rebuilt; and the hospital (1849), which today functions as an administrative building. Occupying the old powder magazine (1750), the **Museum of the Royal 22nd Regiment** contains a collection of military objects from the 17C to the present, including uniformed mannequins posing as soldiers from the various regiments of New France, and several dioramas illustrating the major battles of the 18C. The tour also leads to the Prince of Wales bastion, the highest natural point in the city, from which a sweeping **view** extends over the St. Lawrence River and the Plains of Abraham.

▷ *Leave the citadel by the Durnford gate and take the path to the left, which ascends to the fortifications; continue toward the St. Lawrence River.*

The path leading to the Governor's Walk runs alongside the citadel's outer wall and the National Battlefields Park. One of the Martello towers is visible in the distance.

Promenade des Gouverneurs★★ **(Governor's Walk)**

○*Closed in winter.*

Rising over the park, a belvedere affording magnificent **views**★★ of the St. Lawrence and the Quebec region marks the beginning of this spectacular walk.

Precariously suspended between the heavens and the dark waters of the St. Lawrence along the steep cliff, the boardwalk leads from the belvedere to Dufferin Terrace. The **panorama**★ extends northeast to the Île d'Orléans, Mt. Sainte-Anne and the Laurentians.

Walking Tour of Ramparts★★ 2km/1.2mi.

Map HAUTE-VILLE.

▶ *Begin the tour at Dufferin Terrace.*

Terrasse Dufferin★★★ (Dufferin Terrace)

Stretching 671m/2,200ft above the majestic river, this popular vantage point offers breathtaking **views**★★ of the Lower Town, St. Lawrence River and surrounding region. The terrace, a large wooden boardwalk, is an extension of Lord Dufferin's beautification project. It was constructed to provide a view of the river at a time when the Lower Town was overrun by commercial buildings and warehouses.

The section of the terrace that faces Château Frontenac lies over the remains of the colonial governor's residence, the **Château Saint-Louis**, destroyed by fire in 1834. Governor Durham had a terrace built over the site. It bore his name until the present terrace was built.

Dufferin Terrace rapidly became a focal point of city life. It was electrified in 1885 and, shortly thereafter, ice slides were set up. The terrace's kiosks and public benches introduced Quebecers to urban fixtures akin to those found on Parisian boulevards and created a lively, bustling atmosphere.

Jardin des Gouverneurs (Governor's Garden)

This small park beside the Château Frontenac was created in the mid-17C for the enjoyment of the governor-general of New France. The **Wolfe-Montcalm Monument** (**4**) (1827) is a joint memorial to the two enemies who died in combat and, as was observed at the time, whose meeting resulted in the creation of the Canadian nation. The shape of the monument symbolizes death: Note the

cenotaph forming the base of the structure and, particularly, the dignified obelisk. The inscription reads in translation from Latin: "Valor gave them a common death, history a common fame, posterity a common monument."

▶ *To the right of the garden, follow Rue du Mont-Carmel to the Cavalier du Moulin park. Continue to the end of Dufferin Terrace.*

Erected in 1898, the **Samuel de Champlain Monument** (**5**), by Paul Chevré, honors the "father of New France." Nearby stands a monument made of bronze, granite and glass that commemorates the inscription of Quebec's historic district on UNESCO's World Heritage List, in December 1985. A **funicular** links Dufferin terrace to the Lower Town.

▶ *Take the Frontenac staircase and cross the Prescott gate to Montmorency Park.*

Inaugurated on July 3, 1983 to commemorate the 375th anniversary of the founding of Quebec City, the **Porte Prescott** (Prescott Gate) is a reconstruction of a previous gate that was erected on the same spot in 1797, and demolished in 1871.

Parc Montmorency (Montmorency Park)

It is here, at the summit of Côte de la Montagne, that the intendant of New France, Jean Talon, had a house built in 1667. At the end of the 17C, Msgr. de Saint-Vallier, second bishop of Quebec, purchased the house and constructed a vast episcopal palace (1691–1696). The Legislative Assembly of Lower Canada occupied the building from 1792 onwards. Reconstructed in the early 19C, the structure housed the Parliament of the Union Government, which held sessions intermittently in Quebec City, Kingston, Montreal and Toronto. It was later destroyed by fire.

The park features a **monument** (**6**) to the memory of George-Étienne Cartier, and another (**7**) to Louis Hébert, Marie Rollet and Guillaume Couillard. Created

Address Book

A NIGHT AT LE CAPITOLE

972 Rue Saint-Jean. Information & reservations ☎418-694-4444. Located just steps away from the St. John Gate, this nearly century-old building houses one of Quebec's most prestigious live-performance theatres. With a seating capacity of 1,300, the sumptuous interior lends itself to large-scale productions as well as more intimate concerts. Before or after the show (or even for breakfast), stop in at **Il Teatro** (*in the Capitole building;* ☎ *418-694-9996; www.lecapitole.com*), a charming eatery serving fine Italian cuisine in a modern, welcoming setting. In summer the terrace offers a wonderful view of Rue Saint-Jean.

by sculptor Alfred Laliberté (1918), the latter commemorates the tricentennial of the arrival of the first settlers in New France (their names are inscribed on the back of the monument).

The park provides a good view of the Quebec Seminary, in particular the five-story building currently housing Laval University's School of Architecture. From this vantage point, the visitor can appreciate the elegant **lantern** placed atop the central dome, which has become a familiar landmark in Old Quebec.

Rue des Remparts★

Until approximately 1875, this street was a mere path which ran alongside the ramparts, connecting bastions and batteries. Located across from the seminary buildings, the Sault-au-Matelot and Clergé batteries, erected in 1711, protected the Quebec harbor. Today black cannons overlooking the Lower Town permit the visitor to recapture the atmosphere of the old fortified city.

▸ *Continue along Rue des Remparts to Rue Sainte-Famille.*

Located at the foot of Rue Sainte-Famille until 1871, the Hope gate closed off access to the Upper Town. Branching off Rue des Remparts, the sinuous Côte de la Canoterie has linked the Upper

and Lower towns since 1634; it used to lead to a tiny cove, known as l'Anse à la Canoterie, that served as a merchandise landing and a shipyard for the construction of small crafts.

Maison Montcalm (Montcalm House)

45–49 Rue des Remparts.
Situated in a slightly recessed spot, this majestic residence contains three separate structures. The middle part, built in 1725, was soon flanked by two similar buildings. The house is named for Louis-Joseph de Saint-Véran, **marquis de Montcalm**, who lived on the ground floor of the center section from December 1758 to June 1759. In 1810, the middle structure was raised one story; the two neighboring houses followed suit in 1830.

Across the Montcalm House, the Montcalm Bastion, a small, tranquil square, offers lovely views of Rue des Remparts and the fortifications.

Bastion des Augustines (Augustine Bastion)

Across from Augustine Monastery, 75 Rue des Remparts.
Facing the Saint-Charles River, the northern section of the fortifications was long neglected because the cliff provided an adequate natural defense. After the American invasion of 1775–76, it was decided to complete this section of the walls surrounding the Upper Town. Completed in 1811, the masonry wall was so high that peering through the gun embrasures proved the only way to look out over the countryside.

The Palace Gate, demolished in 1871, once stood before the Augustine Monastery. In the monastery garden, adjacent to the entrance portal, note the former powder magazine, built in 1820 to supply the northern cannon batteries.

A few blocks past the Augustine Bastion, the **Gare du Palais** (Palais Station) and the **Old Post Office** are visible to the right. Constructed of local granite, stone and brick, both buildings reflect the architectural style imposed throughout Canada by the Canadian Pacific Railway on its buildings following the construction of the Château Frontenac

Morrin Centre

The Morrin Centre (*44 Chaussée des Écossais in the Old City;* ☎*418-694-9147; www. morrin.org*) fosters English-speaking culture in Quebec City, shares it with the French-speaking population and tourists, and encourages cultural exchanges in French and English. This anglo-cultural center offers a wide range of activities including library services, guided tours, readings by prominent authors, discussions on stimulating topics, writing workshops, poetry classes, and more. Tours of the Center (☜$6, Fridays at 4pm, early June–mid-September) begin with a descent into the dark prison cells of the Quebec City Common Gaol (1813–1868). There you will understand the daily lives of criminals and political prisoners who were incarcerated (and sometimes hanged) in this building. The tour also explores the anglo-Protestant life of Morrin College (1868–c. 1900) by visiting the former College Hall, classroom for classics, and science lab. The role of learned societies in the 19C is also examined in the beautiful library of the Literary and Historical Society of Quebec. Through this tour, you will understand the evolution of Quebec's English-speaking community, which—believe it or not—formed about 40% of the city's population in the mid-19C. If you need or want a final British fix, you may complete your tour with English tea and biscuits (bring your own clotted cream!).

in 1893. *A 20min detour to the train station is recommended for those wishing to visit the refurbished interior.* Restored to their former splendor, the original porcelain tiles and steel arches adorn a surprisingly modern and functional entrance hall.

▶ *Cross Côte du Palais and take Rue de l'Arsenal leading to the back entrance of the Artillery Park. If renovations are in progress and the back entrance is closed, proceed along Côte du Palais and turn right on to Rue Saint-Jean, then right on Rue D'Auteuil.*

Lieu historique national du Canada du Parc-de-l'Artillerie★ (Artillery Park National Historic Site of Canada)

The main entrance at 2 Rue d'Auteuil is located near the St. John Gate. ⊙*Access to the Artillery Park (Arsenal Foundry, Dauphine Redoubt and Officers' Quarters) Apr–mid-Oct, daily 10am–5pm; late Oct–Mar, by reservation only.* ☜*$3.90.* ♿☎*418-648-4205. www.p.gc.ca/artillery.*

This vast site that includes barracks, a redoubt and an old foundry, commemorates three centuries of military, social and industrial life in Quebec City. Originally a residential district, the area now occupied by the Artillery Park was transformed by the construction of army barracks in 1749. After the Conquest, soldiers of the Royal Artillery Regiment

took up residence here and erected several additional buildings over the years. The area's industrial vocation began in 1879, when the Canadian government acquired the site to convert it into a cartridge factory, later named the Dominion Arsenal. The industrial complex was abandoned in 1964 and in 1972 the Canadian Parks Service began a program of renovations. Today the site features several noteworthy buildings.

Ancienne Fonderie (Old Foundry)

The large windows and skylights of this 1903 foundry recall its original function. Today the building houses a reception and interpretation center for the Artillery Park complex. Focal point of the exhibit, the **scale model**★★ of Quebec City presents a stunning picture of the city as it appeared at the beginning of the 19C. Created between 1806 and 1808 by military engineers, the model reproduces topographical features and public buildings with great precision. On the lower level, visitors can see the ruins of a powder magazine and its protective wall (1808), and objects recovered during archaeological digs at the site.

Dauphine Redoubt

Construction of the impressive white edifice began in 1712 but was interrupted in 1713, following the signature of the Treaty of Utrecht. Remains of the bastioned stone wall along the structure can still be seen today. Completed in 1748 by Chaussegros de Léry, the redoubt was converted into barracks. After the Conquest, the British army built an additional story over part of the structure and also added massive buttresses to contain the masonry and prevent the vaults from collapsing. The informative exhibits combine costumes, paintings and artifacts to offer insight into a soldier's life during the 18C and 19C.

Nouvelles Casernes (Barracks)

Chaussegros de Léry designed this 160m/525ft-long stone structure in 1750 as a succession of row houses, an unusual concept at the time. The barracks contained armories, stockrooms, a guard room and six prison cells. The building was partially reconstructed during the late 19C.

▸ *Exit at the St. John Gate.*

Porte Saint-Jean (St. John Gate)

As of 1867, a larger gate replaced the one designed in the 18C. To facilitate traffic flow between the various parts of the city, this gate was demolished in 1897. The current structure was built in 1936. It is the most famous of the numerous gates giving access to Old Quebec City.

Place d'Youville

Located on the site of the former Montcalm market, this lively square has been a cultural and entertainment center for residents of Quebec City since 1900. Note the Montcalm Palace (*Palais Montcalm*), erected in 1930; the sober architecture and lack of ornamentation testify to the magnitude of the economic crisis that marked that era. Adjacent stands the Capitole Theatre (Théâtre du Capitole); its rounded façade is typical of the Beaux-Arts style popular during the early 20C.

▸ *Return through the St. John Gate and turn right on Rue d'Auteuil.*

Porte Kent (Kent Gate)

Named in honor of the Duchess of Kent, this opening in the western rampart was created in 1879.

Chapelle des Jésuites (Jesuit Chapel)

20 Rue Dauphine, at the junction of Rue d'Auteuil. ◷*Open year-round, Mon–Fri 11.30am–1.30pm.* ⊘*Closed major holidays.* ☎*418-694-9616. www. patrimoine-religieux.com.*

This chapel has been dedicated to Canadian martyrs since 1925. The small structure (1820) stands on land formerly belonging to the Jesuit College. The building was enlarged in 1857 and a new façade added in 1930. The gilded wooden statues of the Virgin and St. Joseph were sculpted by Pierre-Noël Levasseur. Médard Bourgault, of Saint-Jean-Port-Joli, carved the Stations of the Cross.

Lieu historique national du Canada des Fortifications-de-Québec (Fortifications of Québec National Historic Site of Canada)

100 Rue St-Louis, near the St. Louis Gate. ◷*Open early May–mid-Oct, daily 10am–5pm; rest of year by reservation.* ☞*$3.90.* ♿☎*418-648-7016. www.pc.gc.ca/fortifications.*

Contained within the surrounding wall, the **interpretation center** presents the history of Quebec via the evolution of its defence systems and organizes guided tours (👥) of the imposing wall surrounding the city. Near the center, to the right of the St. Louis Gate, lies the **poudrière** (powder magazine), built in 1810 on the Esplanade, a vast field used for military exercises during the 18C.

Porte Saint-Louis (St. Louis Gate)

The St. Louis gate—like its counterparts, the Kent, St. John and Prescott gates—no longer controls access to the city. Instead, it provides a bridge for visitors using the fortifications walkway to tour the old city. Replete with towers, turrets, battlements and machicolations, the gate was designed in 1878 by Irish architect W.H. Lynn, a collaborator of Lord Dufferin. The St. Louis gate influenced the development of a Chateau-style architecture in Quebec City.

Porte Saint-Louis

4 Grande Allée★ *5km/3mi.*
Maps HAUTE-VILLE & QUEBEC AND ENVIRONS.

▶ *Begin the walking tour at the Parliament Building.*

Departing from the St. Louis gate and extending southward of Old Quebec, the Grande Allée is the city's Champs-Élysées. Lined with an abundance of restaurants, bars, outdoor cafés, boutiques and offices, Quebec City's premier thoroughfare provides an elegant setting for the city's nightlife.

Grande Allée developed along the east-west axis that separated the land plots allotted to a few major property holders on the Quebec plateau in the early 17C. Originally a country road, it acquired a sudden popularity in the late 18C when it was transformed into a resort district by the British. In just a few years, magnificent villas appeared along the south side of Grande Allée, and the Faubourg Saint-Louis began taking shape.

Adding to the shift of business activity to Montreal and the move of the Canadian Parliament to Ottawa, the departure of the British garrison in 1871 hastened the decline of Quebec City. Inspired by the new city of Edinburgh, which developed alongside the original medieval town, the municipal engineer Charles Baillairgé suggested that Grande Allée be transformed into one of Quebec City's main arteries.

A major fire destroyed the Faubourg Saint-Louis on July 1, 1876, clearing much of the area and prompting the decision to erect the Parliament Building on this site. Following construction of the imposing edifice in 1886, the boulevard was designed as a corridor for official processions, linking the Parliament Building to Bois-de-Coulonge Park, the official residence of the lieutenant-governor.

The first residents of the remodelled Grande Allée (1886–1890) were the political elite of the city, who built opulent villas in the Second Empire style. Between 1890 and 1900, the upper portion of the boulevard was further developed with the arrival of a new bourgeoisie reaping the benefits of the Lower Town's industrialization. The heyday of Grande Allée continued well after World War I, and came to an end with the opening of the Quebec City Bridge to car travel in 1929, which gradually transformed the elegant residential district into a busy thoroughfare.

Hôtel du Parlement★★ (Parliament Building)
Visit by guided tour (French, English, Spanish, 30min) only, late Jun–Labor Day, Mon–Fri 9am–4.30pm, weekends 10am–4.30pm; rest of the year, Mon–Fri 9am–4.30pm. Photo ID required for security purposes. 418-643-7239 & 1-866-337-8837. www.assnat.qc.ca.

Hôtel du Parlement

Address Book

AVENUE CARTIER

The comings and goings of neighborhood denizens animate this attractive thoroughfare located well away from Quebec City's main tourist areas. Lining the street are a number of interesting restaurants, cafés and small stores well worth taking the time to explore. The menu at **Graffiti** (*1191 Ave. Cartier;* ☎*418-529-4949*) features high-quality Italian and French food accompanied by an excellent wine list. A glass-brick wall enhances the warm, welcoming interior. Down the street, **Bistro-café Krieghoff** (*1089 Ave. Cartier;* ☎*418-522-3711*) serves light meals and excellent breakfasts, attracting a varied clientele to its small, simply decorated dining rooms.

Overlooking the old city, this majestic edifice is the finest example of Second Empire architecture in Quebec City. In 1875 the deputy minister of the Department of Crown Lands, **Eugène-Étienne Taché** (1836–1912), was mandated by the provincial government to draw up the plans of a building to house the parliament and various government ministries. Originally designed to occupy the former site of the Jesuit college in Old Quebec (now City Hall), the project was transferred to the Cricket Field, in the Faubourg Saint-Louis, after the devastating fire of 1876.

The Parliament building forms a quadrangle surrounding an inner courtyard. The imposing **façade** presents a historic tableau featuring bronze figures that commemorate the great names of Quebec history. Some of these sculptures were created by Louis-Philippe Hébert. His *Nigog Fisherman* is encased in a niche before the main entrance; above the niche stands his work entitled *The Amerindian Family,* which was displayed during the 1889 Universal Exhibit in Paris. *In front of the façade is a diagram identifying the various bronze figures and their creators.*

The entrance hall bears the national emblems of various countries, a reminder that, at the time of construction, Quebec was chiefly comprised of immigrants from France, England, Ireland and Scotland. A staircase leads to **Le Parlementaire**, a sumptuous dining room (🕐*open to the public Mon–Fri 8am–2.30pm, reservations recommended* ☎*418-643-6640*) decorated in the Beaux-Arts style (1917). Drawing attention to the restaurant entrance is a stained-glass passageway, flooded with light, which evokes an Atlantic seascape. Reasonably priced, Le Parlementaire menu features Quebec specialties served in a dignified manner by highly competent waiters.

Parliamentary Chambers

On the first floor, an antechamber leads to both parliamentary chambers through finely chiselled doors.

Quebec's bicameral parliamentary system, as established by the Constitution Act of 1867, required two distinct halls: The Chamber of the National Assembly and the Chamber of the Legislative Council. Quebec's National Assembly (elected) now sits in the Chamber of the National Assembly. The Chamber of the Legislative Council, similar in size and décor, was used by the Legislative Council (appointed) until the council was abolished in 1968. Since then, it has hosted meetings of parliamentary committees and official receptions. Following the British parliamentary system, the majority party, which forms the government, sits face to face with the "loyal opposition" made up of one or several parties. Ministers and the principal members of the opposition are separated by a space, which in former times was said to equal "the length of two swords." Above the throne of the National Assembly Speaker hangs a painting by Charles Huot (*The Debate on Languages,* 1910–13) representing the January 21, 1793 sitting of the Legislative Assembly of Lower Canada, during which the historic linguistic debate that granted official status to the French language took place.

Gardens

Several commemorative monuments to Quebec premiers and other notable Québécois are strewn throughout the gardens ("les pelouses") of the Parliament Building.

On the north side, monuments to **Robert Bourassa**, premier of Quebec 1970–76 and 1985–94, father of Quebec's hydropower; **René Lévesque** (1976–85), the great sovereignist premier; and premier **Jean Lesage** (1960–66), leader of the *Quiet Revolution*. There is also an *inukshuk*, monument of stacked stones, paying tribute to the Inuit peoples of Northern Quebec.

On the south side of the gardens, there are monuments to nationalist premier **Maurice Duplessis** (1936–39 and 1944–59); and to premier **Honoré Mercier** (1887–91), a champion of Quebec's autonomy.

On Grande-Allée, near Porte Saint-Louis (St. Louis Gate), stands monuments to **François-Xavier Garneau**, Quebec's first national historian in the 19C; **Louis-Joseph Papineau**, chairman of the Assembly Chamber of Lower Canada (1816–1838); and progressive premier **Adélard Godbout** (1936 and 1939–44).

▶ *Continue south on Grande Allée.*

Manège militaire (Military Hall)
Behind Place George-V.

Constructed between 1884 and 1887 by Eugène-Étienne Taché, the Chateau-style building formerly served as a provincial exhibit pavilion and a military exercise hall. At the turn of the century, an annex was added to the eastern wing of the original structure. More recently, it housed a military regiment and museums.

The Manège Militaire burned down all through the night of April 4, 2008. About 90% of the historic artifacts were saved, fortunately. Only the brick wall facade and two towers where still standing after a blaze that devoured the old wood structure. Clear reconstruction plans were not announced at time of printing.

▶ *Turn right on Rue de la Chevrotière.*

Chapelle historique Bon-Pasteur★ (Historic Good Shepherd Chapel)

1080 Rue de la Chevrotière. Open Jun–Sept, Mon–Fri 2pm–5pm; rest of the year, appointment. Artists' Mass Sun 10.45am. Contribution requested ($2). Closed weeks of Jan 1 & Easter. ☎418-522-6221.

Designed by Charles Baillairgé in 1866, the chapel is located on the second floor of the former convent of the Sisters of the Good Shepherd. The tall, narrow, Baroque-style nave is flanked by superimposed side galleries, enabling occupants on all levels to access the chapel. Resting on the high altar (1730), the gilded retable from the Saint-Louis-de-Lotbinière church was sculpted in the Levasseur workshop in the 1730s. Above it hangs *The Assumption of the Virgin,* by Antoine Plamondon (1868). Several small paintings adorn the pilasters; they were created in the workshop of the Sisters, renowned for their many religious paintings executed for churches in the Quebec diocese in the late 19C. Telephone for a list of summer concerts in this chapel renowned for its acoustics.

Observatoire de la Capitale (Édifice Marie-Guyart)

Entrance at 1037 Rue de la Chevrotière. Open Jun 24–mid-Oct, daily 10am–5pm; rest of the year, Tue–Sun 10am–5pm. $5. Closed Jan 1 & Dec 24, 25 & 31. ☎418-644-9841 & 1-888-497-4322. www.observatoirecapitale.org.

The observatory occupying the 31st floor (221m/685ft up) of this administrative building provides a splendid **view**★★ of Old Quebec, the citadel and fortifications, the St. Lawrence River as well as the surrounding areas. Édifice Marie-Guyart is the tallest building in Quebec City.

▶ *Return to Grande Allée and turn right.*

Église Saint-Cœur-de-Marie (Church of the Sacred Heart of Mary)

At the corner of Rue Scott and Grande Allée (n° 530).

Erected in 1920, the brick edifice was built for the Eudists, also known as the Congregation of Jesus and Mary, founded in the 17C. The quaint steeple distinctly contrasts with the otherwise modern structure.

La Laurentienne
500 Grande Allée Est.

The headquarters of this insurance company occupy a structure (1962) that embodies the functionalist tendency of modern architecture in Quebec City. Towards the rear, a new façade of mirrored glass overlooks the Park of French America (Parc de l'Amérique française).

▶ *Take Ave. Taché on the left to view the Martello tower nº 2 (○open mid-Jun–early Sep & on weekends in Jun, Sep–mid-Oct, 10am–5pm; ⏎$3.50;* 🅿 ☎*418-648-4071). Return to Grande Allée.*

Maison Stewart (Stewart House)
82 Grande Allée Ouest, at the northeast corner of Ave. Cartier.

Surrounded by a small park, this 1849 cottage features large, French windows adorning the façade. Topped by a central chimney stack, the overhanging roof covers the lateral galleries.

At nº 95 stands the **Ladies' Protestant Home**, an elegant example of the Renaissance Revival style exemplified

here by the massive cornice and lantern. To the right of the structure, facing the Avenue Cartier, the **Krieghoff House** (○━ *closed to the public*) was named for the painter Cornelius Krieghoff (1815–72) who lived here intermittently in 1859 and 1860. Built in 1850, this "rustic cottage" is in fact a country house for city dwellers; the style derives from Quebec vernacular architecture.

▶ *Turn left on Ave. Wolfe-Montcalm and follow signs to the Quebec Museum of Fine Arts (Musée national des beaux-arts du Québec).*

The avenue runs alongside a military parade ground used by the British army after they abandoned Place d'Armes in 1823. For years, major events such as the historic parades marking Quebec City's 300th anniversary took place on the site.

Facing the museum, the **Wolfe monument** marks the spot where the victor of the Battle of the Plains of Abraham, General James Wolfe, died on September 13, 1759.

Musée national des beaux-arts du Québec★★ (Quebec Museum of Fine Arts)
Entrance is located between the two main buildings, on ground level. ○Open Jun–early Sept, daily 10am–6pm (Wed 9pm); rest of the year, Tue–Sun 10am–

Musée national des beaux-arts du Québec in the Parc des Champ de-Bataille

©Les Photographes Kedl, 2004/Musée national des beaux-arts du Québec

5pm (Wed 9pm). ○*Closed Dec 25.* ∼*$15.* ✕🚻♿🅿 *($2.50 for first hr, $1 subsequent hours).* ☎*418-643-2150 & 1-866-220-2150. www.mnba.qc.ca.*

Situated on the site of the Parc des Champs-de-Bataille (Battlefields Park), this remarkable museum complex provides a comprehensive overview of Quebec art from the 18C to the present. The greatest visual artists of Quebec are represented, Jean-Paul Riopelle and Jean-Paul Lemieux in particular. Temporary and permanent exhibits drawn from a collection of over 23,000 works of art, including those of the former Brousseau Museum of Inuit Art (**M**¹) are organized throughout three buildings.

Main Hall

Situated between the two other structures, the Main Hall serves as the main entrance to the museum. The modern structure, capped by skylights, houses the reception area, an auditorium and other amenities.

Gérard Morisset Pavilion

The monumental façade of this structure (named for a former museum director), reflects the Beaux-Arts style that was adopted for many of Quebec's government buildings. The granite-clad building features an imposing central staircase leading to an Ionic portico. The sculpted stone pediment evokes the Province's economic history and the history of two groups: The Amerindians (*left side*) and the discoverers and missionaries (*right side*). Aluminium-plated bas-reliefs representing various events in the history of Canada and traditional agricultural scenes adorn the structure's lateral wings. Pieces from the permanent collection are on view here, including ancient, modern and contemporary art; the works offer a sweeping view of the development of Quebec art.

Baillairgé Pavilion

Erected according to plans by Charles Baillairgé, this monumental Renaissance Revival-style structure (1871) housed, until 1967, the old "plains prison." An entire cell block has been preserved as an exhibit of prison life during the last century. One gallery here features

Address Book

RESTAURANT DU MUSÉE

In National Battlefields Park. ☎*418-644-6780; www.mnba.qc.ca.* Located within the Quebec Museum of Fine Arts, this restaurant offers imaginative regional French fare, carefully prepared and served with flair. Natural light floods the vast dining room, where immense windows offer a superb view of the Plains of Abraham. In summer, take a table on the terrace to admire the surrounding countryside.

one of the most important paintings in the history of Canada: The renowned *Assemblée des six comtés* (*Assembly of Six Counties*). A masterpiece of Charles Alexander Smith, this impressive canvas illustrates one of the key moments of the insurrections of 1837–38: In the foreground, Louis-Joseph Papineau, leader of the Patriots, addresses an attentive crowd.

In the tower of this structure (*4th floor*), note the curious statue of a diver sculptured in the late 1960s by David Moore.

▸ *Upon exiting from the museum, turn left on Ave. Georges-VI and continue to Grey Terrace.*

This observatory was named in honor of A.H. Grey, governor-general of Canada from 1904 to 1911, during which time the park was constructed.

▸ *Doubling back, take Ave. Ontario through National Battlefields Park.*

Parc des Champs-de-Bataille★ (Battlefields Park)

○*The park is open daily year-round at no charge. The* **Discovery Pavilion of the Plains of Abraham**★ *presents a multimedia history of the park: 835 Wilfrid-Laurier Avenue.* ○*Open late Jun–Labor Day, daily 10am–5.30pm; rest of the year, daily 10am–5pm.* ∼*$8 ($10 day pass includes access to Martello Tower 1, Louis S. St. Laurent House and a bus tour).* ♿🅿 *($2.50/hr)* ☎*418-648-4071; www.ccbn-nbc.gc.ca. To* *the left of Ave. Ontario, Martello tower 1 is visible (Ⓘopen mid-Jun–early Sept, daily 10am–5.30pm; rest of Sept–mid-Oct, weekends 10am–5.30pm; ⊜$4). Continuing straight ahead, the Ave. du Cap-aux-Diamants leads to the Governor's Walk (promenade des Gouverneurs) belvedere.*

Created in 1908, on the tricentennial of the founding of the city, this national park stretches over 108ha/266 acres along a cliff on the south side of the Quebec City plateau. Overlooking the St. Lawrence River, the site commemorates the battles fought between the British and French armies during the Conquest. The park, completed in 1954, was landscaped by Frederick G. Todd, a student of Frederick Law Olmsted, renowned designer of New York City's Central Park and Montreal's Mt. Royal Park. Inspired by English country gardens, the rambling park introduces a green space into the cityscape, providing a natural-looking environment that contrasts with the structured, rational layout of classical gardens.

The Battle of the Plains of Abraham

A large section of the park occupies the former plains of Abraham, so named after Abraham Martin, a wealthy farmer living on the Quebec City heights in the 17C. On this site, the French and British armies fought the battle that eventually sealed the fate of the French colony.

On September 13, 1759, some 5,000 British troops under the command of General Wolfe scaled the steep cliff and launched an attack on the city. Without waiting for reinforcements, the French general Montcalm urged his ill-prepared army against the British lines, who in turn crushed the attempt in less than 15 minutes. Both generals were mortally wounded during the short, but decisive event. Five days later, Quebec had been completely occupied and the French troops, under the command of François-Gaston de Lévis (1719–1787), retreated to Montreal for the winter.

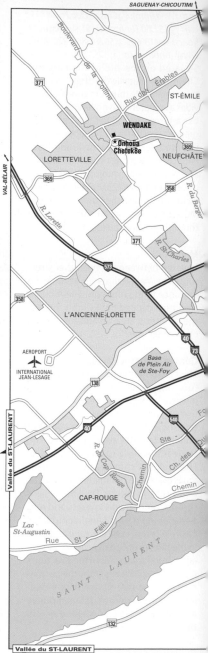

The following April, Lévis and the French army returned to battle the British at Sainte-Foy (a monument located in Braves Park north of Chemin Sainte-Foy commemorates the event). Though the French were victorious, their hopes were

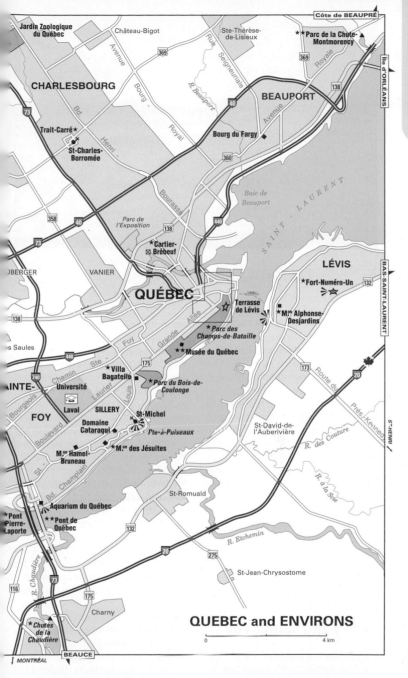

Jardin Zoologique du Québec

Château-Bigot

Ste-Thérèse-de-Lisieux

★★ Parc de la Chute-Montmorency

Côte de BEAUPRÉ

369

Rue Seigneuriale

R. Beauport

369

138

Île d'ORLÉANS

CHARLESBOURG

73

Avenue Bourg-Royal

Bd Henri

40

BEAUPORT

★ Trait-Carré

St-Charles-Borromée

Bourg du Fargy

Avenue

360

358

40

Bourassa

73

Parc de l'Exposition

138

440

Baie de Beauport

SAINT-LAURENT

UBERGER

VANIER

★ Cartier-Brébeuf

QUÉBEC

Terrasse de Lévis

LÉVIS

★ Fort-Numéro-Un

132

BAS-SAINT-LAURENT

138

s Saules

440

Grande Allée

Ste Foy

★ Parc des Champs-de-Bataille

★★ Musée du Québec

M.⁰ⁿ Alphonse-Desjardins

740

Chemin Ste

★ Villa Bagatelle

Louis

175

Université

Laurier

★ Parc du Bois-de-Coulonge

173

Route du

20

AINTE-

Laval

SILLERY

St-Michel

St-David-de-l'Auberivière

FOY

Bourgeois

Boulevard

Domaine Cataraqui

Pte-à-Puiseaux

R. des Couture

St-

M.⁰ⁿ Hamel-Bruneau

M.⁰ⁿ des Jésuites

R. d la Scie

Champlain

St-Romuald

★ Aquarium du Québec

★ Pont Pierre-Laporte

Bd Champlain

★★ Pont de Québec

132

R. Etchemin

Prés. Kenned

ST-HENRI

20

275

St-Jean-Chrysostome

R. Chaudière

73

116

175

Charny

QUEBEC and ENVIRONS

0   4 km

★ Chutes de la Chaudière

BEAUCE

MONTRÉAL

dashed the following month when a ship arrived bearing British reinforcements, sealing the fate of New France. The territory was officially turned over to the British by the Treaty of Paris in 1763.

Fearing that Americans would initiate another invasion following the failed attempt by Bostonians in 1775–76, and still awaiting London's decision regarding the construction of a citadel, the British military erected four **Martello**

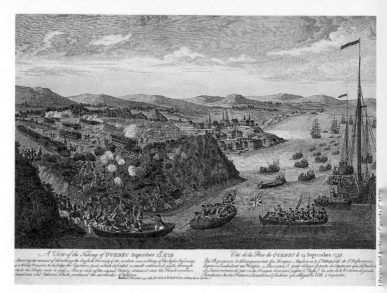

Library and Archive Canada (C 1078)

Battle of the Plains of Abraham

towers between 1808 and 1812 as an advanced defensive line.

Three towers remain, two located in the park and one on Rue Lavigueur (Faubourg Saint-Jean-Baptiste). Named after the Corsican point where they originated, Martello towers are circular defensive outposts, topped by a platform mounted with cannons.

This platform is sometimes protected by a detachable roof that can be quickly dismantled in case of attack. The section of the wall built to resist the enemy is very thick, while the section facing the garrison is much thinner; thus, if the tower were to be overtaken by the enemy, it could be easily destroyed by the besieged troops.

Excursions
Map QUEBEC AND ENVIRONS.

Sillery and Sainte-Foy

Located on the banks of the St. Lawrence barely 1km/.6mi from Quebec, the community of Sillery was named after the French nobleman, Noël Brulart de Sillery. The settlement traces its origins to the Jesuit mission founded in 1637 to evangelize Amerindians. However, ravaging epidemic diseases and alcoholism

led to the abandonment of the settlement in the 1680s. After the Conquest, Jesuits rented the territory to several wealthy merchants. The expanding lumber and shipbuilding industry prompted an economic surge during the mid-19C, as Sillery's coves and bays were used for unloading, squaring off, warehousing and exporting timber. Several of the sumptuous mansions erected during this prosperous era were later acquired by various religious organizations. After World War II, Sillery quickly developed as a residential suburb of Quebec City. Today, the town presents a subtle mix of old world charm and bustling city activities.

Past Battlefields Park, Grande Allée becomes Chemin Saint-Louis. A wooded median divides the boulevard, which is lined with prestigious office buildings.

Parc du Bois-de-Coulonge★ (Bois-de-Coulonge Park)
1215 Grande Allée Ouest, in the borough of Sainte-Foy-Sillery. ○*Open daily year-round.* ◆*Guided tours (French only) Fri–Sun hourly from noon–3pm,* ◎*$5* ◪▣ *($1/hr weekdays, weekends free).* ☎*418-528-0773 & 1-800-442-0773.*

This pleasantly landscaped park constitutes a small part of the old Coulonge seigneury granted to Louis d'Ailleboust,

Sieur de Coulonge, in 1649. During the Conquest, the British temporarily occupied the site. In 1780 the domain was subdivided, and one of the first country homes on this land was erected 10 years later. Built in the Palladian style, the villa was renamed **Spencer Wood** in honor of British prime minister Lord Spencer, in 1811, and would become the residence of Lord Elgin, governor-general of the United Canadas, in 1852. It was rebuilt in 1860 after a fire. Following Confederation, it became the property of the provincial government and served as the residence of the lieutenant-governor. Renamed Bois-de-Coulonge in 1947, the vice-regal residence was destroyed by fire in 1966. Since then, Bois-de-Coulonge Park has been open to the public. The **guardian's house**, a small Chateau-style construction covered with decorative cedar shingles (1891), serves as the park's visitor center. Various old buildings, gardens and a belvedere overlooking the river also await park visitors.

Villa Bagatelle★

1563 Chemin Saint-Louis, in the borough of Sainte-Foy-Sillery. ○*Open Jun–Sept, Tue–Sun 11am–5pm; Apr–May and Oct–Dec, Wed–Sun 1pm–5pm; Jan–Mar, weekends only 1pm–5pm.* ♿☎*418-681-3010.* Villa Bagatelle was constructed in 1927 after a fire the previous year. The villa closely resembles a small Gothic Revival cottage erected in 1848 in the park. The house, surrounded by an English garden, is the Sillery Interpretation Center, housing an exhibit and documentation center and mounts temporary thematic exhibits.

▶ *Continue along Chemin Saint-Louis.*

The road passes by the St. Michael Anglican church, with its squat steeple and large buttresses.

▶ *Turn left on Côte de l'Église.*

Église Saint-Michel (St. Michael Church)

1600 Rue Persico, in Sillery. ○*Open year-round, Mon–Sat 9am–5pm; Sun 10am–noon.* ⤺*Guided tours (French*

and English) from late Jun-Labor Day. ○*Closed Sat from Nov–May.* ♿🅿☎*418-527-3390.*
The Gothic Revival church dates from 1854. Five paintings from the Desjardins collection are preserved in the interior: *Emmaüs' Disciples, Death of St. Francis of Assisi, St. Francis of Assisi Receiving the Stigmata, the Annunciation,* and *The Adoration of the Magi.*

Outside, on a terrace below the church, the lookout at **Pointe-à-Puiseaux** affords a superb **view**★ of Quebec City, Sillery's coves, the Quebec City and Pierre-Laporte bridges and the south shore.

▶ *Return to Chemin Saint-Louis.*

Maison Hamel-Bruneau (Hamel-Bruneau House)

2608 Chemin Saint-Louis, in Sainte-Foy. ○*Open late May-Aug Tue–Sun 11am–5pm, Sept-mid-May 1pm–5pm.* ♿🅿.
This little cottage, a synthesis between the ornate English cottage and the Quebec vernacular style, was built as a country home in 1858. It houses temporary exhibits and offers cultural activities.

▶ *Turn left on Ave. du Parc.*

Aquarium du Québec (Quebec Aquarium) 🅺🅸🅳🆂

1675 Ave. des Hôtels, in borough of Sainte-Foy-Sillery, near to Pont de Québec. ○*Open May–early Oct, 10am–5pm; mid-Oct–Apr 10am–4pm.* ○*Closed Dec 25–Jan 1.* 🎫*$15.50* ♿🅿☎*418-659-5264 & 1-866-659-5264. www.sepaq. com/paq/fr.*
Established in 1959, on a site overlooking the St. Lawrence River, the aquarium houses more than 1,700 specimens of exotic fish, reptiles and sea mammals as well as specimens representing the ecosystems of the St. Lawrence. Of special interest are the outdoor seal pools. Upon leaving the aquarium, stop at the little lookout in the parking lot to enjoy a magnificent **view**★ of the St. Lawrence River, and the Ponts (bridges) de Québec City and Pierre-Laporte.

Quebec Aquarium

▶ *Descend toward the St. Lawrence, take Blvd. Champlain and continue to Côte de Gignac. Turn left, then right onto Chemin du Foulon.*

Maison des Jésuites★ (Jesuit House)

2320 Chemin du Foulon, in Sillery. ○Open Jun–Sept, Tue–Sun 11am–5pm; Apr–May and Oct–Dec, Wed–Sun 1pm–5pm; Feb–Mar, Sun 1pm–5pm. 🅿☎418-654-0259. *www.museocapitale.qc.ca.*

The current early 18C stone house was erected on the site of the St. Joseph mission (the first Jesuit mission in North America), established by Jesuits in 1637 in order to convert the Montagnais, Algonquins and Atikamekw to a sedentary lifestyle. So as to protect themselves from attacks by Iroquois, the Jesuits and Amerindians lived in an enclosure surrounded by stakes, which was later replaced by a stone fort. Facing the house, vestiges of the fort and the Saint-Michel chapel have been unearthed. The British writer, Frances Moore Brookes, lived in this two-story edifice in 1763. In 1769, she published *The History of Emily Montague,* which takes place in this house. By 1929, the Jesuit House was classified as one of the earliest historical monuments in Quebec. It now houses a small museum of exhibits focusing on the history of indigenous peoples, as well as archaeology of the site and local history. In the gardens, note the re-created native camp,

which highlights the site's importance as a meeting place between missionaries and indigenous peoples during the era of New France.

Along Chemin du Foulon, note the old wooden houses, formerly inhabited by shipyard employees.

Université Laval (Laval University)

In Sainte-Foy, 7km/4.3mi from St. Louis Gate by Grande Allée, Chemin Saint-Louis and Blvd. Laurier (Rte. 175).

Founded in 1852 by the Quebec Seminary, Laval University began constructing a campus (*cité universitaire*) in the western suburb of Quebec City in 1949. The north-south axis opens onto a view of the Laurentian Mountains, while the east-west draws attention to the Grand Seminary and the Faculty of Medicine. The university underwent considerable expansion in the 1960s; today its 13 departments, 9 specialty schools and several research centers accommodate a student body of more than 40,000 students.

The Buildings

The **Louis-Jacques Casault Pavilion** (formerly the Grand Seminary) was built in 1958. Inside, the Gothic-style university chapel was redesigned to house the Quebec national archives. Facing the Casault Pavilion are two new buildings, erected in 1990: The

Laurentienne Pavilion and the award-winning, post-Modern **Alexandre-de-Sève Pavilion**.

With its Classic composition, inner courtyard and façades articulated by sunshields of white concrete, the **Charles-de-Koninck Pavilion** (1964) is today considered the main building of the university complex. The **Comtois Pavilion** (1966) also reflects the desire to achieve a Classical appearance through the use of prefabricated modules. With its inner courtyard and pillared structure, it is one of the most interesting buildings in the Quebec City region.

A squat building marked by horizontal lines, the impressive sports complex known as "le PEPS" (Pavillon de l'Éducation Physique et des Sports, 1971) stretches out over terraced grounds covering large underground parking areas. Facilities include an Olympic-size pool, an indoor stadium, skating rinks and several sporting areas.

Cartier-Brébeuf National Historic Site of Canada★

3km/1.8mi from St. John Gate, by Côte d'Abraham, Rue de la Couronne, Drouin Bridge and 1re Ave. Turn left on rue de l'Éspinay. ◷*Open early May–Labor Day, daily 10am–5pm; rest of Sept, daily 1pm–4pm; rest of year by reservation.* ◍*$3.90.* ♿ 🅿 ☎*418-648-4038. www.pc.gc.ca/brebeuf.*

Located on the northern shore of the Lairet Basin, this site commemorates Jacques Cartier, who wintered on this spot in 1535–36, and Jean de Brébeuf, a Jesuit missionary. The interpretation center features insightful displays, which recall Cartier's second voyage to New France and his meetings with the Iroquois, as well as the Jesuits' first mission, established in 1626.

Charlesbourg

▸ *Take Rte. 73 Nord to Exit 150 (80e Rue Ouest).*

Insectarium of Quebec
335 Blvd. du Lac (Charlesbourg District). May–Sept, daily 9am–5pm; rest

of the year, Sat-Sun 9am–5pm. ◍*$7.* ♿ 🅿 ☎*418-841-2828 & 1-866-689-8748. www.insectariumdequebec.ca.*

Do you hate insects and/or arthropods? Or should you like them? Anyhow, you will learn to tell them apart after visiting the Quebec City Insectarium. Four exhibitions halls with live and mounted specimens will quench your thirst for six-legged knowledge. Your hunger might also be taken care of through *entomophagy* (eating insects!); from the crunchy cricket to the juicy worm, you will want to taste them all! And you may save the planet in the process...

Trait-Carré (walking tour)★
Departure point for walking tour of the Trait-Carré: Moulin des Jésuites at 7960 Blvd. Henri-Bourassa, reachable by city Métrobus 801 (◷*open mid-Jun–Sept, Wed–Sun 10am–6pm; early Sept–mid-Jun Sat & Sun 10am–5pm;* ☎*418-624-7720; www.moulindesjesuites.org). Maps/brochures available.*

The heart of old Charlesbourg, commonly referred to as the Trait-Carré historical district, comprises a square lot located in the midst of a star-shaped land division plan. Dating back to 1660, it is the only such design in New France. Throughout Quebec, land concessions traditionally took the form of long, narrow strips of land known as rangs, which prevented large population concentrations.

The Trait-Carré design was devised in Charlesbourg by Jesuit priests and the intendant Jean Talon, who sought to ensure that all homes would be located near the main square, to improve defensibility in case of attack.

Today the center of Trait-Carré is bordered by four streets. In the middle is the institutional center of old Charlesbourg, which includes a church, a municipal library housed in the old Saint Charles College (1903), and the Bon-Pasteur Convent, built in 1883.

Église Saint-Charles-Borromée (St. Charles Borromeo Church)
◷*Visit by guided tour only (by appointment).* ☎*418-624-7720.*
With its two steeples and high façade dominated by a large pediment, this

edifice (1827–1830) exemplifies the influence of English Palladianism on the religious architecture of Quebec.

The focal point of the interior is the imposing triumphal arch adorning the flat apse. Salvaged from an earlier church erected on this site, two statues (1742) by Pierre-Noël Levasseur stand in lateral niches. Also worth noting are works by François Ranvoyzé, Louis Jobin, Charles Vézina and Paul Lambert.

At the southeast corner of the Trait-Carré stands the **Ephraïm Bédard House,** a typical rural dwelling from the early 19C (*7655 Chemin Samuel;* ◷*open Tue, Thu 1.30pm–4pm; otherwise by appointment* ♿🅿☏*418-624-7745; www.societe-historique-charlesbourg.org*). The **Pierre-Lefebvre House,** a representative 19C wood structure, has been converted into the **Trait-Carré Gallery of Visual Arts** (*7985 Trait-Carré Est;* ◷*open mid-Jun–mid-Aug Wed–Sun 11am–6pm; mid-Sept–mid-May Fri 7pm–9pm, weekends 1pm–5pm;* ♿🅿☏*418-623-1877*). Other historic structures in the quarter have also been converted into cultural centers, among them the Magella-Paradis House (1833), which boasts a distinctive roofline.

Wendake

▷ *Take Rte. 73 Nord to Exit 154. Turn left on Rue de la Faune (which becomes Rue des Érables and Rue de la Rivière). Then turn right on Rue Max Gros-Louis.*

Expelled from the Great Lakes region by the Iroquois, and beset by epidemics and famine, the Hurons sought the protection of the French in the mid-17C. Accompanied by Father Chaumonot, a Jesuit missionary, they settled in the Upper Town (near Fort Saint-Louis), and moved on to Île d'Orléans in 1651. In 1668, they emigrated to Sainte-Foy, on the present site of Laval University, and then to Ancienne-Lorette, in 1673. From there they moved one last time to Jeune-Lorette, or Wendake, in 1697. Today a stroll through the streets of the **Huron Village** (Village-des-Hurons) reveals the uniqueness of this place. The

buildings on the reserve were erected on communal land in the Amerindian tradition, without individual land allotments or European cadastral boundaries. The community is located near the Saint Charles (or Kabir-Kouba) River, whose waterfalls have inspired numerous artists.

Site traditionnel huron-wendat Onhoüa Chetek8ᵉ★ (Huron-Wendat Onhoüa Chetek8ᵉ Traditional Site)

575 Rue Stanislas-Kosca, Village-des-Hurons (Wendake). ↝↝*Visit by guided tour (45min) only, May–mid-Oct, daily 8.30am–6pm; rest of the year, daily 9am–5pm.* ☺*$10.* 🍴♿🅿☏ *418-842-4308. www.huron-wendat.qc.ca.*

"Koey Koey ataro…" (Welcome, friend…) Thus begins a visit to this re-created traditional Amerindian village, which offers a fascinating introduction to the history, heritage and customs of the First Nations, and of the Huron Nation in particular. Visitors step inside a longhouse (multi-family dwelling), and view a smokehouse and a traditional sauna, a small structure in which steam is produced by pouring boiling water onto heated stones. From May to October, experience the animation of Huron legends and traditional dance.

Notre-Dame-de-Lorette chapel

Corner of Rues Chef-Maurice-Bastien and Chef-Nicholas-Vincent. ◷*Open May–Oct, Mon–Fri 9am–5pm, weekends 10am–5pm.* 🍴♿🅿☏ *418-845-1241. www.wendake.ca.*

The church occupies the site of the Jesuit Mission of 1697. The present structure (1865) was erected on the site of an earlier church (1730) that was destroyed by a fire in 1862. The very simple décor includes a high altar tabernacle believed to have been made in 1722 by Pierre-Noël Levasseur. Above the altar, a simple sculpture represents the Santa Casa of Loretto, in Italy, supported by two angels. The chapel treasure, which includes religious furnishings left behind by the Jesuit missionaries, is exhibited in the sacristy.

RAWDON ★

LANAUDIÈRE REGION
POPULATION 10,058
MAP: SEE LANAUDIÈRE

Situated in the foothills of the Laurentian Mountains, this small community lies in the heart of a popular recreation area. The Rouge and Ouareau rivers flanking the center of town form spectacular waterfalls and cascades on their journey south to the St. Lawrence.

Originally part of lands granted to Loyalists in 1799, Rawdon was first settled in the late 1810s by Irish immigrants, who were followed by Scots and French Canadians (mainly Acadians). In the course of the 20C, the town has become home to a sizable Eastern European population. To this day, Rawdon remains a multicultural community, as evidenced by the presence of a diverse mix of religious edifices, including a Russian Orthodox Church (*located at the junction of Rue Woodland and 15ᵉ Ave.*). Also of particular interest is the small **Anglican church** (*corner of Rue Metcalfe and 3ᵉ Ave.*). The stone structure (1861), topped by a wooden belfry and bordered on one side by a small cemetery, is perhaps the town's most charming sight.

Information: 3568 Rue Church & Parc des chutes Dorwin, 3102 1ère Avenue. ☎450-834-2551 & 1-800-363-2788. www.municipalite.rwdon.qc.ca/ www.lanaudiere.ca.

▶ **Orient Yourself:** Rawdon is about 75km/46mi north of Montreal by Rtes. 25, 125 and 337.

☺ **Don't Miss:** Dorwin Falls and Parc des Cascades

🕐 **Organizing Your Time:** Rawdon is a nice day trip from Montreal or Trois-Rivières

Kids **Especially for Kids:** Area beaches in public parks

Sights

Parc des Chutes Dorwin★ (Dorwin Falls Park)

Located in a park off Rte. 337 (which is also the 1ère Ave.), just before reaching the center of Rawdon, coming from Montreal. Open May–Oct, daily 9am–7pm. ⚙$4. ✗ ♿ 🅿 ($2), City of Rawdon ☎450-834-2596, a free call from Montreal.

In a wooded site, the Ouareau River cascades over rocks, then plunges 30m/98ft into a small pool and branches off into a narrow, rocky gorge. Enjoy 2.5km/1.5mi of hiking trails.

According to an Amerindian legend, the falls sprang out when Nipissingue, a wicked sorcerer, pushed the beautiful maiden, Hiawitha, into a chasm. He was turned to stone by a clap of thunder, while she was transformed into a waterfall. Popular belief holds that the profile, carved into the rock at the edge of the falls,

is that of the sorcerer (☺*best viewed from the observation deck midway down*).

The Rouge River also drops in a lovely waterfall, the Mason Falls (*on 3ᵉ Ave. and Rue Maple*). ☺*Access to the bottom of the falls is difficult.*

Parc des Cascades★ (Cascades Park)

From Rue Queen, turn onto Rte. 341 toward Saint-Donat. 🕐Open mid-May–Thanksgiving Day daily 9am–6pm. ⚙$8/car. ♿ 🅿 ☎450-834-2596.

The magnificent cascade, tumbling down a broad staircase of rocks, is located at the northern edge of Lake Pontbriand, on the Ouareau River. In summer, visitors can wade into the middle of the stream and enjoy the refreshing water. The paths leading through the pine forest (interpretation signs) and picnic areas make this site an enjoyable resting place. Fishing is permitted.

VALLÉE DU RICHELIEU★★

MONTÉRÉGIE REGION

The majestic Richelieu River constitutes a major link in the waterway flowing between Montreal and New York City. Approximately 130km/81mi long, the river flows from its source in New York State to join the St. Lawrence River at Sorel (now Sorel-Tracy).

Samuel de Champlain discovered the waterway in 1609, and called it the Iroquois River. It was later named after Armand Jean du Plessis, Duke of Richelieu (1585–1642), better known as **Cardinal Richelieu**, chief minister of Louis XIII. Richelieu presided over the destiny of France from the 1620s until his death and actively supported the development of New France.

Settlers moved into the valley in the early 18C to cultivate the fertile land of this region, which remains one of the richest agricultural areas in Quebec. Today a popular weekend retreat for Montrealers, the Richelieu Valley attracts thousands of travelers and tourists every weekend in the summer and fall seasons.

- **Information:** 1080 Chemin des Patriotes Nord (Rte. 133), Mont-Saint-Hilaire. ☎450-746-9441 & 1-888-736-0395. www.vallee-du-richelieu.ca/www.region gourmande.com.
- **Orient Yourself:** Chambly is located approximately 30km/18.6mi east of Montreal by Rte. 10 (Exit 22) or Rte. 112. Itinerary 1 follows the Richelieu River on Rte. 133. Itinerary 2 follows Rte. 223, on the left bank (west side).
- **Don't Miss:** The view of the region, including Montreal, from the summit of Mt. Saint-Hilaire.
- **Organizing Your Time:** Rte. 133 is slow, and Rte. 223 is very slow, so allow plenty of time to accommodate this.
- **Also See:** CHAMBLY.

A Bit of History

Valley of Forts – Owing to its strategic location, the Richelieu Valley was fortified early in the French Regime. Forts were built at Chambly, Saint-Jean-sur-Richelieu, Lennox (on Île aux Noix), and Lacolle. These fortifications were initially built to protect Montreal against attacks by Iroquois, and later by British troops (1759–60) and Americans (1775–76).

In the mid-19C the threat of invasion subsided, marking the beginning of a new era of trade. The objective was no longer to prevent access from the south but to facilitate transportation between Montreal and the United States. An extensive canal system was built to achieve this.

The Patriots' Rebellion (1837–38) – The Richelieu Valley played an important role in the conflict that opposed the Patriots of Lower Canada to the British government. The grave constitutional struggles of the period, combined with a fierce sense of French Canadian nationalism, led Louis-Joseph Papineau and his supporters, the Patriots, to denounce the British regime and to seek self-determination. As patriotic fervor increased, citizens loyal to the British government in power formed armed militias to support the army, and violent confrontations occurred in the Richelieu Valley and around Montreal. British troops under Colonels Charles Gore and Charles Wetherall faced the rebels at Saint-Denis-sur-Richelieu, defeated them at Saint-Charles-sur-Richelieu, and finally crushed them at Saint-Eustache.

Route 133, on the east side of the river, is called the **Patriots' Road** (Chemin des Patriotes). The rifle, knitted hat, woven belt, and sometimes the pipe are symbols of the Patriots and can be seen in numerous illustrations depicting the event. The green, white, and red **Canadian tricolor** was their principal flag.

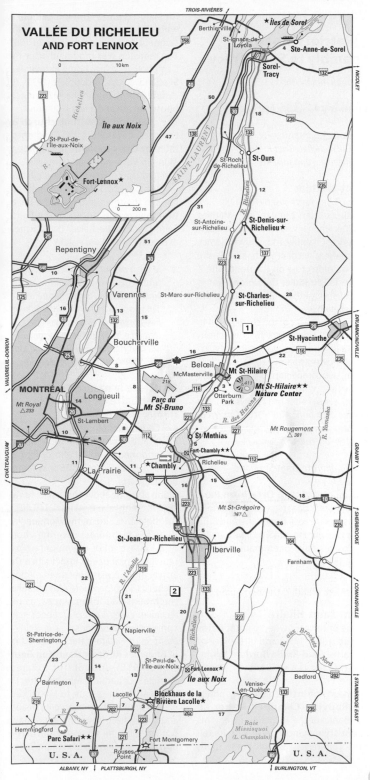

VALLÉE DU RICHELIEU
AND FORT LENNOX

0   10km

Île aux Noix

St-Paul-de-
l'île-aux-Noix

Fort-Lennox ★

0   200 m

TROIS-RIVIÈRES

★ Îles de Sorel

Berthierville

St-Ignace-de-
Loyola

◀ Ste-Anne-de-Sorel

158

Sorel-
Tracy

NICOLET

132

40

50

30

18

239

47

138

133

SAINT-LAURENT

St-Roch
de-Richelieu

St-Ours

31

St-Antoine-
sur-Richelieu

St-Denis-sur-
Richelieu ★

12

235

R. Richelieu

12

137

Repentigny

223

51

30

640

10

Varennes

125

16

13

132

15

St-Marc-sur-Richelieu

St-Charles-
sur-Richelieu

28

DRUMMONDVILLE

40

25

Boucherville

11

1

20

St-Hyacinthe

16

116

22

235

MONTRÉAL

Beloeil

McMasterville

Mt St-Hilaire

Mt St-Hilaire ★★
Nature Center

218

411

Longueuil

Parc du
Mt St-Bruno

116

Otterburn
Park

R. des Hurons

Mt Rougemont
381

R. Yamaska

Mt Royal
233

14

St-Lambert

20

223

9

227

GRANBY

8

10

112

St Mathias

5

Fort-Chambly ★★

★ Chambly

Richelieu

112

La Prairie

11

11

6

30

104

112

132

10

16

15

18

10

235

11

223

Mt St-Grégoire
267

26

104

SHERBROOKE

15

35

5

St-Jean-sur-Richelieu

Iberville

Farnham

COWANSVILLE

22

21

219

R. l'Acadie

223

133

221

2

20

29

227

St-Patrice-de-
Sherrington

4

Napierville

221

R. Richelieu

R. aux Brochets
Nord

23

14

13

St-Paul-de-
l'île-aux-Noix

Fort-Lennox ★

Bedford

202

15

Barrington

9

Île aux Noix

Venise-
en-Québec

133

STANBRIDGE EAST

219

7

Lacolle

Blockhaus de la
Rivière Lacolle ★

202

7

3

223

202

17

Baie
Missisquoi
(L. Champlain)

235

R. Lacolle

7

221

Hemmingford

Parc Safari ★★

87

Fort Montgomery

89

U.S.A.

U.S.A.

Rouses
Point

VAUDREUIL-DORION

CHATEAUGUAY

Driving Tours

1 Patriots' Road – Chambly to Sorel-Tracy

78km/48.4mi by Rte. 133.

Chambly★ – *See Entry Heading.*

▸ *Leave Chambly by Rte. 112, cross the Richelieu River in the village of Richelieu and take Rte. 133 Nord.*

Saint-Mathias

7.4km/4.6mi northeast by Rte. 133.

The first settlers came to Saint-Mathias in 1700, when it was still part of the seigneury of Chambly. Today, lovely homes and marinas border the Chambly Basin. The wayside cross on the right, where Route 133 straddles the Huron River, is one of several that still exist along the Richelieu River.

The interior décor of the **church** (1784), on the east side of Rte. 133, dates from the 1820s and is the work of René Beauvais (known as Saint-James) and Paul Rollin, two companions of Louis-Amable Quévillon, who executed the pulpit and the main altar in 1797 (*visit by guided tour only: May–Oct, Mon, Wed, Fri 9am–noon; contribution requested;* ᗌ🅿☎450-658-1671).

▸ *Continue to Mont-St-Hilaire.*

The municipality of **Otterburn Park** (*9km/5.6mi*) boasts several splendid mansions. Across the river stands the McMasterville industrial complex, where explosives have been manufactured since 1878.

▸ *13.5km/8.4mi northeast by Rte. 133.*

Mont-Saint-Hilaire

Home of the renowned painter **Ozias Leduc** (1864–1955) and birthplace of 20C artist **Paul-Émile Borduas**, Mont-Saint-Hilaire is a well-known artistic centre.

Upon arriving in the community, notice the **Rouville-Campbell Manor** on the banks of the Richelieu River. This Tudor-style manor house with its tall brick chimneys was built in the 1850s for Major Thomas Edmund Campbell, who took over the Hertel de Rouville seigneury after the Rebellion of 1837. The mansion was modelled after the Campbell ancestral home in Inverane, Scotland. Artist Jordi Bonet (1932–79) restored the manor in the 1970s; it now houses an inn and a fine restaurant.

The charming little stone **church** by the river was built in 1837 and decorated by Ozias Leduc in 1898 (◷ *open Mon–Fri 9am–noon, 1.30pm–4.30pm; Sun 1pm–5pm;* ✏*contribution requested;* ᗌ🅿☎450-467-4434). On the opposite bank in the town of Belœil, the beautiful towers and turrets of the Église Saint-Mathieu-de-Belœil (St. Matthew of Belœil Church) are visible.

▸ *Make a detour (10km/6.2mi round-trip) to get to the Mt. Saint-Hilaire Nature Centre. Turn right on Rte. 116 (signposted) and right again on Rue Fortier which becomes Chemin Ozias-Leduc. After 3km/1.8mi, turn left on Chemin de la Montagne, and left again on Chemin des Moulins.*

Centre de la nature du mont Saint-Hilaire★★ (Mt. Saint-Hilaire Nature Centre)

422 Chemin des Moulins. ◷*Open year-round, daily 8am–1hr before dusk, reception manned 9am–4.15pm or longer.* ✏*$5.* ⊀ᗌ🅿☎450-467-1755. www.centrenature.qc.ca

Rising abruptly above the Richelieu Valley, Mt. Saint-Hilaire (411m/1,348.4ft) is the most imposing of the Monteregian Hills. The lush forest covering about 11sq km/4sq mi of the mountain has remained practically intact since the arrival of Europeans in Canada. Apple orchards (*in bloom late May*) blanket the mountain's lower slopes, as the Richelieu Valley is one of Quebec's main apple-growing regions.

Mont Saint-Hilaire is the former estate of Brigadier **Andrew Hamilton Gault** (1882–1958), founder of Princess Patricia's Canadian Light Infantry. He bequeathed his estate to McGill University in order to preserve its beauty and keep it from development. Today a 6sq km/2.3sq mi section of the park is open to the public, while a 5sq km/2sq mi tract is reserved for scientific research. Some 22km/13.6mi of **trails** crisscross the mountain. From the main summit (known as Pain du Sucre, or "Sugarloaf"), visitors can enjoy sweeping **views**★★ of the Richelieu River, the St. Lawrence valley, and the Olympic Tower in Montreal. Some trails lead to Lake Hertel where Gault erected his residence; it has since been converted into a conference center. A small rest area is available for hikers and cross-country skiers.

▶ *Return to Rte. 133.*

Saint-Charles-sur-Richelieu
16km/10mi north on Rte. 133.
It was here that the Patriots were defeated on November 25, 1837, by Colonel Wetherall, two days after the first victory at Saint-Denis (below). In the waterfront park, note the small bas-relief monument dedicated to the Patriots.On the river, the boat L'Escale features theatrical productions during the summer.

Saint-Denis-sur-Richelieu★
11.8km/7.3mi northeast on Rte. 133.
This prosperous agricultural community was the site of the Patriot victory over Colonel Gore, on November 23, 1837. In a pleasant square located in the center of the village, the Canadian tricolor flies above a wooden pedestal, beside a **monument** erected in honor of the Patriots. The inscription written by René Lévesque reads (in translation): "They fought for the recognition of our people, for political liberty and for a democratic system of government." It was placed here in 1987, to commemorate the 150th anniversary of the Rebellion.
Nearby, the **church**★ (Église de Saint-Denis-sur-Richelieu, 1796) is surmounted by large, twin copper towers, one of which contains the liberty bell used to call the Patriots to battle (*visit by guided tour only (1hr); 636 Chemin des Patriotes-Rte. 133;* ℗ ☎*450-787-2020; www.eglisestdenissurrichelieu.com*). The first religious structure in Quebec to have been built with two storeys, it features a double row of windows on the exterior. It is considered to be a "quasi-

cathedral" because a monumental look and size was achieved despite the difficulty of finding construction materials comparable with what was used in Europe. A modern façade has hidden the original structure since 1922. The interior décor of carved wood dates, for the most part, from the 1810s and is attributed to Louis-Amable Quévillon.

Maison Nationale des Patriotes★ (Patriots' National House)
610 Chemin des Patriotes (Rte. 133). ⊙*Open May–Sept, Tue–Sun 10am–noon, 1pm–5pm; Oct Sun 10am–noon, 1pm–5pm; Nov (Patriots' month), Tue–Fri 10am–4pm; Dec–Apr group reservations only.* ☞*$6.* ♿ ℗ ☎*450-787-3623. www.mndp.qc.ca.*
Built in 1810 for Jean-Baptiste Mâsse, a blacksmith, innkeeper, and merchant, this stone house serves as an interpretation centre on the Patriots' Rebellion of 1837–38. Displays and a slide show explain the background of the uprising and highlight the events that led the Patriots in their long fight for freedom and democracy. The battles of Saint-Denis, Saint-Charles, and Saint-Eustache are described. *Note: Displays and slide show in French only.*

Saint-Ours
11.8km/7.3mi northeast on Rte. 133.
In 1672, this seigneury was granted to Pierre de Saint-Ours. The river shoals impeded passing vessels until a dam and lock were completed in 1849. Erected in 1933, the present **Saint-Ours Canal and lock** (⊙*open late Jun–mid-Aug, daily 8.15am–8.15pm; late Aug–Labor Day, Mon–Fri 8.15am–6.15pm, weekends 8.15am–7.15pm; mid-May–mid-Jun & early Sept–mid-Oct, Mon–Fri 8.15am–4.15pm, weekends 8.15am–6.15pm;* ☞*$2.90;* ♿ ℗ *$4/day* ☎*450-785-2212; www.pc.gc.ca/stours*) is 103m/338ft long by 14m/46ft wide, and allows boats to be raised 1.5m/5ft in five minutes. At the turn of the 20C, ships carried timber, hay, and cereals to the US, and returned with coal, iron, copper, and building materials. Today a pleasant park equipped with picnic spots surrounds the lively lock area.

▷ *Beyond the lock (3km/1.8mi), a ferry links Saint-Ours to Saint-Roch. Return to Saint-Ours.*

Sorel-Tracy
18km/11mi.
Located at the confluence of the Richelieu and St. Lawrence rivers, this community was named for Pierre de Saurel, who received the seigneury in 1672. In 1781 Sir Frederick Haldimand, governor of Quebec, granted Sorel a municipal charter and renamed the town William-Henry (in honor of Prince William-Henry, the future King George IV). He also erected a garrison beside the Richelieu to counter the threat of an American invasion and ensure the security of the Loyalists established in the seigneury. Subsequently, the government acquired a large wooden house to lodge the commander of the garrison, General von Riedesel. It was in this house, remodeled several times and today known as the **Governor's House** (*90 Chemin des Patriotes*), that the Riedesels, of German origin, introduced the Christmas tree to Canada.

Carré Royal★ (Royal Square)
Created in 1791 to serve as the parade ground of the military town, this pleasant green space is today a park. Numerous footpaths crisscross it so that, by design, it resembles a British Flag from the air (*bound by Rue du Roi, Rue Charlotte, Rue du Prince, and Rue George*).
Sorel-Tracy is the site of the oldest Anglican mission in Canada (1784). The present **Christ Church** (1842), designed by John Wells in the Gothic Revival style, stands facing the Royal Square on Rue Prince. Between the square and the waterfront (Rue du Roi), a succession of bustling shops, restaurants, and cafés leads to the old market, a yellow brick building constructed in the 1940s. To the east (*Rue Augusta*), a waterfront park with a raised gazebo offers panoramic **views** of the port, the confluence of the Richelieu and St. Lawrence rivers, and the small, lively marina.

Sainte-Anne-de-Sorel
3.7km/2.3mi east by Rte. 132, then right onto Chemin Sainte-Anne.

The vault and walls of the nave of **Église Sainte-Anne** (St. Anne's Church, 1876) are adorned with 13 superb frescoes executed by the painter Suzor-Côté (◷ *open year-round, daily by appointment;* ☎450-743-7909).

Cruise to the Islands of Sorel★
Take Chemin du Chenal-du-Moine; follow signs to "Le Survenant Restaurant." Departs from Sainte-Anne-de-Sorel Jun 24–Labor Day, Tue–Sun 2pm & 4pm. Round-trip 1hr 30min. Commentary. Reservations advised. ◉$22. ⊞*Croisière des Îles de Sorel Inc.* ♿⊞ ☎450-743-7227 & 1-800-361-6420.
This boat trip allows visitors to discover the picturesque and enchanting Sorel Islands, and to see the majestic and powerful St. Lawrence in the distance. Starting at the Du Moine Canal, the boat passes a series of largely undeveloped islands, among them Île du Moine, Île de Grâce and Île d'Embarras. Several of the islands, laced with numerous intricate passageways, are accessible only by boat and are popular with ornithologists, hunters and fishermen.

② From Chambly to Hemmingford

80km/50mi by Rte. 223.

▷ *Leave Chambly by Rte. 223 Sud. The Chambly Canal is visible on the drive south.*

Saint-Jean-sur-Richelieu
– 16km/10mi. ☙*See Entry Heading.*

Île-aux-Noix
20km/12mi. Access by ferry from Saint-Paul-de-l'Île-aux-Noix.
☙*See Entry Heading.*
The Richelieu River widens as it approaches Lake Champlain and the US border. Numerous marinas dot its course.

Blockhaus de la rivière Lacolle★ (Lacolle River Blockhouse)
9km/5.6mi. ◷*Open mid-May–mid-Oct, daily 9am–5pm.* ⊞ ☎450-246-3227.

This two-level log structure was built in 1781 as part of the British defense system to repel American invasion. Standing on the Lacolle River, a tributary of the Richelieu, it is the only defense of its kind remaining in Quebec. During the war of 1812, it withstood attack on three occasions, and bullet holes are still visible on the façade. Recently restored by the Quebec government, the interior houses displays on the military history of the blockhouse. Note the loopholes for muskets and the openings for cannons.

▸ *Continue south on Rte. 223 and turn right on Rte. 202.*

Parc Safari★★ (Safari Park) Kids

35km/21.7mi, before entering Hemmingford. ⊙Open Jun 24–late Aug, daily 10am–7pm; mid-May–mid-Jun & late Aug–early Oct, daily 10am–4pm. ⊜$36 (late Jun–Aug) or $21 (rest of the season and under-17yrs). ⚹♿🅿☎450-247-2727. www.parcsafari.com.

Some 800 animals of 75 different species from Africa, Eurasia and the Americas roam freely in large enclosures in this zoological park. Required to remain in their vehicles, visitors can follow the **Car Safari** (*4km/2.5mi*) along which they can take photographs, touch and feed the animals. The **Enchanted Forest** combines an amusement park and water slides in a zoo-like setting. On the **jungle walk**, visitors can observe the monkeys on their island, walk through the deer compound and cross bridges to look down on lions, tigers and bears. Animal shows at the theatre (*Théâtre sous les Arbres*) and a circus in the stadium (*regular performances*) provide further entertainment; animal rides on elephants or ponies and a petting zoo complete the visit.

RIGAUD

MONTÉRÉGIE REGION

POPULATION 6,888

This small residential town lies at the confluence of the Rigaud and Ottawa rivers, on the border between Ontario and Quebec. Rigaud was originally part of the seigneury granted to Pierre and François Rigaud, sons of the Sieur de Vaudreuil, in 1732. In 1850, members of the Viatorian Clerics came to Rigaud to found a college at the request of Ignace Bourget, Bishop of Montreal. Today, Bourget College is the largest private boarding school in Canada, with more than 1,200 students. **Rigaud Mountain** (213m/699ft), renowned for its shrine and ski center, dominates the town.

🛈 **Information:** ☎1-866-469-0069. www.tourisme-monteregie.qc.ca.
▸ **Orient Yourself:** Rigaud is 70km/43mi west of Montreal by Rte. 40 (Exit 12).
☺ **Don't Miss:** Sanctuaire Notre-Dame-de-Lourdes
Kids **Especially for Kids:** Abraska, la forêt des aventures

Visit

Sanctuaire Notre-Dame de Lourdes★ (Our Lady of Lourdes Shrine)

Rue de Lourdes (at street end). From Rue Saint-Jean-Baptiste, turn left on Rue Saint-Pierre, and follow signs. ⊙Open Jun–mid-Sept, daily (communion at 4.30pm). ⊜Contribution requested. ⚹♿🅿☎450-451-4631. www.viateur.ca.

Built into the rocky hillside, this open-air "Canadian Lourdes" sanctuary was inspired by the shrine of Lourdes in France, site of a 1958 apparition of the Virgin Mary to Bernadette Soubirous, a 14-year-old peasant girl.
In 1874, Brother Ludger Pauzé, a teacher at the Bourget College, placed a statue of Our Lady of Lourdes in a niche on the mountainside. After his death, visitors, encouraged by the college's Superior, Father François-Xavier Chouinard, con-

tinued devotions to the Virgin Mary. In 1887, to accommodate the growing number of faithful, a larger statue was installed in a more accessible site, and a small chapel was built. A second, open-sided chapel was added in 1954.

Immediately upon arrival, the visitor discovers this latest chapel nestled in greenery (*masses are held in the summer months*). A path leads up the hillside past the statue to the original chapel, shaped like an eight-sided belvedere. It offers a remarkable **view**★ of the Ottawa and Rigaud rivers and the surrounding area. The pink rock visible on the hillside is Potsdam sandstone.

RIMOUSKI★

BAS-SAINT-LAURENT REGION
POPULATION 42,516
MAP: SEE CÔTE DE CHARLEVOIX

Built along the banks of the St. Lawrence, this industrial city has developed in a semicircular pattern around the mouth of the Rimouski River. Once a vast forest, the surrounding region long served as hunting grounds for the Micmac Indians. Granted as a seigneury in 1688, the territory was acquired in 1694 by the French merchant René Lepage, who settled here two years later. Rimouski is a Mi'kmaq term meaning "land of the moose."

The local economy, based on agriculture and seasonal fishing, experienced rapid growth during the early 20C, when the Price Brothers Company established sawmills and forestry operations. The city was rebuilt after the great fire of 1950 and is now considered the principal metropolis of eastern Quebec.

- 🛈 **Information:** 50 Rue Saint-Germain Ouest. ☎418-723-2322 & 1-800-746-6875. www.tourismebas-st-laurent.com.
- ▶ **Orient Yourself:** Rimouski is 312km/193mi northeast of Quebec City by Rtes. 73 (Pierre-Laporte Bridge) and 20, and Rte. 132.
- 😊 **Don't Miss:** The Pointe-au-Père Lighthouse and Maritime museum.
- 🕐 **Organizing Your Time:** Rimouski is halfway between Québec City and Gaspé, so it makes sense to stop here for a meal or for an overnight stay.
- Kids **Especially for Kids:** Camp Maritime Ulysse.

Sights

Musée régional de Rimouski (Rimouski Regional Museum)

35 Rue Saint-Germain Ouest. 🕐*Open late Jun–Labor Day, Wed–Fri 9.30am–8pm, Sat–Tue 9.30am–6pm); rest of the year, Wed–Sun noon–5pm (Thu 9pm).* ⬤*$4.* 🍴⬤🅿 ☎*418-724-2272. www.musee rimouski.qc.ca.*

The stone building that has housed the museum since the early 1970s was built in 1824 and served as the parish church until 1862. It was then used as a seminary, a convent, and a primary school. Dedicated to contemporary art, the museum presents mainly temporary exhibits.

Address Book

For price ranges, see the Legend on the cover flap.

WHERE TO STAY

$$–$$$ Hôtel Rimouski – *225 Blvd. René-Lepage Est. SPA-Indoor Pool* 🍴 ℗ ☎418-725-5000 & 1-800-463-0755, www.quebecmaritime.ca/hotelrimouski. *185 rooms, including 52 suites.* Rimouski's biggest and best hotel, with a great view over the river.

MARITIME GAMES

Institut Maritime du Québec Camp Maritime Ulysse – *53 Rue Saint-Germain Oues.* ☎418-724-2822. *www.imq.qc.ca.* Young mariners aged 11 to 18 will have great fun and a truly memo-rable time at Camp Maritime Ulysse. Participants face marine challenges aboard kayaks and sailboats. Camps last 6 or 12 days. Enough time for parents to have adventures of their own!

SPORTS

$–$$ La Cage aux Sports – *130 Ave Belisle.* ☎418-723-7433. Quebec's ultimate chain of sports bar and restaurant, La Cage aux Sports serves hearty, traditional Canadian food, roast chicken, grilled meats, and barbecuedpork ribs. Portions are enormous, just like the multiple TV screens connected to sports around the world.

Maison Lamontagne★ (Lamontagne House)

3km/1.8mi east of the centre of town on Rte. 132; turn right onto Blvd. du Rivage at Rimouski-Est. Follow signs. ⏰*Open late Jun 24–Labor Day, daily 9am–6pm; rest of the year upon reservation.* ☜*$4.* 🍴 ℗ ☎ *418-722-4038.* www.maisonlamontagne.com.

This large house was built in two phases: The longer section, of masonry half-timbering, dates from the second half of the 18C, while the full timbering section was completed around 1810. The structure is one of the few remaining examples of masonry half-timbering in North America; French settlers soon discovered that the stones between the timbering conducted cold and heat into the interior, making this type of construction unsuitable for the harsh Canadian climate. Occupied until 1959, the house was restored in 1981. Expositions mounted inside trace the development of Quebec domestic architecture and re-create rural life in the province during the late 18C. Displays of building materials, artisan craftsmanship, construction techniques and architectural styles, along with a virtual exhibition entitled *De pierre, de bois, de brique*, provide an overview of Québec history .

Musée de la mer et lieu historique national du Canada du phare de Pointe-au-Père★ (Maritime Museum and Pointe-au-Père Lighthouse National Historic Site of Canada)

1034 Rue du Phare, Pointe-au-Père, 10km/6.2mi from Rimouski. Turn left off Rte. 132 onto Rue Père-Nouvel, then right to the museum. ⏰*Open early-Jun–Aug, daily 9am–6pm; Sept–mid-Oct, daily 9am–5pm.* ☜*$10.50.* 🍴 ℗ ☎*418-724-6214. www.museedelamer.qc.ca. www.pc.gc.ca/pointeauperelighthouse. www.shmp.qc.ca.*

The first floor of the keeper's house is dedicated to the Empress of Ireland, nicknamed the "Titanic of the St. Lawrence," which sank close to shore on May 29, 1914, claiming 1,012 lives. Because of the outbreak of World War I shortly thereafter, and the immigrant status of most of the passengers, the disaster lay forgotten for half a century. Since the mid-1960s, hundreds of diving expeditions have recovered numerous objects from the wreck. Many of these artifacts are on display in the museum. A multimedia exhibition re-creates the sinking of the *Empress of Ireland*. In the adjacent **lighthouse** (1909), the second-tallest in Canada, exhibits trace the daily life of a lighthouse keeper at the beginning of the 20C. Climb the 128 steps to the top for a good **view**★ of the coastline.

RIVIÈRE-DU-LOUP★

BAS-SAINT-LAURENT REGION
POPULATION 18,789
MAP: SEE CÔTE DE CHARLEVOIX

Situated in the heart of the Bas-Saint-Laurent region between Quebec City and the Gaspé Peninsula, Rivière-du-Loup commands a geographical position favorable to both commerce and tourism. A ferry links the industrial city to Saint-Siméon, on the north shore of the St. Lawrence in the Charlevoix region, and the Trans-Canada Highway leads south to New Brunswick.

- **Information:** 189 Blvd. de l'Hôtel-de-Ville. ☎418-862-1981 & 1-888-825-1981. www.tourismebas-st-laurent.com.
- **Orient Yourself:** Rivière-du-Loup is located 193km/120mi northeast of Quebec City by Rte. 20 or Rte. 132.
- **Don't Miss:** Chutes de la rivière du Loup.
- **Organizing Your Time:** Rivière-du-Loup marks the end of the freeway (Rte. 20) that splits there into highways leading to Gaspésie and New Brunswick. So it is good idea to pause in Rivière-du-Loup before moving on.

A Bit of History

There are three theories on the origin of the name Rivière-du-Loup (literally "river of the wolf"). According to one, a French ship, named *le Loup,* may have spent the winter here around 1660. Local legend recounts that Champlain encountered an Amerindian tribe called the Mahigans, or wolves, in this area. The third possibility is that the name commemorates the seals, or *loups-marins,* that were commonly sighted at the mouth of the river.

The seigneury of Rivière-du-Loup was granted to Charles Aubert de la Chesnaye, ancestor of writer Philippe-Aubert de Gaspé, in 1673. Together with his companion, Sieur Charles Bazire, he became one of the wealthiest traders in New France, profiting from the furs and fish found in the region. The two partners had so little interest in settling the territory that from 1683 through 1765, the population grew from 4 to only 68. The colony began to expand significantly in 1802, when the seigneury was bought by Alexander Fraser, whose

Address Book

For price ranges, see cover flap.

WHERE TO STAY

$$–$$$ Auberge de la Pointe – 10 Blvd. Cartier. SPA-Indoor Pool ☎418-862-3514 & 1-800-463-1222. www.aubergedelapointe.com. 17 rooms, including 69 with a view on the St. Lawrence River and a private balcony. The Auberge de la Pointe is a true resort accommodation located on the riverside. On site, you can swim, relax in the eight-seat whirlpool, enjoy the spa, be treated at the award-winning restaurant (**$$-$$$**). Close by, you can depart for whale watching cruises and island tours.

BIRD WATCHING

Société Duvetnor Ltée (*200 Rue Hayward;* ☎418-867-1660 (*reservations by phone only); www.duvetnor.com*) provides you with the opportunity to spot Double-crested Cormorants, Great Blue Herons, and even black Guillemots on a nature reserve composed of several islands—Les Pèlerins, Les Îles du Pot-de-l'Eau-de-vie, and l'Île-aux-Lièvres. Accommodation, cruises, and tours organized on your behalf from June to September. Rich wildlife and a secluded environment guarantee a visit accompanied only by the sounds of nature.

involvement in the lumber trade with England brought prosperity to Rivière-du-Loup. In 1860, the arrival of the railway linking the city with Windsor (in the Eastern Townships) to the south provided another important boost to the economy. In 1887 the Témiscouata Railway in turn connected the city to New Brunswick.

The prosperity of the late 19C and early 20C is reflected in the opulent homes and public buildings of this period.

Walking Tour

Town Center★

Hôtel de Ville (Town Hall)
At the corner of Rue Lafontaine and Blvd. Hôtel-de-Ville.
Completed in 1917, the city hall occupies the former site of the market building, destroyed by fire in 1910. An unusual architectural element is the main clock tower, typical of city halls found in the English-speaking provinces.

▶ *After leaving City Hall, turn right on Rue Lafontaine. Cross Rue Lafontaine to Rue de la Cour.*

Located at the corner of Rue Lafontaine and Rue de la Cour, the limestone and brick **Courthouse** was designed by David Ouellet in 1881. It has undergone three major renovations. The **Old Post Office** (1889), a stately dark brick edifice on Rue Iberville (*turn right from Rue Lafontaine*), exemplifies institutional architecture of Anglo-Saxon origin. It is now a community center.

▶ *Continue on Rue Iberville. Turn right on Rue du Domaine, continue to Rue du Rocher and turn right.*

Bibliothèque municipale (Municipal Library)
The Second Empire stone structure was built in 1886 by David Ouellet. For nearly a century, it served as the convent of the Good Shepherd Sisters. After the religious community left in 1978, it was renovated and converted into a library (1983).

Additional Sights

Musée du Bas-Saint-Laurent (Bas-Saint-Laurent Museum)
300 Rue Saint-Pierre. ○Open late Jun–early Oct, daily 10am–6pm; rest of the year, Wed–Sun 1pm–5pm. ○Closed Jan 1 & Dec. 25. ∞$5. 418-862-7547. www.mbsl.qc.ca
Cultural heritage and contemporary art are smartly incorporated into the museum's various temporary exhibits. Works by local artists are also shown.

Chutes de la rivière du Loup★ (Loup River Falls)
Take Rue Lafontaine north to Rue Frontenac and turn right. The falls are two blocks away.
The Loup River drops 90m/295ft before joining the St. Lawrence, and a series of eight cascades interrupts the river flow over a distance of 1,500m/4,920ft. Here, the falls are 38m/125ft high. Steps lead to a lookout providing an expansive view of the town and river. The **illuminated cross** on the cliff overlooking the river is also visible from this point.

Excursion

Cabano
60km/37mi southeast of Rivière-du-Loup by Rte. 185.
This lumbering center occupies a pleasant **site**★ on Lake Témiscouata. The lake was part of an important portage route connecting the St. Lawrence and St. John rivers. In 1839, Fort Ingall was built to protect this route.

Fort Ingall
2km/1.2mi by Rte. 232. ○Open late Jun–Labor Day, daily 9am–5pm; early Jun & rest of Sept, Mon–Fri 10am–4.30pm. ∞$7. 418-854-2375 & 1-866-242-2437. www.roseraie.qc.ca.
Surrounded by a wooden stockade, this lakeside fort complex (1839–42) once housed two hundred soldiers. Among its several reconstructed log buildings are the South Barracks, a blockhouse, and the Officers' Quarters, where displays on regional history are presented.

ROBERVAL

SAGUENAY–LAC SAINT-JEAN REGION
POPULATION 10,767
MAP: SEE LAC SAINT-JEAN

Located on the southwestern shore of Lake Saint-Jean, this city is named after Jean-François de La Rocque, Sieur de Roberval, appointed first-lieutenant of Canada by King François I. It was under Roberval's orders that Jacques Cartier led an ill-fated expedition to colonize the St. Lawrence region in 1541 (Cartier's third voyage to the region). Founded in 1855, Roberval was the site of the prestigious Beemer Hotel at the end of the 19C, owned by the American lumber magnate Horace Jansen Beemer, who also operated two steamships on the lake. The magnificent mansion was destroyed by fire in 1908. Today Roberval is an important service centre for the area and the finish point of the **International Swim Marathon** (Traversée internationale du lac Saint-Jean, *see Calendar of Events*).

- **Information:** ☎1-877-253-8387. www.ville.roberval.qc.ca or www.saguenaylacsaintjean.net.
- ▶ **Orient Yourself:** Roberval is on the west shore of Lac Saint-Jean, 259km/161mi north of Quebec City by Rtes. 175 and 169.
- **Don't Miss:** The Innu community of Mashteuiatsh.

Sights

Église Notre-Dame-de-Roberval★ (Our Lady of Roberval Church)

484 Blvd. Saint-Joseph at the corner of Ave. Lizotte, across from the hospital. ⏱*Open year-round, Sat 9.30am–8pm, Sun 8am–noon.* ♿🅿 ☎*418-275-0272.* Built in 1967, this church resembles a large copper tent topped by a white steeple. The interior is shaped like a pyramid rising above the central altar. The brightly colored stained-glass windows were fashioned by Guy Bruneau.

Excursions

Lac Saint-Jean★★ – *See Entry Heading.*

Mashteuiatsh Innu Reserve (Pointe-Bleue)

9km/5.6mi north of Roberval by Blvd. Saint-Joseph.
This strip of land jutting into Lake Saint-Jean is the site of a reserve created in 1856 for the local indigenous population, mainly Montagnais Indians (also called Innu). Visitors can browse through the shops of the Pointe-Bleue village, featuring Amerindian handicrafts, and walk along the lake. Fur hats and coats are about 50 percent less costly here than in Montreal outlets.
An Amerindian celebration called *Jeux autochtones inter-bandes* (Indigenous Games) is held in July.

Musée amérindien de Mashteuiatsh (Mashteuiatsh Amerindian Museum)

1787 Rue Amishk. ⏱*Open May–Jun, daily 9am–6pm, Jul–mid-Aug, Thu–Tue 9am–6pm & Wed 9am–7.30pm, mid-Aug–mid-Oct, daily 9am–6pm, mid-Oct–mid-May, Mon–Fri 8am–noon & 1pm–4pm.* ☎$9. ♿🅿 ☎*418-275-4842 & 1-888-875-4842; www.museeilnu.ca*
This intriguing museum introduces visitors to the history and culture of the Pekuakamiulnuatsh (Montagnais Indians from the Lake Saint-Jean region)—their traditional lifestyle, customs, language and role in today's society. A small shop offers handicrafts created in the village of Mashteuiatsh.

ROUYN-NORANDA

ABITIBI-TÉMISCAMINGUE REGION
POPULATION 40,478

Located in the heart of the Abitibi region, directly on the watershed line and astride the most mineral-rich portion of the Cadillac Fault, Rouyn-Noranda is both the regional capital of the Abitibi region and its main population center. Abitibi, a relatively uncultivated region of forest, rock, lakes, and rivers, takes its name from an Algonquian term meaning "watershed line." The region rests on a peneplain, or flat land surface created by erosion, gently sloping toward James Bay, carrying along the waters of Lake Abitibi and the Harricana River.

Not just another mining town, the city is the region's cultural center boasting an international film festival and vibrant artistic community. In order to counteract the negative aesthetic effect of mining, residents are dedicated to the development of parks and their prize flower gardens. Rouyn-Noranda proudly claims Richard Desjardins, the popular singer, poet, and activist as its native son.

- **Information:** 155 Ave. Dallaire. ☎819-762-8181 & 1-800-808-0706. www.abitibi-temiscamingue.org.
- ▶ **Orient Yourself:** Rouyn-Noranda is located 638km/396mi northwest of Montreal by Rte. 117. Air Canada flies daily to the city from Montreal; www.aircanada.ca.
- **Don't Miss:** The free guided tour of the Horne Smelter (be sure to wear trousers and enclosed shoes).

A Bit of History

Natural Resources – Since commerce in the area depended entirely on water transportation, settlement only began in 1912, when the first railway line linking Abitibi to nearby Northern Ontario was inaugurated. However, the real catalyst for the sudden and rapid colonization of the Abitibi region was the discovery of the **Cadillac Fault**, a geological structure rich in copper, gold and silver, which traverses the Abitibi region west to east, through Rouyn-Noranda and Val-d'Or. The fault, which splays into innumerable secondary fractures, was the primary focus of mineral prospectors at the turn of the 20C century, resulting in the region's phenomenal development. While the portion of the fault located in Quebec was being explored, mining of the Ontario portion was already underway, notably in Kirkland Lake. The Abitibi region long remained within the commercial sphere of Ontario, where investors and capital were more abundant. In the 1950s, as the veins in the area were being depleted, mining operations moved farther north, yet mining remains one of this region's most important economic resources.

Two mining towns – As its name indicates, Rouyn-Noranda is the result of a merger between the towns of Noranda and Rouyn. Although both are mining towns, their history is quite different. **Noranda** owed its creation to Ontarian interests and was primarily Anglophone: The town's name is a contraction of the words *north* and *Canada*. In its early days, it was essentially a residential town, administered exclusively by the Noranda mine. The town of **Rouyn** was named after Sieur de Rouyn, a captain of the Royal Roussillon regiment, famed for his battle against the English at Sainte-Foy, near Quebec City. Rouyn was originally a meeting place for adventurers in search of a quick fortune; at that time, it was known as the "street of pleasures" (*rue des plaisirs*). The town is truly a product of the gold rush (which in fact became a copper rush) of 1923. Primarily Francophone, it was home to most of the miners and is today the business district of the city.

361

Sights

Maison Dumulon★ (Dumulon House)

191 Ave. du Lac. Approaching from the direction of Val-d'Or, turn left off Rte. 117 onto Ave. du Lac and continue to Lake Osisko, where a tourist information booth is located. ⏲*Open late Jun–Labor Day, daily 8.30am–5pm; rest of the year, Mon–Fri noon–8pm, Sat–Sun noon–5pm.* ⌨*Admission free; guided tours $6.* ♿🅿☎*819-797-712. www.maison-dumulon.ca.*

This reconstructed house re-creates the atmosphere of the 1920s, when it served as Rouyn's first general store and post office. Photographs and various objects reminiscent of bygone days trace the history of the town. The local tourism office is located in the building.

Located in the **Parc des Pionniers** (Pioneer Park) next to the Dumulon House, the Tremoy promenade leads along Lake Osisko to the Centre nautique de Rouyn-Noranda.

Église orthodoxe russe (Russian Orthodox Church)

201 Rue Taschereau Ouest; turn left off Rue Larivière. ⏲*Open late Jun–Labor Day, daily 10am–5pm.* ⌨*Admission is free, guided tour is $3.* ☎*819-797-7125.*

Among the wave of immigrants arriving after World War II to work as miners were about 20 Russian families; to serve them, Father Ustuchenko erected this small church according to the principles of Russian Orthodoxy. The two superimposed cupolas are intended to represent God embracing the earth. The church has been transformed into a small but extensively documented **museum**, full of picturesque details which lead the visitor to the heart of the Russian soul.

Théâtre du Cuivre (Copper Theater)

145 Rue Taschereau.

In 1987 this eminently contemporary building, topped by a copper roof, won the prestigious Felix award for best theater in the province. It hosts movies, plays, and concerts, as well as the popular Abitibi-Témiscamingue *Festival du cinéma international.*

Noranda Metallurgie

101 Rue Portelance.

The discovery of this mine led to the rush of 1923. In 1927, the mine started operations with the help of American and Canadian investors. A total of 51 million tons of high-grade copper and gold ore were mined (on average, five tons of ore are required to produce one ounce of gold). A smelter now occupies the site of the former mine.

Fonderie Horne (Horne Smelter)

101 Ave. Portelance. ☞*Visit by guided tour (2hrs) only, mid-Jun–Labor Day, daily 9am–3pm. Rest of the year by appointment.* ☎*819-762-7764.*

The exhibit here focuses on the entire copper mining and refining process: from extraction to the production of an anode, a large 99 percent copper ingot weighing about 290kg/639lbs. After touring the home of Edmund Horne, discoverer of the Noranda Mine: Visitors enter a railway compartment where a film on mining and the history of the region is presented. Finally, everyone is invited to don helmets and boots to visit the surface installations of the smelter.

Excursion

Angliers

From Rouyn-Noranda head west on Rte. 117. Past Arntfield, turn off Rte. 117 and go south on Rte. 101. About 5km/3mi south of the village of Rollet, turn left onto Rte. 391 to Angliers.

This peaceful village is home to the old **T.E. Draper**, a tugboat used to haul lumber when rivers were the only way to transport materials and reach remote areas (⏲*open Jun 24–Labor Day, daily 10am–6pm;* ⌨*$5;* ♿🅿☎*819-949-4431).* The vessel was in service from 1929 through 1979, dropping off passengers at the southern end of Lake Témiscamingue. You can also tour the Gédéon logging site, a reconstructed logging camp.

FJORD DU SAGUENAY★★★

SAGUENAY-LAC-SAINT-JEAN REGION
MAP: SEE FJORD DU SAGUENAY

Measuring 155km/96mi, the Saguenay River is the only river draining Lake Saint-Jean. Over its first 9km/5.6mi of the section between Alma and Jonquière, the once roaring torrent, which drops about 90m/295ft, has been harnessed and has spawned one of the most industrialized areas in Canada. After 50km/31mi, at Saint-Fulgence, the river flows into the majestic Saguenay fjord that extends to Tadoussac, and empties into the St. Lawrence.

The deep channel through which the Saguenay flows beyond Saint-Fulgence, was gouged in Precambrian rock by glaciers during the last ice age. As the ice receded, the sea swept into the valley, and to this day, tidewaters reach up as far as Chicoutimi. The channel is 1,500m/4,920ft wide in places and has an average depth of 240m/787ft. Rocky cliffs plunge into the dark waters from heights of up to 457m/1,500ft. The Saguenay is the southernmost fjord in the world.

🛈 **Information:** www.saguenaylacsaintjean.net/www.fjord-du-saguenay.qc.ca.

▶ **Orient Yourself:** The fjord is accessible from Quebec City either by Rte. 175 north to Chicoutimi (about 200km/124mi) or by Rte. 138 northeast to Tadoussac (220km/136mi). Route 172 runs along the north shore of the fjord; Rte. 170 follows the south shore.

◉ **Don't Miss:** The drive down the Éternité River valley to the interpretation center on the shore of the fjord.

🕐 **Organizing Your Time:** Although roads circumnavigate the fjord, panoramic views are rare. The best way to see it is by taking one of the cruises from Chicoutimi, Baie Éternité, or Tadoussac. Hikers can get spectacular views of the fjord from trails to cliffs at Baie Éternité and L'Anse-St-Jean.

◔ **Also See:** TADOUSSAC.

A Bit of History

For over 4,000 years the Saguenay has been the *chemin qui cours,* or water route, for the First Nations who paddled upstream to go to their fur-trapping grounds. Upon landing here in 1534, Jacques Cartier first heard of the vast riches of the **Royaume du Saguenay** (Kingdom of the Saguenay). Colonization

View of the Fjord

began in 1838 when William Price created *Société des vingt et un:* 21 hard-working men who left Charlevoix to start new lives in complete wilderness. The area's industrial riches proved illusive until the beginning of the 20C, when the river was finally harnessed for hydroelectricity, giving the local economy an important boost. The Upper Saguenay (Haut-Saguenay) has since been extensively industrialized, and hydroelectric power plants, pulp mills, and aluminum smelters dot its shores. In contrast, the undeveloped Lower Saguenay (Bas-Saguenay) is lined with long stretches of uninhabited land. The Saguenay's stark and untamed beauty has attracted visitors for years. Most choose to take a scenic river cruise, but

the fjord can also be enjoyed by exploring the villages nestled along its shores. A spectacular natural park has been created to preserve part of the shoreline (⊙*difficult access*). The recent popularity of sea kayaking has allowed soft adventure seekers to enjoy fully the beauty of the fjord.

From Tadoussac to l'Anse-Saint-Jean
250km/155mi.

There are several ways to visit this region—by boat, kayak, or car. As there are no bridges that cross the fjord, begin on the north shore at Tadoussac, cross the Saguenay River at Chicoutimi, then explore the southern shore.

Tadoussac★★ –
⊙*See Entry Heading.*

▸ *Take Rte. 138 north for 6km/4mi, then turn left on Rte. 172 and continue for 11km/6.8mi to Sacré-Cœur. Take another left and continue for 8km/5mi.*

L'Anse de Roche (Rock Bay)
25km/15.5mi. Turn left in Sacré-Cœur.

This tiny cove offers a splendid **view**★ of the fjord and the massive power lines that span it, carrying electricity from the Manicouagan region to Montreal and the rest of Southern Quebec.

▸ *Return to Rte. 172.*

Sainte-Rose-du-Nord
69km/43mi. Turn left at sign.
Founded in 1838, this charming village is nestled in a cove between two rocky escarpments. A stroll down to the wharf reveals an exceptional **site**★★, while a walk to the scenic lookout will provide a great view of the village and fjord. The small **nature museum** contains a fascinating collection of nature's oddities, including wood twisted and polished into fantastic shapes, and wild mushrooms (⊙*open daily mid-May–mid-Sept, 8.45am–8.30pm (to 6.30pm mid-Sept–mid-May);* ⊛*$5.50;* ⊕☎*418-675-2348; www.museedelanature.com*).
On its descent towards **Saint-Fulgence** (28km/17.4mi), Rte. 172 affords a magnificent **panorama**★ of the fjord's western end. **Mt. Valin** (968m/3,175ft) rises about 20km/12.4mi to the north of the town. Weather patterns are increasingly difficult to predict in Southern Quebec's ski resorts, but Mt. Valin is a reliable

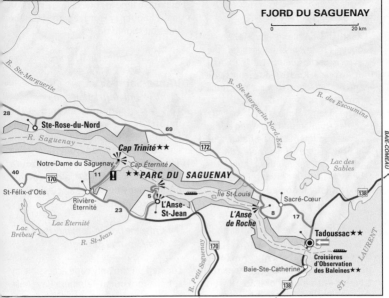

FJORD DU SAGUENAY

source of winter beauty and recreation in wintertime.

▶ *Follow Rtes. 172 and 175 south to Chicoutimi, crossing over the Saguenay.*

Chicoutimi★
16km/10mi from Saint-Fulgence.
🕭 *See Entry Heading.*

La Baie – *19km/11.8mi by Rte. 372.*
🕭 *See Entry Heading.*

▶ *Follow Rte. 170 to Rivière-Éternité (43km/26.7mi). Turn left at sign.*

Parc du Saguenay★★ (Saguenay Park)
🕔*Open mid-May–mid-Oct, daily 8am–8pm; only Baie Éternité sector remains open rest of the year 8.30am–4pm.* ⏗*$3.50.* △ 🗶 🅿 ☎*1-800-665-6527. www.sepaq.com*

Hiking, kayaking, and cross-country skiing. This park was created in 1983 to protect the banks of the fjord. It covers roughly 300sq km/116sq mi and extends about 100km/62mi from La Baie to Tadoussac. Popular areas within the park include Sainte-Marguerite Bay, Tadoussac Dunes, and Éternité Bay. The latter is one of the prettiest coves on the

fjord, dominated by the large twin cliffs, Cape Trinité and Cape Éternité.

The capes are best appreciated by taking a scenic **mini-cruise** (*departs from Baie Éternité late May–late Sept, daily 11.45am; round-trip 1.5hr; commentary;* ⏗ *$20;* 🅿 *Croisières AML* ☎*1-800-563-4643; www.croisieresaml.com*). A footpath beside the bay also affords attractive views. 🏃A superb 25km/15.5mi hiking trail connects Rivière-Éternité to Anse-Saint-Jean (cabins and campgrounds available).

An **interpretation center** located at the end of the Éternité River valley features exhibits tracing the origins of the fjord (🕔 *open early Jun–Aug 24, daily 9am–6pm; rest of Aug–Sept, daily 9am–4pm;* 🗶 ☎*418-272-1509*).

Cap Trinité★★
11km/6.8mi from Rivière-Éternité.
Named so because of its three ledges, this cape rises 518m/1,700ft over the fjord. It is renowned for the impressive statue of the Virgin Mary that stands on the first ledge about 180m/590ft above the black waters of the Saguenay. Known as **Our Lady of the Saguenay**, the statue was created in 1881 by Louis Jobin at the request of a businessman, Charles-Napoléon Robitaille, who had

Sacré Coeur

Another stop along Route 172 that offers an impressive view of the fjord is Sacré-Coeur. Visit the wharf at **Anse-de-Roche**, engage in some aquatic activities or for a real thrill, rent a kayak for whale watching. At Rivière Éternité enjoy the 175 nativity scenes from around the world at the Exposition Internationale de Crèches at the Église de Rivière-Éternité (*☎418-272-2807*). In the winter, each home in the village is decorated with its own nativity scene.

vowed to honor the Virgin after his life was spared on two occasions.
Over 8m/26ft tall, the statue was carved from three huge blocks of pine and then covered with a layer of lead. Hoisting the 3,175kg/7,000lb wood and metal creation into place proved a challenge. After numerous attempts, the statue was separated into pieces and later reassembled. A steep path leads from the interpretation centre to the statue (*about 7km/4.3mi round-trip, allow 4hrs*) and provides dramatic **panoramas★★**. This path requires a good fitness level but it is not technically difficult. If you only have time for one hiking excursion in the Saguenay Fjord region, this is the one you should do.

Return to Rte. 170 (11km/6.8mi).

L'Anse-Saint-Jean

23km/14.3mi. Turn left at sign.
This tiny community located at the mouth of the Saint-Jean River was founded in 1828. A good **view★** of the fjord can be enjoyed from the marina and the wharf. Note also the **Faubourg Bridge** (1929), a 37m/121ft-long covered bridge that spans the Saint-Jean River near the church.

Cross the bridge, continue for 5km/3mi and turn right.

Located on the only cape accessible by car, the lookout at Tabatière Bay (Anse de Tabatière) affords a superb **view** of the surrounding area.

Excursion

Scenic Cruises★★

Departures from Chicoutimi and Tadoussac. *See Entry Headings Chicoutimi and Tadoussac.*

SAINT-CONSTANT

MONTÉRÉGIE REGION
POPULATION 24,449
MAP: SEE MONTREAL

Located on the south shore of the St. Lawrence, this former farming community was thrust into industrialization in 1888 with the construction of the Canadian Pacific Railway bridge across the St. Lawrence. Today a residential suburb of Montreal, Saint-Constant is also the birthplace of Gustave Lanctot (1883–1975), historian, archivist, and author of numerous works on New France.

- **Information:** ☎1-866-469-0069. www.tourisme-monteregie.qc.ca.
- **Orient Yourself:** Saint-Constant is 20km/12.4mi south of Montreal by the Champlain Bridge, Rtes. 15, 132 and 209; or by the Honoré-Mercier Bridge, Rtes. 132 and 209.
- **Organizing Your Time:** Both Honoré-Mercier and Champlain Bridges are extremely busy at rush hours.
- **Especially for Kids:** The railway museum is a must for children and adults.
- **Also See:** CÔTE SAINTE-CATHERINE LOCK.

Sight

Exporail, le Musée Ferroviaire Canadien★ (Canadian Railway Museum) `Kids`

110 Rue Saint-Pierre (Rte. 209), walking distance from the Saint-Constant suburban train station. ◷*Open mid-May–Labor Day, daily 10am–6pm; Sept–Oct, Wed–Sun 10am–5pm; Nov–Apr, weekends 10am–5pm.* ∞*$14; children 4–12yrs $7.* P⊚*450-632-2410. www.exporail.org.*

Established and operated by the Canadian Railroad Historical Association, this large museum site composed of several buildings highlights the important role played by railroads in the development of Canada. In addition to some 6,000 artifacts, 185,000 archival documents, and a restored train station, the museum preserves an exceptional collection of more than 130 locomotives and other railway vehicles (including 44 railway cars in the main building), many of which are in working order. Regular demonstrations on the operation of the trains allow visitors to recapture the past.

Among the steam locomotives is a replica of the tiny **Dorchester**, which pulled the first Canadian train in 1836. Built in England and transported to Saint-Jean-sur-Richelieu by barge, the engine had the power to pull just two cars, and had to be supplemented by horses at even slight inclines. Also on display is an exact replica of the **John Molson**, built in Scotland and shipped to Canada for use from 1850 through 1874 (*demonstrations in summer*). The **CNR 5702**, a locomotive built for passenger service, reached speeds of over 160km/hour (99mph) in 1930. One of the largest locomotives ever constructed, the **CP 5935** hauled trains over the Rockies and the Selkirk Mountains in British Columbia in the 1950s. The **CP 7000**, Canadian Pacific's first electric locomotive with a diesel engine, was used from 1937 through 1964.

Among non-Canadian vehicles is a French locomotive, the **SNCF 030-C-841** "Châteaubriand," dating from 1883, which retired after 83 years of service.

Exporail

A gift from British Rail, the **BR 60010** "Dominion of Canada" belonged to the class that established the world record for steam locomotives with a speed of 204kmph (126.5mph) in 1938.

The museum also owns a large collection of old Montreal streetcars, one of which is used to give tours of the site. The star of the streetcar collection is "the Golden Streetcar," a gold-painted, touring, roofless car that brought Montrealers to large parks on weekends in the early 20C. Locals called it "le tramway observatoire."

Also visible are a bridge-style turntable and an enormous rotary snowplow used to clear the tracks during the long Canadian winters, as well as snowplowing locomotives.

Excursion

Écluse de la Côte Sainte-Catherine (Côte Sainte-Catherine Lock)

About 6km/3.7mi from the Exporail museum. Drive north to Rte. 132 on Rue Saint-Pierre (Rte 209), turn left, then right on Rue Centrale and follow signs. ◷*Open Apr–mid-Nov, daily.* P⊚*450-672-4110 (St. Lawrence Seaway).*

This is the second lock on the St. Lawrence Seaway system. At this point, vessels are raised 9m/30ft, from the level of the La Prairie Basin to that of Lake Saint-Louis, around the Lachine Rapids. The parking lot provides a good **view** of the vessels passing through the lock, and of the Montreal skyline in the distance.

SAINT-EUSTACHE

THE LAURENTIANS REGION
POPULATION 40,062
MAP: SEE MONTREAL

This quiet residential and farming community is situated on the Mille Îles River as it leaves Lake Deux Montagnes and joins the Chêne River. Founded in 1768, it was named for the seigneur of Mille-Îles, Louis-Eustache Lambert-Dumont. In 1837, Saint-Eustache was the site of one of the most crushing defeats of the Patriots' Rebellion.

- **Information:** Travel information bureau of the Lower Laurentians, 600 Rue Dubois (Exit 14 of Rte. 640) ☎450-491-4444 & 1-800-561-6673. www.ville.saint-eustache.qc.ca or www.laurentides.com.
- **Orient Yourself:** Saint-Eustache is about 35km/21.7mi west of Montreal by Rte. 15 and Rte. 640 (Blvd. Arthur-Sauvé Exit). Provincial roads 148 and 344 also traverse Saint-Eustache.
- **Don't Miss:** The Abbey at Oka—and be sure to try some of their Oka cheese.
- **Organizing Your Time:** Saint-Eustache is a pleasant community worth a full day of touring. Don't rush your visit here, especially on a nice, sunny day.

A Bit of History

On December 14, 1837, 200 French-speaking "rebels" led by **Jean-Olivier Chénier** faced 1,200 British soldiers under the command of General Sir John Colborne. The ill-equipped rebels did not expect such a mighty British force and took shelter in the church, which was bombarded and set on fire. Seventy patriots, including Chénier, had died before the rest surrendered. The survivors were imprisoned in Chénier's home, and Colborne burned the then village of Saint-Eustache during what was called "the bloody night" (*la nuit rouge*). Village women and children were thrown out of their homes to face the rigors of winter. This event earned Colborne the nickname "Old Firebrand." The brutality of the repression and the carnage at Saint-Eustache are remembered with sadness.

Sights

Église Saint-Eustache★ (St. Eustache Church)

123 Rue Saint-Louis. ☞Visit by guided tour (45min; English or French) only, Jun 24–Labor Day, Tue–Fri 9.30am–4.30pm, Sun noon–4.30pm; rest of the year by appointment. ☞Contribution requested. ♿ 🅿 ☎450-473-3200, ext. 234.

With its imposing façade and two elegant steeples, the St.-Eustache church was erected in 1783 and enlarged in 1831. Badly damaged in 1837 during the Patriots' battle against the British army, it was carefully rebuilt from the remains in 1841 and enlarged in 1906. Cannonball marks are still visible on the façade. The light and spacious interior contains an ornate barrel vault and is often used by the Montreal Symphony Orchestra for recording sessions because of its excellent acoustics.

To the right is the presbytery; to the left stands a former convent that now serves as the town hall. Behind the church, a pleasant park affords views of the Mille Îles River.

Manoir Globensky (Globensky Manor)

235 Rue Saint-Eustache.

A huge porticoed entrance dominates the façade of this lovely Victorian manor (1903). The second manor erected on this site, this grandiose structure belonged to Charles-Auguste-Maximilien Globensky, last seigneur of the Chêne River seigneury. After his death, two local mayors used it as a residence. The manor became the city hall in 1962 and today still houses municipal offices.

Le Manoir Globensky also houses a permanent exhibit related to the Battle of Saint-Eustache in 1837.

Moulin Légaré (Légaré Mill)

236 Rue Saint-Eustache, across from the manor. ©*Open Jun–mid-Oct, daily 10am–5pm.* ∞*$5.* & P ☎*450-974-5170.* The only building to survive "the bloody night" of December 14, 1837, this seigneurial mill on the Chêne River was built in 1762 and has operated ever since. It is named for the Légaré family who ran it from 1908 through 1978. The original mechanism and equipment can be seen inside, and visitors can purchase wheat and buckwheat flour produced at the mill. From the bridge behind the structure, the turbine gate, the river and the towers of St. Eustache church are visible.

Rue Saint-Eustache

The city's main street is lined with several buildings of historical interest. The former Presbyterian Church (1910) at no. 271 now houses an art gallery presenting temporary exhibits. At n°. 163, the gabled, redbrick Plessis-Bélair House has been converted into a restaurant. The building (1832) at n°. 64, with its distinctive overhanging eaves, belonged to Hubert Globensky, and the store at n°. 40 is the former Paquin House (1889).

Excursions

Parc d'Oka (Oka Park)

14km/8.7mi by Rte. 148 and Rte. 640. Main entrance on Rte 344, other entrance (closed in winter) at the end of Rte. 640. ©*Open year-round, daily 8am–sunset.* ∞*$3.50.* △ ⅙ & P ☎*1-800-665-6527. www.sepaq.com* Set beside Lake Deux Montagnes, this park covers 24sq km/9sq mi of a former seigneury belonging to the Sulpicians. Created in 1962, it was orginally named for Paul Sauvé, premier of Quebec (1959–60) and a representative for the constituency. The park comprises a wide beach and several trails that wind through the magnificent deciduous for-

est (*an information booth is located near the main entrance*). The Oka Beach (plage d'Oka) is one of the few beaches in the Montreal area and is thus extremely popular in summer.

Abbaye cistercienne (Cistercian Abbey)

3km/1.8mi west of the intersection of Rte. 640 and Rte. 344. Parking lot after the main entrance, before the Calvary of Oka. ©*Chapel open year-round, daily 4am–8pm.* & P ☎*450-479-8361.* In 1881 the Sulpicians of Oka donated land to a group of Cistercian monks from the Bellefontaine abbey in France. The Cistercians erected a large monastery, la **Trappe d'Oka**, where, keeping a tradition of hospitality, the monks welcome visitors who wish to participate in their life of retreat.

Calvaire d'Oka★ (Calvary of Oka)

4km/2.5mi from the monastery on Rte. 344.

On the slopes of Oka Mountain (150m/492ft) stand a series of simple whitewashed stone sculptures representing the Stations of the Cross and Calvary. The four oratories and three chapels were built between 1740 and 1744 by Hamon Le Guen, a Sulpician from Brittany, in an effort to evangelize the indigenous population. The mountainside provides a good **view** of the park and of Lake Deux-Montagnes.

▶ *Continue on Rte. 344 to Oka.*

Oka

1km/.6mi from the Calvary; 21km/13mi from Saint-Eustache.

The name of this community on the shores of Lake Deux-Montagnes comes from an Algonquian word for "pike," a ferocious fish once found in abundance in the lake. A mission was founded here in 1717 for Iroquois, Nipissing and Algonquin peoples; the reserve still exists. The community gained international notoriety in the summer of 1990 during the outbreak of the "Oka crisis," an Amerindian uprising centred on the issue of territorial claims of Canada's First Nations.

SAINT-FÉLICIEN

SAGUENAY–LAC SAINT-JEAN REGION
POPULATION 10,441
MAP: SEE LAC SAINT-JEAN

Saint-Félicien is located on the western shore of Lake Saint-Jean, at the confluence of the Mistassini, Ticouapé and Ashuapmushuan rivers, which rush over falls and rapids for 266km/156mi before emptying into the lake. Founded in 1865, Saint-Félicien thrived on agriculture and lumber operations before becoming the gateway to the rich mining area of Chibougamau, to the northwest, in the 1950s. A major paper mill was established here in 1978, and a steam power plant in 1997.

On May 19, 1870, a conflagration known as the **Great Fire** started in Saint-Félicien and eventually ravaged the southern shores of the lake and the forests as far as La Baie. Entire communities were destroyed, and the long process of recovery was arduous.

Today the town is best known for its zoo, created in 1960 by local citizens. Soaring above Boulevard Sacré-Cœur in the centre of town are the twin steeples of Saint-Félicien's large pink-granite church, erected in 1914. Across the street, Sacré-Cœur Park overlooks the Ashuapmushuan River.

- **Information:** 1209 Blvd. Sacré-Coeur. ☎418-679-9888 & 1-877-253-8387, www.ville.stfelicien.qc.ca/www.saguenaylacsaintjean.net.
- ▶ **Orient Yourself:** Saint-Félicien is 285km/177mi north of Quebec City by Rtes. 175 and 169, on the west side of Lac Saint-Jean.
- **Don't Miss:** The Wilderness Zoo.
- ⏱ **Organizing Your Time:** Buy the two-day pass for the zoo so you can see the animals at different times of the day.

Sights

Zoo sauvage de Saint-Félicien★★ (Saint-Félicien Wilderness Zoo) [Kids]

6km/3.7mi on Blvd. du Jardin (Rte. 167). ⏱Open daily Jun–Aug, 9am–6pm (8pm mid-Jul–mid-Aug); May, Sept–Oct, 9am–5pm; rest of year, call ahead. ⬤$32 (children 6–14yrs $21). ✗ ♿ 🅿 ☎418-679-0543 & 1-800-667-5687. www.zoo sauvage.org.

Occupying a rugged, beautiful site on a small island wedged in the Salmon River, the zoo offers a vivid introduction to wild animals native to North America. Close to 1,000 specimens (caribou, wapiti, moose, black bears, wolves, and bison) roam freely in their natural habitat in the **Nature Trails Park**★★ (Parc des Sentiers de la nature) while visitors remain enclosed in a specially designed train. In addition, the pioneer era is recaptured in the authentic buildings on the site: A pioneer home from 1875, a trading post, a Montagnais camp, and a 1930s jobber (lumberjack) camp.

The site is unforgettable because it is not simply landscaped like most zoos, instead, it was carved out of a beautiful piece of boreal forest traversed by a powerful river (Rivière au Doré) that serves as a natural barrier.

In winter, it is moving to see polar bears enjoy a Nordic climate. The northern seals also seem quite pleased with their frigid habitat.

A large aviary allows you to watch the prowess of Bald Eagles. The animal symbol of the United States flies powerfully from Florida to Alaska, and here it is at ease both in the scorching heat of summer and in the polar days of winter.

Excursions

Chute à l'Ours★ (Bear Falls)

After the Saint-Félicien bridge, turn left off Rte. 169 towards Dolbeau onto the road bordering Rte. Saint-Eusèbe Nord and

Along the Ashuapmushuan River

continue on 15km/9.3mi. Follow signs for campground located in Normandin. ⏱*Open late May–late Sept, daily 8am–11pm.* ⊚*$3.* ✗ ♿ ℗ ☏*418-274-3411.*
A footpath leads alongside these Ashuapmushuan River rapids, which extend over a distance of more than 1,500m/4,920ft. The falls were named by the early explorers, whose progress they hindered. Among these was Jesuit father Charles Albanel, the first Frenchman to reach the shores of James Bay, in 1672.

Moulin des Pionniers★ (Pioneers' Mill)
4201 Rue des Peupliers in La Doré, 20km/12mi from Saint-Félicien by Rte. 167. ⏱ ☜*Open mid-Jun–mid-Sept daily 9.30am–5.30pm (last guided tour at 4pm).* ⊚*$12.* ✗ ♿ ℗ ☏*418-256-8242 & 1-866-272-8242. www.moulindespion niers.qc.ca*
Built in 1889 by Belarmain Audet, this wooden mill served to grind wheat, drive the blacksmith's forge, saw wood and cut shingles until 1977; the original mechanism is still in perfect working order, and quite impressive as it slices large pieces of lumber into thin construction wood. The site of the mill, on the Salmon River, is also the largest spawning ground for the landlocked salmon (*ouananiche*), who return to their place of birth each year (*Jul–Oct*) to reproduce.

The pioneer's house (1904), a two-storey log cabin, stands next to the mill. The oldest house in the town of La Doré, it was moved to this site in 1977 and is furnished with period pieces. Hiking trails provide fine **views** of the Salmon River; those interested in fishing can try for salmon and trout in any of the fishing ponds located along the river's banks.

Réserve faunique Ashuapmushuan (Ashuapmushuan Wildlife Reserve)
South entrance is 33km/20.5mi (north entrance: 178km/110.6mi) northwest of Saint-Félicien on Rte. 167, towards Chibougamau (which is 232km/144mi away from Saint-Félicien). ⏱*Open mid-May–Oct, daily 7am–9pm;* ⊚*$3.50.* ⚠ ♿ ℗ ☏*418-256-3806. www.sepaq.com.*
This 4,487sq km/1,732sq mi wildlife reserve is a hunting and fishing paradise, and one of the region's largest spawning grounds for the landlocked salmon (ouananiche). Its name in Montaignais means "place where one stalks moose."
Dedicated to the preservation and promotion of wildlife, the reserve is governed by strict laws intended to protect both animals and visitors to the park. A stop at the welcome center to obtain all necessary information and permits is highly recommended. Simply driving through the reserve requires no special permit.

A Bit of Advice

Route 167 is equipped with security phones, as well as several observation posts and picnic areas. Pets are strictly forbidden in the reserve. Outfitters provide comfortable accommodations and the advice of well-trained guides for a variety of organized hunting and fishing trips. Reserve well in advance. Reservations are required for shelter rentals. Visitors can take part in any of several daily activities, such as fishing, hunting, and canoe-camping (guide services available).

The **Ashuapmushuan River** demarcates the territory of the Wildlife Reserve, which includes over 1,200 bodies of water. The river is 266km/165mi long and is one of the largest tributaries of Lake Saint-Jean. At one time, it served as a route for communication and trade between the Cree and the Montagnais.

Also known as the doorway to Quebec's northern regions, it formed part of the route to James Bay. Fur trading became the principal activity with the arrival of the first Europeans. Several trading posts established along the shores and at the mouth of the river remained in use until the turn of the century.

Chutes de la Chaudière (Chaudière Falls)

68km/42mi, 1hr from Saint-Félicien; 17km/10.5mi are on a dirt road after obtaining a permit at the entrance.
Open mid-Jun–Sept, daily 8am–dusk.
418-256-3806.
A magnificent lookout point on the Chaudière Falls allows visitors to appreciate the magnificent boreal forest comprised of birch, jack pine, black spruce, and fir trees.

Lac Saint-Jean★★ – *See Entry Heading.*

SAINT-HYACINTHE

MONTÉRÉGIE REGION
POPULATION 52,713
MAP: SEE VALLÉE DU RICHELIEU

Set on the western bank of the Yamaska River, Saint-Hyacinthe has become known as the "agro-industrial technopolis of Quebec." Each year in July it hosts a large **Regional Agricultural Fair**. Saint-Hyacinthe is home to Quebec's main college of agriculture. The city is also known for having one of the highest percentages of French-speaking people in the entire province (close to 99 percent).

- **Information:** 2090 Rue Cherrier. ☎450-774-7276 & 1-800-849-7276. www.tourismesainthyacinthe.qc.ca or www.tourisme-monteregie.qc.ca.
- **Orient Yourself:** Saint-Hyacinthe is about 65km/40mi northeast of Montreal by Rte. 20 (Exit 130 Sud) or Rte. 116.

A Bit of History

In 1753, **Jacques-Hyacinthe-Simon Delorme**, a merchant and wood supplier, purchased the Maska seigneury from François-Pierre Rigaud, sieur de Vaudreuil, and the small community was quickly settled. During the late 18C, the Yamaska River was harnessed for power, and in 1848 the railway line from Longueuil reached Saint-Hyacinthe. The

town soon became a religious center: The seminary was established in 1811 and the diocese in 1851.
Fire nearly destroyed the city on three occasions (1854, 1876 and 1903), and a flood carried away three bridges and devastated much of the downtown area in 1864. Nonetheless, by the end of the 19C Saint-Hyacinthe had become a major textile manufacturing center

The Casavant Brothers

In 1879 Joseph-Claver and Samuel-Marie Casavant, sons of the organ-maker, Joseph Casavant, founded the company **Casavant Frères**, now world-renowned for the manufacture of fine organs. The company's most famous organ still graces the Notre Dame Basilica, in Montreal. The Casavant factory (*no visits, 900 Rue Girouard Est; ☎450-773-5001; www.casavant.ca*) produces about 16 organs per year.

Sights

Porte des anciens maires (Gate of the Former Mayors)
Follow Rte. 137 (Rue Laframboise) into town; turn right on Rue Dessaulles (Rte. 116). Turn left on Ave. des Écoles, just before the Rte. 235 interchange. The gate is at the junction of Rue Girouard and Blvd. Laurier, near the banks of the Yamaska River.

Erected in 1927, this unusual brick gate with its two towers commemorates the first 11 mayors of Saint-Hyac inthe. It was inaugurated to celebrate the 100th birthday of the Honorable **Georges-Casimir Dessaulles,** who held the office of mayor from 1868 through 1879 and 1886 to 1897.

Cathédrale de Saint-Hyacinthe-le-Confesseur (Cathedral of St. Hyacinthe the Confessor)
1900 Rue Girouard Ouest. ◷Open year-round, daily 9am–4pm. ♿ 🅿 ☎450-773-8581.

This elegant, Romanesque-inspired cathedral (1878) is flanked by 50m/164ft stone towers topped by slender copper steeples. The Neoclassical interior, featuring an 1885 Casavant organ, was redecorated in 1942, 1964, and 1999. Ozias Leduc painted *The Eternal Father*, hanging in the choir.

Riverfront Walk★
A pleasant walk along Rue Girouard winds along the banks of the Yamaska River, from the Gate of the Former Mayors to downtown. Several lovely Victorian homes line the wide artery, notably between Rue Després and Avenue Desaulniers. Closer to downtown, the street is bordered by imposing public buildings, including the cathedral and city hall dominating the Casimir-Dessaulles Park.

To the south lies Rue des Cascades, a lively street of shops and restaurants. The **Marché-Centre** (public market) (*no. 1555, at the intersection with Rue Saint-Denis*), dates back to 1877, and is considered the province's oldest public market. The Yamaska Rapids are visible from the Barsalou Bridge, at the eastern end of Rue des Cascades.

Marché-Centre

LAC SAINT-JEAN★★

SAGUENAY–LAC SAINT-JEAN REGION

Located north of Quebec City, at the southern tip of the Saguenay region, Lake Saint-Jean fills a shallow glacial basin situated 98m/321ft above sea level. The current body of water, covering an area of 1,350sq km/521sq mi, is a small remnant of the original lake, created by melting glaciers over 10,000 years ago. Nowhere deeper than 63m/207ft, it has an average depth of 20m/66ft. The lake is fed by a number of rivers, including the Péribonka, Mistassini and Ashuapmushuan, but empties into only one: the Saguenay. The Lake Saint-Jean area resembles a crater with walls sloping downward toward the lake, creating spectacular rapids and falls.

Unlike its neighbouring industrial regions, the Saguenay and the Mauricie, the Lake Saint-Jean area supports agriculture; however, farming has only been practiced here since the Great Fire of 1870, which cleared much of the surrounding forest and opened broad tracts of land.

- **Information:** ☎1-877-253-8387. www.saguenaylacsaintjean.net.
- ▶ **Orient Yourself:** Lake Saint-Jean is 180km/112mi north of Quebec City by Rte. 169 or Rte. 175 (via Chicoutimi), from Trois-Rivières by Rte. 155 and from Chicoutimi by Rte. 170.
- **Don't Miss:** Saint-Félicien Zoo and Val-Jalbert
- ⏱ **Organizing Your Time:** Allow several hours more if you intend to explore then orthwest section of Lac Saint-Jean, where fewer attractions are.
- Kids **Especially for Kids:** Dam-en-Terre Recreation Area at Alma has many kid-oriented activities plus heated wading pool.

A Bit of History

First called Piékouagami ("flat lake") by the Montagnais, the lake was renamed for **Jean Dequen**, the first Frenchman to visit its shores in 1647. The fur trade between the Amerindians and the French, initially established at Tadoussac, soon moved into the region. In 1676 a trading post was built on the shores of the lake at the mouth of the Métabetchouane River, a site that later became the village of Desbiens.

The area remained unsettled until the mid-19C, when sawmills and pulp mills were built. The 20C was marked by the harnessing of the rivers for hydroelectricity and the building of an aluminium smelter at Alma. Despite industrialization, the shoreline communities still thrive on agriculture and tourism.

Today Lake Saint-Jean is known for the **granite** found near its shores, notably at Saint-Gédéon, near Alma. Many of the large churches of the region are built of this stone, which has a pinkish hue

once cut. The lake is famous for its abundance of landlocked salmon, known in Québec as **ouananiche**, a favorite catch for sports fishermen. *Gourgane* (a large bean) is among the region's predominant crops, and wild **blueberries**, or *bleuets*, grow so plentifully on the north shore of the lake that inhabitants are often referred to as "Bleuets." These small, wild blueberries are truly delicious and are a folksy symbol of Quebec.

Driving Tour

Around the Lake

220km/132mi by Rte. 169.

Alma

Just east of lake Saint-Jean at the mouth of the Saguenay River lies the regional capital of Alma. Founded in 1864, the city was named in commemoration of that year's Anglo-French victory over the Russian army at the Alma River in the Crimea.

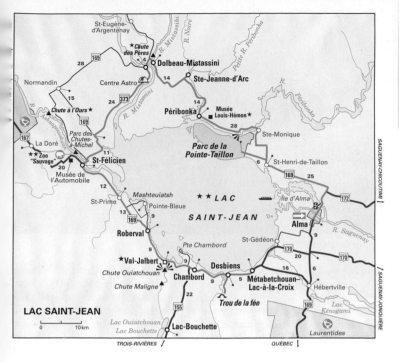

LAC SAINT-JEAN

0   10km

TROIS-RIVIÈRES /   QUÉBEC |

Experience the history of the region from the last ice age though industrialization at **L'Odyssée des Bâtisseurs** (*1671 Ave. du Pont Nord; ◷open mid-Jun– Labor Day, Mon–Fri 9am–5:30pm; early Sept–early Oct, Mon–Fri 9am–4.30pm; rest of the year, Mon–Fri 9am–4.30pm; ◷$11; 🅿 ☎418-668-2606 & 1-866-668- 2606, www.odysseeDesBatisseurs.com*). This historical theme park reviews carefully and completely the fascinating story of the Lac Saint-Jean Region. The "Odyssey of the Builders" present a wide range of hands-on, recreational and learning activities featuring the region's culture and nature. From logging to hydropower plant construction and the ensuing massive industrialisation, l'Odyssée des Bâtisseurs will allow you to grasp, better than anywhere else, how this remote area became one the most vibrant, dynamic, and interesting portions of Quebec. If you enjoy learning about history and industry, allow yourself at least three hours to fully appreciate l'Odyssée des Bâtisseurs.

Complexe touristique Dam-en-Terre

8km/5mi. Exit the city center by Ave. du Pont, heading north, and turn left on Blvd. des Pins; turn right on Chemin de la Dam-en-Terre and right again on Chemin de la Marina. Dam-en-Terre is at 1385 Chemin de la Marina.

The dam constructed between the islands of Alma and Maligne in the early 1950s was designed to harness the river and raise the level of the lake, thereby increasing its hydroelectric potential. Established on the bay in 1979, the **Dam-en-Terre Recreation Area** (◷*open late May–mid-Sept, daily 8am–9pm; rest of the year, Mon–Fri 8am–4pm; ⚠☇🅿 ($5) ☎418-668-3016 & 1-888-289-3016; www.damenterre.qc.ca*) includes a campground, beach, wading pool, picnic shelters, cottages for rent, restaurant and theater, hiking trails and a marina. Visitors can also rent canoes, pedal-boats and bicycles, and during summer there is a theater, cruise and dinner – all can be purchased singly, else a variety of packaged combinations are available. A **scenic cruise** is a particularly good way to visit the Alcan plant,

Point Taillon Park

the Isle-Maligne hydroelectric dam and the numerous villages of Lac Saint-Jean (*departs mid-Jun–Aug, Tue–Sat at various times; round-trip 2hrs; commentary; reservations required;* ⚓ *$26.95; supper and cruise $41.95;* ♿☎*418-668-3016 & 1-888-289-3016; www.damenterre.qc.ca*).

▸ *Take Rte. 169 for 25km/15.5mi to Saint-Henri-de-Taillon and continue 6km/3.7mi to Pointe-Taillon Park (follow signs).*

Parc de la Pointe-Taillon (Pointe-Taillon Park)

31km/19mi. Located at 835 Rang 3 Ouest, Saint-Henri-de-Taillon. 🕐*Opening times vary according to the sector of the park and the weather. South (Taillon) sector May–Oct; north (Sainte-Monique) sector and Véloroute des Bleuets park gatehouse Jun–Oct.* ⚓*$3.50.* ⛺☓♿🅿☎*418-347-5371 & 1-800-665-6527. www.sepaq.com. Interpretation center open mid-Jun–mid-Aug, daily 8am–9pm, end May–mid-Jun & early Sept–mid-Oct, 9am–5pm, mid-Aug–Labor Day, 8am–8pm.*

Located at the mouth of the Péribonka River along the north bank of Lake Saint-Jean, the Pointe-Taillon peninsula was formed by post-glacial alluvial deposits. It stretches for nearly 20km/12.4mi and covers 92sq km/35sq mi. Mainly a land of marshes, swamps and peat bogs, it is also covered with a forest of black spruce and birch. On the shore of the lake, the forest gives way to a fine sandy beach that attracts migrating ducks and geese in the fall. The park offers several hiking trails and a 32km/20mi bike (rentals available) path, as well as canoeing, kayaking, pedal-boating and sailboarding. Pointe-Taillon is the largest and arguably the best beach on Lac Saint-Jean. It is one of very few public beaches in Quebec where night camping is allowed. When you hike, watch for beavers, turtles and all sorts of wildlife.

▸ *Return to Rte. 169 and continue to Péribonka.*

La Véloroute des Bleuets

This 256km/154mi cycling network around Lac Saint-Jean roads, occasionally following the coast along fine sandy beaches and impressive rivers and traverses beautiful agricultural plains. Enjoy small paradises that can only be reached by bicycle on this system of trails and marked sections of road. *For trail information and maps*, contact La Véloroute des Bleuets (*1692 Avenue du PonTNord, Alma, QC, G8B 5G2* ☎*418-668-4541 & 1-866-550-4541; www.veloroute-bleuets.qc.ca*).

After Sainte-Monique, Route 169 crosses the Péribonka River and, 4km/2mi farther along, reaches a charming **viewpoint** and picnic area.

Péribonka

34km/21mi from Pointe-Taillon Park.
This pretty community located on the banks of the Péribonka River, just above its outlet into Lake Saint-Jean, has subsisted on forestry and farming since its foundation in 1887. The mighty Péribonka River, which means "river dug in the sand" in Montagnais, exceeds 460km/285mi in length, making it the largest tributary of Lake Saint-Jean. Today its rushing waters are harnessed by two reservoirs and three power stations.
The French author Louis Hémon (1880–1913) spent a few months in Péribonka in 1912, a visit that inspired the creation of his posthumously published and best-known French-Canadian novel, *Maria Chapdelaine*, a love story of bygone days. The community is also the departure point for the famous Lake Saint-Jean **International Swim Marathon**, which takes place during the last week of July.

Musée Louis-Hémon - Complexe touristique Maria-Chapdeleine

5km/3mi east of Péribonka on Rte. 169 (700 Route 169). ○*Open mid-Jun–Labor Day, daily 9am–5pm; rest of the year, Tue–Fri 9am–4pm.* ✎*Guided tours in French and English, interpretative signs in French only* ∞*$5.50.* ♿⚊*✆418-374-2177. www.museelh.ca.*
Focusing on the life and work of French writer Louis Hémon as well as literature in general, this vast museum complex possesses a collection of some 1,400 works of art, documents and ethnological artifacts from the world of letters. Also open to the public are the house of Samuel Bédard, where young Louis Hémon stayed and worked as a farm hand in 1912, and a new, contemporary pavilion (1986) built of quartz. Exhibits here trace the author's life from his birth in Brittany to his tragic death when he was hit by a train in Chapleau (Northern Ontario).
Maria Chapdelaine (published in 1916) is Hémon's most famous novel and it is a true reflection of the hardships endured by men and particularly by women during Quebec pioneer days around Lac Saint-Jean. Scenes from the novel are recreated in the museum and the film made from the novel can be seen.

▷ *Continue on Rte. 169 to road junction (13km/8mi). Turn right and continue 1km/.6mi.*

Sainte-Jeanne-d'Arc

14km/9mi.
This village is located at the confluence of the Little Péribonka and the Noire rivers. Erected beside a waterfall on the Little Péribonka in 1907, the **old mill** operated until 1974. Visitors can observe the original milling mechanisms and carding machine (○*open mid-Jun–late Aug, daily 9.30am–5pm;* ∞*$3.* ⚊*✆418-276-3166).* At one time, the river was harnessed to run a sawmill, shingle mill and flour mill, in addition to the carding mill.

▷ *Return to Rte. 169.*

Dolbeau-Mistassini

14km/9mi.
Now a shared municipality with Mistassini, Dolbeau was founded in 1927, with the establishment of the Domtar pulp and paper mill. Named after the Récollet missionary Jean Dolbeau, who arrived in Tadoussac in 1615, the town is famous for its **Festival des dix jours western de Dolbeau** (⚊ see Calendar of Events) held in July. Mistassini, meaning "large rock" in Cree, stands on the Mistassibi River beside a lovely waterfall, known as **Chute des Pères**★ (Pères Falls), named after the Trappist monks of Oka who came here in 1892. The twin towers of the original monastery are visible from a spot near the confluence of the Mistassini and Mistassibi rivers. In 1980 the Trappists moved north to Saint-Eugène, but their chocolate and other products are still on sale at the factory near the old monastery. Mistassini is known as Quebec's blueberry capital.

Saint-Félicien – *35km/22mi.*
⚊*See Entry Heading.*

Northern Garden Paradise

In the boreal plain you will find a horticultural challenge, Les Grands Jardins de Normandin (*1515 Avenue du Rocher, Normandin; ☎418-274-1993 & 1-800-920-1993; www.lesgrandsjardinsdenormandin.com; $12*) which has over 55 hectares of beautifully manicured terrain and is sure to please even the most enthusiastic gardeners.

Route 169 passes through Saint-Prime, a village renowned for its cheddar cheese and other dairy products. Saint-Prime's *Perron* cheese is sold accross Canada and is exported to England.

Roberval – *25km/15.5mi.*
🕭*See Entry Heading.*

Route 169 hugs the lake for the entire distance between Roberval and Chambord, revealing a fine panorama.

Val-Jalbert★ – *9km/5.6mi.*
🕭*See Entry Heading.*

Beyond Val-Jalbert, a 2km/1.2mi drive along Route 169 leads to an excellent **viewpoint**★ overlooking the lake.

Chambord
9km/5.6mi.
Established in 1857, this community grew in importance after the arrival of the railway from Quebec City in 1888. It is named after Henry V, count of Chambord, the last of the Bourbon royal line.

Desbiens
9km/5.6mi.
Father Jean Dequen first saw Lake Saint-Jean from this spot in 1647. He established a Jesuit mission five years later, followed by a fur-trading post in 1676. The community is named after Louis Desbiens, who founded the first pulp and paper mill in 1896.
A large wooden wharf just below the small Jean-Dequen Park is a wonderful spot to observe fishermen and admire the lake.

Centre d'histoire et d'archéologie de la Métabetchouane
243 Rue Hébert, right after the bridge that spans the mouth of the Métabetchouane. 🕘*Open late Jun–Labor Day, daily 10am–5pm.* ⊛*$7.* 🕭🅿☎*418-346-5341, www.chamans.com.*
This interpretation center traces the colonial history of Lake Saint-Jean and re-creates living conditions at a 19C fur-trading post. It also features displays on Amerindians and the prehistory of the region. The powder magazine at the entrance marks the exact spot of the original trading post, set on the banks of

Trou de la fée

Charles-David Robitaille/ATR Saguenay-Lac-Saint-Jean

Address Book

For price ranges, see the Legend on the cover flap.

SWIMMING ACROSS THE LAKE

The last week of July marks the beginning of the famous, nine-day international swim marathon (Traversée internationale du lac Saint-Jean), held every July since 1955. The one-way, straightline swim from Péribonka to Roberval is 32km/19mi long and takes about 8hrs to complete. The round-trip, also part of the marathon, is completed by the more stalwart competitors in about 18hrs. In 1990 the marathon's route was lengthened to a 40km/25mi swim along the shore. *For information:* ☎418-275-2851. www.traversee.qc.ca.

WHERE TO STAY

AROUND THE LAKE

$-$$ Almatoit – *755 Rue Price Ouest (close to downtown* **Alma**). ☎418-668-4125 & 1-888-668-4125. www.almatoit.com. *5 rooms.* A large, century-old *maison canadienne* serves as a handsome Bed & Breakfast featuring rustic furniture (even the electrical appliances are old). Surrounded by trees, Almatoit is close to the best portion of the Lac Saint-Jean cycling route and within walking distance from the Alma inter-city bus station. The plentiful breakfast is made of organic fruits, vegetables and local cheeses and eggs.

$$ Auberge du petit cousin – *107 Ave. Boivin (in downtown* **Dolbeau-Mistassini**). ☎418-276-8428 & 1-877-276-8421. www.aubergedupetitcousin.com. *2 rooms.* Just two rooms in a modern house, but a plethora of resources and services are provided at this lodging. There is a good restaurant where you can bring your own wine. There are all sorts of games you (and children) can play, as well as a karaoke system. The staff at the Auberge can direct you to several cottages and cabin rental possibilities along the northern rim of Lake Saint-Jean.

$$ Motel Lac-Saint-Jean – *577 Route 169 (in* **Chambord**, *3km/1.8mi from the VIA Rail train station).* ☎418-342-6334 & 1-877-342-6334. www.motellac saintjean.com. *23 rooms.* This motel looks like a typical North American motel. Yet its location, right on the Lac Saint-Jean with a beach, makes it extraordinary. The rooms and the services (there is a full-service restaurant) are also above what motels sometimes provide, and the price is reasonable. It is best to reserve in advance in this seasonal accommodation on the water. Imagine, you can fish in the lake directly from the motel's quay!

$$-$$$ Hôtel du Jardin – *1400 Blvd. du Jardin (in downtown* **Saint-Félicien**). ☎418-679-8422 & 1-800-463-4927. www.hoteldujardin.com. *85 rooms.* A relatively large business hotel with a restaurant, a bar, a small gym and a beautiful indoor pool.

---

the Métabetchouane River. Note also the memorial honouring Jean de Quen.

Trou de la fée (Fairy Cavern)

Located 6km/3.7mi south of Desbiens. Take 7e Ave. across from city hall (925 Rue Hébert) in Desbiens; ⏰ *open mid-Jun–mid-Aug, daily 9am–5pm; late Aug–Sept, daily 10am–4pm;* ≈*$11;* ☎418-346-5436; www.cavernetroudelafee.ca). Perched 68.5m/225ft above the Métabetchouane River, on the edge of an abrupt cliff, the cavern offers a spectacular **view** of the river. Deserters hiding in the cave during World War II claimed to have been saved by the fairy (fée) of the cavern. The 38m/125ft half-hour guided descent into the 10,000-year-old grotto is impressive, but extremely steep (⏰ sturdy shoes required; helmets provided).

▶ *Return to Route 170.*

Métabetchouan

5km/3mi from Desbiens.
This village, founded in 1861, takes its name from the Métabetchouan River (the name means "waters that unite before flowing in" in Cree). It is the site of a well-known summer music camp, Camp Musical du Lac-Saint-Jean (Sunday evening concerts). The camp provides a view of the lake.

SAINT-JEAN-PORT-JOLI★

CHAUDIÈRE-APPALACHES REGION
POPULATION 3,359
MAP: SEE BAS-ST-LAURENT – CHARLEVOIX

Known as the craft and wood-carving capital of Quebec, the small town of Saint-Jean-Port-Joli boasts the largest concentration of artisans in the province. Numerous craft shops, specializing primarily in wood carvings, line Route 132.

Philippe Aubert de Gaspé (1786–1871) moved to this community in 1824 from Quebec City, intending to write *Les Anciens Canadiens* (*The Canadians of Old*), the novel that ultimately brought him great fame. Saint-Jean-Port-Joli is also the birthplace of a celebrated family of wood carvers, the **Bourgault brothers**: Médard (1897–1967), André (1898–1958), and Jean-Julien (1910–96).

The town holds a Sea Shanty festival, a Winter festival, and an International Sculpture festival. See www.saintjeanportjoli.com for more details.

- **Information:** ☎1-866-598-9465 & 1-888-831-4411. www.saintjeanportjoli.com or www.chaudiereappalaches.com.
- ▸ **Orient Yourself:** Saint-Jean-Port-Joli is 106km/66mi northeast of Quebec City by Rte. 73 (Pierre-Laporte Bridge) and Rte. 20 (Exit 414) or the more scenic Rte. 132.
- **Don't Miss:** The strip of artisans sculptors on Rte. 132 in the middle of town. Also don't forget le Musée des Anciens Canadiens.

Sights

Site archéologique du Manoir du Sieur de Gaspé (Archaeological site of the Sieur de Gaspé Manor)

5km/3mi west of town center on Rte. 132.
On this site stood the manor house where Philippe Aubert de Gaspé wrote *Les Anciens Canadiens,* published in 1863. Fire destroyed the house in 1909, leaving only the bakery (1764), which today serves as a tourist information center. Archaeological excavations take place here every summer.

Saint-Jean-Port-Joli

Musée des Anciens Canadiens (Historical Museum)

3km/1.8mi west of town center on Rte. 132. Located at 332 Ave. de Gaspé Ouest (Route 132). ⏰*Open early May–late Jun, 9am–5.30pm; mid-Jun –Labor Day, 8:30am–9pm; early Sept–early Nov, 8.30am–6pm;*⌨*$6.* ♿📄☏*418-598-3392 & 1-866-598-3392.*

The local history is illustrated by wood carvings crafted by Saint-Jean-Port-Joli's finest artists, including the Bourgault brothers. A video (*15min*) presents the art of sculpture in wood, stone and ice; sculpture demonstrations are held here during the summer.

The museum has expanded and is now considered by many to be the best wood carving museum in North America. Famous wood sculptors have some of their best pieces on display here. The 250-item collection includes life-size replicas of Quebec premier René Lévesque, Canadian prime minister Pierre Elliott Trudeau, singer Félix Leclerc and hockey legend Jean Béliveau.

Église Saint-Jean-Baptiste★ (Church of St. John the Baptist)

In the town center, 3km/1.8mi beyond the Musée des Anciens Canadiens. ⏰*Open early May–mid-Jun, 9am–5pm; mid-Jun –Labor Day, 8.30am–9pm; early Sept–1 Nov, 8.30am–6pm;* ♿📄☏*418-598-3023.*

The slender spires and curved roof contribute to the charm of this edifice (1779). The ornate **interior** features works by Médard and Jean-Julien Bourgault. The main altar tabernacle (1740), attributed to Pierre-Noël Levasseur, stands in the sanctuary, decorated between 1794 and 1798 by Jean Baillairgé and his son, Florent. The barrel vault is composed of small coffers embellished with 4,300 carved flowers to simulate the heavens. The seigneurial pew has been preserved in honour of Philippe Aubert de Gaspé, last seigneur of Saint-Jean-Port-Joli, who is buried in the crypt of the church. In 1987, seventeen local wood carvers pooled their skills to create a magnificent **nativity scene**★ (crèche de Noël). Although each linden figurine was carved by a different artist, the overall effect is remarkably harmonious.

SAINT-JEAN-SUR-RICHELIEU

MONTÉRÉGIE
POPULATION 87,492
MAP: SEE VALLÉE DU RICHELIEU

Birthplace of **Félix-Gabriel Marchand**, premier of Quebec from 1897 to 1900, Saint-Jean-sur-Richelieu is located on the west bank of the Upper Richelieu River, across from its twin city, Iberville. The history of the community can be traced back to 1666, when a small wooden fort was constructed here, forming one of the links in the chain of fortifications established by the French along the Richelieu River during the French-Iroquois wars. After the American Revolution, many Loyalists, faithful to the English Crown, settled in the town, which was then known as Dorchester. It was an important port for commerce with the states surrounding Lake Champlain, namely New York and Vermont.

Today the city is well known for its fascinating balloon festival, the **Festival de montgolfières de Saint-Jean-sur-Richelieu**, which takes place every August.

🛈 **Information:** 31 Rue Frontenac ☏450-542-9090 & 1-866-469-0069. www.tourismehautrichelieu.org/www.tourisme-monteregie.qc.ca

▶ **Orient Yourself:** Saint-Jean-sur-Richelieu is about 40km/25mi southeast of Montreal by Rtes. 10 and 35 (Exit at Blvd. du Séminaire).

📄 **Parking:** Metered parking downtown and near the Richelieu River.

🕑 **Also See:** VALLÉE DU RICHELIEU.

A Bit of History

The 19C was a period of growth and prosperity for Saint-Jean-sur-Richelieu. In 1836, the Champlain and St. Lawrence Railroad Company built the first railway in Canada, connecting the town to La Prairie. The **Chambly Canal** was inaugurated seven years later. Benefiting from these two new transportation routes, Saint-Jean became a manufacturing center for dishes, teapots, jugs and other pieces of white ceramic. In 1840 Moses Farrar opened the first stoneware factory, and one of his relatives began manufacturing glazed white earthenware for hotels and restaurants. With the financial support of several bankers, Moses created the **Saint-John's Stone Chinaware Company** in 1873. Pieces from both this company and the **Farrar** factories are now collectors' items. The industry still exists, producing mainly structural porcelain and fixtures. Crane Canada is the only remaining industrial potter from that era.

Le Vieux-Saint-Jean (Old Saint-Jean)

Musée du Haut-Richelieu (Upper Richelieu Museum)

182 Rue Jacques-Cartier Nord, on the Market Square (Place du Marché). Open late Jun-Labor Day, Mon–Sat 11am–5pm, Sun 1pm–5pm (rest of the year, same hours but closed Mon). $4. 450-347-0649. www.museeduhaut-richelieu.com.

Housed in the former market building (1859), this museum presents interesting displays on the Amerindian presence and the military history of the Upper Richelieu and the "Valley of Forts." It also features a unique collection of pottery and dishes signed "Saint-John's Stone Chinaware Company," notably several settings of the famous **Saint-John's Blue** dinner service, produced about 1890.

▸ *Continue along Place du Marché.*

Adjoining the rear of the market building is the former **Fire Hall** (1877), topped by a small tower.

On the other side of Rue Longueuil, note the **St. John's United Church**, a dark brick structure dating from 1841. Several attractive Victorian-style homes line the neighboring streets. The Neoclassical **courthouse** (1850) stands at the corner of Rue Saint-Charles and Rue Longueuil.

Église anglicane St. James (St. James' Anglican Church)

Corner of Rue Jacques-Cartier and Rue Saint-Georges.

With its white tower and Neoclassical entryway, the structure (1816) resembles a New England church. Today it serves the Roman Catholic parish of St. Thomas More, as well as the Anglican community.

Cathédrale de Saint-Jean-l'Évangéliste (Cathedral of St. John the Evangelist)

Rue Longueuil. Open year-round, Mon–Fri 8.30am–noon, 1pm–4.30pm. Open only for masses on weekends, at 11am on Sat & 4pm on Sun. 450-347-2328.

Originally built between 1828 and 1853, this church features a central copper tower and an elaborate interior. It was enlarged in 1866 by Victor Bourgeau, and became a cathedral when the diocese was created in 1933.

Musée du Fort Saint-Jean (Fort Saint-Jean Museum)

15 Rue Jacques-Cartier Nord. Open May–Sept, Wed–Sun 10am–5pm. $4. 450-358-6500 (ext. 5769). www.cmrsj52.ca/musee.htm

Housed in the former Protestant Chapel (1850) located on the campus of the **Collège militaire royal de Saint-Jean**, this museum traces more than 325 years (1666–1995) of military history in this area. The collection of weapons, uniforms and other military artefacts is bolstered by an exhibit on the development of the fort. A first wooden structure, built by the French in 1666 as a defence against the Iroquois, was replaced by a second in 1748 to protect New France against British forces. In 1759, after the capture of Fort Lennox, Fort Saint-Jean was burned by its

French defenders to avoid capture by the British. The structure was rebuilt by Guy Carleton in 1775 and captured by the Americans the same year, when the fort's small garrison finally surrendered after a long, 45-day siege. Having sustained severe fire damage, the fort was reconstructed after the Patriots' Rebellion of 1837–38.

After visiting the museum, visitors can tour the remains of the old ramparts on the grounds of the campus.

Excursions

Richelieu River Cruises

Departs from 115 Rue du Quai late Jun –August Tues–Sun. Call for depature times, 90mn or 4 hrs cruises. Commentary. Reservations required. $20 (90mn cruise). Croisières Richelieu ☎450-346-2498 & 1-877-346-2498. www.croisieres richelieu.com.

The pleasant cruises begins near the locks and the entrance to the Chambly Canal, and provides lovely **views** of Iberville and the Royal Military College.

SAINT-JOACHIM

RÉGION DE QUÉBEC
POPULATION 1,471
MAP: SEE CÔTE DE BEAUPRÉ

Located north of Quebec City, near the St. Lawrence, the present village of Saint-Joachim was founded soon after the Conquest. On their way to the capital, the British fleet burned the villages along the St. Lawrence shore. Wiser for the experience, the inhabitants of Saint-Joachim established their new community farther inland. Today the peaceful village is known for its lovely church (see below).

- **Information:** ☎1-877-224-3439 & 1-877-783-1608. www.cotedebeaupre.com/ www.quebecregion.com.
- **Orient Yourself:** Saint-Joachim is 40km/25mi northeast of Quebec City. Take Rte. 360 to Beaupré and follow signs.
- **Don't Miss:** The church.
- **Also See:** CÔTE DE CHARLEVOIX (Canyon Sainte-Anne).

Sights

Église Saint-Joachim★★ (St. Joachim Church)

Open mid-May–mid-Oct, daily 9am–5pm. ☎418-827-4020.

Dedicated to the father of the Virgin Mary, this small church (1779) replaced an earlier sanctuary built in 1685 and destroyed by the British during the Conquest. It is one of the oldest churches in Quebec. The façade, designed by David Ouellet in 1895, blocks the view of the more traditional structure, which is best seen from the cemetery.

The church is reputed for its **interior**, fashioned between 1815 and 1825 by **François Baillairgé** and his son,

Thomas, acting here as both architects and sculptors. François had already designed the sumptuous main altar and the chandeliers in 1785, when he was asked to add the finishing touches to the interior. The group of religious themes forms the most elaborate iconographic plan ever conceived for a church in Quebec. These representations, intended to affirm the legitimacy of the Church, depict men and sovereigns bowing to the Saviour, who empowered the Church to represent Him on earth. The parish priest, Father Corbin, left a considerable sum for this project in his will, which explains the extent of the undertaking and the opulence of the design.

Église Saint-Joachim (Interior)

Choir

A sense of unity emanates from the graceful interior. The sculptures blend with the well-defined architectural scheme composed of a storey of pilasters of composite order, an imposing cornice and a finely decorated vault. The painting above the main altar, *St. Joachim and the Virgin*, dates back to 1779. It is one of the few known works by Antoine Aide-Crequy, a parish priest from Baie-Saint-Paul who developed his natural artistic talent to compensate for the lack of trained artists in the region during the mid-18C.

St. Joachim Church long served as the leading model for Neoclassical churches in Quebec. Thomas Baillairgé and his students went on to use the same aesthetic scheme repeatedly, thus helping establish a consistent and unified image of the Catholic Church.

Presbytère (Presbytery)

Across from the church stands the presbytery of Saint-Joachim. The large stone house incorporates a smaller old section (east) built in 1766 and covered with a high roof. The imposing west section and the sculpted Neoclassical wood portals were added in 1830.

Petit-Cap

Just before the Cape Tourmente National Wildlife Reserve.

Petit-Cap is the site of the Seminary, a unique and monumental group of 18C buildings. The main edifice, Château Bellevue, overlooks the St. Lawrence. It dates back to 1779 and was enlarged in the original style in 1875. Adjacent to it are the late 18C chapel and the caretaker's house.

ARCHÉO-VISION

Next to the Saint-Joachim church is an interpretation signpost titled "Archéo-vision", first of a series of eight signposts providing historic context to a region where Amerindians, the French and the British have all played long and significant roles.

LA GRANDE FERME

At the end of Rue de l'Église (Church Street), turn right and drive along the road to Cap Tourmente. Signs will lead you to the Centre d'initiation au patrimoine - La Grande Ferme, a heritage interpretation center focused on the history of land use in this extremely beautiful and significant area.

SAINT-LAMBERT

This residential suburb of Montreal on the south shore of the St. Lawrence was originally part of the seigneury of Longueuil. Because the land was so marshy, the district was commonly called Mouille-pied ("wet feet"). In 1857 the municipality adopted the name Saint-Lambert in honour of an associate of the Sieur de Maisonneuve, **Lambert Closse**, who settled in Montreal in 1642. Today Saint-Lambert is the port of entry to the St. Lawrence Seaway.

- **Information:** ☎450-466-4666 & 1-866-469-0069. www.tourisme-monteregie.qc.ca.
- ▶ **Orient Yourself:** Saint-Lambert is just across the St. Lawrence River from Montreal by Rte. 112 (Victoria Bridge).
- **Parking:** Metered in the downtown core; restricted everywhere else, read parking signs carefully.
- **Don't Miss:** The locks of the St. Lawrence Seaway.
- **Organizing Your Time:** Victoria Bridge (1859) is the oldest and least busy of the Montreal bridges leading to the South Shore area. Try to cross the bridge towards Montreal at dusk; the view on downtown Montreal and on the Montreal islands is then unforgettable.

A Bit of History

St. Lawrence Seaway – The opening of the seaway in 1959 marked the realization of a 400-year-old dream. In the early 16C, Jacques Cartier's quest for the Northwest Passage to the Orient was thwarted by the tumultuous Lachine Rapids, located west of present-day Montreal. The rapids were but the first of a daunting series of natural obstacles that rendered the river unnavigable between Montreal and the Great Lakes. Sadly for Montreal though, the St. Lawrence Seaway allowing ships to go to Toronto marked the start of a major economic shift favoring the Ontario capital.

Conquering the river – Throughout the 300 years that followed Cartier's discoveries, Amerindians, soldiers and settlers repeatedly attempted to conquer the shoals, rapids and falls of the St. Lawrence River upstream from Montreal by constructing canals and locks around such insurmountable obstacles as the mighty Niagara Falls.

The Industrial Revolution engendered an American interest in the creation of a seaway to facilitate the transport of goods between the US and major ports in Canada and Europe. Years of negotiation between the Canadian and American governments led to a joint project to construct, maintain and operate international locks and canals.

Finally, on April 25, 1959, the icebreaker *Iberville* began the first complete voyage through the St. Lawrence Seaway, which was officially inaugurated on Jun 26 of that same year, by Queen Elizabeth II, US president Dwight Eisenhower and Canadian prime minister John Diefenbaker. The seaway is 3,800km/2,361mi long and has a minimum depth of 8m/26ft. Sixteen locks raise and lower vessels a total of 177m/580.7ft, the difference in altitude between Montreal (6m/19.7ft) and Lake Superior (183m/600ft).

The massive seaway ships, known as **lakers,** measure up to 222m/728ft long and 23m/75.4ft wide. They transport ore (principally iron) from Quebec and Labrador to the steel mills of the Great Lakes region, and huge cargoes of grain from the American heartland to ports on the St. Lawrence River.

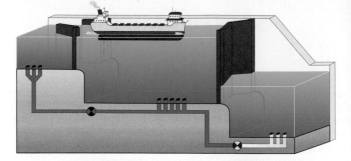

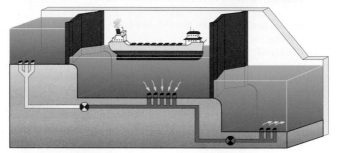

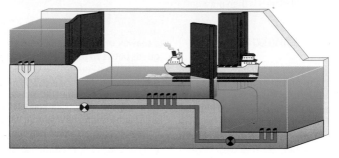

Schematic view of an Operating Lock on the St. Lawrence Seaway

Sight

Écluse de Saint-Lambert★ (Saint-Lambert Lock)

From Victoria Bridge, follow signs for Rte. 20 Sud and turn right immediately, following signs. ⏰*Belvedere open year-round, 8.30am–8.30pm; reservations required 24 hours in advance to tour tower and a minimum of four persons required in the group.* ♿ 🅿 ☎*450-672-4110 ext 2237. www.greatlakes-seaway.com.*

This is the first lock in the St. Lawrence Seaway system. It raises and lowers vessels 4.6m/15ft, enabling them to bypass the treacherous rapids just upstream from the Montreal harbor.

The lock works in conjunction with the **Victoria Bridge**★, an impressive structure built between 1854 and 1859 to carry the Grand Trunk Railway across the river. At the time, the 2,742m/8,996ft bridge was the longest in the world and deemed a great engineering feat. Rebuilt in the late 19C and again in the 1950s, it now carries cars in addition to trains. Drawbridges at each end of the lock allow a flow of road traffic even when the locks are in operation.

From the lock's **observatory**, visitors can watch enormous lakers pass through the lock on their way upriver to the Great Lakes or down to Port-Cartier and Sept-Îles.

VALLÉE DU SAINT-LAURENT

MAURICIE–CENTRE-DU-QUÉBEC–CHAUDIÈRE-APPALACHES-QUEBEC REGIONS
MAP: SEE VALLÉE DU SAINT-LAURENT

A vast agricultural plain in the region of Trois-Rivières, the St. Lawrence Valley narrows as the river flows toward Quebec City, where the foothills of the Laurentian Mountains rise to the north. Many small, older communities hug the shores of the St. Lawrence, and the roads lining the river are quiet and pleasant.

- **Information:** ☎1-877-266-5687. www.bonjourquebec.com.
- **Orient Yourself:** Trois-Rivières is situated halfway between Montreal (85km/52.8mi) and Quebec City (80km/49.7mi) on the north shore of the St. Lawrence and is accessible by Rte. 40 and Rte. 138. The itineraries described below cover the section of the St. Lawrence River Valley between Trois-Rivières and Quebec City, on both the north and south shores of the river.
- **Don't Miss:** Villages of Deschambault in summer, of Sainte-Anne-de-la-Pérade in winter.
- **Organizing Your Time:** The north shore of the Valley is the most interesting, but looping around the Valley on both shores is an excellent itinerary. Drive on this itinerary clockwise in order to keep the car on the river side. And remember to avoid crossing the bridges at peak traffic hours.

Driving Tours

1 North Shore – Trois-Rivières to Quebec City

130km/81mi by Rte. 138 and Rte. 40/440.

Trois-Rivières★★ – *♿See Entry Heading.*

▶ *Leave the city by Rte. 138.*

Cap-de-la-Madeleine – *6km/ 3.7mi. ♿See Entry Heading.*

Along the drive to Batiscan, the Bécancour industrial park can be seen on the opposite shore. It includes the only nuclear power plant in Québec.

Vieux presbytère de Batiscan★ (Old Presbytery of Batiscan)

24km/15mi. On right, before entering the village proper. ◷Open end May– late Sept, daily 10am–5pm. ☞$3.50. ♿ 🅿 ☎418-362-2051.

The first presbytery on this site was erected by Jesuit priests in 1696. In 1816, hoping to obtain the appointment of a resident parish priest, the parishioners replaced the dilapidated structure with the present edifice (built of materials recovered from the original construction). The interior, typical of early 19C rural houses, is furnished with period pieces drawn from the collections of the Museum of Civilization in Quebec City.

▶ *Continue into Batiscan (2km/1.2mi).*

Batiscan's church (1866) stands overlooking the St. Lawrence River. The spires of the church in Saint-Pierre-les-Becquets are visible on the opposite shore. Soon after leaving the village, the road crosses the Batiscan River.

Sainte-Anne-de-la-Pérade

10km/6.2mi from Batiscan.

This community on the Sainte-Anne River is known for its ice fishing. In January and February, millions of tommy cods, known in Quebec as *petits poissons des chenaux*, leave the salt water of the Gulf of St. Lawrence and seek out fresh water to spawn. As the fish settle every year on the same sport at the mouth of the St. Anne River, an actual village of colorful shanties springs up on the frozen surface, inhabited by fishermen from all over the province. The scene is particularly impressive at night. Fishing goes on 24hrs. a day and requires no

Sainte-Anne -de-la-Pérade

special skill. In the off-season, the huts are stacked on the riverbank, creating an unusual site. The large Gothic Revival church (1859) was inspired by Montreal's Notre-Dame Basilica.

After the town of **Grondines,** the road follows the St. Lawrence River, providing views of Lotbinière and of the ferry that crosses to the opposite bank. Quebec's first underwater transmission line passes through a tunnel beneath the St. Lawrence between Grondines and Lotbinière. The line is an important link in the 1,487km/924mi direct-current network between the Radisson substation (La Grande hydroelectric complex) in James Bay, and the Sandy Pond substation in Massachusetts (USA).

Moulins de La Chevrotière (Chevrotière Mills)

20km/12.4mi; after 15km/9.3mi, turn left on Rue de Chavigny. ⊙*Open mid-Jun–late Sept, daily 9.30am–5.30pm.* ⊜*$4.* 🅿️☎*418-286-6862.*

These two mills stand on a lovely site next to the La Chevrotière River. The smaller of the two dates to 1767; the larger, surmounted by a dormered roof, was built in 1802. Within, visitors will find temporary thematic exhibitions on such topics as sculpture, painting, antique tools and others.

Deschambault★
5km/3mi.

Overlooking the river, the **church** (c. 1835, Thomas Baillairgé), distinguished by its wide, lateral galleries, was inspired by Quebec City's Anglican cathedral. Between its twin steeples is a statue of St. Joseph, attributed to Louis Jobin (1845–1928). Inside, the choir is adorned with statues of exceptional quality by François and Thomas Baillairgé (⊙*open mid-Jun–late Sept, daily 9.30am–5.30pm;* ♿🅿️☎*418-286-6891*). In a pleasant park behind the church stands the former **presbytery,** built in 1815 (⊙*open late Jun–late Sept, daily 9.30am–5.30pm;* ⊜*$4.* 🅿️☎*418-286-6891*). Recently restored, the structure contains exhibits, and offers cultural activities in summer. The former **assembly hall** (1840) now houses a café.

After Deschambault, a pleasant drive passes through Portneuf. At **Cap-Santé,** the village church features a lovely façade, modelled on that of Our Lady of Quebec Cathedral. Bordering the riverbank, the Vieux-Chemin extends from the parking lot behind the church. Originally part of the Chemin du Roy, this charming street is lined with 18C homes of French inspiration.

Route 138 then crosses the Jacques-Cartier River and enters **Donnacona,** known for its large pulp mill. From here, the **view** encompasses the river and the countryside around Neuville.

▸ *Continue for 28km/17mi to Rte. 365.*

Detour to Pont-Rouge

18km/11mi round-trip on Rte. 365.
This attractive community is located on the banks of the Jacques-Cartier River, which tumbles in a series of cascades on its descent to the St. Lawrence. Beside the bridge stands the four-storey **Moulin Marcoux** (Marcoux Mill), erected in 1870; restored in 1974, it houses an art gallery, a restaurant and a theater.

▸ *Return to Rte. 138 and continue for 3km/1.8mi.*

Neuville

32km/19.8mi from Deschambault.
Turn left on Rue des Érables.
Originally called Pointe-aux-Trembles, the parish of Neuville supplied freestone, a high-quality form of limestone, to construction sites in Quebec City beginning in the late 17C. Numerous families of stonecutters and masons settled here to work in the local quarries.

Rue des Érables

The availability of both materials and skilled labor explains the exceptional concentration of stone houses in the village. Although only a single main floor is apparent at street level, the houses on Rue des Érables were built to take advantage of the sloping ground, and actually comprise two or three storeys on the river, giving them a mill-like appearance. The Fiset house (*nº. 679*) and the Pothier house (*nº. 549*), both constructed around 1800, are good illustrations of such architecture. The seigneurial manor (*nº. 500*), erected in 1835, reflects Quebec's vernacular architecture.

Église Saint-François de Sales (Church of St. Francis de Sales)

🕐*Open year-round;* ⚑*guided tours in summer 9am–5pm.* ☎418-876-2280.
Neuville's church was erected in several stages: the choir dates from 1761, the nave from 1854 and the façade from 1915. In the sanctuary is a baldachin commissioned in 1695 by Msgr. de Saint-Vallier to ornament the chapel of his episcopal palace in Quebec City. In 1717 the bishop, then in retirement, offered the baldachin to the Neuville parish in exchange for wheat for the community's needy. Four twisted columns encircle the tabernacle, sculpted by François Baillairgé around 1800. The church also contains some 20 paintings by **Antoine Plamondon** (1804–95), a native of Neuville; several of the works

Address Book

♨*For price ranges, see the Legend on the cover flap.*

STAYING ON THE NORTH SHORE

$ La Maison des Leclerc – *2821 Rue Notre-Dame Est (on Rte 138 in* **Sainte-Marthe-sur-le-Lac**, *a rural district of Trois-Rivières).* ♨▣☎819-379-5946 & 1-866-379-5946. www.maisondesleclerc.com. *4 rooms.* Stay on an active dairy farm! The old *maison québécoise* of the Leclerc family is remarkably well preserved. And it was called home by the late Félix Leclerc, Quebec's most famous songwriter; one of the rooms is where Félix Leclerc himself was living... You can ride a bike on the farm or reach a park bench on the river with a private road.

STAYING ON THE SOUTH SHORE

$$$-$$$$ Manoir de Tilly – *3854 Chemin de Tilly (in* **Saint-Antoine-de-Tilly**).* ♨✗▣☎418-886-2407 & 1-888-862-6647. www.manoirdetilly.com. *30 rooms.* A fine resort along the Saint-Lawrence river, only 30 minutes from Quebec City. Some rooms have a river view, some rooms have a fireplace, some rooms have a whirlpool, and some rooms have it all. In 1786, when le Seigneur de Tilly built his Manor, he certainly never thought his house would, 200 and some years later, provide skin treatments by resident masseuses!

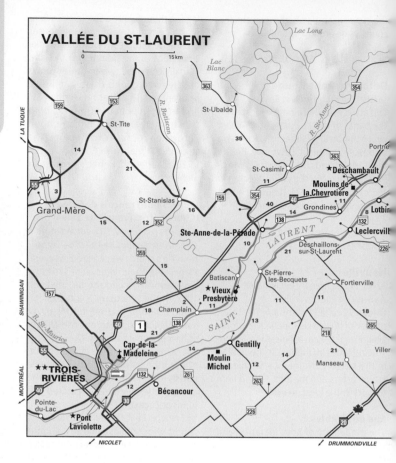

VALLÉE DU ST-LAURENT

were executed when the artist was 80 years old.

The road leaves the banks of the St. Lawrence and heads inland as it approaches the industrial suburbs of Quebec City. Highway 40 leads to **Cap Rouge** (*Exit 302*), where a high trestle railway bridge (1906–12) spans the river of the same name. It was here that Jacques Cartier, under Sieur de Roberval's orders, attempted to establish a settlement in 1541.

Quebec City★★★ – *32km/19.8mi east of Neuville.* 🕭 *See Entry Heading.*

②South Shore – Quebec City to Trois-Rivières

137km/85mi by Rte. 132.

▶ *Cross the St. Lawrence River on the Quebec City Bridge (Rte. 175).*

Le Pont de Québec★★ (Quebec City Bridge)

This remarkable structure, brightly lit at night, has a steel span extending 549m/1,801ft between its two main pylons; it was the world's longest cantilever-type bridge of its day. Construction proved to be a nightmare for the railroad company in charge: the bridge collapsed while under construction in 1907 and, in 1916 the center span fell into the river as it was being installed. Inaugurated in 1917 as a railway bridge, the Quebec City Bridge has been open to vehicular traffic since 1929. Just next to it is the **Pont Pierre-Laporte★**, opened in 1970. Measuring 668m/2,191ft, it is Canada's longest suspension bridge.

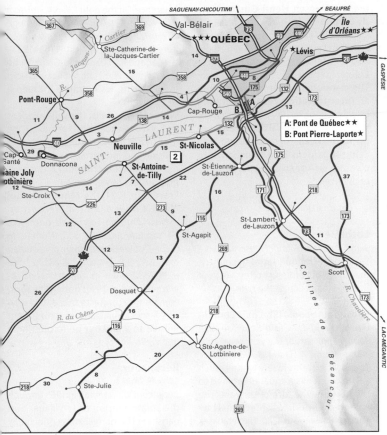

▶ *Take the first exit for Rte. 132.*

Saint-Nicolas

15km/9mi. Turn right on Rue de l'Entente, opposite the water tower. ◔Open year-round Mon–Fri 9am–noon, 1.30pm–4.30pm; &P☎418-831-9622.

Topped by a bell tower shaped like a sail, this intriguing **church** was erected in 1693. The center altar is surrounded by pews and resembles, both visually and symbolically, a ship's helm. Natural light filters into the church at the edges of the dropped ceiling, reflecting on the marble and wood interior. The exterior balcony provides fine **views** of the river and the two bridges leading to Quebec City.

Saint-Antoine-de-Tilly

15km/9mi. Turn right on Chemin de Tilly.
A small road descends from the church (1788) to the St. Lawrence. From here, the view extends across the river to Neuville. The Manoir de Tilly, an old seigneurial manor built during the early 19C, has been converted into a country inn. The road continues through Sainte-Croix with views of Donnacona and the church at Cap-Santé, on the opposite shore.

Domaine Joly de Lotbinière (Joly de Lotbinière Estate)

26km/16mi. After 23km/14mi turn right off Rte. 132 onto Rte. Pointe-Platon and follow signs for another 3km/1.8mi. ◔Open mid-May–mid-Oct, daily 10am–5pm. ⊛$13.50. ⚒P☎418-926-2462. www.domainejoly.com.

This charming white clapboard structure surrounded by wide verandas adorned with a maple-leaf frieze was built in 1840 by Julie-Christine Chartier de Lotbinière and her husband, Pierre Gustave Joly, as a summer residence. It was also used by their son, **Henri-Gustave Joly de Lotbinière** (1829–1908), premier of Quebec (1878–79), Minister of Revenue in Wilfrid Laurier's cabinet (1896–1900) and Lieutenant-Governor of British Columbia (1900–06).

The mansion has been converted into an **interpretation center**, featuring displays on the history of the Lotbinière seigneury and the local natural environment. The beautiful grounds and lush, colorful gardens lend themselves to pleasant walks and picnics with views of the river.

▷ *Return to Rte. 132.*

Lotbinière
9km/5.6mi from Manor House.
Set amidst tranquil farming country, the village of Lotbinière offers views of Deschambault across the river.

Église Saint-Louis (St. Louis Church)
🕐*Open mid-Jun–mid-Sept Tue–Sun 10am–4pm; rest of the year, weekends 10am–4pm.* ♿🅿☎*418-796-2044.*
The façade of this lovely white church (1818) overlooks a square bordered to the north by the former convent. The splendid interior was decorated by Thomas Baillairgé in 1845. The retable—shaped like a triumphant arch over the sanctuary—is surmounted by two Neo-classical statues, *Faith* and *Hope,* both crafted by Baillairgé.

Maison Chavigny de la Chevrotière (Chavigny de la Chevrotière House)
7640 Rue Marie-Victorin.
This monumental structure was erected in 1817 for Ambroise Chavigny, a notary from Chevrotière. Its roof is evocative of the style of the French Regime.

Leclercville
8km/5mi.
First settled by Acadians, this village overlooks the confluence of the Chêne and St. Lawrence rivers. The brick church, dedicated to St. Emmélie, was built in 1863.

The road continues through Deschaillons and Saint-Pierre-les-Becquets, affording expansive views of the St. Lawrence. On the right (*7km/4.3mi from Leclercville*), a plaque marks the huge 272kg/600lb boulder allegedly placed here by Modeste Maillot (1763–1834), the legendary "Canadian Giant," who stood 7'4" (2.25m) tall. Maillot was born in Saint-Pierre-les-Becquets and died in Deschaillons.

West of Leclercville, the valley widens and gives way to plains. Farther on, the road passes through a region both agricultural and industrial, marked by the massive complex of Gentilly 2, Quebec's only nuclear power station.

Erected in 1774, the **Moulin Michel** (*Michel Mill; 675 Blvd. Bécancour, 35km/21.7mi from Leclercville, on the left;* 🕐*open late Jun–Aug, daily 11am–4pm (Sept–Oct weekends only);* ⚲*guided tours*✎*$5;* 🍴♿🅿☎*819-298-2882 & 1-866 -998-2882; www.moulinmichel.qc.ca*) was restored in 1992; during the summer, visitors can taste bread baked on site. A short trail leads up the adjacent hillside to a lookout point offering a fine **view**.

Bécancour
14km/8.7mi.
Bécancour was created in 1965 through the amalgamation of 11 villages and parishes. The name is now principally associated with the industrial park, the site of a huge aluminium smelter and other installations associated with the metallurgical industry.

▷ *Continue on Rte. 132 and Rte. 30.*

From the road, views extend across the river to the Our Lady of the Cape Basilica in Cap-de-la-Madeleine and to the harbor and pulp mills of Trois-Rivières.

▷ *Take Rte. 55 across the Laviolette Bridge and then Rte. 40 to return to Trois-Rivières (17km/10.5mi).*

Pont Laviolette★ (Laviolette Bridge)
Completed in 1967, this elegantly curved bridge is over 3km/1.8mi long. It is the only bridge over the St. Lawrence River between Montreal and Quebec City.

SAINTE-AGATHE-DES-MONTS★

LAURENTIANS REGION
POPULATION 9,024
MAP: SEE LAURENTIDES

Set on the shores of Sables Lake, amidst rolling mountains rising to 580m/1,902ft, this charming community is the main town of the Upper Laurentians region. Settlers founded Sainte-Agathe in 1849, but construction of the Montreal and Occidental railway in 1892 hastened the development of the area, helping the town become the region's earliest tourist center. A lively resort with numerous restaurants and inns, Sainte-Agathe is today home to Le Patriote, the best-known summer theater in the Laurentians (French-language plays only) for decades. The historic downtown area has been renovated and revitalised. Of all the numerous service towns in the tourism-oriented Laurentians Region, Sainte-Agathe-des-Monts is probably the one with the most pleasant environment of montains, lakes and forests. That's is why the town has a very large number of accommodations and restaurants relative to its size.

- **Information:** 24 Rue Saint-Paul Est (Exit 86 of Rte 15) ☎819-326-0457 & 1-800-561-6673. www.sainte-agathe.org or www.laurentides.com.
- **Orient Yourself:** Sainte-Agathe is 86km/53.4mi north of Montreal by Rte. 15 and Rte. 117 (junction with Rte. 329).
- **Don't Miss:** Lac des Sables
- **Especially for Kids:** Year-round outdoor activities in the area, particularly the nice Tessier beach on Lac des Sables (meaning *Sandy Lake*)

Sights

Lac des Sables★★ (Sables Lake)

Located at the foot of Rue Principale, in the downtown area, Lagny Park provides excellent **views**★ of this lake, whose sparkling waters emanate from natural springs. The lake reaches a depth of 25m/82ft and is shaped like a wiggly "H". It offers over 13km/8mi of public (plage Tessier) and private beaches. Among the many celebrities who have sojourned here are Jacqueline Kennedy Onassis, Queen Elizabeth II and Baron von Ribbentrop. The former residence of millionaire Lorne McGibbon was acquired by the Oblate fathers after the stock market crash of 1929. The palatial

Lac des Sables, Sainte-Agathe-des-Monts

Guillaume Pouliot/Tourisme Laurentides

Address Book

☺*For price ranges, see the Legend on the cover flap.*

WHERE TO STAY

SAINTE-AGATHE-DES-MONTS

$$-$$$ Auberge Spa Watell Inn – *250 Rue Saint-Venant (Exit 83 of Highway 15).* ♿ 🍽 P Spa ☎819-326-7016 & 1-800-363-6478. www.watel.ca. 25 rooms. Facing beautiful Lac des Sables, this auberge features comfortable rooms, a good restaurant and a lovely spa (additional cost). Even if you don't pay for the spa, you can enjoy the whirlpool.

$$-$$$ Auberge La Caravelle – *92 Rue Major.* ♿ 🍽 P ☎819-321-2444 & 1-800-661-4272. www.aubergelacaravelle.com. 15 rooms. Very reasonably priced accommodation considering all it offers: restaurant, in-room therapeutic baths (with water jets), heated outdoor pool, play room for children, romantic suites for couples.

$$$ Auberge de la Tour du Lac – *173 Chemin du Tour-du-Lac.* ♿ P Spa ☎819-326-4202 & 1-800-622-1735. www.latourdulac.ca. 11 rooms. A small, cozy inn featuring a spa, Auberge de la Tour-du-Lac is in a large house built a century ago. The fireplace gives it the appropriate feel from the early Laurentians. An excellent breakfast will start the day perfectly.

$$$ Auberge du Lac des Sables – *230 Rue Saint-Venant.* 🍽 ♿ P ☎819-326-3994 & 1-800-567-8329. www.aubergedulac.com. 23 rooms. Location, location, location. This small hotel is located right on the famed Lac des Sables. Although there is no beach, this is still a great place to lift window shades and admire a view of water and mountains.

---

mansion has been transformed into a hospital and rest home for their missionaries.

A **scenic cruise** enables visitors to discover this magnificent lake and the homes lining its shores (*departs from dock at foot of Rue Principale early–late Jun, daily 10.30am, 11.30am, 1.30pm, 2.30pm & 3.30pm; additional departures late Jun–mid-Aug, 5pm & 7.30pm; mid-Aug–mid-Oct, 10.30am, 11.30am, 1.30pm, 2.30pm & 3.30pm; round-trip 50min; commentary;* ∾*$12;* ♿ P *Les Croisières Alouette* ☎819-326-3656; www.croisiere alouette.com*).

Lake Drive★

About 11km/6.8mi. From Rue Principale, before dock, turn right on Rue Saint-Louis, then left on Chemin Tour du Lac. The road crosses a tributary of the Nord River, then reaches a small lookout (*7km/4.3mi*) from which there is a splendid view of the lake. It leads back to the village after passing lovely waterfront estates, a park and a long, sandy beach.

Place Lagny – During the summer season, place Lagny is the gathering place for a non stop programming of outdoors shows and events aimed at keeping visitors busy and happy. In winter, Place Lagny becomes the site of "Hiver en Nord," a season-long festival of snow and ice slides, ice skating on Lac des Sables, snow sculptures and occasional fireworks.

Église de Sainte-Agathe (Church of Ste. Agathe)

Located in the middle of town, at 37 Rue Principale Est. 🕐*Open year-round, hours vary.* ☎819-326-3644.

The Church of Ste. Agathe is classified as a historic site. Like several Catholic churches in Quebec, its size is enormous in comparison with the size of the town.

The monumental stone church was built by architects Gauthier and Daoust, from 1905 to 1907. The stained glass is from Charles Stefanoff. The church boasts tow organs built by the famous Casavant Brothers firm of Saint-Hyacinthe.

SAINTE-ANNE-DE-BEAUPRÉ ★

QUEBEC CITY REGION
POPULATION 2,803
MAP: SEE CÔTE DE BEAUPRÉ

Situated on the north shore of the St. Lawrence overlooking Île d'Orléans, Sainte-Anne-de-Québec is named for the patron saint of Quebec. Its shrine, administered by the Redemptorist fathers, is a major Catholic pilgrimage center, visited by over a million and a half people every year. Sainte-Anne is a logical stop between Quebec City and the Charlevoix Region.

- **Information:** ☎1-877-224-3439 & 1-877-783-1608. www.cotedebeaupre.com/ www.quebecregion.com.
- ▶ **Orient Yourself:** Sainte-Anne-de-Beaupré is 35km/21.7mi northeast of Quebec City by Rtes. 40 and 138.
- **Don't Miss:** The huge Basilica, big like European cathedrals but young and fresh. The Cyclorama of Jerusalem—before the days of cinema, cycloramas were fantastical amusements; this one depicting crucifixion of Christ is the largest in the world.
- **Also See:** CÔTE-DE-BEAUPRÉ (between Sainte-Anne and Quebec City), the cradle of the French colony in North America.

A Bit of History

According to legend, 17C French sailors caught in a storm on the river landed safely on the banks here after praying to St. Anne, the mother of the Virgin Mary. In thanks for their rescue, in 1658 they laid the foundations for a small wooden chapel in her honour. During construction, one of the workmen, Louis Guimont, was miraculously cured of lumbago. His was the first of many healings and, as a result, Sainte-Anne soon became a place of pilgrimage. Throngs of devotees, many seeking healing, came on foot, by canoe, and later by steamboat and by car.

The original wooden chapel was replaced by a sturdier structure in 1661, followed by a stone church in 1676. But so numerous were the pilgrims and parishioners that by the 19C, a larger building was required. Completed in 1876, the immense and imposing new structure was in turn destroyed by fire in 1922 and replaced by the present basilica, which was dedicated in 1934.

The Shrine ★★

Basilica

🕐 *Open Jun–Sept: information desk open year round, daily 8.30am–4.30pm. Church open daily from 7am until the end of the last mass of the day—check website. www.ssadb.qc.ca.* 👣 *Bilingual guided tours Jun–early Sept, Mon–Sat 1pm.* ♿🅿☎*418-827-3781. www.ssadb.qc.ca.* The enormous, twin-spired Medieval-style basilica was designed by the architects Maxime Roisin and Louis-Napoléon Audet. Built in the shape of a Latin cross, with a steel frame and a veneer of white granite, it is 98m/321.5ft long, 60m/196.8ft wide at the transept, and 90m/295ft high. Between the two spires stands a large gilded statue of St. Anne, saved from the fire that destroyed the previous church.

Interior

Inside, the visitor is struck by the immense size of the basilica. The interior is divided into five naves separated by huge columns. Each column is topped by a carved capital, the work of Émile Brunet and Maurice Lord. The interior is lit by 240 **stained-glass windows,** fashioned by the French artist Auguste Laboret, assisted by the master glass-

Address Book

For price ranges, see cover flap.

WHERE TO STAY

NEAR THE BASILICA

$$ Auberge la Grande Ourse – *9717 Ave. Royale.*   *418-827-1244 & 1-877-775-1244. www.quebecweb.com/ grandeourse. 10 rooms.* Cozy, cute and close to the Sainte-Anne-de-Beaupré Basilica, Auberge La Grande Ourse is a B&B. Staying there allows to see and experience a Quebec ancestral home. There are no phones in the rooms; the old furniture and bathroom amenities will bring you back to an era when mobile phones were found only in sci-fi movies. This Auberge has put together smart accommodation/ attractions packages with Beaupré area tourism operators.

maker Pierre Chaudière. Note especially the windows of the transepts and the rose window above the organ. The barrel vault above the main nave is decorated with glimmering **mosaics** portraying the life of St. Anne. Also the work of Auguste Laboret, aided by Jean Gaudin, they combine cream and brown coloring highlighted by red and gold. A particularly beautiful mosaic of the Holy Family is located above the main altar. An ambulatory surrounds the sanctuary with 10 radiating chapels. On a marble pedestal in the left wing of the transept stands a statue of St. Anne cradling the infant Mary in her arms. The chapel behind it contains a relic of St. Anne. Opposite, in the right wing of the transept, note the wooden sculpture (c. 1920) of the Holy Family by Louis Jobin.

Chapelle Commémorative (Memorial Chapel)

Open mid-Apr–mid-Oct, daily 8am–7.30pm.

Built in 1878 on the site of the 1676 parish church, the structure incorporates elements of the original chapel, notably the steeple and its two cupolas.

Chapelle du Saint Escalier (Chapel of the Scala Santa)

Erected in 1891 next to the Memorial Chapel, this sanctuary contains a replica of the Scala Santa (Holy Stairs), which Christ climbed before being sentenced to death by Pontius Pilate. The original staircase was taken to Rome about AD 325 by St. Helena, mother of Emperor Constantine. Many pilgrims mount the steps on their knees.

Chemin de la Croix (The Stations of the Cross)

On the hillside behind the Chapel of the Scala Santa are life-size representations of the Stations of the Cross. They were cast in bronze by French craftsmen between 1913 and 1946.

Additional Sights

Musée de Sainte Anne (Sainte Anne Museum)

9803 Blvd. Sainte-Anne, near the basilica. Open early May–mid-Oct, daily 9am–5pm. $2.   418-827-6873.

Opened in 1997, this museum of religious art presents the life of St. Anne and the development of the community, as well as the history of the shrine.

Cyclorama de Jérusalem★ (Cyclorama of Jerusalem)

8 Rue Régina, beside the basilica. Open May–Oct, daily 9am–6pm. $8. 418-827-3101. www.cyclorama.com.

The large edifice houses an enormous, impressively realistic painting (measuring 1,540sq m/16,576sq ft) showing Jerusalem on the day of the Crucifixion. Painted in Munich (1878–82) by the French panoramist Paul Philippoteaux and five assistants, and installed at Sainte-Anne-de-Beaupré in 1895, it is 14m/46ft high by 110m/361ft in circumference. It remains the largest panoramic painting of its kind in the world.

Atelier Paré - Economuseum of Woodcarving

9269 Ave. Royale. ◷Open mid-May–mid-Oct, daily 9am–5.30pm; rest of the year, Wed–Mon 1pm–4pm. ⬭Free admission, but donations are welcome. ▣ ☎418-827-3583. www.atelierpare.com.

Quebec has been a fertile ground for legends and woodcarving. The two come together at this museum/workshop (this type of establishment is called an economuseum in Quebec). In front of visitors, artists carve and bend (fiberglass is also used) the pieces that will be exposed in the economuseum's garden and the gift shop. Atelier Paré is a family business.

Edison Phonograph Museum

9812 Ave. Royale. ◷Open daily 1pm–8pm; ☺ call in advance; ⬳guided tours in English and French. ⬭$5. ♿ ▣ ☎418-827-5957 & 418-656-2131 ext. 6954. www.phono.org/beaupre.html.

Jean-Paul Agnard has been a passionate phonograph collector since 1970. His museum showcases some 250 phonographs and accessories. The collection is equally divided between American and European phonographs (British, French, German, and Swiss). Edison's 19C hand-driven talking dolls are unforgettable.

SCHEFFERVILLE (KAWAWACHIKAMACH)

DUPLESSIS REGION
POPULATION 249

The mining town of Schefferville abuts the provincial boundary between Quebec and Labrador (province of Newfoundland-and-Labrador). It lies on the northern fringe of the boreal forest, just south of the tundra, on the watershed of the Atlantic and Hudson Strait/Hudson Bay drainage basins. Originally planned for a large population, Schefferville boasts a modern infrastructure. The iron ore mining went on from 1954 to 1982. An extensive road system links the mining sites, their equipment still in place, and leads to a fascinating variety of lakes and mountain ridges. Permission is required to enter the Iron Ore Company grounds (*inquire at municipal office ☎418-585-2471*).

- **Information:** ☎1-888-463-0808. www.tourismeduplessis.com.
- **Orient Yourself: By air:** Air Canada (☎514-393-3333 & 1-888-247-2262; www.aircanada.ca) via Quebec City or Sept-Îles, connecting with Air Inuit (☎418-585-3325 & 1-800-361-2905) to Schefferville. **By train:** Transport ferroviaire Tshiuetin departs twice a week (Mon and Thu at 8am) from Sept-Îles (reservations advised: ☎418-960-9411 & 1-866-962-0988). The interesting train ride (576km/360mi, 12hrs) takes travellers from Sept-Îles across the Canadian Shield to the edge of the tundra. Return trains depart Schefferville Tue and Fri at 8am. Return fare is $171.

A Bit of History

Situated in the heart of the iron-rich **Labrador Trough**, Schefferville was built in 1954 by the Iron Ore Company of Canada, which operated here until 1982. During its heyday, close to 8,000 people lived in this frontier town; a gigantic statue known as the Iron Man recalls the town's former prosperity. Today almost a ghost town, Schefferville is mainly a service center for the Amerindian population; mining continues at a much slower pace. It has also become a departure point for excursions to the Great North of Quebec. Outfitters sell mainly all-inclusive packages (flights, lodgings, meals, fishing/hunting equipment, guides, etc.). For over 40 years, Montreal's McGill University has operated a **Subarctic Research Station** near the airport. The station hosts students and researchers year-round.

Excursions

Kawawachikamach

14.7km/9.1mi northeast of Schefferville. www.naskapi.ca. Unpaved road.
Set amidst small lakes in the hilly region of the Canadian Shield, Kawawachikamach was built between 1981 and 1984, and is settled by Naskapi Indians.

The Naskapis

Related to the Cree and Montagnais (Innu) Indians, the Naskapis are a nomadic people. They originated from the interior of the Ungava region, and followed the migratory route of the caribou. As their traditional hunting activities disappeared, Naskapis settled at the Fort Chimo trading post, now called Kuujjuaq. In 1956, they left Fort Chimo for Schefferville, in the hope of improving their living standards.

When the **Northeastern Quebec Agreement** was signed in 1978, the Naskapis surrendered aboriginal title to their land for financial compensation, land rights and new hunting, fishing and trapping rights. They decided to build their village on the shores of Matemace Lake, leaving behind the reserve of Matimekosh, which they had shared with the Montagnais. This new village was designed to be specifically adapted to the local subarctic climate, one of the harshest in Canada.

Matimekosh

Just north of Schefferville, on foot or by car by municipal road.
Around 1955, Montagnais Indians from the village of Lac-John, created in 1960 on the shore of Lake John. The village later became an Amerindian reserve. The Montagnais, Algonquian-speaking Indians with French as their second language, operate an active crafts center.

SEPT-ÎLES ★

DUPLESSIS REGION
POPULATION 25,276
MAP: SEE CÔTE-NORD

This dynamic city occupies a superb site★★ in a large, almost circular bay on the north shore of the Gulf of St. Lawrence. Protected by the islands at its mouth, the bay remains navigable during all seasons, allowing for industrial activity throughout the year. The Baie des Sept-Îles allows for majestic scenery and fantastic sunsets. Today Sept-Îles is the administrative center of the Côte-Nord, and of one of the largest municipalities in Quebec, covering 2180sq km/842sq mi. A lot of this area is made of forest, lakes and rivers.

- **Information:** 312 Ave. Brochu. ☎418-962-0808 & 1-888-463-0808. www.ville.sept-iles.qc.ca or www.tourismeduplessis.com.
- ▶ **Orient Yourself:** Sept-Îles is 640km/397.6mi northeast of Quebec City by Rte. 138. A ferry service links the community to Rimouski, on the south shore of the St. Lawrence, and to Port-Menier, on Anticosti Island. Service provided by Relais Nordik, Inc. (*mid-Apr–mid-Jan;* ☎1-800-463-0680). The major airport for the Côte-Nord is also located at Sept-Îles, linking this Region to the rest of the world through rugular flights to Montreal.
- **Don't Miss:** A boat tour of the Islands and the Montagnais exhibit at the North Shore Regional Museum. Also try and visit the town of Port Cartier.
- **Organizing Your Time:** Keep in mind that if you will explore the Côte-Nord farther east, Sept-Îles is the last city where you can find and buy a complete array of travel and outdoor gear.

A Bit of History

The earliest known mention of the region of Sept-Îles, or "Seven Islands," dates back to 1535, when Jacques Cartier noted several round islands blocking the entrance to the large bay. In earlier times, Montagnais Indians hunted caribou here. In the 15C, Basque, French and Spanish fishermen came to the area in search of seals and whales from which they extracted oil much in demand in Europe.

In 1651 Father Jean Dequen arrived on these shores and founded the mission of Ange-Gardien. Several years later, the King of France agreed to the establishment of a series of trading posts, to be rented to French merchants. After the Conquest of New France, the King's posts were entrusted to a number of British merchants. The most influential of these, the Hudson's Bay Company, monopolized fishing, hunting and fur-trading rights until 1859, after which the region was opened to settlement. In the early 20C, the paper industry became the principal economic activity, with the construction of a hydroelectric dam and pulp mill at Clarke City, today part of Sept-Îles. The paper mill shut down in 1967, but by the second half of the 20C, the transportation of coal and iron ore had boosted the community's economy. The city's natural deep-water port enables ocean-bound ships to transship coal here. Iron Ore Company of Canada (IOC) owns several wharves in the northeastern sector of the bay, and Wabush Mines Company operates ore-handling facilities in the Pointe-Noire sector.

Sights

Parc du Vieux-Quai (Old Wharf Park)

A boardwalk lines the magnificent bay of Sept-Îles. Seafood enthusiasts can sample shrimp or enjoy a crab sandwich, while enjoying a leisurely stroll along the wharf. The shelters along the boardwalk display crafts by local artisans.

Musée régional de la Côte-Nord (North Shore Regional Museum)

500 Blvd. Laure. ◷*Open late Jun–Labor Day, daily 9am–5pm; rest of the year, Mon–Fri 9am–noon, 1pm–5pm, weekends 1pm–5pm.* ◷*Closed Dec 23–Jan 6.* ⬚*$5.* ♿🅿 ✆*418-968-2070. www.mrcn.qc.ca.*
The museum of art and history was created by the local artist André Michel, as a reminder of the "eternal youth of this ancient land, its roots and the diverse origins of the great men and women who have lived here." The permanent exhibit "A Never-Ending Shore" describes the 1,100km/682mi of shoreline and forests of black spruce, and the successive waves of population growth that resulted from the exploitation of the area's natural resources.

The museum is housed within **Le Vieux-Poste** (Old Trading Post). Reconstructed according to its 18C layout uncovered during archaeological excavations, this group of buildings surrounded by a palisade occupies a historically significant site. Montagnais Indians and European settlers first traded here three centuries ago, and the site was visited by Jacques Cartier, Louis Jolliet and merchants of the Hudson Bay Company. The site recreates the atmosphere of a trading post of years past; other exhibits offer an intriguing introduction to the Montagnais-Innu culture.

Another way to get in touch with the Montagnais-Innu culture is to listen to CKAU (90.1 & 104.5FM; www.ckau.com), Maniutenam/Sept-Îles' **Aboriginal-run community radio station**. You will hear the Innu, French and English languages during programming and understand outright the unique complexities of Amerindian life in Quebec.

Parc Régional de l'Archipel des Sept Îles★ (Sept-Îles Regional Park)

Virée des îles en bateau (Boat Tour of the Islands)

Cruises depart from Old Wharf ticket counter in front of the marina mid-May–mid-Oct, daily 8am–5.15pm (sev-

Lighthouse, Île du Corossol

eral departures a day according to the cruise). Round-trip 3hrs. French and English commentary. Reservations suggested 24hrs in advance, positively required in low season. ⊷$45 (tickets available at the promenade ticket counter in front of the marina). 🅿☎418-968-1818 (during summer season, else contact Tourisme Sept-Îles ☎418-962-1238. www.tourisme septiles.ca).

Scenic **cruises** by ferry, riverboat and raft offer a good introduction to the region, its history and the natural beauty of the Sept-Îles archipelago. The lighthouse indicating the entrance to the bay is located on **Île du Corossol** (Corossol Island), a bird sanctuary with one of the greatest varieties of species in Canada, including gulls, terns and puffins.

Île Grande Basque

Ferry to island departs from Old Wharf ticket counter in front of the marina, mid-May–mid-Oct, daily 9am–6.30pm. One-way 10–20min. Reservations suggested. ⊷$20, rustic camping permitted on the island $10/night. ⚠️♿🅿🏕️*Tourisme Sept-Îles ☎418-962-1238. www.tourisme septiles.ca*

Located closest to the city, La Grande Basque is the only island that has been developed for hiking, picnicking and camping. Numerous trails meander through grandiose and varied landscapes: huge rocky ridges, immense cliffs and a peat bog. Beautiful sandy beaches line the western shore. Islands also reachable by sea kayak (with guided tour or rental kayak).

Centre de la Nature Gallix

3133 Rte 138 (in the Gallix district of Sept-Îles, southwest of the downtown area). 🕐*Open early Jun–early Sept, Mon–Thu 10am–5pm.* ⊷*$8 (13yrs+); $3 (3–12yrs).* 🅿☎*418-766-8345. www. zoocotenord.com.*

It is easy to miss Gallix, the initial Sept-Îles district you go through when you drive from the west, and most tourists do. But a good reason to stop by is the Gallix Nature Center. Here you can find rare North American mammals, including the Canadian lynx, Arctic foxes, wolves, black bears, moose, and the more common white-tailed deer and racoons. Of course, they are behind fences, yet in a more natural and up-close position than in most zoos.

Other activities here include hiking along designated nature trails and fishing for trout (fishing material provided ⊷fee).

SHERBROOKE★

Located on the steep slopes of a valley, at the confluence of the Saint-François and Magog rivers, Sherbrooke was originally called "the great fork" by Abenaki Indians. The first settlers arrived from Vermont about 1800. Soon thereafter, Gilbert Hyatt built a flour mill, and the community became known as Hyatt's Mills. In 1818 the name Sherbrooke was adopted in honour of the governor-in-chief of British North America, **Sir John Coape Sherbrooke** (1764–1830).

Because of its industrial dominance during the 19C, Sherbrooke became the principal city of the Eastern Townships. Mills sprang up on the banks of the Magog River, soon followed by the textile mills. The advent of the railway accelerated Sherbrooke's economic growth, and the Université de Sherbrooke opened in 1954, enhancing the city's position as an important urban center. It is Quebec's sixth-largest city. Originally Anglophone, the population is now overwhelmingly francophone. Today Sherbrooke serves the mining and agricultural concerns of the region. Mt. Bellevue, across the Magog River, is a popular ski center.

- **Information:** 20 Rue Don-Bosco Sud. ☎819-820-2020 & 1-800-355-5755. www.easterntownships.org.
- **Orient Yourself:** Sherbrooke is 150km/93mi east of Montreal by Rte. 10 and Rte. 112.
- **Parking:** Generally easy to find, metered in the downtown core
- **Don't Miss:** Cathédrale Saint-Michel.
- **Organizing Your Time:** From Sherbrooke, you can easily go to either Montreal, Quebec City or Vermont (USA).
- **Especially for Kids:** There are two beaches and a water-ski school on Lac des Nations. It is also possible to rent canoes, kayaks and pedal boats.
- **Also See:** CANTONS DE L'EST (Coaticook).

Town Center

Monument aux morts (War Memorial)
Rue King Ouest between Rue Gordon and Rue Brooks.
This imposing sculpture by George W. Hills stands in the center of Rue King. It was erected in 1926 to commemorate the Sherbrooke residents who gave their lives in World War I. From this vantage point the **view** encompasses the city and the Saint-François River.

- *From the War Memorial, go east down the hill to Rue Wellington, turn left and continue for two blocks.*

Hôtel de Ville (City Hall)
145 Rue Wellington.
Closed to the public.

Completed in 1906 as a courthouse, this imposing edifice exemplifies the Second Empire style. The architect, Elzéar Charest, reused the plans he had submitted to the 1890 city hall competition in Quebec City. Dominating lovely Strathcona Park, the structure has housed the city hall since 1988.

Musée des Beaux-Arts de Sherbrooke (Sherbrooke Museum of Fine Arts)
241 Rue Dufferin. ◷*Open late Jun–Labor Day Tue–Sun 10am–5pm; rest of the year, Tue–Sun 12pm–5pm.* ◷*Closed Jan 1, 2 & Dec 25–26.* ☜*$7.50.* ♿ P ☎819-821-2115. www.mbas.qc.ca.
Housed in a historic structure in downtown Sherbrooke, this museum presents an interesting collection of Quebec art, focusing on the Eastern Townships. Note in particular works by Robert Whale

Address Book

For price ranges, see the Legend on the cover flap.

STAYING, PAMPERING, EATING, WITH OR WITHOUT KIDS

$$$-$$$$ Delta Hotel Sherbrooke
– 2685 Rue King Ouest. KIDS SPA
↻ 819-822-1989 & 1-800-268-1133.
www.deltasherbrooke.com. 178 rooms.
Centrally located, Sherbrooke's largest hotel provides all the services expected from a lodging specializing in both business and family travel.
Set packages also allow you to save significantly on area attractions. Spa devotees will have to choose between

Amma, Californian, Esalen, Swedish, and Rain massages; reflexology and Reiki treatments are also available.
Children will appreciate the small, heated indoor pool, and the *Creative Center*, a room full of toys, arts, crafts and games. A babysitting service is also available. Parents will also love the fact that the excellent restaurant serves meals for free to children 6 and under and at half price to youngsters under 12.
Hotel restaurant **Le Murville** serves creative continental cuisine and is well known for its Saturday night buffet and Sunday brunch.

(1805–87), Suzor-Côté (1869–1937) and Wayne Seese (1918–80). A collection of paintings in the naïve style includes pieces by Arthur Villeneuve, and by such international artists as Dragan Mihailovic and Jean-Marie Godefroy.
The museum also organizes temporary exhibits of works by local artists and offers various educational activities.

Cathédrale Saint-Michel★ (St. Michael's Cathedral)

Rue de la Cathédrale, at the corner of Rue Marquette. ⏱ Open year-round Mon–Fri 7.30am–noon, 1.30pm–4pm, Sat 9am–noon, 2pm–4pm, Sun 9am–noon, 2pm–6pm. ↻ 819-563-9371.
This imposing Gothic Revival structure stands on a hill known as the Marquette Plateau, in the center of Sherbrooke. Consecrated in 1958, the cathedral was built by Louis-Napoléon Audet, who also designed the basilica at Sainte-Anne-de-Beaupré. In the façade's principal stained-glass window hangs a 3m/9.8ft-high aluminium crucifix, by the Montreal artist Cassini. Inside, ceilings over 20m/65.6ft high enclose a light and spacious interior. The large stained-glass windows, by Raphaël Lardeur and Gérard Brassard, portray Biblical scenes. To the left of the altar is a striking oak statue of the Virgin Mary by the 20C artist Sylvia Daoust.

Chapelle des Fondateurs (Founders' Chapel)

Behind main altar to the left.
Added in 1980, this chapel features a mural of enamelled copper by Patricio Rivera, portraying the five founders of the Canadian Catholic Church: Marie de l'Incarnation, Marguerite d'Youville, Msgr. de Laval, Kateri Tekakwitha, and Marguerite Bourgeoys.

The Old North Ward★ (Le Vieux-Nord)

The area north of the Magog River encompasses some of the oldest industries in Sherbrooke, as well as charming streets lined with large, lovely homes. Numerous Colonial and New England-style mansions lend the quarter a stately appearance, enlivened by fanciful examples of the Victorian styles, including Italian Villa, Chateauesque, Queen Anne and Gothic Revival. Their dormers, gables, towers and turrets are set off by splendid gardens dotted with tall trees.

Domaine Howard (Howard Estate)

1300 Blvd. Portland.
↪ *Buildings closed to the public.*
Charles Benjamin Howard (1885–1964), businessman, politician and mayor of Sherbrooke, erected a stone house on this site in 1917, adding a second one a

few years later for his mother. For several years, the buildings housed the offices of the Sherbrooke Historical Society (*now housed at 275 Rue Dufferin*); today both buildings belong to the city and house civic offices. The grounds form a pleasant park surrounding superb French formal gardens.

Excursions

Rocher Mena'Sen (Mena'Sen Rock)

1.5km/1mi north of town. From Rue King Est, turn left on Rue Bowen, then bear left onto Blvd. Saint-François Nord.

An illuminated cross stands on this islet in the Saint-François River, replacing a lone pine tree (*mena'sen* in Abenaki) that was destroyed in a storm in 1913. According to Abenaki folklore, the tree commemorated the Abenaki victory over the Iroquois. Another legend tells of two young Amerindian lovers who, having escaped capture in Massachusetts, stopped here on their way to Odanak.

The girl died at this spot and her lover planted the tree in her memory.

Sanctuaire de Beauvoir (Shrine of Beauvoir)

8km/4mi north of town by Blvd. Saint-François Nord and Chemin Beauvoir. Open May–Nov, daily 9am–10pm; rest of the year, daily 9am–5pm. (summer) 819-569-2535. www.sanctuaire debeauvoir.qc.ca.

In 1915 Abbé Joseph-Arthur Laporte placed a statue of Christ at this spot, 360m/1,181ft above the Saint-François River. A simple stone chapel was constructed in 1920. Today many pilgrims find their way here seeking peace and tranquillity, and to enjoy the **panorama**★ of the Sherbrooke area.

In the woods behind the chapel and the newer church (1945) is the Gospel Walk, consisting of eight **sculptures**★ representing scenes from the life of Christ. These stone sculptures were carved by Joseph Guardo. In summer, mass is celebrated in an outdoor chapel, which can accommodate 1,600 pilgrims.

TADOUSSAC★★

MANICOUAGAN REGION
POPULATION 830
MAP: SEE FJORD DU SAGUENAY

Situated at the mouth of the Saguenay River, Tadoussac occupies a beautiful **site**★★ on the cliffs and sand dunes lining the north shore of the St. Lawrence. Its name is derived from the Montagnais word tatoushak, meaning "knolls," a reference to the pair of small hills west of the community. A boardwalk extends alongside the St. Lawrence linking the old chapel and the Chauvin trading post, just beneath the **Hôtel Tadoussac**, a long, red-roofed structure dating from 1941. Paths circle **Pointe de l'Islet**, which borders the bay, providing fine views of the landscape; others cross the knolls to a small cove (Anse-à-l'eau), where the ferry from Baie-Sainte-Catherine docks. The extremely lively town attracts a growing number of visitors, who come to observe the whales that visit the plankton-rich waters at the mouth of the Saguenay for a few months each year.

- **Information:** 197 Rue des Pionniers. 418-235-4744 & 1-866-235-4744. www.tadoussac.com or www.tourismemanicouagan.com.
- **Orient Yourself:** Tadoussac is about 220km/136.7mi northeast of Quebec City by Rtes. 40 and 138, on the north side of the Saguenay Fjord.
- **Don't Miss:** The Marine Mammal Interpretation Center houses excellent whale exhibits, including skeletons suspended from the ceiling; learn about marine mammals before going to the water to see them. Bring binoculars as you explore the coast as whales can often be spied from shore.
- **Also See:** CÔTE NORD, FJORD DU SAGUENAY.

Address Book

For price ranges, see cover flap.

WHERE TO STAY

$$$-$$$$ Hôtel Tadoussac –
165 Rue Bord de l'Eau. ✗ ⛓ 🅿 🛏 Spa
☎418-235-4421 & 1-800-561-0718.
www.hoteltadoussac.com. 149 rooms.
Recognizable by its striking red roof,
made famous in the film *Hotel New
Hampshire,* cozy Hôtel Tadoussac
invites visitors to choose their own
level of activity. Take a whale-watch-
ing cruise, play tennis, pamper
yourself at the spa, or just relax in
Adirondack chairs on the wide green
lawn and drink in views of the Bay of
Tadoussac. Rooms are furnished with
cottage-country charm; many boast
bay views.

A Bit of History

Tadoussac was a meeting place for
trade well before the arrival of Jacques
Cartier on these shores, in 1535. In 1600,
Pierre Chauvin built Canada's first fur
trading post on this spot, and later the
Jesuits established a mission. Tadous-
sac became a port of call for all vessels
crossing the Atlantic. In 1628 the village
was captured by the Kirke Brothers,
British adventurers, but it later returned
to French hands and remained a trad-
ing center until 1839, when the first per-
manent residents arrived and erected a
sawmill. With the advent of the steam-
ship, Tadoussac the community devel-
oped as a choice resort in the mid-19C.

Mammals of the Deep

Every June, Atlantic Ocean whales swim
up the St. Lawrence River to the mouth
of the Saguenay River. Here, the salty
St. Lawrence and the fresh waters of the
Saguenay combine to create a rich eco-
system for a multitude of flora and fauna.
Krill and caplin, drawn by the plankton
flourishing in these waters, attract the
whales, which consume several tonnes
of the small sea creatures daily.
Many species of whale have been sighted
here, the most common being the **fin**
and **minke**. There is also a significant
population of **belugas**. Occasionally,
humpback whales are sighted, and
lucky tourists may glimpse the huge **blue
whale,** which is known to reach a length
of 25m/82ft (blue whales in the south-
ern hemisphere can grow to 30m/98.4ft),
making it the largest mammal on earth.

Cruises

Whale-Watching Cruises★★
*Depart from the Tadoussac marina Jun–
mid-Sept, at least five departures daily;
rest of the year, call for hours. Round-trip
3hrs. English and French commentary.
☺Reservations required (fee per person*

Hotel Tadoussac

Whale-watching from the shore in Tadoussac

Parc National du Saguenay/Mathieu Dupuis/ Sépaq

$4); ≈$59. ⌘&☐Croisières AML ☎1-800-
563-4643. www.croisieresaml.com.
At Tadoussac, the St. Lawrence is more
than 10km/6.2mi wide. The boats head
for the center, where the whales surface
to breathe and dive to search for food. It
is a magnificent experience to see these
colossal creatures.

The entrance to the Saguenay fjord is
marked by a lighthouse that stands
15m/49ft high and is visible for nearly
50km/31mi.

Scenic Cruises★★

*Depart from the pier mid-Jun–Labor Day,
daily 9.30am & 1.30pm. 3hrs. English and
French commentary. ⌛Reservations
advised. ≈$59. &☐Croisières Dufour
☎1-877-778-8977. www.dufour.ca.*
To fully appreciate the deep and wide
Saguenay fjord, an ancient glacial valley
flanked by precipitous cliffs, visitors are
advised to take a boat trip.

Sights

Marine Mammal Interpretation Center

*108 Rue de la Cale Sèche, near the pier.
◔Open mid-May–mid-Oct, daily 9am–
8pm; mid-May–early Jun & late Sept–mid-
Oct, daily noon–5pm. ≈$8. &☐☎ 418-
235-4701. www.gremm.org.*
This interpretation center (CIMM) presents interesting displays, videos and slide
shows on the marine life of this area, in
particular whales, seals and cormorants.

Petite Chapelle de Tadoussac (Indian Chapel)

*On Rue du Bord-de-l'Eau. ◔Open
mid-Jun–early Sept, daily 9am–8pm,
early Sept–early Oct 9am–6pm. ≈$2.
&☐☎418-235-1415.*
The small chapel, the oldest wooden
church in North America, was built in
1747 by the Jesuit missionary, Claude-
Godefroy Cocquart. The chapel houses a
fine collection of religious objects.

Chauvin Trading Post

*157 Rue du Bord-de-l'Eau. ◔Open
early Jun–mid-Oct, daily 10am–7pm;
early–mid-Jun & rest of Sept–mid-Oct,
daily 10am–6pm. ≈$3. &☐☎ 418-
235-4657.*
This log structure with its steeply
pitched roof is a reconstruction of Pierre
Chauvin's fur trading post of 1600. Inside,
old photographs as well as archaeological and historical displays explain the fur
trade between the Montagnais Indians
and the French. The collection focuses
on the Côte-Nord region.

Maison des dunes (House of the Sand Dunes)

4km/2.5mi east by Rue des Pionniers.
Located in a stone house (1915), an **interpretation center** (◔*open late Jun–mid-
Sept, daily 10am–5pm;* &☐☎418-235-
4238) provides insight into the formation
of the lovely marine terraces of fine sand
lining the Saint Lawrence. Sparrows
and birds of prey are visible here from
August to October.

TERREBONNE★

LANAUDIÈRE REGION
POPULATION 92,972
MAP: SEE LANAUEDIÈRE

This attractive city lies on the north shore of the Mille Îles River, north of Montreal. Terrebonne's refurbished 18C and 19C old quarter, bounded by Rues Saint-Louis and Saint-Pierre, is a delightful place to stroll, with its quaint stone and wooden buildings, many of which house restaurants, cafés, boutiques and galleries. Terrebonne has expanded considerably in recent years as a suburb of Montreal, and it is the main gateway to the Southern Lanaudière region. Terrebonne makes an excellent day trip from Montreal where you can relax, enjoy French Seigneurial architecture and ride a bicycle for the day on a beautiful network of cycle paths inside and outside the city.

- **Information:** 5000 Côte Terrebonne. ☎450-964-0681 & 1-866-964-0681. www.tourismedesmoulins.com/www.lanaudiere.ca.
- ▶ **Orient Yourself:** Terrebonne is 35km/22mi north of Montreal by Rte. 125 (Blvd. Pie-IX) and Rte. 25 (Exit 17). Outside of peak hours, you can reach Terrebonne from Montreal in under then 30 minutes.

A Bit of History

Terrebonne's story begins in 1673 when the seigneury was granted to Daulier des Landes, but settlement only began in the 18C. The community soon became known for its fertile soil, hence the name Terrebonne, meaning "good land." The first mills in the area were built by the abbot Louis Lepage, between 1718 and 1745, on one of the islands (Île des Moulins) in the Mille Îles River.

After the Conquest, Île des Moulins flourished under the Scottish merchants of the Northwest Company. Simon McTavish, one of the stockholders, acquired the Terrebonne seigneury in 1802. Within a few years, he had established an industrial and commercial center on the island, whose fame extended well beyond the region's borders. In 1815 the mills of Terrebonne were reputedly the finest and best equipped in all of Canada. Activity subsided during the 1820s as electricity gradually replaced hydraulic power, and Île des Moulins was reduced to serving the needs of farmers in the area. In 1832, Joseph Masson,

Flour and Sawmills, Île des Moulins

Île des Moulins, Terrebonne

Address Book

⚑ For price ranges, see the Legend
on the cover flap.

WHERE TO STAY

OLD TERREBONNE
$$$-$$$$ Auberge Le Petit St-André
– *211 Rue Saint-André.* ♿🅿📞*450-471-
8822 & 1-888-471-8822. www.auberge
lestandre.ca. 8 rooms.* Sleep peacefully
on the comfortable beds of this large
centennial country home, turned into
a fancy B&B. Every room is decorated
differently and each one has its own
bathroom. Le Petit St-André is located
in Old Terrebonne, one of the most his-
toric areas in Quebec. Yet, Terrebonne
is close enough to Montreal to make
it a sort of town & country retreat for
visitors. Golfing, equestrian, theater
packages and more can be arranged
at the Auberge.

GOLFING AT LE VERSANT
Centre de golf Le Versant - *2075
Côte Terrebonne, just outside of the city.*
🍴🅿📞*450-964-2251. www.golfleversant.
com.* The Montreal area boasts several
excellent golf courses. Le Versant golf
center in Terrebonne is special because
it offers four 18-hole courses (2 cham-
pionship courses, a standard course,
and a par 3 course) at reasonable prices.
With four courses, it is normally pos-
sible to get a chance to play, even with
short notice reservations. There is a vast
and elegant restaurant at Le Versant
offering continental classics and a
remarkable wine list.

a banker from Montreal, acquired the
seigneury and its mills. While he was
unable to restore the village's past
glory, his widow, Geneviève Sophie
Raymond, tried to address the various
needs of the community and created a
road network, the Terrebonne Turnpike,
extending from Saint-Vincent-de-Paul
to Mascouche. However, business con-
tinued to decline and by the end of the
19C, all mills had shut down.

Sights

Situated on high ground above the river,
Rue Saint-Louis is lined with attrac-
tive stone buildings topped by steeply
pitched roofs. At n°. 901, note the former
Masson Manor (1850), built in the Neo-
classical style with a symmetrical façade
and pediments. The former residence of
Geneviève Sophie Raymond, the build-
ing now serves as a school. The church
(Église Saint-Louis-de-France), erected
in 1878, with its tall central steeple and
two side towers, stands nearby.
La Maison de Pays (the old country
house) is a historic jewel on rue Saint-
François-Xavier. Built in 1960 (the year
of the British conquest), la Maison du
Pays offers a glimpse into the cultural

and agricultural past of the Lanaudière
Region through guided tours, ancient
crafts demonstrations and tasting
samples of local products made with
traditional methods. La Maison du Pays
is opened to visitors year round (admis-
sion is free).

Île des Moulins★ (Mill Island)
*From Blvd. des Seigneurs, turn right on
Ave. Moody, left on Rue Saint-Louis and
right on Rue des Braves.* ⏰*Îles aux Mou-
lins is a municipal park open year round
daily 7am–11pm. Activities and exhibi-
tions take place, particularly during the
summer;* 🎟*nominal fees are sometimes
charged.* 🍴📞*450-471-0619. www.ile-des-
moulins.qc.ca.*
The island presents an impressive col-
lection of 19C buildings restored by the
Quebec government. These structures
can best be viewed from Rue des Braves,
on the other side of Masson Pond, which
was used as a reservoir.
Both types of mills that prevailed in Que-
bec in the 18C and 19C can be found
here. The French Regime mills were
often constructed on a causeway or
bridge having supports high enough to
permit the wheel to turn under them.
By the late 18C, English technology
had established mills on land, using

diversion canals to augment the flow of water.

Crossing the causeway, the first building visible is the **flour mill** (*moulin à farine*), built in 1846 on the site of the seigneurial mill of 1721. Both this restored mill and the adjacent **sawmill** (1804) have been converted into the municipal library, an acclaimed example of adaptive building re-use. The pleasant and innovative interior displays remnants of the mills. Visitors can gaze out the large rear windows and observe the pond water trickling down the original wheel mechanism.

The next building, on the island itself, is the **seigneurial office** (*bureau seigneurial*), a stone structure built for the mill foreman's widow around 1850. It houses an **interpretation center** with an exhibit on the history of the site (🕐 *same hours as Mill Island*).

Beside it is the old **bakery** (*boulangerie*). Built in 1803, this massive building is reflects traditional French architecture. The last building, the so-called **new mill** (*moulin neuf*) of 1850, has two floors and an attic and houses a cultural center. The rest of the island is a pleasantly landscaped park dotted with modern sculptures, benches, picnic sites and an outdoor amphitheater. Bike paths meander throughout the park.

The Old Terrebonne sector is the home of **Théâtre du Vieux-Terrebonne** (known as **TVT**), a beautiful and well-appointed 656-seat venue hosting shows year-round. TVT programming accurately portrays the performance arts scene in Quebec, from classics to avant-garde, in theater, singing, humor, classical music, dance, jazz and world beats. TVT presents a summer season of high quality theater (in French).

THETFORD MINES

CHAUDIÈRE-APPALACHES REGION
POPULATION 25,854
MAP: SEE BEAUCE

This community is located in the heart of the largest asbestos-producing region in the Western Hemisphere. Named for a small town in Norfolk, England, Thetford Mines sits in a naturally rolling area drained by the Bécancour River. The town is distinguished by its unique piles of **tailings**, artificial mountains composed of pulverized rock from the mines.

- **Information:** 2600 Blvd. Frontenac. ☎418-423-3333 & 1-877-335-7141. www.tourisme-amiante.com, www.ville.thetfordmines.qc.ca/ www.chaudiereappalaches.com.
- ▶ **Orient Yourself:** Thetford Mines is located 107km/66.4mi southeast of Quebec City by Rte. 73 and Rtes. 173 and 112.
- 😊 **Don't Miss:** The Lookout Point to see mining operations.
- 📏 **Especially for Kids:** The open mine tours.
- 🕐 **Also See:** VICTORIAVILLE.

A Bit of History

In 1876, while ploughing his field, Joseph Fecteau found a strange piece of rock that frayed into silky white fibres: **asbestos.** The mineral had been recognized as "white gold" for over 2,000 years for its heat-resistant and insulating properties. Interest in Fecteau's discovery generated the area's development, particularly after the construction of a railway in 1879, which enabled rapid transport of raw and finished products. Asbestos yields a fibre used today in the construction and aerospace industries. Despite restrictions governing the use of asbestos in recent years, Thetford Mines remains one of the country's largest producing centers, with both underground and open pit mines. A 9km/5.6mi drive south on Route 112 passes through the town of **Black Lake**, and offers unforgettable views of the town's immense open-pit mine at the Asbestos Mine Lookout Point (*Belvédère d'observation de la mine d'amiante*). The Black Lake mine is gigantic, its diameter is 2.1km/1.3mi. and it is 354km/1,155ft deep. The Lookout Point enclosed platform is always open and free of charge.

Musée Minéralogique et Minier

Sight

Open Mine Tours

711 Blvd. Frontenac Ouest (Rte. 112).
Guided tours (2hr) late Jun–Labor Day, daily: Jun & Sept, 1.30pm, July & Aug, 1.30pm, 3.30pm; early Sept–mid-Oct, Sat only at 1.30pm (tours in French and English). Tours depart from the nearby Mining Museum. $18 (tour cost includes visit to the Mining Museum). P ☎418-423-3333 & 1-877-335-7141. www.tourisme-amiante.com.

A well leads you down, way down (354m/1,155ft deep) to the bottom of the mine that gave the town of Thetford its full name. The 2hr guided tour is carried on aboard a specially adapted bus, the Labmobile. You will explore extraction, bagging and expeditions sites. And you will see a 100-ton lorry.

Musée minéralogique et minier de Thetford Mines

711 Blvd. Frontenac Ouest (Rte. 112).
Open late Jun–mid-Aug, daily 9.30am–6pm; mid-Aug–Labor Day, 9.30am–5pm; rest of the year, daily 1pm–5pm (visits by appointment only in January. $7. ☎ P ☎ 418-335-2123. www.musee mineralogique.com.

This museum houses a superb collection of minerals from all over the world, with particular focus on the Appalachians, mountains renowned for the beauty and variety of their minerals. Displays help visitors identify the types of rock and describe their characteristics, such as hardness, translucence, color and lustre. The exhibit highlights asbestos and other minerals found in Quebec.

Excursion

Kinnear's Mills

24km/15mi by Rtes. 112 and 269.
This tiny community in the Osgood River valley is known for the beauty of its site and for the four churches standing side by side (closed to the public) at its center. Around 1842, several Scottish families settled in Kinnear's Mills and built the Presbyterian church. The more modest Methodist church (1876) and the Anglican church with its small steeple, were built by Loyalists after the American Revolution. The Catholic church was built by Irish Catholics who fled Ireland in the 1920s.

TROIS-RIVIÈRES★★

MAURICIE REGION
POPULATION 126,323

Capital of the Mauricie region, this industrial center is located on the north shore of the St. Lawrence River at the mouth of the Saint-Maurice River. Just before it enters the St. Lawrence, the Saint-Maurice River branches around two islands, thereby creating the three "rivers" for which the city is named. Major annual events in Trois-Rivières include an international poetry festival, an international festival of vocal arts, and sports-car racing at Le Grand Prix de Trois-Rivières (*see Calendar of Events*).

- **Information:** 1457 Rue Notre-Dame. ☎819-375-1122 & 1-800-313-1123. www.tourismetroisrivieres.com/www.tourismemauricie.com.
- ▶ **Orient Yourself:** Trois-Rivières is situated about halfway between Montreal (85km/53mi) and Quebec City (80km/50mi) on the north shore of the St. Lawrence. Both Rte. 40 (Center-Ville Exit) and Rte. 138 go through the city.
- **Don't Miss:** Strolling on the Harborfront Park—Trois-Rivières boasts the best urban access to the St. Lawrence River. The small streets of Old Trois-Rivières are also exceptional, and they are not commercialized.
- **Organizing Your Time:** Between Montreal and Quebec City, Trois-Rivières is a pleasant stop. Accommodation is much cheaper here than in the larger cities.
- **Also See:** MAURICIE, VALLÉE DU SAINT-LAURENT.

A Bit of History

First Settlers – In 1634, Samuel de Champlain sent Nicolas Goupil, Sieur de Laviolette (1604–c. 1660), here to establish a fur trading post. For his fort, Laviolette chose an elevated spot (known as the Platon) high above the St. Lawrence. Furs were transported on the Saint-Maurice River until 1737, when the King's Road (Chemin du Roy) was inaugurated, connecting the settlement to the city of Quebec. During New France's heyday, Trois-Rivières was home to many great explorers, including Jean Nicolet and Nicolas Perrot. The joint explorations of **Pierre-Esprit Radisson** and **Médard Chouart, Sieur des Groseilliers**, led to the founding of the Hudson's Bay Company in 1670, and the renowned **Sieur de la Vérendrye** was the first European to reach the Rocky Mountains.

Pulp and Paper Capital – In the 1850s, major logging companies began exploiting the vast forests of the Saint-Maurice River valley. Large lumber mills sprang up in Trois-Rivières, along with a port and, later, hydroelectric installations.

When a process for making paper from wood pulp was developed, a thriving pulp and paper industry took root in the area. By the 1930s, Trois-Rivières was the world capital for the production of newsprint, a distinction the city holds to this day. Three large pulp mills currently operate in the city.

The elegant **Pont Laviolette** across the St. Lawrence was inaugurated in 1967. It is the only bridge linking the river's banks between Montreal and Quebec. Suspended 46m/150ft above the river, it is 3km/1.8mi long. The **Université du Québec à Trois-Rivières** (UQTR) opened outside the downtown district in 1969.

Walking Tour *2.9km/1.8mi.*

A fire in 1908 destroyed or damaged hundreds of buildings, devastating the heart of the old city. The relatively few buildings that survived the disaster have been carefully restored.

- ▶ *Begin the walking tour at the Boucher de Niverville Manor.*

Manoir Boucher-de-Niverville★

168 Rue Bonaventure.
🔒*Closed to the public.*

This whitewashed stone manor house with red shutters was constructed ca. 729 by François Châtelain. His son-in-law, Claude-Joseph Boucher, Sieur de Niverville, gave the manor its name when he inherited it in 1761. The residence is decorated with typical 18C Quebec furniture. Outside stands a **statue** (**1**) of Maurice Duplessis (1890–1959), a native of the city. Premier of Quebec from 1936 to 1939 and from 1944 to 1959, Duplessis lived down the street (*240 Rue Bonaventure*) and graduated from the Trois-Rivières Seminary.

▶ *Walk south on Rue Bonaventure.*

Le Flambeau (Flaming Torch)

On Place Pierre Boucher. The monument is illuminated at night.

The striking obelisk in the center of the Pierre Boucher Square was erected to celebrate Trois-Rivières' 325th anniversary. Pierre Boucher, Sieur de Grosbois (1622–1717), was the governor of Trois-Rivières in 1654 when the settlement was attacked by the Iroquois. He later founded Boucherville.

▶ *Walk south to Rue des Ursulines and turn left.*

Rue des Ursulines★

This charming street is lined with some of the oldest buildings in the city, most spared by the 1908 fire.

Manoir de Tonnancour★

864 Rue des Ursulines. 🕐*Open mid-Jan–mid-Dec, Tue–Fri 10am–1.30pm, weekends 1pm–5pm.* ☎*819-374-2355.* *www.galeriedartduparc.qc.ca.*

This three-story edifice was completed in 1725 by René Godefroy de Tonnancour, seigneur of Pointe-du-Lac, and rebuilt by Judge Pierre-Louis Deschenaux after a fire in 1795. The structure served as an officers' barracks, a presbytery, and a school. It has been restored and now houses the **Galerie d'art du Parc**. Note the unusual style of the pitched roof, which reveals a Loyalist influence. The foundations and stone walls are original.

Opposite the manor house lies the **Place d'Armes**. Prior to 1800, the square served as a camping ground for Algonquin Indians who came to trade furs at the fort. Reserved for military use from 1751 to 1815, the square has now been converted into a pleasant park.

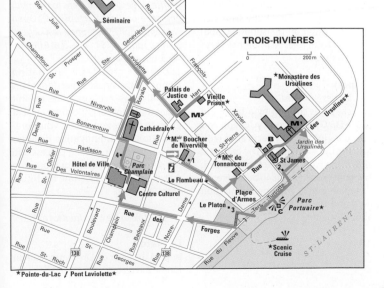

St. James' Church

787 Rue des Ursulines. ✎ Guided tours (1hr) available year-round by appointment only. ♿☎819-378-2071.

The Récollets (reformed Franciscan monks) began construction here on a chapel and monastery in 1693, completing work in 1742. After the Conquest, the building was used as a court of law and a prison. The chapel was converted to an Anglican church in 1823.

Opposite the church, the **Maison de Gannes (A)** (*no. 834; private residence*), built in 1756 by a French officer, is the only structure of French inspiration in the old quarter. At no. 802, note also the historic **Maison Hertel de la Fresnière (B)**, completed in 1829.

Ursulines Monastery★

784 Rue des Ursulines.

This religious complex, replete with a gracious dome and a large wall sundial, is the jewel of Trois-Rivières' old quarter. The Ursuline Sisters arrived in Quebec in 1639 from Tours, France, but were not summoned to Trois-Rivières until 1697. Their first monastery, completed in 1700, was enlarged with a chapel in 1714 and rebuilt after a fire in 1752. A second fire struck in 1806, but the French Regime style of the buildings was maintained during reconstruction. Six subsequent additions were made between 1835 and 1960. The Ursuline Sisters operate a private girls' school, which today has an enrolment of some 1,200 students. The inscription on the sundial (1860) reads, in Latin, *Dies Sicut Umbra* (days flee like shadows).

Chapel★

734 Rue des Ursulines.

The chapel is topped by a beautiful dome (1897) designed by Joseph and Georges Héroux and decorated with frescoes by Luigi Capello. The early 19C altar is the work of François Normand. Paintings executed in 1840 by the French Canadian artists, Antoine Plamondon (*left*) and Joseph Légaré (*right*), hang above the altar.

Musée des Ursulines (Ursuline Museum) (M¹)

734 Rue des Ursulines ◷Open May–Nov, Tue–Sun 10am–5pm; Mar–Apr, Wed–Sun 1pm–5pm; rest of the year by appointment. ☞$3.50 ☎819-375-7922. www.musee-ursulines.qc.ca

The museum features fine collections of ceramics, silver, books, prints, furniture, and decorative arts. Each year, exhibits are compiled on specific themes. A model shows the monastery as it appeared in the 19C. During summer vacations, temporary art exhibits are displayed in the refectory.

▸ *Cross the Ursuline Garden (in front of the monastery).*

A **monument (2)** at the eastern end of the Waterfront Park commemorates Pierre Gaultier de Varennes, **Sieur de la Vérendrye**.

Waterfront Park ★

Once part of the estate of Mayor Joseph-Édouard Turcotte, this attractive terrace affords superb **views** of the river and of the south shore. In 1857 Turcotte gave the land to the city for use as a public park.

Pulp and Paper Industry Exhibition Center (C)

800 Parc Portuaire. Enter from the upper terrace, or descend the steps to the main entrance on Parc Portuaire. ◷Open Jun–Sept, daily 9am–6pm; rest of year by reservation. ☞$4. ✗♿🅿☎819-372-4633; www.ceipp.net.

The center provides a fascinating glimpse of the industry that dominates Trois-Rivières' economy. The exhibit traces the history of paper from ancient China to the present. Audio-visual presentations and innovative displays explain the paper-making process and the different techniques for producing pulp. Large murals illustrate the future of the industry.

▸ *Walk along the waterfront to Le Platon.*

Le Platon

In 1634 the Sieur de Laviolette built his fort on this plateau 35m/115ft above the river. The area's name is derived from the word plateau. A **bust** (**3**) of Laviolette and a plaque were placed here in 1934 to celebrate the city's tricentennial.

Scenic Cruise★

Departs from landing at the foot of Rue des Forges mid-May–Sept. Round-trip 90min. Commentary. Reservations recommended. ≈$18. ✕ P Navire M/V Le Draveur. ☎819-375-3000 & 1-800-567-3737; www.croisieres.qc.ca.

This cruise offers an unequalled **view** of the port of Trois-Rivières and its pulp and paper mills. Visitors can also get a good look at the impressive Laviolette Bridge.

Rue des Forges

Shops and restaurants with outside tables line this busy street, which combines the flavor of the old port with the energy of a bustling university town.

▸ *From Rue des Forges between Rue Hart and Blvd. Royale, turn right between the city hall and the cultural center and climb stairs to Parc Champlain.*

Parc Champlain

The modern, concrete structures of Trois-Rivières' **city hall** and **cultural center** (*hôtel de ville* and *centre culturel*) border this pleasant square dotted with fountains and trees. The center houses a theater, library, and art gallery. Built in 1967 to celebrate the centennial of Canada's confederation, this ensemble has been acclaimed for its architectural design, and it has been thoroughly rejuvenated in 2006.

In the square, a **monument** (**4**) to Benjamin Sulte (1841–1923) commemorates the well-known French-Canadian historian.

Cathédrale de Trois-Rivières★

362 Rue Bonaventure, at the edge of Parc Champlain. ◷ Open year-round Mon–Sat 9am–11.15am, 1pm–5.30pm, Sun 9.30am–noon, 2pm–6pm. ♿ P ☎819-374-2409.

The Gothic Revival cathedral with its copper-clad steeple was designed by Victor Bourgeau. The building was consecrated in 1858, but financial difficulties

delayed the erection of the steeple until 1905. The interior is dominated by Guido Nincheri's richly colored **stained-glass windows**. Produced between 1935 and 1954, they depict the "Lorette Litanies" of the Virgin Mary.

Beside the cathedral stands a statue of Louis-François Laflèche, Bishop of Trois-Rivières from 1870 to 1898.

▸ *Walk along Blvd. Royale. Turn left on Rue Laviolette and continue 400m/437yd.*

Séminaire de Trois-Rivières

858 Rue Laviolette.

Founded in 1860, the St. Joseph Seminary was rebuilt after a fire in 1929. Embellished by columns and a statue of St. Joseph, the main entrance of the long, impressive limestone structure is surmounted by a large, squat copper dome. Untouched by the fire, the Romanesque-style chapel (*behind the reception desk*) is open to visitors and displays the seminary's collection of religious objects, as well as artworks by Jordi Bonet (1932–79). Galleries on each side of the entrance hall make up the **Pierre Boucher Museum** (**M²**), which presents exhibits of the region's historic, ethnographic, and artistic heritage (◷ *open year-round Tue–Sun 1.30pm–4.30pm, 7pm–9pm;* P ☎819-376-4459). On view here are works by Antoine Plamondon, Roy-Audy, Berczy, Ozias Leduc, Suzor-Côté, Rodolphe Duguay, Gaston Petit, and Raymond Lasnier.

▸ *Double back on Rue Laviolette to Rue Hart.*

The old **courthouse** (palais de justice) stands at the corner of Rue Laviolette and Rue Hart. Designed by François Baillairgé and built in 1823, it was enlarged and partially restored in 1913.

▸ *Continue on Rue Hart.*

Musée québécois de culture populaire★ (Quebec Museum of Folk Culture) (M³)

200 Rue Laviolette, at the intersection with Rue Hart. ◷ Open late Jun–Labor Day, daily 10am–6pm; rest of the year,

Tue–Sun 10am–5pm. ⊘*Closed Jan 1 & Dec 24–25.* ⊜*$8.* ✕ ♿ ☎*819-372-0406. www.culturepop.qc.ca.*

Opened in 1996, this large museum offers visitors an opportunity to immerse themselves in Quebec folk culture. Permanent and temporary exhibits display selections from an ethnography collection totalling more than 80,000 objects (tools, furniture, textiles, toys, etc.), illustrating provincial customs and mores; folk arts; traditional occupations; farming methods, and domestic life. The museum also features a permanent archaeological collection of more than 20,000 artifacts of prehistoric Amerindians and European cultures.

Vieille Prison★ (Old Prison)

200 Rue Laviolette. ⊘*Open late Jun–Labor Day, daily 10am–6pm; rest of the year, Tue–Sun 10am–5pm.* ⊘*Closed Jan 1 & Dec 24–25.* ⊜*$8 ($12 combined ticket with the Folk Culture Museum).* ✕ ♿ ☎*819-372-0406. www.enprison.com.*

Linked to the museum by a covered walkway. Designed by François Baillairgé and erected between 1816 and 1822, the imposing stone structure features some of the best surviving examples of Palladianism in Quebec. Note its massive size, three-story framework, severe portal, and wide pediment dominating the central façade, all characteristic of a style that marked the British presence

throughout the Colonial Empire. The nine chimney stacks on the roof are evidence of a concern for the prisoners' comfort. The building ceased to be operated as a jail in 1986. Today it features an interpretation center; 20 of its cells present different aspects of prison life, such as discipline, hygiene, visitation, etc.

Excursions

Pointe-du-Lac★

About 20km/12.4mi from downtown by Rte. 138, on the shores of Lake Saint-Pierre.

In 1721, René Godefroy de Tonnancour established a **seigneurial mill** here, on the banks of the Saint-Charles River. By 1788 the two-story stone structure was Quebec's sixth most productive wheat mill, and ground grain until 1965. The sawmill here operated until 1986. Restored in 1978 by the Quebec government, the *Moulin Seigneurial* has been converted into an art gallery and exhibit hall, presenting changing displays related to milling (⊘*open late May–late Sept, daily 10am–5pm;* ⊜*$3.50;* 🅿 ☎*819-377-1396 & 1-877-377-1396; www.mediat-muse.qc.ca).* Nearby, the Église Notre-Dame-de-la-Visitation (1882) is recognizable by its small steeple.

VAL-D'OR★

ABITIBI-TÉMISCAMINGUE REGION
POPULATION 31,764

Situated in the heart of the Abitibi region, the area around Val-d'Or was the exclusive domain of Algonquin and Cree Amerindians prior to the arrival of Catholic missionaries and trappers in the 17C. The history of the city itself covers less than a century. The town was created in 1922 during the great gold rush that followed the discovery of major mineral deposits in Rouyn-Noranda. Located on the easternmost portion of the Cadillac Fault, Val-d'Or (meaning valley of gold) was the most important gold producer in the region during the 1929 economic crisis.

Today it remains one of the only active mining towns in the Abitibi region, with seven operating gold mines. A thriving logging industry also supports the local economy. In summer, the many saloons, bars, and restaurants light up the Rue Principale with the colorful neon signs reminiscent of 1950s and 1960s western towns.

Information: 1070 3e Avenue Est. ☎819-824-9646 & 1-877-582-5367. www.ville.valdor.qc.ca/www.abitibi-temiscamingue-tourism.org.

▶ **Orient Yourself:** Val-d'Or is accessible by Rte. 113 from Chibougamau (413km/256mi farther northeast) or Rte. 117 northwest from Montreal (531km/329mi). Air Canada Jazz (*www.aircanada.ca*) offers regular flights from Montreal to Val-d'Or; Air Creebec (☎*1-800-567-6567; www.aircreebec.ca*) flies to the James Bay region and Montreal; Pascan Aviation (☎*1-888-313-8777; www.pascan.com*) flies to Montreal with small planes (at the Saint-Hubert regional airport on the South Shore).

🕐 **Organizing Your Time:** The *Cité de l'Or* (a former mine) passport (☞*$37.50*) provides admission to the underground and surface attractions, the mining village, and nearby historical house. Allow 3 hours to visit.

🧒 **Especially for Kids:** Older children will enjoy the visit into the mine at Cité de l'Or; younger ones will probably prefer the simulations and mineral collection at the Malartic museum.

Sights

Cité de l'Or – Village Minier de Bourlamaque (Mining Village)

South of 3e Ave. Upon entering Val-D'Or, take Rue Saint-Jacques, directly opposite the tourist information booth, up to Rue Perreault.

Merged with Val-d'Or in 1965, this mining village was named after François-Charles de Bourlamaque, an aide of French General Montcalm. The village, which was declared a historic district in 1979, was administered exclusively by the Lamaque Mine, one of the main employers on the Cadillac Fault. The mine shaft, hospital, and residence of the mine executives are intact, and the solid log cabins that housed the mine employees are still inhabited.

The **Cité de l'Or** (🧒 🕐 *open late Jun–Labor Day, daily 9am–5pm; rest of the year by appointment;* ☞*$25 (underground or surface visit, 2hrs) or $37.50 (full 4hrs visit can be done over 2 days); tickets available at 90 Ave. Perreault;* 🅿 ☎*819-825-7616 & 1-877-582-5367; www.citedelor.com*) provides guided tours (☞) of the village; in addition, visitors can see the surface buildings of the Lamaque Mine and descend some 91m/300ft into an authentic mine tunnel.

Le parc Belvédère (Rotary Observation Tower)

Rue Sabourin, at the corner of Rue des ...ns. 🕐*Open year-round daily.*

Rising above an attractive forest setting, a tower in Belvédère Park (18m/59ft) overlooks the town and surrounding area, which has been nicknamed the "country of one hundred thousand lakes" (*le pays aux cent mille lacs*).

Excursion

Malartic

25km/15mi west of Val-d'Or, on Rte. 117.

This mining and industrial town was created as a "mushroom city" in 1922, and flourished during the mid-20C, with seven active gold mines. Along the Avenue Royal, false-front buildings recall the city's gold rush days.

Musée minéralogique de l'Abitibi-Témiscamingue★

Arriving from Val-d'Or, turn right on Rue de la Paix (n°. 650). ☞*Visit by guided tour (1hr 30min) only: Jun–mid-Sept, daily 9am–5pm; rest of the year, Mon–Fri 9am–noon, 1pm–5pm, weekends by appointment.* ☞*$6.* ♿ 🅿 ☎*819-757-4677. www.museemalartic.qc.ca.*

This museum was established as a tribute to the mining heritage of the Abitibi-Témiscamingue region. It features a fine collection of mineral samples from the region and from around the world (and the Moon!), as well as an avant-garde exhibit that takes visitors on a simulated journey to the core of the ore.

VAL-JALBERT ★

SAGUENAY–LAC SAINT-JEAN REGION
MAP: SEE LAC ST JEAN

Occupying a dramatic **site**★ near the impressive falls of the Ouiatchouan River, this ghost town conjures up dreams of turn-of-the-century industrial life.
The community began as a company town around a pulp mill built by Damase Jalbert (1804–1904) in 1901. After his death, the mill was taken over and expanded by Alfred Dubuc. At the height of production in 1910, it produced up to 50 tons of pulp a day, and in 1915 the town became a municipality. By 1926, the population had grown to a peak of 950 inhabitants.
Troubles began in 1926. Due to a sudden lack of demand, the price of pulp dropped, and increased competition led the mill to close the following year. The population gradually drifted away, and the village fell into ruin. A program of renovations begun in 1970 saved Val-Jalbert from obscurity. Today a veritable open-air museum, this heritage site offers visitors a wide variety of activities.

- **Information:** www.sepaq.com/ct/val/fr.
- **Orient Yourself:** The Val-Jalbert Historic Village is located in the municipality of Chambord, 245km/162mi northwest of Quebec City by Rtes. 175 and 169.
- **Don't Miss:** Either climb the stairs or take the cable car to the top of the waterfall— and the easy hike farther to the observation deck to look out over the region.
- **Organizing Your Time:** If possible, arrange to stay in one of the renovated houses at the village. Allow at least four hours to walk around the village.

Val-Jalbert Historic Village

Visits on foot or by tram. ◷*Open Jun–early Oct, daily 10am–4.30pm.* ⊚*$18.* ⚠ ✕ ♿ ☐ ⊚*418-275-3132 & 1-888-675-3132; www.sepaq.com.*

Convent

The former convent-school of the Sisters of Our Lady of Good Counsel (1915) serves as an **interpretation center** for the historic village. A slide show (*15min*) and a model of the site recount the history of Val-Jalbert. The nuns' quarters and chapel on the second floor can be visited. Across the street stand the remains of the St. George's Church and its presbytery, overrun with vegetation.

Rue Saint-Georges

Along the village's main artery lies the former **hotel** (*tourist accommodations are available on the second floor*). Destroyed by a fire in 1918, the structure was rebuilt soon after, to house the village's general store. Today a small boutique on the ground floor displays and sells a variety of objects from another era. Behind the general store in the old butcher's stall, a herbarium and a craft store can be visited.

Residential Sector

The residential sector, now deserted, is situated on a plateau bounded by Rues Sainte-Anne, Saint-Joseph, Dubuc, Tremblay, and Labrecque. At its peak, the village counted about 80 employee residences (◷*one is open to the public, on Rue Saint-Georges, near the post office*). When they were built between 1909 and 1920, these houses were considered state-of-the-art, equipped with central heating, electricity, running water, and even telephones. The houses belonged to the company, and were rented to employees for about $10 a month (employees' salaries averaged around $27 a month).

Vieux Moulin (Old Mill)

Standing at the base of the Ouiatchouan falls, this mill produced pulp which was carried south by train. The remains of the rail line are visible.

Village historique de Val-Jalbert/Steve Duschênes/Sépaq

Val-Jalbert Historic Village

The mill now houses an exhibit hall. A model explains the operation of the mill and a film (*20min*) describes the process of transforming wood pulp into paper. The old mill machinery is on display.

Chute Ouiatchouan (Ouiatchouan Falls)

These extremely high 72m/236ft falls were once the sole source of power for the pulp mill and the community. A steep but sturdy stairway (*400 steps*) leads to the top of the falls; visitors can also make the ascent by cable car (👓*$3*). From this spot, visitors can enjoy a magnificent **view**★★ encompassing Lake Saint-Jean and the surrounding countryside. Downstream, the Ouiatchouan River is striking as it carves out a gorge in the rock.

Chute Maligne (Maligne Falls)

4.4km/3mi, allow 1hr 30min for round-trip. Trail begins in campground on west side of river. Note: Steep descent to the falls.

A pleasant wooded trail climbs up above the Ouiatchouan River valley to a point where the river plunges over a second set of falls. A lock and sawmill were once located here to prepare and cut the wood before it was floated down to the mill.

VALCOURT

EASTERN TOWNSHIPS REGION
POPULATION 3,405
MAP: SEE CANTONS DE L'EST

A tiny agricultural community until the 1930s, Valcourt has become famous for the **snowmobile**, the brainchild of one of its residents, and is now the site of a world-class industry.

- **Information:** ☎1-800-355-5755. www.easterntownships.com.
- **Orient Yourself:** Valcourt is 130km/81mi east of Montreal by Rte. 10 (Exit 90) and Rtes. 243 and 222.
- **Organizing Your Time:** Allow 1hr 30min to visit the Bombardier museum.
- **Especially for Kids:** Older children will enjoy the International Snowmobile Exhibit at the Bombardier Museum.

Bit of History

As a boy in Valcourt, **Joseph-Armand Bombardier** (1907–64) envisioned creating an all-terrain vehicle that would travel over snow. He trained as a mechanic and worked in a garage next to his father's farm, inventing in his spare time. In 1937 he received his first patent, for a sprocket wheel/track system, which enabled him to develop vehicles guided by skis. Accommodating several passengers, the vehicle was primarily used for military applications. In 1959 he introduced the **Ski-Doo**, which went on to transform life in the north. A new vehicle and a new sport were born. Today J.-A. Bombardier Industries develops and sells snowmobiles all over the world. It also makes locomotives, airplane engines, and other transportation-related items.

Sight

Musée J.-Armand Bombardier★ [Kids]

1001 Ave. J.-A.-Bombardier. Take Highway 55 south from Quebec, exit 85, then follow blue road signs for the museum. ◷Open May–Labor Day, daily 10am–5pm; rest of the year Tue–Sun 10am–5pm. ⌾$7; children $5 (under 5 free). ☞Group guided tours available by arrangement: Reservations necessary. ♿🅿☎450-532-5300. www.museebombardier.com.

This museum is a fascinating tribute to Valcourt's favorite son. The **J.-Armand Bombardier** Exhibit and the **Bombardier Garage** trace the inventor's life and re-create the atmosphere in which he worked during the early stages of his career.

The **International Snowmobile Exhibit** illustrates the machine's assembly and its usage throughout the world from 1959 through the present.

VAUDREUIL-DORION

MONTÉRÉGIE REGION
POPULATION 26,364
MAP: SEE MONTREAL

Located just west of the island of Montreal, the seigneury of Vaudreuil was granted to Philippe Rigaud de Vaudreuil, Governor of Montreal, in 1702. Barely developed under the French Regime, the community was acquired in 1763 by Michel Chartier de Lotbinière, who furthered growth and established a parish.

On October 25, 1783, he proposed a town plan in which a church and market place in the center would be surrounded by a set of perpendicular streets. The 18C design was never carried out and the village kept its rural character. Engulfed by the Montreal suburbs during the 1970s, the twin communities of Vaudreuil and Dorion were eventually amalgamated, and today form the municipality of Vaudreuil-Dorion.

- 🛈 **Information:** 190 St-Charles Vaudreuil-Dorion. ☎450-455-9480. www.ville.vaudreuil-dorion.qc.ca.
- ▶ **Orient Yourself:** Vaudreuil-Dorion is about 50km/31mi west of Montreal. It is accessible either by Rte. 40 (Exit 35) or by Rte. 20 (Blvd. Saint-Henri Exit).
- ◷ **Organizing Your Time:** Vaudreuil-Dorion can be the westernmost destination in a pleasant day trip from downtown Montreal. Follow the shoreline of Lac St-Louis west to Ste-Anne-de-Bellevue, then explore Île Perrot before crossing to Vaudreuil-Dorion. Stay on Avenue St-Charles northwest under Rte. 40 to follow the shoreline of Lac des Deux-Montagnes. This road brings you t' the ferry to Oka, in order to continue your shoreline circuit back to Montrea'

Sights

Maison Trestler★
(Trestler House)

85 Chemin de la Commune. From Rte. 20, turn right on Blvd. Saint-Henri, and right on Ave. Trestler. ⊙*Open year-round, Mon–Fri 10am–noon, 1pm–4pm, Sun 1pm–4pm.* ⊙ *Closed mid-Dec–early Jan.* ⊛ *$4.* �□☎*450-455-6290. www.trestler.qc.ca*

This enormous stone house stands on a beautiful site overlooking Lake Deux Montagnes. It measures an impressive 44m/144ft long by 13m/42ft wide, and has a total of 14 dormer windows protruding from its wood shingle roof. The center section dates from 1798 and was built by Jean-Joseph Trestler, a German (his original name was Johann Joshef Tröstler) who made his fortune in the fur trade. The wings were added in 1805 and 1806. Several rooms in the house are furnished with exemplary pieces of 18C and 19C furniture. The tour passes through the beautiful curved-ceiling vault, where furs were hung to dry and displayed for purchasers. During the summer, concerts are held in the house.

Maison Valois (Valois House)

331 Ave. Saint-Charles, 1km/.6mi from the Trestler House. From Ave. Trestler, turn right onto Blvd. Saint-Henri, then bear right on Blvd. Saint-Charles. ⊙*Open late Jun–late Aug, daily; hours vary depending on the exhibit.* ☎*450-455-7282.*

Set in a pleasant park overlooking Lake Deux Montagnes, this edifice (1796) is typical of local residences, with its stone base and wooden walls. Note its steep roof, which measures about half the height of the structure and has no overhang. Restored by the municipality, it is used as an art gallery and hosts temporary exhibits.

Musée régional de
Vaudreuil-Soulanges

431 Ave. St-Charles. ⊙*Open Tue–Fri 9.30am–noon, 1.30pm–4.30pm (Tue 7pm–9.30pm), weekends 1pm–4.30pm.* ⊙ *Closed late Dec–early Jan.* ⊛ *$5.* ☎*450-455-2092 & 1-877-455-2092. www. rvs.qc.ca.*

s Old Vaudreuil museum is located
tone school building (1859), where

Lionel Groulx (1878–1967), th
French-Canadian historian, studie
cal of religious architecture of the pe
it features a windowed mansard r
topped by a small lantern. The museu
contains ethnographic objects used in
various facets of domestic and artisanal
life. In addition, the museum presents
thematic and traveling exhibits.

Église Saint-Michel
(St. Michael's Church)

On Blvd. Roche, near the museum. ⊙*Open mid-Jun–late Aug, Sun–Fri 10am–4pm; rest of year by appointment.* ⊛*Donation for guided tour.* ♿□☎*450-455-4282.*

Completed in 1789, this church—one of the oldest in the Montreal region—was declared a historic monument in 1957. The harmonious chevet, composed of an apse and a small sacristy, is best viewed from the cemetery. A new façade was added in 1856. Inside, note the liturgical pieces sculpted by Philippe Liébert in the late 18C: The main altar with its tabernacle, the side tabernacles and the pulpit. The choir paneling and stalls are by Louis-Amable Quévillon. The sculpted décor is complemented by an astonishingly realistic trompe-l'œil by F. E. Meloche, a student of the 19C artist Napoléon Bourassa. The painting of St. Michael above the altar was executed by William Von Moll Berczy. Jean-Joseph Trestler (above) is buried in the crypt.

Excursions

Île Perrot – *About 16km/10mi by Rte. 20.* ⚓ *See Entry Heading.*

Pointe-des-Cascades

Take Rte. 338 from Vaudreuil-Dorion. The village is 7km/4.3mi from the intersection with Rte. 20.

Ancres Park lies near the point where the waters of the St. Lawrence and Ottawa rivers meet, just upstream from Lake Saint-Louis. The park is set beside an old lock on the Soulanges Canal, one of the many canal systems that predated the St. Lawrence Seaway.

VICTORIAVILLE ★ (ARTHABASKA)

CENTER-DU-QUÉBEC REGION
POPULATION OF VICTORIAVILLE 41,316

Incorporated with the city of **Victoriaville**, the former town of Arthabaska lies on the shore of the Nicolet River, at the foot of Mt. Saint-Michel. It is the capital of the Bois-Francs (hardwood) region, so called because of the predominance of maple trees in the area. The town's name is derived from the Amerindian word *ayabaskaw,* meaning "place of bulrushes and reeds." In 1834 the arrival of the first French-speaking settler, Charles Beauchesne, heralded the influx of French Canadians into the southern part of the province, then primarily inhabited by English-speaking Loyalists. Maple products quickly became the backbone of the local economy and remain so today, although forestry and dairy cattle are equally important. After the opening of the railway in 1861, nearby Victoriaville replaced Arthabaska as a major industrial center, although Arthabaska retained its plethora of cultural opportunities and historical sites. The town was home to many notable Quebecers, including Prime Minister **Wilfrid Laurier** and the renowned painter-sculptor **Marc-Aurèle de Foy Suzor-Côté**.

- **Information:** 122 Rue Aqueduc. ☎819-758-0597 & 1-888-816-4007 ext. 300.
- **Orient Yourself:** Victoriaville is located 164km/101mi northeast of Montreal by Rtes. 20 and 161.
- **Parking:** Metered downtown parking is generally easy to find.
- **Don't Miss:** Maison Laurier.

A Bit of History

Victoriaville, nicknamed "Victo," also gets called "Capitale des Bois-Francs" and is noted for its high-quality wood products. There are plenty of cycle paths in Victoriaville, including one going all the way up to Mont Arthabaska. The town also holds The International Actual Music Festival every May, heralding new music. www.fimav.qc.ca.

Sir Wilfrid Laurier – Lawyer, journalist and politician, Wilfrid Laurier (1841–1919) became the first French-Canadian prime minister of Canada (1896–1911) and a legend in his own time. Renowned for his liberalist views, he headed the Canadian Liberal Party from 1887 to 1919, and espoused Canadian unity and the country's emancipation from Great Britain. He also promoted the settlement of the Canadian West by supporting the construction of the Grand Trunk Railway and the creation of the provinces of Alberta and Saskatchewan. Although he was born in the small town of Saint-Lin (now also known as Saint-Lin-Laurentides), 45km/28mi north of Montreal, Laurier spent most of his life in Arthabaska.

Sights

Musée Laurier★ (Laurier Museum)
16 Rue Laurier Ouest. The street intersects Blvd. Bois-Francs Sud just south of the town center. ⊙*Open Jul–Aug, Mon–Fri 10am–5pm, weekends 1pm–5pm; rest of the year, Tue–Fri 10am–noon & 1pm–5pm, weekends 1pm–5pm.* ⊙*Closed Dec 23–early Jan.* ⊜*$5 (entrance to both buildings).* ☎*819-357-8655. www.museelaurier.com.*

This National Historic Site commemorating Arthabaska's beloved native son occupies two separate buildings. The **Sir Wilfrid Laurier House** (*16 Rue Laurier Ouest*), an attractive residence built for Laurier in 1876, features overhanging eaves, decorative brackets, quoins, and bay windows. Laurier lived here until his death in 1919, although he spent m

Musée Laurier

his time in Ottawa after becoming prime minister in 1896.

The ground-floor rooms re-create the era during which Laurier lived here with his wife, Zoé Lafontaine. The bedroom, dining room (boasting a Tiffany lamp), and living room, all appointed in the style of the day, are open to visitors. In the living room is an 1885 Kranick and Bach piano given to Lady Laurier by her husband. Laurier's political career and anecdotes about the couple's life in their home are presented in displays throughout the house. Laurier's study is located in the second floor.

Erected in 1910 in the Second Empire style, the Hôtel des Postes building (*949 Blvd. Bois-Francs Sud*) mounts temporary exhibits of ethnology, history, and art. Outside the museum, note the bust of Sir Wilfrid Laurier by Alfred Laliberté.

Église Saint-Christophe d'Arthabaska (St. Christopher's Church)

40 Rue Laurier Ouest. 🕐 *Open late Jun–late Aug, Tue–Sat 10am–4pm, Sun 1pm–5pm; rest of the year by appointment.* 🔖*$2.* ♿📶⌨️*819-357-2376.*
Restored in 1997, this charming stone church (1873, J. F. Peachy) in the Romanesque style has a remarkable **interior**. The ceiling is decorated with 76 frescoes and paintings, the work of an artist from Saint-Hyacinthe, Joseph Thomas Rousseau, aided by Suzor-Côté. The statue of Christopher, on top of the altar, was [scu]lpted by students of Louis-Philippe [Hébe]rt. Also worth noting are Baroque-

style scrolls, trompe-l'œil paintings, friezes, as well as 43 stained-glass windows by the **Hobbs Company**.

Mont Saint-Michel

From Rue Laurier, take Blvd. Bois-Francs Sud 1.5km/1mi. Turn left on Rue Mont-Saint-Michel.
A small park with benches and picnic tables affords a lovely **view**★ of Victoriaville and the Nicolet River valley. Among the prominent landmarks are the tower of Arthabaska College, operated by the Sacred Heart Brothers (*Frères du Sacré-Cœur*), and the steeples of the churches of St. Christopher and St. Victoria. An iron cross, towering 24m/79ft high, was erected on the summit in 1928.

Excursions

Moulin La Pierre★ (La Pierre Mill)

6km/3.7mi. On Chemin Laurier (nº. 99) between Victoriaville and the village of Norbertville. 📷*Visit by guided group tour (1hr) only: Jun–Sept, Tue–Fri 8.30am–5pm.* 🔖*$4. Call ahead for reservations* 📶⌨️*819-369-9639.*
Straddling the Gosselin River, this is one of the few remaining operating water mills in Quebec. It was built on this site by Jean Goulet in 1845. Visitors can observe the milling process, purchase the high quality organic flour produced here, and enjoy home-made buckwheat biscuits in the café.

Église Sainte-Victoire (Church of St. Victoria)

99 Rue Notre-Dame Ouest, about 5km/3mi by Rte. 161. 🕐*Open late Jun–Aug, Wed–Sat 9am–4pm, Sun 8am–4.30pm; rest of the year by appointment.* ♿📶⌨️*819-752-2112.*
This Neoclassical-style church was completed in 1897; its main steeple measures 60m/197ft tall. The ornate **interior** features elaborate woodwork in the apse, a vault richly decorated with wood sculpture, and imposing lateral galleries. The stained-glass windows were produced in Montreal in 1928. Behind the church, to the left, is the presbytery topped by a mansard roof and a small tower.

VILLE-MARIE
ABITIBI-TÉMISCAMINGUE REGION
POPULATION 2,731

This small, yet vibrant community is the capital of the remote Témiscamingue region, on a vast and fertile plain that runs next to Lake Témiscamingue (an Algonquian word meaning "deep waters"). While farming continues as the town's economic mainstay, forestry and services also figure prominently in the local economy.

- **Information:** 1 Rue Industrielle. ☏819-629-2918 & 1-866-538-3647 & 1-800-808-0706. www.tourismetemiscamingue.ca.
- **Orient Yourself:** Ville-Marie is located 675km/420mi northwest of Montreal. (Rte. 148 west through Gatineau and continue to Rte. 17 in Ontario, travel northwest to Mattawa. Rte. 533 from Mattawa northwest to Rte. 63. Northeast to Témiscaming. Rte. 101 north to Ville-Marie.)
- **Organizing Your Time:** Bring a picnic to Fort Témiscamingue and consider a swim at the nearby beach.
- **Especially for Kids:** The interpretation center at the fort has hands-on exhibits, which are sure to be of interest to children, including samples of the various furs that brought traders to this region.

A Bit of History

Colonization of the region began in 1853 when lumbering laid bare large tracts of farmland. In 1863, the Oblate Fathers took up residence in the Old Fort Mission (Mission du Vieux Fort), located south of Fort Témiscamingue. In 1887 they moved to Baie des Pères, Ville-Marie's former appellation. The Grey Nuns followed shortly thereafter. Since their arrival in the region, both orders have pursued their religious mission in the realms of education and culture. Nicknamed "the father of agriculture in Témiscamingue," Brother **Joseph Moffet** (1852–1932), from the Old Fort Mission, was a well-known organizer and negotiator as well as an intermediary between the settlers and lumber company officials. He also negotiated with produce buyers from Ontario, located on the other side of Lake Témiscamingue. To this day, the region has retained its agricultural vocation while diversifying its forest industry and services. The town boasts golf and tennis facilities and organizes an international regatta on Pères Bay every July.

Sights

Grotte Notre-Dame-de-Lourdes (Our Lady of Lourdes Grotto)
Rue Notre-Dame-de-Lourdes.
This mountain **site**★ reveals a splendid view overlooking Lake Témiscamingue. The pleasant park is dotted with walking trails, picnic areas and Stations of the Cross.
On the corner of Rues Dollard and Notre-Dame-de-Lourdes stands the Medieval-style **town hall**. A school of agriculture from 1939 to 1965, it bears the name of the famed pioneer Brother Moffet.

Maison du Frère-Moffet (Brother Moffet's House)
7 Rue Notre-Dame-de-Lourdes, by the lake.
Open late Jun–Labor Day, daily 10am–6pm. $2.50. ☏819-629-3533.
The oldest house (1881) in the community houses a small museum that presents various objects from the colonization period recounting the unique history of Ville-Marie and Témiscamingue. Facing the house is a small park affording good **views** of the vast and very deep (up to 210m/688ft) Lake Témiscamingue. Stretching over 103km/64mi, the lake is a border between Quebec and Ontario.

L.H.N. Fort-Témiscamingue

Enchanted Forest

Excursions

Fort Témiscamingue National Historic Site of Canada★

8km/5mi south of Ville-Marie, at 834 Chemin du Vieux-Fort. Turn right off Rte. 101 to Témiscamingue. ⊙Open early Jun–Aug, daily 9am–5pm; rest of the year by appointment only. ⊛$5. ⅋ 🅿 ☎819-629-3222. www.pc.gc.ca/forttemiscamingue.

In 1679 the French established a fur trading post on this site; the post was later abandoned. A second post was erected in 1720, and remained active for nearly two centuries. The post changed hands several times as a result of political and commercial fluctuations, passing from the Northwest Company to that company's rival, the Hudson's Bay Company. Today several structures testify to what may have been the region's earliest fur trading post.

The site's **interpretation center** (Kids) offers a glimpse of life at a fur-trading post during the 18C and 19C. Various types of furs and trade items are displayed; the center also houses exhibits on the *voyageurs*. Visitors can relax at the site's large **beach**★, picnic grounds, and recreational areas.

Forêt enchantée★ (Enchanted Forest)

This unusual natural site covers most of [the] site's 4ha/9.8-acres. Here the visi[tor can] admire oddly shaped stands of silverberry, Eastern white cedar, and red pine. It is said that strong northerly winds sweep over the forest at the onset of winter, bending the trees under the forceful gales. Caught by a sudden frost, the small trees stay bent under their cover of snow during the entire winter and retain an irregular shape even after the late thaw. A trail runs alongside the lake, leading to the ruins of old chimneys, remains of the original fort. Tombstones mark the graves of early European settlers.

Route 101 meanders near Lake Témiscamingue, which in some places is visible beyond a forest of oak, beech, maple, poplar, and white or red pine. A few rest areas with picnic grounds and facilities are located along the road.

Témiscaming

Rte. 101 to the Ontario border ends in this small village, 90km/56mi south of Ville-Marie.

In 1917, the Riordon Company, a pulp and paper plant, was established in this charming town, which fostered a prosperous lumber industry.

The picturesque main road, known as the **Kipawa Route**, runs along the hillside to the southern end of Lake Témiscamingue, where it meets the Ottawa River.

NUNAVIK★★

Bounded on the west by Hudson Bay, on the north by the Hudson Strait, and on the east by Labrador, Nunavik ("the land to live" in **Inuktitut**) is the homeland of Quebec's Inuit population. Nunavik covers a total area of some 505,000sq km/194,980sq mi or approximately one-third of the provincial territory, and roughly corresponds to the region formerly known as Nouveau-Québec and still referred to as the "Grand Nord" or Far North.
The socio-cultural region of Nunavik was designated by referendum in the Inuit villages in 1986 and officially accepted by the provincial government two years later. Much of Nunavik's continental territory is situated within **Kativik**, the administrative region created by the James Bay and Northern Quebec Agreement in 1975 to represent the municipalities north of the 55th parallel.

Today modern achievements have considerably transformed the Inuit lifestyle, but the traditional values and heritage of the people survive. In recent years, Nunavik has become a choice destination for adventurous travelers eager to explore one of the world's few remaining frontiers. The region's spectacular expanses of natural wonders offer a truly unique experience, but visitors must be well equipped to cope with harsh conditions (nearly all visitors to Nunavik avail themselves of the services of an outfitter and/or guide).

Geographical Notes

The dominant feature of Nunavik's geography is the long, jagged coastline of the **Ungava Peninsula**, which juts north from the interior of the Quebec-Labrador peninsula, a subcontinental part of the Precambrian Canadian Shield. Most of Nunavik's 14 modern villages are located along this coast.

The northern half of the Ungava Peninsula is divided by the Povungnituk Mountains. This range stretches from east to west and includes the Nouveau-Québec Crater, thought to have been created by a meteorite some 1.4 million years ago. In the east, the **Torngat Mountains**, dominated by Quebec's highest peak, Mt. Iberville

Landscape with Inukshuk

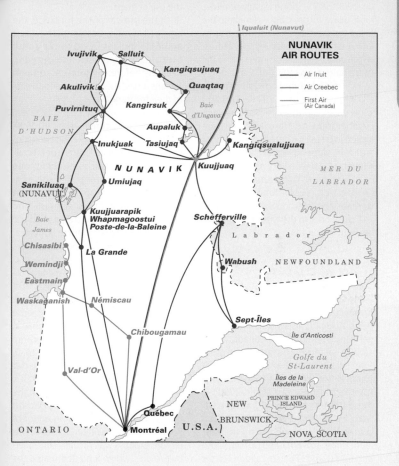

Iqaluit (Nunavut)

**NUNAVIK
AIR ROUTES**

Air Inuit
Air Creebec
First Air
(Air Canada)

Ivujivik   Salluit
                    Kangiqsujuaq
Akulivik   Quaqtaq
Puvirnituq   Kangirsuk   Baie
                                        d'Ungava
BAIE   Aupaluk
D'HUDSON
            Inukjuak   Tasiujaq
                                            Kangiqsualujjuaq
        N U N A V I K   Kuujjuaq
                                        MER DU
            Umiujaq   LABRADOR
Sanikiluaq
(NUNAVUT)
Baie   Kuujjuarapik
James   Whapmagoostui   Schefferville
            Poste-de-la-Baleine
Chisasibi   L a b r a d o r
            La Grande
Wemindji   Wabush   NEWFOUNDLAND
Eastmain
Waskaganish   Némiscau

        Chibougamau   Sept-Îles
                                        Île d'Anticosti

                                        Golfe du
                                        St-Laurent
    Val-d'Or   Îles de la
                                        Madeleine
                                PRINCE EDWARD
                    Québec   NEW   ISLAND
ONTARIO   Montréal   U.S.A.   BRUNSWICK
                                        NOVA SCOTIA

(1,662m/5,451ft), form the boundary between Quebec and Labrador. Nunavik is a land of myriad lakes and rivers. These waterways, draining into Ungava Bay and Hudson Bay, have long been used by the Inuit to transport resources and raw materials such as wood, steatite, and walrus ivory. In the 1950s the Labrador Trough, a mineral-rich geological fault between Kangirsuk in the north and Schefferville/Labrador City/Gagnon in the south, became a major center for iron-ore mining.

Flora – Nunavik comprises three distinct zones of vegetation: To the north, the open **tundra** zone, which is a treeless area rich with lichens, mosses and shrubs; to the south, the northern woodlands or **taiga**, dotted with small stands of black spruce and jack pine; and in between, the **forest tundra**, characterized by spruce, larch, and pine trees. The tree line separating these environments extends from Umiujaq in the west to Tasiujaq, Kuujjuaq and Kangiqsualujjuaq in the northeast. Most of the Ungava Peninsula is under permafrost reaching 275m/902ft in depth at Salluit. Discontinuous permafrost (permafrost that appears in patches), occurs throughout Nunavik.

Climate – The climate of Nunavik is determined by the opposing influences of the cold continental landmass and the warmer Atlantic Ocean. The winters are long and cold; the summers are in general cool, but temperatures can reach up to 30°C/86°F. Spring usually provides long, beautiful days, but—similar to the fall—can be marked by strong storms and unstable weather. Temperatures, which vary between the interior and the coast, range from -40°C/-40°F in January to 20°C/68°F in July. Snowfall is generally high (more than 2m/78.7in) and snow cover can be expected between October and June. The coastal areas are locked in by sea ice between November and June depending on the location, allowing for only a very short boating and shipping season. Nunavik's northern location gives it long days in the summer (about 20 hours of light in June) and short ones in the winter (about five hours in December).

A Bit of History

Early Inhabitants – The Inuit (*Inuit* means "the People": *Inu* means "human being"; *it* means "many") are the aboriginal population of arctic Canada. Some 15,000 or more years ago, hunters from Asia crossed the land bridge that spanned the Bering Strait and settled in Alaska's coastal areas. About 2000 BC, these hunters began migrating eastward, leading to the creation of a second culture that developed along the Labrador Coast, toward Cape Dorset, south of Baffin Island. The so-called "Dorset People" are credited with introducing the igloo to the area. A third culture, known as Thule, developed in Alaska about AD 1000 and invaded the territory of the Dorset People, who eventually disappeared. The present-day Inuit are descendants of the Thule branch.

Like their ancestors, the early Inuit hunted marine mammals (seals, walruses, and whales) along the coast and on the nearby islands. They also ventured inland along rivers and lakes to fish and hunt musk ox, caribou, and waterfowl. Organized in small family groups, they traveled from camp to camp by dogsleds, kayaks, umiaks (large, open boats made from seal skins), or on foot, living in skin tents and sod houses in summer and in igloos in winter. Known for their keen navigational skills, the Inuit were able to travel great distances without the use of maps.

With the growth of the fur trade, the age-old rivalry between the Inuit and Amerindians living to the south escalated. Having been introduced to firearms before the Inuit, Algonquin Indians forced the Inuit to abandon part of their territory.

Arrival of Europeans – About AD 1000, Vikings appeared on the east coast of Canada. Their visits were brief, however, and for several centuries Europe appeared to have forgotten the existence of the American continent, with the exception of Basque, English, and French fishermen who frequented the fish-laden waters of North America. After the early 15C, European explorers probably found their way to the Arctic, but contact with the Inuit remained limited. In 1610, in his quest for the Northwest Passage, Henry Hudson, the British navigator and namesake of the immense bay off the western shores of Nunavik, met the Inuit in what later became known as the Hudson Strait. In 1670, Charles II of England granted a charter to the **Hudson's Bay Company** (HBC), allowing exclusive trading rights in the immense territory surrounding Hudson Bay. Named Rupert's Land in honor of Prince Rupert, cousin of Charles II, this remote expanse was virtually controlled by the HBC, which long dominated the lucrative North American fur trade. After 1750, the Inuit homeland became known to outsiders through subsequent explorations by the HBC. In 1870 Rupert's Land was legally transferred to the young Canadian Confederation in return for certain compensations.

Protestant Moravian missionaries arrived in the early 1810s, and Canadian scientific expeditions took place between the 1880s and 1900. In the early 20C, the French fur company, **Révillon Frères**, established trading posts in the region, thereby competing with the well-established HBC. In 1936, the HBC reaffirmed its economic supremacy in the area by buying out its French competitor. The arrival of European traders and missionaries in the region dramatically transformed the local lifestyle: The economic organization of the indigenous populations shifted from a hunter-gatherer to a barter system, and the religious orders—Protestant, and later, Catholic—introduced European values and education. To a great degree the traders and missionaries brought about the abandonment of the semi-nomadic, self-sufficient existence of the indigenous peoples and the development of permanent, coastal settlements. American whale ships, which frequented the Hudson Strait after 1845, introduced the practice of remuneration, as well as rifles and wooden boats, which led the Inuit to abandon their traditional harpoons and sealskin kayaks. The new, more efficient hunting methods brought walruses and whales near to extinction, and the Inuit were forced to hunt on land to survive. The last whale ship was seen in 1915.

20C Transformations – In 1912 the Canadian government divided the former Rupert's Land among Manitoba, Ontario, and Quebec. The Quebec border was moved up from the Eastmain River to the Hudson Strait, some 1,100km/683.5mi farther north. Federal laws confirming the new border included a clause requiring the province to buy the land belonging to the indigenous peoples. In the 1940s, the Canadian and Quebec governments and the American army began establishing facilities (Fort Chimo, or present-day Kuujjuaq, and Poste-de-la-Baleine, or Kuujjuarapik), and developing mineral and hydroelectric projects in the area. Modern villages with schools and wooden buildings were established by the Canadian federal government as part of its legal obligation toward the local population. Between 1950 and 1963, Inuit family groups became somewhat more sedentary, leaving their hunting and fishing camps for the new villages. In the 1960s, Hydro-Québec launched a monumental hydroelectric project, made effective by the subsequent **James Bay and Northern Quebec greement (JBNQA)**, signed in 1975. is historic accord required the native ‑ulation to surrender certain claims but enabled them to gain other right (see BAIE JAMES).

Since 1975, all 14 coastal villages have experienced major expansions in housing. In addition, airports, health care, and schooling facilities have been upgraded. The HBC operated stores in many of the villages until the mid-1980s; currently these stores are operated by the Northwest Company, and are called Northern Stores. The Inuit have established commercial activities, creating employment opportunities in the villages. These enterprises range from commercial fishing and mining through construction and hotel management. The Inuit-owned Makivik Corporation manages the compensation packages established by the Agreement and has created a variety of subsidiaries, including Air Inuit and First Air airlines.

Nunavik Today – The 1986 grass-roots referendum that created the socio-cultural region of Nunavik sent out a clear signal throughout Quebec for wider acceptance of the distinct cultural identity of the Inuit. Two years later, Nunavik was officially recognized by the provincial government. Today the vast majority of Inuit live in modern, prefabricated houses, and can obtain schooling and professional training. Some Inuit study and have jobs in Montreal or other places outside their homeland. TV, video, telephone, fax machines, and high-speed internet connection (through satellite dishes) are available in all villages. A wide variety of vehicles (motor boats and snowmobiles, for example) have made travel easier and faster.

Despite their settlement in the new coastal villages, the Inuit have generally maintained their traditional economic activities, such as fishing and hunting. The Inuit hope to reap financial benefit from projects undertaken in Nunavik, such as the controversial James Bay project.

As in the past, the Inuit culture finds expression in art and family, and in community festivals. In addition, the Inuit have created projects and organizations to preserve their cultural heritage, such as the **Avataq Cultural Institute** in Inukjuak, which was established in

Stone and Ivory Sculpture by George Kopak Tayarak

R. Corbel/MICHELIN

1980. An active **cooperative movement** has been another characteristic of the community since 1959. Today, the twelve co-ops, under the umbrella of the Fédération des Coopératives du Nouveau-Québec, hold an important position in regional commerce. Each one owns a general store on the local level and regulates the commercialization of crafts, ensuring a livelihood for the many artists, painters, sculptors, and engravers.

Current Population – Nunavik's current population today consists of four different groups: The **Inuit** (about 11,000), occupying some 14 coastal villages; the **Naskapi** (at Kawawachikamach) and the **Cree** (at Whapmagoostui); and the **nonindigenous** or Caucasian, primarily Francophones, most of whom reside in Kuujjuaq, the region's administrative center. The Inuit of Nunavik today are geographically and culturally divided into those living in the northern and western Hudson Strait/Bay area and those in the eastern Ungava Bay area, who have ties with the Inuit on the Labrador coast. The Inuit of Canada have kept their language (some 66 percent still speak Inuktitut), although English and French have become important languages in schools and public life in Nunavik. Since 1978, in accordance with the conditions of the James Bay and Northern Quebec Agreement, the Inuit have created their own school board, and Inuktitut is now taught in all schools.

The people maintain strong ties with other Inuit in Canada, Greenland, Alaska and Russia through cultural exchanges and political activities under the **Inuit Circumpolar Conference,** which was founded in 1977 and is recognized as a non-governmental agency by the United Nations. In late 1992 the Canadian government announced the creation of **Nunavut** ("our land" in Inuktitut), a 2,000,000sq km/770,000sq mi Inuit homeland carved out of the vast eastern expanses of the Northwest Territories, stretching from the Saskatchewan-Manitoba provincial border to Greenland. In 1999 administration of this new nation passed to the Inuit.

East Coast

The villages described in this section are designated by their official names. Former names are given in parentheses and 2006 population figures are shown for the villages.

Kuujjuaq★ (Fort Chimo)

Pop. 2,250

Located on the western shore of the Koksoak River on flat, sandy land some 50km/31mi upstream from Ungava Bay, this regional administrative center is also Nunavik's largest village. Officially named Kuujjuaq, meaning "the great river" in Inuktitut, the settlement has retained its popular name, Fort Chimo. Upon first meeting Europeans, the Inuit would say "Saïmuk! Saïmuk!," which meant "Shake hands!" However, the Europeans understood "Chimo" and so it remained the name of the first post they established. The original fort was founded on the opposite shore of the Koksoak as the first HBC trading post in northern Quebec. The settlement was transferred to its present site in 1945. The traditional red and white buildings of the post have been transported piece by piece to their new location on the western shore of the Koksoak River (*guided tours are available through local guides; check at hotel*).

As the administrative center of Kativik, Kuujjuaq is the seat of regional government offices, health services and hospital, and a base for Air Inuit. A

Practical Information

GETTING THERE

Nunavik is accessible by airplane only (*for more details on airline routes, refer to map p425*). **First Air** (☎*1-800-267-1247; www.firstair.com*) offers a daily jet service between Kuujjuaq and both Montreal and Iqaluit. **Air Inuit** (☎*1-800-361-2965; www.airinuit.com*) offers Dash 8 turboprop service from Montreal to Kuujjuaq twice weekly and, via Kuujjuarapik and Inukjuak, to Puvirnituq five times a week. Air Inuit also flies to the region's villages on a regular basis.

On both the Hudson and Ungava coasts, several airline charter companies stand ready to take you anywhere in the region you like, according to your schedule. A well-known air charter company is **Johnny May's Air Charters** in Kuujjuaq (☎*819-964-2662 & 819-964-2321*); they fly from July through September (landing on floats) and from November through May (landing on skis), and they'll take you anywhere you want.

Nunavik Rotors in Kuujjuaq flies a ASTAR 350, which is a turbine-powered helicopter with a wide-body cabin for versatile payload requirements, for either passagers or cargo.

GENERAL INFORMATION

The villages in the arctic and subarctic regions of Quebec offer limited facilities to tourists, and traveling in these northern areas requires careful preparation. Four different types of travel for individuals or groups are offered: Nature, culture, hunting and fishing, or adventure. Due to government regulations, hunters and anglers must employ the services of a licensed outfitter. A listing can be found on the Nunavik Tourism website. The cost for one week is about $2,500–$3,500 per person, all-inclusive. Before leaving, contact the Nunavik Tourism office for exact information on the availability of accommodations and on different packages offered by adventure operators and outfitters. **Nunavik Tourism Association**, *P.O. Box 779, Kuujjuaq, QC J0M 1C0.* ☎*819-964-2876 & 1-888-594-3424; www.nunavik-tourism.com.*

Inform appropriate people about your movements in the area (location, routes, means of transportation, and times). Never leave villages alone. When going on hikes and/or trips, take along sufficient provisions, proper clothing, shelter, and emergency equipment. Be aware of rapidly changing weather conditions depending on the season and area. When exploring the region during the arctic winter, it is strongly recommended that you hire a guide acquainted with the area.

WHERE TO STAY

It is highly advisable to arrange all accommodations in advance. The *Nunavik Tourist Guide,* available from Nunavik Tourism Association, lists accommodations for Akulivik, Aupaluk, Inukjuak, Ivujivik, Kangiqsualujjuaq, Kangiqsujuaq, Kangirsuk, Kuujjuaq, Kuujjuarapik, Puvirnituq, Quaqtaq, Salluit and Umiujaq. Guest quarters in local homes are sometimes available. Double occupancy rates in hotels and inns range from $180 to $300; private baths are not always available. For reservations, contact **Fédération des Cooperatives du Nouveau-Québec**, *19950 Rue Clark-Graham, Baie D'Urfé, QC H9X 3R8.* ☎*514-457-6580 & 1-800-465-9474* (outfitting services at the same number); *www.articadventures.ca.* Most restaurants serve American fast food. Tourists generally buy and cook their own provisions, as most hotels are equipped with kitchenettes. The local diet consists of caribou, char and other fish, seal, and canned foods; fresh fruits and vegetables are scarce.

SEASONS TO REMEMBER

Nunavik's weather and temperatures have nothing in common with the rest of the travel destinations world. In summer, come prepared for bright sunshine, wind, rain and perhaps, yes, even snow; pack long underwear along with insect repellent! In winter, outdoor activities are impossible without complete snow attire; including mittens, rather than gloves.

Air Force base operated here between 1942 and 1949. Today its two major airfields are part of the current North Warning Systems, and the village serves as the transportation hub for northern Quebec, with several private air charter companies operating here. The present settlement was established around the base in the 1950s. The village has a hotel, restaurants, stores, banks, and art shops. Between the 1960s and 1980s the provincial government maintained a musk-ox farm here; the animals were released in 1985 and now roam Nunavik.

Environs

A number of outfitters are available to arrange wilderness outings around Kuujjuaq for the arctic traveler (char and salmon fishing, as well as caribou hunting). A limited road system (*8km/5mi*) allows travel onto the tundra and to the tree line, in the vicinity of the settlement. These outings take travelers into isolated forested patches on a plateau of rolling hills between 80m/262ft and 250m/820ft in altitude. A highlight of the region is the **Koksoak River**, a tidal river whose character changes continuously with the ebb and flow of the tides. The tides reaching upstream into the river create a variety of fascinating and ever-changing landscapes.

Kangiqsualujjuaq
Pop. 856

This village is located on the eastern shore of **George River**, 25km/15.5mi south of Ungava Bay. It is situated in the shadow of an imposing granite outcrop in a narrow valley at the north end of a bay. Formerly known as George River and Port-Nouveau-Québec, Kangiqsualujjuaq, meaning "very large bay" in Inuktitut, is the northeasternmost permanent settlement in Nunavik. It was established on the initiative of local Inuit, who founded the first co-op in Nunavik, a char fishery, on this site in 1959. In the 1830s, an HBC post operated south of the contemporary village; it closed in the mid-20C.

The settlement hangs on the tree line, and a small lumber (spruce) mill operated here in the 1960s. The area appeals to canoeists, who ride the George River, and to fishermen attracted by the Atlantic salmon populating the river. The George River is also the feeding area of one of Northern Quebec's largest caribou herds. Outfitter camps are found upriver at the beautiful **Helen Falls** (*64km/39.7mi*).

Tasiujaq (Leaf Bay, Baie-aux-Feuilles)
Pop. 277

This small settlement, whose name means "that which resembles a lake" in Inuktitut, is located on low-lying marshy flatland bordering the **Baie-aux-Feuilles**, the westernmost extension of Ungava Bay. The bay is noteworthy for its exceptional tidal movement (up to 17m/56ft), which is considered the highest in the world.

Founded in the 1960s on the western shore of the Bérard River, the settlement was established in the vicinity of early 20C trading posts established by the HBC and the Révillon Frères. Later, its economy was bolstered by mineral exploration that took place in the northern section of the Labrador Trough. The village lies just a few kilometers (a couple of miles) north of the tree line in the southern reaches of the barren tundra. The area is part of the large drainage basin of Feuilles River. Several outfitters' camps provide char, lake trout, and brook trout fishing. Herds of caribou annually pass close to the village on their autumnal trek south.

Aupaluk
Pop. 177

This village is located on the southern shores of Hopes Advance Bay, an inlet on the western coast of Ungava Bay. Aupaluk owes its name, meaning "red place" in Inuktitut, to the reddish color of the soil, which is the result of the high iron-ore content of the northern reaches of the Labrador Trough.

Originally a traditional hunting camp, Aupaluk was established in the late 1970s when Inuit from Kangirsuk and some other villages relocated to this area, which is renowned for its abundance of caribou, fish, and marine mammals. It was incorporated in 1981 and is today the smallest of the Inuit villages in Nunavik. As a new settlement, Aupaluk is the first arctic village in Canada whose town site was planned and conceived by the Inuit themselves. No outfitters operate here.

Kangirsuk (Payne Bay, Bellin)
Pop. 463

Situated on the northern shore of Arnaud River, 13km/8mi upstream from Ungava Bay, Kangirsuk ("the bay" in Inuktitut) began when trading and mission posts were established here in the late 1880s. The HBC established a trading post in 1925. Government services were first introduced in the 1950s. Today there are two stores (Northern Store and a co-op), and several outfitters operate fishing camps on the Ungava Peninsula.

Quaqtaq (Koartac)
Pop. 330

The village of Quaqtaq is located in a small valley on the eastern coast of Diana Bay at Cape Hopes Advance, which protrudes into the Hudson Strait. Frequented by the Inuit and their ancestors for 4,000 years, this region is rich in archaeological sites. Marine resources remain a mainstay of the Inuit to this day. Various trading posts existed here between the 1930s and 1960s, and a government weather station operated in the vicinity between 1927 and 1969. The local co-op store was founded in 1974. Quaqtaq lies on the arctic barrens with rugged mountains to the north and short rocky hills to the south and east. The valleys and other protected places show a little vegetation in summer: Moss, lichens, minuscule flowers in bright colors, berry bushes.

Diana Bay
The region around Diana Bay ("Tuvaaluk," in Inuktitut) is renowned for its rich hunting grounds, where abound land mammals (arctic fox, otter, rabbit, and sometimes the polar bear, which travels on ice for about 80km/50mi from the island of Akpatok) and sea mammals (various species of seals, walruses, beluga whales and some narwhals). Species of bird found here include the partridge; Snow, Canada, and Barnacle geese (Quaqtaq is on their flyway); and the Eider duck. Among the most common fish are the Gray, Red, and Speckled trout, and the Arctic char. Nature enthusiasts might even discover the musk-ox (approximately a million now flourish in the region), the legendary Snowy Owl or the Loon.

© Heiko Wittenborn

sled

Kangiqsujuaq (Wakeham, Maricourt)
Pop. 591

Occupying an exceptional **site**★★ in a valley on the southeastern shore of Wakeham Bay, Kangiqsujuaq was established on the site of an early 20C trading post. In the 1930s the Oblate mission founded a station here. Government services were introduced in the 1960s, and today, the village has a Northern Store, a co-op, and two churches. Its present name, meaning "the great bay" in Inuktitut, replaced the earlier European appellations, Wakeham and Maricourt.

The village is located 88km/55mi northeast of the famous **Nouveau-Québec Crater**★, measuring 3km/1.8mi in diameter and 267m/876ft deep. Outfitters arrange snowmobile excursions to the crater in winter.

Salluit (Saglouc, Sugluk)
Pop. 1,249

Located on the narrow Sugluk Fjord, about 10km/6.2mi from the Hudson Strait, this village is one of the largest settlements in northern Nunavik. The name, Salluit, means "thin ones" in Inuktitut, because, according to tradition, the Inuit had been told that the region abounded in animals to hunt, but when they arrived, they found almost none.

Salluit developed around trading and mission posts, which were established in the area after 1900. Government services were introduced in the 1950s. Today there is an Anglican mission, a co-op and a Northern Store. Salluit is known for the beauty of its **site**★★, surrounded by high, rugged mountains and cliffs rising to 500m/1,640ft.

To the east of Salluit, asbestos mining at Purtuniq (Asbestos Hills) and Deception Bay introduced industrial activities and a modern infrastructure (jet airfield and harbor) in the early 1970s. Full-scale mining and shipping were abandoned in the 1980s.

Nature observation tours afford possibilities for viewing walrus herds, polar bears, and caribou.

Ivujivik
Pop. 327

Located in a cove south of Digges Sound, in a mountainous region near Cape Wolstenholme, Ivujivik is the northernmost settlement in the entire province; its name means "place where ice accumulates during ice break" in Inuktitut. After 1947, the Inuit of the neighboring shores gradually settled in the small village established around the Catholic mission, which was founded in 1938 and closed in the 1960s. Shortly thereafter, government services were introduced and the co-op began operations in 1967. The Inuit of Ivujivik have not signed the James Bay and Northern Quebec Agreement of 1975. Instead, these dissenters have allied themselves with Inuit from Puvirnituq and Salluit to form the Inuit-Tungavingat-Nunamini movement. These groups administer their own schools, under the supervision of a locally elected committee.

Digges Island, north of Ivujivik in the Hudson Strait, was the site of the first recorded encounter between Inuit from the Quebec-Labrador peninsula and Europeans. The historic event took place in 1610 during one of Henry Hudson's expeditions in search of a Northwest Passage to Asia.

West Coast

Akulivik (Cape Smith)
Pop. 536

Located on a peninsula bordered on the north by a deep water port, and on the south by the mouth of the Illukotat River, Akulivik is the westernmost village in Nunavik. Its name, meaning "middle part of a leister (fishing spear)," refers to the geographical aspect of the site.

Just off the coast lies the island of Cape Smith, on which the HBC operated a post between 1924 and 1951. Akulivik was founded by the Inuit in 1976 on the site that served as the summer camp of the Qikirtajuarmiut Inuit group before they moved to Puvirnituq in 195? Qikirtajuarmiut means "the people the island."

The sandy texture of the soil is due to the crumbly, fossilized seashells that are vestiges of the last ice age. The co-op operates a store, a carving shop, and a recreation hall.

Puvirnituq (Puvirnituuq)
Pop. 1,476

The village is situated on the northern shore of the Puvirnituq River, 4km/2.5mi east of Povungnituk Bay. The name Puvirnituq, meaning "place where there is a smell of putrefied meat," refers to a tragic episode in the short history of the village: An epidemic ravaged the settlement, and all the villagers died, leaving no one to bury the dead. When friends and family arrived from nearby camps in the spring, the stench of decaying bodies permeated the air.

As in other villages of the Far North, Puvirnituq developed after the establishment of a HBC fur trading post (1921). The Inuit who came to live in this post after 1951 had occupied, up to that time, summer camps near Akulivik and winter camps on the island of Cape Smith.

In 1975 the citizens of Puvirnituq were joined by those of Ivujivik and 49 percent of those of Salluit in refusing to sign the James Bay and Northern Quebec Agreement. The position taken on this issue has instilled a strong sense of solidarity within the community.

The Hudson Bay Hospital Center, a modern health facility serving the villages of the Hudson Bay coast, is located here. Originating as the Carving Association, created in 1950 by Father André Steinman, a French Oblate missionary, the **Cooperative Association of Puvirnituq** is among the most dynamic co-ops of Nunavik. The Association operates a retail store, a hotel and manages the community's fuel supply. Several local artists have achieved international recognition.

Inukjuak (Port Harrison)
Pop. 1,456

Nunavik's second largest village, Inukjuak, is located at the mouth of the Innuksuac River near the Hopewell Islands. Non-natives arrived in the area in 1909 when the French fur company, Révillon Frères, installed a fur trading post on the site, which they called Port Harrison. The HBC, however, established a post here in 1920 and eventually bought out the French company in 1936. The HBC's monopoly on fur trade with the Inuit continued until 1958. The Anglican Mission arrived in 1927, and in 1935 a postal service for the Far North was established.

Life in Inukjuak maintains a strong link with traditional activities. An important deposit of steatite, stone used for sculp-

Christine Boulez/ MICHELIN

Port Harrison

tures, was discovered here. The find has encouraged the growth of the arts.

Older buildings near the Co-op Hotel include the Anglican Mission, the Northern Store, the co-op store, and the carving shop. The newer constructions of the village are concentrated along the route leading to the airport. On the eastern shore of the river, remnants of the old trading post, settlement, and cemetery can be seen.

Avataq Cultural Institute

Inukjuak is the seat of the head officer of the Avataq Cultural Institute, a non-profit organization devoted to the preservation and development of the linguistic and cultural heritage of the Inuit in Nunavik. Activities linked to toponomy, history, the cultural center, literature, games, traditional music, archaeology, etc., are offered. The Institute also collects various Inuit pieces from other museums and sponsors the annual Conference of the Inuit Elders, whose goal is to collect and preserve oral traditions and knowledge for the benefit of future generations.

Inuit Exhibit

In the lobby of the modern, brick schoolhouse, a series of bas-relief sculptures depicting everyday life in a traditional Inuit community demonstrate the skills of village carvers. The collection of hunting and fishing objects and practical cutting and scraping tools were assembled by a young Inuit archaeologist from Inukjuak, Daniel Weetaluktuk (1951–82), who during his short career greatly contributed to arctic anthropology.

Environs

The gently rolling rock formations dominating the landscape around the village provide a **panorama**★ of the village and port of Inukjuak, the river, the Hopewell Islands and Hudson Bay, and the mountains lying to the north.

A **walk** along the shore of the Innuksuac River toward the airport offers the possibility of discovering many varieties of the tiny wildflowers that miraculously survive in the Arctic climate. The clear waters of the meandering river form cascades and pools along the way.

Umiujaq
Pop. 382

This village was created for those Inuit of Kuujjuarapik who decided to relocate in light of phase 2 of the James Bay project, believing that implementation of the project would necessitate profound changes to their way of life. Archaeological, environmental, and settlement-planning studies were conducted, and construction began during the summer of 1985. At this time, several hundred of the Inuit of Kuujjuarapik moved to the area and lived in temporary quarters until their homes were completed in early 1987.

Today Umiujaq (meaning "which resembles a boat" in Inuktitut, because of a hill that looks like an *umiak,* a large open boat made from seal skins) has a fresh and vibrant quality reflecting the pride of its citizens. This tranquil site near Lake Guillaume-Delisle (Richmond Bay) is remarkable for its escarpments along the seashore.

A municipal building houses the FM radio station, town hall, an Air Inuit bureau, and the post office. A **museum** in the town hall displays a collection of tools, household items, and other artifacts that were unearthed by archaeologists and village elders during the excavation of the site. Beside the municipal building stands the modern and well-equipped clinic, and the co-op, which also contains the carving shop.

Outfitters offer sightseeing trips to nearby islands and excursions on the Nastapoka River.

Kuujjuarapik
Pop. 1,408

Located on Hudson Bay, 172km/106mi north of Radisson, Kuujjuarapik ("little great river") was established as a fur trading post by the Hudson's Bay Company in 1820. The Anglican mission arrived in 1882, but the village did not become a permanent settlement until 1901. The first contacts with Catholic missionaries occurred in 1924. The French fur company, Révillon Frères, set up a post in 1908, at the mouth of the Little Whale River to trade with the

Christine Boulez/MICHELIN

Kuujjuarapik dunes

Cree and Inuit living along the coast of the region. In the 1920s, the village was relocated to the mouth of the Great Whale River.

A weather station was established in 1895, but most government services did not reach the village until after 1949. From 1954 through 1959, Kuujjuarapik became a communication center for northern Quebec through the construction of a series of radar stations known as the "mid-Canada line," between the Atlantic coast and Hudson Bay, north of the 55th parallel. The headquarters was established at Poste-de-la-Baleine. At this time the region around Kuujjuarapik experienced its greatest population growth. In 1965, the installation was evacuated and turned over to the province of Quebec.

A Multiethnic community

Today the village of Kuujjuarapik is home to Inuit, Cree, and non-native populations. This population mix is unusual. The post and village have gone through a number of name changes: First Great Whale River in English, then Poste-de-la-Baleine in French, Kuujjuarapik ("the little big river") in Inuktitut and Whapmagoostui ("Whale River") in Cree. The last three have gained official recognition, making the village one of the few places in Canada with three names.

The Inuit community is located near the mouth of Great Whale River, while the Cree community has settled farther upstream. The Inuit and Cree have separate schools, infirmaries and municipal organizations. The Anglican Church holds services in Inuktitut and Cree. In the old church a collection of tools and typical costumes is on display. The social club provides recreational activities for all members of the community.

The village is bordered on the west by the airstrip which lies parallel to the Hudson Bay. Government offices and non-native housing are located near the airport in the former radar station complex. A research center of the Université Laval (see QUEBEC CITY) is also located here.

Environs

A wide, sandy beach stretches from the mouth of the Great Whale River to the opposite side of the village where high dunes provide good views of the Hudson Bay and the area around Kuujjuarapik, Nunavik's southernmost village.

Approximately 12km/7.4mi upstream from the village, a scenic **waterfall** is accessible by boat in summer or snowmobile in winter.

Northen Lights

Aurora borealis, *arsaniit* in Inuktitut, "aurore boréale" in French, and Northern Lights in English, all describe one of the most spectacular shows in the natural world. Only in the Far North can you see clearly and regularly a wide rippling green, sometimes red and purple, arc across the night sky (from August through March in Nunavik).

A

INDEX

INDEX

INDEX

INDEX

INDEX

MAPS AND PLANS

LIST OF MAPS

THEMATIC MAPS

REGIONAL MAPS

MONTREAL

QUEBEC CITY

COMPANION PUBLICATIONS

NORTH AMERICA ROAD ATLAS

A geographically organized atlas with extensive detailed coverage of the USA, Canada and Mexico. Includes 246 city maps, distance chart, state and provincial driving requirements and a climate chart.

- Comprehensive city and town index
- Easy to follow "Go-to" pointers

MAP 583 NORTHEASTERN USA/ EASTERN CANADA

Large-format map providing detailed road systems; includes driving distances, interstate rest stops, border crossings and interchanges.

- Comprehensive city and town index
- Scale 1:2,400,000
(1 inch = approx. 38 miles

LEGEND

★★★ **Highly recommended**
★★ **Recommended**
★ **Interesting**

Sight symbols

═ ● ═══ Recommended itineraries with departure point

⛪ ✡ ☒ Church, chapel – Synagogue		▭ ▬ Building described
○ Town described		▭ ▭ Other building
AZ B Map co-ordinates locating sights		▪ Small building, statue
▪ ▲ Other points of interest		⊙ ⁂ Fountain – Ruins
⚒ ⌒ Mine – Cave		🛈 Visitor information
⚙ ⚓ Windmill – Lighthouse		⬤ ⚓ Ship – Shipwreck
☆ ⛪ Fort – Mission		☀ ⩔ Panorama – View

Other symbols

🛡 Interstate highway (USA)   🛡 US highway   ⑱⑧⓪ Other route

🍁 Trans-Canada highway   🛡 Canadian highway   🛡 Mexican federal highway

══─══ Highway, bridge		═══ Major city thoroughfare
══►══ Toll highway, interchange		═══ City street with median
═══ Divided highway		──◄── One-way street
─── Major, minor route		═══ Pedestrian Street
↘ **15** Distance in kilometers		⇥∷⇤ Tunnel
╱ 655 ↙ Pass, elevation *(meters)*		▪▪▪▪▪ Steps – Gate
△ 1917 Mtn. peak, elevation *(meters)*		△ 🗼 Drawbridge – Water tower
✈ ✦ Airport – Airfield		🅿 ✉ Parking – Main post office
⛴ Ferry: Cars and passengers		🖼 ✚ University – Hospital
⛴ Ferry: Passengers only		🚂 🚌 Train station – Bus station
←←┌─┐ Waterfall ÷ Lock – Dam		● Ⓢ Subway station
─··─··─ International boundary		⌂ Observatory
─────── Provincial boundary, state boundary		⊥⊥⊥ ≈ Cemetery – Swamp
🍇 Winery		ⅠⅠⅠⅠ Long lines

Recreation

▪─○○○○─▪ Gondola, chairlift		⊂⊃ ► Stadium – Golf course
🚂 Tourist or steam railway		❀ Park, garden
⛴ ⚓ Harbor, lake cruise – Marina		❂ Wildlife reserve
⚓ ⛵ Surfing – Windsurfing		⊙⅄ Wildlife/Safari park, zoo
⊞ ⚓ Diving – Kayaking		─────── Walking path, trail
⛷ ⛷ Ski area – Cross-country skiing		🚶 Hiking trail
	🙂 Sight of special interest for children	

Abbreviations and special symbols

🛡 National Park		Ⓢ Subway station (Montréal)
🄸 Interpretation centre		⊥ Calvary, sanctuary
🄷 Hydroelectric plant		▫ Ghost town
⊠ National historic site		🚌 Covered bridge
	▭ Amerindian reservation	

All maps are oriented north, unless otherwise indicated by a directional arrow.

Michelin Apa Publications Ltd

A joint venture between Michelin and Langenscheidt

Suite 6, Tulip House, 70 Borough High Street, London SE1 1XF, United Kingdom

No part of this publication may be reproduced in any form
without the prior permission of the publisher.

© 2009 Michelin Apa Publications Ltd
ISBN 978-1-906261-44-3
Printed: August 2008
Printed and bound: Himmer, Germany